Almanac
of the
50 States

Basic Data Profiles
with
Comparative Tables

2006

Almanac
of the
50 States

Basic Data Profiles
with
Comparative Tables

2006

State & Municipal Profiles Series™

**information
publications**

Woodside, California

Also from Information Publications

State & Municipal Profiles Series™

Almanac of the 50 States

California Cities, Towns & Counties   *Connecticut Municipal Profiles*

Florida Municipal Profiles   *Massachusetts Municipal Profiles*

The New Jersey Municipal Data Book   *North Carolina Municipal Profiles*

American Profiles Series™

Asian Americans: A Statistical Sourcebook
Black Americans: A Statistical Sourcebook
Hispanic Americans: A Statistical Sourcebook

ISBN 0-931845-91-2 Paper
ISBN 0-931845-92-0 Cloth
Almanac of the 50 States, 2006

©2006 Information Publications, Inc.
Printed in the United States of America

Information Publications, Inc.
2995 Woodside Rd., Suite 400-182
Woodside, CA 94062-2446

www.informationpublications.com

Toll Free Phone 877.544.INFO (4636)
Toll Free Fax 877.544.4635

Direct Dial Phone 650.851.4250
Direct Dial Fax 650.529.9980

17
445
006

Table of Contents

Table of Contents

Comparative Tables

Table of Contents

Introduction

The *Almanac of the Fifty States* provides a comprehensive, easy to use, state statistical reference book. It presents a general overview of every state and the District of Columbia, along with tables of comparative rankings.

The book is divided into two parts. The first, **State Profiles**, is comprised of 52 individual profile sections: one for each of the 50 states, one for the District of Columbia, and one for the US in summary. Each of these profiles is eight pages long, each utilizes the same format organized into 13 subject categories, and each has been compiled from the same sources of information. The result is a set of basic data profiles which are readable, understandable, and provide a strong basis for comparative analysis.

The individual profiles are the heart of the book. Information selected for the profiles has been chosen to include those items which have the greatest general appeal to the broadest cross-section of users. The information comes from the latest reports of federal government agencies, augmented with data from business and trade organizations. No new surveys or original material is included, as the objective is to provide the most vital and significant information about each state, from the most reliable and respected collectors of data. A discussion outlining the data sources for the profiles is provided below.

The second part of the book, **Comparative Tables**, is composed of tables that rank the 50 states, the District of Columbia, and the US as a whole. The 64 tables each list the states in rank order for a selected characteristic chosen from the state profiles. The purpose here is to provide straightforward tabular data on how states compare in regard to a given characteristic. The overall goal of the *Almanac of the 50 States* is to bring together into a single volume a wide variety of diverse information and present it, state by state, in a clear, comprehensible format. It is not intended as a detailed research tool, but rather as a ready reference source, the first place to turn to answer basic questions about the states.

For readers requiring more depth of coverage or a different focus, the full range of federal government resources should be examined. Not only *Statistical Abstract* (and its supplements *City and County Data Book*, and *State and Metropolitan Area Data Book*), but the annual reports and serial publications of individual departments and agencies merit attention as well. The federal government is the largest publishing enterprise in the United States, and once the initial hurdle of access is overcome, the researcher is well rewarded: its materials cover a wide range of topics in great depth and detail.

Additionally, the publications of various trade and professional associations are an excellent source of state information. Most of these organizations produce monographs and annual reports which provide statistical information that is not available elsewhere. Such publications have been useful in compiling this book, and the most pertinent of proprietary information has been reprinted here with permission.

Finally, state governments themselves are publishers of note. Frequently they bring together and make available valuable information on a state and regional level. Most of their

Introduction

material is collected and made available by the respective state libraries.

In order to continue to meet its goals, **Almanac of the 50 States** is revised and updated on an annual basis. The best suggestions for improvement in a ready-reference source such as this come from the regular users of the work. Therefore, your comments and ideas are actively solicited. If you know how this book can become more useful to you, please contact us.

The Editors
Almanac of the 50 States
Information Publications, Inc.
2995 Woodside Road, Suite 400-182
Woodside, CA 94062

info@informationpublications.com

Toll Free Phone: 877-544-4636
Toll Free Fax: 877-544-4635

The Profiles

All information in the profiles has been selected from federal government reports and publications, or from materials published by business and trade organizations. The use of such sources ensures an internal consistency and reliability of data that just would not have been available otherwise. Additionally, it enables the users of this book to go back to the more detailed original source materials, and use the two in combination.

To enhance this consistency, all headings and terms used in the profiles have been carried over as they appear in the original sources. Those unfamiliar with government terminology may at times be puzzled by either the meaning of a specific term , or why the data was gathered in a certain way. Unclear terms are defined (as the data collection agency uses them) in the next section, "The Categories, Headings & Terms." Additionally, the source of origin for each item of information is presented. This allows readers to refer to the original sources themselves which often contain more detailed definitions, and fuller explanations of data collection procedures.

In preparing the format for the profiles, the design has been structured to enable each profile to stand alone. The headings are clear, abbreviations have been avoided whenever possible, and indents have been used to indicate subgroups of the main heading. However, because of the ease of reading, users are cautioned to keep in mind the wording of a heading, and to note whether a dollar amount, median (midway point), mean (average), or percent is being provided. Additionally, it should be pointed out that not all subgroups add to the total shown. This may be due to rounding, or the fact that only selected subgroups are displayed.

Introduction

The Categories, Headings & Terms

A review of the 13 categories which make up each of the profiles appears below. In addition to citing the source of origin, the paragraphs contain a brief identification of terms and some background methodology on the data collection.

State Summary

All information in this box is taken from the other 12 categories, and individual sources are identified below.

Geography & Environment

General coastline data represents the length of the outline of the coast. Tidal shoreline data represents the shoreline of the outer coast, off-shore islands, sounds, bays, rivers, and creeks to the head of the tidewater. The original source of this information is *The Coastline of the United States, 1975*.

Federally owned land data comes from *Federal Real Property Profile*, published in September 30, 2004 by the U.S. General Services Administration, Office of Governmentwide Policy. All other items in this section are from *Statistical Abstract*.

Demographics & Characteristics of the Population

All 1980, 1990, and 2000 items are from the 1980, 1990, and 2000 Decennial Censuses of Population, respectively, conducted by the Bureau of the Census. Other population information in this section comes from ongoing reports published by the Bureau of the Census.

Persons per land square mile is calculated based on the 2004 population estimates and land size estimates.

Metropolitan and non-Metropolitan population data comes from the Bureau of Census, reprinted in the *Statistical Abstract*. The metropolitan area population consists of all persons living in Metropolitan Areas (MAs) in the state. An MA is defined by the Bureau of the Census by fairly complicated criteria, but basically consists of a large population nucleus, together with adjacent communities which have a high degree of economic and social integration with that nucleus. Each MA must include at least: (a) one place with 50,000 or more inhabitants, or (b) a Census Bureau-defined urbanized area and a total MA population of at least 100,000 (75,000 in New England). Non-metropolitan area population is everyone not included in metropolitan area population of the state.

Change in population was calculated from Bureau of the Census data.

Introduction

Racial statistics are provided, although they are a highly sensitive subject. It is important to recognize that the breakdown represents the self-identification of respondents in regard to pre-set census categories. It does not in any way denote any scientific of biological notion of race. Hispanic origin is not racial group as defined by the Bureau, and persons may be of any race and be of Hispanic origin as well.

A household is defined as the person or persons occupying a housing unit. A housing unit is defined below, under "Housing & Construction." Briefly, a housing unit is a separate set of living quarters such as a house, apartment, mobile home, etc. A family is a type of household and consists of a householder and one or more other persons living in the same household who are related to the householder by birth, marriage, or adoption. Married couples, and female heads of household with dependent children and no husband present, are subgroups, or types of families.

Population and age distribution projections are from the Bureau of the Census' World Wide Web site, www.census.gov.

Immigration and naturalization data is from the *Yearbook of Immigration Statistics*, a publication of the US Immigration and Naturalization Service.

Vital Statistics & Health

Birth, death, infant death, marriage, and divorce data comes from the *National Vital Statistics Reports*, publications of the Department of Health & Human Services.

Abortion information comes from *Family Planning Perspectives*, published by the Alan Guttmacher Institute, and is reprinted in *Statistical Abstract*.

Data for physicians are counts of active, non-federally employed practitioners. Physicians exclude doctors of osteopathy. This information comes from the Health Resources and Services Administration, Department of Health and Human Services, reprinted in *Statistical Abstract*. Information on nurses is from the U.S. Department of Health and Human Services, Health Resources and Services Administration and appears in *Statistical Abstract* .

Hospital data comes from *Statistical Abstract*. Data reflects American Hospital Association member hospitals only. The average daily census refers to the average total number of inpatients receiving treatment each day, excluding newborns.

Information on disability status of the population comes from the Bureau of Census. Data covers the civilian non-institutionalized population.

Education

Educational attainment data comes from the U.S. Bureau of the Census.

Most of the other education data is from *Digest of Education Statistics 2004*, compiled by the National Center for Educational Statistics, U.S. Department of Education.

Finance data and public school teacher data is from *Statistical Abstract*. Information on state and local financial support for higher education also comes from *Statistical Abstract*.

Information for Scholastic Aptitude Tests (SAT) scores and percentage of high school graduates who take the test is from www.collegeboard.com.

Social Insurance & Welfare Programs

All items here have been obtained from *Statistical Abstract* and its supplements. It should be noted that detail is provided for three major Social Security programs: those for the retired; for the survivors of enrollees; and for the disabled covered under the program. The original source of Social Security information is the Social Security Administration's *Bulletin* and the *Bulletin's Annual Statistical Supplement*. Medicare and Medicaid data are produced by the U.S. Centers for Medicare and Medicaid Services and are also from *Statistical Abstract*.

Information on persons without health insurance is originated from *Current Population Reports* by the U.S. Census Bureau. Data appears in *Statistical Abstract* .

Housing & Construction

The Bureau of the Census conducts a decennial Census of Housing which is almost as extensive as its Census of Population. The selection of housing information here, taken from the 2000 Census of Housing, represents just a small portion of what is available.

The Bureau defines some key terms as follows: a housing unit is a house, apartment, mobile home or trailer, group of rooms, or single room occupied as separate living quarter or, if vacant, intended as a separate living quarter. Separate living quarters are those in which occupants live and eat separately from any other persons in the building and which have direct access from the outside of the building or from a common hall.

Data for new privately owned housing units and existing home sales comes from *Statistical Abstract*.

Introduction

Government and Elections

Names of State officials and current party in majority have been obtained from web sites for the National Governors Association, the National Lieutenant Governors Association, the National Association of Secretaries of State, the National Association of Attorneys General, the Conference of Chief Justices, and the National Conference of State Legislatures.

Information about the governorship and legislative structure of each state was obtained from respective legislative manuals and annual election reports.

Information on state and local employees is from the Federal, State and Local Government section, *Local Government Employment and Payroll, 2004*, and *State Government Employment and Payroll, 2004,* published by the Bureau of the Census. Figures represent March, 2004, full time equivalent employees, along with March payroll data.

Information on local governments comes from the 2002 *Census of Governments* (conducted by the Bureau of the Census). Readers are cautioned that the data provided concerns governmental units as opposed to geographic entities. For example, in Connecticut there are eight counties, but no county governments, hence a zero appears in the county space in the Connecticut profile.

Voting age population information comes from *Current Population Reports*, published by the U.S. Census Bureau of the Census. Vote for president is from the Federal Election Commission.

Information on women holding public offices comes from press releases provided by the Center for American Women and Politics at the Eagleton Institute of Rutgers University, and is reprinted with permission.

Data concerning black elected officials are from the Joint Center for Political & Economic Studies, Washington, DC, reprinted in *Statistical Abstract*.

Hispanic public officials information is from the National Association of Latino Elected and Appointed Officials, Washington, DC, reprinted in *Statistical Abstract*.

Names of Senators come from the federal web site, www.senate.gov, and the number of Representatives by party comes from clerkweb.house.gov.

Governmental Finance

Revenue, expenditure and debt information comes from the Federal, State and Local Government section, *2004 State Government Finance Data*. Federal government grants information comes from the Federal, State and Local Governments section, *2004 Consolidated Federal Funds Report*. Both are publications of the U.S. Census Bureau and are available on their web site, www.census.gov.

Introduction

Crime, Law Enforcement & Courts

Information on crime, crime rates, police agencies, and arrests comes from *Crime in the United States, 2004*, published by the Federal Bureau of Investigation (FBI), Uniform Crime Reports. Information on number of persons under sentence of death comes from *Sourcebook of Criminal Justice Statistics, 2003* with on-going updates.

Information on prisoners comes from *Prisoners in 2004*. These sources are publications of the U.S. Department of Justice. Readers are cautioned that crime information is based on crimes known to police.

State court information comes from the legislative manuals of the respective states.

Labor & Income

Most of the civilian labor force data comes from *Geographic Profiles of Employment and Unemployment*, published by the Department of Labor, Bureau of Labor Statistics.

The civilian labor force includes all civilians who are either employed or unemployed.

Generally, employed persons are those who: 1) did any work as a paid employee; or 2) worked 15 hours or more as an unpaid employee in a family enterprise; or 3) had jobs but were not working due to illness, vacation, etc.

Unemployed persons are those who: 1) had no paid employment and were both available for and looking for work; or 2) were waiting to be recalled to a job; or 3) were waiting to report to a new job. A full-time employee is one who works at least 35 hours per week.

Unemployed persons are grouped into four categories: a job loser is someone whose employment has ended involuntarily; a job leaver is someone whose employment ended voluntarily; a reentrant is someone who has previously worked, but was out of the labor force prior to seeking employment; and a new entrant is someone who has never worked before and is now seeking employment.

Labor union membership comes from *Union Members* published in the Current Population Summary from the Bureau of Labor Statistics.

Experienced civilian labor force by occupation is from the *Occupational Employment Statistics Survey* published by Bureau of Labor Statistics.

Hours and earnings data comes from *Employment & Earnings*, published by Bureau of Labor Statistics.

Average annual pay and experienced civilian labor force by private industry come from *Employment and Wages, Annual Averages 2004*, published by the Bureau of Labor Statis-

Introduction

tics, and includes the pay of workers who are covered by state unemployment insurance laws, and federal civilian workers covered by federal unemployment. This represents approximately 89% of total civilian employment. It excludes members of the armed forces, elected officials in most states, railroad employees, most self-employed persons, and some others. Pay includes bonuses, the cash value of meals and lodging, and tips and other gratuities.

Household income and poverty information comes from *Income, Poverty, and Health Insurance Coverage in the United States: 2004*, published by the U.S. Bureau of the Census.

Personal income figures come from *Survey of Current Business*, a monthly publication of the Department of Commerce, reprinted in *Statistical Abstract*.

Federal individual income tax data is from *Individual Tax Statistics - State Income for 2002 through 2004*, by the Internal Revenue Service.

Economy, Business, Industry & Agriculture

Fortune 500 companies come from a count of listed corporations found in the annual directory issue of **Fortune**.

Information on patents issued is from U.S. Trademark Office. Bankruptcy information is from Statistical Tables for the Federal Judiciary. Data is republished in *Statistical Abstract*.

Business firm ownership is from the *2002 Survey of Business Owners (SBO)*, published by Bureau of the Census as part of the 2002 Economic Census.

Gross state product is taken from *Survey of Current Business*, a publication of the Department of Commerce, Bureau of Economic Analysis, published on the Bureau of the Census' web site, www.census.gov. The industries represented are major categories under the North American Industry Classification System (NAICS). NAICS is replacing the U.S. SIC (Standard Industrial Classification) system. NAICS was developed jointly by the U.S., Canada, and Mexico to provide new comparability in statistics about business activity across North America. For more information on NAICS and to understand the correspondence between NAICS and SIC, please visit the U.S. Bureau of the Census web site, www.census.gov, and search for NAICS.

Establishment and payroll data are from the 2003 edition of *County Business Patterns*, a 52 volume report issued annually by the Bureau of the Census.

Agricultural data comes from the Department of Agriculture, and is republished in *Statistical Abstract*.

Data on federal economic activity comes from *Consolidated Federal Funds Report, 2003*, and reprinted in *Statistical Abstract*.

Department of Defense information comes from *Atlas/Data Abstract for the United States and Selected Areas*, published by the department and was reprinted in *Statistical Abstract*.

Homeland security information comes from the Department of Homeland Security, State and Local Government Coordination and Preparedness, Office for Domestic Preparedness, and reprinted in *Statistical Abstract*.

FDIC Insured data comes from U.S. Federal Deposit Insurance Corporation, *Statistics on Banking*, and reprinted in *Statistical Abstract*.

Fishing data are from *Fisheries of the United States, 2004*, a publication of the National Oceanic and Atmospheric Administration (NOAA).

Mining information is from the U.S. Bureau of Mines; construction information is from *Statistical Abstract*.

Establishments, receipts, annual payroll and paid employee data come from the 2002 Economic Census, following NAICS classifications.

Communication, Energy & Transportation

The count of daily newspapers and percentages of households with telephones, computers and internet access are from *Statistical Abstract*.

All energy information comes from *State Energy Data Report*, and *Electric Power Annual*, both published by the U.S. Energy Information Administration and American Gas Association Gas Facts and reprinted from *Statistical Abstract*.

All transportation information comes from *Highway Statistics, 2004*, an annual publication of the Department of Transportation.

Alabama   1

State Summary

Capital City. . . . . .Montgomery
Governor. . . . . .Bob Riley
State Capitol
600 Dexter Ave
Montgomery, AL 36130
334-242-7100
Admitted as a state 1819
Area (square miles). 52,419
Population, 2004 (est.) 4,530,182
Largest City. .Birmingham
Population, 2004. 233,000
Personal income per capita, 2004
(in current dollars) $27,795
Gross state product ($ mil), 2004 . . . . . $139,840

Leading industries by payroll, 2003

Manufacturing, Health care/Social assistance, Retail trade

Leading agricultural commodities by receipts, 2003

Broilers, cattle, chicken eggs, greenhouse

Geography & Environment

Total area (sq. mi.). 52,419
land 50,744
water 1,675
Federally-owned land, 2004 (acres) 513,913
percent. 1.6%
Highest point. . . . . Cheaha Mountain
elevation (feet) 2,405
Lowest point . . . . Gulf of Mexico
elevation (feet) . . . . sea level
General coastline (miles). 53
Tidal shoreline (miles). 607
Capital City. .Montgomery
Population 2000 202,000
Population 2004 201,000
Largest City. .Birmingham
Population 2000 243,000
Population 2004 233,000

Number of cities with over 100,000 population

1990 4
2000 4
2004 4

State park and recreation areas, 2003

Area (acres x 1,000). 50
Number of visitors (x 1,000) 4,871
Revenues (x 1,000). $23,897
percent of operating expenditures. 74.7%

National forest system land, 2004

Acres 667,000

Demographics and Characteristics of the Population

Population

1980 3,893,800
1990 4,040,587
2000 4,447,100
2004 (estimate). 4,530,182
persons per sq. mile of land. 89.3
2005 (projection). 4,527,166
Male. 2,186,827
Female. 2,340,339
2010 (projection) 4,596,330
2020 (projection) 4,728,915
2030 (projection) 4,874,243
Male. 2,355,520
Female. 2,518,723

Metropolitan and Non-Metro. area population

	Metro	Non-Metro
1980	2,462,000	1,432,000
1990	2,723,000	1,317,000
2000	3,109,000	1,338,000

Change in population, 2000-2004

Number. 82,831
percent. 1.9%
Natural increase (births minus deaths). . . 62,846
Net internal migration . . . . -703
Net international migration 21,712

Persons by age, 2004

Under 5 years 296,100
18 years and over 3,435,649
65 years and over 597,959
85 years and over 66,170

Persons by age, 2010 (projected)

Total. 4,596,330
Under 5 years 298,302
5 to 17 years 793,882
18 and over 3,504,146
21 and over 3,313,109
65 and over 648,889
85 and over 88,211
Median age 38.5

Race, 2004 (estimate)

One Race
White. 3,234,762
Black or African American 1,194,396
American Indian/Alaska Native. 23,095
Pacific Islander 1,712
Asian Indian. 4,551
Chinese 5,210
Filipino 1,929
Japanese 2,448
Korean. 5,225
Vietnamese. 13,090
Two or more races. 39,419

Persons of Hispanic origin, 2004

Total Hispanic or Latino	86,116
Mexican	66,798
Puerto Rican	5,096
Cuban	1,301
Other Hispanic or Latino	7,121

Marital status, 2000

Population 15 years & over	3,514,199
Never married	839,894
Married	1,950,380
Separated	77,312
Widowed	274,108
Divorced	372,505

Language spoken at home, 2000

Population 5 years & over	4,152,278
English only	3,989,795
Spanish	89,729
Other Indo-European languages	43,812
Asian/Pacific Island languages	22,122

Households & families, 2000

Households	1,737,080
with persons under 18 years	626,857
with persons over 65 years	418,608
persons per household	2.49
Families	1,215,968
persons per family	3.01
Married couples	906,916
Female householder, no husband present	246,466
One-person households	453,898

Nativity, 2000

Number of persons born in state	3,262,053
percent of population	73.4%

Immigration & Naturalization, 2004

Immigrants admitted	2,139
Persons naturalized	734
Asylums granted	23
Asylums denied	3

Vital Statistics and Health

Marriages

2002	44,158
2003	43,139
2004	42,536

Divorces

2002	24,059
2003	23,205
2004	22,405

Births

2003	59,552
Birthrate (per 1,000)	13.2
Low birth weight (2,500g or less)	10.0%
To unmarried mothers	35.0%

2003, continued

White	40,912
Black	17,959
Hispanic	2,907
Asian/Pacific Islander	606
Amer. Indian/Alaska Native	144
2004 (preliminary)	59,549
Birthrate (per 1,000)	13.1
White	40,550
Black	18,057
Hispanic	3,346
Asian/Pacific Islander	762

Deaths

2002

All causes	46,069
rate per 100,000	1,026.8
Heart disease	13,197
rate per 100,000	294.1
Malignant neoplasms	9,698
rate per 100,000	216.2
Cerebrovascular disease	3,201
rate per 100,000	71.3
Chronic lower respiratory disease	2,328
rate per 100,000	51.9
2003	46,726
rate per 100,000	1,038.2
2004 (provisional)	45,986

Infant deaths

2003 (provisional)	502
rate per 1,000	8.5
2004 (provisional)	507
rate per 1,000	8.6

Abortions, 2000

Total	14,000
rate per 1,000 women age 15-44	14.3

Physicians, 2003

Total	9,547
rate per 1,000 persons	212

Nurses, 2001

Total	36,400
rate per 1,000 persons	814

Community Hospitals, 2003

Number	107
Beds (x 1,000)	15.6
Patients admitted (x 1,000)	709
Average daily census (x 1,000)	9.7
Average cost per day	$1,166
Outpatient visits (x mil)	8.9

Disability status of population, 2004

5 to 20 years	7.8%
21 to 64 years	16.8%
65 years and over	46%

Education

Educational attainment, 2004

Population over 25 years 2,906,811
Less than 9th grade 175,932
High school graduates only.......... 884,667
Bachelor's degree only 398,768
Graduate or professional degree..... 236,379
Less than 9th grade percent 6.1%
High school graduate or more 82.4%
College graduate or more............. 22.3%
Graduate or professional degree........ 8.1%

Public school enrollment, Fall 2002

Total.............................. 739,678
Kindergarten through grade 8 533,519
Grades 9 through 12 206,159
Enrollment, 2005 (projected) 725,000

Graduating public high school seniors

2004 (estimate)....................... 37,610

SAT scores, 2005

Average verbal score 567
Average math score 559
Percent of graduates taking test 10%

Public school teachers, 2004

Total (x 1,000) 45.9
Elementary (x 1,000)................... 28.0
Secondary (x 1,000) 20.5
Average salary $38,300
Elementary....................... $37,900
Secondary....................... $38,700

State receipts & expenditures for public schools, 2004

Revenue receipts ($mil)................. $5,328
Expenditures
Total ($mil)......................... $5,499
Per capita $1,221
Per pupil $6,953

Institutions of higher education, 2004

Total.................................... 75
Public................................ 46
Private............................... 29

Enrollment in institutions of higher education, Fall, 2003

Total............................. 255,183
Full-time men 73,432
Full-time women 98,297
Part-time men 32,253
Part-time women................... 51,201

Minority enrollment in institutions of higher education, Fall, 2003

Black, non-hispanic................... 71,208
Hispanic 3,047
Asian/Pacific Islander 3,222
American Indian/Alaska Native.......... 1,876

Earned degrees conferred, 2003

Bachelor's 20,479
Master's............................. 8,441
First-professional..................... 1,019
Doctor's............................. 586

State & local financial support for higher education, 2003-2004

Full-time equivalent enrollment (x 1,000) ..183.3
Appropriations per FTE............... $4,693
as a percent of tax revenue............ 12.0%

Social Insurance & Welfare Programs

Social Security benefits & beneficiaries, 2004

Beneficiaries
Total............................. 884,000
Retired & dependents............... 536,000
Survivors.......................... 142,000
Disabled & dependents............. 207,000
Annual benefit payments ($ mil)
Total............................. $8,697
Retired & dependents............... $5,062
Survivors.......................... $1,686
Disabled & dependents............. $1,949
Average Monthly Benefit
Retired & dependents................. $912
Disabled & dependents............. $866
Widowed......................... $850

Medicare

Enrollment, 2001 (x 1,000) 695
Payments ($ mil, est.) $4,300
Enrollment, 2003 (x 1,000) 719

Medicaid, 2002

Beneficiaries (x 1,000)................... 765
Payments ($ mil) $3,204

State Children's Health Insurance, 2004

Enrollment (x 1,000)................... 79.4
Expenditures ($ mil)................... $19.4

Persons without health insurance, 2003

Number (x 1,000)....................... 629
percent............................ 14.2%
Number of children (x 1,000) 95
percent of children 8.7%

Federal public aid

Temporary Assistance for Needy Families, 2004
Recipients (x 1,000)....................... 45
Families (x 1,000) 19

Supplemental Security Income, 2003
Recipients (x 1,000)..................... 164
Payments ($ mil) $738

Food Stamp Program, 2004

Participants (x 1,000) 498
Benefits ($ mil)......................... $513

Housing & Construction

Housing units

Total 2003 (estimate)	2,035,107
Total 2004 (estimate)	2,058,951
Seasonal or recreational use, 2003	55,000
Owner-occupied single-family, 2003	947,000
Median value	$96,106
Renter-occupied, 2003	484,000
Median rent	$498
Homeownership rate, 2003	76.2%
Homeownership rate, 2004	78.0%

New privately owned housing units, 2004

Number authorized (x 1,000)	27.4
Value ($ mil)	$3,293
Started 2005 (x 1,000, estimate)	20.9
Started 2006 (x 1,000, estimate)	21.1

Existing home sales

2002 (x 1,000)	82.2
2003 (x 1,000)	93.7
2004 (x 1,000)	112.0

Government & Elections

State Officials 2006

Governor (name/party/term expires)
Bob Riley
Republican - 1/07

Lieutenant Governor	Lucy Baxley
Secretary of State	Nancy Worley
Attorney General	Troy King
Chief Justice	Drayton Nabers Jr.

Governorship

Minimum age	30
Length of term	4 years
Consecutive terms permitted	2
Who succeeds	Lt. Governor

State Legislature

Name	Legislature
Upper chamber	Senate
Number of members	35
Length of term	4 years
Party in majority, 2006	Democratic
Lower chamber	House of Representatives
Number of members	105
Length of term	4 years
Party in majority, 2006	Democratic

State Government Employees, 2004

Total	85,647
Payroll	$284,979,309

Local Government Employees, 2004

Total	184,985
Payroll	$500,141,038

Local Governments by Type, 2002

Total	1,171
County	67
Municipal	451
Township	0
School District	128
Special District	525

Voting age population, November 2004

Total	3,332,000
Male	1,568,000
Female	1,764,000
White	2,450,000
Black	799,000
Hispanic	39,000
Asian	40,000

Presidential Election, 2004

Total Popular Vote	1,883,449
Kerry	693,933
Bush	1,176,394
Total Electoral Votes	9

Federal representation, 2006 (109th Congress)

Senator	Jeff Sessions
Party	Republican
Year term expires	2009
Senator	Richard Shelby
Party	Republican
Year term expires	2011
Representatives, total	7
Democrats	2
Republicans	5
Other	0

Votes cast for US Senators

2002

Total vote (x 1,000)	1,353,000
Leading party	Republican
Percent for leading party	58.6%

2004

Total vote (x 1,000)	1,839,000
Leading party	Republican
Percent for leading party	67.5%

Votes cast for US Representatives

2002

Total vote (x 1,000)	1,269
Democratic	507
Republican	695
Leading party	Republican
Percent for leading party	54.7%

2004

Total vote (x 1,000)	1,793
Democratic	708
Republican	1,080
Leading party	Republican
Percent for leading party	60.2%

Women holding public office, 2006

US Congress 0
Statewide elected office..................... 5
State legislature 14

Black public officials, 2001

Total.................................... 756
  US and state legislatures 36
  City/county/regional offices 569
  Judicial/law enforcement................. 57
  Education/school boards................. 94

Hispanic public officials, 2004

Total..................................... 0
  State executives & legislators 0
  City/county/regional offices 0
  Judicial/law enforcement.................. 0
  Education/school boards.................. 0

Governmental Finance

State government revenues, 2004

Total revenue ($1,000) $21,568,441
  Revenue per capita 4,766.51

General Revenue ($ per capita)....... $3,893.06
  Intergovernmental 1,518.53
  Taxes 1,550.99
    general sales 418.25
    individual income tax..............495.81
    corporate income tax 64.54
  Current charges.................... 589.59
  Miscellaneous 233.95

State government expenditure, 2004

Total expenditure (x $1,000) $19,544,560
  Expenditure per capita............. 4,319.24
General Expenditure ($ per capita).... $3,894.30
  Education 1,683.36
  Public welfare..................... 1,009.58
  Health 180.03
  Hospitals......................... 243.21
  Highways 265.10
  Police protection 28.78
  Correction 87.94
  Natural resources 52.51
  Parks & recreation.....................5.09
  Governmental administration 95.83
  Interest on general debt 52.25

State debt & cash, 2004 ($ per capita)

Debt $1,406.38
Cash/security holdings.............. $6,628.09

Federal government grants to state & local government, 2004 (x $1,000)

Total............................$7,007,819

By Federal Agency
  Defense $69,772

By Federal Agency, continued
  Education 618,145
  Energy 34,795
  Environmental Protection Agency 52,581
  Health & Human Services. 3,842,686
  Homeland Security................. 196,475
  Housing & Urban Development...... 391,143
  Justice 97,762
  Labor 122,708
  Transportation 887,492
  Veterans Affairs.................... 13,231

Crime, Law Enforcement & Courts

Crime, 2004 (rates per 100,000 residents)

Property crimes 182,340
  Burglaries......................... 44,666
  Larcenies......................... 123,650
  Motor vehicle thefts 14,024
  Property crime rate................. 4,025.0
Violent crimes....................... 19,324
  Murders........................... 254
  Forcible rape....................... 1,742
  Robberies 6,042
  Aggravated assaults 11,286
  Violent crime rate.................. 426.6

Police Agencies, 2004

Total agencies......................... 307
Total employees 14,476
  Male officers...................... 8,804
  Female officers...................... 668
  Male civilians...................... 1,872
  Female civilians.................... 3,132

Arrests, 2004

Total............................. 208,312
  Persons under 18 years of age 13,596

Prisoners under state & federal jurisdiction, 2004

Total prisoners...................... 25,887
  Percent change, 12/31/03 to 12/31/04 ....-7.3%
Sentenced to more than one year 25,257
  rate per 100,000...................... 556

Persons under sentence of death, 7/1/05

Total............................... 191
  White............................. 97
  Black 92
  Hispanic 2

State's highest court

Name ....Supreme Court
Number of members....................... 9
Length of term .... 6 years
Intermediate appeals court? ....yes

Labor & Income

Civilian labor force, 2004

Total............................ 2,179,000
  Men 1,156,000
  Women 1,023,000
  Persons 16-19 years............... 106,000
  White........................... 1,595,000
  Black 511,000
  Hispanic 50,000
  Asian 0

Civilian labor force as a percent of civilian non-institutional population, 2004

Total................................. 62.5%
  Men 70.0
  Women 55.8
  Persons 16-19 years.................. 39.8
  White................................ 63.4
  Black 60.0
  Hispanic 87.1
  Asian 0.0

Employment, 2004

Total............................ 2,053,000
  Men 1,096,000
  Women 957,000
  Persons 16-19 years................ 89,000
  White........................... 1,535,000
  Black 449,000
  Hispanic 48,000
  Asian 0

Full-time/part-time labor force, 2002

Full-time labor force, employed 1,705,000
Part-time labor force, employed........ 274,000
Unemployed, looking for
  Full-time work..................... 108,000
  Part-time work......................... NA

Unemployment rate, 2004

Total.................................. 5.8%
  Men 5.3
  Women 6.4
  Persons 16-19 years.................. 15.7
  White................................. 3.8
  Black 12.2
  Hispanic 3.7
  Asian .... NA

Unemployed by reason for unemployment (as a percent of total unemployment), 2002

Job losers or completed temp jobs 54.0%
Job leavers.............................. NA
Reentrants............................. NA
New entrants .... NA

Labor unions, 2004

Membership 181,000
  percent of employed 9.7%

Experienced civilian labor force by private industry, first quarter 2004

Total............................ 1,491,717
  Natural Resources & Mining 21,322
  Construction 102,921
  Manufacturing..................... 287,632
  Trade, transportation & utilities 370,738
  Information 31,317
  Finance 94,977
  Professional & business 191,264
  Education & Health 186,285
  Leisure & hospitality................ 157,127
  Other............................. 48,131

Experienced civilian labor force by occupation, 2004

Management......................... 79,070
Business & Financial.................. 56,530
Legal................................ 10,840
Sales............................... 196,150
Office & Admin. Support.............. 297,520
Computers & Math 30,770
Architecture & Engineering 36,910
Arts & Entertainment................. 16,550
Education .... NA
Social Services 16,590
Healthcare Practitioner & Technical.... 104,130
Healthcare support................... 45,040
Maintenance & Repair 92,920
Construction 100,670
Transportation & moving 160,380
Production 212,160
Farming, fishing & forestry............. 6,880

Hours and earnings of production workers on manufacturing payrolls, 2004

Average weekly hours 40.8
Average hourly earnings $14.33
Average weekly earnings $584.66

Average annual pay

2004 .... $33,414
  change from 2003 .... 3.7%

Household income

Median household income, three-year average, 2002-2004........................ $38,111

Personal income, 2004 ($ per capita)

In current dollars.................... $27,795
In constant (2000) dollars $25,778

Poverty

Persons below poverty level, three-year average, 2002-2004........................... 15.5%

Federal individual income tax returns, 2003

Returns filed...................... 1,883,765
Adjusted gross income ($1,000) $74,842,665
Total income tax paid ($1,000) $8,396,882

Economy, Business, Industry & Agriculture

Fortune 500 companies, 2005 2

Patents issued, 2004 412

Bankruptcy cases filed, 2004 42,400

Business firm ownership, 2002

Women-owned. 81,820
   Sales ($ mil) $11,426
Black-owned. 28,684
   Sales ($ mil) $1,749
Hispanic-owned. 2,524
   Sales ($ mil) $756
Asian-owned 4,275
   Sales ($ mil) $1,560
Amer. Indian/Alaska Native-owned 2,908
   Sales ($ mil) $470
Hawaiian/Pacific Isl.-owned 101
   Sales ($ mil) $5

Gross State Product, 2004 ($ mil)

Total Gross State Product $139,840
   Agriculture, forestry, fishing and
      hunting 2,391
   Mining. 1,275
   Utilities 4,224
   Construction 6,249
   Manufacturing, durable goods. 13,528
   Manufacturing, non-durable goods 9,890
   Wholesale trade. 7,961
   Retail trade. 11,528
   Transportation & warehousing 3,977
   Information 4,194
   Finance & insurance. 7,814
   Real estate, rental, leasing 14,362
   Professional and technical services 8,103
   Educational services. 643
   Health care and social assistance. 9,668
   Accommodation/food services. 3,169
   Other services, except government 3,583
   Government 22,543

Establishments, by major industry group, 2003

Total. 99,838
   Forestry, fishing & agriculture 1,063
   Mining. 274
   Construction 9,360
   Manufacturing. 4,980
   Wholesale trade. 5,651
   Retail trade. 19,455
   Transportation & warehousing 3,039
   Information 1,733
   Finance & insurance. 6,330
   Professional/scientific/technical 8,799
   Health care/social assistance 9,493
   Accommodation/food services. 7,178

Annual payroll by major industry group, 2003

Total ($1,000) $47,070,000
   Forestry, fishing & agriculture 205,960
   Mining. 372,045
   Utilities 1,012,597
   Construction 3,067,191
   Manufacturing. 9,723,614
   Wholesale trade. 2,784,545
   Retail trade. 4,478,781
   Transportation & warehousing 1,615,132
   Information 1,639,136
   Finance & insurance. 3,324,450
   Professional/scientific/technical . . . 4,018,506
   Health care/social assistance 7,205,784
   Accommodation/food services. 1,433,874

Agriculture

Number of farms, 2004 44,000
Farm acreage, 2004
   Total. 9,000,000
   Acres per farm, 2004 198
Farm income, 2003 ($mil)
   Net farm income $1,604
   Debt/asset ratio .12.5
Farm marketings, 2003 ($mil)
   Total. $3,415
   Crops. 676
   Livestock. 2,739

Principal commodities, in order by marketing receipts, 2003

   Broilers, cattle, chicken eggs, greenhouse

Federal economic activity in state

Expenditures, 2003
   Total ($ mil) $36,871
   Per capita $8,192
   Defense ($ mil). 7,907
   Non-defense ($ mil) 28,964
Defense department, 2003
   Payroll ($ mil) $2,764
   Contract awards ($ mil). $6,281
   Grants ($ mil). $37
   Homeland security grants ($1,000)
      2004 . . . . $38,723
      2005 . . . . $28,153

FDIC insured financial institutions, 2004

Number 164
   Assets ($bil) $237.3
   Deposits ($bil) 62.6

Fishing, 2004

Catch (x 1,000 lbs) 26,559
Value ($1,000). $37,036

Mining, 2004 ($ mil)

Total non-fuel mineral production $982
Percent of U.S. 2.2%

Construction, 2003 ($ mil)

Total contracts (including non-building). $7,522
    residential........................... 3,231
    non-residential 2,322

Establishments, receipts, payroll & employees, by major industry group, 2002

Mining 282
    Receipts ($1,000) $2,615,060
    Annual payroll ($1,000)........... $346,791
    Paid employees 7,508

Utilities 503
    Receipts ($1,000) .... NA
    Annual payroll ($1,000)........... $948,747
    Paid employees 16,014

Construction........................... 9,345
    Receipts ($1,000) $15,582,292
    Annual payroll ($1,000)......... $2,992,730
    Paid employees 98,555

Manufacturing 5,119
    Receipts ($1,000) $66,686,220
    Annual payroll ($1,000)......... $9,744,347
    Paid employees 284,127

Wholesale trade 5,747
    Receipts ($1,000) $43,641,369
    Annual payroll ($1,000)......... $2,661,974
    Paid employees 74,915

Retail trade 19,608
    Receipts ($1,000) $43,784,342
    Annual payroll ($1,000)......... $4,094,026
    Paid employees 222,416

Transportation....................... 3,048
    Receipts ($1,000) $4,794,369
    Annual payroll ($1,000)......... $1,554,467
    Paid employees 51,940

Information........................... 1,683
    Receipts ($1,000) .... NA
    Annual payroll ($1,000)......... $1,525,854
    Paid employees 40,020

Finance & insurance 6,143
    Receipts ($1,000) .... NA
    Annual payroll ($1,000)......... $3,255,448
    Paid employees 74,238

Professional, scientific & technical 8,679
    Receipts ($1,000) $8,757,629
    Annual payroll ($1,000)......... $3,602,849
    Paid employees 81,275

Health care & social assistance 9,355
    Receipts ($1,000) $16,594,961
    Annual payroll ($1,000).......... $6,660,827
    Paid employees 213,135

Accommodation & food service........... 7,075
    Receipts ($1,000) $4,692,297
    Annual payroll ($1,000).......... $1,321,326
    Paid employees 128,327

Communication, Energy & Transportation

Communication

Daily newspapers, 2004 24
Households with computers, 2003 .... 54%
Households with internet access, 2003 ..... 46%

Energy

Electricity Consumption, 2001
    Total (trillion Btu)..................... 1,943
    Per capita (million Btu) 435
By source of production (trillion Btu)
    Coal 846
    Natural gas 342
    Petroleum............................. 540
    Nuclear electric power 317
    Hydroelectric power.................... 85
By end-use sector (trillion Btu)
    Residential 380
    Commercial 254
    Industrial 863
    Transportation 446
Electric energy, 2003
    Production (billion kWh) 137.5
    Net summer capability (million kW) 30.2
Gas utilities, 2003
    Customers (x1,000).................... 877
    Sales (trillion Btu).................... 105
    Revenues ($mil)....................... $988
Nuclear plants, 2003 5

Transportation, 2004

Public Road & Street Mileage 95,483
    Urban................................ 21,521
    Rural 73,962
    Interstate............................. 904
Vehicle miles of travel per capita 12,926.4
Total motor vehicle registrations...... 4,507,751
    Automobiles...................... 1,693,741
    Buses 9,088
    Trucks 2,804,922
    Motorcycles 81,086
Licensed drivers 3,613,138
    19 years & under 212,749
Deaths from motor vehicle accidents 1,154

State Summary

Capital City......................... Juneau
Governor.................. Frank Murkowski
PO Box 110001
Juneau, AK 99811
907-465-3500
Admitted as a state 1959
Area (square miles).................. 663,267
Population, 2004 (est.) 655,435
Largest City........................Anchorage
Population, 2004................... 273,000
Personal income per capita, 2004
(in current dollars) $34,454
Gross state product ($ mil), 2004 ...... $34,023

Leading industries by payroll, 2003

Health care/Social assistance, Construction,
Transportation & Warehousing

Leading agricultural commodities by receipts, 2003

Greenhouse, hay, dairy products, potatoes

Geography & Environment

Total area (sq. mi.).................... 663,267
land 571,951
water 91,316

Federally-owned land, 2004 (acres) . 252,495,811
percent............................. 69.1%

Highest point....................Mt. McKinley
elevation (feet) 20,320

Lowest point .... Pacific Ocean
elevation (feet) .... sea level

General coastline (miles)................ 6,568

Tidal shoreline (miles)................... 33,904

Capital City..........................Juneau
Population 2000 30,711
Population 2004 31,118

Largest City......................Anchorage
Population 2000 260,000
Population 2004 273,000

Number of cities with over 100,000 population

1990 1
2000 1
2004 1

State park and recreation areas, 2003

Area (acres x 1,000).................... 3,353
Number of visitors (x 1,000) 4,301
Revenues (x 1,000)..................... $1,478
percent of operating expenditures...... 25.4%

National forest system land, 2004

Acres 21,974,000

Demographics and Characteristics of the Population

Population

1980 401,851
1990 550,043
2000 626,932
2004 (estimate)...................... 655,435
persons per sq. mile of land............. 1.1
2005 (projection).................... 661,110
Male............................. 339,795
Female........................... 321,315
2010 (projection) 694,109
2020 (projection) 774,421
2030 (projection).................... 867,674
Male............................. 430,989
Female........................... 436,685

Metropolitan and Non-Metro. area population

	Metro	Non-Metro
1980	174,000	227,000
1990	226,000	324,000
2000	260,000	367,000

Change in population, 2000-2004

Number 28,504
percent............................. 4.5%
Natural increase (births minus deaths)... 28,769
Net internal migration .... -4,481
Net international migration 4,512

Persons by age, 2004

Under 5 years 49,758
18 years and over 467,206
65 years and over 41,887
85 years and over 3,502

Persons by age, 2010 (projected)

Total............................. 694,109
Under 5 years 58,380
5 to 17 years 125,603
18 and over 510,126
21 and over 477,104
65 and over 56,548
85 and over 5,690
Median age 32.5

Race, 2004 (estimate)

One Race
White 463,616
Black or African American 23,842
American Indian/Alaska Native....... 103,617
Pacific Islander 3,768
Asian Indian......................... 433
Chinese 1,338
Filipino 12,649
Japanese 2,467
Korean 3,910
Vietnamese......................... 228
Two or more races..................... 30,809

Persons of Hispanic origin, 2004

Total Hispanic or Latino 30,293
   Mexican............................ 17,142
   Puerto Rican 3,630
   Cuban 1,356
   Other Hispanic or Latino 3,950

Marital status, 2000

Population 15 years & over 468,861
   Never married 133,157
   Married........................... 255,529
   Separated 9,377
   Widowed........................... 15,941
   Divorced 54,857

Language spoken at home, 2000

Population 5 years & over 579,740
   English only 496,982
   Spanish 16,674
   Other Indo-European languages 12,851
   Asian/Pacific Island languages....... 22,186

Households & families, 2000

Households......................... 221,600
   with persons under 18 years 95,129
   with persons over 65 years........... 26,349
   persons per household 2.74
Families........................... 152,337
   persons per family....................3.28
Married couples..................... 116,318
Female householder,
   no husband present................. 23,937
One-person households 52,060

Nativity, 2000

Number of persons born in state 238,613
   percent of population................. 38.1%

Immigration & Naturalization, 2004

Immigrants admitted.................. 1,219
Persons naturalized 777
Asylums granted 23
Asylums denied 3

Vital Statistics and Health

Marriages

2002 5,327
2003 5,237
2004 5,594

Divorces

2002 2,957
2003 2,498
2004 2,829

Births

2003 10,086
   Birthrate (per 1,000)..................15.5
   Low birth weight (2,500g or less)....... 6.0%
   To unmarried mothers................34.6%

2003, continued
   White............................. 6,491
   Black............................... 406
   Hispanic 776
   Asian/Pacific Islander 717
   Amer. Indian/Alaska Native 2,508
2004 (preliminary).................... 10,338
   Birthrate (per 1,000)..................15.8
   White............................. 6,588
   Black............................... 397
   Hispanic 877
   Asian/Pacific Islander 765

Deaths

2002
All causes 3,030
   rate per 100,000.....................470.7
Heart disease 567
   rate per 100,000......................88.1
Malignant neoplasms 715
   rate per 100,000.....................111.1
Cerebrovascular disease.................. 158
   rate per 100,000......................24.5
Chronic lower respiratory disease 142
   rate per 100,000......................22.1
2003 3,185
   rate per 100,000.....................490.9
2004 (provisional) 3,055

Infant deaths

2003 (provisional) 67
   rate per 1,000 ....6.7
2004 (provisional) 65
   rate per 1,000 ....6.3

Abortions, 2000

Total................................. 2,000
   rate per 1,000 women age 15-44..........11.7

Physicians, 2003

Total................................. 1,439
   rate per 1,000 persons.................. 222

Nurses, 2001

Total................................. 4,930
   rate per 1,000 persons................. 778

Community Hospitals, 2003

Number............................... 19
Beds (x 1,000)..........................1.5
Patients admitted (x 1,000) 46
Average daily census (x 1,000) 0.8
Average cost per day $1,952
Outpatient visits (x mil)...................1.4

Disability status of population, 2004

5 to 20 years 8.7%
21 to 64 years 14.2%
65 years and over 47.7%

Education

Educational attainment, 2004

Population over 25 years 381,642
  Less than 9th grade 11,552
  High school graduates only......... 108,482
  Bachelor's degree only 68,615
  Graduate or professional degree...... 35,256
  Less than 9th grade percent 3.0%
  High school graduate or more 90.2%
  College graduate or more............. 25.5%
  Graduate or professional degree........ 9.2%

Public school enrollment, Fall 2002

Total............................... 134,364
  Kindergarten through grade 8 94,380
  Grades 9 through 12 39,984
Enrollment, 2005 (projected) 133,200

Graduating public high school seniors

2004 (estimate)........................ 7,100

SAT scores, 2005

Average verbal score 523
Average math score 519
Percent of graduates taking test 52%

Public school teachers, 2004

Total (x 1,000) 7.8
  Elementary (x 1,000)...................5.1
  Secondary (x 1,000) 2.7
Average salary $51,700
  Elementary $51,500
  Secondary.......................... $52,200

State receipts & expenditures for public schools, 2004

Revenue receipts ($mil)................ $1,285
Expenditures
Total ($mil)........................... $1,418
  Per capita $2,187
  Per pupil $11,432

Institutions of higher education, 2004

Total................................... 8
  Public................................ 5
  Private............................... 3

Enrollment in institutions of higher education, Fall, 2003

Total............................... 31,451
  Full-time men 5,657
  Full-time women 7,364
  Part-time men 6,782
  Part-time women.................... 11,648

Minority enrollment in institutions of higher education, Fall, 2003

Black, non-hispanic.................... 1,029
Hispanic 953
Asian/Pacific Islander 1,218
American Indian/Alaska Native.......... 4,119

Earned degrees conferred, 2003

Bachelor's 1,363
Master's 506
First-professional..................... 0
Doctor's............................... 36

State & local financial support for higher education, 2003-2004

Full-time equivalent enrollment (x 1,000) ...37.6
Appropriations per FTE................ $5,269
  as a percent of tax revenue............ 10.2%

Social Insurance & Welfare Programs

Social Security benefits & beneficiaries, 2004

Beneficiaries
  Total.............................. 63,000
  Retired & dependents................ 41,000
  Survivors........................... 10,000
  Disabled & dependents 13,000
Annual benefit payments ($ mil)
  Total............................... $618
  Retired & dependents................ $388
  Survivors........................... $114
  Disabled & dependents............... $116
Average Monthly Benefit
  Retired & dependents................ $920
  Disabled & dependents............... $868
  Widowed............................ $877

Medicare

Enrollment, 2001 (x 1,000) 44
  Payments ($ mil, est.) $200
Enrollment, 2003 (x 1,000) 48

Medicaid, 2002

Beneficiaries (x 1,000)..................... 110
Payments ($ mil) $687

State Children's Health Insurance, 2004

Enrollment (x 1,000).....................18.9
Expenditures ($ mil).................... $72.8

Persons without health insurance, 2003

Number (x 1,000)....................... 122
  percent...............................18.9%
Number of children (x 1,000) 24
  percent of children 12.3%

Federal public aid

Temporary Assistance for Needy Families, 2004
Recipients (x 1,000)........................ 14
Families (x 1,000) 5

Supplemental Security Income, 2003
Recipients (x 1,000)........................ 11
Payments ($ mil) $47

Food Stamp Program, 2004

Participants (x 1,000) 49
Benefits ($ mil)........................... $64

Housing & Construction

Housing units

Total 2003 (estimate)	268,142
Total 2004 (estimate)	271,533
Seasonal or recreational use, 2003	21,000
Owner-occupied single-family, 2003	112,000
Median value	$174,146
Renter-occupied, 2003	85,000
Median rent	$780
Homeownership rate, 2003	70.0%
Homeownership rate, 2004	67.2%

New privately owned housing units, 2004

Number authorized (x 1,000)	3.1
Value ($ mil)	$540
Started 2005 (x 1,000, estimate)	2.3
Started 2006 (x 1,000, estimate)	2.3

Existing home sales

2002 (x 1,000)	17.2
2003 (x 1,000)	18.4
2004 (x 1,000)	23.0

Government & Elections

State Officials 2006

Governor (name/party/term expires)
Frank Murkowski
Republican - 12/06

Lieutenant Governor	Loren Leman
Secretary of State	(no Secty. of State)
Attorney General	David W. Marquez
Chief Justice	Alexander O. Bryner

Governorship

Minimum age	30
Length of term	4 years
Consecutive terms permitted	2
Who succeeds	Lt. Governor

State Legislature

Name	Legislature
Upper chamber	Senate
Number of members	20
Length of term	4 years
Party in majority, 2006	Republican
Lower chamber	House of Representatives
Number of members	40
Length of term	2 years
Party in majority, 2006	Republican

State Government Employees, 2004

Total	24,657
Payroll	$99,339,309

Local Government Employees, 2004

Total	26,184
Payroll	$104,039,699

Local Governments by Type, 2002

Total	175
County	12
Municipal	149
Township	0
School District	0
Special District	14

Voting age population, November 2004

Total	451,000
Male	224,000
Female	227,000
White	359,000
Black	13,000
Hispanic	22,000
Asian	24,000

Presidential Election, 2004

Total Popular Vote	312,598
Kerry	111,025
Bush	190,889
Total Electoral Votes	3

Federal representation, 2006 (109th Congress)

Senator	Ted Stevens
Party	Republican
Year term expires	2009
Senator	Lisa Murkowski
Party	Republican
Year term expires	2011
Representatives, total	1
Democrats	0
Republicans	1
Other	0

Votes cast for US Senators

2002

Total vote (x 1,000)	230,000
Leading party	Republican
Percent for leading party	78.2%

2004

Total vote (x 1,000)	308,000
Leading party	Republican
Percent for leading party	48.6%

Votes cast for US Representatives

2002

Total vote (x 1,000)	228
Democratic	39
Republican	170
Leading party	Republican
Percent for leading party	74.5%

2004

Total vote (x 1,000)	300
Democratic	67
Republican	213
Leading party	Republican
Percent for leading party	71.1%

Women holding public office, 2006
US Congress 1
Statewide elected office. 0
State legislature 11

Black public officials, 2001
Total. 3
US and state legislatures 1
City/county/regional offices 2
Judicial/law enforcement. 0
Education/school boards 0

Hispanic public officials, 2004
Total. 0
State executives & legislators 0
City/county/regional offices 0
Judicial/law enforcement. 0
Education/school boards 0

Governmental Finance

State government revenues, 2004
Total revenue ($1,000) $8,847,705
Revenue per capita 13,446.36

General Revenue ($ per capita) $10,069.39
Intergovernmental 3,333.71
Taxes 2,034.51
general sales 0
individual income tax. 0
corporate income tax 516.05
Current charges. 573.73
Miscellaneous 4,127.44

State government expenditure, 2004
Total expenditure (x $1,000) $8,089,240
Expenditure per capita. 12,293.68
General Expenditure ($ per capita). . . $10,387.28
Education 2,595.51
Public welfare. 2,236.48
Health 179.80
Hospitals. 35.02
Highways 1,259.63
Police protection 93.74
Correction 268.45
Natural resources 375.38
Parks & recreation. 14.48
Governmental administration 657.81
Interest on general debt 368.45

State debt & cash, 2004 ($ per capita)
Debt $8,708.82
Cash/security holdings. $68,884.23

Federal government grants to state & local government, 2004 (x $1,000)
Total. $3,216,865
By Federal Agency
Defense $70,716

By Federal Agency, continued
Education 336,167
Energy 6,214
Environmental Protection Agency 85,441
Health & Human Services. 1,268,933
Homeland Security. 13,536
Housing & Urban Development. 147,376
Justice 73,382
Labor 54,312
Transportation 747,326
Veterans Affairs. . . . .

Crime, Law Enforcement & Courts

Crime, 2004 (rates per 100,000 residents)
Property crimes 22,172
Burglaries. 3,773
Larcenies. 16,159
Motor vehicle thefts 2,240
Property crime rate. 3,382.8
Violent crimes. 4,159
Murders. 37
Forcible rape. 558
Robberies 447
Aggravated assaults 3,117
Violent crime rate 634.5

Police Agencies, 2004
Total agencies. 41
Total employees 1,896
Male officers. 1,089
Female officers. 124
Male civilians. 218
Female civilians. 465

Arrests, 2004
Total. 36,864
Persons under 18 years of age 4,520

Prisoners under state & federal jurisdiction, 2004
Total prisoners. 4,554
Percent change, 12/31/03 to 12/31/04 . . . . 0.6%
Sentenced to more than one year 2,632
rate per 100,000. 398

Persons under sentence of death, 7/1/05
Total. 0
White. 0
Black 0
Hispanic 0

State's highest court
Name . . . . .Supreme Court
Number of members. 5
Length of term . . . . 10 years
Intermediate appeals court? . . . . .yes

Labor & Income

Civilian labor force, 2004

Total	331,000
Men	179,000
Women	152,000
Persons 16-19 years	18,000
White	247,000
Black	10,000
Hispanic	16,000
Asian	22,000

Civilian labor force as a percent of civilian non-institutional population, 2004

Total	71.1%
Men	76.6
Women	65.6
Persons 16-19 years	47.7
White	72.4
Black	72.5
Hispanic	75.4
Asian	73.1

Employment, 2004

Total	306,000
Men	165,000
Women	141,000
Persons 16-19 years	14,000
White	233,000
Black	9,000
Hispanic	15,000
Asian	20,000

Full-time/part-time labor force, 2002

Full-time labor force, employed	245,000
Part-time labor force, employed	53,000
Unemployed, looking for	
Full-time work	21,000
Part-time work	NA

Unemployment rate, 2004

Total	7.5%
Men	7.9
Women	7.2
Persons 16-19 years	22.5
White	5.7
Black	8.5
Hispanic	7.3
Asian	5.2

Unemployed by reason for unemployment (as a percent of total unemployment), 2002

Job losers or completed temp jobs	48.0%
Job leavers	NA
Reentrants	40
New entrants	NA

Labor unions, 2004

Membership	54,000
percent of employed	20.1%

Experienced civilian labor force by private industry, first quarter 2004

Total	205,751
Natural Resources & Mining	10,327
Construction	14,112
Manufacturing	11,625
Trade, transportation & utilities	57,941
Information	6,753
Finance	12,862
Professional & business	22,369
Education & Health	34,513
Leisure & hospitality	25,850
Other	9,174

Experienced civilian labor force by occupation, 2004

Management	22,510
Business & Financial	8,620
Legal	2,650
Sales	25,410
Office & Admin. Support	50,240
Computers & Math	3,760
Architecture & Engineering	6,150
Arts & Entertainment	2,730
Education	20,320
Social Services	5,700
Healthcare Practitioner & Technical	12,090
Healthcare support	6,670
Maintenance & Repair	15,650
Construction	20,730
Transportation & moving	22,430
Production	10,840
Farming, fishing & forestry	540

Hours and earnings of production workers on manufacturing payrolls, 2004

Average weekly hours	40.6
Average hourly earnings	$12.01
Average weekly earnings	$487.61

Average annual pay

2004	$39,062
change from 2003	3.3%

Household income

Median household income, three-year average, 2002-2004	$54,627

Personal income, 2004 ($ per capita)

In current dollars	$34,454
In constant (2000) dollars	$31,954

Poverty

Persons below poverty level, three-year average, 2002-2004	9.2%

Federal individual income tax returns, 2003

Returns filed	343,032
Adjusted gross income ($1,000)	$14,832,589
Total income tax paid ($1,000)	$1,916,777

Economy, Business, Industry & Agriculture

Fortune 500 companies, 2005 0

Patents issued, 2004 49

Bankruptcy cases filed, 2004 1,500

Business firm ownership, 2002

Women-owned. 16,309
 Sales ($ mil) $2,422
Black-owned. 927
 Sales ($ mil) $88
Hispanic-owned. 1,241
 Sales ($ mil) $171
Asian-owned 1,909
 Sales ($ mil) $436
Amer. Indian/Alaska Native-owned 5,019
 Sales ($ mil) $648
Hawaiian/Pacific Isl.-owned 157
 Sales ($ mil) $10

Gross State Product, 2004 ($ mil)

Total Gross State Product $34,023
 Agriculture, forestry, fishing and
   hunting 346
 Mining. 7,328
 Utilities 408
 Construction 1,725
 Manufacturing, durable goods 156
 Manufacturing, non-durable goods 569
 Wholesale trade. 720
 Retail trade. 1,785
 Transportation & warehousing 3,153
 Information 909
 Finance & insurance. 1,174
 Real estate, rental, leasing 3,209
 Professional and technical services 1,181
 Educational services. 101
 Health care and social assistance 2,017
 Accommodation/food services. 912
 Other services, except government 605
 Government 6,668

Establishments, by major industry group, 2003

Total. 19,176
 Forestry, fishing & agriculture 308
 Mining. 137
 Construction 2,601
 Manufacturing. 511
 Wholesale trade. 758
 Retail trade. 2,668
 Transportation & warehousing 1,105
 Information 419
 Finance & insurance. 718
 Professional/scientific/technical 1,715
 Health care/social assistance 1,902
 Accommodation/food services. 1,895

Annual payroll by major industry group, 2003

Total ($1,000) $8,694,257
 Forestry, fishing & agriculture . . . . NA
 Mining. 637,489
 Utilities 113,488
 Construction 1,006,762
 Manufacturing. 369,312
 Wholesale trade. 325,782
 Retail trade. 852,875
 Transportation & warehousing 881,977
 Information 323,143
 Finance & insurance. 349,805
 Professional/scientific/technical 607,806
 Health care/social assistance 1,550,436
 Accommodation/food services. 422,840

Agriculture

Number of farms, 2004 1,000
Farm acreage, 2004
 Total. 1,000,000
 Acres per farm, 2004 1,452
Farm income, 2003 ($mil)
 Net farm income $10
 Debt/asset ratio 3.7
Farm marketings, 2003 ($mil)
 Total. $51
 Crops 23
 Livestock 28

Principal commodities, in order by marketing receipts, 2003

 Greenhouse, hay, dairy products, potatoes

Federal economic activity in state

Expenditures, 2003
 Total ($ mil) $7,944
 Per capita $12,244
 Defense ($ mil) 2,307
 Non-defense ($ mil) 5,636
Defense department, 2003
 Payroll ($ mil) $1,123
 Contract awards ($ mil) $1,427
 Grants ($ mil). $27
 Homeland security grants ($1,000)
  2004 . . . . $21,218
  2005 . . . . $14,879

FDIC insured financial institutions, 2004

Number 7
 Assets ($bil) $3.9
 Deposits ($bil) 6.0

Fishing, 2004

Catch (x 1,000 lbs) 5,355,281
Value ($1,000). $1,171,976

Mining, 2004 ($ mil)
Total non-fuel mineral production $1,320
Percent of U.S. 3.0%

Construction, 2003 ($ mil)
Total contracts (including non-building). $1,830
   residential............................. 542
   non-residential 638

Establishments, receipts, payroll & employees, by major industry group, 2002

Mining 131
   Receipts ($1,000) $8,254,126
   Annual payroll ($1,000)........... $654,577
   Paid employees 10,300

Utilities 89
   Receipts ($1,000) .... NA
   Annual payroll ($1,000)........... $113,593
   Paid employees 1,721

Construction........................... 2,359
   Receipts ($1,000) $4,417,369
   Annual payroll ($1,000)........... $938,457
   Paid employees 21,357

Manufacturing 514
   Receipts ($1,000) $3,832,024
   Annual payroll ($1,000)........... $362,220
   Paid employees 10,933

Wholesale trade 740
   Receipts ($1,000) $3,616,674
   Annual payroll ($1,000)........... $313,835
   Paid employees 7,425

Retail trade........................... 2,661
   Receipts ($1,000) $7,437,071
   Annual payroll ($1,000)........... $798,468
   Paid employees 32,984

Transportation....................... 1,034
   Receipts ($1,000) $3,205,233
   Annual payroll ($1,000)........... $715,528
   Paid employees 15,457

Information............................ 416
   Receipts ($1,000) .... NA
   Annual payroll ($1,000)........... $316,930
   Paid employees 7,138

Finance & insurance 716
   Receipts ($1,000) .... NA
   Annual payroll ($1,000)........... $330,411
   Paid employees 7,103

Professional, scientific & technical 1,684
   Receipts ($1,000) $1,362,539
   Annual payroll ($1,000)........... $568,143
   Paid employees 11,543

Health care & social assistance 1,820
   Receipts ($1,000) $3,393,974
   Annual payroll ($1,000)........... $1,381,416
   Paid employees 35,623

Accommodation & food service 1,849
   Receipts ($1,000) $1,393,225
   Annual payroll ($1,000)........... $412,784
   Paid employees 23,663

Communication, Energy & Transportation

Communication
Daily newspapers, 2004 7
Households with computers, 2003 ....73%
Households with internet access, 2003 .....68%

Energy
Electricity Consumption, 2001
Total (trillion Btu)....................... 737
Per capita (million Btu) 1,164
By source of production (trillion Btu)
   Coal 16
   Natural gas............................. 413
   Petroleum.............................. 292
   Nuclear electric power 0
   Hydroelectric power.................... 14
By end-use sector (trillion Btu)
   Residential 53
   Commercial 65
   Industrial 413
   Transportation 206
Electric energy, 2003
   Production (billion kWh) 6.3
   Net summer capability (million kW) 1.9
Gas utilities, 2003
   Customers (x1,000).................... 114
   Sales (trillion Btu)..................... 113
   Revenues ($mil)..................... $267
Nuclear plants, 2003 0

Transportation, 2004
Public Road & Street Mileage 14,107
   Urban................................ 2,095
   Rural 12,012
   Interstate............................ 1,082
Vehicle miles of travel per capita 7,630.0
Total motor vehicle registrations....... 659,981
   Automobiles......................... 255,068
   Buses 2,440
   Trucks 402,473
   Motorcycles 21,134
Licensed drivers 482,532
   19 years & under 25,498
Deaths from motor vehicle accidents 101

State Summary

Capital City........................ Phoenix
Governor................... Janet Napolitano
State Capitol
1700 W Washington
Phoenix, AZ 85007
602-542-4331
Admitted as a state 1912
Area (square miles).................. 113,998
Population, 2004 (est.) 5,743,834
Largest City......................... Phoenix
Population, 2004................. 1,418,000
Personal income per capita, 2004
(in current dollars) $28,442
Gross state product ($ mil), 2004...... $199,953

Leading industries by payroll, 2003

Health care/Social assistance, Manufacturing,
Retail trade

Leading agricultural commodities by receipts, 2003

Cattle, dairy products, lettuce, cotton

Geography & Environment

Total area (sq. mi.).................... 113,998
land 113,635
water 364

Federally-owned land, 2004 (acres) .. 34,933,236
percent............................. 48.1%

Highest point................ Humphrey's Peak
elevation (feet) 12,633

Lowest point ....Colorado River
elevation (feet) 70

General coastline (miles)...................... 0

Tidal shoreline (miles)....................... 0

Capital City........................... Phoenix
Population 2000 1,321,000
Population 2004 1,418,000

Largest City........................... Phoenix
Population 2000 1,321,000
Population 2004 1,418,000

Number of cities with over 100,000 population

1990 6
2000 9
2004 9

State park and recreation areas, 2003

Area (acres x 1,000)....................... 61
Number of visitors (x 1,000) 2,201
Revenues (x 1,000)..................... $5,302
percent of operating expenditures...... 31.7%

National forest system land, 2004

Acres 11,263,000

Demographics and Characteristics of the Population

Population

1980 2,718,215
1990 3,665,228
2000 5,130,632
2004 (estimate)...................... 5,743,834
persons per sq. mile of land............. 50.5
2005 (projection)................... 5,868,004
Male.......................... 2,933,877
Female........................ 2,934,127
2010 (projection) 6,637,381
2020 (projection)................... 8,456,448
2030 (projection) 10,712,397
Male.......................... 5,407,629
Female........................ 5,304,768

Metropolitan and Non-Metro. area population

	Metro	Non-Metro
1980	2,040,000	678,000
1990	2,896,000	769,000
2000	4,527,000	604,000

Change in population, 2000-2004

Number............................. 613,202
percent............................. 12.0%
Natural increase (births minus deaths).. 193,305
Net internal migration 281,625
Net international migration 141,175

Persons by age, 2004

Under 5 years 449,904
18 years and over 4,196,574
65 years and over 732,071
85 years and over 85,886

Persons by age, 2010 (projected)

Total........................... 6,637,381
Under 5 years 515,408
5 to 17 years 1,173,056
18 and over 4,948,917
21 and over 4,661,591
65 and over 922,010
85 and over 120,875
Median age 36.4

Race, 2004 (estimate)

One Race
White..................... 5,032,701
Black or African American 203,233
American Indian/Alaska Native...... 288,918
Pacific Islander 10,384
Asian Indian...................... 32,858
Chinese 20,810
Filipino 20,200
Japanese 7,954
Korean......................... 8,498
Vietnamese...................... 19,149
Two or more races.................... 85,665

2   Arizona

Persons of Hispanic origin, 2004
Total Hispanic or Latino 1,584,217
   Mexican. 1,433,823
   Puerto Rican 17,945
   Cuban 5,259
   Other Hispanic or Latino 84,716

Marital status, 2000
Population 15 years & over 3,979,336
   Never married 1,038,607
   Married. 2,188,635
   Separated 71,628
   Widowed. 238,760
   Divorced 441,706

Language spoken at home, 2000
Population 5 years & over 4,752,724
   English only 3,523,487
   Spanish 927,395
   Other Indo-European languages 102,004
   Asian/Pacific Island languages. 62,204

Households & families, 2000
Households. 1,901,327
   with persons under 18 years 673,926
   with persons over 65 years. 465,062
   persons per household 2.64
Families. 1,287,367
   persons per family. 3.18
Married couples. 986,303
Female householder,
   no husband present. 210,781
One-person households 472,006

Nativity, 2000
Number of persons born in state 1,779,492
   percent of population 34.7%

Immigration & Naturalization, 2004
Immigrants admitted 19,297
Persons naturalized 6,500
Asylums granted 64
Asylums denied 10

Vital Statistics and Health

Marriages
2002 36,199
2003 35,873
2004 37,882

Divorces
2002 25,896
2003 24,248
2004 24,403

Births
2003 90,967
   Birthrate (per 1,000). 16.3
   Low birth weight (2,500g or less). 7.1%
   To unmarried mothers. 41.5%

2003, continued
   White. 78,966
   Black. 3,279
   Hispanic 39,798
   Asian/Pacific Islander 2,699
   Amer. Indian/Alaska Native 6,060
2004 (preliminary). 93,672
   Birthrate (per 1,000). 16.3
   White. 81,171
   Black. 3,426
   Hispanic 41,427
   Asian/Pacific Islander 2,801

Deaths
2002
All causes 42,816
   rate per 100,000. . . . . .784.7
Heart disease 10,852
   rate per 100,000. . . . . .198.9
Malignant neoplasms 9,359
   rate per 100,000. . . . . .171.5
Cerebrovascular disease. 2,535
   rate per 100,000. . . . . .46.5
Chronic lower respiratory disease 2,575
   rate per 100,000. . . . . .47.2
2003 43,496
   rate per 100,000. . . . . .779.4
2004 (provisional) 43,054

Infant deaths
2003 (provisional) 591
   rate per 1,000 . . . . .6.5
2004 (provisional) 626
   rate per 1,000 . . . . .6.7

Abortions, 2000
Total 18,000
   rate per 1,000 women age 15-44 . . . . 16.5

Physicians, 2003
Total 11,679
   rate per 1,000 persons. 209

Nurses, 2001
Total 34,880
   rate per 1,000 persons. 657

Community Hospitals, 2003
Number 61
Beds (x 1,000). 10.8
Patients admitted (x 1,000) 603
Average daily census (x 1,000) 7.3
Average cost per day $1,570
Outpatient visits (x mil) 6.7

Disability status of population, 2004
5 to 20 years 6.4%
21 to 64 years 11.9%
65 years and over 37.4%

Education

Educational attainment, 2004

Population over 25 years 3,548,365
  Less than 9th grade 254,306
  High school graduates only......... 946,909
  Bachelor's degree only 551,104
  Graduate or professional degree...... 326,358
  Less than 9th grade percent 7.2%
  High school graduate or more 84.4%
  College graduate or more............. 28.0%
  Graduate or professional degree........ 9.2%

Public school enrollment, Fall 2002

Total............................. 937,755
  Kindergarten through grade 8 660,363
  Grades 9 through 12 277,392
Enrollment, 2005 (projected) 967,300

Graduating public high school seniors

2004 (estimate)....................... 57,010

SAT scores, 2005

Average verbal score 526
Average math score 530
Percent of graduates taking test 33%

Public school teachers, 2004

Total (x 1,000) 45.5
  Elementary (x 1,000).................... 30.8
  Secondary (x 1,000) 14.7
Average salary $41,800
  Elementary...................... $41,800
  Secondary....................... $41,800

State receipts & expenditures for public schools, 2004

Revenue receipts ($mil)................. $7,049
Expenditures
Total ($mil).......................... $6,346
  Per capita $1,137
  Per pupil $5,595

Institutions of higher education, 2004

Total..................................... 74
  Public.................................. 25
  Private................................. 49

Enrollment in institutions of higher education, Fall, 2003

Total............................... 437,620
  Full-time men 115,693
  Full-time women.................... 138,435
  Part-time men 74,560
  Part-time women.................... 108,932

Minority enrollment in institutions of higher education, Fall, 2003

Black, non-hispanic.................... 21,659
Hispanic 63,376
Asian/Pacific Islander 13,483
American Indian/Alaska Native......... 14,490

Earned degrees conferred, 2003

Bachelor's 23,372
Master's 12,618
First-professional....................... 754
Doctor's................................ 803

State & local financial support for higher education, 2003-2004

Full-time equivalent enrollment (x 1,000) ..211.2
Appropriations per FTE................ $5,699
  as a percent of tax revenue.............. 8.5%

Social Insurance & Welfare Programs

Social Security benefits & beneficiaries, 2004

Beneficiaries
  Total............................. 888,000
  Retired & dependents............... 634,000
  Survivors.......................... 108,000
  Disabled & dependents............ 147,000
Annual benefit payments ($ mil)
  Total.............................. $9,282
  Retired & dependents............... $6,377
  Survivors........................... $1,427
  Disabled & dependents.............. $1,478
Average Monthly Benefit
  Retired & dependents............... $973
  Disabled & dependents.............. $924
  Widowed........................... $954

Medicare

Enrollment, 2001 (x 1,000) 691
  Payments ($ mil, est.) $3,300
Enrollment, 2003 (x 1,000) 729

Medicaid, 2002

Beneficiaries (x 1,000).................... 878
Payments ($ mil) $2,882

State Children's Health Insurance, 2004

Enrollment (x 1,000).................... 87.7
Expenditures ($ mil).................. $258.9

Persons without health insurance, 2003

Number (x 1,000)........................ 951
  percent............................ 17.0%
Number of children (x 1,000) 223
  percent of children 14.6%

Federal public aid

Temporary Assistance for Needy Families, 2004
Recipients (x 1,000)...................... 115
Families (x 1,000) 50

Supplemental Security Income, 2003
Recipients (x 1,000)....................... 92
Payments ($ mil) $429

Food Stamp Program, 2004

Participants (x 1,000) 530
Benefits ($ mil)......................... $578

Housing & Construction

Housing units

Total 2003 (estimate) 2,387,735
Total 2004 (estimate) 2,458,231
Seasonal or recreational use, 2003 162,000
Owner-occupied single-family, 2003 .. 1,165,000
    Median value $146,124
Renter-occupied, 2003 646,000
    Median rent $662
Homeownership rate, 2003 .... 67.0%
Homeownership rate, 2004 .... 68.7%

New privately owned housing units, 2004

Number authorized (x 1,000) 90.6
Value ($ mil) $13,531
Started 2005 (x 1,000, estimate) 61.9
Started 2006 (x 1,000, estimate) 60.1

Existing home sales

2002 (x 1,000) 128.2
2003 (x 1,000) 149.6
2004 (x 1,000) 186.8

Government & Elections

State Officials 2006

Governor (name/party/term expires)
            Janet Napolitano
            Democrat - 1/07
Lieutenant Governor .... (no Lt. Governor)
Secretary of State .... Jan Brewer
Attorney General .... Terry Goddard
Chief Justice .... Ruth McGregor

Governorship

Minimum age 25
Length of term .... 4 years
Consecutive terms permitted 2
Who succeeds .... Sec. of State

State Legislature

Name .... Legislature
Upper chamber .... Senate
    Number of members 30
    Length of term .... 2 years
    Party in majority, 2006 .... Republican
Lower chamber .... House of Representatives
    Number of members 60
    Length of term .... 2 years
    Party in majority, 2006 .... Republican

State Government Employees, 2004

Total 66,026
Payroll $216,008,902

Local Government Employees, 2004

Total 204,693
Payroll $687,506,817

Local Governments by Type, 2002

Total 638
    County 15
    Municipal 87
    Township 0
    School District 231
    Special District 305

Voting age population, November 2004

Total 4,122,000
    Male 2,008,000
    Female 2,114,000
    White 3,747,000
    Black 142,000
    Hispanic 1,160,000
    Asian 57,000

Presidential Election, 2004

Total Popular Vote 2,012,585
    Kerry 893,524
    Bush 1,104,294
Total Electoral Votes 10

Federal representation, 2006 (109th Congress)

Senator .... Jon Kyl
    Party .... Republican
    Year term expires 2007
Senator .... John McCain
    Party .... Republican
    Year term expires 2011
Representatives, total 8
    Democrats 2
    Republicans 6
    Other 0

Votes cast for US Senators

2002
Total vote (x 1,000) .... NA
Leading party .... NA
Percent for leading party .... NA

2004
Total vote (x 1,000) 1,962,000
Leading party .... Republican
Percent for leading party 76.7%

Votes cast for US Representatives

2002
Total vote (x 1,000) 1,194
    Democratic 472
    Republican 682
Leading party .... Republican
Percent for leading party 57.1%

2004
Total vote (x 1,000) 1,871
    Democratic 598
    Republican 1,128
Leading party .... Republican
Percent for leading party 60.3%

Women holding public office, 2006

US Congress 0
Statewide elected office 3
State legislature 30

Black public officials, 2001

Total 12
   US and state legislatures 1
   City/county/regional offices 1
   Judicial/law enforcement 5
   Education/school boards 5

Hispanic public officials, 2004

Total 354
   State executives & legislators 15
   City/county/regional offices 135
   Judicial/law enforcement 41
   Education/school boards 163

Governmental Finance

State government revenues, 2004

Total revenue ($1,000) $23,753,397
   Revenue per capita 4,138.22

General Revenue ($ per capita) $3,301.25
   Intergovernmental 1,217.32
   Taxes 1,673.57
      general sales 822.24
      individual income tax 403.46
      corporate income tax 91.58
   Current charges 203.78
   Miscellaneous 206.58

State government expenditure, 2004

Total expenditure (x $1,000) $21,748,803
   Expenditure per capita 3,788.99
General Expenditure ($ per capita) $3,404.44
   Education 1,245.50
   Public welfare 899.34
   Health 197.40
   Hospitals 10.28
   Highways 329.55
   Police protection 32.88
   Correction 137.72
   Natural resources 41.52
   Parks & recreation 29.21
   Governmental administration 84.39
   Interest on general debt 41.36

State debt & cash, 2004 ($ per capita)

Debt $1,180.13
Cash/security holdings $6,766.64

Federal government grants to state & local government, 2004 (x $1,000)

Total $8,363,600
By Federal Agency
   Defense $136,443

By Federal Agency, continued

Education 842,604
Energy 15,219
Environmental Protection Agency 53,534
Health & Human Services 4,974,829
Homeland Security 16,202
Housing & Urban Development 447,625
Justice 139,047
Labor 156,348
Transportation 873,747
Veterans Affairs 5,853

Crime, Law Enforcement & Courts

Crime, 2004 (rates per 100,000 residents)

Property crimes 306,747
   Burglaries 56,885
   Larcenies 194,556
   Motor vehicle thefts 55,306
   Property crime rate 5,340.5
Violent crimes 28,952
   Murders 414
   Forcible rape 1,896
   Robberies 7,721
   Aggravated assaults 18,921
   Violent crime rate 504.1

Police Agencies, 2004

Total agencies 99
Total employees 19,809
   Male officers 10,120
   Female officers 1,197
   Male civilians 3,744
   Female civilians 4,748

Arrests, 2004

Total 315,007
   Persons under 18 years of age 52,893

Prisoners under state & federal jurisdiction, 2004

Total prisoners 32,515
   Percent change, 12/31/03 to 12/31/04 .... 4.3%
Sentenced to more than one year 31,106
   rate per 100,000 534

Persons under sentence of death, 7/1/05

Total 128
   White 91
   Black 12
   Hispanic 21

State's highest court

Name .... Supreme Court
Number of members 5
Length of term .... 6 years
Intermediate appeals court? .... yes

6   Arizona

Labor & Income

Civilian labor force, 2004

Total	2,778,000
Men	1,536,000
Women	1,242,000
Persons 16-19 years	131,000
White	2,526,000
Black	92,000
Hispanic	803,000
Asian	59,000

Civilian labor force as a percent of civilian non-institutional population, 2004

Total	65.1%
Men	73.1
Women	57.4
Persons 16-19 years	47.2
White	65.1
Black	67.6
Hispanic	68.6
Asian	62.8

Employment, 2004

Total	2,637,000
Men	1,458,000
Women	1,179,000
Persons 16-19 years	103,000
White	2,405,000
Black	83,000
Hispanic	752,000
Asian	56,000

Full-time/part-time labor force, 2002

Full-time labor force, employed	2,075,000
Part-time labor force, employed	431,000
Unemployed, looking for	
Full-time work	130,000
Part-time work	NA

Unemployment rate, 2004

Total	5.1%
Men	5.0
Women	5.1
Persons 16-19 years	21.1
White	4.8
Black	10.0
Hispanic	6.4
Asian	4.5

Unemployed by reason for unemployment (as a percent of total unemployment), 2002

Job losers or completed temp jobs	41.8%
Job leavers	NA
Reentrants	34.5
New entrants	NA

Labor unions, 2004

Membership	145,000
percent of employed	6.3%

Experienced civilian labor force by private industry, first quarter 2004

Total	1,958,269
Natural Resources & Mining	43,633
Construction	183,013
Manufacturing	175,699
Trade, transportation & utilities	453,569
Information	48,844
Finance	161,042
Professional & business	327,553
Education & Health	250,573
Leisure & hospitality	244,929
Other	64,915

Experienced civilian labor force by occupation, 2004

Management	116,220
Business & Financial	97,590
Legal	15,540
Sales	254,450
Office & Admin. Support	438,420
Computers & Math	49,070
Architecture & Engineering	57,040
Arts & Entertainment	25,080
Education	133,180
Social Services	24,880
Healthcare Practitioner & Technical	100,880
Healthcare support	52,680
Maintenance & Repair	97,110
Construction	NA
Transportation & moving	154,960
Production	124,640
Farming, fishing & forestry	12,160

Hours and earnings of production workers on manufacturing payrolls, 2004

Average weekly hours	40.5
Average hourly earnings	$14.20
Average weekly earnings	$575.10

Average annual pay

2004	$36,646
change from 2003	4.6%

Household income

Median household income, three-year average, 2002-2004	$42,590

Personal income, 2004 ($ per capita)

In current dollars	$28,442
In constant (2000) dollars	$26,378

Poverty

Persons below poverty level, three-year average, 2002-2004	13.8%

Federal individual income tax returns, 2003

Returns filed	2,285,323
Adjusted gross income ($1,000)	$102,846,339
Total income tax paid ($1,000)	$12,126,455

Economy, Business, Industry & Agriculture

Fortune 500 companies, 2005 3

Patents issued, 2004 1,730

Bankruptcy cases filed, 2004 31,800

Business firm ownership, 2002

Women-owned. 109,749
  Sales ($ mil) $15,762
Black-owned. 6,338
  Sales ($ mil) $538
Hispanic-owned. 35,102
  Sales ($ mil) $4,651
Asian-owned 10,223
  Sales ($ mil) $2,909
Amer. Indian/Alaska Native-owned 6,614
  Sales ($ mil) $960
Hawaiian/Pacific Isl.-owned. 348
  Sales ($ mil) $38

Gross State Product, 2004 ($ mil)

Total Gross State Product $199,953
  Agriculture, forestry, fishing and
    hunting 1,943
  Mining. 1,288
  Utilities 3,585
  Construction 12,273
  Manufacturing, durable goods. 20,634
  Manufacturing, non-durable goods 2,916
  Wholesale trade. 11,378
  Retail trade. 16,795
  Transportation & warehousing 5,606
  Information 6,302
  Finance & insurance. 17,189
  Real estate, rental, leasing 26,327
  Professional and technical services 11,210
  Educational services 1,186
  Health care and social assistance. 13,382
  Accommodation/food services. 6,414
  Other services, except government 3,966
  Government 24,413

Establishments, by major industry group, 2003

Total. 121,533
  Forestry, fishing & agriculture 235
  Mining. 180
  Construction 13,547
  Manufacturing. 4,792
  Wholesale trade. 6,576
  Retail trade. 17,503
  Transportation & warehousing 2,833
  Information 2,210
  Finance & insurance. 8,361
  Professional/scientific/technical 13,870
  Health care/social assistance 12,523
  Accommodation/food services. 9,992

Annual payroll by major industry group, 2003

Total ($1,000) $64,371,697
  Forestry, fishing & agriculture 42,106
  Mining. 349,637
  Utilities 623,232
  Construction 5,673,827
  Manufacturing. 7,137,967
  Wholesale trade. 3,842,446
  Retail trade. 6,321,275
  Transportation & warehousing 3,008,811
  Information 2,672,444
  Finance & insurance. 5,330,178
  Professional/scientific/technical . . . 5,055,840
  Health care/social assistance 8,137,744
  Accommodation/food services. 2,700,302

Agriculture

Number of farms, 2004 10,000
Farm acreage, 2004
  Total. 26,000,000
  Acres per farm, 2004 2,588
Farm income, 2003 ($mil)
  Net farm income $1,078
  Debt/asset ratio 3.6
Farm marketings, 2003 ($mil)
Total. $2,586
  Crops 1,327
  Livestock. 1,259

Principal commodities, in order by marketing receipts, 2003

    Cattle, dairy products, lettuce, cotton

Federal economic activity in state

Expenditures, 2003
  Total ($ mil) $37,801
  Per capita $6,773
  Defense ($ mil). 9,885
  Non-defense ($ mil) 27,916
Defense department, 2003
  Payroll ($ mil) $2,314
  Contract awards ($ mil) $7,505
  Grants ($ mil). $69
  Homeland security grants ($1,000)
    2004 . . . . $53,371
    2005 . . . . $41,705

FDIC insured financial institutions, 2004

Number 49
  Assets ($bil) $59.3
  Deposits ($bil) 61.8

Fishing, 2004

Catch (x 1,000 lbs) 0
Value ($1,000). 0

Mining, 2004 ($ mil)

Total non-fuel mineral production $3,000
Percent of U.S. 6.8%

Construction, 2003 ($ mil)

Total contracts (including non-building) $17,729
  residential............................ 11,507
  non-residential 4,688

Establishments, receipts, payroll & employees, by major industry group, 2002

Mining................................. 280
  Receipts ($1,000).................. $917,469
  Annual payroll ($1,000)........... $156,059
  Paid employees 3,985

Utilities 236
  Receipts ($1,000) .... NA
  Annual payroll ($1,000)............... NA
  Paid employees .... (10k-24k)

Construction........................ 12,991
  Receipts ($1,000) $28,926,214
  Annual payroll ($1,000)......... $5,628,936
  Paid employees 174,871

Manufacturing 4,935
  Receipts ($1,000) $41,910,739
  Annual payroll ($1,000)......... $7,080,603
  Paid employees 168,155

Wholesale trade 6,651
  Receipts ($1,000) $60,976,999
  Annual payroll ($1,000)......... $3,697,812
  Paid employees 88,568

Retail trade 17,238
  Receipts ($1,000) $56,457,863
  Annual payroll ($1,000)......... $6,067,994
  Paid employees 268,584

Transportation....................... 2,760
  Receipts ($1,000) $6,602,709
  Annual payroll ($1,000)......... $2,277,103
  Paid employees 76,124

Information.......................... 2,129
  Receipts ($1,000) .... NA
  Annual payroll ($1,000)......... $2,442,033
  Paid employees 56,781

Finance & insurance 7,966
  Receipts ($1,000) .... NA
  Annual payroll ($1,000)............... NA
  Paid employees ....(100,000+)

Professional, scientific & technical 13,647
  Receipts ($1,000) $11,751,755
  Annual payroll ($1,000)......... $4,791,553
  Paid employees 107,210

Health care & social assistance 12,093
  Receipts ($1,000) $18,821,645
  Annual payroll ($1,000)......... $7,306,947
  Paid employees 212,946

Accommodation & food service.......... 9,944
  Receipts ($1,000) $8,612,730
  Annual payroll ($1,000)......... $2,464,970
  Paid employees 206,402

Communication, Energy & Transportation

Communication

Daily newspapers, 2004 16
Households with computers, 2003 ....64%
Households with internet access, 2003 .....55%

Energy

Electricity Consumption, 2001
  Total (trillion Btu)..................... 1,353
  Per capita (million Btu) 255
By source of production (trillion Btu)
    Coal................................. 424
    Natural gas.......................... 245
    Petroleum........................... 524
    Nuclear electric power 300
    Hydroelectric power................. 80
By end-use sector (trillion Btu)
    Residential 344
    Commercial 312
    Industrial 221
    Transportation 476
Electric energy, 2003
    Production (billion kWh) 94.4
    Net summer capability (million kW) 23.5
Gas utilities, 2003
    Customers (x1,000).................. 1,014
    Sales (trillion Btu)................... 83
    Revenues ($mil)..................... $727
Nuclear plants, 2003 3

Transportation, 2004

Public Road & Street Mileage 58,112
  Urban............................ 22,055
  Rural 36,057
  Interstate......................... 1,168
Vehicle miles of travel per capita 9,981.9
Total motor vehicle registrations 3,776,114
  Automobiles...................... 2,055,202
  Buses 4,787
  Trucks 1,716,125
  Motorcycles 209,048
Licensed drivers 3,783,927
  19 years & under 160,800
Deaths from motor vehicle accidents 1,150

State Summary

Capital City...................... Little Rock
Governor.................... Mike Huckabee
State Capitol
Room 250
Little Rock, AR 72201
501-682-2345
Admitted as a state 1836
Area (square miles).................... 53,179
Population, 2004 (est.) 2,752,629
Largest City....................... Little Rock
Population, 2004................... 184,000
Personal income per capita, 2004
(in current dollars) $25,725
Gross state product ($ mil), 2004 ...... $80,902

Leading industries by payroll, 2003

Manufacturing, Health care/Social assistance, Retail trade

Leading agricultural commodities by receipts, 2003

Broilers, soybeans, rice, cotton

Geography & Environment

Total area (sq. mi.).................... 53,179
land 52,068
water 1,110
Federally-owned land, 2004 (acres) ... 2,407,948
percent............................ 7.2%
Highest point............. Magazine Mountain
elevation (feet) 2,753
Lowest point ....Ouachita River
elevation (feet) 55
General coastline (miles)..................... 0
Tidal shoreline (miles)...................... 0
Capital City...................... Little Rock
Population 2000 183,000
Population 2004 184,000
Largest City...................... Little Rock
Population 2000 183,000
Population 2004 184,000

Number of cities with over 100,000 population

1990 1
2000 1
2004 1

State park and recreation areas, 2003

Area (acres x 1,000)....................... 52
Number of visitors (x 1,000) 9,970
Revenues (x 1,000).................... $14,003
percent of operating expenditures...... 43.4%

National forest system land, 2004

Acres 2,593,000

Demographics and Characteristics of the Population

Population

1980 2,286,435
1990 2,350,725
2000 2,673,400
2004 (estimate)................... 2,752,629
persons per sq. mile of land..............52.9
2005 (projection).................... 2,777,007
Male......................... 1,357,877
Female....................... 1,419,130
2010 (projection) 2,875,039
2020 (projection).................... 3,060,219
2030 (projection).................... 3,240,208
Male......................... 1,588,795
Female....................... 1,651,413

Metropolitan and Non-Metro. area population

	Metro	Non-Metro
1980	885,000	1,401,000
1990	943,000	1,408,000
2000	1,321,000	1,352,000

Change in population, 2000-2004

Number............................. 79,231
percent........................... 3.0%
Natural increase (births minus deaths)... 41,362
Net internal migration................. 20,949
Net international migration 18,427

Persons by age, 2004

Under 5 years 185,555
18 years and over 2,076,079
65 years and over 381,106
85 years and over 47,842

Persons by age, 2010 (projected)

Total............................. 2,875,039
Under 5 years..................... 194,806
5 to 17 years 507,850
18 and over 2,172,383
21 and over 2,056,254
65 and over 412,152
85 and over 58,244
Median age........................37.9

Race, 2004 (estimate)

One Race
White........................... 2,238,490
Black or African American 434,395
American Indian/Alaska Native....... 19,555
Pacific Islander 2,285
Asian Indian....................... 5,606
Chinese 3,922
Filipino 1,198
Japanese 352
Korean............................ 1,260
Vietnamese......................... 5,961
Two or more races..................... 31,997

Persons of Hispanic origin, 2004

Total Hispanic or Latino 117,568
  Mexican............................ 96,232
  Puerto Rican 5,053
  Cuban 0
  Other Hispanic or Latino 9,867

Marital status, 2000

Population 15 years & over 2,111,663
  Never married 447,673
  Married......................... 1,231,100
  Separated 40,122
  Widowed.......................... 160,486
  Divorced 232,283

Language spoken at home, 2000

Population 5 years & over 2,492,205
  English only 2,368,450
  Spanish 82,465
  Other Indo-European languages 22,695
  Asian/Pacific Island languages........ 15,238

Households & families, 2000

Households........................ 1,042,696
  with persons under 18 years 371,331
  with persons over 65 years........... 263,521
  persons per household 2.49
Families........................... 732,261
  persons per family.....................2.99
Married couples..................... 566,401
Female householder,
  no husband present................. 126,561
One-person households 266,585

Nativity, 2000

Number of persons born in state 1,707,529
  percent of population................. 63.9%

Immigration & Naturalization, 2004

Immigrants admitted................... 2,251
Persons naturalized 823
Asylums granted 7
Asylums denied 23

Vital Statistics and Health

Marriages

2002 38,721
2003 36,445
2004 36,806

Divorces

2002 16,708
2003 16,452
2004 16,874

Births

2003 37,784
  Birthrate (per 1,000)....................13.9
  Low birth weight (2,500g or less)........ 8.9%
  To unmarried mothers................. 38.0%

2003, continued
  White............................. 30,048
  Black 7,307
  Hispanic 3,307
  Asian/Pacific Islander 544
  Amer. Indian/Alaska Native........... 260
2004 (preliminary).................... 38,602
  Birthrate (per 1,000)...................14.0
  White............................. 30,363
  Black 7,396
  Hispanic 3,510
  Asian/Pacific Islander 598

Deaths

2002
All causes 28,513
  rate per 100,000.................. 1,052.1
Heart disease 8,330
  rate per 100,000....................307.4
Malignant neoplasms 6,282
  rate per 100,000....................231.8
Cerebrovascular disease................. 2,232
  rate per 100,000.....................82.4
Chronic lower respiratory disease 1,441
  rate per 100,000.....................53.2
2003 27,924
  rate per 100,000.................. 1,024.5
2004 (provisional) 27,597

Infant deaths

2003 (provisional) 333
  rate per 1,000 ....8.7
2004 (provisional) 334
  rate per 1,000 ....8.6

Abortions, 2000

Total................................ 6,000
  rate per 1,000 women age 15-44...........9.8

Physicians, 2003

Total................................ 5,516
  rate per 1,000 persons................... 202

Nurses, 2001

Total............................... 19,860
  rate per 1,000 persons.................. 737

Community Hospitals, 2003

Number 88
Beds (x 1,000)..........................9.9
Patients admitted (x 1,000) 388
Average daily census (x 1,000) 5.7
Average cost per day $1,130
Outpatient visits (x mil)...................4.6

Disability status of population, 2004

5 to 20 years 9%
21 to 64 years 19.9%
65 years and over 49.1%

Education

Educational attainment, 2004

Population over 25 years	1,749,731
Less than 9th grade	127,368
High school graduates only	621,746
Bachelor's degree only	209,179
Graduate or professional degree	107,412
Less than 9th grade percent	7.3%
High school graduate or more	79.2%
College graduate or more	18.8%
Graduate or professional degree	6.1%

Public school enrollment, Fall 2002

Total	450,985
Kindergarten through grade 8	318,828
Grades 9 through 12	132,157
Enrollment, 2005 (projected)	447,500

Graduating public high school seniors

2004 (estimate)	26,890

SAT scores, 2005

Average verbal score	563
Average math score	552
Percent of graduates taking test	6%

Public school teachers, 2004

Total (x 1,000)	32.0
Elementary (x 1,000)	15.6
Secondary (x 1,000)	16.4
Average salary	$39,300
Elementary	$37,400
Secondary	$41,100

State receipts & expenditures for public schools, 2004

Revenue receipts ($mil)	$3,535
Expenditures	
Total ($mil)	$3,160
Per capita	$1,158
Per pupil	$6,663

Institutions of higher education, 2004

Total	47
Public	33
Private	14

Enrollment in institutions of higher education, Fall, 2003

Total	138,407
Full-time men	38,238
Full-time women	54,139
Part-time men	17,461
Part-time women	28,569

Minority enrollment in institutions of higher education, Fall, 2003

Black, non-hispanic	24,052
Hispanic	2,204
Asian/Pacific Islander	1,804
American Indian/Alaska Native	1,361

Earned degrees conferred, 2003

Bachelor's	10,591
Master's	2,384
First-professional	477
Doctor's	180

State & local financial support for higher education, 2003-2004

Full-time equivalent enrollment (x 1,000)	97.7
Appropriations per FTE	$5,233
as a percent of tax revenue	9.6%

Social Insurance & Welfare Programs

Social Security benefits & beneficiaries, 2004

Beneficiaries	
Total	546,000
Retired & dependents	341,000
Survivors	81,000
Disabled & dependents	123,000
Annual benefit payments ($ mil)	
Total	$5,228
Retired & dependents	$3,151
Survivors	$935
Disabled & dependents	$1,142
Average Monthly Benefit	
Retired & dependents	$888
Disabled & dependents	$846
Widowed	$826

Medicare

Enrollment, 2001 (x 1,000)	442
Payments ($ mil, est.)	$2,400
Enrollment, 2003 (x 1,000)	453

Medicaid, 2002

Beneficiaries (x 1,000)	579
Payments ($ mil)	$2,015

State Children's Health Insurance, 2004

Enrollment (x 1,000)	NA
Expenditures ($ mil)	$28.5

Persons without health insurance, 2003

Number (x 1,000)	465
percent	17.4%
Number of children (x 1,000)	71
percent of children	10.5%

Federal public aid

Temporary Assistance for Needy Families, 2004

Recipients (x 1,000)	22
Families (x 1,000)	10

Supplemental Security Income, 2003

Recipients (x 1,000)	87
Payments ($ mil)	$361

Food Stamp Program, 2004

Participants (x 1,000)	346
Benefits ($ mil)	$347

4   Arkansas

Housing & Construction

Housing units
Total 2003 (estimate) 1,217,310
Total 2004 (estimate) 1,233,203
Seasonal or recreational use, 2003 23,000
Owner-occupied single-family, 2003.... 556,000
  Median value $83,699
Renter-occupied, 2003 337,000
  Median rent $513
Homeownership rate, 2003 .... 69.6%
Homeownership rate, 2004 .... 69.1%

New privately owned housing units, 2004
Number authorized (x 1,000) 15.9
Value ($ mil)........................ $1,764
Started 2005 (x 1,000, estimate)...........13.6
Started 2006 (x 1,000, estimate)...........13.6

Existing home sales
2002 (x 1,000)...........................52.2
2003 (x 1,000)...........................53.8
2004 (x 1,000)...........................60.9

Government & Elections

State Officials 2006
Governor (name/party/term expires)
  Mike Huckabee
  Republican - 1/07
Lieutenant Governor......Winthrop Rockefeller
Secretary of State............... Charlie Daniels
Attorney General.................. Mike Beebe
Chief Justice .... Jim Hannah

Governorship
Minimum age............................ 30
Length of term .... 4 years
Consecutive terms permitted 2
Who succeeds....................Lt. Governor

State Legislature
Name .... General Assembly
Upper chamber ....Senate
  Number of members.................... 35
  Length of term..................... 4 years
  Party in majority, 2006 ....Democratic
Lower chamber........House of Representatives
  Number of members................... 100
  Length of term..................... 2 years
  Party in majority, 2006 ....Democratic

State Government Employees, 2004
Total................................ 54,005
Payroll...................... $164,061,412

Local Government Employees, 2004
Total................................ 97,933
Payroll...................... $239,902,608

Local Governments by Type, 2002
Total................................. 1,588
  County................................. 75
  Municipal............................. 499
  Township 0
  School District....................... 310
  Special District 704

Voting age population, November 2004
Total............................. 2,010,000
  Male............................... 962,000
  Female........................... 1,048,000
  White............................ 1,649,000
  Black 295,000
  Hispanic 73,000
  Asian 24,000

Presidential Election, 2004
Total Popular Vote 1,054,945
  Kerry 469,953
  Bush............................... 572,898
Total Electoral Votes....................... 6

Federal representation, 2006 (109th Congress)
Senator.........................Mark Pryor
  Party .... Democrat
  Year term expires 2009
Senator.....................Blanche Lincoln
  Party .... Democrat
  Year term expires 2011
Representatives, total 4
  Democrats............................. 3
  Republicans 1
  Other 0

Votes cast for US Senators
2002
Total vote (x 1,000) 804,000
Leading party.....................Democratic
Percent for leading party 53.9%
2004
Total vote (x 1,000) 1,039,000
Leading party.....................Democratic
Percent for leading party 55.9%

Votes cast for US Representatives
2002
Total vote (x 1,000) 688
  Democratic............................ 392
  Republican 284
Leading party.....................Democratic
Percent for leading party 57.0%
2004
Total vote (x 1,000) 791
  Democratic............................ 426
  Republican 358
Leading party.....................Democratic
Percent for leading party 53.9%

Women holding public office, 2006

US Congress 1
Statewide elected office 0
State legislature 22

Black public officials, 2001

Total 502
  US and state legislatures 15
  City/county/regional offices 298
  Judicial/law enforcement 67
  Education/school boards 122

Hispanic public officials, 2004

Total 0
  State executives & legislators 0
  City/county/regional offices 0
  Judicial/law enforcement 0
  Education/school boards 0

Governmental Finance

State government revenues, 2004

Total revenue ($1,000) $14,225,176
  Revenue per capita 5,172.79

General Revenue ($ per capita) $4,247.17
  Intergovernmental 1,469.78
  Taxes 2,029.34
    general sales 781.65
    individual income tax 612.94
    corporate income tax 66.12
  Current charges 561.40
  Miscellaneous 186.66

State government expenditure, 2004

Total expenditure (x $1,000) $12,674,325
  Expenditure per capita 4,608.85
General Expenditure ($ per capita) $4,248.27
  Education 1,720.02
  Public welfare 1,089.17
  Health 114.93
  Hospitals 193.75
  Highways 405.93
  Police protection 29.02
  Correction 127.92
  Natural resources 81.87
  Parks & recreation 30.21
  Governmental administration 173.19
  Interest on general debt 44.77

State debt & cash, 2004 ($ per capita)

Debt $1,363.38
Cash/security holdings $6,904.80

Federal government grants to state & local government, 2004 (x $1,000)

Total $4,682,798
By Federal Agency
  Defense $37,948

By Federal Agency, continued
  Education 391,889
  Energy 3,366
  Environmental Protection Agency 42,043
  Health & Human Services 2,705,421
  Homeland Security 51,594
  Housing & Urban Development 251,547
  Justice 62,476
  Labor 71,760
  Transportation 706,796
  Veterans Affairs 2,381

Crime, Law Enforcement & Courts

Crime, 2004 (rates per 100,000 residents)

Property crimes 110,464
  Burglaries 30,099
  Larcenies 73,874
  Motor vehicle thefts 6,491
  Property crime rate 4,013.0
Violent crimes 13,737
  Murders 176
  Forcible rape 1,166
  Robberies 2,372
  Aggravated assaults 10,023
  Violent crime rate 499.1

Police Agencies, 2004

Total agencies 242
Total employees 7,826
  Male officers 4,690
  Female officers 544
  Male civilians 1,003
  Female civilians 1,589

Arrests, 2004

Total 98,086
  Persons under 18 years of age 9,358

Prisoners under state & federal jurisdiction, 2004

Total prisoners 13,807
  Percent change, 12/31/03 to 12/31/04 .... 3.7%
Sentenced to more than one year 13,668
  rate per 100,000 495

Persons under sentence of death, 7/1/05

Total 38
  White 16
  Black 22
  Hispanic 0

State's highest court

Name .... .Supreme Court
Number of members 7
Length of term .... 8 years
Intermediate appeals court? .... .yes

Labor & Income

Civilian labor force, 2004

Total............................. 1,308,000
  Men 707,000
  Women 601,000
  Persons 16-19 years................. 65,000
  White........................... 1,066,000
  Black 192,000
  Hispanic 51,000
  Asian 0

Civilian labor force as a percent of civilian non-institutional population, 2004

Total................................. 62.2%
  Men 70.1
  Women 54.9
  Persons 16-19 years................. 45.0
  White.............................. 62.1
  Black 62.4
  Hispanic 73.9
  Asian 0.0

Employment, 2004

Total............................. 1,231,000
  Men 668,000
  Women 562,000
  Persons 16-19 years................. 50,000
  White........................... 1,016,000
  Black 167,000
  Hispanic 49,000
  Asian 0

Full-time/part-time labor force, 2002

Full-time labor force, employed 1,015,000
Part-time labor force, employed........ 201,000
Unemployed, looking for
  Full-time work..................... 60,000
  Part-time work......................... NA

Unemployment rate, 2004

Total................................. 5.9%
  Men 5.5
  Women 6.4
  Persons 16-19 years................. 24.1
  White.............................. 4.7
  Black 12.8
  Hispanic 5.3
  Asian .... NA

Unemployed by reason for unemployment (as a percent of total unemployment), 2002

Job losers or completed temp jobs 44.3%
Job leavers................................ NA
Reentrants................................. NA
New entrants .... NA

Labor unions, 2004

Membership 51,000
  percent of employed 4.8%

Experienced civilian labor force by private industry, first quarter 2004

Total............................... 931,292
  Natural Resources & Mining 17,988
  Construction 49,539
  Manufacturing...................... 203,032
  Trade, transportation & utilities 235,128
  Information 20,243
  Finance 48,520
  Professional & business 106,792
  Education & Health 135,545
  Leisure & hospitality................ 89,127
  Other.............................. 25,378

Experienced civilian labor force by occupation, 2004

Management......................... 44,510
Business & Financial.................. 34,210
Legal................................ 5,410
Sales 113,090
Office & Admin. Support............. 178,200
Computers & Math 13,180
Architecture & Engineering 12,690
Arts & Entertainment................. 8,120
Education 65,930
Social Services 13,110
Healthcare Practitioner & Technical..... 62,460
Healthcare support.................. 30,160
Maintenance & Repair 52,920
Construction 46,850
Transportation & moving 116,930
Production 156,860
Farming, fishing & forestry............. 7,400

Hours and earnings of production workers on manufacturing payrolls, 2004

Average weekly hours..................... 39.9
Average hourly earnings $13.49
Average weekly earnings $538.25

Average annual pay

2004............................... $30,245
  change from 2003 .... 4.7%

Household income

Median household income, three-year average,
  2002-2004......................... $33,948

Personal income, 2004 ($ per capita)

In current dollars.................... $25,725
In constant (2000) dollars $23,858

Poverty

Persons below poverty level, three-year average,
  2002-2004......................... 17.6%

Federal individual income tax returns, 2003

Returns filed....................... 1,121,518
Adjusted gross income ($1,000) $41,364,084
Total income tax paid ($1,000) $4,451,723

Economy, Business, Industry & Agriculture

Fortune 500 companies, 2005 5

Patents issued, 2004 160

Bankruptcy cases filed, 2004 24,200

Business firm ownership, 2002
Women-owned........................ 49,614
  Sales ($ mil) $6,338
Black-owned........................... 8,944
  Sales ($ mil) $481
Hispanic-owned....................... 2,095
  Sales ($ mil) $387
Asian-owned 2,057
  Sales ($ mil) $616
Amer. Indian/Alaska Native-owned 2,283
  Sales ($ mil) $317
Hawaiian/Pacific Isl.-owned.............. NA
  Sales ($ mil) $4

Gross State Product, 2004 ($ mil)
Total Gross State Product $80,902
  Agriculture, forestry, fishing and
    hunting 3,154
  Mining............................... 336
  Utilities............................ 1,782
  Construction 3,647
  Manufacturing, durable goods......... 7,755
  Manufacturing, non-durable goods 7,095
  Wholesale trade..................... 5,333
  Retail trade........................ 6,006
  Transportation & warehousing 3,983
  Information 3,338
  Finance & insurance................. 3,646
  Real estate, rental, leasing 7,417
  Professional and technical services 2,915
  Educational services.................. 319
  Health care and social assistance 6,150
  Accommodation/food services......... 1,784
  Other services, except government 1,923
  Government 10,394

Establishments, by major industry group, 2003
Total................................ 64,285
  Forestry, fishing & agriculture 888
  Mining.............................. 285
  Construction 5,881
  Manufacturing....................... 3,127
  Wholesale trade..................... 3,459
  Retail trade........................ 11,921
  Transportation & warehousing 2,587
  Information 1,038
  Finance & insurance................. 4,138
  Professional/scientific/technical 5,165
  Health care/social assistance 6,588
  Accommodation/food services......... 4,665

Annual payroll by major industry group, 2003
Total ($1,000) $27,035,322
  Forestry, fishing & agriculture .... NA
  Mining............................ 144,642
  Utilities........................... 414,744
  Construction 1,333,999
  Manufacturing.................... 6,386,389
  Wholesale trade................. 1,570,101
  Retail trade..................... 2,500,831
  Transportation & warehousing 1,790,322
  Information 1,246,486
  Finance & insurance............. 1,387,682
  Professional/scientific/technical ... 1,213,345
  Health care/social assistance 4,431,302
  Accommodation/food services....... 798,043

Agriculture
Number of farms, 2004 48,000
Farm acreage, 2004
  Total........................ 14,000,000
  Acres per farm, 2004 303
Farm income, 2003 ($mil)
  Net farm income $1,914
  Debt/asset ratio 18.8
Farm marketings, 2003 ($mil)
Total................................ $5,298
  Crops............................. 2,083
  Livestock.......................... 3,215

Principal commodities, in order by marketing receipts, 2003
Broilers, soybeans, rice, cotton

Federal economic activity in state
Expenditures, 2003
  Total ($ mil) $18,340
  Per capita $6,729
  Defense ($ mil)..................... 1,445
  Non-defense ($ mil) 16,895
Defense department, 2003
  Payroll ($ mil) $888
  Contract awards ($ mil)............... $588
  Grants ($ mil)........................ $39
  Homeland security grants ($1,000)
    2004 .... $28,815
    2005 .... $21,561

FDIC insured financial institutions, 2004
Number............................... 168
  Assets ($bil) $40.7
  Deposits ($bil) 38.7

Fishing, 2004
Catch (x 1,000 lbs) 0
Value ($1,000).......................... 0

8   Arkansas

Mining, 2004 ($ mil)
Total non-fuel mineral production $514
Percent of U.S. 1.2%

Construction, 2003 ($ mil)
Total contracts (including non-building). $3,974
    residential 1,960
    non-residential 1,105

Establishments, receipts, payroll & employees, by major industry group, 2002

Mining 871
    Receipts ($1,000) $7,293,240
    Annual payroll ($1,000). $936,870
    Paid employees 20,321

Utilities 403
    Receipts ($1,000) . . . . NA
    Annual payroll ($1,000). $394,159
    Paid employees 7,354

Construction 5,637
    Receipts ($1,000) $6,623,949
    Annual payroll ($1,000). $1,297,957
    Paid employees 46,644

Manufacturing 3,185
    Receipts ($1,000) $46,721,413
    Annual payroll ($1,000). $6,309,251
    Paid employees 210,394

Wholesale trade 3,498
    Receipts ($1,000) $34,470,795
    Annual payroll ($1,000). $1,437,962
    Paid employees 42,875

Retail trade 12,141
    Receipts ($1,000) $25,611,630
    Annual payroll ($1,000). $2,347,757
    Paid employees 134,197

Transportation 2,514
    Receipts ($1,000) $5,222,960
    Annual payroll ($1,000). $1,678,344
    Paid employees 59,011

Information 1,002
    Receipts ($1,000) . . . . NA
    Annual payroll ($1,000). $1,269,461
    Paid employees 31,437

Finance & insurance 3,953
    Receipts ($1,000) . . . . NA
    Annual payroll ($1,000). $1,285,696
    Paid employees 33,948

Professional, scientific & technical 5,008
    Receipts ($1,000) $2,599,015
    Annual payroll ($1,000). $1,069,003
    Paid employees 30,467

Health care & social assistance 6,428
    Receipts ($1,000) $9,675,926
    Annual payroll ($1,000). $3,927,617
    Paid employees 134,427

Accommodation & food service 4,659
    Receipts ($1,000) $2,766,905
    Annual payroll ($1,000). $751,908
    Paid employees 77,835

Communication, Energy & Transportation

Communication
Daily newspapers, 2004 28
Households with computers, 2003 . . . . .50%
Households with internet access, 2003 . . . . .42%

Energy
Electricity Consumption, 2001
Total (trillion Btu) 1,106
Per capita (million Btu) 411
By source of production (trillion Btu)
    Coal 274
    Natural gas 232
    Petroleum 379
    Nuclear electric power 154
    Hydroelectric power 26
By end-use sector (trillion Btu)
    Residential 219
    Commercial 148
    Industrial 462
    Transportation 278
Electric energy, 2003
    Production (billion kWh) 50.4
    Net summer capability (million kW) 13.5
Gas utilities, 2003
    Customers (x1,000) 625
    Sales (trillion Btu) 72
    Revenues ($mil) $633
Nuclear plants, 2003 2

Transportation, 2004
Public Road & Street Mileage 98,606
    Urban. 10,863
    Rural 87,743
    Interstate. 656
Vehicle miles of travel per capita 11,567.3
Total motor vehicle registrations 1,917,503
    Automobiles. 960,085
    Buses 7,662
    Trucks 949,756
    Motorcycles 43,668
Licensed drivers 1,862,430
    19 years & under 107,035
Deaths from motor vehicle accidents 704

State Summary

Capital City...................Sacramento
Governor.............Arnold Schwarzenegger
Office of the Governor
State Capitol
Sacramento, CA 95814
916-445-2841
Admitted as a state 1850
Area (square miles) 163,696
Population, 2004 (est.) 35,893,799
Largest City......................Los Angeles
Population, 2004................. 3,846,000
Personal income per capita, 2004
(in current dollars) $35,019
Gross state product ($ mil), 2004 .... $1,550,753

Leading industries by payroll, 2003

Manufacturing, Professional/Scientific/Technical, Health care/Social assistance

Leading agricultural commodities by receipts, 2003

Dairy products, greenhouse, grapes, lettuce

Geography & Environment

Total area (sq. mi.)................... 163,696
land 155,959
water 7,736
Federally-owned land, 2004 (acres) .. 45,393,238
percent............................45.3%
Highest point....................Mt. Whitney
elevation (feet) 14,494
Lowest point ....Death Valley
elevation (feet) .... -282
General coastline (miles)................... 840
Tidal shoreline (miles)................... 3,427
Capital City......................Sacramento
Population 2000 407,000
Population 2004 454,000
Largest City......................Los Angeles
Population 2000 3,695,000
Population 2004 3,846,000

Number of cities with over 100,000 population

1990 43
2000 56
2004 62

State park and recreation areas, 2003

Area (acres x 1,000)..................... 1,481
Number of visitors (x 1,000) 85,779
Revenues (x 1,000)................... $58,065
percent of operating expenditures...... 20.0%

National forest system land, 2004

Acres 20,770,000

Demographics and Characteristics of the Population

Population

1980 23,667,902
1990 29,760,021
2000 33,871,648
2004 (estimate).................... 35,893,799
persons per sq. mile of land............230.1
2005 (projection)................. 36,038,859
Male........................... 17,894,166
Female......................... 18,144,693
2010 (projection)................. 38,067,134
2020 (projection)................. 42,206,743
2030 (projection)................. 46,444,861
Male........................... 22,898,523
Female......................... 23,546,338

Metropolitan and Non-Metro. area population

	Metro	Non-Metro
1980	22,689,000	979,000
1990	28,493,000	1,267,000
2000	32,750,000	1,121,000

Change in population, 2000-2004

Number........................... 2,022,146
percent............................6.0%
Natural increase (births minus deaths) 1,260,527
Net internal migration ....-415,313
Net international migration 1,192,430

Persons by age, 2004

Under 5 years 2,633,972
18 years and over 26,297,336
65 years and over 3,822,957
85 years and over 514,013

Persons by age, 2010 (projected)

Total........................... 38,067,134
Under 5 years 2,853,032
5 to 17 years 6,643,946
18 and over 28,570,156
21 and over 26,781,683
65 and over 4,392,708
85 and over 671,624
Median age 34.9

Race, 2004 (estimate)

One Race
White....................... 27,710,227
Black or African American 2,436,678
American Indian/Alaska Native...... 416,646
Pacific Islander 149,134
Asian Indian...................... 405,976
Chinese 1,127,363
Filipino 1,059,512
Japanese 315,549
Korean....................... 411,062
Vietnamese...................... 495,142
Two or more races.................... 854,988

Persons of Hispanic origin, 2004

Total Hispanic or Latino	12,246,122
Mexican	10,069,145
Puerto Rican	165,661
Cuban	72,696
Other Hispanic or Latino	585,414

Marital status, 2000

Population 15 years & over	26,076,163
Never married	7,848,925
Married	13,637,833
Separated	651,904
Widowed	1,460,265
Divorced	2,477,235

Language spoken at home, 2000

Population 5 years & over	31,416,629
English only	19,014,873
Spanish	8,105,505
Other Indo-European languages	1,335,332
Asian/Pacific Island languages	2,709,179

Households & families, 2000

Households	11,502,870
with persons under 18 years	4,569,910
with persons over 65 years	2,570,170
persons per household	2.87
Families	7,920,049
persons per family	3.43
Married couples	5,877,084
Female householder, no husband present	1,448,510
One-person households	2,708,308

Nativity, 2000

Number of persons born in state	17,019,097
percent of population	50.2%

Immigration & Naturalization, 2004

Immigrants admitted	252,920
Persons naturalized	145,593
Asylums granted	2,681
Asylums denied	561

Vital Statistics and Health

Marriages

2002	217,880
2003	194,914
2004	172,302

Divorces

2002	NA
2003	NA
2004	NA

Births

2003	540,997
Birthrate (per 1,000)	15.2
Low birth weight (2,500g or less)	6.6%
To unmarried mothers	33.5%

2003, continued

White	438,035
Black	32,676
Hispanic	268,867
Asian/Pacific Islander	67,603
Amer. Indian/Alaska Native	2,681
2004 (preliminary)	545,071
Birthrate (per 1,000)	15.2
White	441,315
Black	32,106
Hispanic	275,365
Asian/Pacific Islander	68,749

Deaths

2002

All causes	234,565
rate per 100,000	668.0
Heart disease	68,797
rate per 100,000	195.9
Malignant neoplasms	54,143
rate per 100,000	154.2
Cerebrovascular disease	17,626
rate per 100,000	50.2
Chronic lower respiratory disease	12,684
rate per 100,000	36.1
2003	NA
rate per 100,000	NA
2004 (provisional)	238,958

Infant deaths

2003 (provisional)	2,560
rate per 1,000	4.7
2004 (provisional)	2,781
rate per 1,000	5.1

Abortions, 2000

Total	236,000
rate per 1,000 women age 15-44	31.2

Physicians, 2003

Total	92,470
rate per 1,000 persons	261

Nurses, 2001

Total	185,550
rate per 1,000 persons	536

Community Hospitals, 2003

Number	370
Beds (x 1,000)	74.3
Patients admitted (x 1,000)	3,474
Average daily census (x 1,000)	51.5
Average cost per day	$1,763
Outpatient visits (x mil)	48.0

Disability status of population, 2004

5 to 20 years	4.9%
21 to 64 years	10.5%
65 years and over	39.4%

Education

Educational attainment, 2004

Population over 25 years 22,165,726
- Less than 9th grade 2,250,737
- High school graduates only....... 4,789,186
- Bachelor's degree only 4,209,624
- Graduate or professional degree.... 2,297,198
- Less than 9th grade percent 10.2%
- High school graduate or more 81.3%
- College graduate or more............. 31.7%
- Graduate or professional degree....... 10.4%

Public school enrollment, Fall 2002

Total............................. 6,356,348
- Kindergarten through grade 8 4,528,719
- Grades 9 through 12 1,827,629
Enrollment, 2005 (projected) 6,518,000

Graduating public high school seniors

2004 (estimate)....................... 342,580

SAT scores, 2005

Average verbal score 504
Average math score 522
Percent of graduates taking test 50%

Public school teachers, 2004

Total (x 1,000) 305.9
- Elementary (x 1,000)..................220.7
- Secondary (x 1,000) 85.2
Average salary $56,400
- Elementary........................ $56,400
- Secondary......................... $56,400

State receipts & expenditures for public schools, 2004

Revenue receipts ($mil)................ $60,595
Expenditures
Total ($mil)........................... $58,752
- Per capita $1,657
- Per pupil $7,860

Institutions of higher education, 2004

Total................................. 401
- Public.............................. 144
- Private............................. 257

Enrollment in institutions of higher education, Fall, 2003

Total............................. 2,410,306
- Full-time men 541,955
- Full-time women.................. 701,300
- Part-time men 506,006
- Part-time women.................. 661,045

Minority enrollment in institutions of higher education, Fall, 2003

Black, non-hispanic................. 158,772
Hispanic 528,146
Asian/Pacific Islander 390,158
American Indian/Alaska Native........ 19,785

Earned degrees conferred, 2003

Bachelor's 135,844
Master's............................ 48,651
First-professional................... 8,624
Doctor's............................ 5,731

State & local financial support for higher education, 2003-2004

Full-time equivalent enrollment (x 1,000) 1,623.5
Appropriations per FTE................ $6,103
- as a percent of tax revenue............. 9.7%

Social Insurance & Welfare Programs

Social Security benefits & beneficiaries, 2004

Beneficiaries
- Total........................... 4,412,000
- Retired & dependents............. 3,162,000
- Survivors....................... 579,000
- Disabled & dependents............ 671,000
Annual benefit payments ($ mil)
- Total........................... $45,788
- Retired & dependents.............. $31,216
- Survivors....................... $7,760
- Disabled & dependents........... $6,812
Average Monthly Benefit
- Retired & dependents................. $957
- Disabled & dependents............. $910
- Widowed........................... $949

Medicare

Enrollment, 2001 (x 1,000) 3,955
- Payments ($ mil, est.) $24,900
Enrollment, 2003 (x 1,000) 4,078

Medicaid, 2002

Beneficiaries (x 1,000).................. 9,301
Payments ($ mil) $23,636

State Children's Health Insurance, 2004

Enrollment (x 1,000)................. 1,035.8
Expenditures ($ mil)................. $661.6

Persons without health insurance, 2003

Number (x 1,000)..................... 6,499
- percent........................... 18.4%
Number of children (x 1,000) 1,196
- percent of children 12.5%

Federal public aid

Temporary Assistance for Needy Families, 2004
Recipients (x 1,000).................... 1,103
Families (x 1,000) 457

Supplemental Security Income, 2003
Recipients (x 1,000).................... 1,163
Payments ($ mil) $7,573

Food Stamp Program, 2004

Participants (x 1,000) 1,859
Benefits ($ mil)........................ $1,990

Housing & Construction

Housing units

Total 2003 (estimate)	12,635,635
Total 2004 (estimate)	12,804,702
Seasonal or recreational use, 2003	242,000
Owner-occupied single-family, 2003	5,921,000
Median value	$334,426
Renter-occupied, 2003	4,941,000
Median rent	$890
Homeownership rate, 2003	58.9%
Homeownership rate, 2004	59.7%

New privately owned housing units, 2004

Number authorized (x 1,000)	207.4
Value ($ mil)	$36,059
Started 2005 (x 1,000, estimate)	165.0
Started 2006 (x 1,000, estimate)	154.2

Existing home sales

2002 (x 1,000)	565.1
2003 (x 1,000)	577.6
2004 (x 1,000)	610.1

Government & Elections

State Officials 2006

Governor (name/party/term expires)
Arnold Schwarzenegger
Republican - 1/07

Lieutenant Governor	Cruz Bustamante
Secretary of State	Bruce McPherson
Attorney General	Bill Lockyer
Chief Justice	Ronald George

Governorship

Minimum age	18
Length of term	4 years
Consecutive terms permitted	2
Who succeeds	Lt. Governor

State Legislature

Name	Legislature
Upper chamber	Senate
Number of members	40
Length of term	4 years
Party in majority, 2006	Democratic
Lower chamber	Assembly
Number of members	80
Length of term	2 years
Party in majority, 2006	Democratic

State Government Employees, 2004

Total	393,057
Payroll	$1,890,810,935

Local Government Employees, 2004

Total	1,383,075
Payroll	$6,318,048,725

Local Governments by Type, 2002

Total	4,409
County	57
Municipal	475
Township	0
School District	1,047
Special District	2,830

Voting age population, November 2004

Total	26,085,000
Male	12,783,000
Female	13,302,000
White	20,083,000
Black	1,678,000
Hispanic	8,127,000
Asian	3,524,000

Presidential Election, 2004

Total Popular Vote	12,421,852
Kerry	6,745,485
Bush	5,509,826
Total Electoral Votes	55

Federal representation, 2006 (109th Congress)

Senator	Barbara Boxer
Party	Democrat
Year term expires	2011
Senator	Dianne Feinstein
Party	Democrat
Year term expires	2007
Representatives, total	53
Democrats	33
Republicans	20
Other	0

Votes cast for US Senators

2002

Total vote (x 1,000)	NA
Leading party	NA
Percent for leading party	NA

2004

Total vote (x 1,000)	12,053,000
Leading party	Democratic
Percent for leading party	57.7%

Votes cast for US Representatives

2002

Total vote (x 1,000)	7,258
Democratic	3,731
Republican	3,226
Leading party	Democratic
Percent for leading party	51.4%

2004

Total vote (x 1,000)	11,624
Democratic	6,224
Republican	5,031
Leading party	Democratic
Percent for leading party	53.5%

Women holding public office, 2006

US Congress 21
Statewide elected office..................... 0
State legislature 37

Black public officials, 2001

Total.................................... 224
   US and state legislatures 10
   City/county/regional offices 70
   Judicial/law enforcement................. 67
   Education/school boards................. 77

Hispanic public officials, 2004

Total.................................... 981
   State executives & legislators 28
   City/county/regional offices 379
   Judicial/law enforcement................. 39
   Education/school boards............... 535

Governmental Finance

State government revenues, 2004

Total revenue ($1,000) $229,289,356
   Revenue per capita 6,397.23

General Revenue ($ per capita)........ $4,310.16
   Intergovernmental 1,382.62
   Taxes 2,391.65
      general sales 739.55
      individual income tax............ 1,015.54
      corporate income tax 193.23
   Current charges.................... 317.69
   Miscellaneous 218.21

State government expenditure, 2004

Total expenditure (x $1,000) $203,814,714
   Expenditure per capita............ 5,686.48
General Expenditure ($ per capita).... $4,773.13
   Education 1,667.80
   Public welfare..................... 1,308.48
   Health 265.75
   Hospitals.......................... 144.21
   Highways 219.24
   Police protection 35.53
   Correction 163.93
   Natural resources 101.19
   Parks & recreation.................. 22.65
   Governmental administration 231.54
   Interest on general debt 115.55

State debt & cash, 2004 ($ per capita)

Debt $2,868.50
Cash/security holdings............ $12,160.07

Federal government grants to state & local government, 2004 (x $1,000)

Total........................... $54,534,048

By Federal Agency
   Defense $565,788

By Federal Agency, continued
   Education 4,723,920
   Energy 229,234
   Environmental Protection Agency ... 329,222
   Health & Human Services. 33,194,283
   Homeland Security................ 110,664
   Housing & Urban Development.... 4,378,192
   Justice 912,192
   Labor 670,354
   Transportation 4,638,913
   Veterans Affairs.................... 48,519

Crime, Law Enforcement & Courts

Crime, 2004 (rates per 100,000 residents)

Property crimes 1,227,194
   Burglaries....................... 245,903
   Larcenies........................ 728,687
   Motor vehicle thefts 252,604
   Property crime rate................. 3,419.0
Violent crimes..................... 198,070
   Murders......................... 2,392
   Forcible rape...................... 9,615
   Robberies 61,768
   Aggravated assaults 124,295
   Violent crime rate................... 551.8

Police Agencies, 2004

Total agencies.......................... 457
Total employees 112,584
   Male officers..................... 64,511
   Female officers.................... 9,353
   Male civilians..................... 13,604
   Female civilians.................... 25,116

Arrests, 2004

Total........................... 1,414,732
   Persons under 18 years of age 204,602

Prisoners under state & federal jurisdiction, 2004

Total prisoners..................... 166,556
   Percent change, 12/31/03 to 12/31/04 .... 1.3%
Sentenced to more than one year 164,933
   rate per 100,000....................... 456

Persons under sentence of death, 7/1/05

Total.................................. 648
   White........................... 253
   Black 233
   Hispanic 128

State's highest court

Name .... Supreme Court
Number of members..................... 7
Length of term .... 12 years
Intermediate appeals court? .... yes

Labor & Income

Civilian labor force, 2004

Total	17,551,000
Men	9,690,000
Women	7,860,000
Persons 16-19 years	751,000
White	13,660,000
Black	1,065,000
Hispanic	5,456,000
Asian	2,182,000

Civilian labor force as a percent of civilian non-institutional population, 2004

Total	65.6%
Men	73.9
Women	57.6
Persons 16-19 years	37.2
White	66.1
Black	61.9
Hispanic	67.9
Asian	64.0

Employment, 2004

Total	16,466,000
Men	9,076,000
Women	7,390,000
Persons 16-19 years	595,000
White	12,850,000
Black	953,000
Hispanic	5,012,000
Asian	2,071,000

Full-time/part-time labor force, 2002

Full-time labor force, employed	13,347,000
Part-time labor force, employed	2,894,000
Unemployed, looking for	
Full-time work	992,000
Part-time work	171,000

Unemployment rate, 2004

Total	6.2%
Men	6.3
Women	6.0
Persons 16-19 years	20.8
White	5.9
Black	10.6
Hispanic	8.1
Asian	5.1

Unemployed by reason for unemployment (as a percent of total unemployment), 2002

Job losers or completed temp jobs	56.6%
Job leavers	8.2
Reentrants	27.8
New entrants	7.4

Labor unions, 2004

Membership	2,385,000
percent of employed	16.5%

Experienced civilian labor force by private industry, first quarter 2004

Total	12,390,175
Natural Resources & Mining	333,641
Construction	806,863
Manufacturing	1,510,536
Trade, transportation & utilities	2,673,667
Information	486,678
Finance	887,186
Professional & business	2,047,280
Education & Health	1,521,400
Leisure & hospitality	1,400,052
Other	666,452

Experienced civilian labor force by occupation, 2004

Management	765,610
Business & Financial	631,770
Legal	109,330
Sales	1,516,180
Office & Admin. Support	2,673,520
Computers & Math	379,770
Architecture & Engineering	326,000
Arts & Entertainment	289,110
Education	908,450
Social Services	182,760
Healthcare Practitioner & Technical	592,180
Healthcare support	310,520
Maintenance & Repair	502,440
Construction	749,780
Transportation & moving	1,038,330
Production	997,660
Farming, fishing & forestry	171,580

Hours and earnings of production workers on manufacturing payrolls, 2004

Average weekly hours	40.0
Average hourly earnings	$15.35
Average weekly earnings	$614.00

Average annual pay

2004	$44,641
change from 2003	4.8%

Household income

Median household income, three-year average, 2002-2004	$49,894

Personal income, 2004 ($ per capita)

In current dollars	$35,019
In constant (2000) dollars	$32,478

Poverty

Persons below poverty level, three-year average, 2002-2004	13.2%

Federal individual income tax returns, 2003

Returns filed	15,171,832
Adjusted gross income ($1,000)	$803,511,651
Total income tax paid ($1,000)	$108,077,670

Economy, Business, Industry & Agriculture

Fortune 500 companies, 2005 52

Patents issued, 2004 21,601

Bankruptcy cases filed, 2004 132,500

Business firm ownership, 2002
Women-owned. 870,612
  Sales ($ mil) $138,003
Black-owned. 113,003
  Sales ($ mil) $10,184
Hispanic-owned. 427,805
  Sales ($ mil) $57,835
Asian-owned 372,221
  Sales ($ mil) $130,318
Amer. Indian/Alaska Native-owned 40,541
  Sales ($ mil) $4,387
Hawaiian/Pacific Isl.-owned 7,308
  Sales ($ mil) $1,525

Gross State Product, 2004 ($ mil)
Total Gross State Product $1,550,753
  Agriculture, forestry, fishing and
    hunting 21,504
  Mining. 12,730
  Utilities 27,570
  Construction 71,266
  Manufacturing, durable goods. 109,961
  Manufacturing, non-durable goods . . . 65,891
  Wholesale trade. 86,822
  Retail trade. 108,804
  Transportation & warehousing 35,658
  Information 101,556
  Finance & insurance. 110,701
  Real estate, rental, leasing 240,370
  Professional and technical services . . . 121,686
  Educational services. 10,822
  Health care and social assistance. 90,286
  Accommodation/food services. 39,975
  Other services, except government 37,302
  Government 167,709

Establishments, by major industry group, 2003
Total. 827,472
  Forestry, fishing & agriculture 2,303
  Mining. 818
  Construction 70,333
  Manufacturing. 46,919
  Wholesale trade. 59,137
  Retail trade. 110,506
  Transportation & warehousing 19,184
  Information 20,624
  Finance & insurance. 47,929
  Professional/scientific/technical 101,121
  Health care/social assistance 90,038
  Accommodation/food services. 67,732

Annual payroll by major industry group, 2003
Total ($1,000) $520,597,420
  Forestry, fishing & agriculture 729,216
  Mining. 1,013,246
  Utilities 4,463,484
  Construction 33,304,468
  Manufacturing. 67,751,831
  Wholesale trade. 40,649,466
  Retail trade. 39,384,726
  Transportation & warehousing . . . 16,877,905
  Information 37,767,828
  Finance & insurance. 46,807,107
  Professional/scientific/technical . . 64,354,117
  Health care/social assistance 56,238,269
  Accommodation/food services. . . . 17,466,984

Agriculture
Number of farms, 2004 77,000
Farm acreage, 2004
  Total. 27,000,000
  Acres per farm, 2004 347
Farm income, 2003 ($mil)
  Net farm income $8,475
  Debt/asset ratio .20.6
Farm marketings, 2003 ($mil)
  Total. $27,805
  Crops 20,812
  Livestock 6,993

Principal commodities, in order by marketing receipts, 2003
Dairy products, greenhouse, grapes, lettuce

Federal economic activity in state
Expenditures, 2003
  Total ($ mil) $219,706
  Per capita $6,192
  Defense ($ mil). 39,240
  Non-defense ($ mil) 180,466
Defense department, 2003
  Payroll ($ mil) $13,272
  Contract awards ($ mil) $28,681
  Grants ($ mil). $407
  Homeland security grants ($1,000)
    2004 . . . . $349,894
    2005 . . . . $282,622

FDIC insured financial institutions, 2004
Number 295
  Assets ($bil) $838.5
  Deposits ($bil) .671.1

Fishing, 2004
Catch (x 1,000 lbs) 378,565
Value ($1,000). $138,977

Mining, 2004 ($ mil)
Total non-fuel mineral production $3,620
Percent of U.S. 8.2%

Construction, 2003 ($ mil)
Total contracts (including non-building) $59,781
   residential 33,907
   non-residential 17,320

Establishments, receipts, payroll & employees, by major industry group, 2002

Mining 950
   Receipts ($1,000) $5,342,881
   Annual payroll ($1,000) $686,454
   Paid employees 13,448

Utilities 1,144
   Receipts ($1,000) . . . . NA
   Annual payroll ($1,000) $3,814,616
   Paid employees 57,461

Construction 69,023
   Receipts ($1,000) $150,527,556
   Annual payroll ($1,000) $32,986,608
   Paid employees 870,334

Manufacturing 48,478
   Receipts ($1,000) $378,661,414
   Annual payroll ($1,000) $66,468,561
   Paid employees 1,616,504

Wholesale trade 58,770
   Receipts ($1,000) $655,954,708
   Annual payroll ($1,000) $39,060,893
   Paid employees 811,344

Retail trade 108,941
   Receipts ($1,000) $359,120,365
   Annual payroll ($1,000) $37,282,032
   Paid employees 1,525,113

Transportation 19,012
   Receipts ($1,000) $45,507,276
   Annual payroll ($1,000) $13,129,272
   Paid employees 397,266

Information 20,484
   Receipts ($1,000) . . . . NA
   Annual payroll ($1,000) $35,120,863
   Paid employees 563,841

Finance & insurance 45,981
   Receipts ($1,000) . . . . NA
   Annual payroll ($1,000) $42,647,825
   Paid employees 681,626

Professional, scientific & technical 100,284
   Receipts ($1,000) $145,236,098
   Annual payroll ($1,000) $61,995,937
   Paid employees 1,164,306

Health care & social assistance 88,249
   Receipts ($1,000) $136,397,384
   Annual payroll ($1,000) $51,786,504
   Paid employees 1,434,479

Accommodation & food service 66,568
   Receipts ($1,000) $55,559,669
   Annual payroll ($1,000) $15,830,563
   Paid employees 1,145,536

Communication, Energy & Transportation

Communication
Daily newspapers, 2004 90
Households with computers, 2003 . . . . 66%
Households with internet access, 2003 . . . . . 60%

Energy
Electricity Consumption, 2001
Total (trillion Btu) 7,853
Per capita (million Btu) 227
By source of production (trillion Btu)
   Coal 68
   Natural gas 2,514
   Petroleum 3,604
   Nuclear electric power 347
   Hydroelectric power 256
By end-use sector (trillion Btu)
   Residential 1,446
   Commercial 1,509
   Industrial 1,928
   Transportation 2,971
Electric energy, 2003
   Production (billion kWh) 192.8
   Net summer capability (million kW) 57.9
Gas utilities, 2003
   Customers (x1,000) 10,224
   Sales (trillion Btu) 708
   Revenues ($mil) $6,137
Nuclear plants, 2003 4

Transportation, 2004
Public Road & Street Mileage 169,791
   Urban 86,137
   Rural 83,654
   Interstate 2,458
Vehicle miles of travel per capita 9,068.8
Total motor vehicle registrations 31,399,596
   Automobiles 19,255,690
   Buses 53,643
   Trucks 12,090,263
   Motorcycles 626,529
Licensed drivers 22,761,088
   19 years & under 936,015
Deaths from motor vehicle accidents 4,120

Colorado   1

State Summary

Capital City. . . . . Denver
Governor. . . . . Bill Owens
136 State Capitol
Denver, CO 80203
303-866-2471

Admitted as a state 1876
Area (square miles) 104,094
Population, 2004 (est.) 4,601,403
Largest City. . . . . Denver
   Population, 2004. 557,000
Personal income per capita, 2004
   (in current dollars) $36,063
Gross state product ($ mil), 2004 . . . . . . $199,969

Leading industries by payroll, 2003

Professional/Scientific/Technical, Health care/
   Social assistance, Construction

Leading agricultural commodities by receipts, 2003

Cattle, dairy products, greenhouse, corn

Geography & Environment

Total area (sq. mi.) 104,094
   land 103,718
   water 376

Federally-owned land, 2004 (acres) . . 24,354,713
   percent. 36.6%

Highest point. . . . . Mt. Elbert
   elevation (feet) 14,433

Lowest point . . . . Arkansas River
   elevation (feet) 3,350

General coastline (miles). 0
Tidal shoreline (miles). 0

Capital City. . . . . Denver
   Population 2000 555,000
   Population 2004 557,000

Largest City. . . . . Denver
   Population 2000 555,000
   Population 2004 557,000

Number of cities with over 100,000 population

1990 4
2000 8
2004 9

State park and recreation areas, 2003

Area (acres x 1,000). 360
Number of visitors (x 1,000) 11,378
Revenues (x 1,000). . . . .
   percent of operating expenditures. . . . . . . NA

National forest system land, 2004

Acres 14,499,000

Demographics and Characteristics of the Population

Population

1980 2,889,964
1990 3,294,394
2000 4,301,261
2004 (estimate). 4,601,403
   persons per sq. mile of land. 44.4
2005 (projection) 4,617,962
   Male. 2,329,934
   Female 2,288,028
2010 (projection) 4,831,554
2020 (projection) 5,278,867
2030 (projection) 5,792,357
   Male. 2,938,068
   Female 2,854,289

Metropolitan and Non-Metro. area population

	Metro	Non-Metro
1980	2,326,000	563,000
1990	2,686,000	608,000
2000	3,608,000	694,000

Change in population, 2000-2004

Number 299,388
   percent. 7.0%
Natural increase (births minus deaths). . 164,359
Net internal migration 42,100
Net international migration 94,620

Persons by age, 2004

Under 5 years 339,079
18 years and over 3,422,514
65 years and over 450,971
85 years and over 55,636

Persons by age, 2010 (projected)

Total. 4,831,554
   Under 5 years 353,009
   5 to 17 years 835,574
   18 and over 3,642,971
   21 and over 3,438,486
   65 and over 517,419
   85 and over 74,269
   Median age 35.7

Race, 2004 (estimate)

One Race
   White. 4,154,464
   Black or African American 189,159
   American Indian/Alaska Native. 52,334
   Pacific Islander 6,485
   Asian Indian. 15,162
   Chinese 19,573
   Filipino 6,218
   Japanese 13,885
   Korean. 24,964
   Vietnamese. 17,522
Two or more races. 82,478

Persons of Hispanic origin, 2004

Total Hispanic or Latino 862,631
  Mexican........................ 643,235
  Puerto Rican 21,819
  Cuban 5,058
  Other Hispanic or Latino 153,520

Marital status, 2000

Population 15 years & over 3,385,369
  Never married 914,050
  Married....................... 1,882,265
  Separated 54,166
  Widowed........................ 159,112
  Divorced 372,391

Language spoken at home, 2000

Population 5 years & over 4,006,285
  English only 3,402,266
  Spanish 421,670
  Other Indo-European languages 100,148
  Asian/Pacific Island languages....... 63,745

Households & families, 2000

Households........................ 1,658,238
  with persons under 18 years 585,387
  with persons over 65 years......... 292,763
  persons per household 2.53
Families........................ 1,084,461
  persons per family.....................3.09
Married couples....................... 858,671
Female householder,
  no husband present................ 158,979
One-person households 435,778

Nativity, 2000

Number of persons born in state 1,766,731
  percent of population................ 41.1%

Immigration & Naturalization, 2004

Immigrants admitted.................. 10,923
Persons naturalized 6,007
Asylums granted 55
Asylums denied 15

Vital Statistics and Health

Marriages

2002 35,774
2003 35,204
2004 33,826

Divorces

2002 21,055
2003 19,280
2004 20,230

Births

2003 69,339
  Birthrate (per 1,000)....................15.2
  Low birth weight (2,500g or less)........ 9.0%
  To unmarried mothers................ 26.7%

2003, continued
  White......................... 63,189
  Black 2,938
  Hispanic 21,398
  Asian/Pacific Islander 2,672
  Amer. Indian/Alaska Native............. 564

2004 (preliminary)................... 68,520
  Birthrate (per 1,000)...................14.9
  White......................... 62,514
  Black 2,929
  Hispanic 21,746
  Asian/Pacific Islander 2,480

Deaths

2002
All causes 29,210
  rate per 100,000..................... 648.2
Heart disease 6,425
  rate per 100,000.....................142.6
Malignant neoplasms................... 6,384
  rate per 100,000.....................141.7
Cerebrovascular disease............... 1,915
  rate per 100,000..................... 42.5
Chronic lower respiratory disease 1,848
  rate per 100,000..................... 41.0
2003 29,542
  rate per 100,000.....................649.2
2004 (provisional) 28,296

Infant deaths

2003 (provisional) 416
  rate per 1,000 6
2004 (provisional) 442
  rate per 1,000 ....6.5

Abortions, 2000

Total............................. 16,000
  rate per 1,000 women age 15-44..........15.9

Physicians, 2003

Total............................. 11,600
  rate per 1,000 persons................. 255

Nurses, 2001

Total............................. 33,510
  rate per 1,000 persons................. 756

Community Hospitals, 2003

Number 68
Beds (x 1,000).........................9.5
Patients admitted (x 1,000) 444
Average daily census (x 1,000) 6.2
Average cost per day $1,551
Outpatient visits (x mil)....................7.0

Disability status of population, 2004

5 to 20 years 5.3%
21 to 64 years 10.1%
65 years and over 35.4%

Education

Educational attainment, 2004

Population over 25 years 2,894,340
  Less than 9th grade 130,662
  High school graduates only......... 699,826
  Bachelor's degree only 632,753
  Graduate or professional degree...... 343,081
  Less than 9th grade percent 4.5%
  High school graduate or more 88.3%
  College graduate or more............. 35.5%
  Graduate or professional degree....... 11.9%

Public school enrollment, Fall 2002

Total............................... 751,862
  Kindergarten through grade 8 534,465
  Grades 9 through 12 217,397
Enrollment, 2005 (projected) 768,600

Graduating public high school seniors

2004 (estimate)....................... 42,920

SAT scores, 2005

Average verbal score 560
Average math score 560
Percent of graduates taking test 26%

Public school teachers, 2004

Total (x 1,000) 44.9
  Elementary (x 1,000)...................22.4
  Secondary (x 1,000) 22.5
Average salary $43,300
  Elementary $43,300
  Secondary $43,200

State receipts & expenditures for public schools, 2004

Revenue receipts ($mil)................. $6,489
Expenditures
Total ($mil)........................... $7,272
  Per capita $1,599
  Per pupil $8,651

Institutions of higher education, 2004

Total.................................. 74
  Public............................... 28
  Private.............................. 46

Enrollment in institutions of higher education, Fall, 2003

Total............................... 306,370
  Full-time men 85,309
  Full-time women..................... 92,511
  Part-time men 52,617
  Part-time women..................... 75,933

Minority enrollment in institutions of higher education, Fall, 2003

Black, non-hispanic.................... 11,686
Hispanic 30,037
Asian/Pacific Islander 10,136
American Indian/Alaska Native.......... 4,006

Earned degrees conferred, 2003

Bachelor's 23,101
Master's 9,232
First-professional....................... 979
Doctor's................................ 813

State & local financial support for higher education, 2003-2004

Full-time equivalent enrollment (x 1,000) ..161.2
Appropriations per FTE................ $3,202
  as a percent of tax revenue............. 4.6%

Social Insurance & Welfare Programs

Social Security benefits & beneficiaries, 2004

Beneficiaries
  Total............................. 571,000
  Retired & dependents.............. 406,000
  Survivors.......................... 77,000
  Disabled & dependents.............. 88,000
Annual benefit payments ($ mil)
  Total.............................. $5,822
  Retired & dependents............... $3,926
  Survivors.......................... $1,025
  Disabled & dependents................ $871
Average Monthly Benefit
  Retired & dependents................. $935
  Disabled & dependents................ $887
  Widowed.............................. $929

Medicare

Enrollment, 2001 (x 1,000) 476
  Payments ($ mil, est.) $2,700
Enrollment, 2003 (x 1,000) 493

Medicaid, 2002

Beneficiaries (x 1,000)..................... 426
Payments ($ mil) $2,166

State Children's Health Insurance, 2004

Enrollment (x 1,000).....................57.2
Expenditures ($ mil)....................$37.6

Persons without health insurance, 2003

Number (x 1,000)......................... 772
  percent.............................. 17.2%
Number of children (x 1,000) 159
  percent of children 13.7%

Federal public aid

Temporary Assistance for Needy Families, 2004
Recipients (x 1,000)....................... 38
Families (x 1,000) 15

Supplemental Security Income, 2003
Recipients (x 1,000)....................... 54
Payments ($ mil) $246

Food Stamp Program, 2004

Participants (x 1,000) 242
Benefits ($ mil)......................... $251

Housing & Construction

Housing units

Total 2003 (estimate)	1,974,123
Total 2004 (estimate)	2,010,806
Seasonal or recreational use, 2003	24,000
Owner-occupied single-family, 2003	1,062,000
Median value	$210,398
Renter-occupied, 2003	532,000
Median rent	$754
Homeownership rate, 2003	71.3%
Homeownership rate, 2004	71.1%

New privately owned housing units, 2004

Number authorized (x 1,000)	46.5
Value ($ mil)	$8,050
Started 2005 (x 1,000, estimate)	36.8
Started 2006 (x 1,000, estimate)	37.7

Existing home sales

2002 (x 1,000)	109.4
2003 (x 1,000)	112.4
2004 (x 1,000)	126.0

Government & Elections

State Officials 2006

Governor (name/party/term expires)
Bill Owens
Republican - 1/07

Lieutenant Governor	Jane Norton
Secretary of State	Gigi Dennis
Attorney General	John Suthers
Chief Justice	Mary Mullarkey

Governorship

Minimum age	30
Length of term	4 years
Consecutive terms permitted	2
Who succeeds	Lt. Governor

State Legislature

Name	General Assembly
Upper chamber	Senate
Number of members	35
Length of term	4 years
Party in majority, 2006	Democratic
Lower chamber	House of Representatives
Number of members	65
Length of term	2 years
Party in majority, 2006	Democratic

State Government Employees, 2004

Total	65,652
Payroll	$266,515,794

Local Government Employees, 2004

Total	182,752
Payroll	$636,732,609

Local Governments by Type, 2002

Total	1,928
County	62
Municipal	270
Township	0
School District	182
Special District	1,414

Voting age population, November 2004

Total	3,398,000
Male	1,691,000
Female	1,708,000
White	3,098,000
Black	123,000
Hispanic	574,000
Asian	87,000

Presidential Election, 2004

Total Popular Vote	2,130,330
Kerry	1,001,732
Bush	1,101,255
Total Electoral Votes	9

Federal representation, 2006 (109th Congress)

Senator	Wayne Allard
Party	Republican
Year term expires	2009
Senator	Ken Salazar
Party	Democrat
Year term expires	2011
Representatives, total	7
Democrats	3
Republicans	4
Other	0

Votes cast for US Senators

2002

Total vote (x 1,000)	1,416,000
Leading party	Republican
Percent for leading party	50.7%

2004

Total vote (x 1,000)	2,107,000
Leading party	Democratic
Percent for leading party	51.3%

Votes cast for US Representatives

2002

Total vote (x 1,000)	1,397
Democratic	589
Republican	753
Leading party	Republican
Percent for leading party	53.9%

2004

Total vote (x 1,000)	2,039
Democratic	995
Republican	992
Leading party	Democratic
Percent for leading party	48.8%

Women holding public office, 2006
US Congress 2
Statewide elected office 2
State legislature 33

Black public officials, 2001
Total 18
    US and state legislatures 4
    City/county/regional offices 4
    Judicial/law enforcement 9
    Education/school boards 1

Hispanic public officials, 2004
Total 134
    State executives & legislators 8
    City/county/regional offices 92
    Judicial/law enforcement 9
    Education/school boards 25

Governmental Finance

State government revenues, 2004
Total revenue ($1,000) $23,081,951
    Revenue per capita 5,015.63

General Revenue ($ per capita) $3,250.05
    Intergovernmental 998.41
    Taxes 1,532.26
        general sales 414.87
        individual income tax 741.83
        corporate income tax 52.06
    Current charges 403.01
    Miscellaneous 316.37

State government expenditure, 2004
Total expenditure (x $1,000) $18,060,533
    Expenditure per capita 3,924.50
General Expenditure ($ per capita) $3,266.98
    Education 1,367.50
    Public welfare 768.75
    Health 170.44
    Hospitals 70.67
    Highways 298.59
    Police protection 24.41
    Correction 152.48
    Natural resources 44.99
    Parks & recreation 15.97
    Governmental administration 101.13
    Interest on general debt 88.69

State debt & cash, 2004 ($ per capita)
Debt $2,145.75
Cash/security holdings $10,308.79

Federal government grants to state & local government, 2004 (x $1,000)
Total $5,643,498

By Federal Agency
    Defense $80,854

By Federal Agency, continued
    Education 478,121
    Energy 59,023
    Environmental Protection Agency 67,278
    Health & Human Services. 2,667,061
    Homeland Security 17,478
    Housing & Urban Development 398,556
    Justice 127,252
    Labor 113,475
    Transportation 710,868
    Veterans Affairs 8,748

Crime, Law Enforcement & Courts

Crime, 2004 (rates per 100,000 residents)
Property crimes 180,342
    Burglaries 33,008
    Larcenies 123,271
    Motor vehicle thefts 24,063
    Property crime rate 3,919.3
Violent crimes 17,185
    Murders 203
    Forcible rape 1,956
    Robberies 3,750
    Aggravated assaults 11,276
    Violent crime rate 373.5

Police Agencies, 2004
Total agencies 223
Total employees 15,446
    Male officers 9,206
    Female officers 1,322
    Male civilians 1,531
    Female civilians 3,387

Arrests, 2004
Total 229,977
    Persons under 18 years of age 43,373

Prisoners under state & federal jurisdiction, 2004
Total prisoners 20,293
    Percent change, 12/31/03 to 12/31/04 .... 3.2%
Sentenced to more than one year 20,293
    rate per 100,000 438

Persons under sentence of death, 7/1/05
Total 3
    White 0
    Black 2
    Hispanic 1

State's highest court
Name .... Supreme Court
Number of members 7
Length of term .... 10 years
Intermediate appeals court? .... yes

Labor & Income

Civilian labor force, 2004

Total.............................. 2,525,000
   Men 1,383,000
   Women 1,142,000
   Persons 16-19 years................ 116,000
   White........................... 2,319,000
   Black 89,000
   Hispanic 449,000
   Asian 52,000

Civilian labor force as a percent of civilian non-institutional population, 2004

Total................................. 72.8%
   Men 80.5
   Women 65.3
   Persons 16-19 years................ 52.0
   White.............................. 73.2
   Black 69.8
   Hispanic 72.1
   Asian 67.9

Employment, 2004

Total.............................. 2,389,000
   Men 1,305,000
   Women 1,084,000
   Persons 16-19 years................ 92,000
   White........................... 2,202,000
   Black 77,000
   Hispanic 415,000
   Asian 51,000

Full-time/part-time labor force, 2002

Full-time labor force, employed 1,886,000
Part-time labor force, employed........ 411,000
Unemployed, looking for
   Full-time work..................... 115,000
   Part-time work......................... NA

Unemployment rate, 2004

Total................................. 5.4%
   Men 5.7
   Women 5.1
   Persons 16-19 years................ 20.6
   White.............................. 5.1
   Black 12.5
   Hispanic 7.5
   Asian 2.3

Unemployed by reason for unemployment (as a percent of total unemployment), 2002

Job losers or completed temp jobs 53.6%
Job leavers................................ NA
Reentrants................................ 27.1
New entrants .... NA

Labor unions, 2004

Membership 172,000
   percent of employed 8.4%

Experienced civilian labor force by private industry, first quarter 2004

Total............................. 1,766,663
   Natural Resources & Mining 26,162
   Construction 142,651
   Manufacturing..................... 152,853
   Trade, transportation & utilities 394,654
   Information 82,604
   Finance 149,556
   Professional & business 289,306
   Education & Health 214,295
   Leisure & hospitality............... 249,656
   Other............................. 64,631

Experienced civilian labor force by occupation, 2004

Management......................... 104,990
Business & Financial.................. 103,350
Legal............................... 15,670
Sales 247,990
Office & Admin. Support.............. 372,790
Computers & Math 76,000
Architecture & Engineering 52,680
Arts & Entertainment................. 30,360
Education 115,400
Social Services 24,210
Healthcare Practitioner & Technical..... 95,050
Healthcare support 39,580
Maintenance & Repair 86,200
Construction 128,890
Transportation & moving 135,170
Production 106,820
Farming, fishing & forestry............. 5,000

Hours and earnings of production workers on manufacturing payrolls, 2004

Average weekly hours 40.4
Average hourly earnings $16.46
Average weekly earnings $664.98

Average annual pay

2004 .... $40,276
   change from 2003 .... 3.5%

Household income

Median household income, three-year average, 2002-2004........................ $51,022

Personal income, 2004 ($ per capita)

In current dollars.................... $36,063
In constant (2000) dollars $33,446

Poverty

Persons below poverty level, three-year average, 2002-2004........................... 9.8%

Federal individual income tax returns, 2003

Returns filed....................... 2,079,044
Adjusted gross income ($1,000) ... $105,024,784
Total income tax paid ($1,000) $13,501,382

Economy, Business, Industry & Agriculture

Fortune 500 companies, 2005 10

Patents issued, 2004 2,289

Bankruptcy cases filed, 2004 27,400

Business firm ownership, 2002
Women-owned...................... 135,220
  Sales ($ mil) $16,363
Black-owned.......................... 7,067
  Sales ($ mil) $775
Hispanic-owned..................... 24,054
  Sales ($ mil) $5,114
Asian-owned 10,917
  Sales ($ mil) $2,554
Amer. Indian/Alaska Native-owned 3,950
  Sales ($ mil) $490
Hawaiian/Pacific Isl.-owned.............. 413
  Sales ($ mil) $36

Gross State Product, 2004 ($ mil)
Total Gross State Product $199,969
  Agriculture, forestry, fishing and
    hunting 1,629
  Mining............................ 3,928
  Utilities........................... 2,840
  Construction 12,194
  Manufacturing, durable goods........ 8,983
  Manufacturing, non-durable goods 5,546
  Wholesale trade.................... 10,636
  Retail trade....................... 13,250
  Transportation & warehousing 5,530
  Information 17,460
  Finance & insurance................ 13,573
  Real estate, rental, leasing 27,827
  Professional and technical services.... 17,082
  Educational services................. 1,075
  Health care and social assistance..... 11,596
  Accommodation/food services........ 6,018
  Other services, except government 4,790
  Government 24,248

Establishments, by major industry group, 2003
Total............................... 143,949
  Forestry, fishing & agriculture 284
  Mining............................. 924
  Construction 18,202
  Manufacturing...................... 5,240
  Wholesale trade..................... 7,362
  Retail trade....................... 18,954
  Transportation & warehousing 3,088
  Information 3,234
  Finance & insurance................ 9,928
  Professional/scientific/technical 19,858
  Health care/social assistance 11,961
  Accommodation/food services........ 11,003

Annual payroll by major industry group, 2003
Total ($1,000) $67,914,762
  Forestry, fishing & agriculture .... NA
  Mining............................. 848,490
  Utilities........................... 532,770
  Construction 5,904,307
  Manufacturing...................... 5,845,597
  Wholesale trade.................... 4,800,415
  Retail trade....................... 5,704,044
  Transportation & warehousing 1,964,703
  Information 5,264,341
  Finance & insurance............... 5,621,045
  Professional/scientific/technical ... 8,519,145
  Health care/social assistance 7,347,313
  Accommodation/food services..... 2,798,288

Agriculture
Number of farms, 2004 31,000
Farm acreage, 2004
  Total........................ 31,000,000
  Acres per farm, 2004 1,000
Farm income, 2003 ($mil)
  Net farm income $1,172
  Debt/asset ratio 15.3
Farm marketings, 2003 ($mil)
  Total............................. $4,964
  Crops............................. 1,289
  Livestock.......................... 3,676

Principal commodities, in order by marketing receipts, 2003
  Cattle, dairy products, greenhouse, corn

Federal economic activity in state
Expenditures, 2003
  Total ($ mil) $28,874
  Per capita $6,345
  Defense ($ mil)..................... 5,184
  Non-defense ($ mil) 23,690
Defense department, 2003
  Payroll ($ mil) $2,712
  Contract awards ($ mil)............... $2,488
  Grants ($ mil)....................... $44
  Homeland security grants ($1,000)
    2004 .... $45,583
    2005 .... $36,799

FDIC insured financial institutions, 2004
Number...................... 177
  Assets ($bil) $39.4
  Deposits ($bil) 64.5

Fishing, 2004
Catch (x 1,000 lbs).......................... 0
Value ($1,000)............................. 0

Mining, 2004 ($ mil)

Total non-fuel mineral production $762
Percent of U.S. 1.7%

Construction, 2003 ($ mil)

Total contracts (including non-building) $11,574
    residential...................... 7,142
    non-residential 2,699

Establishments, receipts, payroll & employees, by major industry group, 2002

Mining 73
    Receipts ($1,000) $208,448
    Annual payroll ($1,000)............. $42,004
    Paid employees 883

Utilities 396
    Receipts ($1,000) .... NA
    Annual payroll ($1,000)............ $523,457
    Paid employees 8,503

Construction......................... 17,998
    Receipts ($1,000) $32,663,596
    Annual payroll ($1,000).......... $6,219,618
    Paid employees 175,302

Manufacturing 5,349
    Receipts ($1,000) $34,661,144
    Annual payroll ($1,000).......... $6,323,772
    Paid employees 148,824

Wholesale trade 7,339
    Receipts ($1,000) $92,092,155
    Annual payroll ($1,000).......... $4,789,420
    Paid employees 101,108

Retail trade 18,851
    Receipts ($1,000) $52,226,983
    Annual payroll ($1,000).......... $5,595,862
    Paid employees 247,264

Transportation....................... 3,017
    Receipts ($1,000) $4,357,611
    Annual payroll ($1,000).......... $1,485,756
    Paid employees 47,296

Information.......................... 3,200
    Receipts ($1,000) .... NA
    Annual payroll ($1,000).......... $5,090,490
    Paid employees 102,169

Finance & insurance 9,371
    Receipts ($1,000) .... NA
    Annual payroll ($1,000).......... $5,265,862
    Paid employees 101,856

Professional, scientific & technical 19,417
    Receipts ($1,000) $20,547,273
    Annual payroll ($1,000).......... $8,456,503
    Paid employees 155,868

Health care & social assistance 11,629
    Receipts ($1,000) $17,499,334
    Annual payroll ($1,000).......... $7,094,913
    Paid employees 202,409

Accommodation & food service.......... 10,799
    Receipts ($1,000) $8,808,846
    Annual payroll ($1,000).......... $2,617,701
    Paid employees 206,597

Communication, Energy & Transportation

Communication

Daily newspapers, 2004 30
Households with computers, 2003 ....70%
Households with internet access, 2003 ......63%

Energy

Electricity Consumption, 2001
  Total (trillion Btu) 1,270
  Per capita (million Btu) 287
By source of production (trillion Btu)
    Coal 400
    Natural gas............................ 385
    Petroleum............................. 462
    Nuclear electric power 0
    Hydroelectric power.................... 13
By end-use sector (trillion Btu)
    Residential 303
    Commercial 287
    Industrial 294
    Transportation 386
Electric energy, 2003
    Production (billion kWh) 46.6
    Net summer capability (million kW) 10.4
Gas utilities, 2003
    Customers (x1,000)................... 1,593
    Sales (trillion Btu)..................... 198
    Revenues ($mil)..................... $1,224
Nuclear plants, 2003 0

Transportation, 2004

Public Road & Street Mileage 87,096
    Urban............................. 18,465
    Rural 68,631
    Interstate 956
Vehicle miles of travel per capita 9,974.1
Total motor vehicle registrations...... 2,023,292
    Automobiles...................... 894,582
    Buses 5,822
    Trucks 1,122,888
    Motorcycles 8,411
Licensed drivers 3,205,054
    19 years & under 168,499
Deaths from motor vehicle accidents 665

State Summary

Capital City. . . . . Hartford
Governor. . . . . M. Jodi Rell
210 Capitol Ave
Hartford, CT 06106
800-406-1527
Admitted as a state 1788
Area (square miles) 5,543
Population, 2004 (est.) 3,503,604
Largest City. . . . . Bridgeport
Population, 2004. 140,000
Personal income per capita, 2004
(in current dollars) $45,398
Gross state product ($ mil), 2004 . . . . . . $185,802

Leading industries by payroll, 2003

Finance & Insurance, Manufacturing, Health
care/Social assistance

Leading agricultural commodities by receipts, 2003

Greenhouse, dairy products, chicken eggs,
aquaculture

Geography & Environment

Total area (sq. mi.) 5,543
land 4,845
water 699

Federally-owned land, 2004 (acres) 13,938
percent. 0.4%

Highest point. . . . . Mt. Frissell (south slope)
elevation (feet) 2,380

Lowest point . . . . Long Island Sound
elevation (feet) . . . . sea level

General coastline (miles). 0

Tidal shoreline (miles). 618

Capital City. . . . . Hartford
Population 2000 122,000
Population 2004 125,000

Largest City. . . . . Bridgeport
Population 2000 140,000
Population 2004 140,000

Number of cities with over 100,000 population

1990 5
2000 5
2004 5

State park and recreation areas, 2003

Area (acres x 1,000) 202
Number of visitors (x 1,000) 7,033
Revenues (x 1,000). . . . .
percent of operating expenditures. . . . . NA

National forest system land, 2004

Acres . . . . NA

Demographics and Characteristics of the Population

Population

1980 3,107,576
1990 3,287,116
2000 3,405,565
2004 (estimate). 3,503,604
persons per sq. mile of land. 723.1
2005 (projection). 3,503,185
Male. 1,695,922
Female. 1,807,263
2010 (projection) 3,577,490
2020 (projection) 3,675,650
2030 (projection) 3,688,630
Male. 1,769,336
Female. 1,919,294

Metropolitan and Non-Metro. area population

	Metro	Non-Metro
1980	2,879,000	228,000
1990	3,038,000	250,000
2000	3,257,000	149,000

Change in population, 2000-2004

Number. 98,002
percent. 2.9%
Natural increase (births minus deaths). . . 53,997
Net internal migration . . . . -18,255
Net international migration 63,771

Persons by age, 2004

Under 5 years 213,048
18 years and over 2,664,816
65 years and over 473,693
85 years and over 82,075

Persons by age, 2010 (projected)

Total. 3,577,490
Under 5 years 217,712
5 to 17 years 596,296
18 and over 2,763,482
21 and over 2,619,899
65 and over 515,621
85 and over 93,698
Median age 39.6

Race, 2004 (estimate)

One Race
White. 2,983,059
Black or African American 352,272
American Indian/Alaska Native. 11,812
Pacific Islander 2,648
Asian Indian. 29,075
Chinese 23,966
Filipino 10,056
Japanese 7,695
Korean 11,133
Vietnamese. 6,521
Two or more races. 46,051

2   Connecticut

Persons of Hispanic origin, 2004

Total Hispanic or Latino 359,093
    Mexican............................ 41,802
    Puerto Rican 199,695
    Cuban 5,808
    Other Hispanic or Latino 22,759

Marital status, 2000

Population 15 years & over 2,696,250
    Never married 733,380
    Married........................ 1,482,938
    Separated 43,140
    Widowed.......................... 188,738
    Divorced 250,751

Language spoken at home, 2000

Population 5 years & over 3,184,514
    English only 2,600,601
    Spanish 268,044
    Other Indo-European languages 251,335
    Asian/Pacific Island languages....... 47,993

Households & families, 2000

Households...................... 1,301,670
    with persons under 18 years 451,411
    with persons over 65 years.......... 326,743
    persons per household 2.53
Families......................... 881,170
    persons per family....................3.08
Married couples..................... 676,467
Female householder,
    no husband present............... 157,411
One-person households 344,224

Nativity, 2000

Number of persons born in state 1,940,576
    percent of population 57.0%

Immigration & Naturalization, 2004

Immigrants admitted................. 12,138
Persons naturalized 5,957
Asylums granted 44
Asylums denied 6

Vital Statistics and Health

Marriages

2002 19,573
2003 19,216
2004 20,240

Divorces

2002 11,340
2003 11,065
2004 10,942

Births

2003 42,873
    Birthrate (per 1,000)...................12.3
    Low birth weight (2,500g or less)........ 7.5%
    To unmarried mothers................ 30.0%

2003, continued
    White......................... 35,372
    Black 5,184
    Hispanic 7,547
    Asian/Pacific Islander 2,031
    Amer. Indian/Alaska Native............ 261

2004 (preliminary).................... 42,099
    Birthrate (per 1,000)...................12.0
    White......................... 34,454
    Black 5,279
    Hispanic 7,598
    Asian/Pacific Islander 2,116

Deaths

2002
All causes 30,122
    rate per 100,000.....................870.5
Heart disease 8,815
    rate per 100,000..................... 254.7
Malignant neoplasms 7,163
    rate per 100,000.....................207.0
Cerebrovascular disease............... 1,861
    rate per 100,000.....................53.8
Chronic lower respiratory disease 1,453
    rate per 100,000.....................42.0
2003 29,432
    rate per 100,000..................... 844.9
2004 (provisional) 29,196

Infant deaths

2003 (provisional) 222
    rate per 1,000 ....5.1
2004 (provisional) 234
    rate per 1,000 ....5.6

Abortions, 2000

Total................................. 15,000
    rate per 1,000 women age 15-44.........21.1

Physicians, 2003

Total................................. 12,603
    rate per 1,000 persons.................. 362

Nurses, 2001

Total................................. 32,740
    rate per 1,000 persons.................. 953

Community Hospitals, 2003

Number 34
Beds (x 1,000)........................7.2
Patients admitted (x 1,000) 372
Average daily census (x 1,000) 5.6
Average cost per day $1,684
Outpatient visits (x mil)....................6.8

Disability status of population, 2004

5 to 20 years 4.5%
21 to 64 years 9.2%
65 years and over 33.5%

Education

Educational attainment, 2004
Population over 25 years 2,298,043
   Less than 9th grade 92,848
   High school graduates only......... 681,489
   Bachelor's degree only 458,687
   Graduate or professional degree...... 335,954
   Less than 9th grade percent 4.0%
   High school graduate or more 88.8%
   College graduate or more............. 34.5%
   Graduate or professional degree....... 14.6%

Public school enrollment, Fall 2002
Total............................. 570,023
   Kindergarten through grade 8 405,998
   Grades 9 through 12................ 164,025
Enrollment, 2005 (projected) 567,300

Graduating public high school seniors
2004 (estimate)....................... 34,380

SAT scores, 2005
Average verbal score 517
Average math score....................... 517
Percent of graduates taking test 86%

Public school teachers, 2004
Total (x 1,000) 43.0
   Elementary (x 1,000)..................30.3
   Secondary (x 1,000) 12.7
Average salary $57,300
   Elementary.......................$56,900
   Secondary........................$58,100

State receipts & expenditures for public schools, 2004
Revenue receipts ($mil)................ $7,457
Expenditures
Total ($mil)........................... $7,469
   Per capita $2,142
   Per pupil $12,394

Institutions of higher education, 2004
Total................................... 45
   Public............................... 22
   Private.............................. 23

Enrollment in institutions of higher education, Fall, 2003
Total................................ 179,103
   Full-time men 50,103
   Full-time women................... 61,378
   Part-time men 25,051
   Part-time women................... 42,571

Minority enrollment in institutions of higher education, Fall, 2003
Black, non-hispanic.................... 16,046
Hispanic 12,043
Asian/Pacific Islander 6,595
American Indian/Alaska Native........... 673

Earned degrees conferred, 2003
Bachelor's 15,850
Master's 8,252
First-professional...................... 1,008
Doctor's............................... 648

State & local financial support for higher education, 2003-2004
Full-time equivalent enrollment (x 1,000) ...70.0
Appropriations per FTE................ $8,916
   as a percent of tax revenue.............. 5.0%

Social Insurance & Welfare Programs

Social Security benefits & beneficiaries, 2004
Beneficiaries
   Total............................. 584,000
   Retired & dependents.............. 435,000
   Survivors........................... 69,000
   Disabled & dependents............. 80,000
Annual benefit payments ($ mil)
   Total............................... $6,642
   Retired & dependents............... $4,808
   Survivors........................... $1,011
   Disabled & dependents............... $824
Average Monthly Benefit
   Retired & dependents............... $1,044
   Disabled & dependents.............. $932
   Widowed............................ $1,021

Medicare
Enrollment, 2001 (x 1,000) 516
   Payments ($ mil, est.) $3,100
Enrollment, 2003 (x 1,000) 522

Medicaid, 2002
Beneficiaries (x 1,000)..................... 479
Payments ($ mil) $3,245

State Children's Health Insurance, 2004
Enrollment (x 1,000)......................21.4
Expenditures ($ mil)......................$17.2

Persons without health insurance, 2003
Number (x 1,000) 357
   percent............................ 10.4%
Number of children (x 1,000) 71
   percent of children 8.3%

Federal public aid
Temporary Assistance for Needy Families, 2004
Recipients (x 1,000)....................... 43
Families (x 1,000) 21

Supplemental Security Income, 2003
Recipients (x 1,000)....................... 51
Payments ($ mil) $244

Food Stamp Program, 2004
Participants (x 1,000) 196
Benefits ($ mil).......................... $198

Housing & Construction

Housing units

Total 2003 (estimate)	1,406,993
Total 2004 (estimate)	1,414,433
Seasonal or recreational use, 2003	22,000
Owner-occupied single-family, 2003	765,000
Median value	$226,202
Renter-occupied, 2003	427,000
Median rent	$766
Homeownership rate, 2003	73.0%
Homeownership rate, 2004	71.7%

New privately owned housing units, 2004

Number authorized (x 1,000)	11.8
Value ($ mil)	$2,032
Started 2005 (x 1,000, estimate)	8.5
Started 2006 (x 1,000, estimate)	8.5

Existing home sales

2002 (x 1,000)	64.2
2003 (x 1,000)	63.5
2004 (x 1,000)	72.5

Government & Elections

State Officials 2006

Governor (name/party/term expires)
M. Jodi Rell
Republican - 1/07

Lieutenant Governor	Kevin Sullivan
Secretary of State	Susan Bysiewicz
Attorney General	Richard Blumenthal
Chief Justice	William Sullivan

Governorship

Minimum age	30
Length of term	4 years
Consecutive terms permitted	not specified
Who succeeds	Lt. Governor

State Legislature

Name	General Assembly
Upper chamber	Senate
Number of members	36
Length of term	2 years
Party in majority, 2006	Democratic
Lower chamber	House of Representatives
Number of members	151
Length of term	2 years
Party in majority, 2006	Democratic

State Government Employees, 2004

Total	58,648
Payroll	$270,629,334

Local Government Employees, 2004

Total	122,969
Payroll	$496,527,771

Local Governments by Type, 2002

Total	580
County	0
Municipal	30
Township	149
School District	17
Special District	384

Voting age population, November 2004

Total	2,606,000
Male	1,246,000
Female	1,359,000
White	2,278,000
Black	233,000
Hispanic	170,000
Asian	75,000

Presidential Election, 2004

Total Popular Vote	1,578,769
Kerry	857,488
Bush	693,826
Total Electoral Votes	7

Federal representation, 2006 (109th Congress)

Senator	Joseph Lieberman
Party	Democrat
Year term expires	2007
Senator	Christopher J. Dodd
Party	Democrat
Year term expires	2011
Representatives, total	5
Democrats	2
Republicans	3
Other	0

Votes cast for US Senators

2002

Total vote (x 1,000)	NA
Leading party	NA
Percent for leading party	NA

2004

Total vote (x 1,000)	1,425,000
Leading party	Democratic
Percent for leading party	66.4%

Votes cast for US Representatives

2002

Total vote (x 1,000)	989
Democratic	509
Republican	466
Leading party	Democratic
Percent for leading party	51.5%

2004

Total vote (x 1,000)	1,429
Democratic	786
Republican	630
Leading party	Democratic
Percent for leading party	55.0%

Women holding public office, 2006

US Congress 2
Statewide elected office 4
State legislature 55

Black public officials, 2001

Total 72
  US and state legislatures 14
  City/county/regional offices 47
  Judicial/law enforcement 3
  Education/school boards 8

Hispanic public officials, 2004

Total 28
  State executives & legislators 5
  City/county/regional offices 19
  Judicial/law enforcement 0
  Education/school boards 4

Governmental Finance

State government revenues, 2004

Total revenue ($1,000) $19,518,768
  Revenue per capita 5,578.38

General Revenue ($ per capita) $4,979.46
  Intergovernmental 1,180.80
  Taxes 2,941.21
    general sales 893.75
    individual income tax 1,234.51
    corporate income tax 108.55
  Current charges 400.51
  Miscellaneous 456.94

State government expenditure, 2004

Total expenditure (x $1,000) $19,523,465
  Expenditure per capita 5,579.73
General Expenditure ($ per capita) $4,764.04
  Education 1,277.64
  Public welfare 1,262.49
  Health 142.81
  Hospitals 402.67
  Highways 246.38
  Police protection 48.84
  Correction 159.49
  Natural resources 27.55
  Parks & recreation 43.22
  Governmental administration 279.26
  Interest on general debt 356.55

State debt & cash, 2004 ($ per capita)

Debt $6,451.72
Cash/security holdings $9,371.67

Federal government grants to state & local government, 2004 (x $1,000)

Total $5,555,683

By Federal Agency
  Defense $77,737

By Federal Agency, continued
  Education 373,606
  Energy 45,230
  Environmental Protection Agency 65,752
  Health & Human Services 3,346,103
  Homeland Security 21,105
  Housing & Urban Development 580,480
  Justice 80,040
  Labor 107,155
  Transportation 549,112
  Veterans Affairs 8,647

Crime, Law Enforcement & Courts

Crime, 2004 (rates per 100,000 residents)

Property crimes 92,046
  Burglaries 15,570
  Larcenies 65,451
  Motor vehicle thefts 11,025
  Property crime rate 2,627.2
Violent crimes 10,032
  Murders 91
  Forcible rape 724
  Robberies 4,222
  Aggravated assaults 4,995
  Violent crime rate 286.3

Police Agencies, 2004

Total agencies 101
Total employees 9,701
  Male officers 7,201
  Female officers 697
  Male civilians 680
  Female civilians 1,123

Arrests, 2004

Total 116,805
  Persons under 18 years of age 19,671

Prisoners under state & federal jurisdiction, 2004

Total prisoners 19,497
  Percent change, 12/31/03 to 12/31/04 ... -1.8%
Sentenced to more than one year 13,240
  rate per 100,000 377

Persons under sentence of death, 7/1/05

Total 8
  White 3
  Black 3
  Hispanic 2

State's highest court

Name .... .Supreme Court
Number of members 6
Length of term .... 8 years
Intermediate appeals court? .... .yes

Labor & Income

Civilian labor force, 2004
Total............................ 1,790,000
  Men 943,000
  Women 848,000
  Persons 16-19 years................ 89,000
  White........................... 1,562,000
  Black 162,000
  Hispanic 160,000
  Asian 43,000

Civilian labor force as a percent of civilian non-institutional population, 2004
Total.................................66.3%
  Men 73.3
  Women 60.0
  Persons 16-19 years.................42.9
  White.............................66.4
  Black 66.2
  Hispanic 66.2
  Asian 68.8

Employment, 2004
Total............................ 1,702,000
  Men 895,000
  Women 807,000
  Persons 16-19 years............... 75,000
  White........................... 1,490,000
  Black 149,000
  Hispanic 146,000
  Asian 42,000

Full-time/part-time labor force, 2002
Full-time labor force, employed 1,360,000
Part-time labor force, employed........ 336,000
Unemployed, looking for
  Full-time work...................... 63,000
  Part-time work........................ NA

Unemployment rate, 2004
Total................................. 4.9%
  Men 5.1
  Women 4.7
  Persons 16-19 years................16.4
  White.............................4.6
  Black 7.8
  Hispanic 9.3
  Asian 3.4

Unemployed by reason for unemployment (as a percent of total unemployment), 2002
Job losers or completed temp jobs 57.1%
Job leavers.............................. NA
Reentrants............................. NA
New entrants .... NA

Labor unions, 2004
Membership 235,000
  percent of employed 15.3%

Experienced civilian labor force by private industry, first quarter 2004
Total.............................1,370,181
  Natural Resources & Mining 5,141
  Construction 58,600
  Manufacturing.................... 197,250
  Trade, transportation & utilities 300,564
  Information 38,866
  Finance 139,892
  Professional & business 193,447
  Education & Health 261,503
  Leisure & hospitality............... 119,341
  Other............................. 55,368

Experienced civilian labor force by occupation, 2004
Management......................... 82,850
Business & Financial.................. 85,040
Legal................................ 12,560
Sales............................... 175,370
Office & Admin. Support.............. 295,620
Computers & Math 47,140
Architecture & Engineering 36,610
Arts & Entertainment................. 20,060
Education 122,740
Social Services 30,280
Healthcare Practitioner & Technical..... 88,490
Healthcare support 49,790
Maintenance & Repair 54,210
Construction 56,320
Transportation & moving 93,630
Production 116,120
Farming, fishing & forestry............. 1,510

Hours and earnings of production workers on manufacturing payrolls, 2004
Average weekly hours 41.8
Average hourly earnings $18.35
Average weekly earnings $767.03

Average annual pay
2004 .... $51,007
  change from 2003 .... 5.6%

Household income
Median household income, three-year average,
  2002-2004......................... $55,970

Personal income, 2004 ($ per capita)
In current dollars.................... $45,398
In constant (2000) dollars $42,104

Poverty
Persons below poverty level, three-year average,
  2002-2004.......................... 8.8%

Federal individual income tax returns, 2003
Returns filed...................... 1,653,789
Adjusted gross income ($1,000) ... $111,028,777
Total income tax paid ($1,000) $17,986,786

Economy, Business, Industry & Agriculture

Fortune 500 companies, 2005 14

Patents issued, 2004 1,722

Bankruptcy cases filed, 2004 11,800

Business firm ownership, 2002

Women-owned. 82,119
  Sales ($ mil) $12,219
Black-owned. 10,311
  Sales ($ mil) $737
Hispanic-owned. 9,409
  Sales ($ mil) $1,277
Asian-owned 7,182
  Sales ($ mil) $1,945
Amer. Indian/Alaska Native-owned 1,216
  Sales ($ mil) $148
Hawaiian/Pacific Isl.-owned. 185
  Sales ($ mil) $78

Gross State Product, 2004 ($ mil)

Total Gross State Product $185,802
  Agriculture, forestry, fishing and
    hunting 303
  Mining. 54
  Utilities 3,570
  Construction 6,459
  Manufacturing, durable goods. 15,821
  Manufacturing, non-durable goods 6,832
  Wholesale trade. 9,842
  Retail trade. 11,507
  Transportation & warehousing 3,007
  Information 7,360
  Finance & insurance. 30,916
  Real estate, rental, leasing 24,370
  Professional and technical services 13,896
  Educational services. 2,554
  Health care and social assistance. 13,820
  Accommodation/food services. 3,328
  Other services, except government 3,830
  Government 16,348

Establishments, by major industry group, 2003

Total. 91,611
  Forestry, fishing & agriculture 100
  Mining. 74
  Construction 9,363
  Manufacturing. 5,222
  Wholesale trade. 4,668
  Retail trade. 13,786
  Transportation & warehousing 1,681
  Information 1,823
  Finance & insurance. 5,907
  Professional/scientific/technical 10,240
  Health care/social assistance 9,515
  Accommodation/food services. 7,192

Annual payroll by major industry group, 2003

Total ($1,000) $69,742,050
  Forestry, fishing & agriculture 12,712
  Mining. 36,701
  Utilities 731,031
  Construction 3,185,105
  Manufacturing. 9,828,242
  Wholesale trade. 4,329,255
  Retail trade. 4,889,392
  Transportation & warehousing 1,566,108
  Information 2,431,357
  Finance & insurance. 13,818,534
  Professional/scientific/technical . . . 5,905,689
  Health care/social assistance 8,604,864
  Accommodation/food services. 2,184,993

Agriculture

Number of farms, 2004 4,000
Farm acreage, 2004
  Total. . . . . < 500,000
  Acres per farm, 2004 86
Farm income, 2003 ($mil)
  Net farm income $93
  Debt/asset ratio 12
Farm marketings, 2003 ($mil)
  Total. $485
  Crops 320
  Livestock 165

Principal commodities, in order by marketing receipts, 2003

  Greenhouse, dairy products, chicken eggs,
    aquaculture

Federal economic activity in state

Expenditures, 2003
  Total ($ mil) $28,595
  Per capita $8,209
  Defense ($ mil). 8,545
  Non-defense ($ mil) 20,050
Defense department, 2003
  Payroll ($ mil) $623
  Contract awards ($ mil) $8,065
  Grants ($ mil). $43
  Homeland security grants ($1,000)
    2004 . . . . $46,523
    2005 . . . . $24,080

FDIC insured financial institutions, 2004

Number 57
  Assets ($bil) $60.7
  Deposits ($bil) 73.8

Fishing, 2004

Catch (x 1,000 lbs). 21,150
Value ($1,000). $35,787

Mining, 2004 ($ mil)

Total non-fuel mineral production $132
Percent of U.S. 0.3%

Construction, 2003 ($ mil)

Total contracts (including non-building). $4,826
    residential. 2,118
    non-residential 2,294

Establishments, receipts, payroll & employees, by major industry group, 2002

Mining 17
    Receipts ($1,000) $13,860
    Annual payroll ($1,000). $2,491
    Paid employees 86

Utilities 129
    Receipts ($1,000) . . . . NA
    Annual payroll ($1,000). $846,781
    Paid employees 10,575

Construction. 9,187
    Receipts ($1,000) $13,697,394
    Annual payroll ($1,000). $3,052,989
    Paid employees 76,594

Manufacturing 5,384
    Receipts ($1,000) $45,053,345
    Annual payroll ($1,000). $9,877,987
    Paid employees 214,910

Wholesale trade 4,785
    Receipts ($1,000) $86,932,049
    Annual payroll ($1,000). $4,328,971
    Paid employees 79,072

Retail trade 13,861
    Receipts ($1,000) $41,952,682
    Annual payroll ($1,000). $4,531,064
    Paid employees 191,807

Transportation 1,656
    Receipts ($1,000) $4,014,398
    Annual payroll ($1,000). $1,378,167
    Paid employees 40,216

Information. 1,794
    Receipts ($1,000) . . . . NA
    Annual payroll ($1,000). $2,579,445
    Paid employees 48,221

Finance & insurance 5,741
    Receipts ($1,000) . . . . NA
    Annual payroll ($1,000). $11,537,638
    Paid employees 146,016

Professional, scientific & technical 10,330
    Receipts ($1,000) $14,610,345
    Annual payroll ($1,000). $6,261,035
    Paid employees 107,079

Health care & social assistance 9,599
    Receipts ($1,000) $18,512,454
    Annual payroll ($1,000). $8,168,162
    Paid employees 229,548

Accommodation & food service. 7,047
    Receipts ($1,000) $6,681,803
    Annual payroll ($1,000). $1,967,217
    Paid employees 118,337

Communication, Energy & Transportation

Communication

Daily newspapers, 2004 17
Households with computers, 2003 . . . . .69%
Households with internet access, 2003 . . . . . .63%

Energy

Electricity Consumption, 2001
    Total (trillion Btu). 853
    Per capita (million Btu) 249
By source of production (trillion Btu)
    Coal 40
    Natural gas 149
    Petroleum. 439
    Nuclear electric power 161
    Hydroelectric power 3
By end-use sector (trillion Btu)
    Residential 267
    Commercial 215
    Industrial 134
    Transportation 238
Electric energy, 2003
    Production (billion kWh) 29.5
    Net summer capability (million kW) 7.6
Gas utilities, 2003
    Customers (x1,000). 515
    Sales (trillion Btu). 85
    Revenues ($mil) $935
Nuclear plants, 2003 2

Transportation, 2004

Public Road & Street Mileage 21,143
    Urban. 15,006
    Rural 6,137
    Interstate. 346
Vehicle miles of travel per capita 9,072.3
Total motor vehicle registrations 3,041,592
    Automobiles. 2,047,031
    Buses 10,410
    Trucks 984,151
    Motorcycles 64,754
Licensed drivers 2,694,574
    19 years & under 102,238
Deaths from motor vehicle accidents 291

State Summary

Capital City............................Dover
Governor...................Ruth Ann Minner
Legislative Hall
Dover, DE 19902
302-577-3210
Admitted as a state 1787
Area (square miles).................... 2,489
Population, 2004 (est.) 830,364
Largest City..................... Wilmington
Population, 2004.................... 72,784
Personal income per capita, 2004
(in current dollars) $35,861
Gross state product ($ mil), 2004 .... $54,274

Leading industries by payroll, 2003

Finance & Insurance, Health care/Social assistance, Manufacturing

Leading agricultural commodities by receipts, 2003

Broilers, soybeans, corn, greenhouse

Geography & Environment

Total area (sq. mi.)..................... 2,489
land 1,954
water 536
Federally-owned land, 2004 (acres) 25,874
percent............................2.0%
Highest point. Ebright Road (New Castle County)
elevation (feet) 442
Lowest point ....Atlantic Ocean
elevation (feet) .... sea level
General coastline (miles)................... 28
Tidal shoreline (miles).................... 381
Capital City...........................Dover
Population 2000 32,135
Population 2004 33,618
Largest City.................... Wilmington
Population 2000 72,664
Population 2004 72,784

Number of cities with over 100,000 population

1990 0
2000 0
2004 0

State park and recreation areas, 2003

Area (acres x 1,000)....................... 24
Number of visitors (x 1,000) 5,549
Revenues (x 1,000).................... $7,758
percent of operating expenditures...... 42.6%

National forest system land, 2004

Acres .... NA

Demographics and Characteristics of the Population

Population

1980 594,338
1990 666,168
2000 783,600
2004 (estimate)..................... 830,364
persons per sq. mile of land............. 425
2005 (projection)..................... 836,687
Male............................. 404,842
Female............................ 431,845
2010 (projection) 884,342
2020 (projection) 963,209
2030 (projection).................. 1,012,658
Male............................. 483,035
Female............................ 529,623

Metropolitan and Non-Metro. area population

	Metro	Non-Metro
1980	398,000	196,000
1990	442,000	224,000
2000	627,000	157,000

Change in population, 2000-2004

Number............................. 46,764
percent................................6.0%
Natural increase (births minus deaths)... 17,369
Net internal migration................. 20,184
Net international migration 9,621

Persons by age, 2004

Under 5 years 53,781
18 years and over 636,858
65 years and over 108,961
85 years and over 13,259

Persons by age, 2010 (projected)

Total................................ 884,342
Under 5 years...................... 58,179
5 to 17 years 144,029
18 and over 682,134
21 and over 646,656
65 and over 124,972
85 and over 16,636
Median age 39.4

Race, 2004 (estimate)

One Race
White........................... 625,117
Black or African American 169,251
American Indian/Alaska Native........ 3,263
Pacific Islander 453
Asian Indian........................ 6,242
Chinese 4,509
Filipino 4,914
Japanese 304
Korean............................. 1,789
Vietnamese......................... 1,782
Two or more races.................... 10,814

Persons of Hispanic origin, 2004

Total Hispanic or Latino 47,526
    Mexican............................. 21,775
    Puerto Rican 16,926
    Cuban 1,556
    Other Hispanic or Latino 2,068

Marital status, 2000

Population 15 years & over 620,661
    Never married 168,820
    Married............................ 335,157
    Separated 12,413
    Widowed........................... 42,826
    Divorced 60,825

Language spoken at home, 2000

Population 5 years & over 732,378
    English only 662,845
    Spanish 34,690
    Other Indo-European languages 22,584
    Asian/Pacific Island languages........ 9,359

Households & families, 2000

Households.......................... 298,736
    with persons under 18 years 105,833
    with persons over 65 years........... 71,466
    persons per household 2.54
Families............................ 204,590
    persons per family....................3.04
Married couples 153,136
Female householder,
    no husband present................. 38,986
One-person households 74,639

Nativity, 2000

Number of persons born in state 378,840
    percent of population 48.3%

Immigration & Naturalization, 2004

Immigrants admitted.................. 1,671
Persons naturalized 982
Asylums granted 25
Asylums denied 4

Vital Statistics and Health

Marriages

2002 5,171
2003 4,924
2004 5,095

Divorces

2002 2,792
2003 3,178
2004 3,108

Births

2003 11,329
    Birthrate (per 1,000)...................13.9
    Low birth weight (2,500g or less)........ 9.4%
    To unmarried mothers................ 41.9%

2003, continued
    White............................. 7,903
    Black 2,883
    Hispanic 1,369
    Asian/Pacific Islander 446
    Amer. Indian/Alaska Native.............. 31

2004 (preliminary).................... 11,299
    Birthrate (per 1,000)...................13.6
    White............................. 7,919
    Black 2,895
    Hispanic 1,519
    Asian/Pacific Islander 452

Deaths

2002
All causes 6,861
    rate per 100,000....................849.8
Heart disease 1,918
    rate per 100,000....................237.6
Malignant neoplasms 1,621
    rate per 100,000................... 200.8
Cerebrovascular disease.................. 405
    rate per 100,000.....................50.2
Chronic lower respiratory disease 350
    rate per 100,000.....................43.3
2003 7,070
    rate per 100,000................... 864.8
2004 (provisional) 7,111

Infant deaths

2003 (provisional) 97
    rate per 1,000 ....8.5
2004 (provisional) 87
    rate per 1,000 ....7.6

Abortions, 2000

Total................................ 5,000
    rate per 1,000 women age 15-44..........31.3

Physicians, 2003

Total................................ 2,069
    rate per 1,000 persons................... 253

Nurses, 2001

Total................................ 7,280
    rate per 1,000 persons.................. 913

Community Hospitals, 2003

Number 6
Beds (x 1,000)...........................2.0
Patients admitted (x 1,000) 97
Average daily census (x 1,000) 1.7
Average cost per day $1,508
Outpatient visits (x mil)...................2.0

Disability status of population, 2004

5 to 20 years 8.3%
21 to 64 years 12.9%
65 years and over 37.2%

Education

Educational attainment, 2004

Population over 25 years 539,831
  Less than 9th grade 21,446
  High school graduates only 169,552
  Bachelor's degree only 93,678
  Graduate or professional degree 57,873
  Less than 9th grade percent 4.0%
  High school graduate or more 86.5%
  College graduate or more 26.9%
  Graduate or professional degree 10.7%

Public school enrollment, Fall 2002

Total 116,342
  Kindergarten through grade 8 82,221
  Grades 9 through 12 34,121
Enrollment, 2005 (projected) 116,400

Graduating public high school seniors

2004 (estimate) 6,840

SAT scores, 2005

Average verbal score 503
Average math score 502
Percent of graduates taking test 74%

Public school teachers, 2004

Total (x 1,000) 7.8
  Elementary (x 1,000) 3.8
  Secondary (x 1,000) 3.9
Average salary $49,400
  Elementary $49,000
  Secondary $49,700

State receipts & expenditures for public schools, 2004

Revenue receipts ($mil) $1,254
Expenditures
Total ($mil) $1,380
  Per capita $1,687
  Per pupil $10,347

Institutions of higher education, 2004

Total 10
  Public 5
  Private 5

Enrollment in institutions of higher education, Fall 2003

Total 50,319
  Full-time men 13,238
  Full-time women 18,545
  Part-time men 6,542
  Part-time women 11,994

Minority enrollment in institutions of higher education, Fall 2003

Black, non-hispanic 8,100
Hispanic 1,421
Asian/Pacific Islander 1,238
American Indian/Alaska Native 170

Earned degrees conferred, 2003

Bachelor's 5,164
Master's 1,763
First-professional 312
Doctor's 168

State & local financial support for higher education, 2003-2004

Full-time equivalent enrollment (x 1,000) . . . 31.0
Appropriations per FTE $10,907
  as a percent of tax revenue 6.8%

Social Insurance & Welfare Programs

Social Security benefits & beneficiaries, 2004

Beneficiaries
  Total 149,000
  Retired & dependents 105,000
  Survivors 19,000
  Disabled & dependents 25,000
Annual benefit payments ($ mil)
  Total $1,618
  Retired & dependents $1,098
  Survivors $259
  Disabled & dependents $261
Average Monthly Benefit
  Retired & dependents $1,004
  Disabled & dependents $936
  Widowed $988

Medicare

Enrollment, 2001 (x 1,000) 114
  Payments ($ mil, est.) $500
Enrollment, 2003 (x 1,000) 119

Medicaid, 2002

Beneficiaries (x 1,000) 167
Payments ($ mil) $651

State Children's Health Insurance, 2004

Enrollment (x 1,000) 10.3
Expenditures ($ mil) $5.3

Persons without health insurance, 2003

Number (x 1,000) 91
  percent 11.1%
Number of children (x 1,000) 17
  percent of children 8.5%

Federal public aid

Temporary Assistance for Needy Families, 2004
Recipients (x 1,000) 13
Families (x 1,000) 6

Supplemental Security Income, 2003
Recipients (x 1,000) 13
Payments ($ mil) $59

Food Stamp Program, 2004

Participants (x 1,000) 56
Benefits ($ mil) $57

4   Delaware

Housing & Construction

Housing units
Total 2003 (estimate) 359,871
Total 2004 (estimate) 367,448
Seasonal or recreational use, 2003 28,000
Owner-occupied single-family, 2003 185,000
    Median value $165,739
Renter-occupied, 2003 82,000
    Median rent $718
Homeownership rate, 2003 .... 77.2%
Homeownership rate, 2004 .... 77.3%

New privately owned housing units, 2004
Number authorized (x 1,000) 7.9
Value ($ mil) $893
Started 2005 (x 1,000, estimate) 5.9
Started 2006 (x 1,000, estimate) 5.7

Existing home sales
2002 (x 1,000) 14.5
2003 (x 1,000) 15.8
2004 (x 1,000) 18.9

Government & Elections

State Officials 2006
Governor (name/party/term expires)
Ruth Ann Minner
Democrat - 1/09
Lieutenant Governor .... John Carney
Secretary of State ...... Harriet Smith Windsor
Attorney General .... Carl C. Danberg
Chief Justice .... Myron Steele

Governorship
Minimum age 30
Length of term .... 4 years
Consecutive terms permitted ... 2 max. (not nec. consecutive)
Who succeeds .... Lt. Governor

State Legislature
Name .... General Assembly
Upper chamber .... Senate
    Number of members 21
    Length of term .... 4 years
    Party in majority, 2006 .... Democratic
Lower chamber .... House of Representatives
    Number of members 41
    Length of term .... 2 years
    Party in majority, 2006 .... Republican

State Government Employees, 2004
Total 24,254
Payroll $86,929,233

Local Government Employees, 2004
Total 23,625
Payroll $82,621,978

Local Governments by Type, 2002
Total 339
    County 3
    Municipal 57
    Township 0
    School District 19
    Special District 260

Voting age population, November 2004
Total 612,000
    Male 292,000
    Female 320,000
    White 485,000
    Black 108,000
    Hispanic 44,000
    Asian 12,000

Presidential Election, 2004
Total Popular Vote 375,190
    Kerry 200,152
    Bush 171,660
Total Electoral Votes 3

Federal representation, 2006 (109th Congress)
Senator .... Thomas Carper
    Party .... Democrat
    Year term expires 2007
Senator .... Joseph R. Biden Jr.
    Party .... Democrat
    Year term expires 2009
Representatives, total 1
    Democrats 0
    Republicans 1
    Other 0

Votes cast for US Senators
2002
Total vote (x 1,000) 232,000
Leading party .... Democratic
Percent for leading party 58.2%

2004
Total vote (x 1,000) .... NA
Leading party .... NA
Percent for leading party .... NA

Votes cast for US Representatives
2002
Total vote (x 1,000) 228
    Democratic 61
    Republican 165
Leading party .... Republican
Percent for leading party 72.1%

2004
Total vote (x 1,000) 356
    Democratic 106
    Republican 246
Leading party .... Republican
Percent for leading party 69.1%

Delaware 5

Women holding public office, 2006
US Congress 0
Statewide elected office...................... 2
State legislature 21

Black public officials, 2001
Total.................................... 24
  US and state legislatures 4
  City/county/regional offices 16
  Judicial/law enforcement.................. 1
  Education/school boards.................. 3

Hispanic public officials, 2004
Total..................................... 2
  State executives & legislators 1
  City/county/regional offices 1
  Judicial/law enforcement................. 0
  Education/school boards................. 0

Governmental Finance

State government revenues, 2004
Total revenue ($1,000) $5,697,849
  Revenue per capita 6,864.88

General Revenue ($ per capita)....... $6,198.17
  Intergovernmental 1,270.32
  Taxes 2,862.03
    general sales 0
    individual income tax............. 941.22
    corporate income tax 262.37
  Current charges.................... 862.01
  Miscellaneous 1,203.81

State government expenditure, 2004
Total expenditure (x $1,000) $5,387,960
  Expenditure per capita............. 6,491.52
General Expenditure ($ per capita).... $5,921.22
  Education 2,050.46
  Public welfare..................... 1,231.34
  Health 349.19
  Hospitals........................... 68.44
  Highways 472.41
  Police protection.................... 94.29
  Correction 244.32
  Natural resources 99.45
  Parks & recreation...................56.98
  Governmental administration 475.28
  Interest on general debt 274.61

State debt & cash, 2004 ($ per capita)
Debt $5,009.78
Cash/security holdings............. $13,547.23

Federal government grants to state & local government, 2004 (x $1,000)
Total........................... $1,241,092
By Federal Agency
  Defense $24,137

By Federal Agency, continued
  Education 115,962
  Energy 9,008
  Environmental Protection Agency 29,684
  Health & Human Services. 626,906
  Homeland Security.................... 9,048
  Housing & Urban Development....... 92,862
  Justice 35,937
  Labor 27,633
  Transportation 149,234
  Veterans Affairs.................... 3,729

Crime, Law Enforcement & Courts

Crime, 2004 (rates per 100,000 residents)
Property crimes 26,272
  Burglaries........................ 5,383
  Larcenies......................... 18,742
  Motor vehicle thefts 2,147
  Property crime rate................. 3,163.9
Violent crimes........................ 4,720
  Murders............................. 17
  Forcible rape....................... 345
  Robberies 1,218
  Aggravated assaults 3,140
  Violent crime rate.................... 568.4

Police Agencies, 2004
Total agencies............................ 52
Total employees 3,195
  Male officers...................... 1,983
  Female officers 280
  Male civilians...................... 378
  Female civilians...................... 554

Arrests, 2004
Total.................................. 31,048
  Persons under 18 years of age 6,767

Prisoners under state & federal jurisdiction, 2004
Total prisoners........................ 6,927
  Percent change, 12/31/03 to 12/31/04 .... 2.0%
Sentenced to more than one year 4,087
  rate per 100,000....................... 488

Persons under sentence of death, 7/1/05
Total.................................... 19
  White................................ 10
  Black 6
  Hispanic 3

State's highest court
Name ....Supreme Court
Number of members....................... 5
Length of term .... 12 years
Intermediate appeals court? .... no

6   Delaware

Labor & Income

Civilian labor force, 2004

Total 426,000
- Men 220,000
- Women 206,000
- Persons 16-19 years 22,000
- White 333,000
- Black 76,000
- Hispanic 26,000
- Asian 11,000

Civilian labor force as a percent of civilian non-institutional population, 2004

Total 66.3%
- Men 72.0
- Women 61.1
- Persons 16-19 years 48.0
- White 65.9
- Black 66.8
- Hispanic 73.7
- Asian 73.7

Employment, 2004

Total 409,000
- Men 212,000
- Women 198,000
- Persons 16-19 years 20,000
- White 322,000
- Black 71,000
- Hispanic 25,000
- Asian 11,000

Full-time/part-time labor force, 2002

Full-time labor force, employed 345,000
Part-time labor force, employed 60,000
Unemployed, looking for
- Full-time work 16,000
- Part-time work .... NA

Unemployment rate, 2004

Total 3.9%
- Men 3.9
- Women 4.0
- Persons 16-19 years 9.9
- White 3.5
- Black 6.1
- Hispanic 5.5
- Asian 1.0

Unemployed by reason for unemployment (as a percent of total unemployment), 2002

Job losers or completed temp jobs 61.1%
Job leavers .... NA
Reentrants .... NA
New entrants .... NA

Labor unions, 2004

Membership 46,000
- percent of employed 12.4%

Experienced civilian labor force by private industry, first quarter 2004

Total 347,826
- Natural Resources & Mining 1,375
- Construction 24,996
- Manufacturing 35,014
- Trade, transportation & utilities 77,091
- Information 7,267
- Finance 44,264
- Professional & business 62,013
- Education & Health 47,284
- Leisure & hospitality 36,170
- Other 12,352

Experienced civilian labor force by occupation, 2004

Management 21,030
Business & Financial 20,050
Legal 4,180
Sales 46,000
Office & Admin. Support 84,010
Computers & Math 11,080
Architecture & Engineering 6,260
Arts & Entertainment 3,340
Education 21,020
Social Services 6,790
Healthcare Practitioner & Technical 19,940
Healthcare support 9,120
Maintenance & Repair 17,750
Construction 21,530
Transportation & moving 24,540
Production 26,290
Farming, fishing & forestry 870

Hours and earnings of production workers on manufacturing payrolls, 2004

Average weekly hours 40.0
Average hourly earnings $17.68
Average weekly earnings $707.20

Average annual pay

2004 .... $42,487
- change from 2003 .... 3.7%

Household income

Median household income, three-year average, 2002-2004 .... $50,152

Personal income, 2004 ($ per capita)

In current dollars $35,861
In constant (2000) dollars $33,259

Poverty

Persons below poverty level, three-year average, 2002-2004 .... 8.5%

Federal individual income tax returns, 2003

Returns filed 388,288
Adjusted gross income ($1,000) $19,284,435
Total income tax paid ($1,000) $2,415,713

Economy, Business, Industry & Agriculture

Fortune 500 companies, 2005 2

Patents issued, 2004 406

Bankruptcy cases filed, 2004 3,800

Business firm ownership, 2002

Women-owned 15,344
  Sales ($ mil) $2,021
Black-owned 4,258
  Sales ($ mil) $215
Hispanic-owned 880
  Sales ($ mil) $138
Asian-owned 1,899
  Sales ($ mil) $625
Amer. Indian/Alaska Native-owned 333
  Sales ($ mil) . . . . NA
Hawaiian/Pacific Isl.-owned . . . . NA
  Sales ($ mil) $20

Gross State Product, 2004 ($ mil)

Total Gross State Product $54,274
  Agriculture, forestry, fishing and
    hunting 344
  Mining 9
  Utilities 950
  Construction 1,870
  Manufacturing, durable goods 1,681
  Manufacturing, non-durable goods 3,160
  Wholesale trade 2,001
  Retail trade 2,432
  Transportation & warehousing 667
  Information 1,002
  Finance & insurance 17,897
  Real estate, rental, leasing 6,290
  Professional and technical services 3,257
  Educational services 234
  Health care and social assistance 2,709
  Accommodation/food services 833
  Other services, except government 827
  Government 4,510

Establishments, by major industry group, 2003

Total 24,803
  Forestry, fishing & agriculture 46
  Mining 15
  Construction 2,499
  Manufacturing 691
  Wholesale trade 999
  Retail trade 3,785
  Transportation & warehousing 717
  Information 425
  Finance & insurance 2,087
  Professional/scientific/technical 2,359
  Health care/social assistance 2,095
  Accommodation/food services 1,627

Annual payroll by major industry group, 2003

Total ($1,000) $15,079,817
  Forestry, fishing & agriculture . . . . NA
  Mining . . . . NA
  Utilities 209,548
  Construction 871,932
  Manufacturing 1,654,918
  Wholesale trade 1,354,112
  Retail trade 1,194,725
  Transportation & warehousing 338,870
  Information 423,905
  Finance & insurance 2,348,894
  Professional/scientific/technical . . . 1,572,120
  Health care/social assistance 1,794,553
  Accommodation/food services 393,206

Agriculture

Number of farms, 2004 2,000
Farm acreage, 2004
  Total 1,000,000
  Acres per farm, 2004 230
Farm income, 2003 ($mil)
  Net farm income $156
  Debt/asset ratio 22.7
Farm marketings, 2003 ($mil)
Total $760
  Crops 168
  Livestock 593

Principal commodities, in order by marketing receipts, 2003

    Broilers, soybeans, corn, greenhouse

Federal economic activity in state

Expenditures, 2003
  Total ($ mil) $5,061
  Per capita $6,191
  Defense ($ mil) 564
  Non-defense ($ mil) 4,497
Defense department, 2003
  Payroll ($ mil) $383
  Contract awards ($ mil) $168
  Grants ($ mil) $19
  Homeland security grants ($1,000)
    2004 . . . . $20,206
    2005 . . . . $14,984

FDIC insured financial institutions, 2004

Number 34
  Assets ($bil) $436.0
  Deposits ($bil) 105.8

Fishing, 2004

Catch (x 1,000 lbs) 4,286
Value ($1,000) $5,437

8   Delaware

Mining, 2004 ($ mil)
Total non-fuel mineral production $21
Percent of U.S. 0.1%

Construction, 2003 ($ mil)
Total contracts (including non-building). $1,504
   residential............................ 798
   non-residential 446

Establishments, receipts, payroll & employees, by major industry group, 2002

Mining 1
   Receipts ($1,000) .... NA
   Annual payroll ($1,000) .... NA
   Paid employees .... (1-19)

Utilities 37
   Receipts ($1,000) .... NA
   Annual payroll ($1,000) $187,211
   Paid employees 2,670

Construction......................... 2,407
   Receipts ($1,000) $3,882,206
   Annual payroll ($1,000) $907,842
   Paid employees 25,133

Manufacturing 705
   Receipts ($1,000) $16,417,927
   Annual payroll ($1,000) $1,564,801
   Paid employees 37,287

Wholesale trade 997
   Receipts ($1,000) $17,292,794
   Annual payroll ($1,000) $1,286,636
   Paid employees 21,162

Retail trade 3,727
   Receipts ($1,000) $10,912,971
   Annual payroll ($1,000) $1,094,288
   Paid employees 51,889

Transportation......................... 701
   Receipts ($1,000) $749,566
   Annual payroll ($1,000) $270,380
   Paid employees 8,707

Information........................... 390
   Receipts ($1,000) .... NA
   Annual payroll ($1,000) $393,899
   Paid employees 8,167

Finance & insurance 1,827
   Receipts ($1,000) .... NA
   Annual payroll ($1,000) $2,830,272
   Paid employees 48,136

Professional, scientific & technical 2,339
   Receipts ($1,000) $3,135,436
   Annual payroll ($1,000) $1,359,247
   Paid employees 22,964

Health care & social assistance 2,084
   Receipts ($1,000) $3,792,091
   Annual payroll ($1,000) $1,688,979
   Paid employees 47,437

Accommodation & food service........... 1,576
   Receipts ($1,000) $1,231,595
   Annual payroll ($1,000) $355,458
   Paid employees 26,972

Communication, Energy & Transportation

Communication
Daily newspapers, 2004 2
Households with computers, 2003 ....60%
Households with internet access, 2003 ......53%

Energy
Electricity Consumption, 2001
Total (trillion Btu)......................... 293
Per capita (million Btu) 368
By source of production (trillion Btu)
   Coal 38
   Natural gas 52
   Petroleum............................ 147
   Nuclear electric power 0
   Hydroelectric power.................... 0
By end-use sector (trillion Btu)
   Residential 62
   Commercial 52
   Industrial 113
   Transportation 66
Electric energy, 2003
   Production (billion kWh) 7.4
   Net summer capability (million kW) 3.4
Gas utilities, 2003
   Customers (x1,000)................... 142
   Sales (trillion Btu)..................... 21
   Revenues ($mil)..................... $192
Nuclear plants, 2003 0

Transportation, 2004
Public Road & Street Mileage 6,043
   Urban................................ 2,860
   Rural 3,183
   Interstate............................. 41
Vehicle miles of travel per capita 11,233.1
Total motor vehicle registrations........ 711,039
   Automobiles........................ 422,755
   Buses 2,101
   Trucks 286,183
   Motorcycles 17,485
Licensed drivers 533,943
   19 years & under 28,574
Deaths from motor vehicle accidents 134

District Summary

City........................ Washington, DC
Mayor..................... Anthony William
John A. Wilson Building
1350 Pennsylvania Ave NW
Washington, DC 20004
202-727-1000
Founded................................ 1790
Area (square miles)....................... 68
Population, 2004 (est.)................ 553,523
Largest City.................. Washington, DC
Population, 2004................... 554,000
Personal income per capita, 2004
(in current dollars)................ $51,803
Gross state product ($ mil), 2004...... $76,685

Leading industries by payroll, 2003

Professional/scientific/technical, Health care/so-
cial assistance, Information

**Leading agricultural commodities by receipts,
2003**

NA

Geography & Environment

Total area (sq. mi.)........................ 68
land.................................. 61
water................................. 7

Federally-owned land, 2004 (acres)....... 9,631
percent............................24.7%

Highest point.....................Tenleytown
elevation (feet)....................... 410

Lowest point.................. Potomac River
elevation (feet).................... sea level

General coastline (miles)..................... 0

Tidal shoreline (miles)....................... 0

Capital City................. Washington, DC
Population 2000................... 572,000
Population 2004................... 554,000

Largest City................. Washington, DC
Population 2000................... 572,000
Population 2004................... 554,000

Number of cities with over 100,000 population

1990................................. NA
2000................................. 1
2004................................. 1

State park and recreation areas, 2003

Area (acres x 1,000)...................... NA
Number of visitors (x 1,000).............. NA
Revenues (x 1,000)...................... NA
percent of operating expenditures........ NA

National forest system land, 2004

Acres................................. NA

Demographics and Characteristics of the Population

Population

1980............................... 638,333
1990............................... 606,900
2000............................... 572,059
2004 (estimate)...................... 553,523
persons per sq. mile of land...........9074.1
2005 (projection).................... 551,136
Male............................... 260,927
Female............................. 290,209
2010 (projection).................... 529,785
2020 (projection).................... 480,540
2030 (projection).................... 433,414
Male............................... 208,243
Female............................. 225,171

Metropolitan and Non-Metro. area population

	Metro	Non-Metro
1980	638,000	0
1990	607,000	0
2000	572,000	0

Change in population, 2000-2004

Number.............................-18,536
percent.............................. -3.2%
Natural increase (births minus deaths).... 7,994
Net internal migration................-43,304
Net international migration........... 17,156

Persons by age, 2004

Under 5 years........................ 35,029
18 years and over.................... 443,976
65 years and over..................... 67,171
85 years and over...................... 9,288

Persons by age, 2010 (projected)

Total................................ 529,785
Under 5 years..................... 41,737
5 to 17 years...................... 72,327
18 and over....................... 415,721
21 and over....................... 385,635
65 and over....................... 61,036
85 and over....................... 9,812
Median age........................33.8

Race, 2004 (estimate)

One Race
White........................... 207,246
Black or African American.......... 319,196
American Indian/Alaska Native........ 1,873
Pacific Islander...................... 374
Asian Indian........................ 4,243
Chinese............................ 3,105
Filipino............................ 2,073
Japanese........................... 1,752
Korean............................. 1,373
Vietnamese......................... 1,270
Two or more races.................... 8,050

2   District of Columbia

Persons of Hispanic origin, 2004

Total Hispanic or Latino	45,879
Mexican	5,001
Puerto Rican	2,742
Cuban	1,812
Other Hispanic or Latino	4,528

Marital status, 2000

Population 15 years & over	474,417
Never married	229,618
Married	141,851
Separated	19,926
Widowed	37,005
Divorced	46,018

Language spoken at home, 2000

Population 5 years & over	539,658
English only	449,241
Spanish	49,461
Other Indo-European languages	23,721
Asian/Pacific Island languages	8,974

Households & families, 2000

Households	248,338
with persons under 18 years	60,987
with persons over 65 years	53,369
persons per household	2.16
Families	114,166
persons per family	3.07
Married couples	56,631
Female householder,	
no husband present	47,032
One-person households	108,744

Nativity, 2000

Number of persons born in state	224,352
percent of population	39.2%

Immigration & Naturalization, 2004

Immigrants admitted	2,110
Persons naturalized	882
Asylums granted	126
Asylums denied	26

Vital Statistics and Health

Marriages

2002	2,940
2003	2,927
2004	2,497

Divorces

2002	1,384
2003	1,157
2004	1,043

Births

2003	7,619
Birthrate (per 1,000)	13.5
Low birth weight (2,500g or less)	10.9%
To unmarried mothers	53.6%

2003, continued

White	2,125
Black	5,223
Hispanic	954
Asian/Pacific Islander	253
Amer. Indian/Alaska Native	4
2004 (preliminary)	7,932
Birthrate (per 1,000)	14.3
White	2,302
Black	5,392
Hispanic	998
Asian/Pacific Islander	229

Deaths

2002	
All causes	5,851
rate per 100,000	1,024.9
Heart disease	1,666
rate per 100,000	291.8
Malignant neoplasms	1,298
rate per 100,000	227.4
Cerebrovascular disease	279
rate per 100,000	48.9
Chronic lower respiratory disease	133
rate per 100,000	23.3
2003	5,513
rate per 100,000	976.9
2004 (provisional)	5,350

Infant deaths

2003 (provisional)	70
rate per 1,000	9.4
2004 (provisional)	82
rate per 1,000	11

Abortions, 2000

Total	10,000
rate per 1,000 women age 15-44	68.1

Physicians, 2003

Total	4,329
rate per 1,000 persons	768

Nurses, 2001

Total	8,600
rate per 1,000 persons	1,498

Community Hospitals, 2003

Number	10
Beds (x 1,000)	3.4
Patients admitted (x 1,000)	135
Average daily census (x 1,000)	2.5
Average cost per day	$1,824
Outpatient visits (x mil)	1.6

Disability status of population, 2004

5 to 20 years	9.6%
21 to 64 years	10.9%
65 years and over	37.9%

Education

Educational attainment, 2004

Population over 25 years 372,359
  Less than 9th grade 19,451
  High school graduates only. 73,873
  Bachelor's degree only 80,909
  Graduate or professional degree. 96,780
  Less than 9th grade percent 5.2%
  High school graduate or more 86.4%
  College graduate or more. 45.7%
  Graduate or professional degree. 26.0%

Public school enrollment, Fall 2002

Total. 76,166
  Kindergarten through grade 8 58,794
  Grades 9 through 12. 17,372
Enrollment, 2005 (projected) 73,900

Graduating public high school seniors

2004 (estimate). 3,150

SAT scores, 2005

Average verbal score 490
Average math score 478
Percent of graduates taking test 79%

Public school teachers, 2004

Total (x 1,000) 5.7
  Elementary (x 1,000). 4.1
  Secondary (x 1,000) 1.6
Average salary $57,000
  Elementary. $57,000
  Secondary. $57,000

District receipts & expenditures for public schools, 2004

Revenue receipts ($mil). $827
Expenditures
Total ($mil). $1,042
  Per capita $1,869
  Per pupil $14,621

Institutions of higher education, 2004

Total. 16
  Public. 2
  Private. 14

Enrollment in institutions of higher education, Fall, 2003

Total. 96,774
  Full-time men 25,091
  Full-time women. 35,292
  Part-time men 14,666
  Part-time women. 21,725

Minority enrollment in institutions of higher education, Fall, 2003

Black, non-hispanic. 26,628
Hispanic 3,574
Asian/Pacific Islander 5,481
American Indian/Alaska Native. 275

Earned degrees conferred, 2003

Bachelor's 8,900
Master's. 7,460
First-professional. 2,605
Doctor's. 579

State & local financial support for higher education, 2003-2004

Full-time equivalent enrollment (x 1,000) . . . NA
Appropriations per FTE. . . . . NA
  as a percent of tax revenue. . . . . NA

Social Insurance & Welfare Programs

Social Security benefits & beneficiaries, 2004

Beneficiaries
  Total. 72,000
  Retired & dependents. 50,000
  Survivors. 11,000
  Disabled & dependents. 11,000
Annual benefit payments ($ mil)
  Total. $653
  Retired & dependents. $435
  Survivors. $114
  Disabled & dependents. $104
Average Monthly Benefit
  Retired & dependents. $819
  Disabled & dependents. $824
  Widowed. $767

Medicare

Enrollment, 2001 (x 1,000) 75
  Payments ($ mil, est.) $800
Enrollment, 2003 (x 1,000) 74

Medicaid, 2002

Beneficiaries (x 1,000). 193
Payments ($ mil) $1,027

State Children's Health Insurance, 2004

Enrollment (x 1,000). 6.1
Expenditures ($ mil). $7.2

Persons without health insurance, 2003

Number (x 1,000). 79
  percent. 14.3%
Number of children (x 1,000) 12
  percent of children 11.4%

Federal public aid

Temporary Assistance for Needy Families, 2004
Recipients (x 1,000). 44
Families (x 1,000) 17

Supplemental Security Income, 2003
Recipients (x 1,000). 20
Payments ($ mil) $105

Food Stamp Program, 2004

Participants (x 1,000) 89
Benefits ($ mil). $98

Housing & Construction

Housing units

Total 2003 (estimate)	275,925
Total 2004 (estimate)	276,600
Seasonal or recreational use, 2003	2,000
Owner-occupied single-family, 2003	76,000
Median value	$248,171
Renter-occupied, 2003	143,000
Median rent	$721
Homeownership rate, 2003	43.0%
Homeownership rate, 2004	NA

New privately owned housing units, 2004

Number authorized (x 1,000)	1.9
Value ($ mil)	$225
Started 2005 (x 1,000, estimate)	0.4
Started 2006 (x 1,000, estimate)	0.4

Existing home sales

2002 (x 1,000)	11.2
2003 (x 1,000)	12.1
2004 (x 1,000)	13.4

Government & Elections

District Officials 2006

Mayor (name/party/term expires)
Anthony William
Democrat - 2006

Secretary of District	Sherryl Hobbs Newman
Attorney General	Robert J. Spagnoletti
Chief Judge	Eric Washington

Mayorship

Minimum age	NA
Length of term	4 years
Consecutive terms permitted	yes
Who succeeds	NA

District Legislature

Name	NA
Upper chamber	NA
Number of members	NA
Length of term	NA
Party in majority, 2006	NA
Lower chamber	NA
Number of members	NA
Length of term	NA
Party in majority, 2006	NA

Local Government Employees, 2004

Total	44,671
Payroll	$204,379,294

Local Governments by Type, 2002

Total	2
County	0
Municipal	1
Township	0
School District	0
Special District	1

Voting age population, November 2004

Total	435,000
Male	199,000
Female	236,000
White	179,000
Black	240,000
Hispanic	38,000
Asian	9,000

Presidential Election, 2004

Total Popular Vote	227,586
Kerry	202,970
Bush	21,256
Total Electoral Votes	3

Federal representation, 2006 (109th Congress)

Representatives, total	1
Democrats	1
Delegate	Eleanor Holmes Norton
Shadow Representative	Ray Browne
Shadow Senator	Paul Strauss
Party	Democrat
Year term expires	2009
Shadow Senator	Florence Pendleton
Party	Democrat
Year term expires	2007

Votes cast for US Senators

2002

Total vote (x 1,000)	118,259
Leading party	Democratic
Percent for leading party	77.3%

2004

Total vote (x 1,000)	NA
Leading party	NA
Percent for leading party	NA

Votes cast for US Representatives

2002

Total vote (x 1,000)	112,333
Democratic	95,159
Republican	NA
Leading party	Democratic
Percent for leading party	84.7%

2004

Total vote (x 1,000)	195,476
Democratic	168,693
Republican	NA
Leading party	Democratic
Percent for leading party	86.3%

Women holding public office, 2006

US Congress 1
Statewide elected office................... NA
State legislature .... NA

Black public officials, 2001

Total................................... 176
   US and state legislatures 2
   City/county/regional offices 171
   Judicial/law enforcement................. 0
   Education/school boards.................. 3

Hispanic public officials, 2004

Total.................................... 0
   State executives & legislators 0
   City/county/regional offices 0
   Judicial/law enforcement................. 0
   Education/school boards.................. 0

Governmental Finance

District government revenues, 2004

Total revenue ($1,000) .... NA
   Revenue per capita .... NA

General Revenue ($ per capita) .... NA
   Intergovernmental .... NA
   Taxes .... NA
      general sales .... NA
      individual income tax................. NA
      corporate income tax .... NA
   Current charges........................ NA
   Miscellaneous .... NA

District government expenditure, 2004

Total expenditure (x $1,000) .... NA
   Expenditure per capita................. NA
General Expenditure ($ per capita).......... NA
   Education .... NA
   Public welfare......................... NA
   Health .... NA
   Hospitals............................. NA
   Highways .... NA
   Police protection .... NA
   Correction .... NA
   Natural resources .... NA
   Parks & recreation..................... NA
   Governmental administration .... NA
   Interest on general debt .... NA

District debt & cash, 2004 ($ per capita)

Debt .... NA
Cash/security holdings.................... NA

Federal government grants to state & local government, 2004 (x $1,000)

Total............................. $4,204,862
By Federal Agency
   Defense $43,193

By Federal Agency, continued
   Education 348,230
   Energy 23,792
   Environmental Protection Agency 82,334
   Health & Human Services. 1,624,807
   Homeland Security.................. 16,208
   Housing & Urban Development...... 321,134
   Justice 123,272
   Labor 211,972
   Transportation 417,963
   Veterans Affairs..................... 1,417

Crime, Law Enforcement & Courts

Crime, 2004 (rates per 100,000 residents)

Property crimes 26,896
   Burglaries........................... 3,946
   Larcenies........................... 14,542
   Motor vehicle thefts 8,408
   Property crime rate.................. 4,859.1
Violent crimes........................ 7,590
   Murders............................. 198
   Forcible rape........................ 222
   Robberies 3,202
   Aggravated assaults 3,968
   Violent crime rate................... 1,371.2

Police Agencies, 2004

Total agencies............................. 3
Total employees 4,876
   Male officers....................... 3,195
   Female officers...................... 969
   Male civilians....................... 248
   Female civilians..................... 464

Arrests, 2004

Total................................. 5,779
   Persons under 18 years of age 338

Prisoners under district & federal jurisdiction, 2004

Total prisoners.......................... NA
   Percent change, 12/31/03 to 12/31/04 ..... NA
Sentenced to more than one year .... NA
   rate per 100,000...................... NA

Persons under sentence of death, 7/1/05

Total.................................... 0
   White................................ 0
   Black 0
   Hispanic 0

District's highest court

Name .... Court of Appeals
Number of members....................... 9
Length of term..................... 15 years
Intermediate appeals court? .... no

Labor & Income

Civilian labor force, 2004

Total	299,000
Men	150,000
Women	149,000
Persons 16-19 years	7,000
White	140,000
Black	147,000
Hispanic	28,000
Asian	9,000

Civilian labor force as a percent of civilian non-institutional population, 2004

Total	67.6%
Men	73.9
Women	62.3
Persons 16-19 years	28.6
White	79.1
Black	59.5
Hispanic	76.4
Asian	66.3

Employment, 2004

Total	275,000
Men	136,000
Women	138,000
Persons 16-19 years	5,000
White	135,000
Black	128,000
Hispanic	26,000
Asian	8,000

Full-time/part-time labor force, 2002

Full-time labor force, employed	256,000
Part-time labor force, employed	29,000
Unemployed, looking for	
Full-time work	18,000
Part-time work	NA

Unemployment rate, 2004

Total	8.2%
Men	9.0
Women	7.4
Persons 16-19 years	30.4
White	3.5
Black	13.0
Hispanic	7.4
Asian	5.7

Unemployed by reason for unemployment (as a percent of total unemployment), 2002

Job losers or completed temp jobs	50.0%
Job leavers	NA
Reentrants	35.0
New entrants	NA

Labor unions, 2004

Membership	33,000
percent of employed	12.7%

Experienced civilian labor force by private industry, first quarter 2004

Total	424,604
Natural Resources & Mining	28
Construction	12,172
Manufacturing	2,532
Trade, transportation & utilities	27,661
Information	24,180
Finance	26,745
Professional & business	134,122
Education & Health	85,779
Leisure & hospitality	50,322
Other	54,489

Experienced civilian labor force by occupation, 2004

Management	60,800
Business & Financial	62,390
Legal	35,770
Sales	30,050
Office & Admin. Support	124,470
Computers & Math	32,740
Architecture & Engineering	12,430
Arts & Entertainment	22,200
Education	27,340
Social Services	7,840
Healthcare Practitioner & Technical	28,550
Healthcare support	7,770
Maintenance & Repair	8,090
Construction	11,870
Transportation & moving	14,090
Production	8,040
Farming, fishing & forestry	43,180

Hours and earnings of production workers on manufacturing payrolls, 2004

Average weekly hours	NA
Average hourly earnings	NA
Average weekly earnings	NA

Average annual pay

2004	$63,887
change from 2003	5.8%

Household income

Median household income, three-year average, 2002-2004	$43,573

Personal income, 2004 ($ per capita)

In current dollars	$51,803
In constant (2000) dollars	$48,044

Poverty

Persons below poverty level, three-year average, 2002-2004	16.8%

Federal individual income tax returns, 2003

Returns filed	275,645
Adjusted gross income ($1,000)	$16,145,339
Total income tax paid ($1,000)	$2,523,767

Economy, Business, Industry & Agriculture

Fortune 500 companies, 2005 2

Patents issued, 2004 80

Bankruptcy cases filed, 2004 2,100

Business firm ownership, 2002

Women-owned. 15,675
  Sales ($ mil) $2,403
Black-owned. 12,202
  Sales ($ mil) $1,572
Hispanic-owned. 2,162
  Sales ($ mil) $542
Asian-owned 2,415
  Sales ($ mil) $1,097
Amer. Indian/Alaska Native-owned 217
  Sales ($ mil) $42
Hawaiian/Pacific Isl.-owned . . . . NA
  Sales ($ mil) . . . . NA

Gross State Product, 2004 ($ mil)

Total Gross State Product $76,685
  Agriculture, forestry, fishing and
    hunting 2
  Mining. 12
  Utilities 700
  Construction 769
  Manufacturing, durable goods. 99
  Manufacturing, non-durable goods 111
  Wholesale trade. 752
  Retail trade. 1,031
  Transportation & warehousing 483
  Information 5,120
  Finance & insurance. 4,267
  Real estate, rental, leasing 6,068
  Professional and technical services 15,264
  Educational services 1,869
  Health care and social assistance 3,505
  Accommodation/food services. 2,175
  Other services, except government 4,586
  Government 27,106

Establishments, by major industry group, 2003

Total. 19,372
  Forestry, fishing & agriculture 2
  Mining. 7
  Construction 325
  Manufacturing. 150
  Wholesale trade. 367
  Retail trade. 1,813
  Transportation & warehousing 184
  Information 785
  Finance & insurance. 931
  Professional/scientific/technical 4,196
  Health care/social assistance 2,109
  Accommodation/food services. 1,796

Annual payroll by major industry group, 2003

Total ($1,000) $22,456,247
  Forestry, fishing & agriculture . . . . NA
  Mining. . . . . NA
  Utilities 212,532
  Construction 287,475
  Manufacturing. 74,538
  Wholesale trade. 298,193
  Retail trade. 416,274
  Transportation & warehousing 124,534
  Information 1,946,009
  Finance & insurance. 1,672,491
  Professional/scientific/technical . . . 7,029,530
  Health care/social assistance 2,617,617
  Accommodation/food services. 991,879

Agriculture

Number of farms, 2004 . . . . NA
Farm acreage, 2004
  Total. . . . . NA
  Acres per farm, 2004 . . . . NA
Farm income, 2003 ($mil)
  Net farm income . . . . NA
  Debt/asset ratio . . . . NA
Farm marketings, 2003 ($mil)
Total. . . . . NA
  Crops . . . . NA
  Livestock. . . . . NA

Principal commodities, in order by marketing receipts, 2003

NA

Federal economic activity in district

Expenditures, 2003
  Total ($ mil) $34,750
  Per capita $61,681
  Defense ($ mil). 3,321
  Non-defense ($ mil) 31,429
Defense department, 2003
  Payroll ($ mil) $2,163
  Contract awards ($ mil) $1,845
  Grants ($ mil). $33
  Homeland security grants ($1,000)
    2004 . . . . $49,231
    2005 . . . . $96,144

FDIC insured financial institutions, 2004

Number 6
  Assets ($bil) $0.9
  Deposits ($bil) 18.6

Fishing, 2004

Catch (x 1,000 lbs) 0
Value ($1,000). 0

Mining, 2004 ($ mil)

Total non-fuel mineral production .... NA
Percent of U.S. .... NA

Construction, 2003 ($ mil)

Total contracts (including non-building). $1,837
   residential............................ 311
   non-residential 1,222

Establishments, receipts, payroll & employees, by major industry group, 2002

Mining.................................. 283
   Receipts ($1,000) $1,562,949
   Annual payroll ($1,000)........... $252,814
   Paid employees 5,951

Utilities 34
   Receipts ($1,000) .... NA
   Annual payroll ($1,000)................ NA
   Paid employees .... (2,500-4,999)

Construction........................... 359
   Receipts ($1,000) $1,380,689
   Annual payroll ($1,000)........... $273,225
   Paid employees 5,992

Manufacturing 146
   Receipts ($1,000) $246,237
   Annual payroll ($1,000)............. $76,126
   Paid employees 2,021

Wholesale trade 381
   Receipts ($1,000) $2,971,507
   Annual payroll ($1,000)........... $278,233
   Paid employees 5,779

Retail trade 1,877
   Receipts ($1,000) $3,061,401
   Annual payroll ($1,000)........... $383,878
   Paid employees 18,513

Transportation......................... 215
   Receipts ($1,000) $905,612
   Annual payroll ($1,000)........... $209,150
   Paid employees 5,777

Information............................. 796
   Receipts ($1,000) .... NA
   Annual payroll ($1,000).......... $1,820,098
   Paid employees 28,511

Finance & insurance 902
   Receipts ($1,000) .... NA
   Annual payroll ($1,000)................ NA
   Paid employees .... (10k-24k)

Professional, scientific & technical 4,363
   Receipts ($1,000) $17,967,225
   Annual payroll ($1,000).......... $6,679,110
   Paid employees 83,525

Health care & social assistance 2,168
   Receipts ($1,000) $5,772,971
   Annual payroll ($1,000).......... $2,400,594
   Paid employees 62,381

Accommodation & food service.......... 1,799
   Receipts ($1,000) $2,943,078
   Annual payroll ($1,000).......... $873,095
   Paid employees 43,300

Communication, Energy & Transportation

Communication

Daily newspapers, 2004 2
Households with computers, 2003 ....64%
Households with internet access, 2003 .....57%

Energy

Electricity Consumption, 2001
   Total (trillion Btu)......................... 168
   Per capita (million Btu) 294
By source of production (trillion Btu)
   Coal 1
   Natural gas 31
   Petroleum................................ 34
   Nuclear electric power 0
   Hydroelectric power...................... 0
By end-use sector (trillion Btu)
   Residential 34
   Commercial 104
   Industrial 4
   Transportation 26
Electric energy, 2003
   Production (billion kWh) 0.1
   Net summer capability (million kW) 0.8
Gas utilities, 2003
   Customers (x1,000)..................... 121
   Sales (trillion Btu)...................... 16
   Revenues ($mil)........................ $209
Nuclear plants, 2003 0

Transportation, 2004

Public Road & Street Mileage 1,500
   Urban................................. 1,500
   Rural 0
   Interstate............................... 13
Vehicle miles of travel per capita........ 6,754.5
Total motor vehicle registrations........ 238,802
   Automobiles........................ 189,230
   Buses 2,897
   Trucks 46,675
   Motorcycles 1,601
Licensed drivers 349,122
   19 years & under 9,527
Deaths from motor vehicle accidents 43

State Summary

Capital City...................... Tallahassee
Governor............................Jeb Bush
PL 05 The Capitol
400 S Monroe St
Tallahassee, FL 32399
850-488-4441

Admitted as a state 1845
Area (square miles).................... 65,755
Population, 2004 (est.) 17,397,161
Largest City..................... Jacksonville
Population, 2004 778,000
Personal income per capita, 2004
(in current dollars) $31,455
Gross state product ($ mil), 2004 ...... $599,068

Leading industries by payroll, 2003

Health care/Social assistance, Retail trade, Professional/Scientific/Technical

Leading agricultural commodities by receipts, 2003

Greenhouse, oranges, sugar cane, tomatoes

Geography & Environment

Total area (sq. mi.).................... 65,755
land 53,927
water 11,828

Federally-owned land, 2004 (acres) ... 2,858,782
percent............................8.2%

Highest point....... Sec. 30 TGN R20W (Walton County)
elevation (feet) 345

Lowest point .... Atlantic Ocean
elevation (feet) .... sea level

General coastline (miles)................. 1,650

Tidal shoreline (miles)................... 8,426

Capital City...................... Tallahassee
Population 2000 151,000
Population 2004 157,000

Largest City..................... Jacksonville
Population 2000 736,000
Population 2004 778,000

Number of cities with over 100,000 population

1990 9
2000 13
2004 17

State park and recreation areas, 2003

Area (acres x 1,000)..................... 602
Number of visitors (x 1,000) 18,241
Revenues (x 1,000).................... $32,075
percent of operating expenditures...... 45.6%

National forest system land, 2004

Acres 1,157,000

Demographics and Characteristics of the Population

Population

1980 9,746,324
1990 12,937,926
2000 15,982,378
2004 (estimate)..................... 17,397,161
persons per sq. mile of land............322.6
2005 (projection)................... 17,509,827
Male...................... 8,543,474
Female...................... 8,966,353
2010 (projection) 19,251,691
2020 (projection) 23,406,525
2030 (projection) 28,685,769
Male...................... 14,015,012
Female...................... 14,670,757

Metropolitan and Non-Metro. area population

	Metro	Non-Metro
1980	8,885,000	862,000
1990	11,754,000	1,184,000
2000	14,837,000	1,145,000

Change in population, 2000-2004

Number.......................... 1,414,337
percent............................8.8%
Natural increase (births minus deaths).. 185,188
Net internal migration............... 791,904
Net international migration 444,726

Persons by age, 2004

Under 5 years 1,091,292
18 years and over 13,393,871
65 years and over 2,927,583
85 years and over 379,572

Persons by age, 2010 (projected)

Total........................... 19,251,691
Under 5 years 1,195,168
5 to 17 years 2,890,955
18 and over 15,165,568
21 and over 14,441,696
65 and over 3,418,697
85 and over 537,846
Median age 41.9

Race, 2004 (estimate)

One Race

White........................... 14,022,447
Black or African American 2,726,160
American Indian/Alaska Native....... 73,606
Pacific Islander 13,945
Asian Indian....................... 111,565
Chinese 56,823
Filipino 61,743
Japanese 16,218
Korean........................... 21,731
Vietnamese........................ 34,295
Two or more races................... 209,028

2   Florida

Persons of Hispanic origin, 2004

Total Hispanic or Latino	3,250,768
Mexican	465,706
Puerto Rican	656,299
Cuban	985,334
Other Hispanic or Latino	184,399

Marital status, 2000

Population 15 years & over	12,946,990
Never married	3,081,384
Married	7,030,216
Separated	310,728
Widowed	1,022,812
Divorced	1,501,851

Language spoken at home, 2000

Population 5 years & over	15,043,603
English only	11,569,739
Spanish	2,476,528
Other Indo-European languages	755,214
Asian/Pacific Island languages	164,516

Households & families, 2000

Households	6,337,929
with persons under 18 years	1,986,554
with persons over 65 years	1,943,478
persons per household	2.46
Families	4,210,760
persons per family	2.98
Married couples	3,192,266
Female householder, no husband present	759,000
One-person households	1,687,303

Nativity, 2000

Number of persons born in state	5,231,906
percent of population	32.7%

Immigration & Naturalization, 2004

Immigrants admitted	75,644
Persons naturalized	43,795
Asylums granted	5,384
Asylums denied	541

Vital Statistics and Health

Marriages

2002	157,554
2003	153,023
2004	156,370

Divorces

2002	85,181
2003	85,367
2004	82,662

Births

2003	212,250
Birthrate (per 1,000)	12.5
Low birth weight (2,500g or less)	8.5%
To unmarried mothers	39.9%

2003, continued

White	158,053
Black	47,349
Hispanic	54,864
Asian/Pacific Islander	5,795
Amer. Indian/Alaska Native	1,089
2004 (preliminary)	218,034
Birthrate (per 1,000)	12.5
White	157,701
Black	52,758
Hispanic	55,407
Asian/Pacific Islander	6,834

Deaths

2002

All causes	167,814
rate per 100,000	1,004.1
Heart disease	49,235
rate per 100,000	294.6
Malignant neoplasms	39,140
rate per 100,000	234.2
Cerebrovascular disease	10,269
rate per 100,000	61.4
Chronic lower respiratory disease	9,062
rate per 100,000	54.2
2003	168,607
rate per 100,000	990.7
2004 (provisional)	168,939

Infant deaths

2003 (provisional)	1,576
rate per 1,000	7.4
2004 (provisional)	1,505
rate per 1,000	6.9

Abortions, 2000

Total	103,000
rate per 1,000 women age 15-44	31.9

Physicians, 2003

Total	42,213
rate per 1,000 persons	248

Nurses, 2001

Total	129,610
rate per 1,000 persons	792

Community Hospitals, 2003

Number	203
Beds (x 1,000)	50.7
Patients admitted (x 1,000)	2,296
Average daily census (x 1,000)	32.8
Average cost per day	$1,387
Outpatient visits (x mil)	22.0

Disability status of population, 2004

5 to 20 years	6.1%
21 to 64 years	11.9%
65 years and over	36.4%

Education

Educational attainment, 2004
Population over 25 years 11,559,464
   Less than 9th grade 614,412
   High school graduates only. 3,510,067
   Bachelor's degree only 1,881,839
   Graduate or professional degree. . . . 1,054,617
   Less than 9th grade percent 5.3%
   High school graduate or more 85.9%
   College graduate or more. 26.0%
   Graduate or professional degree. 9.1%

Public school enrollment, Fall 2002
Total. 2,539,929
   Kindergarten through grade 8 1,809,279
   Grades 9 through 12 730,650
Enrollment, 2005 (projected) 2,609,100

Graduating public high school seniors
2004 (estimate). 129,020

SAT scores, 2005
Average verbal score 498
Average math score 498
Percent of graduates taking test 65%

Public school teachers, 2004
Total (x 1,000) 148.2
   Elementary (x 1,000). 74.6
   Secondary (x 1,000) 73.6
Average salary $40,600
   Elementary $40,600
   Secondary $40,600

State receipts & expenditures for public schools, 2004
Revenue receipts ($mil) $21,161
Expenditures
Total ($mil). $21,869
   Per capita $1,286
   Per pupil $7,181

Institutions of higher education, 2004
Total. 169
   Public. 40
   Private 129

Enrollment in institutions of higher education, Fall, 2003
Total. 894,088
   Full-time men 216,687
   Full-time women. 283,064
   Part-time men 155,348
   Part-time women. 238,989

Minority enrollment in institutions of higher education, Fall, 2003
Black, non-hispanic. 142,128
Hispanic 139,766
Asian/Pacific Islander 26,603
American Indian/Alaska Native. 3,387

Earned degrees conferred, 2003
Bachelor's 58,933
Master's 20,785
First-professional. 3,235
Doctor's 2,592

State & local financial support for higher education, 2003-2004
Full-time equivalent enrollment (x 1,000) . . 526.7
Appropriations per FTE. $4,293
   as a percent of tax revenue. 5.8%

Social Insurance & Welfare Programs

Social Security benefits & beneficiaries, 2004
Beneficiaries
   Total. 3,382,000
   Retired & dependents. 2,497,000
   Survivors. 407,000
   Disabled & dependents. 478,000
Annual benefit payments ($ mil)
   Total. $34,976
   Retired & dependents. $24,782
   Survivors. $5,437
   Disabled & dependents. $4,757
Average Monthly Benefit
   Retired & dependents. $951
   Disabled & dependents. $895
   Widowed. $948

Medicare
Enrollment, 2001 (x 1,000) 2,838
   Payments ($ mil, est.) $21,600
Enrollment, 2003 (x 1,000) 2,921

Medicaid, 2002
Beneficiaries (x 1,000). 2,676
Payments ($ mil) $9,827

State Children's Health Insurance, 2004
Enrollment (x 1,000). 419.7
Expenditures ($ mil) $176.5

Persons without health insurance, 2003
Number (x 1,000). 3,071
   percent. 18.2%
Number of children (x 1,000) 616
   percent of children 15.5%

Federal public aid
Temporary Assistance for Needy Families, 2004
Recipients (x 1,000). 116
Families (x 1,000) 57

Supplemental Security Income, 2003
Recipients (x 1,000). 409
Payments ($ mil) $1,908

Food Stamp Program, 2004
Participants (x 1,000) 1,202
Benefits ($ mil). $1,269

Housing & Construction

Housing units

Total 2003 (estimate) 7,810,997
Total 2004 (estimate) 8,009,427
Seasonal or recreational use, 2003 582,000
Owner-occupied single-family, 2003 .. 3,508,000
  Median value $144,507
Renter-occupied, 2003 1,971,000
  Median rent $724
Homeownership rate, 2003 .... 69.5%
Homeownership rate, 2004 .... 72.2%

New privately owned housing units, 2004

Number authorized (x 1,000) 255.9
Value ($ mil) $36,959
Started 2005 (x 1,000, estimate) 173.6
Started 2006 (x 1,000, estimate) 165.4

Existing home sales

2002 (x 1,000) 429.3
2003 (x 1,000) 476.1
2004 (x 1,000) 526.5

Government & Elections

State Officials 2006

Governor (name/party/term expires)
Jeb Bush
Republican - 1/07
Lieutenant Governor............. Tori Jennings
Secretary of State....................Sue Cobb
Attorney General.................Charlie Crist
Chief Justice .... Barbara J. Pariente

Governorship

Minimum age............................ 30
Length of term...................... 4 years
Consecutive terms permitted 2
Who succeeds....................Lt. Governor

State Legislature

Name .... Legislature
Upper chamber ....Senate
  Number of members..................... 40
  Length of term...................... 4 years
  Party in majority, 2006 .... Republican
Lower chamber........House of Representatives
  Number of members.................... 120
  Length of term...................... 2 years
  Party in majority, 2006 .... Republican

State Government Employees, 2004

Total............................... 183,265
Payroll......................... $613,716,119

Local Government Employees, 2004

Total............................... 641,072
Payroll..................... $2,085,873,063

Local Governments by Type, 2002

Total................................. 1,191
  County................................ 66
  Municipal 404
  Township 0
  School District........................ 95
  Special District...................... 626

Voting age population, November 2004

Total........................... 13,133,000
  Male............................. 6,266,000
  Female........................... 6,867,000
  White........................... 10,871,000
  Black............................ 1,832,000
  Hispanic 2,422,000
  Asian 260,000

Presidential Election, 2004

Total Popular Vote 7,609,810
  Kerry 3,583,544
  Bush............................. 3,964,522
Total Electoral Votes...................... 27

Federal representation, 2006 (109th Congress)

Senator.......................... Bill Nelson
  Party .... Democrat
  Year term expires 2007
Senator....................... Mel Martinez
  Party .... Republican
  Year term expires 2011
Representatives, total 25
  Democrats........................... 7
  Republicans 18
  Other................................. 0

Votes cast for US Senators

2002
Total vote (x 1,000) .... NA
Leading party........................... NA
Percent for leading party .... NA

2004
Total vote (x 1,000) 7,430,000
Leading party.................... Republican
Percent for leading party 49.4%

Votes cast for US Representatives

2002
Total vote (x 1,000) 3,767
  Democratic......................... 1,537
  Republican 2,161
Leading party.................... Republican
Percent for leading party 57.4%

2004
Total vote (x 1,000) 5,627
  Democratic......................... 2,212
  Republican 3,319
Leading party.................... Republican
Percent for leading party 59.0%

Women holding public office, 2006

US Congress 5
Statewide elected office..................... 1
State legislature 38

Black public officials, 2001

Total.................................. 243
    US and state legislatures 25
    City/county/regional offices 163
    Judicial/law enforcement................. 39
    Education/school boards................. 16

Hispanic public officials, 2004

Total.................................. 109
    State executives & legislators 16
    City/county/regional offices 59
    Judicial/law enforcement................. 28
    Education/school boards................. 6

Governmental Finance

State government revenues, 2004

Total revenue ($1,000) $75,176,415
    Revenue per capita 4,324.21

General Revenue ($ per capita) $3,259.80
    Intergovernmental 962.71
    Taxes 1,756.36
        general sales 985.25
        individual income tax................. 0
        corporate income tax 82.91
    Current charges......................211.55
    Miscellaneous 329.18

State government expenditure, 2004

Total expenditure (x $1,000) $59,943,442
    Expenditure per capita............. 3,448.00
General Expenditure ($ per capita).... $3,120.91
    Education 1,020.26
    Public welfare...................... 886.70
    Health 162.78
    Hospitals............................13.58
    Highways 291.42
    Police protection 23.19
    Correction 125.69
    Natural resources 84.68
    Parks & recreation.....................8.84
    Governmental administration 119.23
    Interest on general debt 64.81

State debt & cash, 2004 ($ per capita)

Debt $1,334.18
Cash/security holdings............. $10,207.14

Federal government grants to state & local government, 2004 (x $1,000)

Total.......................... $19,609,519
By Federal Agency
    Defense $133,382

By Federal Agency, continued
    Education 1,843,862
    Energy 25,558
    Environmental Protection Agency ... 133,905
    Health & Human Services. 11,278,983
    Homeland Security................. 850,333
    Housing & Urban Development.... 1,246,989
    Justice 345,577
    Labor 390,984
    Transportation 1,860,100
    Veterans Affairs.................... 11,751

Crime, Law Enforcement & Courts

Crime, 2004 (rates per 100,000 residents)

Property crimes 727,141
    Burglaries......................... 166,332
    Larcenies......................... 482,484
    Motor vehicle thefts 78,325
    Property crime rate................ 4,179.7
Violent crimes...................... 123,754
    Murders........................... 946
    Forcible rape....................... 6,612
    Robberies 29,997
    Aggravated assaults 86,199
    Violent crime rate 711.3

Police Agencies, 2004

Total agencies.......................... 407
Total employees 72,106
    Male officers....................... 37,869
    Female officers 6,168
    Male civilians...................... 10,346
    Female civilians.................... 17,723

Arrests, 2004

Total............................. 1,028,856
    Persons under 18 years of age 121,143

Prisoners under state & federal jurisdiction, 2004

Total prisoners........................ 85,533
    Percent change, 12/31/03 to 12/31/04 .... 4.3%
Sentenced to more than one year 85,530
    rate per 100,000........................ 486

Persons under sentence of death, 7/1/05

Total................................. 388
    White............................. 219
    Black 133
    Hispanic 34

State's highest court

Name ....Supreme Court
Number of members...................... 7
Length of term .... 6 years
Intermediate appeals court? ....yes

6   Florida

Labor & Income

Civilian labor force, 2004

Total 8,411,000
Men 4,507,000
Women 3,904,000
Persons 16-19 years 353,000
White 6,860,000
Black 1,245,000
Hispanic 1,654,000
Asian 184,000

Civilian labor force as a percent of civilian non-institutional population, 2004

Total 62.2%
Men 69.6
Women 55.4
Persons 16-19 years 39.8
White 61.5
Black 65.3
Hispanic 65.3
Asian 67.0

Employment, 2004

Total 8,021,000
Men 4,302,000
Women 3,719,000
Persons 16-19 years 299,000
White 6,591,000
Black 1,137,000
Hispanic 1,572,000
Asian 177,000

Full-time/part-time labor force, 2002

Full-time labor force, employed 6,490,000
Part-time labor force, employed 1,152,000
Unemployed, looking for
Full-time work 376,000
Part-time work 67,000

Unemployment rate, 2004

Total 4.6%
Men 4.5
Women 4.7
Persons 16-19 years 15.4
White 3.9
Black 8.6
Hispanic 5.0
Asian 3.8

Unemployed by reason for unemployment (as a percent of total unemployment), 2002

Job losers or completed temp jobs 56.3%
Job leavers 11.8
Reentrants 26.5
New entrants . . . . NA

Labor unions, 2004

Membership 414,000
percent of employed 6.0%

Experienced civilian labor force by private industry, first quarter 2004

Total 6,400,666
Natural Resources & Mining 123,076
Construction 480,027
Manufacturing 388,420
Trade, transportation & utilities . . . 1,478,653
Information 168,904
Finance 494,792
Professional & business 1,264,786
Education & Health 880,276
Leisure & hospitality 868,988
Other 237,656

Experienced civilian labor force by occupation, 2004

Management 240,710
Business & Financial 302,570
Legal 66,460
Sales 903,910
Office & Admin. Support 1,460,180
Computers & Math 145,670
Architecture & Engineering 116,420
Arts & Entertainment 88,740
Education . . . . NA
Social Services 79,370
Healthcare Practitioner & Technical 384,610
Healthcare support 184,740
Maintenance & Repair 299,130
Construction 451,710
Transportation & moving 548,270
Production 339,700
Farming, fishing & forestry 14,240

Hours and earnings of production workers on manufacturing payrolls, 2004

Average weekly hours 41.1
Average hourly earnings $13.84
Average weekly earnings $568.82

Average annual pay

2004 . . . . $35,186
change from 2003 . . . . 5.0%

Household income

Median household income, three-year average,
2002-2004 . . . . $40,171

Personal income, 2004 ($ per capita)

In current dollars $31,455
In constant (2000) dollars $29,173

Poverty

Persons below poverty level, three-year average,
2002-2004 . . . . 12.3%

Federal individual income tax returns, 2003

Returns filed 7,849,542
Adjusted gross income ($1,000) . . . $350,664,124
Total income tax paid ($1,000) $46,603,954

Economy, Business, Industry & Agriculture

Fortune 500 companies, 2005 14

Patents issued, 2004 2,989

Bankruptcy cases filed, 2004 92,200

Business firm ownership, 2002
Women-owned....................... 437,415
   Sales ($ mil) $61,327
Black-owned........................ 102,074
   Sales ($ mil) $6,037
Hispanic-owned.................... 266,828
   Sales ($ mil) $41,029
Asian-owned 41,342
   Sales ($ mil) $11,576
Amer. Indian/Alaska Native-owned 10,105
   Sales ($ mil) $647
Hawaiian/Pacific Isl.-owned 1,798
   Sales ($ mil) $122

Gross State Product, 2004 ($ mil)
Total Gross State Product $599,068
   Agriculture, forestry, fishing and
     hunting 5,339
   Mining............................... 694
   Utilities........................... 11,815
   Construction 36,332
   Manufacturing, durable goods...... 20,693
   Manufacturing, non-durable goods ... 11,659
   Wholesale trade.................... 39,285
   Retail trade....................... 49,063
   Transportation & warehousing 16,952
   Information 26,719
   Finance & insurance................ 43,919
   Real estate, rental, leasing 93,036
   Professional and technical services.... 36,865
   Educational services................ 3,882
   Health care and social assistance..... 44,590
   Accommodation/food services........ 22,060
   Other services, except government 16,087
   Government....................... 71,400

Establishments, by major industry group, 2003
Total................................ 460,746
   Forestry, fishing & agriculture 1,142
   Mining............................... 274
   Construction 43,992
   Manufacturing...................... 14,750
   Wholesale trade.................... 31,820
   Retail trade....................... 70,306
   Transportation & warehousing 11,474
   Information 8,021
   Finance & insurance................ 29,822
   Professional/scientific/technical 59,015
   Health care/social assistance 45,486
   Accommodation/food services........ 30,970

Annual payroll by major industry group, 2003
Total ($1,000) $202,370,528
   Forestry, fishing & agriculture 292,406
   Mining............................ 300,264
   Utilities......................... 1,819,466
   Construction 13,676,214
   Manufacturing................... 14,044,609
   Wholesale trade................. 12,369,943
   Retail trade.................... 19,663,247
   Transportation & warehousing 6,731,276
   Information 8,689,955
   Finance & insurance............ 17,501,489
   Professional/scientific/technical ... 18,447,119
   Health care/social assistance 28,552,200
   Accommodation/food services..... 8,780,095

Agriculture
Number of farms, 2004 43,000
Farm acreage, 2004
   Total.......................... 10,000,000
   Acres per farm, 2004 235
Farm income, 2003 ($mil)
   Net farm income $1,831
   Debt/asset ratio 15.6
Farm marketings, 2003 ($mil)
   Total............................... $6,450
   Crops 5,244
   Livestock........................... 1,206

Principal commodities, in order by marketing receipts, 2003
   Greenhouse, oranges, sugar cane, tomatoes

Federal economic activity in state
Expenditures, 2003
   Total ($ mil) $113,341
   Per capita $6,660
   Defense ($ mil)..................... 15,969
   Non-defense ($ mil) 97,372
Defense department, 2003
   Payroll ($ mil) $8,105
   Contract awards ($ mil).............. $8,108
   Grants ($ mil)........................ $184
   Homeland security grants ($1,000)
     2004 .... $142,667
     2005 .... $101,285

FDIC insured financial institutions, 2004
Number............................... 295
   Assets ($bil) $127.3
   Deposits ($bil) 301.0

Fishing, 2004
Catch (x 1,000 lbs) 124,546
Value ($1,000)...................... $190,588

Mining, 2004 ($ mil)

Total non-fuel mineral production $2,220
Percent of U.S. 5.1%

Construction, 2003 ($ mil)

Total contracts (including non-building) $48,876
    residential 32,217
    non-residential 9,941

Establishments, receipts, payroll & employees, by major industry group, 2002

Mining 235
    Receipts ($1,000) $1,635,358
    Annual payroll ($1,000) $257,432
    Paid employees 6,550

Utilities 563
    Receipts ($1,000) . . . . NA
    Annual payroll ($1,000) $1,644,351
    Paid employees 28,476

Construction 40,830
    Receipts ($1,000) $79,384,681
    Annual payroll ($1,000) $13,252,374
    Paid employees 424,868

Manufacturing 15,202
    Receipts ($1,000) $78,474,770
    Annual payroll ($1,000) $14,082,395
    Paid employees 377,137

Wholesale trade 31,332
    Receipts ($1,000) $219,490,896
    Annual payroll ($1,000) $11,884,840
    Paid employees 299,340

Retail trade 69,543
    Receipts ($1,000) $191,805,685
    Annual payroll ($1,000) $18,371,874
    Paid employees 902,760

Transportation 11,193
    Receipts ($1,000) $25,805,912
    Annual payroll ($1,000) $5,674,523
    Paid employees 176,357

Information 7,758
    Receipts ($1,000) . . . . NA
    Annual payroll ($1,000) $8,088,549
    Paid employees 184,701

Finance & insurance 28,053
    Receipts ($1,000) . . . . NA
    Annual payroll ($1,000) $15,993,236
    Paid employees 341,471

Professional, scientific & technical 56,822
    Receipts ($1,000) $42,457,665
    Annual payroll ($1,000) $17,197,105
    Paid employees 378,593

Health care & social assistance 44,372
    Receipts ($1,000) $70,972,374
    Annual payroll ($1,000) $27,074,198
    Paid employees 807,392

Accommodation & food service 30,215
    Receipts ($1,000) $29,366,940
    Annual payroll ($1,000) $7,940,944
    Paid employees 621,207

Communication, Energy & Transportation

Communication

Daily newspapers, 2004 40
Households with computers, 2003 . . . . .61%
Households with internet access, 2003 . . . . .56%

Energy

Electricity Consumption, 2001
    Total (trillion Btu) 4,135
    Per capita (million Btu) 253
By source of production (trillion Btu)
    Coal 726
    Natural gas 570
    Petroleum 1,990
    Nuclear electric power 330
    Hydroelectric power 2
By end-use sector (trillion Btu)
    Residential 1,193
    Commercial 958
    Industrial 598
    Transportation 1,386
Electric energy, 2003
    Production (billion kWh) 212.6
    Net summer capability (million kW) 49.4
Gas utilities, 2003
    Customers (x1,000) 649
    Sales (trillion Btu) 45
    Revenues ($mil) $520
Nuclear plants, 2003 5

Transportation, 2004

Public Road & Street Mileage 119,529
    Urban 78,272
    Rural 41,257
    Interstate 1,471
Vehicle miles of travel per capita 11,214.5
Total motor vehicle registrations 15,057,473
    Automobiles 8,440,792
    Buses 47,337
    Trucks 6,569,344
    Motorcycles 461,935
Licensed drivers 13,146,357
    19 years & under 468,099
Deaths from motor vehicle accidents 3,244

Georgia　1

State Summary

Capital City.........................Atlanta
Governor...................... Sonny Perdue
203 State Capitol
Atlanta, GA 30334
404-656-1776
Admitted as a state 1788
Area (square miles)................... 59,425
Population, 2004 (est.) 8,829,383
Largest City..........................Atlanta
Population, 2004................... 419,000
Personal income per capita, 2004
(in current dollars) $30,051
Gross state product ($ mil), 2004 ..... $343,125

Leading industries by payroll, 2003

Manufacturing, Health care/Social assistance,
Professional/Scientific/Technical

Leading agricultural commodities by receipts, 2003

Broilers, cotton, chicken eggs, peanuts

Geography & Environment

Total area (sq. mi.).................... 59,425
land 57,906
water 1,519

Federally-owned land, 2004 (acres) ... 1,409,406
percent.............................. 3.8%

Highest point................. Brasstown Bald
elevation (feet) 4,784

Lowest point ....Atlantic Ocean
elevation (feet) .... sea level

General coastline (miles)................. 100

Tidal shoreline (miles)................. 2,344

Capital City..........................Atlanta
Population 2000 416,000
Population 2004 419,000

Largest City..........................Atlanta
Population 2000 416,000
Population 2004 419,000

Number of cities with over 100,000 population

1990 4
2000 5
2004 5

State park and recreation areas, 2003

Area (acres x 1,000)...................... 84
Number of visitors (x 1,000) 12,405
Revenues (x 1,000)................... $27,114
percent of operating expenditures...... 47.4%

National forest system land, 2004

Acres 865,000

Demographics and Characteristics of the Population

Population

1980 5,463,105
1990 6,478,216
2000 8,186,453
2004 (estimate)................. 8,829,383
persons per sq. mile of land............152.5
2005 (projection)................... 8,925,796
Male...................... 4,416,845
Female...................... 4,508,951
2010 (projection) 9,589,080
2020 (projection) 10,843,753
2030 (projection) 12,017,838
Male...................... 5,989,343
Female...................... 6,028,495

Metropolitan and Non-Metro. area population

	Metro	Non-Metro
1980	3,403,000	2,060,000
1990	4,212,000	2,266,000
2000	5,667,000	2,520,000

Change in population, 2000-2004

Number 642,567
percent............................ 7.8%
Natural increase (births minus deaths).. 298,562
Net internal migration.................181,296
Net international migration 161,522

Persons by age, 2004

Under 5 years 679,064
18 years and over 6,496,816
65 years and over 847,082
85 years and over 95,273

Persons by age, 2010 (projected)

Total.......................... 9,589,080
Under 5 years 730,521
5 to 17 years 1,771,865
18 and over 7,086,694
21 and over 6,660,839
65 and over 980,824
85 and over 122,818
Median age 34.7

Race, 2004 (estimate)

One Race
White........................... 5,862,978
Black or African American 2,612,936
American Indian/Alaska Native....... 27,457
Pacific Islander 6,768
Asian Indian........................ 52,486
Chinese 42,130
Filipino 17,282
Japanese 12,362
Korean 40,178
Vietnamese........................ 29,762
Two or more races.................... 89,503

Persons of Hispanic origin, 2004

Total Hispanic or Latino	576,113
Mexican	390,672
Puerto Rican	46,017
Cuban	14,622
Other Hispanic or Latino	27,760

Marital status, 2000

Population 15 years & over	6,366,625
Never married	1,738,089
Married	3,437,978
Separated	146,432
Widowed	388,364
Divorced	655,762

Language spoken at home, 2000

Population 5 years & over	7,594,476
English only	6,843,038
Spanish	426,115
Other Indo-European languages	168,629
Asian/Pacific Island languages	116,456

Households & families, 2000

Households	3,006,369
with persons under 18 years	1,174,114
with persons over 65 years	563,830
persons per household	2.65
Families	2,111,647
persons per family	3.14
Married couples	1,548,800
Female householder, no husband present	435,410
One-person households	710,523

Nativity, 2000

Number of persons born in state	4,735,652
percent of population	57.8%

Immigration & Naturalization, 2004

Immigrants admitted	16,286
Persons naturalized	6,880
Asylums granted	151
Asylums denied	12

Vital Statistics and Health

Marriages

2002	55,432
2003	60,252
2004	68,897

Divorces

2002	21,308
2003	27,693
2004	NA

Births

2003	135,979
Birthrate (per 1,000)	15.7
Low birth weight (2,500g or less)	9.0%
To unmarried mothers	38.1%

2003, continued

White	88,085
Black	43,059
Hispanic	18,266
Asian/Pacific Islander	4,549
Amer. Indian/Alaska Native	319

2004 (preliminary)	138,851
Birthrate (per 1,000)	15.7
White	89,771
Black	44,001
Hispanic	20,113
Asian/Pacific Islander	4,804

Deaths

2002

All causes	65,449
rate per 100,000	764.6
Heart disease	17,529
rate per 100,000	204.8
Malignant neoplasms	13,975
rate per 100,000	163.3
Cerebrovascular disease	4,261
rate per 100,000	49.8
Chronic lower respiratory disease	3,163
rate per 100,000	36.9
2003	66,473
rate per 100,000	765.4
2004 (provisional)	65,842

Infant deaths

2003 (provisional)	1,158
rate per 1,000	8.5
2004 (provisional)	1,173
rate per 1,000	8.4

Abortions, 2000

Total	32,000
rate per 1,000 women age 15-44	16.9

Physicians, 2003

Total	19,222
rate per 1,000 persons	221

Nurses, 2001

Total	58,600
rate per 1,000 persons	697

Community Hospitals, 2003

Number	146
Beds (x 1,000)	24.6
Patients admitted (x 1,000)	926
Average daily census (x 1,000)	16.5
Average cost per day	$1,044
Outpatient visits (x mil)	12.8

Disability status of population, 2004

5 to 20 years	5.9%
21 to 64 years	11.7%
65 years and over	45%

Education

Educational attainment, 2004

Population over 25 years	5,451,333
Less than 9th grade	378,850
High school graduates only	1,618,013
Bachelor's degree only	927,149
Graduate or professional degree	467,394
Less than 9th grade percent	6.9%
High school graduate or more	85.2%
College graduate or more	27.6%
Graduate or professional degree	8.6%

Public school enrollment, Fall 2002

Total	1,496,012
Kindergarten through grade 8	1,088,561
Grades 9 through 12	407,451
Enrollment, 2005 (projected)	1,530,700

Graduating public high school seniors

2004 (estimate)	69,720

SAT scores, 2005

Average verbal score	497
Average math score	496
Percent of graduates taking test	75%

Public school teachers, 2004

Total (x 1,000)	103.6
Elementary (x 1,000)	62.5
Secondary (x 1,000)	41.1
Average salary	$46,000
Elementary	$45,400
Secondary	$46,900

State receipts & expenditures for public schools, 2004

Revenue receipts ($mil)	$13,883
Expenditures	
Total ($mil)	$14,299
Per capita	$1,648
Per pupil	$8,671

Institutions of higher education, 2004

Total	126
Public	74
Private	52

Enrollment in institutions of higher education, Fall, 2003

Total	422,067
Full-time men	117,696
Full-time women	162,146
Part-time men	52,762
Part-time women	89,463

Minority enrollment in institutions of higher education, Fall, 2003

Black, non-hispanic	120,029
Hispanic	8,583
Asian/Pacific Islander	14,127
American Indian/Alaska Native	1,147

Earned degrees conferred, 2003

Bachelor's	31,974
Master's	12,059
First-professional	2,108
Doctor's	1,122

State & local financial support for higher education, 2003-2004

Full-time equivalent enrollment (x 1,000)	210.0
Appropriations per FTE	$8,231
as a percent of tax revenue	8.6%

Social Insurance & Welfare Programs

Social Security benefits & beneficiaries, 2004

Beneficiaries	
Total	1,192,000
Retired & dependents	771,000
Survivors	181,000
Disabled & dependents	239,000
Annual benefit payments ($ mil)	
Total	$11,958
Retired & dependents	$7,464
Survivors	$2,167
Disabled & dependents	$2,326
Average Monthly Benefit	
Retired & dependents	$929
Disabled & dependents	$878
Widowed	$864

Medicare

Enrollment, 2001 (x 1,000)	933
Payments ($ mil, est.)	$4,400
Enrollment, 2003 (x 1,000)	974

Medicaid, 2002

Beneficiaries (x 1,000)	1,637
Payments ($ mil)	$4,796

State Children's Health Insurance, 2004

Enrollment (x 1,000)	280.1
Expenditures ($ mil)	$215.0

Persons without health insurance, 2003

Number (x 1,000)	1,409
percent	16.4%
Number of children (x 1,000)	314
percent of children	13.7%

Federal public aid

Temporary Assistance for Needy Families, 2004

Recipients (x 1,000)	124
Families (x 1,000)	53

Supplemental Security Income, 2003

Recipients (x 1,000)	200
Payments ($ mil)	$888

Food Stamp Program, 2004

Participants (x 1,000)	867
Benefits ($ mil)	$924

Housing & Construction

Housing units

Total 2003 (estimate)	3,583,937
Total 2004 (estimate)	3,672,677
Seasonal or recreational use, 2003	98,000
Owner-occupied single-family, 2003	1,745,000
Median value	$140,734
Renter-occupied, 2003	989,000
Median rent	$687
Homeownership rate, 2003	71.4%
Homeownership rate, 2004	70.9%

New privately owned housing units, 2004

Number authorized (x 1,000)	108.4
Value ($ mil)	$12,884
Started 2005 (x 1,000, estimate)	86.1
Started 2006 (x 1,000, estimate)	84.1

Existing home sales

2002 (x 1,000)	173.9
2003 (x 1,000)	174.0
2004 (x 1,000)	215.8

Government & Elections

State Officials 2006

Governor (name/party/term expires)
Sonny Perdue
Republican - 1/07

Lieutenant Governor	Mark Taylor
Secretary of State	Cathy Cox
Attorney General	Thurbert Baker
Chief Justice	Leah Ward Sears

Governorship

Minimum age	30
Length of term	4 years
Consecutive terms permitted	2
Who succeeds	Lt. Governor

State Legislature

Name	General Assembly
Upper chamber	Senate
Number of members	56
Length of term	2 years
Party in majority, 2006	Republican
Lower chamber	House of Representatives
Number of members	180
Length of term	2 years
Party in majority, 2006	Republican

State Government Employees, 2004

Total	121,526
Payroll	$391,417,151

Local Government Employees, 2004

Total	378,779
Payroll	$1,102,538,647

Local Governments by Type, 2002

Total	1,448
County	156
Municipal	531
Township	0
School District	180
Special District	581

Voting age population, November 2004

Total	6,338,000
Male	3,070,000
Female	3,268,000
White	4,390,000
Black	1,688,000
Hispanic	376,000
Asian	194,000

Presidential Election, 2004

Total Popular Vote	3,301,875
Kerry	1,366,149
Bush	1,914,254
Total Electoral Votes	15

Federal representation, 2006 (109th Congress)

Senator	Saxby Chambliss
Party	Republican
Year term expires	2009
Senator	Johnny Isakson
Party	Republican
Year term expires	2011
Representatives, total	13
Democrats	6
Republicans	7
Other	0

Votes cast for US Senators

2002

Total vote (x 1,000)	2,032,000
Leading party	Republican
Percent for leading party	52.7%

2004

Total vote (x 1,000)	3,221,000
Leading party	Republican
Percent for leading party	57.8%

Votes cast for US Representatives

2002

Total vote (x 1,000)	1,919
Democratic	814
Republican	1,105
Leading party	Republican
Percent for leading party	57.6%

2004

Total vote (x 1,000)	2,961
Democratic	1,141
Republican	1,820
Leading party	Republican
Percent for leading party	61.5%

Women holding public office, 2006

US Congress 1
Statewide elected office...................... 3
State legislature 44

Black public officials, 2001

Total.................................... 611
   US and state legislatures 53
   City/county/regional offices 395
   Judicial/law enforcement................. 43
   Education/school boards................ 120

Hispanic public officials, 2004

Total..................................... 7
   State executives & legislators 3
   City/county/regional offices 2
   Judicial/law enforcement.................. 2
   Education/school boards.................. 0

Governmental Finance

State government revenues, 2004

Total revenue ($1,000) $34,814,306
   Revenue per capita 3,903.82

General Revenue ($ per capita)....... $3,162.68
   Intergovernmental 1,019.94
   Taxes 1,633.84
      general sales 551.84
      individual income tax.............. 765.92
      corporate income tax 55.47
   Current charges...................... 267.84
   Miscellaneous 241.06

State government expenditure, 2004

Total expenditure (x $1,000) $34,196,775
   Expenditure per capita............... 3,834.58
General Expenditure ($ per capita).... $3,461.45
   Education 1,491.96
   Public welfare..................... 1,033.37
   Health 112.49
   Hospitals.......................... 77.13
   Highways 156.29
   Police protection..................... 27.02
   Correction 146.23
   Natural resources.................... 58.10
   Parks & recreation.................... 15.60
   Governmental administration.......... 85.11
   Interest on general debt 51.71

State debt & cash, 2004 ($ per capita)

Debt $971.56
Cash/security holdings............... $7,183.50

Federal government grants to state & local government, 2004 (x $1,000)

Total........................... $11,758,731
By Federal Agency
   Defense $51,984

By Federal Agency, continued
   Education 1,059,737
   Energy............................ 43,440
   Environmental Protection Agency 80,824
   Health & Human Services......... 6,962,809
   Homeland Security.................. 20,550
   Housing & Urban Development...... 759,810
   Justice 222,873
   Labor 172,887
   Transportation 1,297,302
   Veterans Affairs.................... 11,639

Crime, Law Enforcement & Courts

Crime, 2004 (rates per 100,000 residents)

Property crimes 376,656
   Burglaries......................... 82,992
   Larcenies......................... 249,426
   Motor vehicle thefts 44,238
   Property crime rate................. 4,265.9
Violent crimes........................ 40,217
   Murders 613
   Forcible rape...................... 2,387
   Robberies 13,656
   Aggravated assaults 23,561
   Violent crime rate.................... 455.5

Police Agencies, 2004

Total agencies............................ 466
Total employees 29,302
   Male officers...................... 18,377
   Female officers..................... 2,893
   Male civilians...................... 2,735
   Female civilians.................... 5,297

Arrests, 2004

Total 205,472
   Persons under 18 years of age 24,054

Prisoners under state & federal jurisdiction, 2004

Total prisoners....................... 51,104
   Percent change, 12/31/03 to 12/31/04 .... 8.3%
Sentenced to more than one year 51,089
   rate per 100,000...................... 574

Persons under sentence of death, 7/1/05

Total................................. 112
   White............................. 54
   Black 54
   Hispanic 3

State's highest court

Name .... Supreme Court
Number of members........................ 7
Length of term .... 6 years
Intermediate appeals court? .... yes

Labor & Income

Civilian labor force, 2004

Total	4,399,000
Men	2,389,000
Women	2,010,000
Persons 16-19 years	160,000
White	3,052,000
Black	1,178,000
Hispanic	299,000
Asian	118,000

Civilian labor force as a percent of civilian non-institutional population, 2004

Total	67.3%
Men	76.0
Women	59.2
Persons 16-19 years	36.7
White	67.0
Black	67.8
Hispanic	78.1
Asian	71.5

Employment, 2004

Total	4,194,000
Men	2,280,000
Women	1,914,000
Persons 16-19 years	134,000
White	2,946,000
Black	1,087,000
Hispanic	285,000
Asian	113,000

Full-time/part-time labor force, 2002

Full-time labor force, employed	3,567,000
Part-time labor force, employed	504,000
Unemployed, looking for	
Full-time work	200,000
Part-time work	NA

Unemployment rate, 2004

Total	4.7%
Men	4.6
Women	4.8
Persons 16-19 years	16.3
White	3.5
Black	7.7
Hispanic	4.6
Asian	3.8

Unemployed by reason for unemployment (as a percent of total unemployment), 2002

Job losers or completed temp jobs	55.7%
Job leavers	NA
Reentrants	NA
New entrants	NA

Labor unions, 2004

Membership	242,000
percent of employed	6.4%

Experienced civilian labor force by private industry, first quarter 2004

Total	3,179,318
Natural Resources & Mining	30,114
Construction	196,150
Manufacturing	449,510
Trade, transportation & utilities	816,742
Information	120,532
Finance	213,039
Professional & business	503,165
Education & Health	386,284
Leisure & hospitality	352,226
Other	98,582

Experienced civilian labor force by occupation, 2004

Management	229,230
Business & Financial	144,270
Legal	25,950
Sales	401,170
Office & Admin. Support	679,330
Computers & Math	95,480
Architecture & Engineering	54,640
Arts & Entertainment	33,400
Education	NA
Social Services	38,120
Healthcare Practitioner & Technical	176,960
Healthcare support	77,660
Maintenance & Repair	178,890
Construction	166,300
Transportation & moving	325,580
Production	341,220
Farming, fishing & forestry	1,000

Hours and earnings of production workers on manufacturing payrolls, 2004

Average weekly hours	39.2
Average hourly earnings	$14.53
Average weekly earnings	$569.58

Average annual pay

2004	$37,866
change from 2003	3.4%

Household income

Median household income, three-year average, 2002-2004	$43,217

Personal income, 2004 ($ per capita)

In current dollars	$30,051
In constant (2000) dollars	$27,870

Poverty

Persons below poverty level, three-year average, 2002-2004	12.0%

Federal individual income tax returns, 2003

Returns filed	3,709,312
Adjusted gross income ($1,000)	$168,864,213
Total income tax paid ($1,000)	$20,246,950

Economy, Business, Industry & Agriculture

Fortune 500 companies, 2005 17

Patents issued, 2004 1,492

Bankruptcy cases filed, 2004 79,800

Business firm ownership, 2002

Women-owned...................... 196,195
  Sales ($ mil) $30,029
Black-owned......................... 90,480
  Sales ($ mil) $5,925
Hispanic-owned..................... 18,375
  Sales ($ mil) $4,215
Asian-owned 26,923
  Sales ($ mil) $8,604
Amer. Indian/Alaska Native-owned 4,472
  Sales ($ mil) $662
Hawaiian/Pacific Isl.-owned.............. 203
  Sales ($ mil) $29

Gross State Product, 2004 ($ mil)

Total Gross State Product $343,125
  Agriculture, forestry, fishing and
    hunting 3,263
  Mining............................ 1,047
  Utilities........................... 6,819
  Construction 17,163
  Manufacturing, durable goods....... 19,831
  Manufacturing, non-durable goods ... 27,846
  Wholesale trade.................... 25,847
  Retail trade....................... 22,996
  Transportation & warehousing 12,963
  Information 22,445
  Finance & insurance................ 21,864
  Real estate, rental, leasing 38,293
  Professional and technical services.... 20,690
  Educational services................ 2,519
  Health care and social assistance..... 19,585
  Accommodation/food services........ 8,707
  Other services, except government 7,152
  Government 44,099

Establishments, by major industry group, 2003

Total............................... 209,137
  Forestry, fishing & agriculture 1,119
  Mining............................ 224
  Construction 20,957
  Manufacturing...................... 8,652
  Wholesale trade.................... 13,713
  Retail trade....................... 34,012
  Transportation & warehousing 5,686
  Information 4,172
  Finance & insurance................ 13,922
  Professional/scientific/technical 24,249
  Health care/social assistance 18,312
  Accommodation/food services........ 16,177

Annual payroll by major industry group, 2003

Total ($1,000) $116,311,049
  Forestry, fishing & agriculture....... 241,673
  Mining............................ 281,155
  Utilities........................... 1,602,099
  Construction 7,107,410
  Manufacturing..................... 15,839,451
  Wholesale trade................... 9,361,536
  Retail trade....................... 9,258,742
  Transportation & warehousing 5,471,125
  Information 7,280,684
  Finance & insurance.............. 9,248,920
  Professional/scientific/technical .. 10,212,542
  Health care/social assistance 13,504,306
  Accommodation/food services..... 3,880,971

Agriculture

Number of farms, 2004 49,000
Farm acreage, 2004
  Total........................... 11,000,000
  Acres per farm, 2004 218
Farm income, 2003 ($mil)
  Net farm income $2,971
  Debt/asset ratio 13.7
Farm marketings, 2003 ($mil)
Total............................... $5,246
  Crops............................. 2,024
  Livestock.......................... 3,222

Principal commodities, in order by marketing receipts, 2003

    Broilers, cotton, chicken eggs, peanuts

Federal economic activity in state

Expenditures, 2003
  Total ($ mil) $51,910
  Per capita $5,977
  Defense ($ mil)...................... 9,003
  Non-defense ($ mil) 42,907
Defense department, 2003
  Payroll ($ mil) $5,971
  Contract awards ($ mil).............. $3,447
  Grants ($ mil)........................ $54
  Homeland security grants ($1,000)
    2004 .... $70,815
    2005 .... $54,918

FDIC insured financial institutions, 2004

Number............................... 344
  Assets ($bil) $224.7
  Deposits ($bil) 132.0

Fishing, 2004

Catch (x 1,000 lbs)..................... 6,341
Value ($1,000)....................... $11,320

Mining, 2004 ($ mil)

Total non-fuel mineral production $1,830
Percent of U.S. 4.2%

Construction, 2003 ($ mil)

Total contracts (including non-building) $20,084
　residential......................... 12,027
　non-residential 5,254

Establishments, receipts, payroll & employees, by major industry group, 2002

Mining.................................. 8
　Receipts ($1,000).................... $25,581
　Annual payroll ($1,000)............. $7,284
　Paid employees 122

Utilities 572
　Receipts ($1,000).................... NA
　Annual payroll ($1,000)......... $1,658,725
　Paid employees 25,455

Construction........................ 20,257
　Receipts ($1,000)............ $41,366,986
　Annual payroll ($1,000).......... $6,852,101
　Paid employees 221,292

Manufacturing 8,805
　Receipts ($1,000)........... $126,156,636
　Annual payroll ($1,000)........ $15,709,628
　Paid employees 452,625

Wholesale trade 13,794
　Receipts ($1,000)............ $201,091,040
　Annual payroll ($1,000).......... $9,177,276
　Paid employees 201,018

Retail trade 34,050
　Receipts ($1,000)............ $90,098,578
　Annual payroll ($1,000).......... $8,850,581
　Paid employees 447,618

Transportation....................... 5,525
　Receipts ($1,000)............. $10,586,256
　Annual payroll ($1,000)......... $3,734,646
　Paid employees 117,182

Information........................... 4,081
　Receipts ($1,000)..................... NA
　Annual payroll ($1,000)......... $7,140,428
　Paid employees 145,370

Finance & insurance 13,137
　Receipts ($1,000)..................... NA
　Annual payroll ($1,000)......... $8,555,209
　Paid employees 178,920

Professional, scientific & technical 23,679
　Receipts ($1,000)............ $25,165,914
　Annual payroll ($1,000)......... $9,890,670
　Paid employees 192,587

Health care & social assistance 17,927
　Receipts ($1,000).............. $31,478,319
　Annual payroll ($1,000)........ $12,470,539
　Paid employees 374,902

Accommodation & food service......... 15,463
　Receipts ($1,000) $12,740,423
　Annual payroll ($1,000).......... $3,515,727
　Paid employees 293,064

Communication, Energy & Transportation

Communication

Daily newspapers, 2004 34
Households with computers, 2003.......... 61%
Households with internet access, 2003 ..... 54%

Energy

Electricity Consumption, 2001
Total (trillion Btu)..................... 2,881
Per capita (million Btu) 343
By source of production (trillion Btu)
　Coal 772
　Natural gas 363
　Petroleum........................... 1,034
　Nuclear electric power 352
　Hydroelectric power................. 21
By end-use sector (trillion Btu)
　Residential 642
　Commercial 503
　Industrial 876
　Transportation 860
Electric energy, 2003
　Production (billion kWh) 124.1
　Net summer capability (million kW) 34.8
Gas utilities, 2003
　Customers (x1,000)................... 353
　Sales (trillion Btu)................... 56
　Revenues ($mil)..................... $480
Nuclear plants, 2003 4

Transportation, 2004

Public Road & Street Mileage 116,916
　Urban............................. 36,413
　Rural 80,503
　Interstate......................... 1,244
Vehicle miles of travel per capita....... 12,668.2
Total motor vehicle registrations...... 7,882,365
　Automobiles....................... 4,222,236
　Buses 20,171
　Trucks 3,639,958
　Motorcycles 129,439
Licensed drivers 5,793,143
　19 years & under 269,453
Deaths from motor vehicle accidents 1,634

State Summary

Capital City . . . . Honolulu
Governor . . . . Linda Lingle
Executive Chambers
State Capitol
Honolulu, HI 96813
808-586-0034

Admitted as a state 1959
Area (square miles) 10,931
Population, 2004 (est.) 1,262,840
Largest City . . . . Honolulu
Population, 2004 377,000
Personal income per capita, 2004
(in current dollars) $32,160
Gross state product ($ mil), 2004 . . . . . . $50,322

Leading industries by payroll, 2003

Health care/Social assistance, Accommodation &
Food services, Retail trade

Leading agricultural commodities by receipts, 2003

Pineapples, greenhouse, sugar cane, macadamia
nuts

Geography & Environment

Total area (sq. mi.) 10,931
  land 6,423
  water 4,508

Federally-owned land, 2004 (acres) 796,726
  percent 19.4%

Highest point . . . . Mauna Kea
  elevation (feet) 13,796

Lowest point . . . . Pacific Ocean
  elevation (feet) . . . . sea level

General coastline (miles) 750

Tidal shoreline (miles) 1,052

Capital City . . . . Honolulu
  Population 2000 372,000
  Population 2004 377,000

Largest City . . . . Honolulu
  Population 2000 372,000
  Population 2004 377,000

Number of cities with over 100,000 population

1990 1
2000 1
2004 1

State park and recreation areas, 2003

Area (acres x 1,000) 28
Number of visitors (x 1,000) 4,499
Revenues (x 1,000) $1,759
  percent of operating expenditures 25.2%

National forest system land, 2004

Acres . . . . NA

Demographics and Characteristics of the Population

Population

1980 964,691
1990 1,108,229
2000 1,211,537
2004 (estimate) 1,262,840
  persons per sq. mile of land 196.6
2005 (projection) 1,276,552
  Male 638,447
  Female 638,105
2010 (projection) 1,340,674
2020 (projection) 1,412,373
2030 (projection) 1,466,046
  Male 734,781
  Female 731,265

Metropolitan and Non-Metro. area population

	Metro	Non-Metro
1980	763,000	202,000
1990	836,000	272,000
2000	876,000	335,000

Change in population, 2000-2004

Number 51,303
  percent 4.2%
Natural increase (births minus deaths) . . . 39,637
Net internal migration . . . . -11,986
Net international migration 24,204

Persons by age, 2004

Under 5 years 88,759
18 years and over 964,147
65 years and over 172,008
85 years and over 25,344

Persons by age, 2010 (projected)

Total 1,340,674
  Under 5 years 101,347
  5 to 17 years 214,916
  18 and over 1,024,411
  21 and over 964,238
  65 and over 191,065
  85 and over 27,645
  Median age 37.4

Race, 2004 (estimate)

One Race
  White 334,752
  Black or African American 28,105
  American Indian/Alaska Native 4,299
  Pacific Islander 114,346
  Asian Indian 1,255
  Chinese 51,462
  Filipino 188,759
  Japanese 206,331
  Korean 25,382
  Vietnamese 9,833
Two or more races 253,792

Persons of Hispanic origin, 2004

Total Hispanic or Latino 96,778
 Mexican............................ 27,478
 Puerto Rican 33,833
 Cuban 1,886
 Other Hispanic or Latino 29,356

Marital status, 2000

Population 15 years & over 965,875
 Never married 292,660
 Married........................... 512,880
 Separated 15,454
 Widowed........................... 57,953
 Divorced 86,929

Language spoken at home, 2000

Population 5 years & over 1,134,351
 English only 832,226
 Spanish 18,820
 Other Indo-European languages 14,242
 Asian/Pacific Island languages...... 267,157

Households & families, 2000

Households........................... 403,240
 with persons under 18 years 153,008
 with persons over 65 years........... 110,475
 persons per household 2.92
Families............................. 287,068
 persons per family.....................3.42
Married couples 216,077
Female householder,
 no husband present................. 49,923
One-person households 88,153

Nativity, 2000

Number of persons born in state 689,056
 percent of population................56.9%

Immigration & Naturalization, 2004

Immigrants admitted.................. 6,347
Persons naturalized 2,050
Asylums granted .... NA
Asylums denied 0

Vital Statistics and Health

Marriages

2002 25,795
2003 27,495
2004 28,843

Divorces

2002 4,612
2003 .... NA
2004 .... NA

Births

2003 18,100
 Birthrate (per 1,000)...................14.4
 Low birth weight (2,500g or less)........ 8.6%
 To unmarried mothers................ 33.5%

2003, continued
 White............................... 4,831
 Black 519
 Hispanic 2,619
 Asian/Pacific Islander 12,700
 Amer. Indian/Alaska Native............. 64
2004 (preliminary).................... 18,280
 Birthrate (per 1,000)...................14.5
 White............................... 5,177
 Black 573
 Hispanic 2,679
 Asian/Pacific Islander 12,463

Deaths

2002
All causes 8,801
 rate per 100,000.....................707.0
Heart disease 2,512
 rate per 100,000.....................201.8
Malignant neoplasms 1,945
 rate per 100,000.....................156.2
Cerebrovascular disease................... 812
 rate per 100,000.....................65.2
Chronic lower respiratory disease 265
 rate per 100,000.....................21.3
2003 8,987
 rate per 100,000.....................714.6
2004 (provisional) 8,741

Infant deaths

2003 (provisional) 139
 rate per 1,000 .... 7.7
2004 (provisional) 95
 rate per 1,000 .... 5.2

Abortions, 2000

Total................................ 6,000
 rate per 1,000 women age 15-44.........22.1

Physicians, 2003

Total................................ 3,901
 rate per 1,000 persons................... 310

Nurses, 2001

Total................................ 8,680
 rate per 1,000 persons................... 707

Community Hospitals, 2003

Number 24
Beds (x 1,000)..........................3.1
Patients admitted (x 1,000) 112
Average daily census (x 1,000) 2.2
Average cost per day $1,350
Outpatient visits (x mil)...................1.9

Disability status of population, 2004

5 to 20 years 5.3%
21 to 64 years 10%
65 years and over 35.9%

Education

Educational attainment, 2004

Population over 25 years 821,711
Less than 9th grade 46,146
High school graduates only 243,867
Bachelor's degree only 160,198
Graduate or professional degree....... 79,110
Less than 9th grade percent 5.6%
High school graduate or more 88.0%
College graduate or more............. 26.6%
Graduate or professional degree........ 9.6%

Public school enrollment, Fall 2002

Total............................... 183,829
Kindergarten through grade 8 130,862
Grades 9 through 12 52,967
Enrollment, 2005 (projected) 181,700

Graduating public high school seniors

2004 (estimate)...................... 10,300

SAT scores, 2005

Average verbal score 490
Average math score 516
Percent of graduates taking test 61%

Public school teachers, 2004

Total (x 1,000) 11.3
Elementary (x 1,000)................... 6.0
Secondary (x 1,000) 5.3
Average salary $45,500
Elementary.......................... $45,500
Secondary........................... $45,500

State receipts & expenditures for public schools, 2004

Revenue receipts ($mil) $2,106
Expenditures
Total ($mil)......................... $1,683
Per capita $1,347
Per pupil $9,019

Institutions of higher education, 2004

Total................................... 20
Public............................... 10
Private.............................. 10

Enrollment in institutions of higher education, Fall 2003

Total............................... 68,072
Full-time men 17,160
Full-time women................... 23,649
Part-time men 11,215
Part-time women.................... 16,048

Minority enrollment in institutions of higher education, Fall, 2003

Black, non-hispanic.................... 1,539
Hispanic 1,869
Asian/Pacific Islander 38,917
American Indian/Alaska Native........... 332

Earned degrees conferred, 2003

Bachelor's 5,047
Master's............................ 1,728
First-professional..................... 126
Doctor's.............................. 146

State & local financial support for higher education, 2003-2004

Full-time equivalent enrollment (x 1,000) ...35.4
Appropriations per FTE................ $9,566
as a percent of tax revenue.............. 8.7%

Social Insurance & Welfare Programs

Social Security benefits & beneficiaries, 2004

Beneficiaries
Total............................. 199,000
Retired & dependents............. 154,000
Survivors........................ 23,000
Disabled & dependents.............. 23,000
Annual benefit payments ($ mil)
Total............................. $2,039
Retired & dependents.............. $1,516
Survivors.......................... $291
Disabled & dependents.............. $232
Average Monthly Benefit
Retired & dependents............... $945
Disabled & dependents.............. $915
Widowed............................ $899

Medicare

Enrollment, 2001 (x 1,000) 168
Payments ($ mil, est.) $700
Enrollment, 2003 (x 1,000) 175

Medicaid, 2002

Beneficiaries (x 1,000)................. 200
Payments ($ mil) $695

State Children's Health Insurance, 2004

Enrollment (x 1,000).................... 19.2
Expenditures ($ mil)................... $10.5

Persons without health insurance, 2003

Number (x 1,000)....................... 127
percent........................... 10.1%
Number of children (x 1,000) 23
percent of children 7.4%

Federal public aid

Temporary Assistance for Needy Families, 2004
Recipients (x 1,000)..................... 23
Families (x 1,000) 9

Supplemental Security Income, 2003
Recipients (x 1,000)..................... 22
Payments ($ mil) $113

Food Stamp Program, 2004

Participants (x 1,000).................... 99
Benefits ($ mil)....................... $152

Housing & Construction

Housing units

Total 2003 (estimate)	476,380
Total 2004 (estimate)	482,873
Seasonal or recreational use, 2003	27,000
Owner-occupied single-family, 2003	185,000
Median value	$324,661
Renter-occupied, 2003	181,000
Median rent	$863
Homeownership rate, 2003	58.3%
Homeownership rate, 2004	60.9%

New privately owned housing units, 2004

Number authorized (x 1,000)	9.0
Value ($ mil)	$1,742
Started 2005 (x 1,000, estimate)	6.5
Started 2006 (x 1,000, estimate)	6.2

Existing home sales

2002 (x 1,000)	28.1
2003 (x 1,000)	34.4
2004 (x 1,000)	35.5

Government & Elections

State Officials 2006

Governor (name/party/term expires)
Linda Lingle
Republican - 12/06

Lieutenant Governor	James Aiona
Secretary of State	(no Secty. of State)
Attorney General	Mark Bennett
Chief Justice	Ronald Moon

Governorship

Minimum age	30
Length of term	4 years
Consecutive terms permitted	2
Who succeeds	Lt. Governor

State Legislature

Name	Legislature
Upper chamber	Senate
Number of members	25
Length of term	4 years
Party in majority, 2006	Democratic
Lower chamber	House of Representatives
Number of members	51
Length of term	2 years
Party in majority, 2006	Democratic

State Government Employees, 2004

Total	56,540
Payroll	$191,079,945

Local Government Employees, 2004

Total	14,392
Payroll	$54,276,798

Local Governments by Type, 2002

Total	19
County	3
Municipal	1
Township	0
School District	0
Special District	15

Voting age population, November 2004

Total	938,000
Male	448,000
Female	490,000
White	208,000
Black	17,000
Hispanic	55,000
Asian	475,000

Presidential Election, 2004

Total Popular Vote	429,013
Kerry	231,708
Bush	194,191
Total Electoral Votes	4

Federal representation, 2006 (109th Congress)

Senator	Daniel Akata
Party	Democrat
Year term expires	2007
Senator	Daniel K. Inouye
Party	Democrat
Year term expires	2011
Representatives, total	2
Democrats	2
Republicans	0
Other	0

Votes cast for US Senators

2002

Total vote (x 1,000)	NA
Leading party	NA
Percent for leading party	NA

2004

Total vote (x 1,000)	415,000
Leading party	Democratic
Percent for leading party	75.5%

Votes cast for US Representatives

2002

Total vote (x 1,000)	360
Democratic	232
Republican	117
Leading party	Democratic
Percent for leading party	64.5%

2004

Total vote (x 1,000)	417
Democratic	262
Republican	148
Leading party	Democratic
Percent for leading party	62.9%

Women holding public office, 2006

US Congress 0
Statewide elected office...................... 1
State legislature 22

Black public officials, 2001

Total....................................... 0
   US and state legislatures 0
   City/county/regional offices 0
   Judicial/law enforcement................... 0
   Education/school boards................... 0

Hispanic public officials, 2004

Total....................................... 1
   State executives & legislators 1
   City/county/regional offices 0
   Judicial/law enforcement................... 0
   Education/school boards................... 0

Governmental Finance

State government revenues, 2004

Total revenue ($1,000) $8,229,259
   Revenue per capita 6,520.81

General Revenue ($ per capita) $5,289.60
   Intergovernmental 1,299.42
   Taxes 3,050.03
      general sales 1,505.85
      individual income tax............. 926.47
      corporate income tax 46.05
   Current charges..................... 699.07
   Miscellaneous 241.08

State government expenditure, 2004

Total expenditure (x $1,000) $7,856,134
   Expenditure per capita............. 6,225.15
General Expenditure ($ per capita).... $5,610.91
   Education 1,971.18
   Public welfare..................... 1,067.01
   Health 329.83
   Hospitals.......................... 193.40
   Highways 169.61
   Police protection 10.92
   Correction 125.22
   Natural resources 86.78
   Parks & recreation................... 45.72
   Governmental administration 351.01
   Interest on general debt 282.36

State debt & cash, 2004 ($ per capita)

Debt $4,553.24
Cash/security holdings............. $10,455.94

Federal government grants to state & local government, 2004 (x $1,000)

Total $2,158,313
By Federal Agency
   Defense $57,236

By Federal Agency, continued
   Education 249,624
   Energy 4,320
   Environmental Protection Agency 29,475
   Health & Human Services. 1,006,912
   Homeland Security................... 3,816
   Housing & Urban Development..... 141,756
   Justice 46,889
   Labor 47,160
   Transportation 276,835
   Veterans Affairs.................... 20,006

Crime, Law Enforcement & Courts

Crime, 2004 (rates per 100,000 residents)

Property crimes 60,525
   Burglaries......................... 10,827
   Larcenies......................... 41,078
   Motor vehicle thefts 8,620
   Property crime rate................ 4,792.8
Violent crimes....................... 3,213
   Murders............................. 33
   Forcible rape........................ 333
   Robberies 944
   Aggravated assaults 1,903
   Violent crime rate 254.4

Police Agencies, 2004

Total agencies........................... 4
Total employees 3,427
   Male officers..................... 2,447
   Female officers...................... 265
   Male civilians....................... 207
   Female civilians..................... 508

Arrests, 2004

Total.................................. 49,456
   Persons under 18 years of age 9,542

Prisoners under state & federal jurisdiction, 2004

Total prisoners........................ 5,960
   Percent change, 12/31/03 to 12/31/04 .... 2.3%
Sentenced to more than one year 4,174
   rate per 100,000....................... 329

Persons under sentence of death, 7/1/05

Total.................................... 0
   White................................ 0
   Black 0
   Hispanic 0

State's highest court

Name ....Supreme Court
Number of members...................... 5
Length of term .... 10 years
Intermediate appeals court? ....yes

Labor & Income

Civilian labor force, 2004

Total 612,000
  Men 317,000
  Women 295,000
  Persons 16-19 years 21,000
  White 138,000
  Black 0
  Hispanic 38,000
  Asian 297,000

Civilian labor force as a percent of civilian non-institutional population, 2004

Total 64.7%
  Men 69.7
  Women 60.1
  Persons 16-19 years 36.5
  White 67.1
  Black 0.0
  Hispanic 69.7
  Asian 61.7

Employment, 2004

Total 591,000
  Men 304,000
  Women 287,000
  Persons 16-19 years 18,000
  White 134,000
  Black 0
  Hispanic 35,000
  Asian 290,000

Full-time/part-time labor force, 2002

Full-time labor force, employed 457,000
Part-time labor force, employed 100,000
Unemployed, looking for
  Full-time work 21,000
  Part-time work . . . . NA

Unemployment rate, 2004

Total 3.4%
  Men 4.1
  Women 2.7
  Persons 16-19 years 15.0
  White 2.7
  Black . . . . NA
  Hispanic 6.7
  Asian 2.3

Unemployed by reason for unemployment (as a percent of total unemployment), 2002

Job losers or completed temp jobs . . . . NA
Job leavers . . . . NA
Reentrants . . . . NA
New entrants . . . . NA

Labor unions, 2004

Membership 126,000
  percent of employed 23.7%

Experienced civilian labor force by private industry, first quarter 2004

Total 461,064
  Natural Resources & Mining 8,042
  Construction 27,273
  Manufacturing 15,264
  Trade, transportation & utilities 109,134
  Information 10,652
  Finance 28,627
  Professional & business 70,624
  Education & Health 65,473
  Leisure & hospitality 102,563
  Other 23,376

Experienced civilian labor force by occupation, 2004

Management 25,850
Business & Financial 20,770
Legal 4,000
Sales 59,240
Office & Admin. Support 100,670
Computers & Math 8,180
Architecture & Engineering 8,090
Arts & Entertainment 9,300
Education 37,310
Social Services 9,560
Healthcare Practitioner & Technical 22,740
Healthcare support 11,950
Maintenance & Repair 22,620
Construction 27,730
Transportation & moving 37,560
Production 19,120
Farming, fishing & forestry 4,520

Hours and earnings of production workers on manufacturing payrolls, 2004

Average weekly hours 37.9
Average hourly earnings $13.48
Average weekly earnings $510.89

Average annual pay

2004 . . . . $35,198
  change from 2003 . . . . 4.3%

Household income

Median household income, three-year average,
  2002-2004 . . . . $53,123

Personal income, 2004 ($ per capita)

In current dollars $32,160
In constant (2000) dollars $29,826

Poverty

Persons below poverty level, three-year average,
  2002-2004 . . . . 9.7%

Federal individual income tax returns, 2003

Returns filed 591,084
Adjusted gross income ($1,000) $25,718,250
Total income tax paid ($1,000) $2,936,112

Economy, Business, Industry & Agriculture

Fortune 500 companies, 2005 0

Patents issued, 2004 86

Bankruptcy cases filed, 2004 3,500

Business firm ownership, 2002

Women-owned. 29,897
  Sales ($ mil) $4,562
Black-owned. 831
  Sales ($ mil) $89
Hispanic-owned. 3,096
  Sales ($ mil) $483
Asian-owned 44,980
  Sales ($ mil) $12,649
Amer. Indian/Alaska Native-owned 953
  Sales ($ mil) $114
Hawaiian/Pacific Isl.-owned 8,470
  Sales ($ mil) $1,489

Gross State Product, 2004 ($ mil)

Total Gross State Product $50,322
  Agriculture, forestry, fishing and
    hunting 311
  Mining. 20
  Utilities 961
  Construction 2,526
  Manufacturing, durable goods. 290
  Manufacturing, non-durable goods 656
  Wholesale trade. 1,751
  Retail trade. 3,741
  Transportation & warehousing 1,753
  Information 1,496
  Finance & insurance. 2,426
  Real estate, rental, leasing 8,331
  Professional and technical services 2,274
  Educational services. 489
  Health care and social assistance 3,422
  Accommodation/food services. 4,239
  Other services, except government 1,290
  Government 11,384

Establishments, by major industry group, 2003

Total. 31,061
  Forestry, fishing & agriculture 46
  Mining. 10
  Construction 2,475
  Manufacturing. 924
  Wholesale trade. 1,895
  Retail trade. 4,893
  Transportation & warehousing 810
  Information 621
  Finance & insurance. 1,495
  Professional/scientific/technical 3,084
  Health care/social assistance 3,307
  Accommodation/food services. 3,191

Annual payroll by major industry group, 2003

Total ($1,000) $14,138,996
  Forestry, fishing & agriculture . . . . NA
  Mining. . . . . NA
  Utilities 166,916
  Construction 1,241,356
  Manufacturing. 455,119
  Wholesale trade. 698,785
  Retail trade. 1,451,356
  Transportation & warehousing 851,921
  Information 701,531
  Finance & insurance. 957,863
  Professional/scientific/technical 961,950
  Health care/social assistance 2,100,102
  Accommodation/food services. 1,810,529

Agriculture

Number of farms, 2004 6,000
Farm acreage, 2004
  Total. 1,000,000
  Acres per farm, 2004 236
Farm income, 2003 ($mil)
  Net farm income $122
  Debt/asset ratio 6.3
Farm marketings, 2003 ($mil)
  Total. $549
  Crops. 464
  Livestock. 86

Principal commodities, in order by marketing receipts, 2003

Pineapples, greenhouse, sugar cane, macadamia nuts

Federal economic activity in state

Expenditures, 2003
  Total ($ mil) $11,269
  Per capita $8,961
  Defense ($ mil). 4,484
  Non-defense ($ mil) 6,785
Defense department, 2003
  Payroll ($ mil) $3,038
  Contract awards ($ mil) $1,808
  Grants ($ mil). $42
  Homeland security grants ($1,000)
    2004 . . . . $26,865
    2005 . . . . $23,130

FDIC insured financial institutions, 2004

Number 8
  Assets ($bil) $33.8
  Deposits ($bil) 23.1

Fishing, 2004

Catch (x 1,000 lbs) 24,265
Value ($1,000). $57,202

Mining, 2004 ($ mil)

Total non-fuel mineral production $75
Percent of U.S. 0.2%

Construction, 2003 ($ mil)

Total contracts (including non-building). $2,245
    residential. 1,363
    non-residential 467

Establishments, receipts, payroll & employees, by major industry group, 2002

Mining 104
    Receipts ($1,000) $284,619
    Annual payroll ($1,000) $76,128
    Paid employees 1,841

Utilities 40
    Receipts ($1,000) . . . . NA
    Annual payroll ($1,000) $180,207
    Paid employees 2,445

Construction 2,350
    Receipts ($1,000) $5,640,054
    Annual payroll ($1,000) $1,139,031
    Paid employees 27,287

Manufacturing 929
    Receipts ($1,000) $3,460,199
    Annual payroll ($1,000) $421,269
    Paid employees 13,200

Wholesale trade 1,876
    Receipts ($1,000) $9,986,355
    Annual payroll ($1,000) $683,396
    Paid employees 19,412

Retail trade 4,924
    Receipts ($1,000) $13,008,182
    Annual payroll ($1,000) $1,333,809
    Paid employees 63,794

Transportation 771
    Receipts ($1,000) $1,293,826
    Annual payroll ($1,000) $487,193
    Paid employees 16,177

Information 594
    Receipts ($1,000) . . . . NA
    Annual payroll ($1,000) $581,426
    Paid employees 11,665

Finance & insurance 1,421
    Receipts ($1,000) . . . . NA
    Annual payroll ($1,000) $874,184
    Paid employees 18,257

Professional, scientific & technical 2,982
    Receipts ($1,000) $2,290,675
    Annual payroll ($1,000) $882,817
    Paid employees 21,208

Health care & social assistance 3,256
    Receipts ($1,000) $4,686,323
    Annual payroll ($1,000) $1,983,971
    Paid employees 56,169

Accommodation & food service 3,138
    Receipts ($1,000) $5,551,380
    Annual payroll ($1,000) $1,604,706
    Paid employees 85,641

Communication, Energy & Transportation

Communication

Daily newspapers, 2004 6
Households with computers, 2003 . . . . .63%
Households with internet access, 2003 . . . . . .55%

Energy

Electricity Consumption, 2001
    Total (trillion Btu). 282
    Per capita (million Btu) 230
By source of production (trillion Btu)
    Coal 18
    Natural gas 3
    Petroleum 240
    Nuclear electric power 0
    Hydroelectric power 1
By end-use sector (trillion Btu)
    Residential 35
    Commercial 39
    Industrial 77
    Transportation 132
Electric energy, 2003
    Production (billion kWh) 11
    Net summer capability (million kW) 2.3
Gas utilities, 2003
    Customers (x1,000). 33
    Sales (trillion Btu). 3
    Revenues ($mil) $54
Nuclear plants, 2003 0

Transportation, 2004

Public Road & Street Mileage 4,318
    Urban. 2,136
    Rural 2,182
    Interstate. 55
Vehicle miles of travel per capita 7,773.8
Total motor vehicle registrations 947,412
    Automobiles. 539,845
    Buses 5,268
    Trucks 402,299
    Motorcycles 23,106
Licensed drivers 843,876
    19 years & under 29,487
Deaths from motor vehicle accidents 142

State Summary

Capital City............................Boise
Governor.................. Dirk Kempthorne
700 West Jefferson
Second Floor
Boise, ID 83702
208-334-2100
Admitted as a state 1890
Area (square miles).................. 83,570
Population, 2004 (est.) 1,393,262
Largest City...........................Boise
Population, 2004................. 190,000
Personal income per capita, 2004
(in current dollars) $27,098
Gross state product ($ mil), 2004 ...... $43,571

Leading industries by payroll, 2003

Manufacturing, Health care/Social assistance,
Retail trade

Leading agricultural commodities by receipts, 2003

Cattle, dairy products, potatoes, wheat

Geography & Environment

Total area (sq. mi.).................... 83,570
land 82,747
water 823
Federally-owned land, 2004 (acres) .. 26,565,412
percent.............................50.2%
Highest point.....................Borah Peak
elevation (feet) 12,662
Lowest point ....Snake River
elevation (feet) 710
General coastline (miles).................... 0
Tidal shoreline (miles)....................... 0
Capital City..........................Boise
Population 2000 186,000
Population 2004 190,000
Largest City..........................Boise
Population 2000 186,000
Population 2004 190,000

Number of cities with over 100,000 population

1990 1
2000 1
2004 1

State park and recreation areas, 2003

Area (acres x 1,000)...................... 45
Number of visitors (x 1,000) 2,438
Revenues (x 1,000).................... $4,055
percent of operating expenditures...... 20.5%

National forest system land, 2004

Acres 20,716,000

Demographics and Characteristics of the Population

Population

1980 943,935
1990 1,006,749
2000 1,293,953
2004 (estimate)..................... 1,393,262
persons per sq. mile of land............16.8
2005 (projection)................. 1,407,060
Male............................. 705,161
Female 701,899
2010 (projection) 1,517,291
2020 (projection) 1,741,333
2030 (projection) 1,969,624
Male............................. 985,253
Female........................... 984,371

Metropolitan and Non-Metro. area population

	Metro	Non-Metro
1980	173,000	771,000
1990	206,000	801,000
2000	508,000	786,000

Change in population, 2000-2004

Number............................. 99,306
percent............................. 7.7%
Natural increase (births minus deaths)... 45,760
Net internal migration..................40,761
Net international migration 12,208

Persons by age, 2004

Under 5 years 103,482
18 years and over 1,020,851
65 years and over 158,695
85 years and over.................... 22,478

Persons by age, 2010 (projected)

Total....................... 1,517,291
Under 5 years 115,880
5 to 17 years 284,357
18 and over 1,117,054
21 and over 1,057,335
65 and over 181,416
85 and over 26,239
Median age 34.8

Race, 2004 (estimate)

One Race
White..................... 1,331,057
Black or African American............ 7,863
American Indian/Alaska Native....... 19,891
Pacific Islander 1,640
Asian Indian........................ 2,546
Chinese 3,590
Filipino 1,027
Japanese 2,475
Korean............................. 3,022
Vietnamese......................... 1,264
Two or more races.................... 18,645

Persons of Hispanic origin, 2004

Total Hispanic or Latino 121,398
  Mexican. 104,980
  Puerto Rican 1,086
  Cuban 260
  Other Hispanic or Latino 12,334

Marital status, 2000

Population 15 years & over 991,624
  Never married 226,090
  Married. 594,974
  Separated 11,899
  Widowed. 52,556
  Divorced 105,112

Language spoken at home, 2000

Population 5 years & over 1,196,793
  English only 1,084,914
  Spanish 80,241
  Other Indo-European languages 19,460
  Asian/Pacific Island languages. 8,105

Households & families, 2000

Households 469,645
  with persons under 18 years 181,967
  with persons over 65 years. 100,742
  persons per household 2.69
Families. 335,588
  persons per family. 3.17
Married couples. 276,511
Female householder,
  no husband present. 40,849
One-person households 105,175

Nativity, 2000

Number of persons born in state 610,929
  percent of population 47.2%

Immigration & Naturalization, 2004

Immigrants admitted 2,229
Persons naturalized 864
Asylums granted 8
Asylums denied 0

Vital Statistics and Health

Marriages

2002 14,684
2003 14,867
2004 14,997

Divorces

2002 7,088
2003 7,082
2004 6,922

Births

2003 21,800
  Birthrate (per 1,000). 16.0
  Low birth weight (2,500g or less). 6.5%
  To unmarried mothers. 22.3%

2003, continued
  White. 20,972
  Black 108
  Hispanic 2,940
  Asian/Pacific Islander 353
  Amer. Indian/Alaska Native 369

2004 (preliminary). 22,527
  Birthrate (per 1,000). 16.2
  White. 21,710
  Black 109
  Hispanic 3,241
  Asian/Pacific Islander 309

Deaths

2002
All causes 9,923
  rate per 100,000. . . . . .739.9
Heart disease 2,532
  rate per 100,000. . . . . .188.8
Malignant neoplasms 2,138
  rate per 100,000. . . . . .159.4
Cerebrovascular disease. 736
  rate per 100,000. .54.9
Chronic lower respiratory disease 595
  rate per 100,000. .44.4
2003 10,385
  rate per 100,000. . . . . .760.1
2004 (provisional) 10,071

Infant deaths

2003 (provisional) 158
  rate per 1,000 . . . . .7.2
2004 (provisional) 152
  rate per 1,000 . . . . .6.8

Abortions, 2000

Total. 2,000
  rate per 1,000 women age 15-44 . . . . .7.0

Physicians, 2003

Total. 2,324
  rate per 1,000 persons. 170

Nurses, 2001

Total. 8,400
  rate per 1,000 persons. 636

Community Hospitals, 2003

Number 39
Beds (x 1,000). 3.4
Patients admitted (x 1,000) 136
Average daily census (x 1,000) 1.9
Average cost per day $1,235
Outpatient visits (x mil) 2.8

Disability status of population, 2004

5 to 20 years 6.9%
21 to 64 years 13.3%
65 years and over 46.1%

Education

Educational attainment, 2004

Population over 25 years 843,345
  Less than 9th grade 36,703
  High school graduates only.......... 238,291
  Bachelor's degree only 134,483
  Graduate or professional degree...... 66,086
  Less than 9th grade percent 4.4%
  High school graduate or more 87.9%
  College graduate or more.............. 23.8%
  Graduate or professional degree........ 7.8%

Public school enrollment, Fall 2002

Total............................... 248,515
  Kindergarten through grade 8 173,200
  Grades 9 through 12 75,315
Enrollment, 2005 (projected) 254,200

Graduating public high school seniors

2004 (estimate)....................... 15,460

SAT scores, 2005

Average verbal score 544
Average math score 542
Percent of graduates taking test 21%

Public school teachers, 2004

Total (x 1,000) 14.1
  Elementary (x 1,000)...................... 7.2
  Secondary (x 1,000) 6.9
Average salary $41,100
  Elementary........................ $41,100
  Secondary......................... $41,100

State receipts & expenditures for public schools, 2004

Revenue receipts ($mil)................. $1,650
Expenditures
Total ($mil)........................... $1,700
  Per capita $1,244
  Per pupil $6,779

Institutions of higher education, 2004

Total.................................... 14
  Public................................. 7
  Private................................ 7

Enrollment in institutions of higher education, Fall, 2003

Total................................ 76,442
  Full-time men 24,577
  Full-time women..................... 28,397
  Part-time men 9,438
  Part-time women..................... 14,030

Minority enrollment in institutions of higher education, Fall, 2003

Black, non-hispanic........................ 547
Hispanic 2,922
Asian/Pacific Islander 1,295
American Indian/Alaska Native............ 982

Earned degrees conferred, 2003

Bachelor's 5,975
Master's................................ 1,487
First-professional......................... 154
Doctor's.................................. 131

State & local financial support for higher education, 2003-2004

Full-time equivalent enrollment (x 1,000) ...49.8
Appropriations per FTE................ $6,050
  as a percent of tax revenue............. 10.1%

Social Insurance & Welfare Programs

Social Security benefits & beneficiaries, 2004

Beneficiaries
  Total............................. 219,000
  Retired & dependents............... 156,000
  Survivors........................... 28,000
  Disabled & dependents............... 35,000
Annual benefit payments ($ mil)
  Total............................. $2,202
  Retired & dependents............... $1,495
  Survivors............................ $369
  Disabled & dependents................ $338
Average Monthly Benefit
  Retired & dependents................. $931
  Disabled & dependents................ $879
  Widowed............................. $938

Medicare

Enrollment, 2001 (x 1,000) 169
  Payments ($ mil, est.)................ $700
Enrollment, 2003 (x 1,000) 178

Medicaid, 2002

Beneficiaries (x 1,000)................... 176
Payments ($ mil) $792

State Children's Health Insurance, 2004

Enrollment (x 1,000)..................... 17.4
Expenditures ($ mil)................... $14.4

Persons without health insurance, 2003

Number (x 1,000)........................ 253
  percent............................. 18.6%
Number of children (x 1,000) 51
  percent of children 13.7%

Federal public aid

Temporary Assistance for Needy Families, 2004
Recipients (x 1,000)........................ 3
Families (x 1,000) 2

Supplemental Security Income, 2003
Recipients (x 1,000)....................... 20
Payments ($ mil) $91

Food Stamp Program, 2004

Participants (x 1,000) 91
Benefits ($ mil).......................... $91

Housing & Construction

Housing units

Total 2003 (estimate)	564,754
Total 2004 (estimate)	578,774
Seasonal or recreational use, 2003	27,000
Owner-occupied single-family, 2003	284,000
Median value	$118,174
Renter-occupied, 2003	125,000
Median rent	$565
Homeownership rate, 2003	74.4%
Homeownership rate, 2004	73.7%

New privately owned housing units, 2004

Number authorized (x 1,000)	18.1
Value ($ mil)	$2,624
Started 2005 (x 1,000, estimate)	13.1
Started 2006 (x 1,000, estimate)	12.8

Existing home sales

2002 (x 1,000)	25.7
2003 (x 1,000)	27.6
2004 (x 1,000)	32.0

Government & Elections

State Officials 2006

Governor (name/party/term expires)
Dirk Kempthorne
Republican - 1/07

Lieutenant Governor	Jim Risch
Secretary of State	Ben Ysursa
Attorney General	Lawrence Wasden
Chief Justice	Gerald F. Schroeder

Governorship

Minimum age	30
Length of term	4 years
Consecutive terms permitted	not specified
Who succeeds	Lt. Governor

State Legislature

Name	Legislature
Upper chamber	Senate
Number of members	35
Length of term	2 years
Party in majority, 2006	Republican
Lower chamber	House of Representatives
Number of members	70
Length of term	2 years
Party in majority, 2006	Republican

State Government Employees, 2004

Total	23,198
Payroll	$72,917,168

Local Government Employees, 2004

Total	55,112
Payroll	$151,380,588

Local Governments by Type, 2002

Total	1,158
County	44
Municipal	200
Township	0
School District	116
Special District	798

Voting age population, November 2004

Total	996,000
Male	487,000
Female	509,000
White	942,000
Black	5,000
Hispanic	89,000
Asian	15,000

Presidential Election, 2004

Total Popular Vote	598,447
Kerry	181,098
Bush	409,235
Total Electoral Votes	4

Federal representation, 2006 (109th Congress)

Senator	Larry Craig
Party	Republican
Year term expires	2009
Senator	Mike Crapo
Party	Republican
Year term expires	2011
Representatives, total	2
Democrats	0
Republicans	2
Other	0

Votes cast for US Senators

2002

Total vote (x 1,000)	409,000
Leading party	Republican
Percent for leading party	65.2%

2004

Total vote (x 1,000)	504,000
Leading party	Republican
Percent for leading party	99.2%

Votes cast for US Representatives

2002

Total vote (x 1,000)	405
Democratic	138
Republican	256
Leading party	Republican
Percent for leading party	63.3%

2004

Total vote (x 1,000)	572
Democratic	171
Republican	401
Leading party	Republican
Percent for leading party	70.1%

Women holding public office, 2006
US Congress 0
Statewide elected office 1
State legislature 29

Black public officials, 2001
Total 2
   US and state legislatures 0
   City/county/regional offices 2
   Judicial/law enforcement 0
   Education/school boards 0

Hispanic public officials, 2004
Total 1
   State executives & legislators 1
   City/county/regional offices 0
   Judicial/law enforcement 0
   Education/school boards 0

Governmental Finance

State government revenues, 2004
Total revenue ($1,000) $7,112,364
   Revenue per capita 5,098.47

General Revenue ($ per capita) $3,806.38
   Intergovernmental 1,248.31
   Taxes 1,898.06
      general sales 743.31
      individual income tax 650.75
      corporate income tax 74.40
   Current charges 336.94
   Miscellaneous 323.07

State government expenditure, 2004
Total expenditure (x $1,000) $5,762,624
   Expenditure per capita 4,130.91
General Expenditure ($ per capita) $3,650.92
   Education 1,443.68
   Public welfare 858.37
   Health 80.60
   Hospitals 28.09
   Highways 375.80
   Police protection 30.97
   Correction 122.57
   Natural resources 128.18
   Parks & recreation 18.68
   Governmental administration 192.46
   Interest on general debt 95.91

State debt & cash, 2004 ($ per capita)
Debt $1,708.85
Cash/security holdings $8,412.48

Federal government grants to state & local government, 2004 (x $1,000)
Total $1,994,706
By Federal Agency
   Defense $33,730

By Federal Agency, continued
   Education 179,965
   Energy 14,145
   Environmental Protection Agency 49,525
   Health & Human Services 994,872
   Homeland Security 7,910
   Housing & Urban Development 82,193
   Justice 48,470
   Labor 55,188
   Transportation 270,150
   Veterans Affairs 10,966

Crime, Law Enforcement & Courts

Crime, 2004 (rates per 100,000 residents)
Property crimes 38,933
   Burglaries 7,626
   Larcenies 28,583
   Motor vehicle thefts 2,724
   Property crime rate 2,794.4
Violent crimes 3,412
   Murders 30
   Forcible rape 570
   Robberies 240
   Aggravated assaults 2,572
   Violent crime rate 244.9

Police Agencies, 2004
Total agencies 118
Total employees 3,620
   Male officers 2,289
   Female officers 155
   Male civilians 208
   Female civilians 968

Arrests, 2004
Total 72,204
   Persons under 18 years of age 15,567

Prisoners under state & federal jurisdiction, 2004
Total prisoners 6,375
   Percent change, 12/31/03 to 12/31/04 .... 11.1%
Sentenced to more than one year 6,375
   rate per 100,000 454

Persons under sentence of death, 7/1/05
Total 21
   White 21
   Black 0
   Hispanic 0

State's highest court
Name .... Supreme Court
Number of members 5
Length of term .... 6 years
Intermediate appeals court? .... yes

6   Idaho

Labor & Income

Civilian labor force, 2004
```
Total....................................706,000
  Men ................................383,000
  Women .............................323,000
  Persons 16-19 years................45,000
  White..............................674,000
  Black ...................................0
  Hispanic ...........................56,000
  Asian ...................................0
```

Civilian labor force as a percent of civilian non-institutional population, 2004
```
Total.....................................68.0%
  Men ...................................74.8
  Women ................................61.3
  Persons 16-19 years...................55.0
  White..................................68.7
  Black ..................................0.0
  Hispanic ..............................70.1
  Asian ..................................0.0
```

Employment, 2004
```
Total....................................669,000
  Men ................................361,000
  Women .............................307,000
  Persons 16-19 years................38,000
  White..............................640,000
  Black ...................................0
  Hispanic ...........................51,000
  Asian ...................................0
```

Full-time/part-time labor force, 2002
```
Full-time labor force, employed .......509,000
Part-time labor force, employed........135,000
Unemployed, looking for
  Full-time work.....................34,000
  Part-time work.........................NA
```

Unemployment rate, 2004
```
Total......................................5.3%
  Men ....................................5.8
  Women .................................4.7
  Persons 16-19 years...................16.9
  White...................................5.0
  Black ...................................NA
  Hispanic ...............................8.0
  Asian ...................................NA
```

Unemployed by reason for unemployment (as a percent of total unemployment), 2002
```
Job losers or completed temp jobs ........60.0%
Job leavers................................NA
Reentrants.................................NA
New entrants ..............................NA
```

Labor unions, 2004
```
Membership ...........................33,000
  percent of employed ..................5.8%
```

Experienced civilian labor force by private industry, first quarter 2004
```
Total..................................462,135
  Natural Resources & Mining .........18,614
  Construction .......................35,482
  Manufacturing.......................60,671
  Trade, transportation & utilities .....113,522
  Information ..........................9,304
  Finance .............................25,381
  Professional & business .............69,782
  Education & Health ..................60,948
  Leisure & hospitality................53,831
  Other ...............................14,358
```

Experienced civilian labor force by occupation, 2004
```
Management...............................40,230
Business & Financial....................19,110
Legal....................................3,550
Sales...................................56,960
Office & Admin. Support................97,460
Computers & Math .......................9,700
Architecture & Engineering ............14,090
Arts & Entertainment....................6,400
Education ..............................35,210
Social Services ........................7,970
Healthcare Practitioner & Technical.....26,590
Healthcare support .....................15,750
Maintenance & Repair ..................27,350
Construction ..........................34,860
Transportation & moving ...............44,590
Production ............................39,040
Farming, fishing & forestry............2,760
```

Hours and earnings of production workers on manufacturing payrolls, 2004
```
Average weekly hours .....................40.5
Average hourly earnings ...............$14.15
Average weekly earnings ..............$573.08
```

Average annual pay
```
2004...................................$29,871
  change from 2003 .......................4.2%
```

Household income
```
Median household income, three-year average,
  2002-2004.........................$42,519
```

Personal income, 2004 ($ per capita)
```
In current dollars.....................$27,098
In constant (2000) dollars ............$25,132
```

Poverty
```
Persons below poverty level, three-year average,
  2002-2004...........................10.5%
```

Federal individual income tax returns, 2003
```
Returns filed.........................577,926
Adjusted gross income ($1,000) ....$22,254,112
Total income tax paid ($1,000) ......$2,338,746
```

Economy, Business, Industry & Agriculture

Fortune 500 companies, 2005 2

Patents issued, 2004 1,822

Bankruptcy cases filed, 2004 9,700

Business firm ownership, 2002

Women-owned 28,824
    Sales ($ mil) $3,216
Black-owned 373
    Sales ($ mil) $58
Hispanic-owned 2,780
    Sales ($ mil) $352
Asian-owned 1,115
    Sales ($ mil) $361
Amer. Indian/Alaska Native-owned 1,143
    Sales ($ mil) $204
Hawaiian/Pacific Isl.-owned 99
    Sales ($ mil) $9

Gross State Product, 2004 ($ mil)

Total Gross State Product $43,571
    Agriculture, forestry, fishing and
        hunting 2,075
    Mining 134
    Utilities 924
    Construction 2,903
    Manufacturing, durable goods 4,299
    Manufacturing, non-durable goods 1,932
    Wholesale trade 2,326
    Retail trade 3,616
    Transportation & warehousing 1,212
    Information 999
    Finance & insurance 1,865
    Real estate, rental, leasing 5,191
    Professional and technical services 2,780
    Educational services 212
    Health care and social assistance 2,914
    Accommodation/food services 1,048
    Other services, except government 856
    Government 6,074

Establishments, by major industry group, 2003

Total 39,839
    Forestry, fishing & agriculture 557
    Mining 109
    Construction 6,352
    Manufacturing 1,778
    Wholesale trade 2,001
    Retail trade 5,915
    Transportation & warehousing 1,520
    Information 693
    Finance & insurance 2,512
    Professional/scientific/technical 3,418
    Health care/social assistance 3,775
    Accommodation/food services 3,076

Annual payroll by major industry group, 2003

Total ($1,000) $13,106,885
    Forestry, fishing & agriculture 107,344
    Mining 69,775
    Utilities 200,998
    Construction 1,163,819
    Manufacturing 2,338,478
    Wholesale trade 828,677
    Retail trade 1,443,807
    Transportation & warehousing 378,082
    Information 480,406
    Finance & insurance 740,275
    Professional/scientific/technical 1,177,310
    Health care/social assistance 1,818,480
    Accommodation/food services 488,432

Agriculture

Number of farms, 2004 25,000
Farm acreage, 2004
    Total 12,000,000
    Acres per farm, 2004 472
Farm income, 2003 ($mil)
    Net farm income $1,218
    Debt/asset ratio 17.4
Farm marketings, 2003 ($mil)
    Total $3,953
    Crops 1,776
    Livestock 2,177

Principal commodities, in order by marketing receipts, 2003

    Cattle, dairy products, potatoes, wheat

Federal economic activity in state

Expenditures, 2003
    Total ($ mil) $8,654
    Per capita $6,334
    Defense ($ mil) 653
    Non-defense ($ mil) 8,002
Defense department, 2003
    Payroll ($ mil) $439
    Contract awards ($ mil) $213
    Grants ($ mil) $21
    Homeland security grants ($1,000)
        2004 .... $22,621
        2005 .... $16,805

FDIC insured financial institutions, 2004

Number 17
    Assets ($bil) $5.5
    Deposits ($bil) 13.8

Fishing, 2004

Catch (x 1,000 lbs) 0
Value ($1,000) 0

8   Idaho

Mining, 2004 ($ mil)
Total non-fuel mineral production $322
Percent of U.S. 0.7%

Construction, 2003 ($ mil)
Total contracts (including non-building). $3,050
   residential............................ 2,130
   non-residential 621

**Establishments, receipts, payroll & employees,
by major industry group, 2002**

Mining.................................. 593
   Receipts ($1,000) $2,276,094
   Annual payroll ($1,000)........... $424,757
   Paid employees 9,091

Utilities 184
   Receipts ($1,000)...................... NA
   Annual payroll ($1,000) $199,812
   Paid employees 3,703

Construction........................... 5,745
   Receipts ($1,000) $5,507,211
   Annual payroll ($1,000).......... $1,036,778
   Paid employees 36,097

Manufacturing 1,814
   Receipts ($1,000) $15,174,196
   Annual payroll ($1,000)......... $2,192,645
   Paid employees 61,538

Wholesale trade 1,989
   Receipts ($1,000) $11,458,012
   Annual payroll ($1,000).......... $768,806
   Paid employees 22,947

Retail trade 5,874
   Receipts ($1,000) $13,540,952
   Annual payroll ($1,000).......... $1,372,177
   Paid employees 69,641

Transportation....................... 1,474
   Receipts ($1,000) $1,183,968
   Annual payroll ($1,000)........... $333,747
   Paid employees 12,902

Information........................... 655
   Receipts ($1,000) .... NA
   Annual payroll ($1,000)........... $351,785
   Paid employees 10,996

Finance & insurance 2,403
   Receipts ($1,000) .... NA
   Annual payroll ($1,000).......... $658,617
   Paid employees 17,789

Professional, scientific & technical 3,244
   Receipts ($1,000) $2,309,182
   Annual payroll ($1,000).......... $1,167,979
   Paid employees 31,826

Health care & social assistance 3,589
   Receipts ($1,000) $4,251,492
   Annual payroll ($1,000).......... $1,747,910
   Paid employees 61,124

Accommodation & food service........... 3,088
   Receipts ($1,000) $1,653,671
   Annual payroll ($1,000)........... $450,236
   Paid employees 45,435

Communication, Energy & Transportation

Communication
Daily newspapers, 2004 12
Households with computers, 2003 ....69%
Households with internet access, 2003 .....56%

Energy
Electricity Consumption, 2001
Total (trillion Btu)......................... 501
Per capita (million Btu) 379
By source of production (trillion Btu)
   Coal 11
   Natural gas........................... 82
   Petroleum............................ 155
   Nuclear electric power 0
   Hydroelectric power.................... 74
By end-use sector (trillion Btu)
   Residential 105
   Commercial 95
   Industrial 180
   Transportation 122
Electric energy, 2003
   Production (billion kWh) 10.4
   Net summer capability (million kW) 3
Gas utilities, 2003
   Customers (x1,000)................... 307
   Sales (trillion Btu)..................... 31
   Revenues ($mil)...................... $218
Nuclear plants, 2003 0

Transportation, 2004
Public Road & Street Mileage 47,100
   Urban.............................. 4,620
   Rural 42,480
   Interstate............................ 612
Vehicle miles of travel per capita....... 10,774.7
Total motor vehicle registrations...... 1,344,124
   Automobiles........................ 574,825
   Buses 3,801
   Trucks 765,498
   Motorcycles 49,578
Licensed drivers 942,983
   19 years & under 60,795
Deaths from motor vehicle accidents 260

State Summary

Capital City...................... Springfield
Governor.....................Rod Blagojevich
State Capitol
207 Statehouse
Springfield, IL 62706
217-782-6830
Admitted as a state 1818
Area (square miles).................... 57,914
Population, 2004 (est.) 12,713,634
Largest City......................... Chicago
Population, 2004................. 2,862,000
Personal income per capita, 2004
(in current dollars) $34,351
Gross state product ($ mil), 2004...... $521,900

Leading industries by payroll, 2003

Manufacturing, Health care/Social assistance,
Finance & Insurance

Leading agricultural commodities by receipts, 2003

Corn, soybeans, hogs, cattle

Geography & Environment

Total area (sq. mi.).................... 57,914
land 55,584
water 2,331

Federally-owned land, 2004 (acres) 641,959
percent............................1.8%

Highest point.................. Charles Mound
elevation (feet) 1,235

Lowest point .... Mississippi River
elevation (feet) 279

General coastline (miles)..................... 0

Tidal shoreline (miles)....................... 0

Capital City....................... Springfield
Population 2000 111,000
Population 2004 115,000

Largest City......................... Chicago
Population 2000 2,896,000
Population 2004 2,862,000

Number of cities with over 100,000 population

1990 4
2000 7
2004 7

State park and recreation areas, 2003

Area (acres x 1,000)...................... 327
Number of visitors (x 1,000) 37,137
Revenues (x 1,000).................... $16,851
percent of operating expenditures...... 29.8%

National forest system land, 2004

Acres 293,000

Demographics and Characteristics of the Population

Population

1980 11,426,518
1990 11,430,602
2000 12,419,293
2004 (estimate)................... 12,713,634
persons per sq. mile of land............228.7
2005 (projection).................. 12,699,336
Male....................... 6,235,749
Female....................... 6,463,587
2010 (projection) 12,916,894
2020 (projection)................. 13,236,720
2030 (projection)................. 13,432,892
Male....................... 6,630,355
Female....................... 6,802,537

Metropolitan and Non-Metro. area population

	Metro	Non-Metro
1980	9,339,000	2,088,000
1990	9,450,000	1,981,000
2000	10,542,000	1,878,000

Change in population, 2000-2004

Number............................. 293,987
percent............................2.4%
Natural increase (births minus deaths).. 321,232
Net internal migration................-304,775
Net international migration 276,890

Persons by age, 2004

Under 5 years 890,545
18 years and over 9,475,484
65 years and over 1,520,629
85 years and over 219,387

Persons by age, 2010 (projected)

Total........................... 12,916,894
Under 5 years 926,650
5 to 17 years 2,270,256
18 and over 9,719,988
21 and over 9,174,856
65 and over 1,600,863
85 and over 259,377
Median age 36

Race, 2004 (estimate)

One Race

White................... 10,101,163
Black or African American........ 1,926,010
American Indian/Alaska Native....... 38,997
Pacific Islander 8,062
Asian Indian....................... 152,598
Chinese 84,960
Filipino 106,909
Japanese 21,576
Korean 73,151
Vietnamese..................... 14,736
Two or more races................... 134,784

Persons of Hispanic origin, 2004

Total Hispanic or Latino 1,739,870
   Mexican........................ 1,361,997
   Puerto Rican 145,452
   Cuban 20,720
   Other Hispanic or Latino 76,039

Marital status, 2000

Population 15 years & over 9,707,837
   Never married 2,805,565
   Married........................ 5,203,401
   Separated 174,741
   Widowed........................ 650,425
   Divorced 863,997

Language spoken at home, 2000

Population 5 years & over 11,547,505
   English only 9,326,786
   Spanish 1,253,676
   Other Indo-European languages 640,237
   Asian/Pacific Island languages...... 248,800

Households & families, 2000

Households....................... 4,591,779
   with persons under 18 years 1,663,878
   with persons over 65 years........ 1,064,919
   persons per household 2.63
Families......................... 3,105,513
   persons per family....................3.23
Married couples.................... 2,353,892
Female householder,
   no husband present................ 563,718
One-person households 1,229,807

Nativity, 2000

Number of persons born in state 8,335,553
   percent of population 67.1%

Immigration & Naturalization, 2004

Immigrants admitted.................. 46,314
Persons naturalized 29,432
Asylums granted 225
Asylums denied 32

Vital Statistics and Health

Marriages

2002 83,208
2003 82,076
2004 77,845

Divorces

2002 36,854
2003 34,553
2004 33,076

Births

2003 182,495
   Birthrate (per 1,000)..................14.4
   Low birth weight (2,500g or less)........8.3%
   To unmarried mothers................ 35.3%

2003, continued
   White........................... 142,216
   Black 31,602
   Hispanic 42,486
   Asian/Pacific Islander 8,530
   Amer. Indian/Alaska Native 243

2004 (preliminary)................... 180,934
   Birthrate (per 1,000)..................14.2
   White........................... 140,867
   Black 30,874
   Hispanic 42,608
   Asian/Pacific Islander 8,903

Deaths

2002
All causes 106,667
   rate per 100,000..................... 846.5
Heart disease 30,821
   rate per 100,000..................... 244.6
Malignant neoplasms 24,737
   rate per 100,000.....................196.3
Cerebrovascular disease................. 7,183
   rate per 100,000......................57.0
Chronic lower respiratory disease 4,827
   rate per 100,000......................38.3
2003 .... NA
   rate per 100,000..................... NA
2004 (provisional) 101,752

Infant deaths

2003 (provisional) 1,361
   rate per 1,000 ....7.5
2004 (provisional) 1,253
   rate per 1,000 7

Abortions, 2000

Total.............................. 64,000
   rate per 1,000 women age 15-44..........23.2

Physicians, 2003

Total.............................. 34,461
   rate per 1,000 persons................. 272

Nurses, 2001

Total.............................. 104,830
   rate per 1,000 persons................. 837

Community Hospitals, 2003

Number 192
Beds (x 1,000)..........................35.0
Patients admitted (x 1,000) 1,594
Average daily census (x 1,000) 22.4
Average cost per day $1,497
Outpatient visits (x mil) 27.0

Disability status of population, 2004

5 to 20 years 5.2%
21 to 64 years 9.3%
65 years and over 38.1%

Education

Educational attainment, 2004

Population over 25 years 8,013,790
  Less than 9th grade 503,482
  High school graduates only........ 2,268,652
  Bachelor's degree only 1,435,776
  Graduate or professional degree...... 893,724
  Less than 9th grade percent 6.3%
  High school graduate or more 86.8%
  College graduate or more.............. 27.4%
  Graduate or professional degree........ 11.2%

Public school enrollment, Fall 2002

Total............................. 2,084,187
  Kindergarten through grade 8 1,487,654
  Grades 9 through 12................ 596,533
Enrollment, 2005 (projected) 2,091,000

Graduating public high school seniors

2004 (estimate)...................... 121,270

SAT scores, 2005

Average verbal score 594
Average math score....................... 606
Percent of graduates taking test 10%

Public school teachers, 2004

Total (x 1,000) 130
  Elementary (x 1,000)...................89.9
  Secondary (x 1,000) 40.1
Average salary $54,200
  Elementary $50,900
  Secondary........................... $61,800

State receipts & expenditures for public schools, 2004

Revenue receipts ($mil)................ $18,240
Expenditures
Total ($mil)........................... $29,528
  Per capita $2,334
  Per pupil $10,866

Institutions of higher education, 2004

Total..................................... 173
  Public................................ 60
  Private............................... 113

Enrollment in institutions of higher education, Fall, 2003

Total................................. 809,721
  Full-time men 206,794
  Full-time women................... 246,958
  Part-time men 139,710
  Part-time women................... 216,259

Minority enrollment in institutions of higher education, Fall 2003

Black, non-hispanic................... 103,764
Hispanic 89,283
Asian/Pacific Islander 44,424
American Indian/Alaska Native.......... 2,475

Earned degrees conferred, 2003

Bachelor's 59,569
Master's 30,240
First-professional...................... 4,359
Doctor's.............................. 2,582

State & local financial support for higher education, 2003-2004

Full-time equivalent enrollment (x 1,000) ..378.1
Appropriations per FTE................ $6,777
  as a percent of tax revenue.............. 8.1%

Social Insurance & Welfare Programs

Social Security benefits & beneficiaries, 2004

Beneficiaries
  Total........................... 1,884,000
  Retired & dependents............. 1,337,000
  Survivors......................... 276,000
  Disabled & dependents 271,000
Annual benefit payments ($ mil)
  Total........................... $20,456
  Retired & dependents............. $13,869
  Survivors......................... $3,826
  Disabled & dependents.............. $2,761
Average Monthly Benefit
  Retired & dependents................. $993
  Disabled & dependents................ $924
  Widowed............................. $984

Medicare

Enrollment, 2001 (x 1,000) 1,640
  Payments ($ mil, est.) $8,000
Enrollment, 2003 (x 1,000) 1,661

Medicaid, 2002

Beneficiaries (x 1,000).................. 1,731
Payments ($ mil) $9,122

State Children's Health Insurance, 2004

Enrollment (x 1,000)................... 234.0
Expenditures ($ mil).................. $309.8

Persons without health insurance, 2003

Number (x 1,000)...................... 1,818
  percent............................. 14.4%
Number of children (x 1,000) 320
  percent of children 10.0%

Federal public aid

Temporary Assistance for Needy Families, 2004
Recipients (x 1,000)...................... 89
Families (x 1,000) 36

Supplemental Security Income, 2003
Recipients (x 1,000)...................... 255
Payments ($ mil) $1,267

Food Stamp Program, 2004

Participants (x 1,000) 1,070
Benefits ($ mil)....................... $1,211

Housing & Construction

Housing units

Total 2003 (estimate)	5,040,347
Total 2004 (estimate)	5,094,186
Seasonal or recreational use, 2003	30,000
Owner-occupied single-family, 2003	2,563,000
Median value	$160,551
Renter-occupied, 2003	1,438,000
Median rent	$699
Homeownership rate, 2003	70.7%
Homeownership rate, 2004	72.7%

New privately owned housing units, 2004

Number authorized (x 1,000)	59.8
Value ($ mil)	$9,551
Started 2005 (x 1,000, estimate)	58.5
Started 2006 (x 1,000, estimate)	56.6

Existing home sales

2002 (x 1,000)	269.0
2003 (x 1,000)	275.1
2004 (x 1,000)	307.5

Government & Elections

State Officials 2006

Governor (name/party/term expires)
Rod Blagojevich
Democrat - 1/07

Lieutenant Governor	Patrick Quinn
Secretary of State	Jesse White
Attorney General	Lisa Madigan
Chief Justice	Robert R. Thomas

Governorship

Minimum age	25
Length of term	4 years
Consecutive terms permitted	not specified
Who succeeds	Lt. Governor

State Legislature

Name	General Assembly
Upper chamber	Senate
Number of members	59
Length of term	4 years
Party in majority, 2006	Democratic
Lower chamber	House of Representatives
Number of members	118
Length of term	2 years
Party in majority, 2006	Democratic

State Government Employees, 2004

Total	133,672
Payroll	$504,647,035

Local Government Employees, 2004

Total	502,088
Payroll	$1,811,287,821

Local Governments by Type, 2002

Total	6,903
County	102
Municipal	1,291
Township	1,431
School District	934
Special District	3,145

Voting age population, November 2004

Total	9,303,000
Male	4,469,000
Female	4,835,000
White	7,648,000
Black	1,277,000
Hispanic	1,031,000
Asian	277,000

Presidential Election, 2004

Total Popular Vote	5,274,322
Kerry	2,891,550
Bush	2,345,946
Total Electoral Votes	21

Federal representation, 2006 (109th Congress)

Senator	Richard Durbin
Party	Democrat
Year term expires	2009
Senator	Barack Obama
Party	Democrat
Year term expires	2011
Representatives, total	19
Democrats	10
Republicans	9
Other	0

Votes cast for US Senators

2002

Total vote (x 1,000)	3,487,000
Leading party	Democratic
Percent for leading party	60.3%

2004

Total vote (x 1,000)	5,142,000
Leading party	Democratic
Percent for leading party	70.0%

Votes cast for US Representatives

2002

Total vote (x 1,000)	3,429
Democratic	1,741
Republican	1,657
Leading party	Democratic
Percent for leading party	50.8%

2004

Total vote (x 1,000)	4,989
Democratic	2,675
Republican	2,272
Leading party	Democratic
Percent for leading party	53.6%

Women holding public office, 2006
US Congress 3
Statewide elected office...................... 2
State legislature 49

Black public officials, 2001
Total................................... 624
    US and state legislatures 28
    City/county/regional offices 318
    Judicial/law enforcement.................. 55
    Education/school boards................ 223

Hispanic public officials, 2004
Total................................... 70
    State executives & legislators 11
    City/county/regional offices 46
    Judicial/law enforcement................. 5
    Education/school boards................. 8

Governmental Finance

State government revenues, 2004
Total revenue ($1,000) $61,255,138
    Revenue per capita 4,818.69

General Revenue ($ per capita)....... $3,659.43
    Intergovernmental 1,114.90
    Taxes 2,005.24
        general sales 544.57
        individual income tax............. 640.31
        corporate income tax 162.73
    Current charges..................... 252.65
    Miscellaneous 286.65

State government expenditure, 2004
Total expenditure (x $1,000) $53,429,176
    Expenditure per capita............. 4,203.05
General Expenditure ($ per capita).... $3,603.59
    Education 1,201.45
    Public welfare....................... 998.59
    Health 212.15
    Hospitals.......................... 78.24
    Highways 243.62
    Police protection 31.39
    Correction 101.04
    Natural resources 31.08
    Parks & recreation....................29.35
    Governmental administration 109.81
    Interest on general debt 211.24

State debt & cash, 2004 ($ per capita)
Debt $3,833.08
Cash/security holdings............. $8,242.84

Federal government grants to state & local government, 2004 (x $1,000)
Total...........................$16,531,175
By Federal Agency
    Defense $106,418

By Federal Agency, continued
    Education 1,524,116
    Energy.......................... 61,430
    Environmental Protection Agency ... 157,069
    Health & Human Services. 9,318,522
    Homeland Security.................. 37,803
    Housing & Urban Development.... 1,778,448
    Justice 219,871
    Labor 420,744
    Transportation 1,674,450
    Veterans Affairs................... 25,100

Crime, Law Enforcement & Courts

Crime, 2004 (rates per 100,000 residents)
Property crimes 405,070
    Burglaries......................... 75,944
    Larcenies......................... 288,771
    Motor vehicle thefts 40,355
    Property crime rate................. 3,186.1
Violent crimes....................... 69,026
    Murders............................ 776
    Forcible rape........................ 4,216
    Robberies 22,532
    Aggravated assaults 41,502
    Violent crime rate 542.9

Police Agencies, 2004
Total agencies........................ 753
Total employees 50,174
    Male officers...................... 30,889
    Female officers...................... 5,543
    Male civilians....................... 6,235
    Female civilians..................... 7,507

Arrests, 2004
Total................................ 200,447
    Persons under 18 years of age 36,581

Prisoners under state & federal jurisdiction, 2004
Total prisoners....................... 44,054
    Percent change, 12/31/03 to 12/31/04 .... 1.5%
Sentenced to more than one year 44,054
    rate per 100,000....................... 346

Persons under sentence of death, 7/1/05
Total................................. 10
    White.............................. 5
    Black 3
    Hispanic 2

State's highest court
Name ....Supreme Court
Number of members....................... 7
Length of term .... 10 years
Intermediate appeals court? ....yes

Labor & Income

Civilian labor force, 2004

Total	6,386,000
Men	3,408,000
Women	2,979,000
Persons 16-19 years	316,000
White	5,282,000
Black	825,000
Hispanic	752,000
Asian	223,000

Civilian labor force as a percent of civilian non-institutional population, 2004

Total	66.2%
Men	73.3
Women	59.7
Persons 16-19 years	44.8
White	66.9
Black	62.0
Hispanic	69.3
Asian	67.1

Employment, 2004

Total	5,997,000
Men	3,203,000
Women	2,794,000
Persons 16-19 years	259,000
White	5,011,000
Black	718,000
Hispanic	704,000
Asian	214,000

Full-time/part-time labor force, 2002

Full-time labor force, employed	4,987,000
Part-time labor force, employed	976,000
Unemployed, looking for	
Full-time work	363,000
Part-time work	52,000

Unemployment rate, 2004

Total	6.1%
Men	6.0
Women	6.2
Persons 16-19 years	18.0
White	5.1
Black	12.9
Hispanic	6.4
Asian	3.9

Unemployed by reason for unemployment (as a percent of total unemployment), 2002

Job losers or completed temp jobs	59.0%
Job leavers	NA
Reentrants	26.5
New entrants	NA

Labor unions, 2004

Membership	908,000
percent of employed	16.8%

Experienced civilian labor force by private industry, first quarter 2004

Total	4,796,827
Natural Resources & Mining	22,428
Construction	245,151
Manufacturing	694,126
Trade, transportation & utilities	1,142,385
Information	121,810
Finance	391,984
Professional & business	772,030
Education & Health	717,319
Leisure & hospitality	483,653
Other	196,587

Experienced civilian labor force by occupation, 2004

Management	303,110
Business & Financial	279,370
Legal	43,600
Sales	605,970
Office & Admin. Support	986,650
Computers & Math	132,710
Architecture & Engineering	85,600
Arts & Entertainment	63,290
Education	375,960
Social Services	65,280
Healthcare Practitioner & Technical	284,420
Healthcare support	125,850
Maintenance & Repair	204,810
Construction	239,450
Transportation & moving	492,450
Production	508,030
Farming, fishing & forestry	4,950

Hours and earnings of production workers on manufacturing payrolls, 2004

Average weekly hours	41.0
Average hourly earnings	$15.61
Average weekly earnings	$640.01

Average annual pay

2004	$42,277
change from 2003	4.2%

Household income

Median household income, three-year average, 2002-2004	$45,787

Personal income, 2004 ($ per capita)

In current dollars	$34,351
In constant (2000) dollars	$31,858

Poverty

Persons below poverty level, three-year average, 2002-2004	12.5%

Federal individual income tax returns, 2003

Returns filed	5,722,755
Adjusted gross income ($1,000)	$290,425,049
Total income tax paid ($1,000)	$39,138,546

Economy, Business, Industry & Agriculture

Fortune 500 companies, 2005 33

Patents issued, 2004 3,754

Bankruptcy cases filed, 2004 81,300

Business firm ownership, 2002
Women-owned....................... 284,950
   Sales ($ mil) $46,860
Black-owned.......................... 68,708
   Sales ($ mil) $5,244
Hispanic-owned....................... 39,553
   Sales ($ mil) $7,516
Asian-owned 44,501
   Sales ($ mil) $14,888
Amer. Indian/Alaska Native-owned 3,393
   Sales ($ mil) $452
Hawaiian/Pacific Isl.-owned.............. 693
   Sales ($ mil) $30

Gross State Product, 2004 ($ mil)
Total Gross State Product $521,900
   Agriculture, forestry, fishing and
     hunting 3,802
   Mining............................. 1,113
   Utilities.......................... 12,139
   Construction 24,587
   Manufacturing, durable goods........ 39,042
   Manufacturing, non-durable goods ... 31,986
   Wholesale trade.................... 36,794
   Retail trade....................... 31,515
   Transportation & warehousing 18,638
   Information 21,802
   Finance & insurance................ 52,311
   Real estate, rental, leasing....... 64,434
   Professional and technical services.... 42,671
   Educational services................ 5,122
   Health care and social assistance..... 34,115
   Accommodation/food services........ 11,825
   Other services, except government 12,988
   Government 44,812

Establishments, by major industry group, 2003
Total............................... 311,714
   Forestry, fishing & agriculture 395
   Mining............................... 587
   Construction 30,931
   Manufacturing..................... 16,363
   Wholesale trade.................... 20,228
   Retail trade....................... 43,303
   Transportation & warehousing 10,266
   Information 5,837
   Finance & insurance................ 23,258
   Professional/scientific/technical 36,890
   Health care/social assistance 28,401
   Accommodation/food services........ 24,629

Annual payroll by major industry group, 2003
Total ($1,000) $201,040,291
   Forestry, fishing & agriculture 101,842
   Mining............................ 501,403
   Utilities...................... 2,664,549
   Construction 12,824,517
   Manufacturing................. 29,092,534
   Wholesale trade................ 16,446,506
   Retail trade................... 13,821,148
   Transportation & warehousing 8,212,055
   Information 7,800,490
   Finance & insurance............ 22,622,582
   Professional/scientific/technical .. 20,640,929
   Health care/social assistance 23,015,222
   Accommodation/food services..... 5,663,291

Agriculture
Number of farms, 2004 73,000
Farm acreage, 2004
   Total........................ 28,000,000
   Acres per farm, 2004 377
Farm income, 2003 ($mil)
   Net farm income $1,657
   Debt/asset ratio 12
Farm marketings, 2003 ($mil)
Total................................. $8,290
   Crops............................. 6,490
   Livestock........................... 1,800

Principal commodities, in order by marketing receipts, 2003
Corn, soybeans, hogs, cattle

Federal economic activity in state
Expenditures, 2003
   Total ($ mil) $73,020
   Per capita $5,771
   Defense ($ mil)..................... 4,938
   Non-defense ($ mil) 68,082
Defense department, 2003
   Payroll ($ mil) $2,497
   Contract awards ($ mil) $2,565
   Grants ($ mil)........................ $86
   Homeland security grants ($1,000)
     2004 .... $114,925
     2005 .... $102,593

FDIC insured financial institutions, 2004
Number............................... 746
   Assets ($bil) $340.6
   Deposits ($bil) 281.9

Fishing, 2004
Catch (x 1,000 lbs) .... NA
Value ($1,000)......................... NA

Mining, 2004 ($ mil)

Total non-fuel mineral production $1,030
Percent of U.S. 2.4%

Construction, 2003 ($ mil)

Total contracts (including non-building) $19,034
   residential 9,921
   non-residential 5,916

Establishments, receipts, payroll & employees, by major industry group, 2002

Mining 345
   Receipts ($1,000) $1,359,560
   Annual payroll ($1,000) $274,443
   Paid employees 5,794

Utilities 466
   Receipts ($1,000) . . . . NA
   Annual payroll ($1,000) $2,576,932
   Paid employees 34,964

Construction 30,555
   Receipts ($1,000) $55,308,836
   Annual payroll ($1,000) $12,878,044
   Paid employees 309,386

Manufacturing 16,860
   Receipts ($1,000) $188,365,216
   Annual payroll ($1,000) $29,841,718
   Paid employees 741,908

Wholesale trade 20,520
   Receipts ($1,000) $317,467,059
   Annual payroll ($1,000) $15,493,128
   Paid employees 331,527

Retail trade 43,022
   Receipts ($1,000) $131,469,518
   Annual payroll ($1,000) $12,514,264
   Paid employees 601,465

Transportation 9,923
   Receipts ($1,000) $19,329,778
   Annual payroll ($1,000) $5,936,581
   Paid employees 181,908

Information 5,716
   Receipts ($1,000) . . . . NA
   Annual payroll ($1,000) $7,669,139
   Paid employees 150,002

Finance & insurance 21,802
   Receipts ($1,000) . . . . NA
   Annual payroll ($1,000) $20,602,525
   Paid employees 348,764

Professional, scientific & technical 36,633
   Receipts ($1,000) $45,533,746
   Annual payroll ($1,000) $19,945,923
   Paid employees 349,039

Health care & social assistance 28,084
   Receipts ($1,000) $52,394,634
   Annual payroll ($1,000) $22,300,109
   Paid employees 661,268

Accommodation & food service 24,245
   Receipts ($1,000) $19,072,168
   Annual payroll ($1,000) $5,227,014
   Paid employees 420,801

Communication, Energy & Transportation

Communication

Daily newspapers, 2004 67
Households with computers, 2003 . . . . .60%
Households with internet access, 2003 . . . . . .51%

Energy

Electricity Consumption, 2001
   Total (trillion Btu) 3,870
   Per capita (million Btu) 309
By source of production (trillion Btu)
   Coal 994
   Natural gas 971
   Petroleum 1,304
   Nuclear electric power 965
   Hydroelectric power 2
By end-use sector (trillion Btu)
   Residential 928
   Commercial 829
   Industrial 1,173
   Transportation 939
Electric energy, 2003
   Production (billion kWh) 189.1
   Net summer capability (million kW) 45.5
Gas utilities, 2003
   Customers (x1,000) 3,787
   Sales (trillion Btu) 555
   Revenues ($mil) $4,627
Nuclear plants, 2003 11

Transportation, 2004

Public Road & Street Mileage 138,624
   Urban 37,550
   Rural 101,074
   Interstate 2,169
Vehicle miles of travel per capita 8,584.5
Total motor vehicle registrations 9,231,541
   Automobiles 5,652,494
   Buses 17,944
   Trucks 3,561,103
   Motorcycles 276,122
Licensed drivers 8,057,683
   19 years & under 455,443
Deaths from motor vehicle accidents 1,356

State Summary

Capital City . . . . Indianapolis
Governor . . . . Mitch Daniels
State House
Room 206
Indianapolis, IN 46204
317-232-4567
Admitted as a state 1816
Area (square miles) 36,418
Population, 2004 (est.) 6,237,569
Largest City . . . . Indianapolis
Population, 2004 784,000
Personal income per capita, 2004
(in current dollars) $30,094
Gross state product ($ mil), 2004 . . . . . . $227,569

Leading industries by payroll, 2003

Manufacturing, Health care/Social assistance,
Retail trade

Leading agricultural commodities by receipts, 2003

Corn, soybeans, hogs, dairy products

Geography & Environment

Total area (sq. mi.) 36,418
land 35,867
water 551

Federally-owned land, 2004 (acres) 463,245
percent 2.0%

Highest point . . . . . Franklin Twp., Wayne County
elevation (feet) 1,257

Lowest point . . . . Ohio River
elevation (feet) 320

General coastline (miles) 0

Tidal shoreline (miles) 0

Capital City . . . . Indianapolis
Population 2000 782,000
Population 2004 784,000

Largest City . . . . Indianapolis
Population 2000 782,000
Population 2004 784,000

Number of cities with over 100,000 population

1990 5
2000 5
2004 4

State park and recreation areas, 2003

Area (acres x 1,000) 179
Number of visitors (x 1,000) 14,798
Revenues (x 1,000) $35,683
percent of operating expenditures 81.6%

National forest system land, 2004

Acres 201,000

Demographics and Characteristics of the Population

Population

1980 5,490,224
1990 5,544,159
2000 6,080,485
2004 (estimate) 6,237,569
persons per sq. mile of land 173.9
2005 (projection) 6,249,617
Male 3,073,597
Female 3,176,020
2010 (projection) 6,392,139
2020 (projection) 6,627,008
2030 (projection) 6,810,108
Male 3,360,646
Female 3,449,462

Metropolitan and Non-Metro. area population

	Metro	Non-Metro
1980	3,719,000	1,771,000
1990	3,796,000	1,748,000
2000	4,390,000	1,691,000

Change in population, 2000-2004

Number 157,052
percent 2.6%
Natural increase (births minus deaths) . . 128,284
Net internal migration . . . . -18,818
Net international migration 47,067

Persons by age, 2004

Under 5 years 430,557
18 years and over 4,637,274
65 years and over 772,010
85 years and over 104,873

Persons by age, 2010 (projected)

Total 6,392,139
Under 5 years 436,614
5 to 17 years 1,159,571
18 and over 4,795,954
21 and over 4,516,063
65 and over 811,290
85 and over 124,184
Median age 36.5

Race, 2004 (estimate)

One Race
White 5,529,707
Black or African American 548,269
American Indian/Alaska Native 17,532
Pacific Islander 2,833
Asian Indian 17,602
Chinese 16,025
Filipino 7,835
Japanese 4,771
Korean 9,388
Vietnamese 6,503
Two or more races 66,215

Persons of Hispanic origin, 2004

Total Hispanic or Latino 264,936
   Mexican. 214,553
   Puerto Rican 16,864
   Cuban 2,431
   Other Hispanic or Latino 21,282

Marital status, 2000

Population 15 years & over 4,771,040
   Never married 1,183,218
   Married. 2,690,867
   Separated 62,024
   Widowed. 314,889
   Divorced 520,043

Language spoken at home, 2000

Population 5 years & over 5,657,818
   English only 5,295,736
   Spanish 185,576
   Other Indo-European languages 126,530
   Asian/Pacific Island languages. 36,707

Households & families, 2000

Households. 2,336,306
   with persons under 18 years 834,826
   with persons over 65 years. 524,632
   persons per household 2.53
Families. 1,602,501
   persons per family. 3.05
Married couples. 1,251,458
Female householder,
   no husband present. 259,372
One-person households 605,428

Nativity, 2000

Number of persons born in state 4,215,694
   percent of population 69.3%

Immigration & Naturalization, 2004

Immigrants admitted. 5,929
Persons naturalized 2,455
Asylums granted 88
Asylums denied 25

Vital Statistics and Health

Marriages

2002 48,342
2003 43,974
2004 48,354

Divorces

2002 . . . . NA
2003 . . . . NA
2004 . . . . NA

Births

2003 86,434
   Birthrate (per 1,000). 14.0
   Low birth weight (2,500g or less). 7.9%
   To unmarried mothers. 37.1%

2003, continued
   White. 75,688
   Black 9,387
   Hispanic 6,764
   Asian/Pacific Islander 1,389
   Amer. Indian/Alaska Native 136

2004 (preliminary). 86,733
   Birthrate (per 1,000). 13.9
   White. 75,418
   Black 9,655
   Hispanic 7,257
   Asian/Pacific Islander 1,543

Deaths

2002
All causes 55,396
   rate per 100,000. . . . . .899.4
Heart disease 15,321
   rate per 100,000. . . . . 248.8
Malignant neoplasms 12,865
   rate per 100,000. . . . . 208.9
Cerebrovascular disease. 3,717
   rate per 100,000. .60.4
Chronic lower respiratory disease 3,138
   rate per 100,000. .50.9
2003 56,193
   rate per 100,000. . . . . .907.0
2004 (provisional) 54,288

Infant deaths

2003 (provisional) 672
   rate per 1,000 . . . . .7.7
2004 (provisional) 726
   rate per 1,000 . . . . .8.3

Abortions, 2000

Total. 12,000
   rate per 1,000 women age 15-44. . . . . 9.4

Physicians, 2003

Total. 13,346
   rate per 1,000 persons. 215

Nurses, 2001

Total. 49,590
   rate per 1,000 persons. 809

Community Hospitals, 2003

Number 112
Beds (x 1,000). 18.9
Patients admitted (x 1,000) 712
Average daily census (x 1,000) 11.0
Average cost per day $1,352
Outpatient visits (x mil). 15.0

Disability status of population, 2004

5 to 20 years 7.2%
21 to 64 years 12.5%
65 years and over 40.8%

Education

Educational attainment, 2004

Population over 25 years 3,899,357
   Less than 9th grade 198,283
   High school graduates only........ 1,433,721
   Bachelor's degree only 529,925
   Graduate or professional degree...... 308,510
   Less than 9th grade percent 5.1%
   High school graduate or more 87.2%
   College graduate or more............. 21.1%
   Graduate or professional degree........ 7.9%

Public school enrollment, Fall 2002

Total........................... 1,003,875
   Kindergarten through grade 8 714,013
   Grades 9 through 12 289,862
Enrollment, 2005 (projected) 1,015,900

Graduating public high school seniors

2004 (estimate)....................... 57,610

SAT scores, 2005

Average verbal score 504
Average math score 508
Percent of graduates taking test 66%

Public school teachers, 2004

Total (x 1,000) 59.8
   Elementary (x 1,000)....................32.1
   Secondary (x 1,000) 27.7
Average salary $45,800
   Elementary......................... $45,800
   Secondary.......................... $45,800

State receipts & expenditures for public schools, 2004

Revenue receipts ($mil)................. $9,763
Expenditures
Total ($mil)......................... $10,191
   Per capita $1,644
   Per pupil $9,138

Institutions of higher education, 2004

Total................................... 101
   Public................................. 29
   Private................................ 72

Enrollment in institutions of higher education, Fall, 2003

Total............................... 353,158
   Full-time men 112,667
   Full-time women.................... 131,371
   Part-time men 44,236
   Part-time women.................... 64,884

Minority enrollment in institutions of higher education, Fall, 2003

Black, non-hispanic.................... 26,925
Hispanic 9,091
Asian/Pacific Islander 6,605
American Indian/Alaska Native.......... 1,282

Earned degrees conferred, 2003

Bachelor's 35,284
Master's 9,503
First-professional...................... 1,638
Doctor's............................... 1,147

State & local financial support for higher education, 2003-2004

Full-time equivalent enrollment (x 1,000) ..218.4
Appropriations per FTE................ $5,103
   as a percent of tax revenue.............. 7.8%

Social Insurance & Welfare Programs

Social Security benefits & beneficiaries, 2004

Beneficiaries
   Total........................... 1,038,000
   Retired & dependents............... 719,000
   Survivors.......................... 147,000
   Disabled & dependents............. 173,000
Annual benefit payments ($ mil)
   Total............................. $11,259
   Retired & dependents............... $7,520
   Survivors........................... $2,037
   Disabled & dependents.............. $1,702
Average Monthly Benefit
   Retired & dependents............... $1,003
   Disabled & dependents............. $899
   Widowed............................ $981

Medicare

Enrollment, 2001 (x 1,000) 858
   Payments ($ mil, est.) $5,000
Enrollment, 2003 (x 1,000) 878

Medicaid, 2002

Beneficiaries (x 1,000).................... 849
Payments ($ mil) $3,725

State Children's Health Insurance, 2004

Enrollment (x 1,000)....................80.7
Expenditures ($ mil)....................$65.4

Persons without health insurance, 2003

Number (x 1,000)........................ 853
   percent............................. 13.9%
Number of children (x 1,000) 143
   percent of children 9.0%

Federal public aid

Temporary Assistance for Needy Families, 2004
Recipients (x 1,000)...................... 131
Families (x 1,000) 51

Supplemental Security Income, 2003
Recipients (x 1,000)....................... 94
Payments ($ mil) $441

Food Stamp Program, 2004

Participants (x 1,000) 526
Benefits ($ mil)..........................$550

Housing & Construction

Housing units

Total 2003 (estimate)	2,655,036
Total 2004 (estimate)	2,690,619
Seasonal or recreational use, 2003	69,000
Owner-occupied single-family, 2003	1,419,000
Median value	$106,840
Renter-occupied, 2003	646,000
Median rent	$581
Homeownership rate, 2003	74.4%
Homeownership rate, 2004	75.8%

New privately owned housing units, 2004

Number authorized (x 1,000)	39.2
Value ($ mil)	$5,610
Started 2005 (x 1,000, estimate)	39.4
Started 2006 (x 1,000, estimate)	38.8

Existing home sales

2002 (x 1,000)	125.2
2003 (x 1,000)	120.4
2004 (x 1,000)	130.5

Government & Elections

State Officials 2006

Governor (name/party/term expires)
Mitch Daniels
Republican - 1/09

Lieutenant Governor	Becky Skillman
Secretary of State	Todd Rokita
Attorney General	Steve Carter
Chief Justice	Randall T. Shepard

Governorship

Minimum age	30
Length of term	4 years
Consecutive terms permitted	8 out of any 12 yrs
Who succeeds	Lt. Governor

State Legislature

Name	General Assembly
Upper chamber	Senate
Number of members	50
Length of term	4 years
Party in majority, 2006	Republican
Lower chamber	House of Representatives
Number of members	100
Length of term	2 years
Party in majority, 2006	Republican

State Government Employees, 2004

Total	90,404
Payroll	$286,110,796

Local Government Employees, 2004

Total	239,177
Payroll	$719,626,784

Local Governments by Type, 2002

Total	3,085
County	91
Municipal	567
Township	1,008
School District	294
Special District	1,125

Voting age population, November 2004

Total	4,536,000
Male	2,182,000
Female	2,354,000
White	4,088,000
Black	368,000
Hispanic	182,000
Asian	22,000

Presidential Election, 2004

Total Popular Vote	2,468,002
Kerry	969,011
Bush	1,479,438
Total Electoral Votes	11

Federal representation, 2006 (109th Congress)

Senator	Richard G. Lugar
Party	Republican
Year term expires	2007
Senator	Evan Bayh
Party	Democrat
Year term expires	2011
Representatives, total	9
Democrats	2
Republicans	7
Other	0

Votes cast for US Senators

2002

Total vote (x 1,000)	NA
Leading party	NA
Percent for leading party	NA

2004

Total vote (x 1,000)	2,428,000
Leading party	Democratic
Percent for leading party	61.6%

Votes cast for US Representatives

2002

Total vote (x 1,000)	1,521
Democratic	641
Republican	841
Leading party	Republican
Percent for leading party	55.3%

2004

Total vote (x 1,000)	2,416
Democratic	999
Republican	1,382
Leading party	Republican
Percent for leading party	57.2%

Women holding public office, 2006

US Congress 1
Statewide elected office 3
State legislature 25

Black public officials, 2001

Total 86
　US and state legislatures 13
　City/county/regional offices 52
　Judicial/law enforcement 13
　Education/school boards 8

Hispanic public officials, 2004

Total 12
　State executives & legislators 1
　City/county/regional offices 7
　Judicial/law enforcement 3
　Education/school boards 1

Governmental Finance

State government revenues, 2004

Total revenue ($1,000) $26,917,365
　Revenue per capita 4,322.69

General Revenue ($ per capita) $3,768.25
　Intergovernmental 1,133.36
　Taxes 1,920.26
　　general sales 764.32
　　individual income tax 611.51
　　corporate income tax 103.55
　Current charges 429.29
　Miscellaneous 285.33

State government expenditure, 2004

Total expenditure (x $1,000) $25,373,330
　Expenditure per capita 4,074.73
General Expenditure ($ per capita) $3,780.79
　Education 1,451.92
　Public welfare 911.48
　Health 94.83
　Hospitals 45.66
　Highways 308.48
　Police protection 36.30
　Correction 108.43
　Natural resources 43.23
　Parks & recreation 10.16
　Governmental administration 96.47
　Interest on general debt 71.85

State debt & cash, 2004 ($ per capita)

Debt $2,100.50
Cash/security holdings $5,933.52

Federal government grants to state & local government, 2004 (x $1,000)

Total $7,436,310
By Federal Agency
　Defense $92,038

By Federal Agency, continued
　Education 642,599
　Energy 37,327
　Environmental Protection Agency 71,274
　Health & Human Services 4,321,705
　Homeland Security 45,671
　Housing & Urban Development 527,817
　Justice 100,256
　Labor 139,572
　Transportation 863,239
　Veterans Affairs 6,600

Crime, Law Enforcement & Courts

Crime, 2004 (rates per 100,000 residents)

Property crimes 211,929
　Burglaries 42,168
　Larcenies 148,670
　Motor vehicle thefts 21,091
　Property crime rate 3,397.6
Violent crimes 20,294
　Murders 316
　Forcible rape 1,803
　Robberies 6,373
　Aggravated assaults 11,802
　Violent crime rate 325.4

Police Agencies, 2004

Total agencies 249
Total employees 17,109
　Male officers 9,963
　Female officers 806
　Male civilians 2,915
　Female civilians 3,425

Arrests, 2004

Total 215,441
　Persons under 18 years of age 34,024

Prisoners under state & federal jurisdiction, 2004

Total prisoners 24,008
　Percent change, 12/31/03 to 12/31/04 .... 4.1%
Sentenced to more than one year 23,939
　rate per 100,000 383

Persons under sentence of death, 7/1/05

Total 30
　White 22
　Black 8
　Hispanic 0

State's highest court

Name .... Supreme Court
Number of members 5
Length of term .... 10 years
Intermediate appeals court? .... yes

Labor & Income

Civilian labor force, 2004

Total	3,160,000
Men	1,674,000
Women	1,486,000
Persons 16-19 years	162,000
White	2,855,000
Black	233,000
Hispanic	126,000
Asian	0

Civilian labor force as a percent of civilian non-institutional population, 2004

Total	66.9%
Men	73.1
Women	61.0
Persons 16-19 years	46.8
White	67.2
Black	64.4
Hispanic	75.6
Asian	0.0

Employment, 2004

Total	2,993,000
Men	1,588,000
Women	1,406,000
Persons 16-19 years	138,000
White	2,717,000
Black	209,000
Hispanic	114,000
Asian	0

Full-time/part-time labor force, 2002

Full-time labor force, employed	2,494,000
Part-time labor force, employed	517,000
Unemployed, looking for	
Full-time work	135,000
Part-time work	NA

Unemployment rate, 2004

Total	5.3%
Men	5.2
Women	5.4
Persons 16-19 years	14.4
White	4.8
Black	10.0
Hispanic	9.2
Asian	NA

Unemployed by reason for unemployment (as a percent of total unemployment), 2002

Job losers or completed temp jobs	54.6%
Job leavers	NA
Reentrants	28.8
New entrants	NA

Labor unions, 2004

Membership	311,000
percent of employed	11.4%

Experienced civilian labor force by private industry, first quarter 2004

Total	2,397,703
Natural Resources & Mining	17,143
Construction	136,544
Manufacturing	567,009
Trade, transportation & utilities	557,079
Information	40,941
Finance	136,610
Professional & business	256,760
Education & Health	340,012
Leisure & hospitality	262,512
Other	82,608

Experienced civilian labor force by occupation, 2004

Management	117,200
Business & Financial	89,350
Legal	11,980
Sales	282,830
Office & Admin. Support	446,940
Computers & Math	38,030
Architecture & Engineering	49,310
Arts & Entertainment	28,400
Education	NA
Social Services	29,500
Healthcare Practitioner & Technical	150,990
Healthcare support	64,510
Maintenance & Repair	132,000
Construction	141,440
Transportation & moving	261,050
Production	396,040
Farming, fishing & forestry	2,780

Hours and earnings of production workers on manufacturing payrolls, 2004

Average weekly hours	42.1
Average hourly earnings	$17.92
Average weekly earnings	$754.43

Average annual pay

2004	$34,694
change from 2003	3.9%

Household income

Median household income, three-year average, 2002-2004	$43,003

Personal income, 2004 ($ per capita)

In current dollars	$30,094
In constant (2000) dollars	$27,910

Poverty

Persons below poverty level, three-year average, 2002-2004	10.2%

Federal individual income tax returns, 2003

Returns filed	2,816,535
Adjusted gross income ($1,000)	$119,764,629
Total income tax paid ($1,000)	$13,703,703

Economy, Business, Industry & Agriculture

Fortune 500 companies, 2005 6

Patents issued, 2004 1,485

Bankruptcy cases filed, 2004 55,700

Business firm ownership, 2002

Women-owned....................... 118,857
  Sales ($ mil) $16,481
Black-owned.......................... 14,062
  Sales ($ mil) $1,689
Hispanic-owned........................ 5,487
  Sales ($ mil) $797
Asian-owned 6,088
  Sales ($ mil) $2,629
Amer. Indian/Alaska Native-owned 1,974
  Sales ($ mil) $288
Hawaiian/Pacific Isl.-owned............... 127
  Sales ($ mil) $86

Gross State Product, 2004 ($ mil)

Total Gross State Product $227,569
  Agriculture, forestry, fishing and
    hunting 2,192
  Mining............................. 821
  Utilities........................... 5,362
  Construction 10,618
  Manufacturing, durable goods........ 42,517
  Manufacturing, non-durable goods ... 20,960
  Wholesale trade.................... 11,937
  Retail trade....................... 14,886
  Transportation & warehousing 7,615
  Information 5,497
  Finance & insurance................ 13,791
  Real estate, rental, leasing........... 22,197
  Professional and technical services..... 8,319
  Educational services................. 1,545
  Health care and social assistance...... 16,035
  Accommodation/food services........ 4,869
  Other services, except government 5,247
  Government 21,982

Establishments, by major industry group, 2003

Total................................ 147,547
  Forestry, fishing & agriculture 258
  Mining............................. 328
  Construction 16,109
  Manufacturing...................... 9,045
  Wholesale trade.................... 8,122
  Retail trade....................... 23,994
  Transportation & warehousing 4,933
  Information 2,304
  Finance & insurance................ 9,857
  Professional/scientific/technical 12,321
  Health care/social assistance 13,789
  Accommodation/food services........ 11,898

Annual payroll by major industry group, 2003

Total ($1,000) $81,408,367
  Forestry, fishing & agriculture .... NA
  Mining............................ 277,624
  Utilities........................... 855,207
  Construction 5,404,236
  Manufacturing.................. 22,906,270
  Wholesale trade.................. 4,504,884
  Retail trade..................... 6,559,305
  Transportation & warehousing 3,249,673
  Information 2,063,374
  Finance & insurance............. 5,139,889
  Professional/scientific/technical ... 4,377,358
  Health care/social assistance 11,015,791
  Accommodation/food services..... 2,778,852

Agriculture

Number of farms, 2004 59,000
Farm acreage, 2004
  Total......................... 15,000,000
  Acres per farm, 2004 253
Farm income, 2003 ($mil)
  Net farm income $1,328
  Debt/asset ratio 13.9
Farm marketings, 2003 ($mil)
Total............................... $5,162
  Crops 3,363
  Livestock.......................... 1,799

Principal commodities, in order by marketing receipts, 2003

Corn, soybeans, hogs, dairy products

Federal economic activity in state

Expenditures, 2003
  Total ($ mil) $35,525
  Per capita $5,734
  Defense ($ mil)..................... 3,650
  Non-defense ($ mil) 31,874
Defense department, 2003
  Payroll ($ mil) $1,106
  Contract awards ($ mil)............. $2,607
  Grants ($ mil)........................ $40
  Homeland security grants ($1,000)
    2004 .... $55,534
    2005 .... $38,996

FDIC insured financial institutions, 2004

Number............................... 197
  Assets ($bil) $102.8
  Deposits ($bil) 81.1

Fishing, 2004

Catch (x 1,000 lbs)..................... 0
Value ($1,000)......................... 0

Mining, 2004 ($ mil)
Total non-fuel mineral production $774
Percent of U.S. 1.8%

Construction, 2003 ($ mil)
Total contracts (including non-building) $12,673
  residential......................... 6,472
  non-residential 4,307

**Establishments, receipts, payroll & employees,
by major industry group, 2002**

Mining 208
  Receipts ($1,000) $333,227
  Annual payroll ($1,000)............. $73,139
  Paid employees 2,005
Utilities 508
  Receipts ($1,000) .... NA
  Annual payroll ($1,000)............ $860,761
  Paid employees 15,324
Construction......................... 15,512
  Receipts ($1,000) $23,435,911
  Annual payroll ($1,000)......... $5,284,119
  Paid employees 148,230
Manufacturing 9,223
  Receipts ($1,000) $160,924,188
  Annual payroll ($1,000)......... $22,852,682
  Paid employees 565,559
Wholesale trade 8,213
  Receipts ($1,000) $79,806,006
  Annual payroll ($1,000).......... $4,202,096
  Paid employees 109,600
Retail trade 24,322
  Receipts ($1,000) $67,261,298
  Annual payroll ($1,000).......... $6,403,730
  Paid employees 343,551
Transportation....................... 4,842
  Receipts ($1,000) $10,601,332
  Annual payroll ($1,000).......... $2,939,057
  Paid employees 97,095
Information.......................... 2,267
  Receipts ($1,000) .... NA
  Annual payroll ($1,000).......... $1,983,316
  Paid employees 49,621
Finance & insurance 9,509
  Receipts ($1,000) .... NA
  Annual payroll ($1,000).......... $4,888,992
  Paid employees 108,401
Professional, scientific & technical 12,090
  Receipts ($1,000) $9,154,500
  Annual payroll ($1,000).......... $3,981,215
  Paid employees 97,860

Health care & social assistance 13,638
  Receipts ($1,000) $25,539,903
  Annual payroll ($1,000)......... $10,441,904
  Paid employees 335,043
Accommodation & food service......... 11,788
  Receipts ($1,000) $9,409,270
  Annual payroll ($1,000).......... $2,547,617
  Paid employees 231,071

Communication, Energy & Transportation

Communication
Daily newspapers, 2004 68
Households with computers, 2003 .... 60%
Households with internet access, 2003 ..... 51%

Energy
Electricity Consumption, 2001
Total (trillion Btu) 2,802
Per capita (million Btu) 457
By source of production (trillion Btu)
  Coal 1,567
  Natural gas 514
  Petroleum 837
  Nuclear electric power 0
  Hydroelectric power 6
By end-use sector (trillion Btu)
  Residential 504
  Commercial 397
  Industrial 1,296
  Transportation 604
Electric energy, 2003
  Production (billion kWh) 124.9
  Net summer capability (million kW) 25.6
Gas utilities, 2003
  Customers (x1,000).................. 1,737
  Sales (trillion Btu)................. 264
  Revenues ($mil).................... $2,209
Nuclear plants, 2003 0

Transportation, 2004
Public Road & Street Mileage 94,597
  Urban............................. 20,600
  Rural 73,997
  Interstate 1,169
Vehicle miles of travel per capita 13,113.3
Total motor vehicle registrations...... 5,524,752
  Automobiles....................... 3,067,260
  Buses 31,344
  Trucks 2,426,148
  Motorcycles 153,566
Licensed drivers 4,521,329
  19 years & under 227,897
Deaths from motor vehicle accidents 947

State Summary

Capital City...................... Des Moines
Governor....................... Tom Vilsack
State Capitol
Des Moines, IA 50319
515-281-5211
Admitted as a state 1846
Area (square miles).................... 56,272
Population, 2004 (est.) 2,954,451
Largest City...................... Des Moines
Population, 2004.................. 194,000
Personal income per capita, 2004
(in current dollars)................ $30,560
Gross state product ($ mil), 2004...... $111,114

Leading industries by payroll, 2003

Manufacturing, Health care/Social assistance,
Finance & Insurance

Leading agricultural commodities by receipts, 2003

Corn, hogs, soybeans, cattle

Geography & Environment

Total area (sq. mi.).................... 56,272
land 55,869
water 402

Federally-owned land, 2004 (acres) 273,954
percent............................ 0.8%

*Highest point*Sec. 29 T 100N R 41W (Oscealo Co.)
elevation (feet) 1,670

Lowest point .... Mississippi River
elevation (feet) 480

General coastline (miles)..................... 0

Tidal shoreline (miles)....................... 0

Capital City...................... Des Moines
Population 2000 199,000
Population 2004 194,000

Largest City...................... Des Moines
Population 2000 199,000
Population 2004 194,000

Number of cities with over 100,000 population

1990 2
2000 2
2004 2

State park and recreation areas, 2003

Area (acres x 1,000)....................... 63
Number of visitors (x 1,000) 14,534
Revenues (x 1,000)..................... $3,431
percent of operating expenditures...... 29.4%

National forest system land, 2004

Acres .... NA

Demographics and Characteristics of the Population

Population

1980 2,913,808
1990 2,776,755
2000 2,926,324
2004 (estimate)................. 2,954,451
persons per sq. mile of land............ 52.9
2005 (projection)................. 2,973,700
Male........................... 1,462,832
Female......................... 1,510,868
2010 (projection) 3,009,907
2020 (projection) 3,020,496
2030 (projection) 2,955,172
Male........................... 1,453,789
Female......................... 1,501,383

Metropolitan and Non-Metro. area population

	Metro	Non-Metro
1980	1,223,000	1,691,000
1990	1,223,000	1,554,000
2000	1,326,000	1,600,000

Change in population, 2000-2004

Number............................. 28,069
percent............................. 1.0%
Natural increase (births minus deaths)... 41,208
Net internal migration .... -37,315
Net international migration 24,975

Persons by age, 2004

Under 5 years 180,839
18 years and over 2,274,014
65 years and over 433,139
85 years and over 72,373

Persons by age, 2010 (projected)

Total............................. 3,009,907
Under 5 years 193,313
5 to 17 years 517,743
18 and over 2,298,851
21 and over 2,174,268
65 and over 449,887
85 and over 85,204
Median age 38.3

Race, 2004 (estimate)

One Race
White........................... 2,806,633
Black or African American 67,596
American Indian/Alaska Native....... 10,338
Pacific Islander 1,275
Asian Indian....................... 3,939
Chinese 9,308
Filipino 3,228
Japanese 323
Korean........................... 2,423
Vietnamese....................... 4,007
Two or more races..................... 26,231

Persons of Hispanic origin, 2004

Total Hispanic or Latino 104,688
   Mexican.......................... 84,044
   Puerto Rican 1,951
   Cuban 981
   Other Hispanic or Latino 10,989

Marital status, 2000

Population 15 years & over 2,324,863
   Never married 578,891
   Married....................... 1,343,771
   Separated 23,249
   Widowed.......................... 167,390
   Divorced 211,563

Language spoken at home, 2000

Population 5 years & over 2,738,499
   English only 2,578,477
   Spanish 79,491
   Other Indo-European languages 49,032
   Asian/Pacific Island languages........ 25,335

Households & families, 2000

Households......................... 1,149,276
   with persons under 18 years 382,455
   with persons over 65 years........... 291,420
   persons per household 2.46
Families............................. 769,684
   persons per family........................ 3
Married couples..................... 633,254
Female householder,
   no husband present.................. 98,270
One-person households 313,083

Nativity, 2000

Number of persons born in state 2,188,424
   percent of population................. 74.8%

Immigration & Naturalization, 2004

Immigrants admitted................... 3,984
Persons naturalized 1,314
Asylums granted 30
Asylums denied 5

Vital Statistics and Health

Marriages

2002 20,406
2003 20,371
2004 20,455

Divorces

2002 9,113
2003 8,285
2004 8,305

Births

2003 38,174
   Birthrate (per 1,000)....................13.0
   Low birth weight (2,500g or less)........ 6.6%
   To unmarried mothers................ 29.9%

2003, continued
   White............................. 35,692
   Black 1,287
   Hispanic 2,521
   Asian/Pacific Islander 941
   Amer. Indian/Alaska Native............ 262
2004 (preliminary).................... 38,439
   Birthrate (per 1,000)....................13.0
   White............................. 35,727
   Black 1,478
   Hispanic 2,835
   Asian/Pacific Islander 983

Deaths

2002
All causes 27,978
   rate per 100,000......................952.7
Heart disease 8,181
   rate per 100,000......................278.6
Malignant neoplasms 6,473
   rate per 100,000......................220.4
Cerebrovascular disease................. 2,226
   rate per 100,000.......................75.8
Chronic lower respiratory disease 1,580
   rate per 100,000.......................53.8
2003 28,080
   rate per 100,000......................953.8
2004 (provisional) 26,940

Infant deaths

2003 (provisional) 207
   rate per 1,000 ....5.4
2004 (provisional) 198
   rate per 1,000 ....5.2

Abortions, 2000

Total................................. 6,000
   rate per 1,000 women age 15-44...........9.8

Physicians, 2003

Total................................. 5,544
   rate per 1,000 persons................... 188

Nurses, 2001

Total................................ 30,190
   rate per 1,000 persons............... 1,030

Community Hospitals, 2003

Number 116
Beds (x 1,000)..........................11.0
Patients admitted (x 1,000) 363
Average daily census (x 1,000) 6.5
Average cost per day $952
Outpatient visits (x mil)...................9.7

Disability status of population, 2004

5 to 20 years 6.3%
21 to 64 years 10.8%
65 years and over 39.7%

Education

Educational attainment, 2004

Population over 25 years	1,898,918
Less than 9th grade	70,593
High school graduates only	674,614
Bachelor's degree only	317,182
Graduate or professional degree	136,933
Less than 9th grade percent	3.7%
High school graduate or more	89.8%
College graduate or more	24.3%
Graduate or professional degree	7.2%

Public school enrollment, Fall 2002

Total	482,210
Kindergarten through grade 8	325,879
Grades 9 through 12	156,331
Enrollment, 2005 (projected)	466,700

Graduating public high school seniors

2004 (estimate)	33,820

SAT scores, 2005

Average verbal score	596
Average math score	608
Percent of graduates taking test	5%

Public school teachers, 2004

Total (x 1,000)	34.8
Elementary (x 1,000)	16.5
Secondary (x 1,000)	18.3
Average salary	$39,400
Elementary	$38,600
Secondary	$40,200

State receipts & expenditures for public schools, 2004

Revenue receipts ($mil)	$4,251
Expenditures	
Total ($mil)	$4,139
Per capita	$1,407
Per pupil	$7,696

Institutions of higher education, 2004

Total	63
Public	19
Private	44

Enrollment in institutions of higher education, Fall 2003

Total	215,624
Full-time men	68,383
Full-time women	79,016
Part-time men	26,490
Part-time women	41,735

Minority enrollment in institutions of higher education, Fall 2003

Black, non-hispanic	6,635
Hispanic	4,218
Asian/Pacific Islander	4,091
American Indian/Alaska Native	971

Earned degrees conferred, 2003

Bachelor's	20,034
Master's	3,948
First-professional	1,579
Doctor's	506

State & local financial support for higher education, 2003-2004

Full-time equivalent enrollment (x 1,000)	117.7
Appropriations per FTE	$5,255
as a percent of tax revenue	9.8%

Social Insurance & Welfare Programs

Social Security benefits & beneficiaries, 2004

Beneficiaries	
Total	546,000
Retired & dependents	396,000
Survivors	77,000
Disabled & dependents	73,000
Annual benefit payments ($ mil)	
Total	$5,689
Retired & dependents	$3,926
Survivors	$1,061
Disabled & dependents	$702
Average Monthly Benefit	
Retired & dependents	$952
Disabled & dependents	$857
Widowed	$940

Medicare

Enrollment, 2001 (x 1,000)	478
Payments ($ mil, est.)	$1,600
Enrollment, 2003 (x 1,000)	482

Medicaid, 2002

Beneficiaries (x 1,000)	353
Payments ($ mil)	$1,856

State Children's Health Insurance, 2004

Enrollment (x 1,000)	40.8
Expenditures ($ mil)	$37.3

Persons without health insurance, 2003

Number (x 1,000)	329
percent	11.3%
Number of children (x 1,000)	60
percent of children	8.6%

Federal public aid

Temporary Assistance for Needy Families, 2004

Recipients (x 1,000)	45
Families (x 1,000)	18

Supplemental Security Income, 2003

Recipients (x 1,000)	42
Payments ($ mil)	$176

Food Stamp Program, 2004

Participants (x 1,000)	179
Benefits ($ mil)	$176

4   Iowa

Housing & Construction

Housing units

Total 2003 (estimate)	1,272,179
Total 2004 (estimate)	1,292,976
Seasonal or recreational use, 2003	20,000
Owner-occupied single-family, 2003	688,000
Median value	$91,427
Renter-occupied, 2003	293,000
Median rent	$531
Homeownership rate, 2003	73.4%
Homeownership rate, 2004	73.2%

New privately owned housing units, 2004

Number authorized (x 1,000)	16.3
Value ($ mil)	$2,231
Started 2005 (x 1,000, estimate)	14.6
Started 2006 (x 1,000, estimate)	14.1

Existing home sales

2002 (x 1,000)	58.4
2003 (x 1,000)	62.4
2004 (x 1,000)	71.1

Government & Elections

State Officials 2006

Governor (name/party/term expires)
Tom Vilsack
Democrat - 1/07

Lieutenant Governor	Sally Pedersen
Secretary of State	Chet Culver
Attorney General	Tom Miller
Chief Justice	Louis Lavorato

Governorship

Minimum age	30
Length of term	4 years
Consecutive terms permitted	not specified
Who succeeds	Lt. Governor

State Legislature

Name	General Assembly
Upper chamber	Senate
Number of members	50
Length of term	4 years
Party in majority, 2006	50/50
Lower chamber	House of Representatives
Number of members	100
Length of term	2 years
Party in majority, 2006	Republican

State Government Employees, 2004

Total	53,291
Payroll	$213,162,907

Local Government Employees, 2004

Total	131,261
Payroll	$369,077,059

Local Governments by Type, 2002

Total	1,975
County	99
Municipal	948
Township	0
School District	386
Special District	542

Voting age population, November 2004

Total	2,212,000
Male	1,073,000
Female	1,139,000
White	2,120,000
Black	37,000
Hispanic	69,000
Asian	27,000

Presidential Election, 2004

Total Popular Vote	1,506,908
Kerry	741,898
Bush	751,957
Total Electoral Votes	7

Federal representation, 2006 (109th Congress)

Senator	Tom Harkin
Party	Democrat
Year term expires	2009
Senator	Charles E. Grassley
Party	Republican
Year term expires	2011
Representatives, total	5
Democrats	1
Republicans	4
Other	0

Votes cast for US Senators

2002

Total vote (x 1,000)	1,023,000
Leading party	Democratic
Percent for leading party	54.2%

2004

Total vote (x 1,000)	1,479,000
Leading party	Republican
Percent for leading party	70.2%

Votes cast for US Representatives

2002

Total vote (x 1,000)	1,013
Democratic	454
Republican	546
Leading party	Republican
Percent for leading party	54.0%

2004

Total vote (x 1,000)	1,458
Democratic	625
Republican	823
Leading party	Republican
Percent for leading party	56.4%

Women holding public office, 2006

US Congress 0
Statewide elected office..................... 2
State legislature 30

Black public officials, 2001

Total.................................... 13
  US and state legislatures 1
  City/county/regional offices 8
  Judicial/law enforcement.................. 1
  Education/school boards.................. 3

Hispanic public officials, 2004

Total..................................... 0
  State executives & legislators 0
  City/county/regional offices 0
  Judicial/law enforcement.................. 0
  Education/school boards................. 0

Governmental Finance

State government revenues, 2004

Total revenue ($1,000) $15,291,539
  Revenue per capita 5,178.31

General Revenue ($ per capita) $4,011.25
  Intergovernmental 1,367.50
  Taxes 1,741.66
    general sales 547.75
    individual income tax............. 663.29
    corporate income tax 30.42
  Current charges..................... 601.48
  Miscellaneous 300.61

State government expenditure, 2004

Total expenditure (x $1,000) $13,424,350
  Expenditure per capita............. 4,546.00
General Expenditure ($ per capita).... $4,074.18
  Education 1,581.62
  Public welfare..................... 1,054.09
  Health 66.29
  Hospitals.......................... 304.39
  Highways 462.50
  Police protection 24.18
  Correction 74.45
  Natural resources 76.00
  Parks & recreation.................... 6.88
  Governmental administration 159.49
  Interest on general debt 54.68

State debt & cash, 2004 ($ per capita)

Debt $1,644.98
Cash/security holdings.............. $9,164.62

Federal government grants to state & local government, 2004 (x $1,000)

Total........................... $4,038,677
By Federal Agency
  Defense $64,620

By Federal Agency, continued
  Education 328,767
  Energy 65,889
  Environmental Protection Agency 75,358
  Health & Human Services. 2,275,823
  Homeland Security.................. 42,380
  Housing & Urban Development...... 230,746
  Justice 72,934
  Labor 73,274
  Transportation 446,741
  Veterans Affairs.................. 13,681

Crime, Law Enforcement & Courts

Crime, 2004 (rates per 100,000 residents)

Property crimes 85,836
  Burglaries....................... 18,174
  Larcenies........................ 62,258
  Motor vehicle thefts 5,404
  Property crime rate................. 2,905.3
Violent crimes...................... 8,003
  Murders. 46
  Forcible rape...................... 790
  Robberies 1,124
  Aggravated assaults 6,043
  Violent crime rate.................. 270.9

Police Agencies, 2004

Total agencies......................... 231
Total employees 7,449
  Male officers...................... 4,598
  Female officers.................... 361
  Male civilians..................... 887
  Female civilians.................... 1,603

Arrests, 2004

Total............................... 110,513
  Persons under 18 years of age 18,872

Prisoners under state & federal jurisdiction, 2004

Total prisoners........................ 8,525
  Percent change, 12/31/03 to 12/31/04 ... -0.2%
Sentenced to more than one year 8,525
  rate per 100,000...................... 288

Persons under sentence of death, 7/1/05

Total.................................... 0
  White.................................. 0
  Black 0
  Hispanic 0

State's highest court

Name .... Supreme Court
Number of members....................... 9
Length of term .... 8 years
Intermediate appeals court? .... yes

Labor & Income

Civilian labor force, 2004

Total.............................. 1,620,000
Men 846,000
Women 774,000
Persons 16-19 years.............. 104,000
White............................ 1,542,000
Black 28,000
Hispanic 64,000
Asian 30,000

Civilian labor force as a percent of civilian non-institutional population, 2004

Total................................70.2%
Men 75.3
Women 65.4
Persons 16-19 years..............61.1
White............................70.3
Black 63.5
Hispanic 79.0
Asian 75.9

Employment, 2004

Total.............................. 1,545,000
Men 809,000
Women 736,000
Persons 16-19 years.............. 91,000
White............................ 1,474,000
Black 22,000
Hispanic 59,000
Asian 30,000

Full-time/part-time labor force, 2002

Full-time labor force, employed 1,260,000
Part-time labor force, employed....... 341,000
Unemployed, looking for
Full-time work..................... 49,000
Part-time work..................... NA

Unemployment rate, 2004

Total................................4.6%
Men 4.4
Women 4.9
Persons 16-19 years..............12.2
White............................4.4
Black 19.6
Hispanic 7.4
Asian 1.4

Unemployed by reason for unemployment (as a percent of total unemployment), 2002

Job losers or completed temp jobs .... NA
Job leavers............................. NA
Reentrants.............................. NA
New entrants .... NA

Labor unions, 2004

Membership 141,000
percent of employed 10.5%

Experienced civilian labor force by private industry, first quarter 2004

Total.............................. 1,162,383
Natural Resources & Mining 13,893
Construction 59,688
Manufacturing..................... 219,237
Trade, transportation & utilities 295,658
Information 33,374
Finance 95,362
Professional & business 105,267
Education & Health 179,864
Leisure & hospitality............... 120,273
Other............................ 39,767

Experienced civilian labor force by occupation, 2004

Management........................ 57,190
Business & Financial................. 56,570
Legal............................. 6,830
Sales 149,420
Office & Admin. Support 236,850
Computers & Math 23,600
Architecture & Engineering 15,840
Arts & Entertainment............... 16,280
Education 88,260
Social Services 20,110
Healthcare Practitioner & Technical..... 71,790
Healthcare support 42,380
Maintenance & Repair 60,010
Construction 65,410
Transportation & moving 120,450
Production 163,050
Farming, fishing & forestry.......... 4,510

Hours and earnings of production workers on manufacturing payrolls, 2004

Average weekly hours 42.2
Average hourly earnings $16.17
Average weekly earnings $682.37

Average annual pay

2004................................ $32,097
change from 2003 .... 4.4%

Household income

Median household income, three-year average, 2002-2004......................... $43,042

Personal income, 2004 ($ per capita)

In current dollars..................... $30,560
In constant (2000) dollars $28,342

Poverty

Persons below poverty level, three-year average, 2002-2004.......................... 9.7%

Federal individual income tax returns, 2003

Returns filed....................... 1,324,876
Adjusted gross income ($1,000) $54,107,442
Total income tax paid ($1,000) $5,865,511

Economy, Business, Industry & Agriculture

Fortune 500 companies, 2005 2

Patents issued, 2004 736

Bankruptcy cases filed, 2004 13,000

Business firm ownership, 2002

Women-owned. 63,821
  Sales ($ mil) $7,399
Black-owned. 1,619
  Sales ($ mil) $287
Hispanic-owned. 1,535
  Sales ($ mil) $289
Asian-owned 1,778
  Sales ($ mil) $464
Amer. Indian/Alaska Native-owned 644
  Sales ($ mil) $86
Hawaiian/Pacific Isl.-owned. 30
  Sales ($ mil) $10

Gross State Product, 2004 ($ mil)

Total Gross State Product $111,114
  Agriculture, forestry, fishing and
     hunting 5,147
  Mining. 197
  Utilities 2,849
  Construction 4,555
  Manufacturing, durable goods. 12,678
  Manufacturing, non-durable goods . . . 10,181
  Wholesale trade. 6,413
  Retail trade. 7,274
  Transportation & warehousing 3,771
  Information 3,672
  Finance & insurance. 11,878
  Real estate, rental, leasing. 9,834
  Professional and technical services 3,332
  Educational services. 878
  Health care and social assistance. 7,475
  Accommodation/food services. 2,132
  Other services, except government 2,403
  Government. 12,568

Establishments, by major industry group, 2003

Total. 81,078
  Forestry, fishing & agriculture 287
  Mining. 203
  Construction 8,844
  Manufacturing. 3,767
  Wholesale trade. 4,821
  Retail trade. 13,828
  Transportation & warehousing 3,566
  Information 1,627
  Finance & insurance. 5,912
  Professional/scientific/technical 5,923
  Health care/social assistance 7,288
  Accommodation/food services. 6,568

Annual payroll by major industry group, 2003

Total ($1,000) $35,989,231
  Forestry, fishing & agriculture 58,965
  Mining. 72,858
  Utilities 443,318
  Construction 2,264,763
  Manufacturing. 8,241,660
  Wholesale trade. 2,216,003
  Retail trade. 3,300,420
  Transportation & warehousing 1,507,471
  Information 1,445,856
  Finance & insurance. 3,916,989
  Professional/scientific/technical . . . 1,633,351
  Health care/social assistance 5,345,655
  Accommodation/food services. 1,045,108

Agriculture

Number of farms, 2004 90,000
Farm acreage, 2004
  Total. 32,000,000
  Acres per farm, 2004 353
Farm income, 2003 ($mil)
  Net farm income $2,023
  Debt/asset ratio .17.3
Farm marketings, 2003 ($mil)
Total. $12,633
  Crops. 6,560
  Livestock. 6,073

Principal commodities, in order by marketing receipts, 2003

Corn, hogs, soybeans, cattle

Federal economic activity in state

Expenditures, 2003
  Total ($ mil) $17,550
  Per capita $5,961
  Defense ($ mil). 1,008
  Non-defense ($ mil) 16,542
Defense department, 2003
  Payroll ($ mil) $339
  Contract awards ($ mil) $667
  Grants ($ mil). $34
  Homeland security grants ($1,000)
    2004 . . . . $29,918
    2005 . . . . $22,291

FDIC insured financial institutions, 2004

Number. 414
  Assets ($bil) $51.1
  Deposits ($bil) .51.2

Fishing, 2004

Catch (x 1,000 lbs). 0
Value ($1,000). 0

Mining, 2004 ($ mil)
Total non-fuel mineral production $533
Percent of U.S. 1.2%

Construction, 2003 ($ mil)
Total contracts (including non-building). $6,517
    residential 2,097
    non-residential 1,706

Establishments, receipts, payroll & employees, by major industry group, 2002

Mining 856
    Receipts ($1,000) $3,247,527
    Annual payroll ($1,000) $272,254
    Paid employees 6,956

Utilities 330
    Receipts ($1,000) . . . . NA
    Annual payroll ($1,000) $435,623
    Paid employees 8,127

Construction 8,538
    Receipts ($1,000) $9,940,503
    Annual payroll ($1,000) $2,242,375
    Paid employees 67,213

Manufacturing 3,804
    Receipts ($1,000) $65,042,043
    Annual payroll ($1,000) $8,125,864
    Paid employees 222,968

Wholesale trade 4,926
    Receipts ($1,000) $33,546,948
    Annual payroll ($1,000) $2,145,460
    Paid employees 62,023

Retail trade 13,859
    Receipts ($1,000) $31,195,012
    Annual payroll ($1,000) $3,175,923
    Paid employees 176,251

Transportation 3,452
    Receipts ($1,000) $5,063,344
    Annual payroll ($1,000) $1,416,591
    Paid employees 43,765

Information 1,567
    Receipts ($1,000) . . . . NA
    Annual payroll ($1,000) $1,413,851
    Paid employees 44,210

Finance & insurance 5,795
    Receipts ($1,000) . . . . NA
    Annual payroll ($1,000) $3,778,140
    Paid employees 95,040

Professional, scientific & technical 5,798
    Receipts ($1,000) $3,580,073
    Annual payroll ($1,000) $1,419,050
    Paid employees 37,820

Health care & social assistance 7,330
    Receipts ($1,000) $11,441,141
    Annual payroll ($1,000) $5,096,574
    Paid employees 181,388

Accommodation & food service 6,586
    Receipts ($1,000) $3,698,955
    Annual payroll ($1,000) $1,017,109
    Paid employees 104,638

Communication, Energy & Transportation

Communication
Daily newspapers, 2004 37
Households with computers, 2003 . . . . 65%
Households with internet access, 2003 . . . . . 57%

Energy
Electricity Consumption, 2001
Total (trillion Btu) 1,151
Per capita (million Btu) 392
By source of production (trillion Btu)
    Coal 445
    Natural gas 225
    Petroleum 401
    Nuclear electric power 40
    Hydroelectric power 9
By end-use sector (trillion Btu)
    Residential 229
    Commercial 179
    Industrial 472
    Transportation 270
Electric energy, 2003
    Production (billion kWh) 42.1
    Net summer capability (million kW) 10.1
Gas utilities, 2003
    Customers (x1,000) 929
    Sales (trillion Btu) 120
    Revenues ($mil) $1,021
Nuclear plants, 2003 1

Transportation, 2004
Public Road & Street Mileage 113,835
    Urban 10,961
    Rural 102,874
    Interstate 782
Vehicle miles of travel per capita 10,593.9
Total motor vehicle registrations 3,369,431
    Automobiles 1,882,364
    Buses 8,357
    Trucks 1,478,710
    Motorcycles 140,000
Licensed drivers 2,003,723
    19 years & under 122,414
Deaths from motor vehicle accidents 390

Kansas   1

State Summary

Capital City. . . . . Topeka
Governor. . . . . Kathleen Sebelius
Capitol
300 SW 10th Ave
Suite 212S
Topeka, KS 66612
785-296-3232

Admitted as a state 1861
Area (square miles) 82,277
Population, 2004 (est.) 2,735,502
Largest City. . . . . Wichita
Population, 2004. 354,000
Personal income per capita, 2004
(in current dollars) $30,811
Gross state product ($ mil), 2004 . . . . . . $98,946

Leading industries by payroll, 2003

Manufacturing, Health care/Social assistance,
Retail trade

Leading agricultural commodities by receipts, 2003

Cattle, wheat, corn, soybeans

Geography & Environment

Total area (sq. mi.). 82,277
land 81,815
water 462

Federally-owned land, 2004 (acres) 631,351
percent. 1.2%

Highest point. . . . . .Mt. Sunflower
elevation (feet) 4,039

Lowest point . . . . .Verdigris River
elevation (feet) 679

General coastline (miles). 0

Tidal shoreline (miles). 0

Capital City. . . . . Topeka
Population 2000 122,000
Population 2004 122,000

Largest City. . . . . Wichita
Population 2000 344,000
Population 2004 354,000

Number of cities with over 100,000 population

1990 4
2000 4
2004 5

State park and recreation areas, 2003

Area (acres x 1,000). 32
Number of visitors (x 1,000) 8,250
Revenues (x 1,000). $5,736
percent of operating expenditures. 68.9%

National forest system land, 2004

Acres 108,000

Demographics and Characteristics of the Population

Population

1980 2,363,679
1990 2,477,574
2000 2,688,418
2004 (estimate). 2,735,502
persons per sq. mile of land. 33.4
2005 (projection). 2,751,509
Male. 1,366,070
Female. 1,385,439
2010 (projection) 2,805,470
2020 (projection) 2,890,566
2030 (projection) 2,940,084
Male. 1,470,977
Female. 1,469,107

Metropolitan and Non-Metro. area population

	Metro	Non-Metro
1980	1,184,000	1,180,000
1990	1,333,000	1,145,000
2000	1,521,000	1,167,000

Change in population, 2000-2004

Number. 46,678
percent. 1.7%
Natural increase (births minus deaths). . . 61,630
Net internal migration . . . . -48,141
Net international migration 32,289

Persons by age, 2004

Under 5 years 188,782
18 years and over 2,052,011
65 years and over 354,579
85 years and over 55,055

Persons by age, 2010 (projected)

Total. 2,805,470
Under 5 years 199,534
5 to 17 years 499,462
18 and over 2,106,474
21 and over 1,985,141
65 and over 375,315
85 and over 66,506
Median age 36.4

Race, 2004 (estimate)

One Race
White. 2,444,815
Black or African American 161,305
American Indian/Alaska Native. 26,193
Pacific Islander 1,870
Asian Indian. 6,656
Chinese 8,399
Filipino 7,068
Japanese 2,261
Korean 5,129
Vietnamese. 13,433
Two or more races. 44,460

2   Kansas

Persons of Hispanic origin, 2004

Total Hispanic or Latino	160,808
Mexican	128,640
Puerto Rican	7,456
Cuban	3,659
Other Hispanic or Latino	9,318

Marital status, 2000

Population 15 years & over	2,100,656
Never married	506,258
Married	1,220,481
Separated	25,208
Widowed	138,643
Divorced	212,166

Language spoken at home, 2000

Population 5 years & over	2,500,360
English only	2,281,705
Spanish	137,247
Other Indo-European languages	41,207
Asian/Pacific Island languages	33,203

Households & families, 2000

Households	1,037,891
with persons under 18 years	368,875
with persons over 65 years	241,686
persons per household	2.51
Families	701,547
persons per family	3.07
Married couples	567,924
Female householder, no husband present	96,661
One-person households	280,387

Nativity, 2000

Number of persons born in state	1,600,274
percent of population	59.5%

Immigration & Naturalization, 2004

Immigrants admitted	4,041
Persons naturalized	2,093
Asylums granted	40
Asylums denied	11

Vital Statistics and Health

Marriages

2002	19,783
2003	18,781
2004	19,072

Divorces

2002	9,645
2003	8,946
2004	9,102

Births

2003	39,476
Birthrate (per 1,000)	14.5
Low birth weight (2,500g or less)	7.4%
To unmarried mothers	31.6%

2003, continued

White	35,019
Black	2,765
Hispanic	5,443
Asian/Pacific Islander	1,226
Amer. Indian/Alaska Native	483
2004 (preliminary)	39,581
Birthrate (per 1,000)	14.5
White	35,089
Black	2,837
Hispanic	5,472
Asian/Pacific Islander	1,156

Deaths

2002

All causes	25,021
rate per 100,000	921.3
Heart disease	6,680
rate per 100,000	246.0
Malignant neoplasms	5,362
rate per 100,000	197.4
Cerebrovascular disease	1,845
rate per 100,000	67.9
Chronic lower respiratory disease	1,367
rate per 100,000	50.3
2003	24,596
rate per 100,000	903.1
2004 (provisional)	23,935

Infant deaths

2003 (provisional)	261
rate per 1,000	6.4
2004 (provisional)	290
rate per 1,000	7.2

Abortions, 2000

Total	12,000
rate per 1,000 women age 15-44	21.4

Physicians, 2003

Total	5,947
rate per 1,000 persons	218

Nurses, 2001

Total	24,680
rate per 1,000 persons	913

Community Hospitals, 2003

Number	134
Beds (x 1,000)	10.6
Patients admitted (x 1,000)	331
Average daily census (x 1,000)	5.9
Average cost per day	$952
Outpatient visits (x mil)	6.0

Disability status of population, 2004

5 to 20 years	6.8%
21 to 64 years	11.8%
65 years and over	37.9%

Education

Educational attainment, 2004

Population over 25 years 1,715,460
  Less than 9th grade 65,624
  High school graduates only 516,480
  Bachelor's degree only 323,567
  Graduate or professional degree 161,486
  Less than 9th grade percent 3.8%
  High school graduate or more 89.6%
  College graduate or more 30.0%
  Graduate or professional degree 9.4%

Public school enrollment, Fall 2002

Total 470,957
  Kindergarten through grade 8 321,886
  Grades 9 through 12 149,071
Enrollment, 2005 (projected) 459,400

Graduating public high school seniors

2004 (estimate) 30,040

SAT scores, 2005

Average verbal score 585
Average math score 588
Percent of graduates taking test 9%

Public school teachers, 2004

Total (x 1,000) 32.6
  Elementary (x 1,000) 16.0
  Secondary (x 1,000) 16.6
Average salary $38,600
  Elementary $38,600
  Secondary $38,600

State receipts & expenditures for public schools, 2004

Revenue receipts ($mil) $4,274
Expenditures
Total ($mil) $3,863
  Per capita $1,418
  Per pupil $8,189

Institutions of higher education, 2004

Total 63
  Public 36
  Private 27

Enrollment in institutions of higher education, Fall, 2003

Total 194,422
  Full-time men 54,385
  Full-time women 60,426
  Part-time men 31,669
  Part-time women 47,942

Minority enrollment in institutions of higher education, Fall, 2003

Black, non-hispanic 10,231
Hispanic 7,450
Asian/Pacific Islander 5,407
American Indian/Alaska Native 2,890

Earned degrees conferred, 2003

Bachelor's 15,744
Master's 5,604
First-professional 666
Doctor's 414

State & local financial support for higher education, 2003-2004

Full-time equivalent enrollment (x 1,000) . . 110.2
Appropriations per FTE $5,940
  as a percent of tax revenue 10.1%

Social Insurance & Welfare Programs

Social Security benefits & beneficiaries, 2004

Beneficiaries
  Total 447,000
  Retired & dependents 319,000
  Survivors 62,000
  Disabled & dependents 66,000
Annual benefit payments ($ mil)
  Total $4,745
  Retired & dependents $3,260
  Survivors $860
  Disabled & dependents $625
Average Monthly Benefit
  Retired & dependents $979
  Disabled & dependents $866
  Widowed $976

Medicare

Enrollment, 2001 (x 1,000) 391
  Payments ($ mil, est.) $2,100
Enrollment, 2003 (x 1,000) 394

Medicaid, 2002

Beneficiaries (x 1,000) 289
Payments ($ mil) $1,501

State Children's Health Insurance, 2004

Enrollment (x 1,000) 44.4
Expenditures ($ mil) $39.6

Persons without health insurance, 2003

Number (x 1,000) 294
  percent 11.0%
Number of children (x 1,000) 45
  percent of children 6.4%

Federal public aid

Temporary Assistance for Needy Families, 2004
Recipients (x 1,000) 44
Families (x 1,000) 17

Supplemental Security Income, 2003
Recipients (x 1,000) 38
Payments ($ mil) $170

Food Stamp Program, 2004

Participants (x 1,000) 170
Benefits ($ mil) $158

Housing & Construction

Housing units
Total 2003 (estimate) 1,171,973
Total 2004 (estimate) 1,185,114
Seasonal or recreational use, 2003 13,000
Owner-occupied single-family, 2003 611,000
    Median value $100,257
Renter-occupied, 2003 322,000
    Median rent $535
Homeownership rate, 2003 .... 70.3%
Homeownership rate, 2004 .... 69.9%

New privately owned housing units, 2004
Number authorized (x 1,000) 13.3
Value ($ mil) $1,926
Started 2005 (x 1,000, estimate) 13.8
Started 2006 (x 1,000, estimate) 13.8

Existing home sales
2002 (x 1,000) 60.0
2003 (x 1,000) 65.3
2004 (x 1,000) 73.4

Government & Elections

State Officials 2006
Governor (name/party/term expires)
        Kathleen Sebelius
        Democrat - 1/07
Lieutenant Governor .... John Moore
Secretary of State .... Ron Thornburgh
Attorney General .... Phill Kline
Chief Justice .... Kay McFarland

Governorship
Minimum age .... not specified
Length of term .... 4 years
Consecutive terms permitted 2
Who succeeds .... Lt. Governor

State Legislature
Name .... Legislature
Upper chamber .... Senate
    Number of members 40
    Length of term .... 4 years
    Party in majority, 2006 .... Republican
Lower chamber .... House of Representatives
    Number of members 125
    Length of term .... 2 years
    Party in majority, 2006 .... Republican

State Government Employees, 2004
Total 43,787
Payroll $146,063,124

Local Government Employees, 2004
Total 135,759
Payroll $382,282,500

Local Governments by Type, 2002
Total 3,887
    County 104
    Municipal 627
    Township 1,299
    School District 324
    Special District 1,533

Voting age population, November 2004
Total 1,990,000
    Male 970,000
    Female 1,019,000
    White 1,768,000
    Black 99,000
    Hispanic 132,000
    Asian 73,000

Presidential Election, 2004
Total Popular Vote 1,187,756
    Kerry 434,993
    Bush 736,456
Total Electoral Votes 6

Federal representation, 2006 (109th Congress)
Senator .... Pat Roberts
    Party .... Republican
    Year term expires 2009
Senator .... Sam Brownback
    Party .... Republican
    Year term expires 2011
Representatives, total 4
    Democrats 1
    Republicans 3
    Other 0

Votes cast for US Senators
2002
Total vote (x 1,000) 767,000
Leading party .... Republican
Percent for leading party 83.6%

2004
Total vote (x 1,000) 1,129,000
Leading party .... Republican
Percent for leading party 69.2%

Votes cast for US Representatives
2002
Total vote (x 1,000) 830
Democratic 260
Republican 536
Leading party .... Republican
Percent for leading party 64.6%

2004
Total vote (x 1,000) 1,156
Democratic 387
Republican 724
Leading party .... Republican
Percent for leading party 62.6%

Women holding public office, 2006

US Congress 0
Statewide elected office...................... 3
State legislature 54

Black public officials, 2001

Total................................... 17
  US and state legislatures 7
  City/county/regional offices 4
  Judicial/law enforcement................. 3
  Education/school boards.................. 3

Hispanic public officials, 2004

Total..................................... 8
  State executives & legislators 2
  City/county/regional offices 6
  Judicial/law enforcement................. 0
  Education/school boards................. 0

Governmental Finance

State government revenues, 2004

Total revenue ($1,000) $11,044,146
  Revenue per capita 4,039.56

General Revenue ($ per capita) $3,609.71
  Intergovernmental 1,097.31
  Taxes 1,932.58
    general sales 707.00
    individual income tax............. 700.63
    corporate income tax 60.94
  Current charges.................... 328.39
  Miscellaneous 251.44

State government expenditure, 2004

Total expenditure (x $1,000) $11,207,121
  Expenditure per capita.............. 4,099.17
General Expenditure ($ per capita).... $3,695.25
  Education 1,625.71
  Public welfare..................... 905.28
  Health 105.13
  Hospitals...........................39.42
  Highways 448.25
  Police protection 27.14
  Correction 115.83
  Natural resources...................67.91
  Parks & recreation.....................2.73
  Governmental administration 153.73
  Interest on general debt 60.87

State debt & cash, 2004 ($ per capita)

Debt $1,672.06
Cash/security holdings.............. $5,149.08

Federal government grants to state & local government, 2004 (x $1,000)

Total............................ $3,468,608
By Federal Agency
  Defense $91,360

By Federal Agency, continued
  Education 380,600
  Energy............................ 11,537
  Environmental Protection Agency 42,449
  Health & Human Services. 1,770,890
  Homeland Security.................. 20,711
  Housing & Urban Development...... 199,849
  Justice 63,827
  Labor 61,055
  Transportation 438,043
  Veterans Affairs.................... 14,829

Crime, Law Enforcement & Courts

Crime, 2004 (rates per 100,000 residents)

Property crimes 108,694
  Burglaries........................ 19,999
  Larcenies.......................... 80,260
  Motor vehicle thefts 8,435
  Property crime rate................. 3,973.5
Violent crimes...................... 10,245
  Murders.......................... 123
  Forcible rape....................... 1,104
  Robberies 1,813
  Aggravated assaults 7,205
  Violent crime rate 374.5

Police Agencies, 2004

Total agencies......................... 337
Total employees 9,966
  Male officers 6,504
  Female officers..................... 640
  Male civilians...................... 975
  Female civilians.................... 1,847

Arrests, 2004

Total................................. 80,262
  Persons under 18 years of age 12,426

Prisoners under state & federal jurisdiction, 2004

Total prisoners....................... 8,966
  Percent change, 12/31/03 to 12/31/04 ... -1.8%
Sentenced to more than one year 8,966
  rate per 100,000..................... 327

Persons under sentence of death, 7/1/05

Total..................................... 7
  White................................. 5
  Black 2
  Hispanic 0

State's highest court

Name ....Supreme Court
Number of members...................... 7
Length of term .... 6 years
Intermediate appeals court? ....yes

Labor & Income

Civilian labor force, 2004

Total............................. 1,480,000
  Men 795,000
  Women 685,000
  Persons 16-19 years................. 91,000
  White........................... 1,321,000
  Black 71,000
  Hispanic 86,000
  Asian 40,000

Civilian labor force as a percent of civilian non-institutional population, 2004

Total................................. 71.5%
  Men 78.9
  Women 64.5
  Persons 16-19 years..................56.3
  White................................72.0
  Black 66.3
  Hispanic 78.6
  Asian 70.1

Employment, 2004

Total............................. 1,398,000
  Men 754,000
  Women 644,000
  Persons 16-19 years................ 77,000
  White........................... 1,259,000
  Black 59,000
  Hispanic 80,000
  Asian 38,000

Full-time/part-time labor force, 2002

Full-time labor force, employed 1,074,000
Part-time labor force, employed....... 268,000
Unemployed, looking for
  Full-time work..................... 54,000
  Part-time work........................ NA

Unemployment rate, 2004

Total................................. 5.5%
  Men 5.2
  Women 5.9
  Persons 16-19 years.................15.2
  White.................................4.7
  Black 17.4
  Hispanic 7.0
  Asian 5.8

Unemployed by reason for unemployment (as a percent of total unemployment), 2002

Job losers or completed temp jobs 50.0%
Job leavers............................... NA
Reentrants................................ NA
New entrants .... NA

Labor unions, 2004

Membership 103,000
  percent of employed 8.4%

Experienced civilian labor force by private industry, first quarter 2004

Total............................. 1,039,461
  Natural Resources & Mining 15,583
  Construction 58,910
  Manufacturing..................... 174,817
  Trade, transportation & utilities 253,550
  Information 42,473
  Finance 69,618
  Professional & business 125,723
  Education & Health 154,794
  Leisure & hospitality.............. 106,608
  Other............................. 37,385

Experienced civilian labor force by occupation, 2004

Management......................... 57,360
Business & Financial.................. 49,590
Legal............................... 7,820
Sales.............................. 133,110
Office & Admin. Support............. 224,220
Computers & Math 27,220
Architecture & Engineering 26,760
Arts & Entertainment................. 14,160
Education 84,120
Social Services 16,430
Healthcare Practitioner & Technical..... 67,550
Healthcare support................. 41,240
Maintenance & Repair 57,210
Construction 63,470
Transportation & moving 96,540
Production 122,820
Farming, fishing & forestry............. 5,720

Hours and earnings of production workers on manufacturing payrolls, 2004

Average weekly hours 41.0
Average hourly earnings $16.57
Average weekly earnings $679.37

Average annual pay

2004............................... $32,738
  change from 2003 .... 4.0%

Household income

Median household income, three-year average, 2002-2004........................ $43,725

Personal income, 2004 ($ per capita)

In current dollars.................... $30,811
In constant (2000) dollars $28,575

Poverty

Persons below poverty level, three-year average, 2002-2004......................... 10.7%

Federal individual income tax returns, 2003

Returns filed....................... 1,218,580
Adjusted gross income ($1,000) $52,503,139
Total income tax paid ($1,000) $6,124,669

Economy, Business, Industry & Agriculture

Fortune 500 companies, 2005 2

Patents issued, 2004 540

Bankruptcy cases filed, 2004 16,300

Business firm ownership, 2002
Women-owned. 59,635
  Sales ($ mil) $6,949
Black-owned. 4,468
  Sales ($ mil) $376
Hispanic-owned. 4,188
  Sales ($ mil) $674
Asian-owned 3,568
  Sales ($ mil) $913
Amer. Indian/Alaska Native-owned 1,727
  Sales ($ mil) $353
Hawaiian/Pacific Isl.-owned. 57
  Sales ($ mil) $34

Gross State Product, 2004 ($ mil)
Total Gross State Product $98,946
  Agriculture, forestry, fishing and
    hunting 2,052
  Mining. 1,224
  Utilities 2,367
  Construction 4,164
  Manufacturing, durable goods. 9,328
  Manufacturing, non-durable goods 5,569
  Wholesale trade. 6,209
  Retail trade. 7,241
  Transportation & warehousing 3,758
  Information 7,739
  Finance & insurance. 6,234
  Real estate, rental, leasing 8,790
  Professional and technical services 4,408
  Educational services. 496
  Health care and social assistance. 6,930
  Accommodation/food services. 2,323
  Other services, except government 2,396
  Government 13,854

Establishments, by major industry group, 2003
Total. 74,972
  Forestry, fishing & agriculture 217
  Mining. 864
  Construction 7,722
  Manufacturing. 3,159
  Wholesale trade. 4,590
  Retail trade. 11,834
  Transportation & warehousing 2,576
  Information 1,516
  Finance & insurance. 5,569
  Professional/scientific/technical 6,793
  Health care/social assistance 7,129
  Accommodation/food services. 5,635

Annual payroll by major industry group, 2003
Total ($1,000) $34,040,946
  Forestry, fishing & agriculture 17,247
  Mining. 290,652
  Utilities 378,157
  Construction 2,282,021
  Manufacturing. 6,691,611
  Wholesale trade. 2,622,701
  Retail trade. 2,773,674
  Transportation & warehousing 1,316,655
  Information 2,378,673
  Finance & insurance. 2,608,579
  Professional/scientific/technical . . . 2,052,712
  Health care/social assistance 4,939,323
  Accommodation/food services. 992,313

Agriculture
Number of farms, 2004 65,000
Farm acreage, 2004
  Total. 47,000,000
  Acres per farm, 2004 732
Farm income, 2003 ($mil)
  Net farm income $1,387
  Debt/asset ratio .20.4
Farm marketings, 2003 ($mil)
Total. $9,046
  Crops 2,867
  Livestock 6,179

Principal commodities, in order by marketing receipts, 2003
Cattle, wheat, corn, soybeans

Federal economic activity in state
Expenditures, 2003
  Total ($ mil) $18,208
  Per capita $6,686
  Defense ($ mil). 2,520
  Non-defense ($ mil) 15,688
Defense department, 2003
  Payroll ($ mil) $1,341
  Contract awards ($ mil) $1,222
  Grants ($ mil). $27
  Homeland security grants ($1,000)
    2004 . . . . $29,064
    2005 . . . . $21,784

FDIC insured financial institutions, 2004
Number 372
  Assets ($bil) $57.8
  Deposits ($bil) 46.5

Fishing, 2004
Catch (x 1,000 lbs) 0
Value ($1,000). 0

Mining, 2004 ($ mil)
Total non-fuel mineral production $741
Percent of U.S. 1.7%

Construction, 2003 ($ mil)
Total contracts (including non-building). $4,529
    residential 2,306
    non-residential 1,224

Establishments, receipts, payroll & employees,
    by major industry group, 2002

Mining 654
    Receipts ($1,000) $4,948,381
    Annual payroll ($1,000) $868,444
    Paid employees 19,814

Utilities 263
    Receipts ($1,000) . . . . NA
    Annual payroll ($1,000) $368,601
    Paid employees 6,603

Construction 7,518
    Receipts ($1,000) $10,341,081
    Annual payroll ($1,000) $2,297,820
    Paid employees 68,670

Manufacturing 3,218
    Receipts ($1,000) $50,897,796
    Annual payroll ($1,000) $6,877,335
    Paid employees 177,825

Wholesale trade 4,705
    Receipts ($1,000) $44,117,100
    Annual payroll ($1,000) $2,177,130
    Paid employees 57,926

Retail trade 11,890
    Receipts ($1,000) $26,505,396
    Annual payroll ($1,000) $2,687,657
    Paid employees 144,874

Transportation 2,513
    Receipts ($1,000) $3,963,169
    Annual payroll ($1,000) $1,239,945
    Paid employees 40,578

Information 1,528
    Receipts ($1,000) . . . . NA
    Annual payroll ($1,000) $2,349,449
    Paid employees 49,738

Finance & insurance 5,423
    Receipts ($1,000) . . . . NA
    Annual payroll ($1,000) $2,303,574
    Paid employees 55,258

Professional, scientific & technical 6,745
    Receipts ($1,000) $6,285,201
    Annual payroll ($1,000) $2,047,912
    Paid employees 53,263

Health care & social assistance 7,095
    Receipts ($1,000) $11,162,607
    Annual payroll ($1,000) $4,709,065
    Paid employees 163,540

Accommodation & food service 5,584
    Receipts ($1,000) $3,196,947
    Annual payroll ($1,000) $910,771
    Paid employees 92,125

Communication, Energy & Transportation

Communication
Daily newspapers, 2004 43
Households with computers, 2003 . . . . 64%
Households with internet access, 2003 . . . . . 54%

Energy
Electricity Consumption, 2001
Total (trillion Btu) 1,044
Per capita (million Btu) 387
By source of production (trillion Btu)
    Coal 355
    Natural gas 274
    Petroleum 391
    Nuclear electric power 108
    Hydroelectric power . . . . < 0.5
By end-use sector (trillion Btu)
    Residential 215
    Commercial 192
    Industrial 385
    Transportation 252
Electric energy, 2003
    Production (billion kWh) 46.6
    Net summer capability (million kW) 10.9
Gas utilities, 2003
    Customers (x1,000) 935
    Sales (trillion Btu) 102
    Revenues ($mil) $861
Nuclear plants, 2003 1

Transportation, 2004
Public Road & Street Mileage 135,016
    Urban 10,859
    Rural 124,157
    Interstate 874
Vehicle miles of travel per capita 10,979.3
Total motor vehicle registrations 2,346,522
    Automobiles 852,648
    Buses 3,889
    Trucks 1,489,985
    Motorcycles 61,678
Licensed drivers 1,979,746
    19 years & under 137,854
Deaths from motor vehicle accidents 461

State Summary

Capital City....................... Frankfort
Governor.......................Ernie Fletcher
700 Capitol Ave
Suite 100
Frankfort, KY 40601
502-564-2611
Admitted as a state 1792
Area (square miles)................... 40,409
Population, 2004 (est.) 4,145,922
Largest City........................ Louisville
Population, 2004.................. 256,231
Personal income per capita, 2004
(in current dollars) $27,709
Gross state product ($ mil), 2004 ..... $136,446

Leading industries by payroll, 2003

Manufacturing, Health care/Social assistance,
Retail trade

Leading agricultural commodities by receipts, 2003

Horses/mules, cattle, broilers, tobacco

Geography & Environment

Total area (sq. mi.).................... 40,409
land 39,728
water 681
Federally-owned land, 2004 (acres) ... 1,378,677
percent............................. 5.4%
Highest point.................. Black Mountain
elevation (feet) 4,139
Lowest point .... Mississippi River
elevation (feet) 257
General coastline (miles)..................... 0
Tidal shoreline (miles)...................... 0
Capital City........................ Frankfort
Population 2000 27,741
Population 2004 27,281
Largest City........................ Louisville
Population 2000 256,000
Population 2004 256,231

Number of cities with over 100,000 population

1990 2
2000 2
2004 2

State park and recreation areas, 2003

Area (acres x 1,000)....................... 45
Number of visitors (x 1,000) 7,668
Revenues (x 1,000).................... $47,559
percent of operating expenditures...... 62.2%

National forest system land, 2004

Acres 811,000

Demographics and Characteristics of the Population

Population

1980 3,660,777
1990 3,685,296
2000 4,041,769
2004 (estimate)..................... 4,145,922
persons per sq. mile of land............104.4
2005 (projection)................... 4,163,360
Male............................. 2,042,653
Female............................ 2,120,707
2010 (projection)................... 4,265,117
2020 (projection)................... 4,424,431
2030 (projection)................... 4,554,998
Male............................. 2,253,512
Female............................ 2,301,486

Metropolitan and Non-Metro. area population

	Metro	Non-Metro
1980	1,677,000	1,984,000
1990	1,714,000	1,971,000
2000	1,973,000	2,069,000

Change in population, 2000-2004

Number............................. 103,637
percent............................. 2.6%
Natural increase (births minus deaths)... 60,299
Net internal migration................. 22,512
Net international migration 22,745

Persons by age, 2004

Under 5 years 266,614
18 years and over 3,165,735
65 years and over 519,327
85 years and over 59,024

Persons by age, 2010 (projected)

Total.............................. 4,265,117
Under 5 years 275,053
5 to 17 years 727,254
18 and over 3,262,810
21 and over 3,085,501
65 and over 557,471
85 and over 73,633
Median age 38

Race, 2004 (estimate)

One Race
White........................... 3,746,921
Black or African American 310,996
American Indian/Alaska Native........ 9,220
Pacific Islander 1,927
Asian Indian....................... 6,113
Chinese 8,439
Filipino 3,127
Japanese 2,834
Korean 5,493
Vietnamese......................... 6,076
Two or more races.................... 39,872

Persons of Hispanic origin, 2004

Total Hispanic or Latino 74,613
Mexican............................ 47,527
Puerto Rican 5,702
Cuban 5,310
Other Hispanic or Latino 4,408

Marital status, 2000

Population 15 years & over 3,217,167
Never married 730,297
Married......................... 1,846,654
Separated 57,909
Widowed......................... 231,636
Divorced 353,888

Language spoken at home, 2000

Population 5 years & over 3,776,230
English only 3,627,757
Spanish 70,061
Other Indo-European languages 51,025
Asian/Pacific Island languages....... 21,031

Households & families, 2000

Households....................... 1,590,647
with persons under 18 years 564,175
with persons over 65 years.......... 363,000
persons per household 2.47
Families......................... 1,104,398
persons per family.....................2.97
Married couples...................... 857,944
Female householder,
no husband present............... 187,957
One-person households 414,095

Nativity, 2000

Number of persons born in state 2,980,272
percent of population 73.7%

Immigration & Naturalization, 2004

Immigrants admitted.................. 3,624
Persons naturalized 1,307
Asylums granted 32
Asylums denied 13

Vital Statistics and Health

Marriages

2002 36,909
2003 37,345
2004 36,391

Divorces

2002 21,086
2003 20,468
2004 20,298

Births

2003 55,236
Birthrate (per 1,000).....................13.4
Low birth weight (2,500g or less)........ 8.7%
To unmarried mothers................ 33.8%

2003, continued
White............................. 49,457
Black 4,859
Hispanic 1,964
Asian/Pacific Islander 867
Amer. Indian/Alaska Native.............. 99

2004 (preliminary).................... 54,451
Birthrate (per 1,000)....................13.1
White............................. 48,665
Black 4,878
Hispanic 2,177
Asian/Pacific Islander 813

Deaths

2002

All causes 40,697
rate per 100,000..................... 994.3
Heart disease 11,696
rate per 100,000..................... 285.8
Malignant neoplasms 9,438
rate per 100,000.....................230.6
Cerebrovascular disease................. 2,554
rate per 100,000.....................62.4
Chronic lower respiratory disease 2,401
rate per 100,000.....................58.7
2003 40,236
rate per 100,000.....................977.1
2004 (provisional) 38,412

Infant deaths

2003 (provisional) 341
rate per 1,000 ....6.2
2004 (provisional) 348
rate per 1,000 ....6.3

Abortions, 2000

Total................................. 5,000
rate per 1,000 women age 15-44...........5.3

Physicians, 2003

Total................................. 9,348
rate per 1,000 persons................... 227

Nurses, 2001

Total................................ 34,920
rate per 1,000 persons................. 858

Community Hospitals, 2003

Number............................... 103
Beds (x 1,000)..........................14.9
Patients admitted (x 1,000) 600
Average daily census (x 1,000) 9.3
Average cost per day $1,106
Outpatient visits (x mil)...................8.5

Disability status of population, 2004

5 to 20 years 8.1%
21 to 64 years 20.1%
65 years and over 47.5%

Education

Educational attainment, 2004
Population over 25 years 2,692,934
Less than 9th grade 257,856
High school graduates only 939,716
Bachelor's degree only 300,476
Graduate or professional degree...... 211,955
Less than 9th grade percent 9.6%
High school graduate or more 81.8%
College graduate or more.............. 21.0%
Graduate or professional degree........ 7.9%

Public school enrollment, Fall 2002
Total................................ 660,782
Kindergarten through grade 8 476,758
Grades 9 through 12 184,024
Enrollment, 2005 (projected) 642,500

Graduating public high school seniors
2004 (estimate)....................... 36,170

SAT scores, 2005
Average verbal score 561
Average math score 559
Percent of graduates taking test 12%

Public school teachers, 2004
Total (x 1,000) 39.3
Elementary (x 1,000).................27.7
Secondary (x 1,000) 11.6
Average salary $40,200
Elementary $40,000
Secondary........................... $40,800

State receipts & expenditures for public schools, 2004
Revenue receipts ($mil)................ $5,196
Expenditures
Total ($mil)........................... $5,203
Per capita $1,263
Per pupil $8,298

Institutions of higher education, 2004
Total.................................... 77
Public................................... 34
Private.................................. 43

Enrollment in institutions of higher education, Fall, 2003
Total................................ 237,766
Full-time men 64,012
Full-time women..................... 87,425
Part-time men 37,094
Part-time women..................... 49,235

Minority enrollment in institutions of higher education, Fall, 2003
Black, non-hispanic.................... 18,257
Hispanic 2,169
Asian/Pacific Islander 2,584
American Indian/Alaska Native........... 653

Earned degrees conferred, 2003
Bachelor's 16,254
Master's 5,430
First-professional....................... 1,031
Doctor's................................ 404

State & local financial support for higher education, 2003-2004
Full-time equivalent enrollment (x 1,000) ..144.7
Appropriations per FTE................. $6,360
as a percent of tax revenue.............. 9.9%

Social Insurance & Welfare Programs

Social Security benefits & beneficiaries, 2004
Beneficiaries
Total............................. 785,000
Retired & dependents.............. 459,000
Survivors......................... 125,000
Disabled & dependents............. 201,000
Annual benefit payments ($ mil)
Total............................. $7,656
Retired & dependents.............. $4,247
Survivors.......................... $1,502
Disabled & dependents.............. $1,907
Average Monthly Benefit
Retired & dependents.............. $903
Disabled & dependents.............. $879
Widowed........................... $838

Medicare
Enrollment, 2001 (x 1,000) 630
Payments ($ mil, est.) $3,600
Enrollment, 2003 (x 1,000) 648

Medicaid, 2002
Beneficiaries (x 1,000)..................... 808
Payments ($ mil) $3,459

State Children's Health Insurance, 2004
Enrollment (x 1,000)....................94.5
Expenditures ($ mil)....................$71.5

Persons without health insurance, 2003
Number (x 1,000)........................ 574
percent........................... 14.0%
Number of children (x 1,000) 107
percent of children 10.5%

Federal public aid
Temporary Assistance for Needy Families, 2004
Recipients (x 1,000)....................... 78
Families (x 1,000) 36

Supplemental Security Income, 2003
Recipients (x 1,000)....................... 179
Payments ($ mil) $819

Food Stamp Program, 2004
Participants (x 1,000) 545
Benefits ($ mil)........................... $543

Housing & Construction

Housing units

Total 2003 (estimate) 1,822,075
Total 2004 (estimate) 1,842,971
Seasonal or recreational use, 2003 39,000
Owner-occupied single-family, 2003.... 812,000
    Median value $104,103
Renter-occupied, 2003 459,000
    Median rent $491
Homeownership rate, 2003 .... 74.4%
Homeownership rate, 2004 .... 74.3%

New privately owned housing units, 2004

Number authorized (x 1,000) 22.6
Value ($ mil).......................... $2,679
Started 2005 (x 1,000, estimate) 20.4
Started 2006 (x 1,000, estimate) 20.5

Existing home sales

2002 (x 1,000)............................73.5
2003 (x 1,000)............................81.1
2004 (x 1,000)............................89.3

Government & Elections

State Officials 2006

Governor (name/party/term expires)
Ernie Fletcher
Republican - 12/07
Lieutenant Governor........... Stephen Pence
Secretary of State............... Trey Grayson
Attorney General..........Gregory D. Stumbo
Chief Justice ....Joseph E. Lambert

Governorship

Minimum age........................... 30
Length of term....................... 4 years
Consecutive terms permitted 2
Who succeeds....................Lt. Governor

State Legislature

Name .... General Assembly
Upper chamber ....Senate
    Number of members..................... 38
    Length of term...................... 4 years
    Party in majority, 2006 .... Republican
Lower chamber........House of Representatives
    Number of members................... 100
    Length of term...................... 2 years
    Party in majority, 2006 .... Democratic

State Government Employees, 2004

Total................................. 79,481
Payroll......................... $260,018,917

Local Government Employees, 2004

Total................................ 157,736
Payroll......................... $421,554,443

Local Governments by Type, 2002

Total.............................. 1,439
    County.............................. 119
    Municipal 424
    Township 0
    School District........................ 176
    Special District 720

Voting age population, November 2004

Total............................. 3,042,000
    Male............................. 1,454,000
    Female........................... 1,588,000
    White............................ 2,775,000
    Black............................. 204,000
    Hispanic 44,000
    Asian 27,000

Presidential Election, 2004

Total Popular Vote 1,795,882
    Kerry 712,733
    Bush.......................... 1,069,439
Total Electoral Votes........................ 8

Federal representation, 2006 (109th Congress)

Senator.................... Mitch McConnell
    Party .... Republican
    Year term expires 2009
Senator.......................Jim Bunning
    Party .... Republican
    Year term expires 2011
Representatives, total 6
    Democrats....................... 1
    Republicans 5
    Other................................. 0

Votes cast for US Senators

2002
Total vote (x 1,000) 1,131,000
Leading party...................... Republican
Percent for leading party 64.7%

2004
Total vote (x 1,000) 1,724,000
Leading party...................... Republican
Percent for leading party 50.7%

Votes cast for US Representatives

2002
Total vote (x 1,000) 1,094
    Democratic........................... 351
    Republican 694
Leading party...................... Republican
Percent for leading party 63.4%

2004
Total vote (x 1,000) 1,635
    Democratic........................... 602
    Republican 1,017
Leading party...................... Republican
Percent for leading party 62.2%

Women holding public office, 2006

US Congress 1
Statewide elected office. 1
State legislature 17

Black public officials, 2001

Total. 60
  US and state legislatures 5
  City/county/regional offices 44
  Judicial/law enforcement. 5
  Education/school boards. 6

Hispanic public officials, 2004

Total. 0
  State executives & legislators 0
  City/county/regional offices 0
  Judicial/law enforcement. 0
  Education/school boards. 0

Governmental Finance

State government revenues, 2004

Total revenue ($1,000) $20,180,416
  Revenue per capita 4,872.14

General Revenue ($ per capita). $4,196.55
  Intergovernmental 1,399.23
  Taxes 2,043.31
    general sales 595.37
    individual income tax. 680.68
    corporate income tax 92.11
  Current charges. 457.59
  Miscellaneous 296.41

State government expenditure, 2004

Total expenditure (x $1,000) $20,072,526
  Expenditure per capita. 4,846.10
General Expenditure ($ per capita). . . . $4,259.19
  Education 1,543.34
  Public welfare. 1,273.52
  Health 129.29
  Hospitals. 164.77
  Highways 417.90
  Police protection 37.49
  Correction 109.24
  Natural resources 83.32
  Parks & recreation. 32.49
  Governmental administration 161.15
  Interest on general debt 103.31

State debt & cash, 2004 ($ per capita)

Debt $1,959.55
Cash/security holdings. $8,206.25

Federal government grants to state & local government, 2004 (x $1,000)

Total. $6,743,285
By Federal Agency
  Defense $18,199

By Federal Agency, continued
  Education 574,246
  Energy 13,834
  Environmental Protection Agency 59,971
  Health & Human Services. 4,053,926
  Homeland Security. 68,730
  Housing & Urban Development. 450,887
  Justice 107,194
  Labor 125,919
  Transportation 711,514
  Veterans Affairs. 10,554

Crime, Law Enforcement & Courts

Crime, 2004 (rates per 100,000 residents)

Property crimes 105,209
  Burglaries. 25,902
  Larcenies. 70,535
  Motor vehicle thefts 8,772
  Property crime rate. 2,537.7
Violent crimes. 10,152
  Murders. 236
  Forcible rape. 1,238
  Robberies 3,268
  Aggravated assaults 5,410
  Violent crime rate 244.9

Police Agencies, 2004

Total agencies. 361
Total employees 10,164
  Male officers. 7,083
  Female officers. 572
  Male civilians. 954
  Female civilians. 1,555

Arrests, 2004

Total. 69,483
  Persons under 18 years of age 7,829

Prisoners under state & federal jurisdiction, 2004

Total prisoners. 17,814
  Percent change, 12/31/03 to 12/31/04 . . . . 7.2%
Sentenced to more than one year 17,140
  rate per 100,000. 412

Persons under sentence of death, 7/1/05

Total. 37
  White. 28
  Black 8
  Hispanic 1

State's highest court

Name . . . . .Supreme Court
Number of members. 7
Length of term . . . . 6 years
Intermediate appeals court? . . . . .yes

Labor & Income

Civilian labor force, 2004

Total	1,977,000
Men	1,057,000
Women	920,000
Persons 16-19 years	113,000
White	1,781,000
Black	147,000
Hispanic	33,000
Asian	0

Civilian labor force as a percent of civilian non-institutional population, 2004

Total	61.9%
Men	68.9
Women	55.4
Persons 16-19 years	47.6
White	61.6
Black	64.6
Hispanic	68.7
Asian	0.0

Employment, 2004

Total	1,874,000
Men	998,000
Women	876,000
Persons 16-19 years	88,000
White	1,698,000
Black	131,000
Hispanic	30,000
Asian	0

Full-time/part-time labor force, 2002

Full-time labor force, employed	1,548,000
Part-time labor force, employed	308,000
Unemployed, looking for	
Full-time work	92,000
Part-time work	NA

Unemployment rate, 2004

Total	5.2%
Men	5.6
Women	4.8
Persons 16-19 years	21.7
White	4.7
Black	11.2
Hispanic	7.2
Asian	NA

Unemployed by reason for unemployment (as a percent of total unemployment), 2002

Job losers or completed temp jobs	50.9%
Job leavers	NA
Reentrants	32.7
New entrants	NA

Labor unions, 2004

Membership	164,000
percent of employed	9.6%

Experienced civilian labor force by private industry, first quarter 2004

Total	1,412,336
Natural Resources & Mining	25,752
Construction	78,675
Manufacturing	263,268
Trade, transportation & utilities	363,020
Information	29,011
Finance	84,902
Professional & business	156,223
Education & Health	208,689
Leisure & hospitality	154,693
Other	44,856

Experienced civilian labor force by occupation, 2004

Management	80,300
Business & Financial	47,750
Legal	11,080
Sales	177,370
Office & Admin. Support	284,560
Computers & Math	23,720
Architecture & Engineering	23,550
Arts & Entertainment	15,550
Education	104,760
Social Services	20,680
Healthcare Practitioner & Technical	96,860
Healthcare support	48,200
Maintenance & Repair	79,000
Construction	83,570
Transportation & moving	153,400
Production	203,850
Farming, fishing & forestry	2,540

Hours and earnings of production workers on manufacturing payrolls, 2004

Average weekly hours	40.8
Average hourly earnings	$16.51
Average weekly earnings	$673.61

Average annual pay

2004	$33,165
change from 2003	4.1%

Household income

Median household income, three-year average, 2002-2004	$37,396

Personal income, 2004 ($ per capita)

In current dollars	$27,709
In constant (2000) dollars	$25,698

Poverty

Persons below poverty level, three-year average, 2002-2004	15.4%

Federal individual income tax returns, 2003

Returns filed	1,740,856
Adjusted gross income ($1,000)	$68,275,688
Total income tax paid ($1,000)	$7,474,532

Economy, Business, Industry & Agriculture

Fortune 500 companies, 2005 6

Patents issued, 2004 463

Bankruptcy cases filed, 2004 29,300

Business firm ownership, 2002

Women-owned........................	77,159
Sales ($ mil)	$9,451
Black-owned...........................	7,595
Sales ($ mil)	$1,091
Hispanic-owned........................	2,082
Sales ($ mil)	$783
Asian-owned	3,243
Sales ($ mil)	$1,474
Amer. Indian/Alaska Native-owned	1,324
Sales ($ mil)	$79
Hawaiian/Pacific Isl.-owned..............	NA
Sales ($ mil)	$11

Gross State Product, 2004 ($ mil)

Total Gross State Product	$136,446
Agriculture, forestry, fishing and hunting	1,838
Mining...............................	2,547
Utilities.............................	2,103
Construction	5,849
Manufacturing, durable goods........	17,397
Manufacturing, non-durable goods ...	11,311
Wholesale trade.....................	8,043
Retail trade.........................	9,529
Transportation & warehousing	6,414
Information	3,514
Finance & insurance..................	6,909
Real estate, rental, leasing	12,306
Professional and technical services.....	5,856
Educational services..................	697
Health care and social assistance......	10,484
Accommodation/food services.........	3,435
Other services, except government	2,957
Government........................	20,107

Establishments, by major industry group, 2003

Total................................	90,651
Forestry, fishing & agriculture	313
Mining...............................	641
Construction	8,998
Manufacturing........................	4,202
Wholesale trade.....................	4,583
Retail trade.........................	16,672
Transportation & warehousing	3,028
Information	1,641
Finance & insurance..................	6,087
Professional/scientific/technical	7,611
Health care/social assistance	9,789
Accommodation/food services.........	6,713

Annual payroll by major industry group, 2003

Total ($1,000)....................	$43,768,132
Forestry, fishing & agriculture	46,295
Mining.............................	811,512
Utilities............................	501,355
Construction	2,626,031
Manufacturing....................	10,091,395
Wholesale trade..................	2,668,455
Retail trade......................	4,029,569
Transportation & warehousing	2,776,816
Information	1,083,481
Finance & insurance..............	2,719,418
Professional/scientific/technical ...	2,155,301
Health care/social assistance	6,846,913
Accommodation/food services.....	1,550,387

Agriculture

Number of farms, 2004 85,000
Farm acreage, 2004

Total........................	14,000,000
Acres per farm, 2004	162

Farm income, 2003 ($mil)

Net farm income	$864
Debt/asset ratio	13.1

Farm marketings, 2003 ($mil)

Total..............................	$3,469
Crops.............................	1,243
Livestock..........................	2,226

Principal commodities, in order by marketing receipts, 2003

Horses/mules, cattle, broilers, tobacco

Federal economic activity in state

Expenditures, 2003

Total ($ mil)	$31,153
Per capita	$7,565
Defense ($ mil)...................	5,289
Non-defense ($ mil)	25,864

Defense department, 2003

Payroll ($ mil)	$2,215
Contract awards ($ mil).............	$3,897
Grants ($ mil).....................	$17
Homeland security grants ($1,000)	
2004	$45,537
2005	$31,419

FDIC insured financial institutions, 2004

Number.............................	237
Assets ($bil)	$51.5
Deposits ($bil)	56.9

Fishing, 2004

Catch (x 1,000 lbs).....................	0
Value ($1,000).......................	0

Mining, 2004 ($ mil)

Total non-fuel mineral production $674
Percent of U.S. 1.5%

Construction, 2003 ($ mil)

Total contracts (including non-building). $7,157
    residential. 3,250
    non-residential 2,139

Establishments, receipts, payroll & employees, by major industry group, 2002

Mining 1,503
    Receipts ($1,000) $30,181,037
    Annual payroll ($1,000). $1,993,512
    Paid employees 46,871

Utilities 342
    Receipts ($1,000) . . . . NA
    Annual payroll ($1,000). $529,109
    Paid employees 9,113

Construction. 8,814
    Receipts ($1,000) $12,644,444
    Annual payroll ($1,000). $2,637,092
    Paid employees 83,946

Manufacturing 4,283
    Receipts ($1,000) $88,513,497
    Annual payroll ($1,000). $10,077,029
    Paid employees 263,202

Wholesale trade 4,630
    Receipts ($1,000) $51,838,719
    Annual payroll ($1,000). $2,536,575
    Paid employees 69,192

Retail trade 16,847
    Receipts ($1,000) $40,062,561
    Annual payroll ($1,000). $3,827,629
    Paid employees 214,192

Transportation 3,040
    Receipts ($1,000) $8,249,830
    Annual payroll ($1,000). $2,017,584
    Paid employees 67,163

Information. 1,546
    Receipts ($1,000) . . . . NA
    Annual payroll ($1,000). $921,919
    Paid employees 29,450

Finance & insurance 5,841
    Receipts ($1,000) . . . . NA
    Annual payroll ($1,000). $2,584,566
    Paid employees 68,764

Professional, scientific & technical 7,503
    Receipts ($1,000) $5,190,416
    Annual payroll ($1,000). $1,998,857
    Paid employees 55,537

Health care & social assistance 9,635
    Receipts ($1,000) $16,633,446
    Annual payroll ($1,000). $6,705,258
    Paid employees 218,732

Accommodation & food service 6,660
    Receipts ($1,000) $4,908,331
    Annual payroll ($1,000). $1,397,143
    Paid employees 136,442

Communication, Energy & Transportation

Communication

Daily newspapers, 2004 23
Households with computers, 2003 . . . . .58%
Households with internet access, 2003 . . . . .50%

Energy

Electricity Consumption, 2001
Total (trillion Btu). 1,880
Per capita (million Btu) 462
By source of production (trillion Btu)
    Coal 1,011
    Natural gas 217
    Petroleum 704
    Nuclear electric power 0
    Hydroelectric power 39
By end-use sector (trillion Btu)
    Residential 339
    Commercial 246
    Industrial 846
    Transportation 449
Electric energy, 2003
    Production (billion kWh) 91.7
    Net summer capability (million kW) 19.1
Gas utilities, 2003
    Customers (x1,000). 800
    Sales (trillion Btu). 111
    Revenues ($mil). $919
Nuclear plants, 2003 0

Transportation, 2004

Public Road & Street Mileage 77,363
    Urban. 11,977
    Rural 65,386
    Interstate. 762
Vehicle miles of travel per capita 11,413.9
Total motor vehicle registrations 3,319,034
    Automobiles. 1,881,213
    Buses 14,188
    Trucks 1,423,633
    Motorcycles 53,478
Licensed drivers 2,823,454
    19 years & under 130,104
Deaths from motor vehicle accidents 964

State Summary

Capital City..................... Baton Rouge
Governor.................... Kathleen Blanco
PO Box 94004
Baton Rouge, LA 70804
225-342-0991
Admitted as a state 1812
Area (square miles) 51,840
Population, 2004 (est.) 4,515,770
Largest City...................... New Orleans
Population, 2004 462,000
Personal income per capita, 2004
(in current dollars) $27,581
Gross state product ($ mil), 2004 ...... $152,944

Leading industries by payroll, 2003

Health care/Social assistance, Manufacturing,
Retail trade

Leading agricultural commodities by receipts, 2003

Sugar cane, cotton, cattle, rice

Geography & Environment

Total area (sq. mi.).................... 51,840
land 43,562
water 8,278

Federally-owned land, 2004 (acres) ... 1,474,788
percent............................. 5.1%

Highest point............... Driskill Mountain
elevation (feet) 535

Lowest point .... New Orleans
elevation (feet) .... -8

General coastline (miles)................... 397

Tidal shoreline (miles)................... 7,721

Capital City..................... Baton Rouge
Population 2000 228,000
Population 2004 224,000

Largest City.................... New Orleans
Population 2000 485,000
Population 2004 462,000

Number of cities with over 100,000 population

1990 4
2000 4
2004 4

State park and recreation areas, 2003

Area (acres x 1,000)....................... 41
Number of visitors (x 1,000) 2,064
Revenues (x 1,000)....................... $200
percent of operating expenditures....... 1.1%

National forest system land, 2004

Acres 604,000

Demographics and Characteristics of the Population

Population

1980 4,205,900
1990 4,219,973
2000 4,468,976
2004 (estimate)................... 4,515,770
persons per sq. mile of land............ 103.7
2005 (projection).................... 4,534,310
Male 2,200,497
Female....................... 2,333,813
2010 (projection) 4,612,679
2020 (projection) 4,719,160
2030 (projection) 4,802,633
Male......................... 2,351,302
Female....................... 2,451,331

Metropolitan and Non-Metro. area population

	Metro	Non-Metro
1980	2,892,000	1,314,000
1990	2,935,000	1,285,000
2000	3,370,000	1,099,000

Change in population, 2000-2004

Number............................. 46,812
percent............................. 1.0%
Natural increase (births minus deaths).. 106,769
Net internal migration................. -74,776
Net international migration 16,680

Persons by age, 2004

Under 5 years 323,991
18 years and over 3,350,809
65 years and over 527,644
85 years and over 60,321

Persons by age, 2010 (projected)

Total............................. 4,612,679
Under 5 years 337,954
5 to 17 years 833,548
18 and over 3,441,177
21 and over 3,237,912
65 and over 582,340
85 and over 82,653
Median age 35.7

Race, 2004 (estimate)

One Race
White.......................... 2,896,096
Black or African American 1,492,298
American Indian/Alaska Native....... 27,331
Pacific Islander 1,576
Asian Indian....................... 8,390
Chinese 11,888
Filipino 2,933
Japanese 1,370
Korean 3,492
Vietnamese........................ 20,861
Two or more races.................... 36,666

Persons of Hispanic origin, 2004

Total Hispanic or Latino 118,273
  Mexican. 31,442
  Puerto Rican 5,537
  Cuban 8,752
  Other Hispanic or Latino 25,183

Marital status, 2000

Population 15 years & over 3,466,380
  Never married 991,385
  Married. 1,774,787
  Separated 90,126
  Widowed. 256,512
  Divorced 353,571

Language spoken at home, 2000

Population 5 years & over 4,153,367
  English only 3,771,003
  Spanish 105,189
  Other Indo-European languages 225,750
  Asian/Pacific Island languages. 41,963

Households & families, 2000

Households. 1,656,053
  with persons under 18 years 649,314
  with persons over 65 years. 372,354
  persons per household 2.62
Families. 1,156,438
  persons per family. 3.16
Married couples. 809,498
Female householder,
  no husband present. 275,075
One-person households 419,200

Nativity, 2000

Number of persons born in state 3,546,980
  percent of population 79.4%

Immigration & Naturalization, 2004

Immigrants admitted. 2,998
Persons naturalized 1,458
Asylums granted 7
Asylums denied 19

Vital Statistics and Health

Marriages

2002 36,543
2003 37,288
2004 36,282

Divorces

2002 14,767
2003 15,230
2004 . . . . NA

Births

2003 65,040
  Birthrate (per 1,000). 14.5
  Low birth weight (2,500g or less). 10.7%
  To unmarried mothers. 47.5%

2003, continued
  White. 37,459
  Black. 26,328
  Hispanic 1,684
  Asian/Pacific Islander 1,106
  Amer. Indian/Alaska Native 406

2004 (preliminary). 65,399
  Birthrate (per 1,000). 14.5
  White. 37,144
  Black. 26,732
  Hispanic 1,954
  Asian/Pacific Islander 1,096

Deaths

2002
All causes 41,984
  rate per 100,000. . . . . .936.6
Heart disease 11,185
  rate per 100,000. . . . . .249.5
Malignant neoplasms 9,441
  rate per 100,000. . . . . .210.6
Cerebrovascular disease. 2,595
  rate per 100,000. .57.9
Chronic lower respiratory disease 1,696
  rate per 100,000. .37.8
2003 42,893
  rate per 100,000. . . . . 954.0
2004 (provisional) 42,048

Infant deaths

2003 (provisional) 596
  rate per 1,000 . . . . .9.2
2004 (provisional) 653
  rate per 1,000 10

Abortions, 2000

Total. 13,000
  rate per 1,000 women age 15-44 . . . . .13.0

Physicians, 2003

Total. 11,904
  rate per 1,000 persons. 265

Nurses, 2001

Total. 36,690
  rate per 1,000 persons. 821

Community Hospitals, 2003

Number 127
Beds (x 1,000). 17.8
Patients admitted (x 1,000) 690
Average daily census (x 1,000) 10.6
Average cost per day $1,177
Outpatient visits (x mil) 10.8

Disability status of population, 2004

5 to 20 years 7.8%
21 to 64 years 14.6%
65 years and over 46.3%

Education

Educational attainment, 2004

Population over 25 years	2,763,102
Less than 9th grade	195,656
High school graduates only	944,854
Bachelor's degree only	397,260
Graduate or professional degree	197,709
Less than 9th grade percent	7.1%
High school graduate or more	78.7%
College graduate or more	22.4%
Graduate or professional degree	7.2%

Public school enrollment, Fall 2002

Total	730,464
Kindergarten through grade 8	536,881
Grades 9 through 12	193,583
Enrollment, 2005 (projected)	709,100

Graduating public high school seniors

2004 (estimate)	36,220

SAT scores, 2005

Average verbal score	565
Average math score	562
Percent of graduates taking test	8%

Public school teachers, 2004

Total (x 1,000)	50.4
Elementary (x 1,000)	35.3
Secondary (x 1,000)	15.1
Average salary	$37,900
Elementary	$37,900
Secondary	$37,900

State receipts & expenditures for public schools, 2004

Revenue receipts ($mil)	$5,779
Expenditures	
Total ($mil)	$6,144
Per capita	$1,367
Per pupil	$7,840

Institutions of higher education, 2004

Total	90
Public	62
Private	28

Enrollment in institutions of higher education, Fall, 2003

Total	252,063
Full-time men	74,749
Full-time women	108,609
Part-time men	24,595
Part-time women	44,110

Minority enrollment in institutions of higher education, Fall, 2003

Black, non-hispanic	71,115
Hispanic	5,359
Asian/Pacific Islander	4,886
American Indian/Alaska Native	1,493

Earned degrees conferred, 2003

Bachelor's	21,182
Master's	5,813
First-professional	1,592
Doctor's	491

State & local financial support for higher education, 2003-2004

Full-time equivalent enrollment (x 1,000)	183.3
Appropriations per FTE	$5,037
as a percent of tax revenue	8.7%

Social Insurance & Welfare Programs

Social Security benefits & beneficiaries, 2004

Beneficiaries	
Total	739,000
Retired & dependents	440,000
Survivors	148,000
Disabled & dependents	151,000
Annual benefit payments ($ mil)	
Total	$7,121
Retired & dependents	$3,960
Survivors	$1,759
Disabled & dependents	$1,403
Average Monthly Benefit	
Retired & dependents	$888
Disabled & dependents	$887
Widowed	$846

Medicare

Enrollment, 2001 (x 1,000)	605
Payments ($ mil, est.)	$4,900
Enrollment, 2003 (x 1,000)	620

Medicaid, 2002

Beneficiaries (x 1,000)	899
Payments ($ mil)	$3,234

State Children's Health Insurance, 2004

Enrollment (x 1,000)	105.6
Expenditures ($ mil)	$94.4

Persons without health insurance, 2003

Number (x 1,000)	912
percent	20.6%
Number of children (x 1,000)	182
percent of children	15.2%

Federal public aid

Temporary Assistance for Needy Families, 2004	
Recipients (x 1,000)	46
Families (x 1,000)	19
Supplemental Security Income, 2003	
Recipients (x 1,000)	168
Payments ($ mil)	$769

Food Stamp Program, 2004

Participants (x 1,000)	706
Benefits ($ mil)	$754

4   Louisiana

Housing & Construction

Housing units

Total 2003 (estimate)	1,898,992
Total 2004 (estimate)	1,919,859
Seasonal or recreational use, 2003	25,000
Owner-occupied single-family, 2003	892,000
Median value	$99,215
Renter-occupied, 2003	546,000
Median rent	$525
Homeownership rate, 2003	67.5%
Homeownership rate, 2004	70.6%

New privately owned housing units, 2004

Number authorized (x 1,000)	23.0
Value ($ mil)	$2,626
Started 2005 (x 1,000, estimate)	18.0
Started 2006 (x 1,000, estimate)	17.7

Existing home sales

2002 (x 1,000)	71.7
2003 (x 1,000)	76.2
2004 (x 1,000)	79.6

Government & Elections

State Officials 2006

Governor (name/party/term expires)
Kathleen Blanco
Democrat - 1/08

Lieutenant Governor	Mitch Landrieu
Secretary of State	Al Ater
Attorney General	Charles C. Foti Jr.
Chief Justice	Pascal Calagero Jr.

Governorship

Minimum age	25
Length of term	4 years
Consecutive terms permitted	2
Who succeeds	Lt. Governor

State Legislature

Name	Legislature
Upper chamber	Senate
Number of members	39
Length of term	4 years
Party in majority, 2006	Democratic
Lower chamber	House of Representatives
Number of members	105
Length of term	4 years
Party in majority, 2006	Democratic

State Government Employees, 2004

Total	90,600
Payroll	$289,111,367

Local Government Employees, 2004

Total	191,711
Payroll	$482,714,562

Local Governments by Type, 2002

Total	473
County	60
Municipal	302
Township	0
School District	66
Special District	45

Voting age population, November 2004

Total	3,277,000
Male	1,528,000
Female	1,749,000
White	2,260,000
Black	976,000
Hispanic	68,000
Asian	8,000

Presidential Election, 2004

Total Popular Vote	1,943,106
Kerry	820,299
Bush	1,102,169
Total Electoral Votes	9

Federal representation, 2006 (109th Congress)

Senator	Mary Landrieu
Party	Democrat
Year term expires	2009
Senator	David Vitter
Party	Republican
Year term expires	2011
Representatives, total	7
Democrats	2
Republicans	5
Other	0

Votes cast for US Senators

2002

Total vote (x 1,000)	1,235,000
Leading party	Democratic
Percent for leading party	51.7%

2004

Total vote (x 1,000)	1,848,000
Leading party	Republican
Percent for leading party	51.0%

Votes cast for US Representatives

2002

Total vote (x 1,000)	1,140
Democratic	391
Republican	668
Leading party	Republican
Percent for leading party	58.6%

2004

Total vote (x 1,000)	1,259
Democratic	478
Republican	780
Leading party	Republican
Percent for leading party	62.0%

Women holding public office, 2006

US Congress 1
Statewide elected office..................... 1
State legislature 24

Black public officials, 2001

Total..................................... 705
   US and state legislatures 32
   City/county/regional offices 388
   Judicial/law enforcement................ 122
   Education/school boards 163

Hispanic public officials, 2004

Total..................................... 2
   State executives & legislators 0
   City/county/regional offices 0
   Judicial/law enforcement.................. 2
   Education/school boards 0

Governmental Finance

State government revenues, 2004

Total revenue ($1,000) $23,730,239
   Revenue per capita 5,265.20

General Revenue ($ per capita) $4,250.31
   Intergovernmental 1,552.23
   Taxes 1,781.78
      general sales 594.79
      individual income tax............. 486.36
      corporate income tax 52.53
   Current charges.................... 530.47
   Miscellaneous 385.83

State government expenditure, 2004

Total expenditure (x $1,000) $20,471,959
   Expenditure per capita............ 4,542.26
General Expenditure ($ per capita).... $3,995.50
   Education 1,427.53
   Public welfare...................... 914.67
   Health 104.70
   Hospitals.......................... 365.71
   Highways 252.55
   Police protection.................... 57.49
   Correction 135.06
   Natural resources 87.99
   Parks & recreation.................... 47.57
   Governmental administration 149.16
   Interest on general debt 150.75

State debt & cash, 2004 ($ per capita)

Debt $2,259.36
Cash/security holdings.............. $9,568.67

Federal government grants to state & local government, 2004 (x $1,000)

Total............................. $7,786,693
By Federal Agency
   Defense $111,676

By Federal Agency, continued
   Education 711,018
   Energy 9,852
   Environmental Protection Agency 58,652
   Health & Human Services. 4,790,508
   Homeland Security.................. 38,236
   Housing & Urban Development...... 486,638
   Justice 117,022
   Labor 105,195
   Transportation 623,269
   Veterans Affairs.................... 30,395

Crime, Law Enforcement & Courts

Crime, 2004 (rates per 100,000 residents)

Property crimes 199,153
   Burglaries........................ 45,359
   Larcenies......................... 134,080
   Motor vehicle thefts 19,714
   Property crime rate................ 4,410.2
Violent crimes........................ 28,844
   Murders 574
   Forcible rape....................... 1,616
   Robberies 6,564
   Aggravated assaults 20,090
   Violent crime rate 638.7

Police Agencies, 2004

Total agencies............................ 199
Total employees 21,439
   Male officers 13,477
   Female officers 3,086
   Male civilians...................... 1,307
   Female civilians.................... 3,569

Arrests, 2004

Total................................. 232,704
   Persons under 18 years of age 35,055

Prisoners under state & federal jurisdiction, 2004

Total prisoners....................... 36,939
   Percent change, 12/31/03 to 12/31/04 .... 2.5%
Sentenced to more than one year 36,939
   rate per 100,000....................... 816

Persons under sentence of death, 7/1/05

Total..................................... 89
   White................................. 29
   Black 57
   Hispanic 2

State's highest court

Name ....Supreme Court
Number of members........................ 7
Length of term .... 10 years
Intermediate appeals court? ....yes

Labor & Income

Civilian labor force, 2004

Total 2,058,000
  Men 1,075,000
  Women 982,000
  Persons 16-19 years 90,000
  White 1,434,000
  Black 594,000
  Hispanic 48,000
  Asian 0

Civilian labor force as a percent of civilian non-institutional population, 2004

Total 60.9%
  Men 67.7
  Women 54.9
  Persons 16-19 years 34.2
  White 62.2
  Black 58.5
  Hispanic 69.7
  Asian 0.0

Employment, 2004

Total 1,934,000
  Men 1,008,000
  Women 926,000
  Persons 16-19 years 71,000
  White 1,372,000
  Black 533,000
  Hispanic 46,000
  Asian 0

Full-time/part-time labor force, 2002

Full-time labor force, employed 1,606,000
Part-time labor force, employed 277,000
Unemployed, looking for
  Full-time work 110,000
  Part-time work .... NA

Unemployment rate, 2004

Total 6.0%
  Men 6.3
  Women 5.7
  Persons 16-19 years 21.2
  White 4.4
  Black 10.3
  Hispanic 5.6
  Asian .... NA

Unemployed by reason for unemployment (as a percent of total unemployment), 2002

Job losers or completed temp jobs 43.9%
Job leavers .... NA
Reentrants 34.1
New entrants .... NA

Labor unions, 2004

Membership 129,000
  percent of employed 7.6%

Experienced civilian labor force by private industry, first quarter 2004

Total 1,495,713
  Natural Resources & Mining 53,456
  Construction 120,048
  Manufacturing 151,838
  Trade, transportation & utilities 375,132
  Information 29,265
  Finance 97,149
  Professional & business 184,848
  Education & Health 229,921
  Leisure & hospitality 201,475
  Other 50,483

Experienced civilian labor force by occupation, 2004

Management 94,820
Business & Financial 54,380
Legal 14,030
Sales 195,800
Office & Admin. Support 310,900
Computers & Math 19,660
Architecture & Engineering 27,920
Arts & Entertainment 17,950
Education 110,000
Social Services 24,170
Healthcare Practitioner & Technical 108,200
Healthcare support 53,060
Maintenance & Repair 92,980
Construction 111,710
Transportation & moving 152,820
Production 124,520
Farming, fishing & forestry 2,360

Hours and earnings of production workers on manufacturing payrolls, 2004

Average weekly hours 43.9
Average hourly earnings $16.40
Average weekly earnings $719.96

Average annual pay

2004 .... $31,880
  change from 2003 .... 3.5%

Household income

Median household income, three-year average,
  2002-2004 .... $35,523

Personal income, 2004 ($ per capita)

In current dollars $27,581
In constant (2000) dollars $25,580

Poverty

Persons below poverty level, three-year average,
  2002-2004 .... 17.0%

Federal individual income tax returns, 2003

Returns filed 1,879,651
Adjusted gross income ($1,000) $70,865,204
Total income tax paid ($1,000) $8,050,240

Economy, Business, Industry & Agriculture

Fortune 500 companies, 2005 1

Patents issued, 2004 387

Bankruptcy cases filed, 2004 30,200

Business firm ownership, 2002

Women-owned.	86,876
Sales ($ mil)	$12,253
Black-owned.	40,252
Sales ($ mil)	$1,995
Hispanic-owned.	7,646
Sales ($ mil)	$1,947
Asian-owned	8,224
Sales ($ mil)	$1,820
Amer. Indian/Alaska Native-owned	2,707
Sales ($ mil)	$283
Hawaiian/Pacific Isl.-owned	NA
Sales ($ mil)	NA

Gross State Product, 2004 ($ mil)

Total Gross State Product	$152,944
Agriculture, forestry, fishing and hunting	1,356
Mining.	19,669
Utilities	4,492
Construction	6,554
Manufacturing, durable goods.	5,089
Manufacturing, non-durable goods . . .	11,014
Wholesale trade.	7,854
Retail trade.	10,768
Transportation & warehousing	5,649
Information	4,043
Finance & insurance.	6,066
Real estate, rental, leasing	15,354
Professional and technical services	7,003
Educational services.	1,140
Health care and social assistance	10,555
Accommodation/food services.	4,620
Other services, except government	3,705
Government	19,839

Establishments, by major industry group, 2003

Total.	102,245
Forestry, fishing & agriculture	748
Mining.	1,411
Construction	8,305
Manufacturing.	3,459
Wholesale trade.	5,763
Retail trade.	17,671
Transportation & warehousing	3,733
Information	1,499
Finance & insurance.	7,422
Professional/scientific/technical	10,895
Health care/social assistance	10,923
Accommodation/food services.	7,720

Annual payroll by major industry group, 2003

Total ($1,000)	$47,137,015
Forestry, fishing & agriculture	129,381
Mining.	2,507,323
Utilities	772,432
Construction	4,062,760
Manufacturing.	6,591,992
Wholesale trade.	2,697,344
Retail trade.	4,326,189
Transportation & warehousing	2,347,667
Information	1,229,446
Finance & insurance.	2,715,998
Professional/scientific/technical . . .	3,143,300
Health care/social assistance	7,368,696
Accommodation/food services.	2,132,160

Agriculture

Number of farms, 2004 27,000
Farm acreage, 2004

Total.	8,000,000
Acres per farm, 2004	289

Farm income, 2003 ($mil)

Net farm income	$711
Debt/asset ratio	15.3

Farm marketings, 2003 ($mil)

Total.	$1,993
Crops	1,296
Livestock.	697

Principal commodities, in order by marketing receipts, 2003

Sugar cane, cotton, cattle, rice

Federal economic activity in state

Expenditures, 2003

Total ($ mil)	$31,646
Per capita	$7,038
Defense ($ mil).	3,605
Non-defense ($ mil)	28,042

Defense department, 2003

Payroll ($ mil)	$1,647
Contract awards ($ mil)	$1,914
Grants ($ mil).	$80
Homeland security grants ($1,000)	
2004	$76,005
2005	$42,670

FDIC insured financial institutions, 2004

Number	166
Assets ($bil)	$59.8
Deposits ($bil)	55.2

Fishing, 2004

Catch (x 1,000 lbs)	1,095,821
Value ($1,000).	$274,419

Mining, 2004 ($ mil)

Total non-fuel mineral production $364
Percent of U.S. 0.8%

Construction, 2003 ($ mil)

Total contracts (including non-building). $6,541
   residential 2,895
   non-residential 2,080

**Establishments, receipts, payroll & employees,
by major industry group, 2002**

Mining 33
   Receipts ($1,000) . . . . NA
   Annual payroll ($1,000) . . . . NA
   Paid employees . . . . (100-249)
Utilities 566
   Receipts ($1,000) . . . . NA
   Annual payroll ($1,000) $706,341
   Paid employees 11,899
Construction 7,986
   Receipts ($1,000) $15,288,176
   Annual payroll ($1,000) $4,008,618
   Paid employees 123,766
Manufacturing 3,524
   Receipts ($1,000) $89,540,799
   Annual payroll ($1,000) $6,427,378
   Paid employees 150,401
Wholesale trade 5,904
   Receipts ($1,000) $47,192,153
   Annual payroll ($1,000) $2,676,924
   Paid employees 73,548
Retail trade 17,613
   Receipts ($1,000) $41,885,192
   Annual payroll ($1,000) $4,069,984
   Paid employees 228,290
Transportation 3,642
   Receipts ($1,000) $7,847,325
   Annual payroll ($1,000) $2,228,474
   Paid employees 64,409
Information 1,426
   Receipts ($1,000) . . . . NA
   Annual payroll ($1,000) $1,097,832
   Paid employees 31,405
Finance & insurance 7,170
   Receipts ($1,000) . . . . NA
   Annual payroll ($1,000) $2,554,625
   Paid employees 65,103
Professional, scientific & technical 10,718
   Receipts ($1,000) $8,243,267
   Annual payroll ($1,000) $2,993,298
   Paid employees 79,983

Health care & social assistance 10,708
   Receipts ($1,000) $18,169,655
   Annual payroll ($1,000) $6,956,703
   Paid employees 244,912
Accommodation & food service 7,535
   Receipts ($1,000) $7,411,702
   Annual payroll ($1,000) $2,034,265
   Paid employees 170,158

Communication, Energy & Transportation

Communication

Daily newspapers, 2004 26
Households with computers, 2003 . . . . .52%
Households with internet access, 2003 . . . . . .44%

Energy

Electricity Consumption, 2001
Total (trillion Btu) 3,500
Per capita (million Btu) 784
By source of production (trillion Btu)
   Coal 240
   Natural gas 1,340
   Petroleum 1,491
   Nuclear electric power 181
   Hydroelectric power 7
By end-use sector (trillion Btu)
   Residential 348
   Commercial 264
   Industrial 2,135
   Transportation 753
Electric energy, 2003
   Production (billion kWh) 94.9
   Net summer capability (million kW) 25.7
Gas utilities, 2003
   Customers (x1,000) 1,023
   Sales (trillion Btu) 185
   Revenues ($mil) $1,290
Nuclear plants, 2003 2

Transportation, 2004

Public Road & Street Mileage 60,942
   Urban 14,814
   Rural 46,128
   Interstate 903
Vehicle miles of travel per capita 9,728.9
Total motor vehicle registrations 3,766,793
   Automobiles 1,973,399
   Buses 21,889
   Trucks 1,771,505
   Motorcycles 55,846
Licensed drivers 3,169,627
   19 years & under 116,298
Deaths from motor vehicle accidents 904

State Summary

Capital City......................Augusta
Governor.....................John Baldacci
#1 State House Station
Augusta, ME 04333
207-287-3531
Admitted as a state 1820
Area (square miles) 35,385
Population, 2004 (est.) 1,317,253
Largest City....................... Portland
Population, 2004.................... 63,905
Personal income per capita, 2004
(in current dollars) $30,566
Gross state product ($ mil), 2004 ...... $43,336

Leading industries by payroll, 2003

Health care/Social assistance, Manufacturing,
Retail trade

Leading agricultural commodities by receipts, 2003

Potatoes, dairy products, chicken eggs, aquaculture

Geography & Environment

Total area (sq. mi.)................... 35,385
land 30,862
water 4,523
Federally-owned land, 2004 (acres) 208,422
percent............................ 1.1%
Highest point................ Mount Katahdin
elevation (feet) 5,267
Lowest point ....Atlantic Ocean
elevation (feet) .... sea level
General coastline (miles)................ 228
Tidal shoreline (miles)................ 3,478
Capital City....................... Augusta
Population 2000 18,560
Population 2004 18,631
Largest City....................... Portland
Population 2000 64,249
Population 2004 63,905

Number of cities with over 100,000 population

1990 0
2000 0
2004 0

State park and recreation areas, 2003

Area (acres x 1,000)...................... 99
Number of visitors (x 1,000) 2,542
Revenues (x 1,000).........................
percent of operating expenditures........ NA

National forest system land, 2004

Acres 53,000

Demographics and Characteristics of the Population

Population

1980 1,124,660
1990 1,227,928
2000 1,274,923
2004 (estimate)................... 1,317,253
persons per sq. mile of land.............42.7
2005 (projection)................. 1,318,557
Male.............................. 642,021
Female............................ 676,536
2010 (projection) 1,357,134
2020 (projection) 1,408,665
2030 (projection) 1,411,097
Male.............................. 679,419
Female............................ 731,678

Metropolitan and Non-Metro. area population

	Metro	Non-Metro
1980	404,000	720,000
1990	441,000	787,000
2000	467,000	808,000

Change in population, 2000-2004

Number 42,330
percent............................. 3.3%
Natural increase (births minus deaths).... 4,338
Net internal migration 34,356
Net international migration 4,182

Persons by age, 2004

Under 5 years 67,628
18 years and over 1,035,124
65 years and over 189,751
85 years and over 25,091

Persons by age, 2010 (projected)

Total............................. 1,357,134
Under 5 years 72,829
5 to 17 years 196,403
18 and over 1,087,902
21 and over 1,039,586
65 and over 212,278
85 and over 32,770
Median age 42.2

Race, 2004 (estimate)

One Race
White........................... 1,277,026
Black or African American 9,560
American Indian/Alaska Native........ 7,454
Pacific Islander 459
Asian Indian....................... 1,452
Chinese 1,077
Filipino 2,155
Japanese 1,106
Korean............................ 451
Vietnamese......................... 527
Two or more races..................... 11,900

Persons of Hispanic origin, 2004

Total Hispanic or Latino	11,419
Mexican	3,071
Puerto Rican	3,112
Cuban	624
Other Hispanic or Latino	1,124

Marital status, 2000

Population 15 years & over	1,028,823
Never married	245,889
Married	579,227
Separated	12,346
Widowed	73,046
Divorced	118,315

Language spoken at home, 2000

Population 5 years & over	1,204,164
English only	1,110,198
Spanish	9,611
Other Indo-European languages	76,079
Asian/Pacific Island languages	5,737

Households & families, 2000

Households	518,200
with persons under 18 years	167,685
with persons over 65 years	128,137
persons per household	2.39
Families	340,685
persons per family	2.9
Married couples	272,152
Female householder, no husband present	49,022
One-person households	139,969

Nativity, 2000

Number of persons born in state	857,515
percent of population	67.3%

Immigration & Naturalization, 2004

Immigrants admitted	1,264
Persons naturalized	548
Asylums granted	13
Asylums denied	0

Vital Statistics and Health

Marriages

2002	10,887
2003	11,005
2004	11,234

Divorces

2002	5,937
2003	5,776
2004	5,677

Births

2003	13,855
Birthrate (per 1,000)	10.6
Low birth weight (2,500g or less)	6.5%
To unmarried mothers	33.5%

2003, continued

White	13,371
Black	184
Hispanic	167
Asian/Pacific Islander	208
Amer. Indian/Alaska Native	98
2004 (preliminary)	13,945
Birthrate (per 1,000)	10.6
White	13,382
Black	225
Hispanic	180
Asian/Pacific Islander	222

Deaths

2002

All causes	12,694
rate per 100,000	980.6
Heart disease	3,170
rate per 100,000	244.9
Malignant neoplasms	3,206
rate per 100,000	247.7
Cerebrovascular disease	823
rate per 100,000	63.6
Chronic lower respiratory disease	791
rate per 100,000	61.1
2003	12,534
rate per 100,000	959.9
2004 (provisional)	12,372

Infant deaths

2003 (provisional)	64
rate per 1,000	4.6
2004 (provisional)	81
rate per 1,000	5.8

Abortions, 2000

Total	3,000
rate per 1,000 women age 15-44	9.9

Physicians, 2003

Total	3,485
rate per 1,000 persons	267

Nurses, 2001

Total	13,390
rate per 1,000 persons	1,043

Community Hospitals, 2003

Number	37
Beds (x 1,000)	3.7
Patients admitted (x 1,000)	149
Average daily census (x 1,000)	2.2
Average cost per day	$1,416
Outpatient visits (x mil)	3.9

Disability status of population, 2004

5 to 20 years	10.4%
21 to 64 years	15.3%
65 years and over	37.8%

Education

Educational attainment, 2004

Population over 25 years 888,030
Less than 9th grade 36,040
High school graduates only......... 319,933
Bachelor's degree only 158,939
Graduate or professional degree....... 72,735
Less than 9th grade percent 4.1%
High school graduate or more 87.1%
College graduate or more............. 24.2%
Graduate or professional degree........ 8.2%

Public school enrollment, Fall 2002

Total.............................. 204,337
Kindergarten through grade 8 141,785
Grades 9 through 12................. 62,552
Enrollment, 2005 (projected) 192,500

Graduating public high school seniors

2004 (estimate)...................... 13,380

SAT scores, 2005

Average verbal score 509
Average math score 505
Percent of graduates taking test 75%

Public school teachers, 2004

Total (x 1,000) 15.7
Elementary (x 1,000)................. 10.7
Secondary (x 1,000) 5.0
Average salary $39,900
Elementary....................... $39,800
Secondary........................ $40,000

State receipts & expenditures for public schools, 2004

Revenue receipts ($mil)................ $2,132
Expenditures
Total ($mil)......................... $2,247
Per capita $1,716
Per pupil $10,961

Institutions of higher education, 2004

Total................................. 30
Public............................... 15
Private.............................. 15

Enrollment in institutions of higher education, Fall, 2003

Total................................ 65,107
Full-time men 17,519
Full-time women................... 22,127
Part-time men 7,956
Part-time women................... 17,505

Minority enrollment in institutions of higher education, Fall, 2003

Black, non-hispanic...................... 730
Hispanic 572
Asian/Pacific Islander 818
American Indian/Alaska Native........... 840

Earned degrees conferred, 2003

Bachelor's 6,158
Master's 1,349
First-professional..................... 172
Doctor's.............................. 56

State & local financial support for higher education, 2003-2004

Full-time equivalent enrollment (x 1,000) ...34.5
Appropriations per FTE................ $5,900
as a percent of tax revenue............. 5.2%

Social Insurance & Welfare Programs

Social Security benefits & beneficiaries, 2004

Beneficiaries
Total............................. 265,000
Retired & dependents.............. 175,000
Survivors......................... 33,000
Disabled & dependents............. 57,000
Annual benefit payments ($ mil)
Total............................. $2,548
Retired & dependents.............. $1,617
Survivors......................... $425
Disabled & dependents............. $506
Average Monthly Benefit
Retired & dependents.............. $882
Disabled & dependents............. $819
Widowed........................ $875

Medicare

Enrollment, 2001 (x 1,000) 219
Payments ($ mil, est.) $900
Enrollment, 2003 (x 1,000) 227

Medicaid, 2002

Beneficiaries (x 1,000)................. 276
Payments ($ mil) $1,717

State Children's Health Insurance, 2004

Enrollment (x 1,000)................... 29.2
Expenditures ($ mil)................. $25.2

Persons without health insurance, 2003

Number (x 1,000)...................... 133
percent........................... 10.4%
Number of children (x 1,000) 17
percent of children 6.0%

Federal public aid

Temporary Assistance for Needy Families, 2004
Recipients (x 1,000)..................... 27
Families (x 1,000) 10

Supplemental Security Income, 2003
Recipients (x 1,000)..................... 31
Payments ($ mil) $136

Food Stamp Program, 2004

Participants (x 1,000) 142
Benefits ($ mil)........................ $140

4   Maine

Housing & Construction

Housing units

Total 2003 (estimate) 669,928
Total 2004 (estimate) 676,667
Seasonal or recreational use, 2003 102,000
Owner-occupied single-family, 2003.... 267,000
    Median value $134,846
Renter-occupied, 2003 154,000
    Median rent $562
Homeownership rate, 2003 .... 73.7%
Homeownership rate, 2004 .... 74.7%

New privately owned housing units, 2004

Number authorized (x 1,000) 8.8
Value ($ mil) $1,249
Started 2005 (x 1,000, estimate) 6.8
Started 2006 (x 1,000, estimate) 6.5

Existing home sales

2002 (x 1,000) 28.8
2003 (x 1,000) 30.7
2004 (x 1,000) 33.6

Government & Elections

State Officials 2006

Governor (name/party/term expires)
John Baldacci
Democrat - 1/07
Lieutenant Governor........... Beth Edmonds
Secretary of State.............. Mathew Dunlap
Attorney General................. Steve Rowe
Chief Justice .... Leigh Saufley

Governorship

Minimum age........................... 30
Length of term .... 4 years
Consecutive terms permitted 2
Who succeeds.............. Pres. of the Senate

State Legislature

Name .... Legislature
Upper chamber ....Senate
    Number of members.................... 35
    Length of term.................... 2 years
    Party in majority, 2006 ....Democratic
Lower chamber.......House of Representatives
    Number of members................... 151
    Length of term................... 2 years
    Party in majority, 2006 ....Democratic

State Government Employees, 2004

Total................................. 21,720
Payroll $74,918,521

Local Government Employees, 2004

Total................................. 55,335
Payroll $149,271,376

Local Governments by Type, 2002

Total................................... 826
    County................................ 16
    Municipal 22
    Township 467
    School District....................... 99
    Special District 222

Voting age population, November 2004

Total............................. 1,022,000
    Male............................. 493,000
    Female 529,000
    White............................. 990,000
    Black 8,000
    Hispanic 9,000
    Asian 9,000

Presidential Election, 2004

Total Popular Vote 740,752
    Kerry 396,842
    Bush.............................. 330,201
Total Electoral Votes....................... 4

Federal representation, 2006 (109th Congress)

Senator..................... Olympia Snowe
    Party .... Republican
    Year term expires 2007
Senator...................... Susan Collins
    Party .... Republican
    Year term expires 2009
Representatives, total 2
    Democrats........................... 2
    Republicans 0
    Other 0

Votes cast for US Senators

2002
Total vote (x 1,000) 505,000
Leading party..................... Republican
Percent for leading party 58.4%

2004
Total vote (x 1,000) .... NA
Leading party........................... NA
Percent for leading party .... NA

Votes cast for US Representatives

2002
Total vote (x 1,000) 495
    Democratic........................... 290
    Republican 206
Leading party................... Democratic
Percent for leading party 58.5%

2004
Total vote (x 1,000) 710
    Democratic........................... 418
    Republican 283
Leading party................... Democratic
Percent for leading party 58.9%

Women holding public office, 2006

US Congress 2
Statewide elected office..................... 0
State legislature 43

Black public officials, 2001

Total..................................... 1
   US and state legislatures 0
   City/county/regional offices 0
   Judicial/law enforcement.................. 0
   Education/school boards 1

Hispanic public officials, 2004

Total..................................... 0
   State executives & legislators 0
   City/county/regional offices 0
   Judicial/law enforcement.................. 0
   Education/school boards 0

Governmental Finance

State government revenues, 2004

Total revenue ($1,000) $8,309,930
   Revenue per capita 6,319.34

General Revenue ($ per capita) $5,167.56
   Intergovernmental 1,957.06
   Taxes 2,202.86
      general sales 697.53
      individual income tax............. 882.15
      corporate income tax 84.88
   Current charges..................... 408.48
   Miscellaneous 599.17

State government expenditure, 2004

Total expenditure (x $1,000) $7,322,061
   Expenditure per capita............... 5,568.11
General Expenditure ($ per capita).... $5,073.12
   Education 1,257.49
   Public welfare..................... 1,738.69
   Health 332.43
   Hospitals......................... 41.46
   Highways 408.20
   Police protection 47.03
   Correction 85.23
   Natural resources 142.12
   Parks & recreation.................... 8.54
   Governmental administration 195.26
   Interest on general debt 191.66

State debt & cash, 2004 ($ per capita)

Debt $3,531.55
Cash/security holdings............. $10,610.21

Federal government grants to state & local government, 2004 (x $1,000)

Total............................ $2,757,942
By Federal Agency
   Defense $46,174

By Federal Agency, continued
   Education 174,385
   Energy 5,793
   Environmental Protection Agency 37,581
   Health & Human Services. 1,806,184
   Homeland Security.................. 14,378
   Housing & Urban Development...... 187,212
   Justice 49,389
   Labor 54,097
   Transportation 203,945
   Veterans Affairs.................... 7,618

Crime, Law Enforcement & Courts

Crime, 2004 (rates per 100,000 residents)

Property crimes 31,740
   Burglaries......................... 6,341
   Larcenies......................... 24,096
   Motor vehicle thefts 1,303
   Property crime rate................. 2,409.6
Violent crimes...................... 1,364
   Murders 18
   Forcible rape....................... 315
   Robberies 289
   Aggravated assaults 742
   Violent crime rate 103.5

Police Agencies, 2004

Total agencies........................... 131
Total employees 2,892
   Male officers....................... 2,060
   Female officers..................... 134
   Male civilians...................... 304
   Female civilians..................... 394

Arrests, 2004

Total................................. 55,345
   Persons under 18 years of age 8,580

Prisoners under state & federal jurisdiction, 2004

Total prisoners........................ 2,024
   Percent change, 12/31/03 to 12/31/04 .... 0.5%
Sentenced to more than one year 1,961
   rate per 100,000...................... 148

Persons under sentence of death, 7/1/05

Total..................................... 0
   White..................................... 0
   Black 0
   Hispanic 0

State's highest court

Name ....Supreme Court
Number of members........................ 7
Length of term .... 7 years
Intermediate appeals court? .... no

Labor & Income

Civilian labor force, 2004

Total	696,000
Men	362,000
Women	334,000
Persons 16-19 years	36,000
White	674,000
Black	0
Hispanic	0
Asian	0

Civilian labor force as a percent of civilian non-institutional population, 2004

Total	66.0%
Men	71.4
Women	61.0
Persons 16-19 years	51.3
White	66.3
Black	0.0
Hispanic	0.0
Asian	0.0

Employment, 2004

Total	664,000
Men	344,000
Women	320,000
Persons 16-19 years	31,000
White	644,000
Black	0
Hispanic	0
Asian	0

Full-time/part-time labor force, 2002

Full-time labor force, employed	516,000
Part-time labor force, employed	141,000
Unemployed, looking for	
Full-time work	24,000
Part-time work	NA

Unemployment rate, 2004

Total	4.7%
Men	5.1
Women	4.2
Persons 16-19 years	13.9
White	4.6
Black	NA
Hispanic	NA
Asian	NA

Unemployed by reason for unemployment (as a percent of total unemployment), 2002

Job losers or completed temp jobs	53.3%
Job leavers	NA
Reentrants	NA
New entrants	NA

Labor unions, 2004

Membership	64,000
percent of employed	11.3%

Experienced civilian labor force by private industry, first quarter 2004

Total	473,994
Natural Resources & Mining	5,079
Construction	28,306
Manufacturing	62,010
Trade, transportation & utilities	118,937
Information	10,961
Finance	33,573
Professional & business	48,457
Education & Health	101,473
Leisure & hospitality	48,953
Other	16,185

Experienced civilian labor force by occupation, 2004

Management	32,980
Business & Financial	19,210
Legal	3,470
Sales	59,660
Office & Admin. Support	101,030
Computers & Math	7,270
Architecture & Engineering	9,210
Arts & Entertainment	6,040
Education	42,770
Social Services	13,510
Healthcare Practitioner & Technical	34,220
Healthcare support	18,540
Maintenance & Repair	25,600
Construction	30,910
Transportation & moving	43,130
Production	42,640
Farming, fishing & forestry	2,350

Hours and earnings of production workers on manufacturing payrolls, 2004

Average weekly hours	39.6
Average hourly earnings	$16.97
Average weekly earnings	$672.01

Average annual pay

2004	$31,906
change from 2003	3.9%

Household income

Median household income, three-year average, 2002-2004	$39,395

Personal income, 2004 ($ per capita)

In current dollars	$30,566
In constant (2000) dollars	$28,348

Poverty

Persons below poverty level, three-year average, 2002-2004	12.2%

Federal individual income tax returns, 2003

Returns filed	615,092
Adjusted gross income ($1,000)	$24,727,190
Total income tax paid ($1,000)	$2,719,153

Economy, Business, Industry & Agriculture

Fortune 500 companies, 2005 0

Patents issued, 2004 138

Bankruptcy cases filed, 2004 4,600

Business firm ownership, 2002

Women-owned. 32,512
   Sales ($ mil) $3,282
Black-owned. 328
   Sales ($ mil) $33
Hispanic-owned. 730
   Sales ($ mil) $81
Asian-owned 835
   Sales ($ mil) $283
Amer. Indian/Alaska Native-owned 680
   Sales ($ mil) $47
Hawaiian/Pacific Isl.-owned . . . . NA
   Sales ($ mil) . . . . NA

Gross State Product, 2004 ($ mil)

Total Gross State Product $43,336
   Agriculture, forestry, fishing and
     hunting 575
   Mining. 5
   Utilities 941
   Construction 2,021
   Manufacturing, durable goods. 2,612
   Manufacturing, non-durable goods 2,565
   Wholesale trade. 2,303
   Retail trade. 4,073
   Transportation & warehousing 1,031
   Information 1,272
   Finance & insurance. 2,991
   Real estate, rental, leasing 5,821
   Professional and technical services 1,943
   Educational services 396
   Health care and social assistance 4,554
   Accommodation/food services 1,329
   Other services, except government 970
   Government 6,159

Establishments, by major industry group, 2003

Total. 40,701
   Forestry, fishing & agriculture 780
   Mining. 30
   Construction 5,076
   Manufacturing. 1,857
   Wholesale trade. 1,690
   Retail trade. 7,019
   Transportation & warehousing 1,269
   Information 765
   Finance & insurance. 1,825
   Professional/scientific/technical 3,355
   Health care/social assistance 4,496
   Accommodation/food services. 3,811

Annual payroll by major industry group, 2003

Total ($1,000) $14,790,889
   Forestry, fishing & agriculture 103,481
   Mining. . . . . NA
   Utilities 141,668
   Construction 957,263
   Manufacturing. 2,559,924
   Wholesale trade. 714,284
   Retail trade. 1,685,470
   Transportation & warehousing 408,933
   Information 463,473
   Finance & insurance. 1,245,511
   Professional/scientific/technical 889,028
   Health care/social assistance 2,906,230
   Accommodation/food services. 666,380

Agriculture

Number of farms, 2004 7,000
Farm acreage, 2004
   Total. 1,000,000
   Acres per farm, 2004 190
Farm income, 2003 ($mil)
   Net farm income $84
   Debt/asset ratio 19.1
Farm marketings, 2003 ($mil)
Total. $499
   Crops 227
   Livestock 272

Principal commodities, in order by marketing receipts, 2003

Potatoes, dairy products, chicken eggs, aquaculture

Federal economic activity in state

Expenditures, 2003
   Total ($ mil) $9,966
   Per capita $7,632
   Defense ($ mil). 1,813
   Non-defense ($ mil) 8,152
Defense department, 2003
   Payroll ($ mil) $692
   Contract awards ($ mil) $1,182
   Grants ($ mil). $20
   Homeland security grants ($1,000)
     2004 . . . . $23,776
     2005 . . . . $16,609

FDIC insured financial institutions, 2004

Number 39
   Assets ($bil) $43.0
   Deposits ($bil) 16.7

Fishing, 2004

Catch (x 1,000 lbs) 208,405
Value ($1,000). $315,766

Mining, 2004 ($ mil)

Total non-fuel mineral production $122
Percent of U.S. 0.3%

Construction, 2003 ($ mil)

Total contracts (including non-building) . $2,058
  residential 1,068
  non-residential 598

Establishments, receipts, payroll & employees, by major industry group, 2002

Mining 90
  Receipts ($1,000) $417,336
  Annual payroll ($1,000) $74,564
  Paid employees 1,804

Utilities 109
  Receipts ($1,000) . . . . NA
  Annual payroll ($1,000) $131,894
  Paid employees 2,857

Construction 4,797
  Receipts ($1,000) $4,256,279
  Annual payroll ($1,000) $944,905
  Paid employees 30,406

Manufacturing 1,880
  Receipts ($1,000) $13,851,915
  Annual payroll ($1,000) $2,627,814
  Paid employees 67,738

Wholesale trade 1,669
  Receipts ($1,000) $10,371,084
  Annual payroll ($1,000) $715,028
  Paid employees 19,434

Retail trade 7,050
  Receipts ($1,000) $16,053,515
  Annual payroll ($1,000) $1,568,308
  Paid employees 80,251

Transportation 1,293
  Receipts ($1,000) $1,118,787
  Annual payroll ($1,000) $369,315
  Paid employees 13,234

Information 739
  Receipts ($1,000) . . . . NA
  Annual payroll ($1,000) $424,162
  Paid employees 11,785

Finance & insurance 1,795
  Receipts ($1,000) . . . . NA
  Annual payroll ($1,000) $1,121,474
  Paid employees 27,008

Professional, scientific & technical 3,275
  Receipts ($1,000) $2,252,787
  Annual payroll ($1,000) $862,952
  Paid employees 21,917

Health care & social assistance 4,403
  Receipts ($1,000) $6,237,132
  Annual payroll ($1,000) $2,719,483
  Paid employees 93,921

Accommodation & food service 3,726
  Receipts ($1,000) $2,045,841
  Annual payroll ($1,000) $606,880
  Paid employees 44,966

Communication, Energy & Transportation

Communication

Daily newspapers, 2004 7
Households with computers, 2003 . . . . .68%
Households with internet access, 2003 . . . . .58%

Energy

Electricity Consumption, 2001
Total (trillion Btu) 491
Per capita (million Btu) 382
By source of production (trillion Btu)
  Coal 8
  Natural gas 101
  Petroleum 233
  Nuclear electric power 0
  Hydroelectric power 27
By end-use sector (trillion Btu)
  Residential 111
  Commercial 74
  Industrial 199
  Transportation 107
Electric energy, 2003
  Production (billion kWh) 19
  Net summer capability (million kW) 4.3
Gas utilities, 2003
  Customers (x1,000) 26
  Sales (trillion Btu) 5
  Revenues ($mil) $57
Nuclear plants, 2003 0

Transportation, 2004

Public Road & Street Mileage 22,749
  Urban 2,641
  Rural 20,108
  Interstate 367
Vehicle miles of travel per capita 11,376.0
Total motor vehicle registrations 1,068,064
  Automobiles 608,700
  Buses 3,306
  Trucks 456,058
  Motorcycles 38,712
Licensed drivers 984,829
  19 years & under 45,584
Deaths from motor vehicle accidents 194

Maryland   1

State Summary

Capital City . . . . Annapolis
Governor . . . . Robert Ehrlich
100 State Circle
Annapolis, MD 21401
410-974-3591

Admitted as a state 1788
Area (square miles) 12,407
Population, 2004 (est.) 5,558,058
Largest City . . . . Baltimore
Population, 2004 636,000
Personal income per capita, 2004
(in current dollars) $39,247
Gross state product ($ mil), 2004 . . . . . $227,991

Leading industries by payroll, 2003

Professional/Scientific/Technical, Health care/
Social assistance, Finance & Insurance

**Leading agricultural commodities by receipts,
2003**

Broilers, greenhouse, dairy products, corn

Geography & Environment

Total area (sq. mi.) 12,407
land 9,774
water 2,633

Federally-owned land, 2004 (acres) 178,527
percent 2.8%

Highest point . . . . Backbone Mountain
elevation (feet) 3,360

Lowest point . . . . Atlantic Ocean
elevation (feet) . . . . sea level

General coastline (miles) 31

Tidal shoreline (miles) 3,190

Capital City . . . . Annapolis
Population 2000 35,838
Population 2004 36,217

Largest City . . . . Baltimore
Population 2000 651,000
Population 2004 636,000

Number of cities with over 100,000 population

1990 1
2000 1
2004 1

State park and recreation areas, 2003

Area (acres x 1,000) 266
Number of visitors (x 1,000) 10,219
Revenues (x 1,000) $14,361
percent of operating expenditures 33.8%

National forest system land, 2004

Acres . . . . NA

Demographics and Characteristics of the Population

Population

1980 4,216,975
1990 4,781,468
2000 5,296,486
2004 (estimate) 5,558,058
persons per sq. mile of land 568.7
2005 (projection) 5,600,563
Male 2,698,759
Female 2,901,804
2010 (projection) 5,904,970
2020 (projection) 6,497,626
2030 (projection) 7,022,251
Male 3,340,447
Female 3,681,804

Metropolitan and Non-Metro. area population

	Metro	Non-Metro
1980	3,920,000	287,000
1990	4,439,000	343,000
2000	4,911,000	385,000

Change in population, 2000-2004

Number 261,552
percent 4.9%
Natural increase (births minus deaths) . . 129,652
Net internal migration 21,969
Net international migration 91,278

Persons by age, 2004

Under 5 years 374,578
18 years and over 4,163,250
65 years and over 634,743
85 years and over 82,752

Persons by age, 2010 (projected)

Total 5,904,970
Under 5 years 412,152
5 to 17 years 994,142
18 and over 4,498,676
21 and over 4,244,241
65 and over 717,987
85 and over 105,097
Median age 36.8

Race, 2004 (estimate)

One Race
White 3,583,210
Black or African American 1,615,036
American Indian/Alaska Native 17,860
Pacific Islander 3,319
Asian Indian 69,608
Chinese 63,693
Filipino 25,440
Japanese 7,616
Korean 39,492
Vietnamese 16,030
Two or more races 80,757

Persons of Hispanic origin, 2004

Total Hispanic or Latino 294,052
  Mexican............................ 61,734
  Puerto Rican 27,453
  Cuban 11,172
  Other Hispanic or Latino 33,937

Marital status, 2000

Population 15 years & over 4,159,636
  Never married 1,197,975
  Married......................... 2,200,447
  Separated 128,949
  Widowed.......................... 270,376
  Divorced 366,048

Language spoken at home, 2000

Population 5 years & over 4,945,043
  English only 4,322,329
  Spanish 230,829
  Other Indo-European languages 198,932
  Asian/Pacific Island languages...... 135,899

Households & families, 2000

Households......................... 1,980,859
  with persons under 18 years 739,048
  with persons over 65 years........... 429,316
  persons per household 2.61
Families........................... 1,359,318
  persons per family....................3.13
Married couples...................... 994,549
Female householder,
  no husband present................ 279,876
One-person households 495,459

Nativity, 2000

Number of persons born in state 2,610,963
  percent of population 49.3%

Immigration & Naturalization, 2004

Immigrants admitted................. 20,253
Persons naturalized 12,295
Asylums granted 1,279
Asylums denied 160

Vital Statistics and Health

Marriages

2002 38,877
2003 38,176
2004 38,318

Divorces

2002 18,448
2003 17,642
2004 17,802

Births

2003 74,930
  Birthrate (per 1,000)..................13.6
  Low birth weight (2,500g or less)........ 9.1%
  To unmarried mothers................34.8%

2003, continued
  White........................... 45,780
  Black........................... 24,776
  Hispanic 6,296
  Asian/Pacific Islander 4,052
  Amer. Indian/Alaska Native............ 248
2004 (preliminary)..................... 74,605
  Birthrate (per 1,000)..................13.4
  White........................... 43,909
  Black 25,721
  Hispanic 7,637
  Asian/Pacific Islander 4,806

Deaths

2002
All causes 43,970
  rate per 100,000..................... 805.6
Heart disease 12,008
  rate per 100,000..................... 220.0
Malignant neoplasms 10,395
  rate per 100,000.....................190.4
Cerebrovascular disease............. 2,811
  rate per 100,000.....................51.5
Chronic lower respiratory disease 1,944
  rate per 100,000.....................35.6
2003 44,500
  rate per 100,000.....................807.8
2004 (provisional) 43,300

Infant deaths

2003 (provisional) 645
  rate per 1,000 ....8.5
2004 (provisional) 657
  rate per 1,000 ....8.7

Abortions, 2000

Total................................ 35,000
  rate per 1,000 women age 15-44..........29.0

Physicians, 2003

Total................................ 22,819
  rate per 1,000 persons.................. 414

Nurses, 2001

Total................................ 43,340
  rate per 1,000 persons.................. 805

Community Hospitals, 2003

Number................................ 51
Beds (x 1,000)...........................11.6
Patients admitted (x 1,000) 645
Average daily census (x 1,000) 8.7
Average cost per day $1,571
Outpatient visits (x mil)...................6.5

Disability status of population, 2004

5 to 20 years 6.8%
21 to 64 years 10.5%
65 years and over 39.3%

Education

Educational attainment, 2004

Population over 25 years 3,557,398
  Less than 9th grade 153,071
  High school graduates only......... 979,727
  Bachelor's degree only 687,119
  Graduate or professional degree..... 551,770
  Less than 9th grade percent 4.3%
  High school graduate or more 87.4%
  College graduate or more............. 35.2%
  Graduate or professional degree....... 15.5%

Public school enrollment, Fall 2002

Total................................ 866,743
  Kindergarten through grade 8 610,384
  Grades 9 through 12 256,359
Enrollment, 2005 (projected) 862,600

Graduating public high school seniors

2004 (estimate)....................... 53,030

SAT scores, 2005

Average verbal score 511
Average math score 515
Percent of graduates taking test 71%

Public school teachers, 2004

Total (x 1,000) 55.2
  Elementary (x 1,000)...................32.7
  Secondary (x 1,000) 22.5
Average salary $50,300
  Elementary......................... $50,200
  Secondary.......................... $48,500

State receipts & expenditures for public schools, 2004

Revenue receipts ($mil)................. $9,074
Expenditures
Total ($mil)......................... $8,971
  Per capita $1,627
  Per pupil $9,824

Institutions of higher education, 2004

Total..................................... 62
  Public.................................. 29
  Private................................. 33

Enrollment in institutions of higher education, Fall, 2003

Total............................... 316,307
  Full-time men 76,332
  Full-time women..................... 94,001
  Part-time men 54,242
  Part-time women..................... 91,732

Minority enrollment in institutions of higher education, Fall, 2003

Black, non-hispanic..................... 78,822
Hispanic 10,889
Asian/Pacific Islander 18,537
American Indian/Alaska Native.......... 1,315

Earned degrees conferred, 2003

Bachelor's 23,556
Master's.............................. 12,057
First-professional...................... 1,046
Doctor's................................. 969

State & local financial support for higher education, 2003-2004

Full-time equivalent enrollment (x 1,000) ..165.5
Appropriations per FTE................ $5,378
  as a percent of tax revenue............. 7.2%

Social Insurance & Welfare Programs

Social Security benefits & beneficiaries, 2004

Beneficiaries
  Total............................. 761,000
  Retired & dependents............... 541,000
  Survivors.......................... 113,000
  Disabled & dependents.............. 108,000
Annual benefit payments ($ mil)
  Total.............................. $8,076
  Retired & dependents................ $5,460
  Survivors........................... $1,490
  Disabled & dependents............... $1,127
Average Monthly Benefit
  Retired & dependents................. $962
  Disabled & dependents................ $926
  Widowed.............................. $939

Medicare

Enrollment, 2001 (x 1,000) 655
  Payments ($ mil, est.) $4,600
Enrollment, 2003 (x 1,000) 674

Medicaid, 2002

Beneficiaries (x 1,000).................... 693
Payments ($ mil) $3,662

State Children's Health Insurance, 2004

Enrollment (x 1,000).....................111.5
Expenditures ($ mil)...................$106.4

Persons without health insurance, 2003

Number (x 1,000)......................... 762
  percent........................... 13.9%
Number of children (x 1,000) 114
  percent of children 8.1%

Federal public aid

Temporary Assistance for Needy Families, 2004
Recipients (x 1,000)....................... 59
Families (x 1,000) 25

Supplemental Security Income, 2003
Recipients (x 1,000)....................... 91
Payments ($ mil) $441

Food Stamp Program, 2004

Participants (x 1,000) 274
Benefits ($ mil)......................... $287

Housing & Construction

Housing units

Total 2003 (estimate)	2,224,551
Total 2004 (estimate)	2,250,339
Seasonal or recreational use, 2003	38,000
Owner-occupied single-family, 2003. .	1,255,000
Median value	$186,139
Renter-occupied, 2003	623,000
Median rent	$817
Homeownership rate, 2003	71.6%
Homeownership rate, 2004	72.1%

New privately owned housing units, 2004

Number authorized (x 1,000)	27.4
Value ($ mil)	$3,823
Started 2005 (x 1,000, estimate)	27.1
Started 2006 (x 1,000, estimate)	27.0

Existing home sales

2002 (x 1,000)	117.6
2003 (x 1,000)	120.8
2004 (x 1,000)	140.6

Government & Elections

State Officials 2006

Governor (name/party/term expires)
Robert Ehrlich
Republican - 1/07

Lieutenant Governor.	Michael Steele
Secretary of State	Mary Kane
Attorney General	Joseph Curran
Chief Justice	Robert Bell

Governorship

Minimum age............................	30
Length of term	4 years
Consecutive terms permitted	2
Who succeeds....................	Lt. Governor

State Legislature

Name	Legislature
Upper chamber	Senate
Number of members....................	47
Length of term....................	4 years
Party in majority, 2006	Democratic
Lower chamber.............	House of Delegates
Number of members..................	141
Length of term....................	4 years
Party in majority, 2006	Democratic

State Government Employees, 2004

Total..............................	90,682
Payroll	$346,870,911

Local Government Employees, 2004

Total..............................	191,680
Payroll	$758,066,612

Local Governments by Type, 2002

Total.................................	265
County..............................	23
Municipal	157
Township	0
School District.......................	0
Special District	85

Voting age population, November 2004

Total.............................	4,043,000
Male..............................	1,906,000
Female............................	2,137,000
White.............................	2,737,000
Black	1,070,000
Hispanic	282,000
Asian	168,000

Presidential Election, 2004

Total Popular Vote	2,386,678
Kerry	1,334,493
Bush	1,024,703
Total Electoral Votes......................	10

Federal representation, 2006 (109th Congress)

Senator.......................	Paul S. Sarbanes
Party	Democrat
Year term expires	2007
Senator....................	Barbara Mikulski
Party	Democrat
Year term expires	2011
Representatives, total	8
Democrats...........................	6
Republicans	2
Other................................	0

Votes cast for US Senators

2002

Total vote (x 1,000)	NA
Leading party..........................	NA
Percent for leading party	NA

2004

Total vote (x 1,000)	2,322,000
Leading party.....................	Democratic
Percent for leading party	64.8%

Votes cast for US Representatives

2002

Total vote (x 1,000)	1,659
Democratic...........................	904
Republican	753
Leading party.....................	Democratic
Percent for leading party	54.5%

2004

Total vote (x 1,000)	2,254
Democratic...........................	1,311
Republican	896
Leading party.....................	Democratic
Percent for leading party	58.2%

Maryland 5

Women holding public office, 2006
US Congress 1
Statewide elected office. 0
State legislature 64

Black public officials, 2001
Total. 175
US and state legislatures 40
City/county/regional offices 93
Judicial/law enforcement. 33
Education/school boards 9

Hispanic public officials, 2004
Total. 6
State executives & legislators 4
City/county/regional offices 1
Judicial/law enforcement. 0
Education/school boards 1

Governmental Finance

State government revenues, 2004
Total revenue ($1,000) $28,395,564
Revenue per capita 5,106.20

General Revenue ($ per capita) $4,107.48
Intergovernmental 1,161.10
Taxes 2,214.49
general sales 529.59
individual income tax. 949.08
corporate income tax 80.47
Current charges. 414.49
Miscellaneous .317.40

State government expenditure, 2004
Total expenditure (x $1,000) $25,343,680
Expenditure per capita. 4,557.40
General Expenditure ($ per capita). . . . $4,009.89
Education 1,324.60
Public welfare. 987.30
Health 274.08
Hospitals. 72.85
Highways 297.75
Police protection 75.32
Correction 191.35
Natural resources 87.06
Parks & recreation. 46.00
Governmental administration 141.32
Interest on general debt 156.68

State debt & cash, 2004 ($ per capita)
Debt $2,445.74
Cash/security holdings. $7,914.89

Federal government grants to state & local government, 2004 (x $1,000)
Total $8,836,910
By Federal Agency
Defense $168,512

By Federal Agency, continued
Education 586,581
Energy 32,569
Environmental Protection Agency 99,337
Health & Human Services. 5,504,259
Homeland Security. 73,084
Housing & Urban Development. 706,744
Justice 147,039
Labor 191,664
Transportation 647,236
Veterans Affairs. 4,298

Crime, Law Enforcement & Courts

Crime, 2004 (rates per 100,000 residents)
Property crimes 202,326
Burglaries. 36,682
Larcenies. 129,786
Motor vehicle thefts 35,858
Property crime rate. 3,640.2
Violent crimes. 38,932
Murders. 521
Forcible rape. 1,316
Robberies 12,761
Aggravated assaults 24,334
Violent crime rate 700.5

Police Agencies, 2004
Total agencies. 147
Total employees 19,483
Male officers. 12,817
Female officers. 2,080
Male civilians. 1,713
Female civilians. 2,873

Arrests, 2004
Total. 309,630
Persons under 18 years of age 52,191

Prisoners under state & federal jurisdiction, 2004
Total prisoners. 23,285
Percent change, 12/31/03 to 12/31/04 . . . -2.1%
Sentenced to more than one year 22,696
rate per 100,000. 406

Persons under sentence of death, 7/1/05
Total. 9
White. 3
Black 6
Hispanic 0

State's highest court
Name . . . . Court of Appeals
Number of members. 7
Length of term . . . . 10 years
Intermediate appeals court? . . . . .yes

6   Maryland

Labor & Income

Civilian labor force, 2004
Total	2,883,000
Men	1,489,000
Women	1,394,000
Persons 16-19 years	137,000
White	1,939,000
Black	773,000
Hispanic	232,000
Asian	123,000

Civilian labor force as a percent of civilian non-institutional population, 2004
Total	68.3%
Men	75.0
Women	62.3
Persons 16-19 years	44.7
White	67.7
Black	69.1
Hispanic	80.3
Asian	69.4

Employment, 2004
Total	2,762,000
Men	1,431,000
Women	1,331,000
Persons 16-19 years	117,000
White	1,871,000
Black	725,000
Hispanic	222,000
Asian	120,000

Full-time/part-time labor force, 2002
Full-time labor force, employed	2,335,000
Part-time labor force, employed	437,000
Unemployed, looking for	
Full-time work	104,000
Part-time work	NA

Unemployment rate, 2004
Total	4.2%
Men	3.9
Women	4.6
Persons 16-19 years	14.6
White	3.5
Black	6.2
Hispanic	4.4
Asian	2.5

Unemployed by reason for unemployment (as a percent of total unemployment), 2002
Job losers or completed temp jobs	46.8%
Job leavers	NA
Reentrants	NA
New entrants	NA

Labor unions, 2004
Membership	272,000
percent of employed	10.9%

Experienced civilian labor force by private industry, first quarter 2004
Total	1,975,618
Natural Resources & Mining	6,235
Construction	169,209
Manufacturing	142,399
Trade, transportation & utilities	454,027
Information	50,509
Finance	154,954
Professional & business	364,168
Education & Health	332,622
Leisure & hospitality	211,471
Other	87,799

Experienced civilian labor force by occupation, 2004
Management	153,090
Business & Financial	119,350
Legal	22,960
Sales	258,280
Office & Admin. Support	437,540
Computers & Math	93,250
Architecture & Engineering	56,550
Arts & Entertainment	30,240
Education	159,200
Social Services	32,110
Healthcare Practitioner & Technical	131,760
Healthcare support	56,010
Maintenance & Repair	99,460
Construction	137,640
Transportation & moving	150,240
Production	103,560
Farming, fishing & forestry	4,960

Hours and earnings of production workers on manufacturing payrolls, 2004
Average weekly hours	40.1
Average hourly earnings	$16.48
Average weekly earnings	$660.85

Average annual pay
2004	$42,579
change from 2003	4.7%

Household income
Median household income, three-year average, 2002-2004	$56,763

Personal income, 2004 ($ per capita)
In current dollars	$39,247
In constant (2000) dollars	$36,399

Poverty
Persons below poverty level, three-year average, 2002-2004	8.6%

Federal individual income tax returns, 2003
Returns filed	2,601,859
Adjusted gross income ($1,000)	$145,388,987
Total income tax paid ($1,000)	$18,763,983

Economy, Business, Industry & Agriculture

Fortune 500 companies, 2005 6

Patents issued, 2004 1,436

Bankruptcy cases filed, 2004 32,000

Business firm ownership, 2002
Women-owned. 137,410
  Sales ($ mil) $17,333
Black-owned. 69,428
  Sales ($ mil) $4,790
Hispanic-owned. 15,364
  Sales ($ mil) $2,404
Asian-owned 26,315
  Sales ($ mil) $7,104
Amer. Indian/Alaska Native-owned 3,634
  Sales ($ mil) $344
Hawaiian/Pacific Isl.-owned . . . . NA
  Sales ($ mil) $52

Gross State Product, 2004 ($ mil)
Total Gross State Product $227,991
  Agriculture, forestry, fishing and
      hunting 747
  Mining. 163
  Utilities 6,195
  Construction 13,396
  Manufacturing, durable goods. 6,387
  Manufacturing, non-durable goods 7,675
  Wholesale trade. 12,025
  Retail trade. 15,358
  Transportation & warehousing 4,843
  Information 8,462
  Finance & insurance. 15,525
  Real estate, rental, leasing 34,763
  Professional and technical services 22,780
  Educational services 2,574
  Health care and social assistance 16,815
  Accommodation/food services. 6,106
  Other services, except government 6,006
  Government 38,348

Establishments, by major industry group, 2003
Total. 133,304
  Forestry, fishing & agriculture 228
  Mining. 92
  Construction 15,763
  Manufacturing. 3,875
  Wholesale trade. 6,062
  Retail trade. 19,461
  Transportation & warehousing 3,611
  Information 2,605
  Finance & insurance. 7,765
  Professional/scientific/technical 18,077
  Health care/social assistance 14,146
  Accommodation/food services. 9,589

Annual payroll by major industry group, 2003
Total ($1,000) $78,882,222
  Forestry, fishing & agriculture 28,761
  Mining. 74,517
  Utilities 749,866
  Construction 6,977,530
  Manufacturing. 6,669,622
  Wholesale trade. 4,569,503
  Retail trade. 6,597,387
  Transportation & warehousing 1,978,202
  Information 3,813,837
  Finance & insurance. 7,304,970
  Professional/scientific/technical . . . 11,957,327
  Health care/social assistance 10,367,886
  Accommodation/food services. 2,408,879

Agriculture
Number of farms, 2004 12,000
Farm acreage, 2004
  Total. 2,000,000
  Acres per farm, 2004 169
Farm income, 2003 ($mil)
  Net farm income $327
  Debt/asset ratio 14
Farm marketings, 2003 ($mil)
Total. $1,467
  Crops 620
  Livestock. 847

Principal commodities, in order by marketing receipts, 2003
  Broilers, greenhouse, dairy products, corn

Federal economic activity in state
Expenditures, 2003
  Total ($ mil) $57,646
  Per capita $10,464
  Defense ($ mil). 11,412
  Non-defense ($ mil) 46,235
Defense department, 2003
  Payroll ($ mil) $4,548
  Contract awards ($ mil) $7,570
  Grants ($ mil). $151
  Homeland security grants ($1,000)
    2004 . . . . $64,014
    2005 . . . . $42,250

FDIC insured financial institutions, 2004
Number 116
  Assets ($bil) $46.2
  Deposits ($bil) 82.1

Fishing, 2004
Catch (x 1,000 lbs) 49,507
Value ($1,000). $49,185

Mining, 2004 ($ mil)

Total non-fuel mineral production $478
Percent of U.S. 1.1%

Construction, 2003 ($ mil)

Total contracts (including non-building). $8,972
  residential. 4,287
  non-residential 3,086

Establishments, receipts, payroll & employees, by major industry group, 2002

Mining 104
  Receipts ($1,000) $297,738
  Annual payroll ($1,000) $77,352
  Paid employees 1,731

Utilities 105
  Receipts ($1,000) . . . . NA
  Annual payroll ($1,000) $817,161
  Paid employees 12,237

Construction 15,433
  Receipts ($1,000) $29,735,639
  Annual payroll ($1,000) $6,589,271
  Paid employees 181,255

Manufacturing 3,999
  Receipts ($1,000) $36,363,340
  Annual payroll ($1,000) $6,475,210
  Paid employees 151,294

Wholesale trade 6,104
  Receipts ($1,000) $60,679,602
  Annual payroll ($1,000) $4,443,829
  Paid employees 93,474

Retail trade 19,394
  Receipts ($1,000) $60,039,971
  Annual payroll ($1,000) $6,208,963
  Paid employees 285,561

Transportation 3,589
  Receipts ($1,000) $4,635,726
  Annual payroll ($1,000) $1,717,554
  Paid employees 56,042

Information 2,554
  Receipts ($1,000) . . . . NA
  Annual payroll ($1,000) $3,570,867
  Paid employees 72,686

Finance & insurance 7,468
  Receipts ($1,000) . . . . NA
  Annual payroll ($1,000) $6,539,055
  Paid employees 122,276

Professional, scientific & technical 17,867
  Receipts ($1,000) $28,059,470
  Annual payroll ($1,000) $10,871,910
  Paid employees 198,351

Health care & social assistance 13,923
  Receipts ($1,000) $23,785,022
  Annual payroll ($1,000) $9,546,615
  Paid employees 280,257

Accommodation & food service 9,406
  Receipts ($1,000) $7,832,268
  Annual payroll ($1,000) $2,173,737
  Paid employees 176,495

Communication, Energy & Transportation

Communication

Daily newspapers, 2004 13
Households with computers, 2003 . . . . .66%
Households with internet access, 2003 . . . . . .59%

Energy

Electricity Consumption, 2001
  Total (trillion Btu). 1,420
  Per capita (million Btu) 264
By source of production (trillion Btu)
  Coal 317
  Natural gas 191
  Petroleum. 568
  Nuclear electric power 143
  Hydroelectric power. 12
By end-use sector (trillion Btu)
  Residential 391
  Commercial 372
  Industrial 252
  Transportation 405
Electric energy, 2003
  Production (billion kWh) 52.2
  Net summer capability (million kW) 12.5
Gas utilities, 2003
  Customers (x1,000). 886
  Sales (trillion Btu). 98
  Revenues ($mil). $1,054
Nuclear plants, 2003 2

Transportation, 2004

Public Road & Street Mileage 30,808
  Urban. 16,893
  Rural 13,915
  Interstate. 481
Vehicle miles of travel per capita 9,946.7
Total motor vehicle registrations 4,119,664
  Automobiles. 2,547,973
  Buses 11,860
  Trucks 1,559,831
  Motorcycles 72,844
Licensed drivers 3,594,251
  19 years & under 159,071
Deaths from motor vehicle accidents 643

Massachusetts 1

State Summary

Capital City.......................... Boston
Governor...................... Mitt Romney
State House
Office of the Governor
Room 360
Boston, MA 02133
617-727-6250
Admitted as a state 1788
Area (square miles)................... 10,555
Population, 2004 (est.) 6,416,505
Largest City.......................... Boston
Population, 2004................... 569,000
Personal income per capita, 2004
(in current dollars) $41,801
Gross state product ($ mil), 2004 ..... $317,798

Leading industries by payroll, 2003

Health care/Social assistance, Professional/Scientific/Technical, Manufacturing

Leading agricultural commodities by receipts, 2003

Greenhouse, cranberries, dairy products, sweet corn

Geography & Environment

Total area (sq. mi.).................... 10,555
land 7,840
water 2,715
Federally-owned land, 2004 (acres) 93,950
percent............................. 1.9%
Highest point.....................Mt. Greylock
elevation (feet) 3,487
Lowest point ....Atlantic Ocean
elevation (feet) .... sea level
General coastline (miles)................... 192
Tidal shoreline (miles)................... 1,519
Capital City........................... Boston
Population 2000 589,000
Population 2004 569,000
Largest City........................... Boston
Population 2000 589,000
Population 2004 569,000

Number of cities with over 100,000 population

1990 3
2000 5
2004 5

State park and recreation areas, 2003

Area (acres x 1,000)...................... 295
Number of visitors (x 1,000) 10,512
Revenues (x 1,000)................... $2,199
percent of operating expenditures....... 7.1%

National forest system land, 2004

Acres .... NA

Demographics and Characteristics of the Population

Population

1980 5,737,037
1990 6,016,425
2000 6,349,097
2004 (estimate)..................... 6,416,505
persons per sq. mile of land............818.4
2005 (projection)................... 6,518,868
Male............................. 3,138,781
Female 3,380,087
2010 (projection) 6,649,441
2020 (projection) 6,855,546
2030 (projection) 7,012,009
Male............................. 3,330,034
Female 3,681,975

Metropolitan and Non-Metro. area population

	Metro	Non-Metro
1980	5,231,000	506,000
1990	5,438,000	578,000
2000	6,088,000	261,000

Change in population, 2000-2004

Number 67,400
percent............................ 1.1%
Natural increase (births minus deaths).. 105,859
Net internal migration ....-173,062
Net international migration 137,394

Persons by age, 2004

Under 5 years 395,662
18 years and over 4,952,316
65 years and over 854,343
85 years and over 136,125

Persons by age, 2010 (projected)

Total............................. 6,649,441
Under 5 years 400,704
5 to 17 years 1,083,149
18 and over 5,165,588
21 and over 4,868,790
65 and over 908,565
85 and over 157,950
Median age..........................38.8

Race, 2004 (estimate)

One Race
White 5,581,053
Black or African American 434,545
American Indian/Alaska Native....... 18,404
Pacific Islander 5,223
Asian Indian...................... 62,661
Chinese 110,984
Filipino 10,792
Japanese 11,894
Korean........................... 14,836
Vietnamese....................... 40,743
Two or more races..................... 82,579

2   Massachusetts

Persons of Hispanic origin, 2004

Total Hispanic or Latino 478,929
  Mexican. 18,614
  Puerto Rican 218,763
  Cuban 6,198
  Other Hispanic or Latino 27,007

Marital status, 2000

Population 15 years & over 5,091,369
  Never married 1,583,416
  Married. 2,632,238
  Separated 101,827
  Widowed. 356,396
  Divorced 422,584

Language spoken at home, 2000

Population 5 years & over 5,954,249
  English only 4,838,679
  Spanish 370,011
  Other Indo-European languages 529,784
  Asian/Pacific Island languages. 171,253

Households & families, 2000

Households. 2,443,580
  with persons under 18 years 804,940
  with persons over 65 years. 604,481
  persons per household 2.51
Families. 1,576,696
  persons per family. 3.11
Married couples. 1,197,917
Female householder,
  no husband present. 289,944
One-person households 684,345

Nativity, 2000

Number of persons born in state 4,196,702
  percent of population 66.1%

Immigration & Naturalization, 2004

Immigrants admitted. 27,676
Persons naturalized 16,263
Asylums granted 283
Asylums denied 22

Vital Statistics and Health

Marriages

2002 37,738
2003 36,225
2004 41,549

Divorces

2002 16,253
2003 15,903
2004 14,148

Births

2003 80,184
  Birthrate (per 1,000). 12.5
  Low birth weight (2,500g or less). 7.6%
  To unmarried mothers. 27.8%

2003, continued
  White. 66,061
  Black 8,606
  Hispanic 9,809
  Asian/Pacific Islander 5,398
  Amer. Indian/Alaska Native. 184

2004 (preliminary). 78,566
  Birthrate (per 1,000). 12.2
  White. 64,031
  Black 8,720
  Hispanic 9,847
  Asian/Pacific Islander 5,650

Deaths

2002
All causes 56,928
  rate per 100,000. . . . . .885.7
Heart disease 14,736
  rate per 100,000. . . . . .229.3
Malignant neoplasms 13,914
  rate per 100,000. . . . . .216.5
Cerebrovascular disease. 3,559
  rate per 100,000. .55.4
Chronic lower respiratory disease 2,745
  rate per 100,000. .42.7
2003 56,297
  rate per 100,000. . . . . .875.1
2004 (provisional) 52,611

Infant deaths

2003 (provisional) 425
  rate per 1,000 . . . . .5.3
2004 (provisional) 341
  rate per 1,000 . . . . .4.3

Abortions, 2000

Total. 30,000
  rate per 1,000 women age 15-44. . . . . . . .21.4

Physicians, 2003

Total. 28,474
  rate per 1,000 persons. 443

Nurses, 2001

Total. 75,580
  rate per 1,000 persons. 1,181

Community Hospitals, 2003

Number. 79
Beds (x 1,000). 16.0
Patients admitted (x 1,000) 785
Average daily census (x 1,000) 11.9
Average cost per day $1,631
Outpatient visits (x mil) 19.6

Disability status of population, 2004

5 to 20 years 6.5%
21 to 64 years 9.8%
65 years and over 35.2%

Education

Educational attainment, 2004

Population over 25 years 4,254,378
Less than 9th grade 195,532
High school graduates only 1,184,840
Bachelor's degree only 926,453
Graduate or professional degree 664,786
Less than 9th grade percent 4.6%
High school graduate or more 86.9%
College graduate or more 36.7%
Graduate or professional degree 15.6%

Public school enrollment, Fall 2002

Total 982,989
Kindergarten through grade 8 701,050
Grades 9 through 12 281,939
Enrollment, 2005 (projected) 966,400

Graduating public high school seniors

2004 (estimate) 57,930

SAT scores, 2005

Average verbal score 520
Average math score 527
Percent of graduates taking test 86%

Public school teachers, 2004

Total (x 1,000) 65.2
Elementary (x 1,000) 28.0
Secondary (x 1,000) 37.2
Average salary $53,200
Elementary $53,200
Secondary $53,200

State receipts & expenditures for public schools, 2004

Revenue receipts ($mil) $12,227
Expenditures
Total ($mil) $11,602
Per capita $1,807
Per pupil $11,445

Institutions of higher education, 2004

Total 122
Public 31
Private 91

Enrollment in institutions of higher education, Fall, 2003

Total 445,633
Full-time men 134,518
Full-time women 167,523
Part-time men 53,410
Part-time women 90,182

Minority enrollment in institutions of higher education, Fall, 2003

Black, non-hispanic 27,311
Hispanic 21,696
Asian/Pacific Islander 25,978
American Indian/Alaska Native 1,597

Earned degrees conferred, 2003

Bachelor's 44,726
Master's 26,946
First-professional 4,076
Doctor's 2,320

State & local financial support for higher education, 2003-2004

Full-time equivalent enrollment (x 1,000) .. 137.5
Appropriations per FTE $7,021
as a percent of tax revenue 4.8%

Social Insurance & Welfare Programs

Social Security benefits & beneficiaries, 2004

Beneficiaries
Total 1,067,000
Retired & dependents 748,000
Survivors 130,000
Disabled & dependents 189,000
Annual benefit payments ($ mil)
Total $11,195
Retired & dependents $7,561
Survivors $1,798
Disabled & dependents $1,837
Average Monthly Benefit
Retired & dependents $961
Disabled & dependents $883
Widowed $952

Medicare

Enrollment, 2001 (x 1,000) 961
Payments ($ mil, est.) $6,000
Enrollment, 2003 (x 1,000) 966

Medicaid, 2002

Beneficiaries (x 1,000) 1,066
Payments ($ mil) $6,387

State Children's Health Insurance, 2004

Enrollment (x 1,000) 166.5
Expenditures ($ mil) $119.1

Persons without health insurance, 2003

Number (x 1,000) 682
percent 10.7%
Number of children (x 1,000) 118
percent of children 7.9%

Federal public aid

Temporary Assistance for Needy Families, 2004
Recipients (x 1,000) 108
Families (x 1,000) 50

Supplemental Security Income, 2003
Recipients (x 1,000) 168
Payments ($ mil) $855

Food Stamp Program, 2004

Participants (x 1,000) 335
Benefits ($ mil) $304

Housing & Construction

Housing units

Total 2003 (estimate) 2,658,275
Total 2004 (estimate) 2,672,061
Seasonal or recreational use, 2003 101,000
Owner-occupied single-family, 2003 .. 1,259,000
    Median value $309,736
Renter-occupied, 2003 862,000
    Median rent $820
Homeownership rate, 2003 .... 64.3%
Homeownership rate, 2004 .... 63.8%

New privately owned housing units, 2004

Number authorized (x 1,000) 22.5
Value ($ mil) $3,790
Started 2005 (x 1,000, estimate) 16.0
Started 2006 (x 1,000, estimate) 16.0

Existing home sales

2002 (x 1,000) 115.9
2003 (x 1,000) 118.3
2004 (x 1,000) 141.7

Government & Elections

State Officials 2006

Governor (name/party/term expires)
Mitt Romney
Republican - 1/07
Lieutenant Governor............. Kerry Healey
Secretary of State.............. William Galvin
Attorney General................Thomas Reilly
Chief Justice .... Margaret Marshall

Governorship

Minimum age.................... not specified
Length of term .... 4 years
Consecutive terms permitted ..... not specified
Who succeeds....................Lt. Governor

State Legislature

Name .... General Court
Upper chamber ....Senate
    Number of members..................... 40
    Length of term...................... 2 years
    Party in majority, 2006 ....Democratic
Lower chamber.......House of Representatives
    Number of members................... 160
    Length of term...................... 2 years
    Party in majority, 2006 ....Democratic

State Government Employees, 2004

Total................................ 88,051
Payroll $373,001,987

Local Government Employees, 2004

Total............................... 235,016
Payroll $915,331,110

Local Governments by Type, 2002

Total................................... 841
    County................................. 5
    Municipal 45
    Township 306
    School District....................... 82
    Special District..................... 403

Voting age population, November 2004

Total............................... 4,840,000
    Male............................... 2,299,000
    Female............................. 2,541,000
    White.............................. 4,297,000
    Black............................... 292,000
    Hispanic 323,000
    Asian 199,000

Presidential Election, 2004

Total Popular Vote 2,912,388
    Kerry 1,803,800
    Bush.............................. 1,071,109
Total Electoral Votes....................... 12

Federal representation, 2006 (109th Congress)

Senator...................Edward M. Kennedy
    Party .... Democrat
    Year term expires 2007
Senator....................... John F. Kerry
    Party .... Democrat
    Year term expires 2009
Representatives, total 10
    Democrats........................... 10
    Republicans 0
    Other................................ 0

Votes cast for US Senators

2002
Total vote (x 1,000) 2,220,000
Leading party....................Democratic
Percent for leading party 72.3%

2004
Total vote (x 1,000) .... NA
Leading party.............................. NA
Percent for leading party .... NA

Votes cast for US Representatives

2002
Total vote (x 1,000) 2,220
    Democratic......................... 1,529
    Republican 290
Leading party....................Democratic
Percent for leading party 68.8%

2004
Total vote (x 1,000) 2,927
    Democratic......................... 2,060
    Republican 435
Leading party....................Democratic
Percent for leading party 70.4%

Massachusetts 5

Women holding public office, 2006

US Congress 0
Statewide elected office 1
State legislature 49

Black public officials, 2001

Total 60
    US and state legislatures 6
    City/county/regional offices 44
    Judicial/law enforcement 2
    Education/school boards 8

Hispanic public officials, 2004

Total 18
    State executives & legislators 4
    City/county/regional offices 11
    Judicial/law enforcement 0
    Education/school boards 3

Governmental Finance

State government revenues, 2004

Total revenue ($1,000) $41,615,765
    Revenue per capita 6,495.36

General Revenue ($ per capita) $5,147.48
    Intergovernmental 1,404.29
    Taxes 2,628.26
        general sales 584.24
        individual income tax 1,378.23
        corporate income tax 203.07
    Current charges 404.92
    Miscellaneous 710.01

State government expenditure, 2004

Total expenditure (x $1,000) $38,405,514
    Expenditure per capita 5,994.31
General Expenditure ($ per capita) $5,251.53
    Education 1,183.20
    Public welfare 1,647.08
    Health 107.19
    Hospitals 64.72
    Highways 470.65
    Police protection 63.67
    Correction 151.75
    Natural resources 42.48
    Parks & recreation 47.68
    Governmental administration 216.92
    Interest on general debt 400.52

State debt & cash, 2004 ($ per capita)

Debt $7,957.10
Cash/security holdings $10,162.42

Federal government grants to state & local government, 2004 (x $1,000)

Total $13,876,126
By Federal Agency
    Defense $251,119

By Federal Agency, continued
    Education 805,137
    Energy 141,440
    Environmental Protection Agency ... 128,340
    Health & Human Services 8,582,655
    Homeland Security 35,191
    Housing & Urban Development 1,685,156
    Justice 167,504
    Labor 205,894
    Transportation 834,230
    Veterans Affairs 25,933

Crime, Law Enforcement & Courts

Crime, 2004 (rates per 100,000 residents)

Property crimes 157,825
    Burglaries 34,469
    Larcenies 101,303
    Motor vehicle thefts 22,053
    Property crime rate 2,459.7
Violent crimes 29,437
    Murders 169
    Forcible rape 1,799
    Robberies 7,467
    Aggravated assaults 20,002
    Violent crime rate 458.8

Police Agencies, 2004

Total agencies 332
Total employees 19,466
    Male officers 14,809
    Female officers 1,315
    Male civilians 1,444
    Female civilians 1,898

Arrests, 2004

Total 101,430
    Persons under 18 years of age 14,460

Prisoners under state & federal jurisdiction, 2004

Total prisoners 10,144
    Percent change, 12/31/03 to 12/31/04 ... -0.9%
    Sentenced to more than one year 8,688
    rate per 100,000 232

Persons under sentence of death, 7/1/05

Total 0
    White 0
    Black 0
    Hispanic 0

State's highest court

Name .... Supreme Court
Number of members 7
Length of term .... to age 70
Intermediate appeals court? .... yes

Labor & Income

Civilian labor force, 2004

Total	3,399,000
Men	1,769,000
Women	1,629,000
Persons 16-19 years	171,000
White	3,041,000
Black	201,000
Hispanic	235,000
Asian	127,000

Civilian labor force as a percent of civilian non-institutional population, 2004

Total	67.5%
Men	73.7
Women	61.9
Persons 16-19 years	47.2
White	67.9
Black	65.2
Hispanic	73.1
Asian	62.3

Employment, 2004

Total	3,226,000
Men	1,665,000
Women	1,562,000
Persons 16-19 years	148,000
White	2,900,000
Black	181,000
Hispanic	214,000
Asian	119,000

Full-time/part-time labor force, 2002

Full-time labor force, employed	2,661,000
Part-time labor force, employed	641,000
Unemployed, looking for	
Full-time work	159,000
Part-time work	NA

Unemployment rate, 2004

Total	5.1%
Men	5.9
Women	4.2
Persons 16-19 years	13.4
White	4.6
Black	9.7
Hispanic	8.7
Asian	6.7

Unemployed by reason for unemployment (as a percent of total unemployment), 2002

Job losers or completed temp jobs	65.4%
Job leavers	NA
Reentrants	20.0
New entrants	NA

Labor unions, 2004

Membership	393,000
percent of employed	13.5%

Experienced civilian labor force by private industry, first quarter 2004

Total	2,676,095
Natural Resources & Mining	7,188
Construction	124,768
Manufacturing	313,107
Trade, transportation & utilities	560,095
Information	87,412
Finance	215,805
Professional & business	435,514
Education & Health	548,652
Leisure & hospitality	267,296
Other	116,258

Experienced civilian labor force by occupation, 2004

Management	207,690
Business & Financial	149,200
Legal	24,660
Sales	318,160
Office & Admin. Support	539,340
Computers & Math	108,940
Architecture & Engineering	73,890
Arts & Entertainment	43,980
Education	203,560
Social Services	55,780
Healthcare Practitioner & Technical	189,110
Healthcare support	91,850
Maintenance & Repair	100,210
Construction	118,040
Transportation & moving	170,720
Production	184,380
Farming, fishing & forestry	4,630

Hours and earnings of production workers on manufacturing payrolls, 2004

Average weekly hours	41.1
Average hourly earnings	$16.89
Average weekly earnings	$694.18

Average annual pay

2004	$48,916
change from 2003	5.6%

Household income

Median household income, three-year average, 2002-2004	$52,354

Personal income, 2004 ($ per capita)

In current dollars	$41,801
In constant (2000) dollars	$38,768

Poverty

Persons below poverty level, three-year average, 2002-2004	9.8%

Federal individual income tax returns, 2003

Returns filed	3,051,697
Adjusted gross income ($1,000)	$178,243,921
Total income tax paid ($1,000)	$25,774,812

Economy, Business, Industry & Agriculture

Fortune 500 companies, 2005 11

Patents issued, 2004 3,904

Bankruptcy cases filed, 2004 18,200

Business firm ownership, 2002

Women-owned.	161,919
Sales ($ mil)	$23,138
Black-owned.	12,820
Sales ($ mil)	$1,290
Hispanic-owned.	15,940
Sales ($ mil)	$2,075
Asian-owned	18,071
Sales ($ mil)	$5,147
Amer. Indian/Alaska Native-owned	2,220
Sales ($ mil)	$340
Hawaiian/Pacific Isl.-owned.	283
Sales ($ mil)	$33

Gross State Product, 2004 ($ mil)

Total Gross State Product	$317,798
Agriculture, forestry, fishing and hunting	751
Mining.	124
Utilities	3,833
Construction	15,870
Manufacturing, durable goods.	25,262
Manufacturing, non-durable goods	9,650
Wholesale trade.	18,774
Retail trade.	17,795
Transportation & warehousing	5,267
Information	14,813
Finance & insurance.	37,768
Real estate, rental, leasing	43,439
Professional and technical services	31,729
Educational services.	7,289
Health care and social assistance	26,353
Accommodation/food services.	7,676
Other services, except government	6,538
Government	27,313

Establishments, by major industry group, 2003

Total.	178,675
Forestry, fishing & agriculture	438
Mining.	109
Construction	17,790
Manufacturing.	8,509
Wholesale trade.	9,066
Retail trade.	25,755
Transportation & warehousing	3,607
Information	3,783
Finance & insurance.	9,572
Professional/scientific/technical	21,858
Health care/social assistance	17,429
Accommodation/food services.	15,230

Annual payroll by major industry group, 2003

Total ($1,000)	$127,099,808
Forestry, fishing & agriculture	31,486
Mining.	75,562
Utilities	1,044,351
Construction	6,664,896
Manufacturing.	15,797,582
Wholesale trade.	8,633,432
Retail trade.	8,429,063
Transportation & warehousing	2,703,267
Information	7,264,674
Finance & insurance.	15,702,301
Professional/scientific/technical . .	16,563,733
Health care/social assistance	17,422,569
Accommodation/food services.	3,817,583

Agriculture

Number of farms, 2004 6,000
Farm acreage, 2004

Total.	1,000,000
Acres per farm, 2004	85

Farm income, 2003 ($mil)

Net farm income	$40
Debt/asset ratio	10.5

Farm marketings, 2003 ($mil)

Total.	$385
Crops	298
Livestock.	87

Principal commodities, in order by marketing receipts, 2003

Greenhouse, cranberries, dairy products, sweet corn

Federal economic activity in state

Expenditures, 2003

Total ($ mil)	$51,265
Per capita	$7,969
Defense ($ mil).	7,422
Non-defense ($ mil)	43,843

Defense department, 2003

Payroll ($ mil)	$980
Contract awards ($ mil)	$6,800
Grants ($ mil).	$156
Homeland security grants ($1,000)	
2004	$69,288
2005	$62,436

FDIC insured financial institutions, 2004

Number	200
Assets ($bil)	$224.2
Deposits ($bil)	172.7

Fishing, 2004

Catch (x 1,000 lbs)	336,948
Value ($1,000).	$326,067

Mining, 2004 ($ mil)

Total non-fuel mineral production $221
Percent of U.S. 0.5%

Construction, 2003 ($ mil)

Total contracts (including non-building) . $8,751
    residential. 3,983
    non-residential 3,659

**Establishments, receipts, payroll & employees,
by major industry group, 2002**

Mining 446
    Receipts ($1,000) $1,427,350
    Annual payroll ($1,000) $257,997
    Paid employees 5,747

Utilities 249
    Receipts ($1,000) . . . . NA
    Annual payroll ($1,000) $1,019,363
    Paid employees 14,206

Construction 17,107
    Receipts ($1,000) $31,547,604
    Annual payroll ($1,000) $6,772,400
    Paid employees 165,596

Manufacturing 8,859
    Receipts ($1,000) $77,996,586
    Annual payroll ($1,000) $15,573,734
    Paid employees 349,184

Wholesale trade 9,333
    Receipts ($1,000) $127,129,789
    Annual payroll ($1,000) $8,536,677
    Paid employees 154,939

Retail trade 25,761
    Receipts ($1,000) $73,903,837
    Annual payroll ($1,000) $7,874,188
    Paid employees 359,149

Transportation 3,597
    Receipts ($1,000) $5,919,533
    Annual payroll ($1,000) $2,186,001
    Paid employees 71,350

Information 3,888
    Receipts ($1,000) . . . . NA
    Annual payroll ($1,000) $7,258,735
    Paid employees 124,642

Finance & insurance 9,340
    Receipts ($1,000) . . . . NA
    Annual payroll ($1,000) $15,147,886
    Paid employees 215,893

Professional, scientific & technical 21,906
    Receipts ($1,000) $37,329,788
    Annual payroll ($1,000) $15,613,290
    Paid employees 239,737

Health care & social assistance 17,348
    Receipts ($1,000) $37,307,723
    Annual payroll ($1,000) $16,636,676
    Paid employees 476,297

Accommodation & food service 15,175
    Receipts ($1,000) $11,789,582
    Annual payroll ($1,000) $3,466,882
    Paid employees 241,451

Communication, Energy & Transportation

Communication

Daily newspapers, 2004 32
Households with computers, 2003 . . . . .64%
Households with internet access, 2003 . . . . .58%

Energy

Electricity Consumption, 2001
    Total (trillion Btu) 1,549
    Per capita (million Btu) 242
By source of production (trillion Btu)
    Coal 109
    Natural gas 364
    Petroleum 762
    Nuclear electric power 54
    Hydroelectric power . . . . < 0.5
By end-use sector (trillion Btu)
    Residential 461
    Commercial 379
    Industrial 261
    Transportation 447
Electric energy, 2003
    Production (billion kWh) 48.4
    Net summer capability (million kW) 13.9
Gas utilities, 2003
    Customers (x1,000) 1,438
    Sales (trillion Btu) 230
    Revenues ($mil) $2,415
Nuclear plants, 2003 1

Transportation, 2004

Public Road & Street Mileage 35,783
    Urban. 27,856
    Rural 7,927
    Interstate. 573
Vehicle miles of travel per capita 8,535.3
Total motor vehicle registrations 5,456,267
    Automobiles. 3,504,943
    Buses 11,400
    Trucks 1,939,924
    Motorcycles 136,887
Licensed drivers 4,645,857
    19 years & under 195,400
Deaths from motor vehicle accidents 476

State Summary

Capital City.......................... Lansing
Governor................. Jennifer Granholm
PO Box 30013
Lansing, MI 48909
517-335-7858
Admitted as a state 1837
Area (square miles)................... 96,716
Population, 2004 (est.) 10,112,620
Largest City...........................Detroit
Population, 2004 900,000
Personal income per capita, 2004
(in current dollars) $31,954
Gross state product ($ mil), 2004 ...... $372,169

Leading industries by payroll, 2003

Manufacturing, Health care/Social assistance,
Professional/Scientific/Technical

Leading agricultural commodities by receipts, 2003

Dairy products, greenhouse, corn, soybeans

Geography & Environment

Total area (sq. mi.)..................... 96,716
land 56,804
water 39,912

Federally-owned land, 2004 (acres) ... 3,637,873
percent............................. 10.0%

Highest point....................... Mt. Avron
elevation (feet) 1,979

*Lowest point ....*Lake Erie
elevation (feet) 572

General coastline (miles)..................... 0

Tidal shoreline (miles)....................... 0

Capital City......................... Lansing
Population 2000 119,000
Population 2004 117,000

*Largest City........................*Detroit
Population 2000 951,000
Population 2004 900,000

Number of cities with over 100,000 population

1990 7
2000 8
2004 7

State park and recreation areas, 2003

Area (acres x 1,000)...................... 286
Number of visitors (x 1,000) 22,430
Revenues (x 1,000).................... $24,098
percent of operating expenditures...... 46.7%

National forest system land, 2004

Acres 2,868,000

Demographics and Characteristics of the Population

Population

1980 9,262,078
1990 9,295,297
2000 9,938,444
2004 (estimate)..................... 10,112,620
persons per sq. mile of land............. 178
2005 (projection).................. 10,207,421
Male....................... 5,022,145
Female....................... 5,185,276
2010 (projection) 10,428,683
2020 (projection) 10,695,993
2030 (projection) 10,694,172
Male....................... 5,286,727
Female....................... 5,407,445

Metropolitan and Non-Metro. area population

	Metro	Non-Metro
1980	7,481,000	1,782,000
1990	7,446,000	1,850,000
2000	8,169,000	1,769,000

Change in population, 2000-2004

Number 174,140
percent............................. 1.8%
Natural increase (births minus deaths).. 190,164
Net internal migration................ -116,477
Net international migration 103,785

Persons by age, 2004

Under 5 years 649,842
18 years and over 7,579,181
65 years and over 1,246,595
85 years and over 175,067

Persons by age, 2010 (projected)

Total........................... 10,428,683
Under 5 years 681,154
5 to 17 years 1,805,904
18 and over 7,941,625
21 and over 7,489,009
65 and over 1,334,491
85 and over 205,188
Median age 37.4

Race, 2004 (estimate)

One Race
White........................... 8,232,138
Black or African American 1,450,583
American Indian/Alaska Native....... 60,462
Pacific Islander 3,770
Asian Indian...................... 93,681
Chinese 32,664
Filipino 21,436
Japanese 9,908
Korean 26,624
Vietnamese...................... 11,780
Two or more races..................... 145,648

Persons of Hispanic origin, 2004

Total Hispanic or Latino	359,111
Mexican	260,030
Puerto Rican	35,229
Cuban	7,275
Other Hispanic or Latino	32,452

Marital status, 2000

Population 15 years & over	7,775,603
Never married	2,161,618
Married	4,183,274
Separated	108,858
Widowed	513,190
Divorced	800,887

Language spoken at home, 2000

Population 5 years & over	9,268,782
English only	8,487,401
Spanish	246,688
Other Indo-European languages	303,122
Asian/Pacific Island languages	104,467

Households & families, 2000

Households	3,785,661
with persons under 18 years	1,347,469
with persons over 65 years	862,730
persons per household	2.56
Families	2,575,699
persons per family	3.1
Married couples	1,947,710
Female householder, no husband present	473,802
One-person households	993,607

Nativity, 2000

Number of persons born in state	7,490,125
percent of population	75.4%

Immigration & Naturalization, 2004

Immigrants admitted	18,334
Persons naturalized	14,615
Asylums granted	211
Asylums denied	46

Vital Statistics and Health

Marriages

2002	65,164
2003	62,911
2004	61,932

Divorces

2002	37,836
2003	35,598
2004	34,701

Births

2003	131,094
Birthrate (per 1,000)	13.0
Low birth weight (2,500g or less)	8.2%
To unmarried mothers	34.6%

2003, continued

White	103,042
Black	22,574
Hispanic	7,666
Asian/Pacific Islander	4,682
Amer. Indian/Alaska Native	639
2004 (preliminary)	129,768
Birthrate (per 1,000)	12.8
White	102,802
Black	21,705
Hispanic	7,826
Asian/Pacific Islander	4,580

Deaths

2002

All causes	87,795
rate per 100,000	873.5
Heart disease	26,659
rate per 100,000	265.3
Malignant neoplasms	19,985
rate per 100,000	198.8
Cerebrovascular disease	5,814
rate per 100,000	57.8
Chronic lower respiratory disease	4,431
rate per 100,000	44.1
2003	86,710
rate per 100,000	860.2
2004 (provisional)	85,216

Infant deaths

2003 (provisional)	1,130
rate per 1,000	8.6
2004 (provisional)	997
rate per 1,000	7.7

Abortions, 2000

Total	46,000
rate per 1,000 women age 15-44	21.6

Physicians, 2003

Total	24,004
rate per 1,000 persons	238

Nurses, 2001

Total	83,950
rate per 1,000 persons	839

Community Hospitals, 2003

Number	144
Beds (x 1,000)	25.8
Patients admitted (x 1,000)	1,168
Average daily census (x 1,000)	17.1
Average cost per day	$1,382
Outpatient visits (x mil)	27.0

Disability status of population, 2004

5 to 20 years	8%
21 to 64 years	13%
65 years and over	39.5%

Education

Educational attainment, 2004

Population over 25 years 6,429,992
  Less than 9th grade 219,304
  High school graduates only........ 2,020,893
  Bachelor's degree only 971,776
  Graduate or professional degree..... 609,728
  Less than 9th grade percent 3.4%
  High school graduate or more 87.9%
  College graduate or more............. 24.4%
  Graduate or professional degree........ 9.5%

Public school enrollment, Fall 2002

Total............................ 1,785,160
  Kindergarten through grade 8 1,253,811
  Grades 9 through 12 531,349
Enrollment, 2005 (projected) 1,789,700

Graduating public high school seniors

2004 (estimate)....................... 106,320

SAT scores, 2005

Average verbal score 568
Average math score 579
Percent of graduates taking test 10%

Public school teachers, 2004

Total (x 1,000) 95.2
  Elementary (x 1,000)....................49.2
  Secondary (x 1,000) 45.9
Average salary $54,400
  Elementary........................... $54,400
  Secondary............................ $54,400

State receipts & expenditures for public schools, 2004

Revenue receipts ($mil)................ $16,713
Expenditures
Total ($mil)......................... $18,954
  Per capita $1,880
  Per pupil $9,416

Institutions of higher education, 2004

Total................................... 110
  Public................................. 45
  Private................................ 65

Enrollment in institutions of higher education, Fall, 2003

Total............................... 627,358
  Full-time men 160,180
  Full-time women.................... 201,062
  Part-time men 104,584
  Part-time women.................... 161,532

Minority enrollment in institutions of higher education, Fall, 2003

Black, non-hispanic.................... 71,286
Hispanic 15,053
Asian/Pacific Islander 19,330
American Indian/Alaska Native.......... 4,665

Earned degrees conferred, 2003

Bachelor's 50,178
Master's.............................. 23,196
First-professional....................... 2,481
Doctor's................................ 1,525

State & local financial support for higher education, 2003-2004

Full-time equivalent enrollment (x 1,000) ..357.6
Appropriations per FTE................ $5,950
  as a percent of tax revenue.............. 8.5%

Social Insurance & Welfare Programs

Social Security benefits & beneficiaries, 2004

Beneficiaries
  Total........................... 1,716,000
  Retired & dependents............. 1,172,000
  Survivors......................... 251,000
  Disabled & dependents............. 293,000
Annual benefit payments ($ mil)
  Total............................ $19,067
  Retired & dependents.............. $12,497
  Survivors.......................... $3,522
  Disabled & dependents.............. $3,048
Average Monthly Benefit
  Retired & dependents................. $1,029
  Disabled & dependents.............. $950
  Widowed............................ $992

Medicare

Enrollment, 2001 (x 1,000) 1,414
  Payments ($ mil, est.) $7,000
Enrollment, 2003 (x 1,000) 1,445

Medicaid, 2002

Beneficiaries (x 1,000).................. 1,450
Payments ($ mil) $5,919

State Children's Health Insurance, 2004

Enrollment (x 1,000)..................... NA
Expenditures ($ mil)....................$159.5

Persons without health insurance, 2003

Number (x 1,000)....................... 1,080
  percent............................ 10.9%
Number of children (x 1,000) 147
  percent of children 5.8%

Federal public aid

Temporary Assistance for Needy Families, 2004
Recipients (x 1,000)..................... 212
Families (x 1,000) 79

Supplemental Security Income, 2003
Recipients (x 1,000)..................... 217
Payments ($ mil) $1,086

Food Stamp Program, 2004

Participants (x 1,000) 944
Benefits ($ mil)..........................$896

Housing & Construction

Housing units

Total 2003 (estimate)	4,386,452
Total 2004 (estimate)	4,433,482
Seasonal or recreational use, 2003	211,000
Owner-occupied single-family, 2003	2,417,000
Median value	$141,413
Renter-occupied, 2003	977,000
Median rent	$608
Homeownership rate, 2003	75.6%
Homeownership rate, 2004	77.1%

New privately owned housing units, 2004

Number authorized (x 1,000)	54.7
Value ($ mil)	$7,625
Started 2005 (x 1,000, estimate)	51.7
Started 2006 (x 1,000, estimate)	50.7

Existing home sales

2002 (x 1,000)	203.5
2003 (x 1,000)	207.4
2004 (x 1,000)	213.4

Government & Elections

State Officials 2006

Governor (name/party/term expires)
Jennifer Granholm
Democrat - 1/07

Lieutenant Governor	John Cherry
Secretary of State	Terri Lynn Land
Attorney General	Mike Cox
Chief Justice	Clifford W. Taylor

Governorship

Minimum age	30
Length of term	4 years
Consecutive terms permitted	2
Who succeeds	Lt. Governor

State Legislature

Name	Legislature
Upper chamber	Senate
Number of members	38
Length of term	4 years
Party in majority, 2006	Republican
Lower chamber	House of Representatives
Number of members	110
Length of term	2 years
Party in majority, 2006	Republican

State Government Employees, 2004

Total	132,825
Payroll	$520,648,390

Local Government Employees, 2004

Total	371,447
Payroll	$1,338,733,279

Local Governments by Type, 2002

Total	2,804
County	83
Municipal	533
Township	1,242
School District	580
Special District	366

Voting age population, November 2004

Total	7,452,000
Male	3,604,000
Female	3,848,000
White	6,163,000
Black	957,000
Hispanic	201,000
Asian	173,000

Presidential Election, 2004

Total Popular Vote	4,839,252
Kerry	2,479,183
Bush	2,313,746
Total Electoral Votes	17

Federal representation, 2006 (109th Congress)

Senator	Debbie Stabenow
Party	Democrat
Year term expires	2007
Senator	Carl Levin
Party	Democrat
Year term expires	2009
Representatives, total	15
Democrats	6
Republicans	9
Other	0

Votes cast for US Senators

2002

Total vote (x 1,000)	3,129,000
Leading party	Democratic
Percent for leading party	60.6%

2004

Total vote (x 1,000)	NA
Leading party	NA
Percent for leading party	NA

Votes cast for US Representatives

2002

Total vote (x 1,000)	3,056
Democratic	1,507
Republican	1,474
Leading party	Democratic
Percent for leading party	49.3%

2004

Total vote (x 1,000)	4,631
Democratic	2,242
Republican	2,289
Leading party	Republican
Percent for leading party	49.4%

Women holding public office, 2006

US Congress 3
Statewide elected office 2
State legislature 30

Black public officials, 2001

Total 346
    US and state legislatures 25
    City/county/regional offices 147
    Judicial/law enforcement 55
    Education/school boards 119

Hispanic public officials, 2004

Total 15
    State executives & legislators 1
    City/county/regional offices 5
    Judicial/law enforcement 3
    Education/school boards 6

Governmental Finance

State government revenues, 2004

Total revenue ($1,000) $57,461,347
    Revenue per capita 5,686.99

General Revenue ($ per capita) $4,629.86
    Intergovernmental 1,360.84
    Taxes 2,381.34
        general sales 781.32
        individual income tax 650.84
        corporate income tax 182.21
    Current charges 532.98
    Miscellaneous 354.69

State government expenditure, 2004

Total expenditure (x $1,000) $52,684,622
    Expenditure per capita 5,214.23
General Expenditure ($ per capita) $4,602.86
    Education 2,013.19
    Public welfare 984.77
    Health 331.58
    Hospitals 179.41
    Highways 322.60
    Police protection 29.25
    Correction 162.05
    Natural resources 44.84
    Parks & recreation 12.41
    Governmental administration 92.05
    Interest on general debt 108.57

State debt & cash, 2004 ($ per capita)

Debt $2,074.42
Cash/security holdings $7,016.18

Federal government grants to state & local government, 2004 (x $1,000)

Total $13,227,411
By Federal Agency
    Defense $81,021

    Education 1,187,632
    Energy 64,029
    Environmental Protection Agency ... 158,510
    Health & Human Services 8,040,554
    Homeland Security 129,668
    Housing & Urban Development 875,663
    Justice 169,540
    Labor 346,446
    Transportation 1,159,870
    Veterans Affairs 17,252

Crime, Law Enforcement & Courts

Crime, 2004 (rates per 100,000 residents)

Property crimes 309,208
    Burglaries 64,394
    Larcenies 194,259
    Motor vehicle thefts 50,555
    Property crime rate 3,057.6
Violent crimes 49,577
    Murders 643
    Forcible rape 5,486
    Robberies 11,320
    Aggravated assaults 32,128
    Violent crime rate 490.2

Police Agencies, 2004

Total agencies 631
Total employees 27,656
    Male officers 17,418
    Female officers 2,802
    Male civilians 3,280
    Female civilians 4,156

Arrests, 2004

Total 331,479
    Persons under 18 years of age 39,224

Prisoners under state & federal jurisdiction, 2004

Total prisoners 48,883
    Percent change, 12/31/03 to 12/31/04 ... -1.0%
Sentenced to more than one year 48,883
    rate per 100,000 483

Persons under sentence of death, 7/1/05

Total 0
    White 0
    Black 0
    Hispanic 0

State's highest court

Name .... .Supreme Court
Number of members 7
Length of term .... 8 years
Intermediate appeals court? .... .yes

Labor & Income

Civilian labor force, 2004

Total	5,114,000
Men	2,720,000
Women	2,394,000
Persons 16-19 years	283,000
White	4,291,000
Black	610,000
Hispanic	159,000
Asian	121,000

Civilian labor force as a percent of civilian non-institutional population, 2004

Total	66.0%
Men	72.8
Women	59.7
Persons 16-19 years	49.9
White	66.7
Black	60.7
Hispanic	69.4
Asian	71.7

Employment, 2004

Total	4,758,000
Men	2,516,000
Women	2,241,000
Persons 16-19 years	230,000
White	4,041,000
Black	523,000
Hispanic	140,000
Asian	114,000

Full-time/part-time labor force, 2002

Full-time labor force, employed	3,728,000
Part-time labor force, employed	963,000
Unemployed, looking for	
Full-time work	265,000
Part-time work	45,000

Unemployment rate, 2004

Total	7.0%
Men	7.5
Women	6.4
Persons 16-19 years	18.9
White	5.8
Black	14.4
Hispanic	12.3
Asian	6.1

Unemployed by reason for unemployment (as a percent of total unemployment), 2002

Job losers or completed temp jobs	60.3%
Job leavers	NA
Reentrants	27.1
New entrants	NA

Labor unions, 2004

Membership	930,000
percent of employed	21.6%

Experienced civilian labor force by private industry, first quarter 2004

Total	3,575,075
Natural Resources & Mining	25,055
Construction	165,032
Manufacturing	700,973
Trade, transportation & utilities	783,587
Information	68,138
Finance	209,665
Professional & business	562,617
Education & Health	534,673
Leisure & hospitality	378,384
Other	131,278

Experienced civilian labor force by occupation, 2004

Management	182,650
Business & Financial	188,840
Legal	24,230
Sales	451,600
Office & Admin. Support	680,180
Computers & Math	85,330
Architecture & Engineering	130,700
Arts & Entertainment	53,990
Education	256,320
Social Services	47,520
Healthcare Practitioner & Technical	226,720
Healthcare support	120,750
Maintenance & Repair	180,500
Construction	176,290
Transportation & moving	309,690
Production	491,710
Farming, fishing & forestry	6,440

Hours and earnings of production workers on manufacturing payrolls, 2004

Average weekly hours	42.4
Average hourly earnings	$21.53
Average weekly earnings	$912.87

Average annual pay

2004	$40,373
change from 2003	2.4%

Household income

Median household income, three-year average, 2002-2004	$44,476

Personal income, 2004 ($ per capita)

In current dollars	$31,954
In constant (2000) dollars	$29,635

Poverty

Persons below poverty level, three-year average, 2002-2004	12.1%

Federal individual income tax returns, 2003

Returns filed	4,546,347
Adjusted gross income ($1,000)	$209,645,953
Total income tax paid ($1,000)	$25,201,784

Economy, Business, Industry & Agriculture

Fortune 500 companies, 2005 22

Patents issued, 2004 4,122

Bankruptcy cases filed, 2004 63,000

Business firm ownership, 2002

Women-owned 217,674
   Sales ($ mil) $29,287
Black-owned 44,367
   Sales ($ mil) $4,346
Hispanic-owned 9,848
   Sales ($ mil) $3,206
Asian-owned 15,299
   Sales ($ mil) $5,528
Amer. Indian/Alaska Native-owned 5,365
   Sales ($ mil) $773
Hawaiian/Pacific Isl.-owned 239
   Sales ($ mil) $57

Gross State Product, 2004 ($ mil)

Total Gross State Product $372,169
   Agriculture, forestry, fishing and
     hunting 1,891
   Mining 721
   Utilities 8,158
   Construction 16,593
   Manufacturing, durable goods 61,943
   Manufacturing, non-durable goods . . . 14,318
   Wholesale trade 21,422
   Retail trade 25,790
   Transportation & warehousing 9,369
   Information 10,634
   Finance & insurance 21,967
   Real estate, rental, leasing 42,930
   Professional and technical services 28,977
   Educational services 1,952
   Health care and social assistance 26,332
   Accommodation/food services 7,925
   Other services, except government 8,408
   Government 38,742

Establishments, by major industry group, 2003

Total 237,122
   Forestry, fishing & agriculture 639
   Mining 440
   Construction 26,403
   Manufacturing 14,780
   Wholesale trade 12,507
   Retail trade 38,620
   Transportation & warehousing 5,385
   Information 3,945
   Finance & insurance 13,876
   Professional/scientific/technical 22,255
   Health care/social assistance 24,790
   Accommodation/food services 19,095

Annual payroll by major industry group, 2003

Total ($1,000) $143,974,115
   Forestry, fishing & agriculture 89,232
   Mining 295,112
   Utilities 1,501,211
   Construction 7,455,886
   Manufacturing 32,036,706
   Wholesale trade 8,559,369
   Retail trade 10,712,001
   Transportation & warehousing 4,003,859
   Information 4,763,527
   Finance & insurance 8,589,779
   Professional/scientific/technical . . 17,328,041
   Health care/social assistance 18,006,152
   Accommodation/food services 3,691,191

Agriculture

Number of farms, 2004 53,000
Farm acreage, 2004
   Total 10,000,000
   Acres per farm, 2004 190
Farm income, 2003 ($mil)
   Net farm income $444
   Debt/asset ratio 11.6
Farm marketings, 2003 ($mil)
Total $3,821
   Crops 2,422
   Livestock 1,399

Principal commodities, in order by marketing receipts, 2003

   Dairy products, greenhouse, corn, soybeans

Federal economic activity in state

Expenditures, 2003
   Total ($ mil) $57,870
   Per capita $5,741
   Defense ($ mil) 3,462
   Non-defense ($ mil) 54,408
Defense department, 2003
   Payroll ($ mil) $1,040
   Contract awards ($ mil) $2,524
   Grants ($ mil) $116
   Homeland security grants ($1,000)
     2004 . . . . $76,981
     2005 . . . . $64,075

FDIC insured financial institutions, 2004

Number 173
   Assets ($bil) $194.6
   Deposits ($bil) 136.1

Fishing, 2004

Catch (x 1,000 lbs) 8,540
Value ($1,000) $6,161

Mining, 2004 ($ mil)

Total non-fuel mineral production $1,530
Percent of U.S. 3.5%

Construction, 2003 ($ mil)

Total contracts (including non-building) $13,918
  residential.......................... 7,199
  non-residential 4,400

Establishments, receipts, payroll & employees, by major industry group, 2002

Mining................................ 165
  Receipts ($1,000) $1,649,882
  Annual payroll ($1,000)........... $282,257
  Paid employees 5,419

Utilities 399
  Receipts ($1,000) .... NA
  Annual payroll ($1,000)................. NA
  Paid employees .... (10k-24k)

Construction........................ 26,014
  Receipts ($1,000) $36,536,275
  Annual payroll ($1,000)......... $8,108,488
  Paid employees 219,032

Manufacturing 15,193
  Receipts ($1,000) $221,433,262
  Annual payroll ($1,000)......... $33,171,232
  Paid employees 736,259

Wholesale trade 12,876
  Receipts ($1,000) $165,958,945
  Annual payroll ($1,000)......... $8,306,473
  Paid employees 177,963

Retail trade......................... 38,876
  Receipts ($1,000) $109,350,139
  Annual payroll ($1,000)........ $10,413,480
  Paid employees 520,958

Transportation....................... 5,340
  Receipts ($1,000) $9,189,132
  Annual payroll ($1,000)......... $3,163,042
  Paid employees 91,458

Information.......................... 3,906
  Receipts ($1,000) .... NA
  Annual payroll ($1,000)......... $4,677,078
  Paid employees 97,088

Finance & insurance 13,652
  Receipts ($1,000) .... NA
  Annual payroll ($1,000)......... $8,394,958
  Paid employees 177,479

Professional, scientific & technical 22,337
  Receipts ($1,000) $24,220,096
  Annual payroll ($1,000)........ $14,814,019
  Paid employees 272,167

Health care & social assistance 24,596
  Receipts ($1,000) $39,441,794
  Annual payroll ($1,000)......... $17,191,187
  Paid employees 512,425

Accommodation & food service......... 19,084
  Receipts ($1,000) $12,248,269
  Annual payroll ($1,000)......... $3,488,978
  Paid employees 329,499

Communication, Energy & Transportation

Communication

Daily newspapers, 2004 48
Households with computers, 2003.......... 60%
Households with internet access, 2003 ..... 52%

Energy

Electricity Consumption, 2001
  Total (trillion Btu).................... 3,120
  Per capita (million Btu)............... 312
By source of production (trillion Btu)
  Coal 797
  Natural gas............................ 929
  Petroleum.......................... 1,042
  Nuclear electric power 279
  Hydroelectric power................... 4
By end-use sector (trillion Btu)
  Residential 790
  Commercial 598
  Industrial 928
  Transportation 804
Electric energy, 2003
  Production (billion kWh) 111.3
  Net summer capability (million kW) 30.4
Gas utilities, 2003
  Customers (x1,000)................... 3,251
  Sales (trillion Btu)................... 522
  Revenues ($mil)..................... $3,617
Nuclear plants, 2003 4

Transportation, 2004

Public Road & Street Mileage 122,382
  Urban............................. 35,561
  Rural 86,821
  Interstate........................... 1,243
Vehicle miles of travel per capita....... 10,249.6
Total motor vehicle registrations...... 8,398,621
  Automobiles...................... 4,680,729
  Buses 26,173
  Trucks 3,691,719
  Motorcycles 228,856
Licensed drivers 7,103,404
  19 years & under 377,513
Deaths from motor vehicle accidents 1,159

State Summary

Capital City.........................St. Paul
Governor......................Tim Pawlenty

130 State Capitol
75 Rev Dr MLK Jr Blvd
St Paul, MN 55155
651-296-3391

Admitted as a state 1858
Area (square miles).................. 86,939
Population, 2004 (est.) 5,100,958
Largest City.....................Minneapolis
  Population, 2004................... 374,000
Personal income per capita, 2004
  (in current dollars) $35,861
Gross state product ($ mil), 2004 ..... $223,822

Leading industries by payroll, 2003

  Manufacturing, Health care/Social assistance,
      Finance & Insurance

**Leading agricultural commodities by receipts,
2003**

  Corn, soybeans, hogs, dairy products

Geography & Environment

Total area (sq. mi.).................... 86,939
  land 79,610
  water 7,329
Federally-owned land, 2004 (acres) ... 2,873,517
  percent............................. 5.6%
Highest point.................. Eagle Mountain
  elevation (feet) 2,301
Lowest point ....Lake Superior
  elevation (feet) 602
General coastline (miles)..................... 0
Tidal shoreline (miles)....................... 0
Capital City.........................St. Paul
  Population 2000 287,000
  Population 2004 277,000
Largest City.....................Minneapolis
  Population 2000 383,000
  Population 2004 374,000

Number of cities with over 100,000 population

1990 2
2000 2
2004 2

State park and recreation areas, 2003

Area (acres x 1,000)...................... 220
Number of visitors (x 1,000) 7,782
Revenues (x 1,000)..................... $7,588
  percent of operating expenditures...... 26.5%

National forest system land, 2004

Acres 2,840,000

Demographics and Characteristics of the Population

Population

1980 4,075,970
1990 4,375,099
2000 4,919,479
2004 (estimate)................... 5,100,958
  persons per sq. mile of land.............64.1
2005 (projection)................... 5,174,743
  Male.......................... 2,572,306
  Female........................ 2,602,437
2010 (projection) 5,420,636
2020 (projection) 5,900,769
2030 (projection) 6,306,130
  Male.......................... 3,159,076
  Female........................ 3,147,054

Metropolitan and Non-Metro. area population

	Metro	Non-Metro
1980	2,621,000	1,455,000
1990	2,960,000	1,415,000
2000	3,463,000	1,456,000

Change in population, 2000-2004

Number........................... 181,466
  percent................................. 3.7%
Natural increase (births minus deaths).. 126,925
Net internal migration .... -7,728
Net international migration 60,274

Persons by age, 2004

Under 5 years 332,024
18 years and over 3,860,678
65 years and over 615,179
85 years and over 98,215

Persons by age, 2010 (projected)

Total............................ 5,420,636
  Under 5 years 369,571
  5 to 17 years 920,392
  18 and over 4,130,673
  21 and over 3,905,704
  65 and over 670,429
  85 and over 114,909
  Median age 36.5

Race, 2004 (estimate)

One Race
  White........................ 4,583,418
  Black or African American 211,628
  American Indian/Alaska Native....... 59,411
  Pacific Islander 2,669
  Asian Indian...................... 19,508
  Chinese 25,378
  Filipino 6,897
  Japanese 5,717
  Korean.......................... 22,550
  Vietnamese...................... 15,729
Two or more races.................... 71,520

Persons of Hispanic origin, 2004

Total Hispanic or Latino 173,124
   Mexican............................ 119,358
   Puerto Rican 7,276
   Cuban 3,778
   Other Hispanic or Latino 11,421

Marital status, 2000

Population 15 years & over 3,857,755
   Never married 1,084,029
   Married......................... 2,171,916
   Separated 38,578
   Widowed.......................... 223,750
   Divorced......................... 335,625

Language spoken at home, 2000

Population 5 years & over 4,591,491
   English only 4,201,503
   Spanish 132,066
   Other Indo-European languages 110,644
   Asian/Pacific Island languages...... 103,520

Households & families, 2000

Households........................ 1,895,127
   with persons under 18 years 658,565
   with persons over 65 years.......... 402,837
   persons per household 2.52
Families.......................... 1,255,141
   persons per family.....................3.09
Married couples.................... 1,018,245
Female householder,
   no husband present................ 168,782
One-person households 509,468

Nativity, 2000

Number of persons born in state 3,451,522
   percent of population................. 70.2%

Immigration & Naturalization, 2004

Immigrants admitted.................. 11,708
Persons naturalized 7,713
Asylums granted 281
Asylums denied 64

Vital Statistics and Health

Marriages

2002 32,836
2003 31,638
2004 30,359

Divorces

2002 15,722
2003 14,991
2004 14,235

Births

2003 70,050
   Birthrate (per 1,000).................... 13.8
   Low birth weight (2,500g or less)........ 6.2%
   To unmarried mothers................ 27.7%

2003, continued
   White............................. 59,491
   Black 5,378
   Hispanic 4,937
   Asian/Pacific Islander 3,871
   Amer. Indian/Alaska Native.......... 1,417
2004 (preliminary)..................... 70,615
   Birthrate (per 1,000)................... 13.8
   White............................. 59,565
   Black 4,646
   Hispanic 5,330
   Asian/Pacific Islander 4,710

Deaths

2002
All causes 38,510
   rate per 100,000...................... 767.2
Heart disease 8,602
   rate per 100,000...................... 171.4
Malignant neoplasms................. 9,210
   rate per 100,000...................... 183.5
Cerebrovascular disease............... 2,706
   rate per 100,000....................... 53.9
Chronic lower respiratory disease 1,971
   rate per 100,000....................... 39.3
2003 37,636
   rate per 100,000...................... 743.9
2004 (provisional) 36,930

Infant deaths

2003 (provisional) 325
   rate per 1,000 .... 4.6
2004 (provisional) 348
   rate per 1,000 .... 4.9

Abortions, 2000

Total............................... 15,000
   rate per 1,000 women age 15-44.......... 13.5

Physicians, 2003

Total............................... 14,088
   rate per 1,000 persons.................. 278

Nurses, 2001

Total............................... 6,990
   rate per 1,000 persons.................. 943

Community Hospitals, 2003

Number 131
Beds (x 1,000)........................ 16.4
Patients admitted (x 1,000) 615
Average daily census (x 1,000) 11.3
Average cost per day $1,109
Outpatient visits (x mil)................... 9.1

Disability status of population, 2004

5 to 20 years 5.7%
21 to 64 years 9.7%
65 years and over 33.9%

Education

Educational attainment, 2004

Population over 25 years	3,257,128
Less than 9th grade	116,802
High school graduates only	937,895
Bachelor's degree only	685,433
Graduate or professional degree	281,475
Less than 9th grade percent	3.6%
High school graduate or more	92.3%
College graduate or more	32.5%
Graduate or professional degree	8.6%

Public school enrollment, Fall 2002

Total	846,891
Kindergarten through grade 8	567,701
Grades 9 through 12	279,190
Enrollment, 2005 (projected)	822,600

Graduating public high school seniors

2004 (estimate)	59,780

SAT scores, 2005

Average verbal score	592
Average math score	597
Percent of graduates taking test	11%

Public school teachers, 2004

Total (x 1,000)	52.2
Elementary (x 1,000)	26.6
Secondary (x 1,000)	25.7
Average salary	$45,400
Elementary	$45,800
Secondary	$44,300

State receipts & expenditures for public schools, 2004

Revenue receipts ($mil)	$8,612
Expenditures	
Total ($mil)	$9,417
Per capita	$1,860
Per pupil	$9,513

Institutions of higher education, 2004

Total	113
Public	52
Private	61

Enrollment in institutions of higher education, Fall 2003

Total	339,731
Full-time men	97,432
Full-time women	120,187
Part-time men	49,400
Part-time women	72,712

Minority enrollment in institutions of higher education, Fall 2003

Black, non-hispanic	15,399
Hispanic	4,748
Asian/Pacific Islander	11,858
American Indian/Alaska Native	3,427

Earned degrees conferred, 2003

Bachelor's	25,783
Master's	9,185
First-professional	1,596
Doctor's	941

State & local financial support for higher education, 2003-2004

Full-time equivalent enrollment (x 1,000)	189.8
Appropriations per FTE	$5,564
as a percent of tax revenue	7.2%

Social Insurance & Welfare Programs

Social Security benefits & beneficiaries, 2004

Beneficiaries	
Total	775,000
Retired & dependents	567,000
Survivors	101,000
Disabled & dependents	106,000
Annual benefit payments ($ mil)	
Total	$8,080
Retired & dependents	$5,640
Survivors	$1,394
Disabled & dependents	$1,046
Average Monthly Benefit	
Retired & dependents	$955
Disabled & dependents	$879
Widowed	$938

Medicare

Enrollment, 2001 (x 1,000)	660
Payments ($ mil, est.)	$3,100
Enrollment, 2003 (x 1,000)	676

Medicaid, 2002

Beneficiaries (x 1,000)	621
Payments ($ mil)	$4,439

State Children's Health Insurance, 2004

Enrollment (x 1,000)	4.8
Expenditures ($ mil)	$72.7

Persons without health insurance, 2003

Number (x 1,000)	444
percent	8.7%
Number of children (x 1,000)	77
percent of children	6.2%

Federal public aid

Temporary Assistance for Needy Families, 2004

Recipients (x 1,000)	88
Families (x 1,000)	34

Supplemental Security Income, 2003

Recipients (x 1,000)	69
Payments ($ mil)	$316

Food Stamp Program, 2004

Participants (x 1,000)	247
Benefits ($ mil)	$249

Housing & Construction

Housing units

Total 2003 (estimate) 2,173,825
Total 2004 (estimate) 2,212,701
Seasonal or recreational use, 2003 54,000
Owner-occupied single-family, 2003 . . 1,259,000
  Median value $169,778
Renter-occupied, 2003 455,000
  Median rent $657
Homeownership rate, 2003 .... 77.2%
Homeownership rate, 2004 .... 76.4%

New privately owned housing units, 2004

Number authorized (x 1,000) 41.8
Value ($ mil)......................... $6,583
Started 2005 (x 1,000, estimate)...........39.0
Started 2006 (x 1,000, estimate)...........37.1

Existing home sales

2002 (x 1,000).........................122.6
2003 (x 1,000).........................126.7
2004 (x 1,000).........................137.4

Government & Elections

State Officials 2006

Governor (name/party/term expires)
         Tim Pawlenty
         Republican - 1/07
Lieutenant Governor.............Carol Molnau
Secretary of State............. Mary Kiffmeyer
Attorney General..................Mike Hatch
Chief Justice .... Kathleen Blatz

Governorship

Minimum age......................... 25
Length of term....................... 4 years
Consecutive terms permitted ..... not specified
Who succeeds....................Lt. Governor

State Legislature

Name .... Legislature
Upper chamber ....Senate
  Number of members.................... 67
  Length of term.................... 4 years
  Party in majority, 2006 ....Democratic
Lower chamber.......House of Representatives
  Number of members.................... 134
  Length of term.................... 2 years
  Party in majority, 2006 .... Republican

State Government Employees, 2004

Total............................. 74,543
Payroll $309,848,728

Local Government Employees, 2004

Total............................ 200,524
Payroll $705,702,098

Local Governments by Type, 2002

Total................................ 3,482
  County............................... 87
  Municipal............................ 854
  Township 1,793
  School District...................... 345
  Special District 403

Voting age population, November 2004

Total................................ 3,766,000
  Male............................... 1,858,000
  Female............................. 1,908,000
  White.............................. 3,435,000
  Black 128,000
  Hispanic 108,000
  Asian 137,000

Presidential Election, 2004

Total Popular Vote 2,828,387
  Kerry 1,445,014
  Bush.............................. 1,346,695
Total Electoral Votes....................... 10

Federal representation, 2006 (109th Congress)

Senator........................ Mark Dayton
  Party .... Democrat
  Year term expires 2007
Senator....................... Norm Coleman
  Party .... Republican
  Year term expires 2009
Representatives, total 8
  Democrats........................... 4
  Republicans 4
  Other 0

Votes cast for US Senators

2002
Total vote (x 1,000) 2,255,000
Leading party..................... Republican
Percent for leading party 49.5%

2004
Total vote (x 1,000) .... NA
Leading party......................... NA
Percent for leading party .... NA

Votes cast for US Representatives

2002
Total vote (x 1,000) 2,202
  Democratic.......................... 1,098
  Republican 1,030
Leading party....................Democratic
Percent for leading party 49.9%

2004
Total vote (x 1,000) 2,722
  Democratic.......................... 1,400
  Republican 1,236
Leading party....................Democratic
Percent for leading party 51.4%

Women holding public office, 2006
US Congress 1
Statewide elected office 3
State legislature 60

Black public officials, 2001
Total 20
  US and state legislatures 2
  City/county/regional offices 4
  Judicial/law enforcement 9
  Education/school boards 5

Hispanic public officials, 2004
Total 4
  State executives & legislators 1
  City/county/regional offices 1
  Judicial/law enforcement 1
  Education/school boards 1

Governmental Finance

State government revenues, 2004
Total revenue ($1,000) $29,708,220
  Revenue per capita 5,828.57

General Revenue ($ per capita) $4,751.23
  Intergovernmental 1,251.68
  Taxes 2,890.90
    general sales 797.88
    individual income tax 1,120.19
    corporate income tax 125.01
  Current charges 373.49
  Miscellaneous 235.17

State government expenditure, 2004
Total expenditure (x $1,000) $28,831,675
  Expenditure per capita 5,656.60
General Expenditure ($ per capita) $4,980.13
  Education 1,936.92
  Public welfare 1,578.96
  Health 101.33
  Hospitals 37.60
  Highways 357.69
  Police protection 41.70
  Correction 80.65
  Natural resources 91.31
  Parks & recreation 31.56
  Governmental administration 128.53
  Interest on general debt 74.16

State debt & cash, 2004 ($ per capita)
Debt $1,307.76
Cash/security holdings $9,914.35

Federal government grants to state & local government, 2004 (x $1,000)
Total $7,208,781
By Federal Agency
  Defense $91,873

By Federal Agency, continued
  Education 538,856
  Energy 31,527
  Environmental Protection Agency 77,106
  Health & Human Services 4,324,656
  Homeland Security 26,894
  Housing & Urban Development 558,686
  Justice 111,433
  Labor 133,860
  Transportation 697,540
  Veterans Affairs 14,208

Crime, Law Enforcement & Courts

Crime, 2004 (rates per 100,000 residents)
Property crimes 155,019
  Burglaries 28,048
  Larcenies 113,453
  Motor vehicle thefts 13,518
  Property crime rate 3,039.0
Violent crimes 13,751
  Murders 113
  Forcible rape 2,123
  Robberies 4,070
  Aggravated assaults 7,445
  Violent crime rate 269.6

Police Agencies, 2004
Total agencies 303
Total employees 12,572
  Male officers 7,234
  Female officers 913
  Male civilians 1,749
  Female civilians 2,676

Arrests, 2004
Total 132,255
  Persons under 18 years of age 30,905

Prisoners under state & federal jurisdiction, 2004
Total prisoners 8,758
  Percent change, 12/31/03 to 12/31/04 ... 11.4%
Sentenced to more than one year 8,758
  rate per 100,000 171

Persons under sentence of death, 7/1/05
Total 0
  White 0
  Black 0
  Hispanic 0

State's highest court
Name .... .Supreme Court
Number of members 9
Length of term .... 6 years
Intermediate appeals court? .... no

Labor & Income

Civilian labor force, 2004

Total	2,941,000
Men	1,556,000
Women	1,384,000
Persons 16-19 years	173,000
White	2,681,000
Black	94,000
Hispanic	81,000
Asian	123,000

Civilian labor force as a percent of civilian non-institutional population, 2004

Total	74.6%
Men	80.3
Women	69.0
Persons 16-19 years	59.7
White	74.7
Black	75.7
Hispanic	78.9
Asian	74.4

Employment, 2004

Total	2,800,000
Men	1,470,000
Women	1,330,000
Persons 16-19 years	152,000
White	2,566,000
Black	82,000
Hispanic	76,000
Asian	117,000

Full-time/part-time labor force, 2002

Full-time labor force, employed	2,149,000
Part-time labor force, employed	641,000
Unemployed, looking for	
Full-time work	103,000
Part-time work	NA

Unemployment rate, 2004

Total	4.8%
Men	5.5
Women	3.9
Persons 16-19 years	12.4
White	4.3
Black	12.9
Hispanic	6.4
Asian	5.0

Unemployed by reason for unemployment (as a percent of total unemployment), 2002

Job losers or completed temp jobs	57.8%
Job leavers	NA
Reentrants	NA
New entrants	NA

Labor unions, 2004

Membership	424,000
percent of employed	17.5%

Experienced civilian labor force by private industry, first quarter 2004

Total	2,146,734
Natural Resources & Mining	18,802
Construction	105,526
Manufacturing	334,888
Trade, transportation & utilities	502,065
Information	60,755
Finance	172,528
Professional & business	291,860
Education & Health	355,460
Leisure & hospitality	219,237
Other	85,613

Experienced civilian labor force by occupation, 2004

Management	126,800
Business & Financial	141,490
Legal	18,290
Sales	277,570
Office & Admin. Support	433,470
Computers & Math	69,200
Architecture & Engineering	52,360
Arts & Entertainment	33,310
Education	149,330
Social Services	46,320
Healthcare Practitioner & Technical	136,790
Healthcare support	74,930
Maintenance & Repair	94,870
Construction	118,210
Transportation & moving	175,530
Production	229,800
Farming, fishing & forestry	4,080

Hours and earnings of production workers on manufacturing payrolls, 2004

Average weekly hours	40.9
Average hourly earnings	$16.04
Average weekly earnings	$656.04

Average annual pay

2004	$40,398
change from 2003	4.7%

Household income

Median household income, three-year average, 2002-2004	$55,914

Personal income, 2004 ($ per capita)

In current dollars	$35,861
In constant (2000) dollars	$33,259

Poverty

Persons below poverty level, three-year average, 2002-2004	7.0%

Federal individual income tax returns, 2003

Returns filed	2,383,813
Adjusted gross income ($1,000)	$119,929,752
Total income tax paid ($1,000)	$14,961,640

Economy, Business, Industry & Agriculture

Fortune 500 companies, 2005 18

Patents issued, 2004 2,996

Bankruptcy cases filed, 2004 19,100

Business firm ownership, 2002

Women-owned....................... 123,905
  Sales ($ mil) $16,252
Black-owned.......................... 7,852
  Sales ($ mil) .... NA
Hispanic-owned....................... 3,988
  Sales ($ mil) $463
Asian-owned 7,699
  Sales ($ mil) $1,910
Amer. Indian/Alaska Native-owned 2,742
  Sales ($ mil) $321
Hawaiian/Pacific Isl.-owned............. 124
  Sales ($ mil) $12

Gross State Product, 2004 ($ mil)

Total Gross State Product $223,822
  Agriculture, forestry, fishing and
    hunting 3,147
  Mining............................. 528
  Utilities........................... 3,574
  Construction 11,468
  Manufacturing, durable goods....... 19,605
  Manufacturing, non-durable goods ... 11,065
  Wholesale trade.................... 15,668
  Retail trade....................... 14,910
  Transportation & warehousing 7,250
  Information 8,231
  Finance & insurance................ 23,448
  Real estate, rental, leasing 24,875
  Professional and technical services.... 13,026
  Educational services............... 1,629
  Health care and social assistance...... 17,637
  Accommodation/food services........ 4,892
  Other services, except government 5,423
  Government 22,635

Establishments, by major industry group, 2003

Total.............................. 145,861
  Forestry, fishing & agriculture 481
  Mining............................. 162
  Construction 17,324
  Manufacturing...................... 7,963
  Wholesale trade.................... 8,770
  Retail trade....................... 21,086
  Transportation & warehousing 4,507
  Information 2,754
  Finance & insurance................ 9,727
  Professional/scientific/technical 15,776
  Health care/social assistance 12,753
  Accommodation/food services........ 10,363

Annual payroll by major industry group, 2003

Total ($1,000) $87,297,655
  Forestry, fishing & agriculture 57,415
  Mining............................ 251,565
  Utilities.......................... 859,831
  Construction 5,882,366
  Manufacturing................. 14,458,139
  Wholesale trade.................. 6,903,472
  Retail trade...................... 6,657,030
  Transportation & warehousing 2,926,177
  Information 3,493,845
  Finance & insurance............. 8,987,744
  Professional/scientific/technical ... 6,575,527
  Health care/social assistance 11,934,900
  Accommodation/food services..... 2,512,398

Agriculture

Number of farms, 2004 80,000
Farm acreage, 2004
  Total........................ 28,000,000
  Acres per farm, 2004 346
Farm income, 2003 ($mil)
  Net farm income $1,568
  Debt/asset ratio 17.6
Farm marketings, 2003 ($mil)
Total............................... $8,588
  Crops............................ 4,516
  Livestock......................... 4,072

Principal commodities, in order by marketing receipts, 2003

    Corn, soybeans, hogs, dairy products

Federal economic activity in state

Expenditures, 2003
  Total ($ mil) $27,580
  Per capita $5,451
  Defense ($ mil).................... 2,120
  Non-defense ($ mil) 25,460
Defense department, 2003
  Payroll ($ mil) $541
  Contract awards ($ mil).............. $1,565
  Grants ($ mil)........................ $52
  Homeland security grants ($1,000)
    2004 .... $60,236
    2005 .... $35,311

FDIC insured financial institutions, 2004

Number............................. 478
  Assets ($bil) $63.5
  Deposits ($bil) 94.4

Fishing, 2004

Catch (x 1,000 lbs)...................... 323
Value ($1,000)........................ $187

Mining, 2004 ($ mil)
Total non-fuel mineral production $1,590
Percent of U.S. 3.6%

Construction, 2003 ($ mil)
Total contracts (including non-building) $10,446
    residential. 6,059
    non-residential 2,408

Establishments, receipts, payroll & employees, by major industry group, 2002

Mining 333
  Receipts ($1,000) $988,177
  Annual payroll ($1,000) $180,056
  Paid employees 4,913

Utilities 279
  Receipts ($1,000) . . . . NA
  Annual payroll ($1,000) $835,871
  Paid employees 12,474

Construction 16,952
  Receipts ($1,000) $29,296,756
  Annual payroll ($1,000) $5,840,385
  Paid employees 148,430

Manufacturing 8,139
  Receipts ($1,000) $80,623,873
  Annual payroll ($1,000) $14,077,260
  Paid employees 351,884

Wholesale trade 8,884
  Receipts ($1,000) $108,388,816
  Annual payroll ($1,000) $6,318,228
  Paid employees 126,735

Retail trade 21,129
  Receipts ($1,000) $60,015,531
  Annual payroll ($1,000) $6,040,265
  Paid employees 306,571

Transportation 4,341
  Receipts ($1,000) $6,735,513
  Annual payroll ($1,000) $1,714,042
  Paid employees 57,425

Information. 2,771
  Receipts ($1,000) . . . . NA
  Annual payroll ($1,000) $3,307,413
  Paid employees 70,155

Finance & insurance 9,357
  Receipts ($1,000) . . . . NA
  Annual payroll ($1,000) $8,490,179
  Paid employees 152,795

Professional, scientific & technical 15,557
  Receipts ($1,000) $14,652,614
  Annual payroll ($1,000) $6,338,987
  Paid employees 125,217

Health care & social assistance 12,413
  Receipts ($1,000) $24,337,547
  Annual payroll ($1,000) $11,072,056
  Paid employees 350,188

Accommodation & food service 10,232
  Receipts ($1,000) $7,959,590
  Annual payroll ($1,000) $2,362,446
  Paid employees 203,062

Communication, Energy & Transportation

Communication
Daily newspapers, 2004 25
Households with computers, 2003 . . . . .68%
Households with internet access, 2003 . . . . . .62%

Energy
Electricity Consumption, 2001
  Total (trillion Btu). 1,745
  Per capita (million Btu) 350
By source of production (trillion Btu)
  Coal 353
  Natural gas 345
  Petroleum. 674
  Nuclear electric power 123
  Hydroelectric power 9
By end-use sector (trillion Btu)
  Residential 381
  Commercial 336
  Industrial 526
  Transportation 502
Electric energy, 2003
  Production (billion kWh) 55.1
  Net summer capability (million kW) 11.5
Gas utilities, 2003
  Customers (x1,000). 1,433
  Sales (trillion Btu). 280
  Revenues ($mil) $2,170
Nuclear plants, 2003 3

Transportation, 2004
Public Road & Street Mileage 131,937
  Urban. 16,293
  Rural 115,644
  Interstate. 914
Vehicle miles of travel per capita 11,109.6
Total motor vehicle registrations 4,593,349
  Automobiles. 2,502,190
  Buses 16,947
  Trucks 2,074,212
  Motorcycles 188,903
Licensed drivers 3,083,007
  19 years & under 193,317
Deaths from motor vehicle accidents 567

State Summary

Capital City......................... Jackson
Governor...................... Haley Barbour
PO Box 139
Jackson, MS 39205
601-359-3100
Admitted as a state 1817
Area (square miles) 48,430
Population, 2004 (est.) 2,902,966
Largest City.......................... Jackson
Population, 2004................... 179,000
Personal income per capita, 2004
(in current dollars) $24,650
Gross state product ($ mil), 2004 ...... $76,166

Leading industries by payroll, 2003

Manufacturing, Health care/Social assistance,
Retail trade

Leading agricultural commodities by receipts, 2003

Broilers, cotton, soybeans, aquaculture

Geography & Environment

Total area (sq. mi.).................... 48,430
land 46,907
water 1,523

Federally-owned land, 2004 (acres) ... 2,196,940
percent............................. 7.3%

Highest point.............. Woodall Mountain
elevation (feet) 806

Lowest point .... Gulf of Mexico
elevation (feet) .... sea level

General coastline (miles)................... 44

Tidal shoreline (miles)..................... 359

Capital City......................... Jackson
Population 2000 184,000
Population 2004 179,000

Largest City......................... Jackson
Population 2000 184,000
Population 2004 179,000

Number of cities with over 100,000 population

1990 1
2000 1
2004 1

State park and recreation areas, 2003

Area (acres x 1,000)...................... 24
Number of visitors (x 1,000) 3,051
Revenues (x 1,000)................... $6,542
percent of operating expenditures...... 48.0%

National forest system land, 2004

Acres 1,171,000

Demographics and Characteristics of the Population

Population

1980 2,520,638
1990 2,573,216
2000 2,844,658
2004 (estimate)................... 2,902,966
persons per sq. mile of land............61.9
2005 (projection)................... 2,915,696
Male..................... 1,413,742
Female.................... 1,501,954
2010 (projection)................... 2,971,412
2020 (projection)................... 3,044,812
2030 (projection)................... 3,092,410
Male..................... 1,510,555
Female..................... 1,581,855

Metropolitan and Non-Metro. area population

	Metro	Non-Metro
1980	716,000	1,804,000
1990	776,000	1,798,000
2000	1,024,000	1,821,000

Change in population, 2000-2004

Number............................. 58,310
percent............................2.0%
Natural increase (births minus deaths)... 61,539
Net internal migration .... -10,423
Net international migration 8,717

Persons by age, 2004

Under 5 years 208,354
18 years and over 2,153,397
65 years and over 352,867
85 years and over 39,632

Persons by age, 2010 (projected)

Total............................. 2,971,412
Under 5 years 211,215
5 to 17 years 548,235
18 and over 2,211,962
21 and over 2,082,747
65 and over 379,025
85 and over 52,056
Median age 36.5

Race, 2004 (estimate)

One Race
White...................... 1,780,313
Black or African American ... 1,068,990
American Indian/Alaska Native....... 13,448
Pacific Islander 844
Asian Indian...................... 4,083
Chinese 1,559
Filipino 2,656
Japanese 405
Korean............................. 1,266
Vietnamese........................ 373
Two or more races.................... 17,962

Persons of Hispanic origin, 2004

Total Hispanic or Latino	41,706
Mexican	27,573
Puerto Rican	1,597
Cuban	801
Other Hispanic or Latino	6,652

Marital status, 2000

Population 15 years & over	2,203,615
Never married	610,401
Married	1,134,862
Separated	63,905
Widowed	174,086
Divorced	222,565

Language spoken at home, 2000

Population 5 years & over	2,641,453
English only	2,545,931
Spanish	50,515
Other Indo-European languages	23,700
Asian/Pacific Island languages	13,558

Households & families, 2000

Households	1,046,434
with persons under 18 years	414,602
with persons over 65 years	248,129
persons per household	2.63
Families	747,159
persons per family	3.14
Married couples	520,844
Female householder, no husband present	180,705
One-person households	257,708

Nativity, 2000

Number of persons born in state	2,113,883
percent of population	74.3%

Immigration & Naturalization, 2004

Immigrants admitted	1,252
Persons naturalized	557
Asylums granted	5
Asylums denied	NA

Vital Statistics and Health

Marriages

2002	18,360
2003	17,798
2004	17,705

Divorces

2002	14,066
2003	13,283
2004	13,077

Births

2003	42,380
Birthrate (per 1,000)	14.7
Low birth weight (2,500g or less)	11.4%
To unmarried mothers	47.0%

2003, continued

White	23,575
Black	18,367
Hispanic	461
Asian/Pacific Islander	289
Amer. Indian/Alaska Native	131

2004 (preliminary)	42,810
Birthrate (per 1,000)	14.7
White	23,558
Black	18,516
Hispanic	1,052
Asian/Pacific Islander	431

Deaths

2002

All causes	28,853
rate per 100,000	1,004.7
Heart disease	9,061
rate per 100,000	315.5
Malignant neoplasms	6,069
rate per 100,000	211.3
Cerebrovascular disease	1,926
rate per 100,000	67.1
Chronic lower respiratory disease	1,378
rate per 100,000	48.0
2003	28,535
rate per 100,000	990.4
2004 (provisional)	27,626

Infant deaths

2003 (provisional)	425
rate per 1,000	10.1
2004 (provisional)	391
rate per 1,000	9.2

Abortions, 2000

Total	4,000
rate per 1,000 women age 15-44	5.9

Physicians, 2003

Total	5,240
rate per 1,000 persons	182

Nurses, 2001

Total	22,290
rate per 1,000 persons	779

Community Hospitals, 2003

Number	92
Beds (x 1,000)	13.0
Patients admitted (x 1,000)	416
Average daily census (x 1,000)	7.4
Average cost per day	$882
Outpatient visits (x mil)	4.0

Disability status of population, 2004

5 to 20 years	8.5%
21 to 64 years	19%
65 years and over	52.1%

Education

Educational attainment, 2004

Population over 25 years 1,774,048
   Less than 9th grade 141,985
   High school graduates only.......... 554,246
   Bachelor's degree only 220,683
   Graduate or professional degree...... 113,970
   Less than 9th grade percent 8.0%
   High school graduate or more......... 83.0%
   College graduate or more.............. 20.1%
   Graduate or professional degree........ 6.4%

Public school enrollment, Fall 2002

Total................................ 492,645
   Kindergarten through grade 8 360,287
   Grades 9 through 12 132,358
Enrollment, 2005 (projected) 484,000

Graduating public high school seniors

2004 (estimate)....................... 23,610

SAT scores, 2005

Average verbal score 564
Average math score 554
Percent of graduates taking test 4%

Public school teachers, 2004

Total (x 1,000) 30.7
   Elementary (x 1,000)................... 18.3
   Secondary (x 1,000) 12.4
Average salary $35,700
   Elementary........................ $35,700
   Secondary $35,700

State receipts & expenditures for public schools, 2004

Revenue receipts ($mil)................. $3,436
Expenditures
Total ($mil).......................... $3,394
   Per capita $1,178
   Per pupil $6,556

Institutions of higher education, 2004

Total.................................... 40
   Public................................ 26
   Private............................... 14

Enrollment in institutions of higher education, Fall, 2003

Total............................... 149,665
   Full-time men 46,214
   Full-time women.................... 68,574
   Part-time men 11,695
   Part-time women.................... 23,182

Minority enrollment in institutions of higher education, Fall, 2003

Black, non-hispanic.................... 55,232
Hispanic 1,008
Asian/Pacific Islander 1,112
American Indian/Alaska Native........... 650

Earned degrees conferred, 2003

Bachelor's 11,797
Master's.............................. 3,417
First-professional....................... 520
Doctor's................................ 340

State & local financial support for higher education, 2003-2004

Full-time equivalent enrollment (x 1,000) ..145.9
Appropriations per FTE................ $3,980
   as a percent of tax revenue............. 11.9%

Social Insurance & Welfare Programs

Social Security benefits & beneficiaries, 2004

Beneficiaries
   Total............................. 546,000
   Retired & dependents............... 319,000
   Survivors.......................... 88,000
   Disabled & dependents............. 139,000
Annual benefit payments ($ mil)
   Total.............................. $5,092
   Retired & dependents............... $2,889
   Survivors............................ $964
   Disabled & dependents.............. $1,239
Average Monthly Benefit
   Retired & dependents................. $875
   Disabled & dependents................ $835
   Widowed............................. $793

Medicare

Enrollment, 2001 (x 1,000) 423
   Payments ($ mil, est.) $2,100
Enrollment, 2003 (x 1,000) 437

Medicaid, 2002

Beneficiaries (x 1,000)................... 712
Payments ($ mil) $2,500

State Children's Health Insurance, 2004

Enrollment (x 1,000)................... 82.9
Expenditures ($ mil) $101.9

Persons without health insurance, 2003

Number (x 1,000)....................... 511
   percent........................... 17.9%
Number of children (x 1,000) 92
   percent of children 12.1%

Federal public aid

Temporary Assistance for Needy Families, 2004
Recipients (x 1,000)...................... 42
Families (x 1,000) 19

Supplemental Security Income, 2003
Recipients (x 1,000)..................... 126
Payments ($ mil) $550

Food Stamp Program, 2004

Participants (x 1,000) 377
Benefits ($ mil)......................... $361

Housing & Construction

Housing units

Total 2003 (estimate)	1,208,331
Total 2004 (estimate)	1,221,240
Seasonal or recreational use, 2003	24,000
Owner-occupied single-family, 2003	560,000
Median value	$85,142
Renter-occupied, 2003	309,000
Median rent	$525
Homeownership rate, 2003	73.4%
Homeownership rate, 2004	74.0%

New privately owned housing units, 2004

Number authorized (x 1,000)	14.5
Value ($ mil)	$1,517
Started 2005 (x 1,000, estimate)	12.8
Started 2006 (x 1,000, estimate)	12.9

Existing home sales

2002 (x 1,000)	48.0
2003 (x 1,000)	51.5
2004 (x 1,000)	58.1

Government & Elections

State Officials 2006

Governor (name/party/term expires)
Haley Barbour
Republican - 1/08

Lieutenant Governor	Amy Tuck
Secretary of State	Eric Clark
Attorney General	Jim Hood
Chief Justice	James W. Smith Jr.

Governorship

Minimum age	30
Length of term	4 years
Consecutive terms permitted	2
Who succeeds	Lt. Governor

State Legislature

Name	Legislature
Upper chamber	Senate
Number of members	52
Length of term	4 years
Party in majority, 2006	Democratic
Lower chamber	House of Representatives
Number of members	122
Length of term	4 years
Party in majority, 2006	Democratic

State Government Employees, 2004

Total	56,968
Payroll	$164,643,155

Local Government Employees, 2004

Total	131,401
Payroll	$321,649,892

Local Governments by Type, 2002

Total	1,000
County	82
Municipal	296
Township	0
School District	164
Special District	458

Voting age population, November 2004

Total	2,081,000
Male	972,000
Female	1,109,000
White	1,335,000
Black	698,000
Hispanic	46,000
Asian	8,000

Presidential Election, 2004

Total Popular Vote	1,152,145
Kerry	458,094
Bush	684,981
Total Electoral Votes	6

Federal representation, 2006 (109th Congress)

Senator	Trent Lott
Party	Republican
Year term expires	2007
Senator	Thad Cochran
Party	Republican
Year term expires	2009
Representatives, total	4
Democrats	2
Republicans	2
Other	0

Votes cast for US Senators

2002

Total vote (x 1,000)	630,000
Leading party	Republican
Percent for leading party	84.6%

2004

Total vote (x 1,000)	NA
Leading party	NA
Percent for leading party	NA

Votes cast for US Representatives

2002

Total vote (x 1,000)	678
Democratic	320
Republican	339
Leading party	Republican
Percent for leading party	50.0%

2004

Total vote (x 1,000)	1,116
Democratic	335
Republican	659
Leading party	Republican
Percent for leading party	59.0%

Women holding public office, 2006

US Congress 0
Statewide elected office..................... 1
State legislature 22

Black public officials, 2001

Total................................... 892
  US and state legislatures 46
  City/county/regional offices 607
  Judicial/law enforcement................ 109
  Education/school boards 130

Hispanic public officials, 2004

Total...................................... 0
  State executives & legislators 0
  City/county/regional offices 0
  Judicial/law enforcement.................. 0
  Education/school boards.................. 0

Governmental Finance

State government revenues, 2004

Total revenue ($1,000) $15,351,077
  Revenue per capita 5,291.65

General Revenue ($ per capita) $4,204.14
  Intergovernmental 1,869.98
  Taxes 1,766.54
    general sales 855.88
    individual income tax............. 365.98
    corporate income tax 84.06
  Current charges.......................417.53
  Miscellaneous 150.09

State government expenditure, 2004

Total expenditure (x $1,000) $14,330,205
  Expenditure per capita............. 4,939.75
General Expenditure ($ per capita).... $4,423.77
  Education 1,485.94
  Public welfare.................... 1,395.60
  Health 102.60
  Hospitals.........................239.69
  Highways 348.96
  Police protection 25.94
  Correction 105.65
  Natural resources 81.18
  Parks & recreation.....................15.81
  Governmental administration 97.67
  Interest on general debt 69.07

State debt & cash, 2004 ($ per capita)

Debt $1,473.62
Cash/security holdings.............. $8,027.61

Federal government grants to state & local government, 2004 (x $1,000)

Total............................. $5,378,932
By Federal Agency
  Defense $44,898

By Federal Agency, continued
  Education 474,736
  Energy 10,535
  Environmental Protection Agency 44,523
  Health & Human Services. 3,382,313
  Homeland Security.................. 37,032
  Housing & Urban Development...... 271,308
  Justice 59,466
  Labor 89,123
  Transportation 429,788
  Veterans Affairs.................. 13,646

Crime, Law Enforcement & Courts

Crime, 2004 (rates per 100,000 residents)

Property crimes 100,980
  Burglaries....................... 27,661
  Larcenies....................... 65,440
  Motor vehicle thefts 7,879
  Property crime rate................. 3,478.5
Violent crimes......................... 8,568
  Murders........................ 227
  Forcible rape..................... 1,161
  Robberies 2,503
  Aggravated assaults 4,677
  Violent crime rate 295.1

Police Agencies, 2004

Total agencies........................... 191
Total employees 8,857
  Male officers..................... 5,071
  Female officers..................... 456
  Male civilians..................... 1,308
  Female civilians.................... 2,022

Arrests, 2004

Total............................... 113,350
  Persons under 18 years of age 12,514

Prisoners under state & federal jurisdiction, 2004

Total prisoners....................... 20,983
  Percent change, 12/31/03 to 12/31/04 .... 1.9%
Sentenced to more than one year 19,469
  rate per 100,000...................... 669

Persons under sentence of death, 7/1/05

Total.................................... 70
  White................................ 33
  Black 36
  Hispanic 0

State's highest court

Name ....Supreme Court
Number of members....................... 9
Length of term .... 6 years
Intermediate appeals court? .... no

Labor & Income

Civilian labor force, 2004

Total.............................. 1,335,000
  Men 698,000
  Women 637,000
  Persons 16-19 years............... 57,000
  White............................ 862,000
  Black 441,000
  Hispanic 26,000
  Asian 0

Civilian labor force as a percent of civilian non-institutional population, 2004

Total................................ 61.6%
  Men 68.4
  Women 55.5
  Persons 16-19 years............... 34.5
  White............................. 62.6
  Black 59.4
  Hispanic 76.2
  Asian 0.0

Employment, 2004

Total.............................. 1,252,000
  Men 659,000
  Women 593,000
  Persons 16-19 years............... 45,000
  White............................. 827,000
  Black 396,000
  Hispanic 25,000
  Asian 0

Full-time/part-time labor force, 2002

Full-time labor force, employed 1,037,000
Part-time labor force, employed........ 173,000
Unemployed, looking for
  Full-time work..................... 75,000
  Part-time work........................ NA

Unemployment rate, 2004

Total................................. 6.2%
  Men 5.6
  Women 6.8
  Persons 16-19 years................ 20.7
  White.............................. 4.1
  Black 10.3
  Hispanic 6.2
  Asian .... NA

Unemployed by reason for unemployment (as a percent of total unemployment), 2002

Job losers or completed temp jobs 45.5%
Job leavers.............................. NA
Reentrants............................... 38.6
New entrants .... NA

Labor unions, 2004

Membership 53,000
  percent of employed 4.8%

Experienced civilian labor force by private industry, first quarter 2004

Total................................ 863,474
  Natural Resources & Mining 19,510
  Construction 47,717
  Manufacturing....................... 179,116
  Trade, transportation & utilities 216,984
  Information 14,800
  Finance 44,705
  Professional & business 81,439
  Education & Health 111,554
  Leisure & hospitality............... 123,009
  Other.............................. 24,640

Experienced civilian labor force by occupation, 2004

Management......................... 51,590
Business & Financial.................. 23,320
Legal................................ 5,950
Sales................................ 112,710
Office & Admin. Support.............. 168,930
Computers & Math 8,890
Architecture & Engineering 15,440
Arts & Entertainment................. 9,030
Education 73,120
Social Services 9,870
Healthcare Practitioner & Technical..... 63,750
Healthcare support 30,480
Maintenance & Repair 48,140
Construction 53,020
Transportation & moving 95,780
Production 132,870
Farming, fishing & forestry............. 2,350

Hours and earnings of production workers on manufacturing payrolls, 2004

Average weekly hours 40.1
Average hourly earnings $13.12
Average weekly earnings $526.11

Average annual pay

2004 .... $28,535
  change from 2003 .... 3.4%

Household income

Median household income, three-year average,
  2002-2004......................... $33,659

Personal income, 2004 ($ per capita)

In current dollars..................... $24,650
In constant (2000) dollars $22,861

Poverty

Persons below poverty level, three-year average,
  2002-2004......................... 17.7%

Federal individual income tax returns, 2003

Returns filed....................... 1,169,646
Adjusted gross income ($1,000) $40,609,782
Total income tax paid ($1,000) $4,154,587

Economy, Business, Industry & Agriculture

Fortune 500 companies, 2005 0

Patents issued, 2004 159

Bankruptcy cases filed, 2004 21,200

Business firm ownership, 2002

Women-owned. 47,102
  Sales ($ mil) $6,728
Black-owned. 25,004
  Sales ($ mil) $1,333
Hispanic-owned. 1,327
  Sales ($ mil) $274
Asian-owned 2,916
  Sales ($ mil) $1,266
Amer. Indian/Alaska Native-owned 689
  Sales ($ mil) $64
Hawaiian/Pacific Isl.-owned . . . . NA
  Sales ($ mil) $7

Gross State Product, 2004 ($ mil)

Total Gross State Product $76,166
  Agriculture, forestry, fishing and
     hunting 2,121
  Mining. 1,074
  Utilities 2,218
  Construction 3,082
  Manufacturing, durable goods. 7,013
  Manufacturing, non-durable goods 5,148
  Wholesale trade. 3,956
  Retail trade. 6,603
  Transportation & warehousing 2,678
  Information 1,909
  Finance & insurance. 3,404
  Real estate, rental, leasing 7,221
  Professional and technical services 2,639
  Educational services 416
  Health care and social assistance 5,497
  Accommodation/food services. 3,155
  Other services, except government 1,855
  Government 13,261

Establishments, by major industry group, 2003

Total. 59,827
  Forestry, fishing & agriculture 832
  Mining. 323
  Construction 4,741
  Manufacturing. 2,706
  Wholesale trade. 2,950
  Retail trade. 12,387
  Transportation & warehousing 2,281
  Information 1,136
  Finance & insurance. 4,465
  Professional/scientific/technical 4,550
  Health care/social assistance 5,462
  Accommodation/food services. 4,450

Annual payroll by major industry group, 2003

Total ($1,000) $23,647,163
  Forestry, fishing & agriculture . . . . NA
  Mining. . . . . NA
  Utilities 461,807
  Construction 1,397,245
  Manufacturing. 5,289,692
  Wholesale trade. 1,211,454
  Retail trade. 2,471,516
  Transportation & warehousing 1,014,739
  Information 634,161
  Finance & insurance. 1,269,471
  Professional/scientific/technical . . . 1,142,227
  Health care/social assistance 4,249,042
  Accommodation/food services. 1,608,613

Agriculture

Number of farms, 2004 42,000
Farm acreage, 2004
  Total. 11,000,000
  Acres per farm, 2004 262
Farm income, 2003 ($mil)
  Net farm income $1,148
  Debt/asset ratio .18.6
Farm marketings, 2003 ($mil)
Total. $3,411
  Crops 1,246
  Livestock 2,165

Principal commodities, in order by marketing receipts, 2003

    Broilers, cotton, soybeans, aquaculture

Federal economic activity in state

Expenditures, 2003
  Total ($ mil) $21,741
  Per capita $7,545
  Defense ($ mil). 3,644
  Non-defense ($ mil) 18,096
Defense department, 2003
  Payroll ($ mil) $1,601
  Contract awards ($ mil) $2,326
  Grants ($ mil). $53
  Homeland security grants ($1,000)
    2004 . . . . $31,795
    2005 . . . . $22,081

FDIC insured financial institutions, 2004

Number 102
  Assets ($bil) $42.1
  Deposits ($bil) 33.5

Fishing, 2004

Catch (x 1,000 lbs) 183,762
Value ($1,000). $43,791

Mining, 2004 ($ mil)

Total non-fuel mineral production $189
Percent of U.S. 0.4%

Construction, 2003 ($ mil)

Total contracts (including non-building). $3,654
   residential 1,700
   non-residential 1,146

Establishments, receipts, payroll & employees, by major industry group, 2002

Mining 295
   Receipts ($1,000) $773,258
   Annual payroll ($1,000) $160,144
   Paid employees 4,261

Utilities 592
   Receipts ($1,000) . . . . NA
   Annual payroll ($1,000) $432,184
   Paid employees 8,614

Construction 4,588
   Receipts ($1,000) $7,212,182
   Annual payroll ($1,000) $1,434,567
   Paid employees 49,180

Manufacturing 2,796
   Receipts ($1,000) $38,276,054
   Annual payroll ($1,000) $5,476,928
   Paid employees 182,822

Wholesale trade 2,948
   Receipts ($1,000) $19,215,751
   Annual payroll ($1,000) $1,170,055
   Paid employees 35,316

Retail trade 12,561
   Receipts ($1,000) $25,017,531
   Annual payroll ($1,000) $2,375,319
   Paid employees 135,838

Transportation 2,289
   Receipts ($1,000) $2,801,650
   Annual payroll ($1,000) $888,398
   Paid employees 29,548

Information 1,000
   Receipts ($1,000) . . . . NA
   Annual payroll ($1,000) $648,499
   Paid employees 19,859

Finance & insurance 4,480
   Receipts ($1,000) . . . . NA
   Annual payroll ($1,000) $1,163,724
   Paid employees 33,700

Professional, scientific & technical 4,473
   Receipts ($1,000) $2,922,664
   Annual payroll ($1,000) $1,040,705
   Paid employees 29,023

Health care & social assistance 5,484
   Receipts ($1,000) $10,092,701
   Annual payroll ($1,000) $3,917,187
   Paid employees 131,976

Accommodation & food service 4,329
   Receipts ($1,000) $5,486,105
   Annual payroll ($1,000) $1,473,389
   Paid employees 109,405

Communication, Energy & Transportation

Communication

Daily newspapers, 2004 23
Households with computers, 2003 . . . . .48%
Households with internet access, 2003 . . . . . .39%

Energy

Electricity Consumption, 2001
Total (trillion Btu) 1,173
Per capita (million Btu) 410
By source of production (trillion Btu)
   Coal 198
   Natural gas 341
   Petroleum 486
   Nuclear electric power 104
   Hydroelectric power 0
By end-use sector (trillion Btu)
   Residential 234
   Commercial 163
   Industrial 427
   Transportation 349
Electric energy, 2003
   Production (billion kWh) 40.1
   Net summer capability (million kW) 17.3
Gas utilities, 2003
   Customers (x1,000) 491
   Sales (trillion Btu) 85
   Revenues ($mil) $642
Nuclear plants, 2003 1

Transportation, 2004

Public Road & Street Mileage 74,129
   Urban 10,621
   Rural 63,508
   Interstate 685
Vehicle miles of travel per capita 13,587.5
Total motor vehicle registrations 1,964,488
   Automobiles 1,123,242
   Buses 9,320
   Trucks 831,926
   Motorcycles 27,162
Licensed drivers 1,896,008
   19 years & under 132,457
Deaths from motor vehicle accidents 900

State Summary

Capital City.................... Jefferson City
Governor..........................Matt Blunt
Capitol Building
Room 218
PO Box 720
Jefferson City, MO 65102
573-751-3222
Admitted as a state 1821
Area (square miles)................... 69,704
Population, 2004 (est.) 5,754,618
Largest City.....................Kansas City
Population, 2004............... 444,000
Personal income per capita, 2004
(in current dollars) $30,608
Gross state product ($ mil), 2004...... $203,294

Leading industries by payroll, 2003

Manufacturing, Health care/Social assistance,
Finance & Insurance

Leading agricultural commodities by receipts, 2003

Cattle, soybeans, corn, hogs

Geography & Environment

Total area (sq. mi.).................... 69,704
land 68,886
water 818
Federally-owned land, 2004 (acres) ... 2,224,788
percent............................. 5.0%
Highest point............Taum Sauk Mountain
elevation (feet) 1,772
Lowest point ....St. Francis River
elevation (feet) 230
General coastline (miles)..................... 0
Tidal shoreline (miles)..................... 0
Capital City.................... Jefferson City
Population 2000 39,636
Population 2004 38,671
Largest City.....................Kansas City
Population 2000 442,000
Population 2004 444,000

Number of cities with over 100,000 population

1990 4
2000 4
2004 4

State park and recreation areas, 2003

Area (acres x 1,000)....................... 140
Number of visitors (x 1,000) 17,016
Revenues (x 1,000).................... $3,949
percent of operating expenditures...... 14.1%

National forest system land, 2004

Acres 1,489,000

Demographics and Characteristics of the Population

Population

1980 4,916,686
1990 5,117,073
2000 5,595,211
2004 (estimate)..................... 5,754,618
persons per sq. mile of land............. 83.5
2005 (projection)................... 5,765,166
Male................................ 2,810,125
Female............................. 2,955,041
2010 (projection) 5,922,078
2020 (projection)................... 6,199,882
2030 (projection)................... 6,430,173
Male................................ 3,138,910
Female............................. 3,291,263

Metropolitan and Non-Metro. area population

	Metro	Non-Metro
1980	3,226,000	1,690,000
1990	3,387,000	1,730,000
2000	3,795,000	1,800,000

Change in population, 2000-2004

Number............................. 157,935
percent.............................. 2.8%
Natural increase (births minus deaths)... 88,807
Net internal migration 20,077
Net international migration 35,880

Persons by age, 2004

Under 5 years 371,469
18 years and over 4,370,076
65 years and over 765,692
85 years and over 100,379

Persons by age, 2010 (projected)

Total............................. 5,922,078
Under 5 years 394,878
5 to 17 years 1,016,516
18 and over 4,510,684
21 and over 4,260,677
65 and over 821,645
85 and over 124,961
Median age 37.6

Race, 2004 (estimate)

One Race
White........................... 4,915,696
Black or African American 661,233
American Indian/Alaska Native....... 26,493
Pacific Islander 3,811
Asian Indian....................... 12,967
Chinese 18,178
Filipino 8,845
Japanese 1,850
Korean....................... 9,918
Vietnamese....................... 7,743
Two or more races..................... 72,800

2   Missouri

Persons of Hispanic origin, 2004

Total Hispanic or Latino	143,729
Mexican	99,936
Puerto Rican	11,889
Cuban	3,342
Other Hispanic or Latino	15,721

Marital status, 2000

Population 15 years & over	4,414,391
Never married	1,094,769
Married	2,445,573
Separated	79,459
Widowed	313,422
Divorced	476,754

Language spoken at home, 2000

Population 5 years & over	5,226,022
English only	4,961,741
Spanish	110,752
Other Indo-European languages	97,816
Asian/Pacific Island languages	41,970

Households & families, 2000

Households	2,194,594
with persons under 18 years	762,492
with persons over 65 years	525,811
persons per household	2.48
Families	1,476,516
persons per family	3.02
Married couples	1,140,866
Female householder, no husband present	253,760
One-person households	599,808

Nativity, 2000

Number of persons born in state	3,792,261
percent of population	67.8%

Immigration & Naturalization, 2004

Immigrants admitted	6,782
Persons naturalized	3,999
Asylums granted	48
Asylums denied	19

Vital Statistics and Health

Marriages

2002	41,552
2003	41,295
2004	40,824

Divorces

2002	22,593
2003	22,166
2004	21,700

Births

2003	77,045
Birthrate (per 1,000)	13.5
Low birth weight (2,500g or less)	8.0%
To unmarried mothers	35.6%

2003, continued

White	63,814
Black	11,163
Hispanic	3,480
Asian/Pacific Islander	1,736
Amer. Indian/Alaska Native	366
2004 (preliminary)	77,780
Birthrate (per 1,000)	13.5
White	64,152
Black	11,455
Hispanic	3,844
Asian/Pacific Islander	1,790

Deaths

2002

All causes	55,940
rate per 100,000	986.1
Heart disease	16,708
rate per 100,000	294.5
Malignant neoplasms	12,322
rate per 100,000	217.2
Cerebrovascular disease	3,885
rate per 100,000	68.5
Chronic lower respiratory disease	2,867
rate per 100,000	50.5
2003	55,569
rate per 100,000	974.1
2004 (provisional)	53,904

Infant deaths

2003 (provisional)	587
rate per 1,000	7.7
2004 (provisional)	557
rate per 1,000	7.2

Abortions, 2000

Total	8,000
rate per 1,000 women age 15-44	6.6

Physicians, 2003

Total	13,732
rate per 1,000 persons	241

Nurses, 2001

Total	52,970
rate per 1,000 persons	940

Community Hospitals, 2003

Number	119
Beds (x 1,000)	19.3
Patients admitted (x 1,000)	831
Average daily census (x 1,000)	11.9
Average cost per day	$1,403
Outpatient visits (x mil)	15.7

Disability status of population, 2004

5 to 20 years	6.5%
21 to 64 years	13.7%
65 years and over	41%

Education

Educational attainment, 2004

Population over 25 years	3,674,818
Less than 9th grade	164,224
High school graduates only	1,220,483
Bachelor's degree only	561,313
Graduate or professional degree	330,902
Less than 9th grade percent	4.5%
High school graduate or more	87.9%
College graduate or more	28.1%
Graduate or professional degree	9.0%

Public school enrollment, Fall 2002

Total	924,445
Kindergarten through grade 8	652,632
Grades 9 through 12	271,813
Enrollment, 2005 (projected)	911,800

Graduating public high school seniors

2004 (estimate)	56,980

SAT scores, 2005

Average verbal score	588
Average math score	588
Percent of graduates taking test	7%

Public school teachers, 2004

Total (x 1,000)	65.0
Elementary (x 1,000)	33.2
Secondary (x 1,000)	31.8
Average salary	$38,000
Elementary	$38,100
Secondary	$37,900

State receipts & expenditures for public schools, 2004

Revenue receipts ($mil)	$7,972
Expenditures	
Total ($mil)	$7,366
Per capita	$1,288
Per pupil	$7,548

Institutions of higher education, 2004

Total	123
Public	34
Private	89

Enrollment in institutions of higher education, Fall, 2003

Total	363,792
Full-time men	96,717
Full-time women	121,055
Part-time men	57,550
Part-time women	88,470

Minority enrollment in institutions of higher education, Fall, 2003

Black, non-hispanic	39,240
Hispanic	8,826
Asian/Pacific Islander	8,189
American Indian/Alaska Native	2,151

Earned degrees conferred, 2003

Bachelor's	33,291
Master's	15,591
First-professional	2,490
Doctor's	1,182

State & local financial support for higher education, 2003-2004

Full-time equivalent enrollment (x 1,000)	138.1
Appropriations per FTE	$7,031
as a percent of tax revenue	7.0%

Social Insurance & Welfare Programs

Social Security benefits & beneficiaries, 2004

Beneficiaries	
Total	1,046,000
Retired & dependents	703,000
Survivors	145,000
Disabled & dependents	198,000
Annual benefit payments ($ mil)	
Total	$10,686
Retired & dependents	$6,918
Survivors	$1,879
Disabled & dependents	$1,889
Average Monthly Benefit	
Retired & dependents	$944
Disabled & dependents	$872
Widowed	$918

Medicare

Enrollment, 2001 (x 1,000)	867
Payments ($ mil, est.)	$4,800
Enrollment, 2003 (x 1,000)	884

Medicaid, 2002

Beneficiaries (x 1,000)	1,036
Payments ($ mil)	$4,072

State Children's Health Insurance, 2004

Enrollment (x 1,000)	176.0
Expenditures ($ mil)	$80.2

Persons without health insurance, 2003

Number (x 1,000)	620
percent	11.0%
Number of children (x 1,000)	103
percent of children	7.3%

Federal public aid

Temporary Assistance for Needy Families, 2004	
Recipients (x 1,000)	100
Families (x 1,000)	41
Supplemental Security Income, 2003	
Recipients (x 1,000)	115
Payments ($ mil)	$528

Food Stamp Program, 2004

Participants (x 1,000)	700
Benefits ($ mil)	$663

Housing & Construction

Housing units

Total 2003 (estimate)	2,533,723
Total 2004 (estimate)	2,564,340
Seasonal or recreational use, 2003	23,000
Owner-occupied single-family, 2003	1,256,000
Median value	$108,625
Renter-occupied, 2003	656,000
Median rent	$556
Homeownership rate, 2003	74.0%
Homeownership rate, 2004	72.4%

New privately owned housing units, 2004

Number authorized (x 1,000)	32.8
Value ($ mil)	$4,286
Started 2005 (x 1,000, estimate)	27.5
Started 2006 (x 1,000, estimate)	27.5

Existing home sales

2002 (x 1,000)	115.2
2003 (x 1,000)	131.1
2004 (x 1,000)	141.8

Government & Elections

State Officials 2006

Governor (name/party/term expires)
Matt Blunt
Republican - 1/09

Lieutenant Governor	Peter Kinder
Secretary of State	Robin Carnahan
Attorney General	Jay Nixon
Chief Justice	Michael A. Wolff

Governorship

Minimum age	30
Length of term	4 years
Consecutive terms permitted	2 max. (not nec. consecutive)
Who succeeds	Lt. Governor

State Legislature

Name	Legislature
Upper chamber	Senate
Number of members	34
Length of term	4 years
Party in majority, 2006	Republican
Lower chamber	House of Representatives
Number of members	163
Length of term	2 years
Party in majority, 2006	Republican

State Government Employees, 2004

Total	90,730
Payroll	$259,788,960

Local Government Employees, 2004

Total	220,476
Payroll	$630,330,260

Local Governments by Type, 2002

Total	3,422
County	114
Municipal	946
Township	312
School District	536
Special District	1,514

Voting age population, November 2004

Total	4,243,000
Male	2,023,000
Female	2,219,000
White	3,636,000
Black	433,000
Hispanic	115,000
Asian	55,000

Presidential Election, 2004

Total Popular Vote	2,731,364
Kerry	1,259,171
Bush	1,455,713
Total Electoral Votes	11

Federal representation, 2006 (109th Congress)

Senator	James Talent
Party	Republican
Year term expires	2007
Senator	Christopher Bond
Party	Republican
Year term expires	2011
Representatives, total	9
Democrats	4
Republicans	5
Other	0

Votes cast for US Senators

2002

Total vote (x 1,000)	NA
Leading party	NA
Percent for leading party	NA

2004

Total vote (x 1,000)	2,706,000
Leading party	Republican
Percent for leading party	56.1%

Votes cast for US Representatives

2002

Total vote (x 1,000)	1,854
Democratic	829
Republican	986
Leading party	Republican
Percent for leading party	53.2%

2004

Total vote (x 1,000)	2,667
Democratic	1,193
Republican	1,430
Leading party	Republican
Percent for leading party	53.6%

Women holding public office, 2006
US Congress 1
Statewide elected office...................... 3
State legislature 42

Black public officials, 2001
Total................................... 201
  US and state legislatures 19
  City/county/regional offices 142
  Judicial/law enforcement................. 16
  Education/school boards................. 24

Hispanic public officials, 2004
Total..................................... 1
  State executives & legislators 0
  City/county/regional offices 1
  Judicial/law enforcement.................. 0
  Education/school boards................. 0

Governmental Finance

State government revenues, 2004
Total revenue ($1,000) $26,320,416
  Revenue per capita 4,569.52

General Revenue ($ per capita) $3,522.12
  Intergovernmental 1,286.82
  Taxes 1,583.28
    general sales 512.16
    individual income tax.............. 645.96
    corporate income tax 38.95
  Current charges....................341.47
  Miscellaneous 310.55

State government expenditure, 2004
Total expenditure (x $1,000) $22,038,965
  Expenditure per capita............. 3,826.21
General Expenditure ($ per capita).... $3,383.16
  Education 1,192.42
  Public welfare...................... 982.28
  Health 115.51
  Hospitals...........................180.79
  Highways 321.76
  Police protection 23.41
  Correction 105.78
  Natural resources 56.48
  Parks & recreation......................9.12
  Governmental administration 107.05
  Interest on general debt 110.96

State debt & cash, 2004 ($ per capita)
Debt $2,815.69
Cash/security holdings.............. $10,317.87

Federal government grants to state & local government, 2004 (x $1,000)
Total........................... $8,734,296
By Federal Agency
  Defense $84,996

By Federal Agency, continued
  Education 655,606
  Energy............................. 13,114
  Environmental Protection Agency 88,676
  Health & Human Services. 5,481,317
  Homeland Security.................. 27,759
  Housing & Urban Development...... 542,818
  Justice 123,103
  Labor 150,157
  Transportation 924,927
  Veterans Affairs.................... 25,717

Crime, Law Enforcement & Courts

Crime, 2004 (rates per 100,000 residents)
Property crimes 224,629
  Burglaries.......................... 40,472
  Larcenies......................... 158,264
  Motor vehicle thefts 25,893
  Property crime rate................. 3,903.5
Violent crimes........................ 28,226
  Murders............................. 354
  Forcible rape........................ 1,479
  Robberies 6,630
  Aggravated assaults 19,763
  Violent crime rate 490.5

Police Agencies, 2004
Total agencies.......................... 560
Total employees 19,073
  Male officers....................... 12,184
  Female officers...................... 1,266
  Male civilians....................... 2,169
  Female civilians..................... 3,454

Arrests, 2004
Total............................... 273,415
  Persons under 18 years of age 36,935

Prisoners under state & federal jurisdiction, 2004
Total prisoners........................ 31,081
  Percent change, 12/31/03 to 12/31/04 ....2.6%
Sentenced to more than one year 31,061
  rate per 100,000........................ 538

Persons under sentence of death, 7/1/05
Total................................... 55
  White.............................. 32
  Black 23
  Hispanic 0

State's highest court
Name ....Supreme Court
Number of members...................... 7
Length of term .... 12 years
Intermediate appeals court? ....yes

6   Missouri

Labor & Income

Civilian labor force, 2004

Total	3,017,000
Men	1,572,000
Women	1,445,000
Persons 16-19 years	175,000
White	2,606,000
Black	325,000
Hispanic	97,000
Asian	36,000

Civilian labor force as a percent of civilian non-institutional population, 2004

Total	68.2%
Men	74.1
Women	62.7
Persons 16-19 years	55.9
White	68.0
Black	70.9
Hispanic	77.9
Asian	61.1

Employment, 2004

Total	2,844,000
Men	1,479,000
Women	1,365,000
Persons 16-19 years	145,000
White	2,479,000
Black	282,000
Hispanic	90,000
Asian	36,000

Full-time/part-time labor force, 2002

Full-time labor force, employed	2,337,000
Part-time labor force, employed	488,000
Unemployed, looking for	
Full-time work	131,000
Part-time work	NA

Unemployment rate, 2004

Total	5.7%
Men	5.9
Women	5.6
Persons 16-19 years	17.4
White	4.9
Black	13.1
Hispanic	7.1
Asian	1.7

Unemployed by reason for unemployment (as a percent of total unemployment), 2002

Job losers or completed temp jobs	51.5%
Job leavers	NA
Reentrants	32.7
New entrants	NA

Labor unions, 2004

Membership	315,000
percent of employed	12.4%

Experienced civilian labor force by private industry, first quarter 2004

Total	2,172,452
Natural Resources & Mining	14,636
Construction	133,623
Manufacturing	310,902
Trade, transportation & utilities	522,129
Information	66,289
Finance	153,964
Professional & business	302,320
Education & Health	334,039
Leisure & hospitality	253,136
Other	81,414

Experienced civilian labor force by occupation, 2004

Management	97,400
Business & Financial	101,400
Legal	18,920
Sales	286,580
Office & Admin. Support	468,680
Computers & Math	59,460
Architecture & Engineering	37,400
Arts & Entertainment	34,740
Education	150,310
Social Services	28,900
Healthcare Practitioner & Technical	149,130
Healthcare support	73,780
Maintenance & Repair	108,070
Construction	132,960
Transportation & moving	201,840
Production	227,410
Farming, fishing & forestry	3,000

Hours and earnings of production workers on manufacturing payrolls, 2004

Average weekly hours	40.2
Average hourly earnings	$17.92
Average weekly earnings	$720.38

Average annual pay

2004	$34,845
change from 2003	3.1%

Household income

Median household income, three-year average, 2002-2004	$43,988

Personal income, 2004 ($ per capita)

In current dollars	$30,608
In constant (2000) dollars	$28,387

Poverty

Persons below poverty level, three-year average, 2002-2004	10.9%

Federal individual income tax returns, 2003

Returns filed	2,563,895
Adjusted gross income ($1,000)	$107,992,455
Total income tax paid ($1,000)	$12,583,497

Economy, Business, Industry & Agriculture

Fortune 500 companies, 2005 11

Patents issued, 2004 895

Bankruptcy cases filed, 2004 38,000

Business firm ownership, 2002

Women-owned....................... 120,438
  Sales ($ mil) $18,596
Black-owned......................... 16,758
  Sales ($ mil) $1,537
Hispanic-owned....................... 3,652
  Sales ($ mil) $682
Asian-owned 6,386
  Sales ($ mil) $1,989
Amer. Indian/Alaska Native-owned 3,298
  Sales ($ mil) $340
Hawaiian/Pacific Isl.-owned.............. 100
  Sales ($ mil) $37

Gross State Product, 2004 ($ mil)

Total Gross State Product $203,294
  Agriculture, forestry, fishing and
    hunting 2,658
  Mining.............................. 447
  Utilities........................... 3,885
  Construction 9,867
  Manufacturing, durable goods....... 17,445
  Manufacturing, non-durable goods ... 14,036
  Wholesale trade.................... 12,759
  Retail trade....................... 14,611
  Transportation & warehousing 7,538
  Information 9,963
  Finance & insurance................ 12,878
  Real estate, rental, leasing 19,529
  Professional and technical services.... 11,586
  Educational services................ 2,269
  Health care and social assistance..... 15,149
  Accommodation/food services........ 5,216
  Other services, except government 5,335
  Government........................ 23,686

Establishments, by major industry group, 2003

Total............................... 150,415
  Forestry, fishing & agriculture 296
  Mining............................. 287
  Construction 15,969
  Manufacturing...................... 7,042
  Wholesale trade..................... 8,412
  Retail trade....................... 23,778
  Transportation & warehousing 4,993
  Information 2,607
  Finance & insurance................ 10,331
  Professional/scientific/technical 12,957
  Health care/social assistance 14,256
  Accommodation/food services........ 11,390

Annual payroll by major industry group, 2003

Total ($1,000).................... $75,594,931
  Forestry, fishing & agriculture 30,669
  Mining........................... 159,229
  Utilities........................ 1,009,931
  Construction 5,578,451
  Manufacturing................. 11,294,741
  Wholesale trade................. 4,896,122
  Retail trade.................... 6,368,513
  Transportation & warehousing 2,683,466
  Information 3,754,952
  Finance & insurance............. 6,619,593
  Professional/scientific/technical ... 5,843,031
  Health care/social assistance 10,461,671
  Accommodation/food services..... 2,706,747

Agriculture

Number of farms, 2004 106,000
Farm acreage, 2004
  Total......................... 30,000,000
  Acres per farm, 2004 284
Farm income, 2003 ($mil)
  Net farm income $1,539
  Debt/asset ratio 12.5
Farm marketings, 2003 ($mil)
Total............................... $4,973
  Crops.............................. 2,344
  Livestock.......................... 2,628

Principal commodities, in order by marketing receipts, 2003

Cattle, soybeans, corn, hogs

Federal economic activity in state

Expenditures, 2003
  Total ($ mil) $43,874
  Per capita $7,691
  Defense ($ mil)...................... 7,991
  Non-defense ($ mil) 35,883
Defense department, 2003
  Payroll ($ mil) $1,804
  Contract awards ($ mil).............. $6,558
  Grants ($ mil)........................ $50
  Homeland security grants ($1,000)
    2004 .... $66,618
    2005 .... $46,952

FDIC insured financial institutions, 2004

Number 373
  Assets ($bil) $91.8
  Deposits ($bil) 87.1

Fishing, 2004

Catch (x 1,000 lbs)...................... 0
Value ($1,000)........................... 0

8 Missouri

Mining, 2004 ($ mil)
Total non-fuel mineral production $1,540
Percent of U.S. 3.5%

Construction, 2003 ($ mil)
Total contracts (including non-building). $9,358
    residential........................... 4,834
    non-residential 2,509

Establishments, receipts, payroll & employees, by major industry group, 2002

Mining 266
    Receipts ($1,000) $1,226,555
    Annual payroll ($1,000) $227,513
    Paid employees 4,622

Utilities 399
    Receipts ($1,000) .... NA
    Annual payroll ($1,000) $1,332,168
    Paid employees 19,540

Construction 15,448
    Receipts ($1,000) $26,103,729
    Annual payroll ($1,000) $5,670,754
    Paid employees 153,890

Manufacturing 7,210
    Receipts ($1,000) $92,909,173
    Annual payroll ($1,000) $12,463,436
    Paid employees 319,974

Wholesale trade 8,491
    Receipts ($1,000) $95,603,561
    Annual payroll ($1,000) $4,610,387
    Paid employees 127,340

Retail trade 23,837
    Receipts ($1,000) $61,861,163
    Annual payroll ($1,000) $6,072,036
    Paid employees 311,593

Transportation 5,063
    Receipts ($1,000) $9,216,811
    Annual payroll ($1,000) $2,389,922
    Paid employees 78,787

Information.......................... 2,641
    Receipts ($1,000) .... NA
    Annual payroll ($1,000) $3,824,283
    Paid employees 82,200

Finance & insurance 9,905
    Receipts ($1,000) .... NA
    Annual payroll ($1,000) $6,241,678
    Paid employees 136,764

Professional, scientific & technical 12,858
    Receipts ($1,000) $14,379,844
    Annual payroll ($1,000) $5,633,426
    Paid employees 119,950

Health care & social assistance 13,828
    Receipts ($1,000) $24,944,155
    Annual payroll ($1,000)......... $10,136,127
    Paid employees 336,115

Accommodation & food service 11,280
    Receipts ($1,000) $8,607,025
    Annual payroll ($1,000) $2,432,448
    Paid employees 215,792

Communication, Energy & Transportation

Communication
Daily newspapers, 2004 42
Households with computers, 2003 .... 61%
Households with internet access, 2003 ..... 53%

Energy
Electricity Consumption, 2001
    Total (trillion Btu)..................... 1,815
    Per capita (million Btu) 322
By source of production (trillion Btu)
    Coal 716
    Natural gas........................... 289
    Petroleum............................ 719
    Nuclear electric power 88
    Hydroelectric power.................... 9
By end-use sector (trillion Btu)
    Residential 496
    Commercial 389
    Industrial 374
    Transportation 556
Electric energy, 2003
    Production (billion kWh) 87.2
    Net summer capability (million kW) 20
Gas utilities, 2003
    Customers (x1,000)................... 1,486
    Sales (trillion Btu).................... 176
    Revenues ($mil)..................... $1,588
Nuclear plants, 2003 1

Transportation, 2004
Public Road & Street Mileage 125,923
    Urban............................. 18,331
    Rural 107,592
    Interstate........................... 1,181
Vehicle miles of travel per capita....... 11,830.2
Total motor vehicle registrations...... 4,812,096
    Automobiles..................... 2,698,085
    Buses 11,514
    Trucks 2,102,497
    Motorcycles 77,519
Licensed drivers 4,047,652
    19 years & under 232,470
Deaths from motor vehicle accidents 1,130

State Summary

Capital City. . . . . Helena
Governor. . . . . Brian Schweitzer
State Capitol
Helena, MT 59620
406-444-3111
Admitted as a state 1889
Area (square miles). 147,042
Population, 2004 (est.) 926,865
Largest City. . . . . Billings
Population, 2004. 96,977
Personal income per capita, 2004
(in current dollars) $26,857
Gross state product ($ mil), 2004 . . . . $27,482

Leading industries by payroll, 2003

Health care/Social assistance, Retail trade,
Construction

Leading agricultural commodities by receipts, 2003

Cattle, wheat, barley, hay

Geography & Environment

Total area (sq. mi.). 147,042
land 145,552
water 1,490

Federally-owned land, 2004 (acres) . . . 27,910,152
percent. 29.9%

Highest point. . . . . .Granite Peak
elevation (feet) 12,799

Lowest point . . . . Kootenal River
elevation (feet). 1,800

General coastline (miles). 0

Tidal shoreline (miles). 0

Capital City. . . . . Helena
Population 2000 25,780
Population 2004 27,196

Largest City. . . . . Billings
Population 2000 89,847
Population 2004 96,977

Number of cities with over 100,000 population

1990 0
2000 0
2004 0

State park and recreation areas, 2003

Area (acres x 1,000). 71
Number of visitors (x 1,000) 1,575
Revenues (x 1,000). $1,228
percent of operating expenditures. 20.1%

National forest system land, 2004

Acres 16,924,000

Demographics and Characteristics of the Population

Population

1980 786,690
1990 799,065
2000 902,195
2004 (estimate). 926,865
persons per sq. mile of land. 6.4
2005 (projection) 933,005
Male. 464,920
Female. 468,085
2010 (projection) 968,598
2020 (projection) 1,022,735
2030 (projection) 1,044,898
Male. 514,942
Female. 529,956

Metropolitan and Non-Metro. area population

	Metro	Non-Metro
1980	189,000	598,000
1990	191,000	608,000
2000	306,000	597,000

Change in population, 2000-2004

Number. 24,670
percent. 2.7%
Natural increase (births minus deaths). . . 10,279
Net internal migration. 13,014
Net international migration 1,741

Persons by age, 2004

Under 5 years 52,510
18 years and over 718,772
65 years and over 126,549
85 years and over 18,233

Persons by age, 2010 (projected)

Total. 968,598
Under 5 years 59,714
5 to 17 years 152,598
18 and over 756,286
21 and over 720,124
65 and over 144,961
85 and over 21,973
Median age 40.4

Race, 2004 (estimate)

One Race
White. 844,461
Black or African American 3,471
American Indian/Alaska Native. 59,514
Pacific Islander 511
Asian Indian. 364
Chinese 543
Filipino 1,246
Japanese 496
Korean. 431
Vietnamese. . . . . -
Two or more races. 13,864

Persons of Hispanic origin, 2004

Total Hispanic or Latino 20,227
  Mexican........................ 15,974
  Puerto Rican 859
  Cuban 246
  Other Hispanic or Latino 1,982

Marital status, 2000

Population 15 years & over 715,915
  Never married 171,820
  Married......................... 410,219
  Separated 9,307
  Widowed......................... 46,534
  Divorced 78,035

Language spoken at home, 2000

Population 5 years & over 847,362
  English only 803,031
  Spanish 12,953
  Other Indo-European languages 17,978
  Asian/Pacific Island languages........ 3,066

Households & families, 2000

Households...................... 358,667
  with persons under 18 years 119,550
  with persons over 65 years........... 83,982
  persons per household 2.45
Families......................... 237,407
  persons per family.....................2.99
Married couples..................... 192,067
Female householder,
  no husband present................ 32,016
One-person households 98,422

Nativity, 2000

Number of persons born in state 505,966
  percent of population 56.1%

Immigration & Naturalization, 2004

Immigrants admitted..................... 419
Persons naturalized 285
Asylums granted 0
Asylums denied 0

Vital Statistics and Health

Marriages

2002 6,511
2003 6,640
2004 6,946

Divorces

2002 3,634
2003 3,582
2004 3,516

Births

2003 11,422
  Birthrate (per 1,000)....................12.4
  Low birth weight (2,500g or less)........6.8%
  To unmarried mothers................32.2%

2003, continued
  White................................ 9,833
  Black 51
  Hispanic 381
  Asian/Pacific Islander 133
  Amer. Indian/Alaska Native 1,399

2004 (preliminary)................... 11,525
  Birthrate (per 1,000)....................12.4
  White................................ 9,827
  Black 53
  Hispanic 374
  Asian/Pacific Islander 125

Deaths

2002
All causes 8,506
  rate per 100,000.....................935.3
Heart disease 1,944
  rate per 100,000.....................213.8
Malignant neoplasms 1,911
  rate per 100,000.....................210.1
Cerebrovascular disease................. 639
  rate per 100,000......................70.3
Chronic lower respiratory disease 576
  rate per 100,000......................63.3
2003 8,467
  rate per 100,000.....................922.7
2004 (provisional) 8,046

Infant deaths

2003 (provisional) 79
  rate per 1,000 ....6.9
2004 (provisional) 50
  rate per 1,000 ....4.3

Abortions, 2000

Total................................. 3,000
  rate per 1,000 women age 15-44.........13.5

Physicians, 2003

Total................................. 2,079
  rate per 1,000 persons................. 227

Nurses, 2001

Total................................. 7,620
  rate per 1,000 persons.................. 842

Community Hospitals, 2003

Number 53
Beds (x 1,000).........................4.3
Patients admitted (x 1,000) 107
Average daily census (x 1,000) 2.9
Average cost per day $733
Outpatient visits (x mil)....................2.7

Disability status of population, 2004

5 to 20 years 6.1%
21 to 64 years 13.2%
65 years and over 38.5%

Education

Educational attainment, 2004

Population over 25 years 605,632
  Less than 9th grade 17,569
  High school graduates only 193,097
  Bachelor's degree only 118,944
  Graduate or professional degree 47,334
  Less than 9th grade percent 2.9%
  High school graduate or more 91.9%
  College graduate or more 25.5%
  Graduate or professional degree 7.8%

Public school enrollment, Fall 2002

Total 149,995
  Kindergarten through grade 8 101,177
  Grades 9 through 12 48,818
Enrollment, 2005 (projected) 142,900

Graduating public high school seniors

2004 (estimate) 10,520

SAT scores, 2005

Average verbal score 540
Average math score 540
Percent of graduates taking test 31%

Public school teachers, 2004

Total (x 1,000) 10.3
  Elementary (x 1,000) 6.9
  Secondary (x 1,000) 3.4
Average salary $37,200
  Elementary $37,200
  Secondary $37,200

State receipts & expenditures for public schools, 2004

Revenue receipts ($mil) $1,251
Expenditures
Total ($mil) $1,205
  Per capita $1,312
  Per pupil $8,631

Institutions of higher education, 2004

Total 23
  Public 18
  Private 5

Enrollment in institutions of higher education, Fall, 2003

Total 47,412
  Full-time men 17,086
  Full-time women 18,904
  Part-time men 4,397
  Part-time women 7,025

Minority enrollment in institutions of higher education, Fall, 2003

Black, non-hispanic 230
Hispanic 683
Asian/Pacific Islander 436
American Indian/Alaska Native 4,432

Earned degrees conferred, 2003

Bachelor's 5,238
Master's 979
First-professional 118
Doctor's 75

State & local financial support for higher education, 2003-2004

Full-time equivalent enrollment (x 1,000) . . . 35.8
Appropriations per FTE $3,915
  as a percent of tax revenue 7.0%

Social Insurance & Welfare Programs

Social Security benefits & beneficiaries, 2004

Beneficiaries
  Total 166,000
  Retired & dependents 119,000
  Survivors 23,000
  Disabled & dependents 24,000
Annual benefit payments ($ mil)
  Total $1,653
  Retired & dependents $1,122
  Survivors $298
  Disabled & dependents $233
Average Monthly Benefit
  Retired & dependents $916
  Disabled & dependents $863
  Widowed $907

Medicare

Enrollment, 2001 (x 1,000) 138
  Payments ($ mil, est.) $700
Enrollment, 2003 (x 1,000) 142

Medicaid, 2002

Beneficiaries (x 1,000) 104
Payments ($ mil) $533

State Children's Health Insurance, 2004

Enrollment (x 1,000) 15.3
Expenditures ($ mil) $14.3

Persons without health insurance, 2003

Number (x 1,000) 177
  percent 19.4%
Number of children (x 1,000) 38
  percent of children 17.7%

Federal public aid

Temporary Assistance for Needy Families, 2004
Recipients (x 1,000) 14
Families (x 1,000) 5

Supplemental Security Income, 2003
Recipients (x 1,000) 14
Payments ($ mil) $64

Food Stamp Program, 2004

Participants (x 1,000) 77
Benefits ($ mil) $79

4   Montana

Housing & Construction

Housing units
Total 2003 (estimate) 420,330
Total 2004 (estimate) 423,262
Seasonal or recreational use, 2003 21,000
Owner-occupied single-family, 2003.... 173,000
    Median value $118,887
Renter-occupied, 2003 107,000
    Median rent $506
Homeownership rate, 2003 .... 71.5%
Homeownership rate, 2004 .... 72.4%

New privately owned housing units, 2004
Number authorized (x 1,000) 5.0
Value ($ mil)............................. $645
Started 2005 (x 1,000, estimate) 2.9
Started 2006 (x 1,000, estimate) 2.8

Existing home sales
2002 (x 1,000).........................22.6
2003 (x 1,000).........................23.2
2004 (x 1,000).........................24.2

Government & Elections

State Officials 2006
Governor (name/party/term expires)
               Brian Schweitzer
               Democrat - 1/09
Lieutenant Governor...........John Bohlinger
Secretary of State............... Brad Johnson
Attorney General.............. Mike Magrath
Chief Justice .... Karla Gray

Governorship
Minimum age............................ 25
Length of term .... 4 years
Consecutive terms permitted ..... 8 out of 16 yrs
Who succeeds....................Lt. Governor

State Legislature
Name .... Legislature
Upper chamber ....Senate
    Number of members.................... 50
    Length of term..................... 4 years
    Party in majority, 2006 ....Democratic
Lower chamber.......House of Representatives
    Number of members................... 100
    Length of term..................... 2 years
    Party in majority, 2006 .... 50/50

State Government Employees, 2004
Total................................ 18,571
Payroll.......................... $57,591,291

Local Government Employees, 2004
Total................................ 35,701
Payroll.......................... $93,362,258

Local Governments by Type, 2002
Total................................. 1,127
    County................................. 54
    Municipal 129
    Township 0
    School District........................ 352
    Special District 592

Voting age population, November 2004
Total............................... 690,000
    Male............................... 339,000
    Female............................. 352,000
    White.............................. 647,000
    Black ....
    Hispanic 12,000
    Asian 3,000

Presidential Election, 2004
Total Popular Vote 450,445
    Kerry 173,710
    Bush.............................. 266,063
Total Electoral Votes........................ 3

Federal representation, 2006 (109th Congress)
Senator........................Conrad Burns
    Party .... Republican
    Year term expires 2007
Senator....................... Max Baucus
    Party .... Democrat
    Year term expires 2009
Representatives, total 1
    Democrats........................... 0
    Republicans 1
    Other................................. 0

Votes cast for US Senators
2002
Total vote (x 1,000) 327,000
Leading party.....................Democratic
Percent for leading party 62.7%
2004
Total vote (x 1,000) .... NA
Leading party.......................... NA
Percent for leading party .... NA

Votes cast for US Representatives
2002
Total vote (x 1,000) 331
    Democratic........................... 108
    Republican 214
Leading party..................... Republican
Percent for leading party 64.6%
2004
Total vote (x 1,000) 444
    Democratic........................... 146
    Republican 286
Leading party..................... Republican
Percent for leading party 64.4%

Women holding public office, 2006
US Congress 0
Statewide elected office 1
State legislature 37

Black public officials, 2001
Total 0
   US and state legislatures 0
   City/county/regional offices 0
   Judicial/law enforcement 0
   Education/school boards 0

Hispanic public officials, 2004
Total 1
   State executives & legislators 0
   City/county/regional offices 0
   Judicial/law enforcement 1
   Education/school boards 0

Governmental Finance

State government revenues, 2004
Total revenue ($1,000) $5,451,685
   Revenue per capita 5,881.00

General Revenue ($ per capita) $4,579.62
   Intergovernmental 1,839.36
   Taxes 1,753.71
     general sales 0
     individual income tax 653.27
     corporate income tax 73.06
   Current charges 532.32
   Miscellaneous 454.23

State government expenditure, 2004
Total expenditure (x $1,000) $4,691,318
   Expenditure per capita 5,060.75
General Expenditure ($ per capita) $4,444.37
   Education 1,486.43
   Public welfare 822.04
   Health 245.83
   Hospitals 42.57
   Highways 580.16
   Police protection 49.56
   Correction 130.70
   Natural resources 301.93
   Parks & recreation 15.67
   Governmental administration 243.92
   Interest on general debt 133.17

State debt & cash, 2004 ($ per capita)
Debt $3,288.96
Cash/security holdings $12,647.45

Federal government grants to state & local government, 2004 (x $1,000)
Total $1,997,362
By Federal Agency
   Defense $58,647

By Federal Agency, continued
Education 215,546
Energy 6,632
Environmental Protection Agency 36,197
Health & Human Services 831,614
Homeland Security 8,108
Housing & Urban Development 108,635
Justice 44,713
Labor 40,201
Transportation 338,929
Veterans Affairs 3,318

Crime, Law Enforcement & Courts

Crime, 2004 (rates per 100,000 residents)
Property crimes 27,215
   Burglaries 3,515
   Larcenies 22,082
   Motor vehicle thefts 1,618
   Property crime rate 2,936.2
Violent crimes 2,723
   Murders 30
   Forcible rape 273
   Robberies 233
   Aggravated assaults 2,187
   Violent crime rate 293.8

Police Agencies, 2004
Total agencies 107
Total employees 2,761
   Male officers 1,524
   Female officers 102
   Male civilians 485
   Female civilians 650

Arrests, 2004
Total .... NA
   Persons under 18 years of age .... NA

Prisoners under state & federal jurisdiction, 2004
Total prisoners 3,877
   Percent change, 12/31/03 to 12/31/04 .... 7.1%
Sentenced to more than one year 3,877
   rate per 100,000 416

Persons under sentence of death, 7/1/05
Total 4
   White 4
   Black 0
   Hispanic 0

State's highest court
Name .... Supreme Court
Number of members 7
Length of term .... 8 years
Intermediate appeals court? .... no

Labor & Income

Civilian labor force, 2004

Total 486,000
  Men 256,000
  Women 230,000
  Persons 16-19 years 30,000
  White 449,000
  Black 0
  Hispanic 11,000
  Asian 0

Civilian labor force as a percent of civilian non-institutional population, 2004

Total 66.5%
  Men 71.2
  Women 62.0
  Persons 16-19 years 49.6
  White 66.8
  Black 0.0
  Hispanic 66.5
  Asian 0.0

Employment, 2004

Total 462,000
  Men 242,000
  Women 220,000
  Persons 16-19 years 26,000
  White 430,000
  Black 0
  Hispanic 10,000
  Asian 0

Full-time/part-time labor force, 2002

Full-time labor force, employed 349,000
Part-time labor force, employed 93,000
Unemployed, looking for
  Full-time work 17,000
  Part-time work .... NA

Unemployment rate, 2004

Total 4.9%
  Men 5.6
  Women 4.3
  Persons 16-19 years 11.0
  White 4.3
  Black .... NA
  Hispanic 6.4
  Asian .... NA

Unemployed by reason for unemployment (as a percent of total unemployment), 2002

Job losers or completed temp jobs 57.1%
Job leavers .... NA
Reentrants .... NA
New entrants .... NA

Labor unions, 2004

Membership 43,000
  percent of employed 11.7%

Experienced civilian labor force by private industry, first quarter 2004

Total 310,463
  Natural Resources & Mining 9,789
  Construction 21,147
  Manufacturing 18,668
  Trade, transportation & utilities 81,693
  Information 7,644
  Finance 20,505
  Professional & business 31,514
  Education & Health 53,561
  Leisure & hospitality 50,096
  Other 15,546

Experienced civilian labor force by occupation, 2004

Management 22,890
Business & Financial 12,910
Legal 2,850
Sales 43,140
Office & Admin. Support 68,320
Computers & Math 5,050
Architecture & Engineering 5,730
Arts & Entertainment 5,300
Education 26,280
Social Services 6,970
Healthcare Practitioner & Technical 20,850
Healthcare support 11,370
Maintenance & Repair 18,880
Construction 25,810
Transportation & moving 28,430
Production 16,690
Farming, fishing & forestry 830

Hours and earnings of production workers on manufacturing payrolls, 2004

Average weekly hours 38.3
Average hourly earnings $14.87
Average weekly earnings $569.52

Average annual pay

2004 .... $27,830
  change from 2003 .... 3.5%

Household income

Median household income, three-year average,
  2002-2004 .... $35,201

Personal income, 2004 ($ per capita)

In current dollars $26,857
In constant (2000) dollars $24,908

Poverty

Persons below poverty level, three-year average,
  2002-2004 .... 14.3%

Federal individual income tax returns, 2003

Returns filed 433,522
Adjusted gross income ($1,000) $15,198,027
Total income tax paid ($1,000) $1,622,526

Economy, Business, Industry & Agriculture

Fortune 500 companies, 2005 0

Patents issued, 2004 131

Bankruptcy cases filed, 2004 4,400

Business firm ownership, 2002

Women-owned	24,519
Sales ($ mil)	$2,139
Black-owned	220
Sales ($ mil)	$12
Hispanic-owned	964
Sales ($ mil)	$99
Asian-owned	512
Sales ($ mil)	$100
Amer. Indian/Alaska Native-owned	1,990
Sales ($ mil)	$215
Hawaiian/Pacific Isl.-owned	NA
Sales ($ mil)	$2

Gross State Product, 2004 ($ mil)

Total Gross State Product	$27,482
Agriculture, forestry, fishing and hunting	1,091
Mining	916
Utilities	1,005
Construction	1,627
Manufacturing, durable goods	807
Manufacturing, non-durable goods	608
Wholesale trade	1,523
Retail trade	2,187
Transportation & warehousing	1,158
Information	856
Finance & insurance	1,422
Real estate, rental, leasing	3,229
Professional and technical services	1,291
Educational services	100
Health care and social assistance	2,491
Accommodation/food services	906
Other services, except government	715
Government	4,488

Establishments, by major industry group, 2003

Total	33,831
Forestry, fishing & agriculture	444
Mining	265
Construction	4,530
Manufacturing	1,227
Wholesale trade	1,500
Retail trade	5,196
Transportation & warehousing	1,187
Information	620
Finance & insurance	1,878
Professional/scientific/technical	3,016
Health care/social assistance	3,088
Accommodation/food services	3,294

Annual payroll by major industry group, 2003

Total ($1,000)	$7,727,630
Forestry, fishing & agriculture	49,442
Mining	236,608
Utilities	168,572
Construction	712,007
Manufacturing	616,090
Wholesale trade	441,147
Retail trade	1,064,024
Transportation & warehousing	291,952
Information	263,742
Finance & insurance	539,689
Professional/scientific/technical	556,361
Health care/social assistance	1,479,785
Accommodation/food services	436,213

Agriculture

Number of farms, 2004 28,000

Farm acreage, 2004

Total	60,000,000
Acres per farm, 2004	2,146

Farm income, 2003 ($mil)

Net farm income	$576
Debt/asset ratio	10.7

Farm marketings, 2003 ($mil)

Total	$1,892
Crops	787
Livestock	1,105

Principal commodities, in order by marketing receipts, 2003

Cattle, wheat, barley, hay

Federal economic activity in state

Expenditures, 2003

Total ($ mil)	$7,092
Per capita	$7,729
Defense ($ mil)	556
Non-defense ($ mil)	6,536

Defense department, 2003

Payroll ($ mil)	$353
Contract awards ($ mil)	$200
Grants ($ mil)	$25
Homeland security grants ($1,000)	
2004	$20,689
2005	$15,318

FDIC insured financial institutions, 2004

Number	80
Assets ($bil)	$14.6
Deposits ($bil)	11.9

Fishing, 2004

Catch (x 1,000 lbs)	0
Value ($1,000)	0

8   Montana

Mining, 2004 ($ mil)
Total non-fuel mineral production $582
Percent of U.S. 1.3%

Construction, 2003 ($ mil)
Total contracts (including non-building). . . $974
    residential. 405
    non-residential 243

Establishments, receipts, payroll & employees, by major industry group, 2002

Mining 131
    Receipts ($1,000) $163,244
    Annual payroll ($1,000) $34,162
    Paid employees 912

Utilities 221
    Receipts ($1,000) . . . . NA
    Annual payroll ($1,000) $177,740
    Paid employees 3,057

Construction 4,025
    Receipts ($1,000) $3,372,837
    Annual payroll ($1,000) $658,456
    Paid employees . . . . 22,506 ◂

Manufacturing 1,234
    Receipts ($1,000) $4,987,577
    Annual payroll ($1,000) $638,834
    Paid employees 18,582

Wholesale trade 1,485
    Receipts ($1,000) $7,223,420
    Annual payroll ($1,000) $430,384
    Paid employees 13,728

Retail trade 5,145
    Receipts ($1,000) $10,122,625
    Annual payroll ($1,000) $988,009
    Paid employees 52,891

Transportation 1,148
    Receipts ($1,000) $996,647
    Annual payroll ($1,000) $234,545
    Paid employees 9,094

Information 633
    Receipts ($1,000) . . . . NA
    Annual payroll ($1,000) $261,550
    Paid employees 9,357

Finance & insurance 1,803
    Receipts ($1,000) . . . . NA
    Annual payroll ($1,000) $468,021
    Paid employees 13,596

Professional, scientific & technical 2,886
    Receipts ($1,000) $1,249,057
    Annual payroll ($1,000) $498,313
    Paid employees 15,617

Health care & social assistance 3,032
    Receipts ($1,000) $3,432,698
    Annual payroll ($1,000) $1,428,942
    Paid employees 51,770

Accommodation & food service 3,260
    Receipts ($1,000) $1,537,986
    Annual payroll ($1,000) $408,977
    Paid employees 40,918

Communication, Energy & Transportation

Communication
Daily newspapers, 2004 11
Households with computers, 2003 . . . . .60%
Households with internet access, 2003 . . . . .50%

Energy
Electricity Consumption, 2001
Total (trillion Btu) 366
Per capita (million Btu) 404
By source of production (trillion Btu)
    Coal 184
    Natural gas 67
    Petroleum 168
    Nuclear electric power 0
    Hydroelectric power 67
By end-use sector (trillion Btu)
    Residential 70
    Commercial 60
    Industrial 128
    Transportation 108
Electric energy, 2003
    Production (billion kWh) 26.3
    Net summer capability (million kW) 5.2
Gas utilities, 2003
    Customers (x1,000) 264
    Sales (trillion Btu) 32
    Revenues ($mil) $220
Nuclear plants, 2003 0

Transportation, 2004
Public Road & Street Mileage 69,452
    Urban. 2,754
    Rural 66,698
    Interstate. 1,192
Vehicle miles of travel per capita 12,115.7
Total motor vehicle registrations 1,008,701
    Automobiles. 433,160
    Buses 2,597
    Trucks 572,944
    Motorcycles 47,967
Licensed drivers 712,880
    19 years & under 48,923
Deaths from motor vehicle accidents 229

State Summary

Capital City. . . . . Lincoln
Governor. . . . . Dave Heineman
PO Box 94848
Lincoln, NE 68509
402-471-2244
Admitted as a state 1867
Area (square miles). 77,354
Population, 2004 (est.) 1,747,214
Largest City. . . . . .Omaha
Population, 2004. 409,000
Personal income per capita, 2004
(in current dollars) $31,339
Gross state product ($ mil), 2004 . . . . . . $68,183

Leading industries by payroll, 2003

Manufacturing, Health care/Social assistance,
Finance & Insurance

Leading agricultural commodities by receipts, 2003

Cattle, corn, soybeans, hogs

Geography & Environment

Total area (sq. mi.). 77,354
land 76,872
water 481
Federally-owned land, 2004 (acres) 665,481
percent. 1.4%
Highest point. . . Johnson Twp. (Kimball County)
elevation (feet) 5,426
Lowest point . . . . southeast corner of state
elevation (feet) 840
General coastline (miles). 0
Tidal shoreline (miles). 0
Capital City. . . . . Lincoln
Population 2000 226,000
Population 2004 236,000
Largest City. . . . . .Omaha
Population 2000 390,000
Population 2004 409,000

Number of cities with over 100,000 population

1990 2
2000 2
2004 2

State park and recreation areas, 2003

Area (acres x 1,000). 135
Number of visitors (x 1,000) 9,726
Revenues (x 1,000). $12,697
percent of operating expenditures. 63.1%

National forest system land, 2004

Acres 352,000

Demographics and Characteristics of the Population

Population

1980 1,569,825
1990 1,578,385
2000 1,711,263
2004 (estimate). 1,747,214
persons per sq. mile of land. 22.7
2005 (projection). 1,744,370
Male. 861,879
Female. 882,491
2010 (projection) 1,768,997
2020 (projection). 1,802,678
2030 (projection). 1,820,247
Male. 899,957
Female. 920,290

Metropolitan and Non-Metro. area population

	Metro	Non-Metro
1980	708,000	862,000
1990	766,000	812,000
2000	900,000	811,000

Change in population, 2000-2004

Number. 35,949
percent. 2.1%
Natural increase (births minus deaths). . . 41,632
Net internal migration . . . . -23,672
Net international migration 18,789

Persons by age, 2004

Under 5 years 122,049
18 years and over 1,312,648
65 years and over 231,803
85 years and over. 35,910

Persons by age, 2010 (projected)

Total. 1,768,997
Under 5 years 127,806
5 to 17 years 318,450
18 and over 1,322,741
21 and over 1,247,471
65 and over 243,313
85 and over 43,230
Median age 36.7

Race, 2004 (estimate)

One Race
White. 1,609,056
Black or African American 74,815
American Indian/Alaska Native. 16,562
Pacific Islander 1,176
Asian Indian. 2,464
Chinese 4,645
Filipino 3,185
Japanese 675
Korean. 3,568
Vietnamese. 6,846
Two or more races. 18,859

Persons of Hispanic origin, 2004

Total Hispanic or Latino 118,227
  Mexican........................... 96,251
  Puerto Rican 3,996
  Cuban 1,357
  Other Hispanic or Latino 7,054

Marital status, 2000

Population 15 years & over 1,342,422
  Never married 346,345
  Married........................... 770,550
  Separated 14,767
  Widowed........................... 89,942
  Divorced 120,818

Language spoken at home, 2000

Population 5 years & over 1,594,700
  English only 1,469,046
  Spanish 77,655
  Other Indo-European languages 27,905
  Asian/Pacific Island languages....... 15,014

Households & families, 2000

Households.......................... 666,184
  with persons under 18 years 229,980
  with persons over 65 years.......... 157,560
  persons per household 2.49
Families............................ 443,411
  persons per family....................3.06
Married couples..................... 360,996
Female householder,
  no husband present................. 60,343
One-person households 183,550

Nativity, 2000

Number of persons born in state 1,147,815
  percent of population................ 67.1%

Immigration & Naturalization, 2004

Immigrants admitted................... 2,954
Persons naturalized 1,537
Asylums granted 70
Asylums denied 34

Vital Statistics and Health

Marriages

2002................................. 12,889
2003................................. 12,240
2004................................. 12,489

Divorces

2002................................. 6,186
2003................................. 5,940
2004................................. 5,962

Births

2003 25,917
  Birthrate (per 1,000)....................14.9
  Low birth weight (2,500g or less)........ 6.9%
  To unmarried mothers................ 29.7%

2003, continued
  White............................. 23,382
  Black 1,467
  Hispanic 3,449
  Asian/Pacific Islander 604
  Amer. Indian/Alaska Native........... 470
2004 (preliminary)..................... 26,331
  Birthrate (per 1,000)....................15.1
  White............................. 23,703
  Black 1,573
  Hispanic 3,446
  Asian/Pacific Islander 606

Deaths

2002
All causes 15,738
  rate per 100,000......................910.1
Heart disease 4,242
  rate per 100,000.................... 245.3
Malignant neoplasms 3,433
  rate per 100,000....................198.5
Cerebrovascular disease................. 1,103
  rate per 100,000......................63.8
Chronic lower respiratory disease 934
  rate per 100,000......................54.0
2003 15,466
  rate per 100,000......................889.2
2004 (provisional) 14,673

Infant deaths

2003 (provisional) 145
  rate per 1,000 ....5.6
2004 (provisional) 176
  rate per 1,000 ....6.7

Abortions, 2000

Total................................. 4,000
  rate per 1,000 women age 15-44..........11.6

Physicians, 2003

Total................................. 4,216
  rate per 1,000 persons................... 242

Nurses, 2001

Total................................. 15,970
  rate per 1,000 persons................... 928

Community Hospitals, 2003

Number................................. 85
Beds (x 1,000)...........................7.5
Patients admitted (x 1,000) 212
Average daily census (x 1,000) 4.4
Average cost per day $1,043
Outpatient visits (x mil)....................3.7

Disability status of population, 2004

5 to 20 years 6.6%
21 to 64 years 11.9%
65 years and over 38.8%

Education

Educational attainment, 2004

Population over 25 years 1,097,070
Less than 9th grade 46,676
High school graduates only......... 341,424
Bachelor's degree only 200,928
Graduate or professional degree...... 90,645
Less than 9th grade percent 4.3%
High school graduate or more 91.3%
College graduate or more............. 24.8%
Graduate or professional degree........ 8.3%

Public school enrollment, Fall 2002

Total................................. 285,402
Kindergarten through grade 8 195,113
Grades 9 through 12 90,289
Enrollment, 2005 (projected) 279,800

Graduating public high school seniors

2004 (estimate)...................... 20,020

SAT scores, 2005

Average verbal score 574
Average math score 579
Percent of graduates taking test 8%

Public school teachers, 2004

Total (x 1,000) 20.7
Elementary (x 1,000).................... 13.5
Secondary (x 1,000) 7.1
Average salary $38,400
Elementary......................... $38,400
Secondary $38,400

State receipts & expenditures for public schools, 2004

Revenue receipts ($mil)................. $2,209
Expenditures
Total ($mil)......................... $2,385
Per capita $1,373
Per pupil $7,947

Institutions of higher education, 2004

Total.................................. 39
Public................................ 15
Private............................... 24

Enrollment in institutions of higher education, Fall 2003

Total............................. 120,305
Full-time men 36,151
Full-time women..................... 42,656
Part-time men 17,095
Part-time women..................... 24,403

Minority enrollment in institutions of higher education, Fall 2003

Black, non-hispanic.................... 4,717
Hispanic 3,441
Asian/Pacific Islander 2,739
American Indian/Alaska Native........... 917

Earned degrees conferred, 2003

Bachelor's 11,025
Master's 3,533
First-professional....................... 809
Doctor's............................... 434

State & local financial support for higher education, 2003-2004

Full-time equivalent enrollment (x 1,000) ...71.3
Appropriations per FTE................ $5,475
as a percent of tax revenue............. 11.1%

Social Insurance & Welfare Programs

Social Security benefits & beneficiaries, 2004

Beneficiaries
Total............................. 291,000
Retired & dependents.............. 211,000
Survivors.......................... 39,000
Disabled & dependents............. 41,000
Annual benefit payments ($ mil)
Total.............................. $2,963
Retired & dependents.............. $2,049
Survivors........................... $535
Disabled & dependents.............. $379
Average Monthly Benefit
Retired & dependents............... $937
Disabled & dependents.............. $847
Widowed............................ $946

Medicare

Enrollment, 2001 (x 1,000) 255
Payments ($ mil, est.) $1,400
Enrollment, 2003 (x 1,000) 257

Medicaid, 2002

Beneficiaries (x 1,000)................. 256
Payments ($ mil) $1,255

State Children's Health Insurance, 2004

Enrollment (x 1,000)..................... 33.3
Expenditures ($ mil).................... $35.3

Persons without health insurance, 2003

Number (x 1,000)....................... 195
percent............................ 11.3%
Number of children (x 1,000) 31
percent of children 7.0%

Federal public aid

Temporary Assistance for Needy Families, 2004
Recipients (x 1,000)..................... 27
Families (x 1,000) 11

Supplemental Security Income, 2003
Recipients (x 1,000)..................... 22
Payments ($ mil) $95

Food Stamp Program, 2004

Participants (x 1,000) 114
Benefits ($ mil)........................ $109

4   Nebraska

Housing & Construction

Housing units

Total 2003 (estimate)	748,813
Total 2004 (estimate)	757,743
Seasonal or recreational use, 2003	15,000
Owner-occupied single-family, 2003	389,000
Median value	$100,539
Renter-occupied, 2003	209,000
Median rent	$540
Homeownership rate, 2003	69.5%
Homeownership rate, 2004	71.2%

New privately owned housing units, 2004

Number authorized (x 1,000)	10.9
Value ($ mil)	$1,373
Started 2005 (x 1,000, estimate)	10.0
Started 2006 (x 1,000, estimate)	9.7

Existing home sales

2002 (x 1,000)	34.3
2003 (x 1,000)	38.0
2004 (x 1,000)	39.8

Government & Elections

State Officials 2006

Governor (name/party/term expires)
Dave Heineman
Republican - 1/07

Lieutenant Governor	Nick Sheehy
Secretary of State	John Gale
Attorney General	Jon Bruning
Chief Justice	John V. Hendry

Governorship

Minimum age	30
Length of term	4 years
Consecutive terms permitted	2
Who succeeds	Lt. Governor

State Legislature

Name	Unicameral Legislature
Upper chamber	NA
Number of members	49
Length of term	4 year
Party in majority, 2006	NA
Lower chamber	NA
Number of members	NA
Length of term	NA
Party in majority, 2006	NA

State Government Employees, 2004

Total	33,662
Payroll	$95,148,741

Local Government Employees, 2004

Total	81,105
Payroll	$254,893,945

Local Governments by Type, 2002

Total	2,791
County	93
Municipal	531
Township	446
School District	575
Special District	1,146

Voting age population, November 2004

Total	1,294,000
Male	628,000
Female	667,000
White	1,181,000
Black	51,000
Hispanic	119,000
Asian	16,000

Presidential Election, 2004

Total Popular Vote	778,186
Kerry	254,328
Bush	512,814
Total Electoral Votes	5

Federal representation, 2006 (109th Congress)

Senator	Ben Nelson
Party	Democrat
Year term expires	2007
Senator	Charles Hagel
Party	Republican
Year term expires	2009
Representatives, total	3
Democrats	0
Republicans	3
Other	0

Votes cast for US Senators

2002

Total vote (x 1,000)	480,000
Leading party	Republican
Percent for leading party	82.8%

2004

Total vote (x 1,000)	NA
Leading party	NA
Percent for leading party	NA

Votes cast for US Representatives

2002

Total vote (x 1,000)	474
Democratic	47
Republican	387
Leading party	Republican
Percent for leading party	81.6%

2004

Total vote (x 1,000)	765
Democratic	231
Republican	515
Leading party	Republican
Percent for leading party	67.3%

Women holding public office, 2006

US Congress 0
Statewide elected office 2
State legislature 12

Black public officials, 2001

Total 8
   US and state legislatures 1
   City/county/regional offices 4
   Judicial/law enforcement 0
   Education/school boards 3

Hispanic public officials, 2004

Total 2
   State executives & legislators 1
   City/county/regional offices 1
   Judicial/law enforcement 0
   Education/school boards 0

Governmental Finance

State government revenues, 2004

Total revenue ($1,000) $8,316,470
   Revenue per capita 4,757.71

General Revenue ($ per capita) $4,197.84
   Intergovernmental 1,363.50
   Taxes 2,082.27
     general sales 872.19
     individual income tax 710.87
     corporate income tax 95.78
   Current charges 373.41
   Miscellaneous 378.67

State government expenditure, 2004

Total expenditure (x $1,000) $6,979,917
   Expenditure per capita 3,993.09
General Expenditure ($ per capita) $3,801.85
   Education 1,329.77
   Public welfare 1,086.44
   Health 176.61
   Hospitals 116.00
   Highways 340.46
   Police protection 39.85
   Correction 107.81
   Natural resources 84.08
   Parks & recreation 17.38
   Governmental administration 101.93
   Interest on general debt 54.94

State debt & cash, 2004 ($ per capita)

Debt $1,115.36
Cash/security holdings $5,876.99

Federal government grants to state & local government, 2004 (x $1,000)

Total $2,530,936
By Federal Agency
   Defense $35,510

By Federal Agency, continued
   Education 242,153
   Energy 5,738
   Environmental Protection Agency 31,482
   Health & Human Services 1,355,822
   Homeland Security 22,172
   Housing & Urban Development 143,383
   Justice 65,415
   Labor 36,901
   Transportation 285,606
   Veterans Affairs 11,889

Crime, Law Enforcement & Courts

Crime, 2004 (rates per 100,000 residents)

Property crimes 61,512
   Burglaries 9,826
   Larcenies 46,399
   Motor vehicle thefts 5,287
   Property crime rate 3,520.6
Violent crimes 5,393
   Murders 40
   Forcible rape 620
   Robberies 1,138
   Aggravated assaults 3,595
   Violent crime rate 308.7

Police Agencies, 2004

Total agencies 163
Total employees 4,803
   Male officers 3,070
   Female officers 373
   Male civilians 380
   Female civilians 980

Arrests, 2004

Total 93,098
   Persons under 18 years of age 14,577

Prisoners under state & federal jurisdiction, 2004

Total prisoners 4,130
   Percent change, 12/31/03 to 12/31/04 .... 2.2%
Sentenced to more than one year 4,038
   rate per 100,000 230

Persons under sentence of death, 7/1/05

Total 10
   White 6
   Black 1
   Hispanic 3

State's highest court

Name .... Supreme Court
Number of members 7
Length of term .... 6 years
Intermediate appeals court? .... no

Labor & Income

Civilian labor force, 2004

Total	990,000
Men	524,000
Women	467,000
Persons 16-19 years	64,000
White	914,000
Black	32,000
Hispanic	62,000
Asian	0

Civilian labor force as a percent of civilian non-institutional population, 2004

Total	74.4%
Men	80.7
Women	68.5
Persons 16-19 years	63.9
White	74.8
Black	66.9
Hispanic	78.5
Asian	0.0

Employment, 2004

Total	953,000
Men	504,000
Women	449,000
Persons 16-19 years	56,000
White	885,000
Black	29,000
Hispanic	58,000
Asian	0

Full-time/part-time labor force, 2002

Full-time labor force, employed	739,000
Part-time labor force, employed	186,000
Unemployed, looking for	
Full-time work	27,000
Part-time work	NA

Unemployment rate, 2004

Total	3.8%
Men	3.7
Women	3.8
Persons 16-19 years	12.6
White	3.2
Black	11.5
Hispanic	7.3
Asian	NA

Unemployed by reason for unemployment (as a percent of total unemployment), 2002

Job losers or completed temp jobs	NA
Job leavers	NA
Reentrants	NA
New entrants	NA

Labor unions, 2004

Membership	69,000
percent of employed	8.3%

Experienced civilian labor force by private industry, first quarter 2004

Total	715,276
Natural Resources & Mining	9,791
Construction	43,674
Manufacturing	100,481
Trade, transportation & utilities	181,711
Information	21,304
Finance	59,731
Professional & business	92,306
Education & Health	105,943
Leisure & hospitality	74,497
Other	25,838

Experienced civilian labor force by occupation, 2004

Management	33,010
Business & Financial	34,070
Legal	4,270
Sales	92,390
Office & Admin. Support	156,430
Computers & Math	20,770
Architecture & Engineering	10,830
Arts & Entertainment	10,770
Education	53,310
Social Services	12,830
Healthcare Practitioner & Technical	48,660
Healthcare support	24,390
Maintenance & Repair	39,520
Construction	43,580
Transportation & moving	78,220
Production	80,420
Farming, fishing & forestry	980

Hours and earnings of production workers on manufacturing payrolls, 2004

Average weekly hours	41.6
Average hourly earnings	$15.19
Average weekly earnings	$631.90

Average annual pay

2004	$31,507
change from 2003	3.8%

Household income

Median household income, three-year average, 2002-2004	$44,623

Personal income, 2004 ($ per capita)

In current dollars	$31,339
In constant (2000) dollars	$29,065

Poverty

Persons below poverty level, three-year average, 2002-2004	9.9%

Federal individual income tax returns, 2003

Returns filed	802,709
Adjusted gross income ($1,000)	$33,043,454
Total income tax paid ($1,000)	$3,758,628

Economy, Business, Industry & Agriculture

Fortune 500 companies, 2005 4

Patents issued, 2004 229

Bankruptcy cases filed, 2004 8,800

Business firm ownership, 2002

Women-owned	38,681
Sales ($ mil)	$5,793
Black-owned	2,092
Sales ($ mil)	$154
Hispanic-owned	1,966
Sales ($ mil)	$434
Asian-owned	1,459
Sales ($ mil)	$702
Amer. Indian/Alaska Native-owned	425
Sales ($ mil)	$47
Hawaiian/Pacific Isl.-owned	9
Sales ($ mil)	$0

Gross State Product, 2004 ($ mil)

Total Gross State Product	$68,183
Agriculture, forestry, fishing and hunting	3,403
Mining	57
Utilities	912
Construction	3,028
Manufacturing, durable goods	4,136
Manufacturing, non-durable goods	4,169
Wholesale trade	4,547
Retail trade	4,588
Transportation & warehousing	4,788
Information	2,491
Finance & insurance	5,742
Real estate, rental, leasing	5,872
Professional and technical services	2,897
Educational services	516
Health care and social assistance	4,919
Accommodation/food services	1,394
Other services, except government	1,608
Government	10,075

Establishments, by major industry group, 2003

Total	50,394
Forestry, fishing & agriculture	189
Mining	125
Construction	5,839
Manufacturing	1,966
Wholesale trade	2,866
Retail trade	8,102
Transportation & warehousing	2,294
Information	922
Finance & insurance	3,968
Professional/scientific/technical	3,915
Health care/social assistance	4,413
Accommodation/food services	4,046

Annual payroll by major industry group, 2003

Total ($1,000)	$23,091,980
Forestry, fishing & agriculture	NA
Mining	31,982
Utilities	63,544
Construction	1,453,967
Manufacturing	3,458,375
Wholesale trade	1,336,864
Retail trade	2,005,062
Transportation & warehousing	1,035,831
Information	925,619
Finance & insurance	2,653,687
Professional/scientific/technical . . .	2,166,051
Health care/social assistance	3,269,394
Accommodation/food services	637,748

Agriculture

Number of farms, 2004 48,000
Farm acreage, 2004

Total	46,000,000
Acres per farm, 2004	950

Farm income, 2003 ($mil)

Net farm income	$3,228
Debt/asset ratio	21

Farm marketings, 2003 ($mil)

Total	$10,621
Crops	3,754
Livestock	6,867

Principal commodities, in order by marketing receipts, 2003

Cattle, corn, soybeans, hogs

Federal economic activity in state

Expenditures, 2003

Total ($ mil)	$11,000
Per capita	$6,324
Defense ($ mil)	1,099
Non-defense ($ mil)	9,901

Defense department, 2003

Payroll ($ mil)	$779
Contract awards ($ mil)	$315
Grants ($ mil)	$38
Homeland security grants ($1,000)	
2004	$24,376
2005	$23,656

FDIC insured financial institutions, 2004

Number	263
Assets ($bil)	$46.1
Deposits ($bil)	32.9

Fishing, 2004

Catch (x 1,000 lbs)	0
Value ($1,000)	0

8   Nebraska

Mining, 2004 ($ mil)
Total non-fuel mineral production $95
Percent of U.S. 0.2%

Construction, 2003 ($ mil)
Total contracts (including non-building). $3,457
    residential............................ 1,563
    non-residential 1,085

Establishments, receipts, payroll & employees, by major industry group, 2002

Mining................................ 185
    Receipts ($1,000) $2,570,066
    Annual payroll ($1,000)............ $511,978
    Paid employees 9,007

Utilities 132
    Receipts ($1,000) .... NA
    Annual payroll ($1,000)............ $92,741
    Paid employees 1,199

Construction........................ 5,579
    Receipts ($1,000) $6,700,924
    Annual payroll ($1,000).......... $1,407,899
    Paid employees 46,004

Manufacturing 1,976
    Receipts ($1,000) $30,610,970
    Annual payroll ($1,000).......... $3,386,495
    Paid employees 103,029

Wholesale trade 2,907
    Receipts ($1,000) $26,155,770
    Annual payroll ($1,000).......... $1,309,945
    Paid employees 36,805

Retail trade 8,157
    Receipts ($1,000) $20,249,200
    Annual payroll ($1,000)......... $1,932,506
    Paid employees 105,634

Transportation........................ 2,244
    Receipts ($1,000) $4,452,719
    Annual payroll ($1,000)............ $946,814
    Paid employees 29,243

Information........................... 896
    Receipts ($1,000) .... NA
    Annual payroll ($1,000)............ $879,246
    Paid employees 22,542

Finance & insurance 3,887
    Receipts ($1,000) .... NA
    Annual payroll ($1,000)......... $2,488,731
    Paid employees 57,353

Professional, scientific & technical 3,888
    Receipts ($1,000) $3,020,944
    Annual payroll ($1,000).......... $1,270,570
    Paid employees 31,036

Health care & social assistance 4,379
    Receipts ($1,000) $7,492,496
    Annual payroll ($1,000)........... $3,141,103
    Paid employees 105,183

Accommodation & food service........... 3,992
    Receipts ($1,000) $2,088,710
    Annual payroll ($1,000)............ $590,533
    Paid employees 62,662

Communication, Energy & Transportation

Communication
Daily newspapers, 2004 17
Households with computers, 2003 .... .66%
Households with internet access, 2003 ..... 55%

Energy
Electricity Consumption, 2001
Total (trillion Btu) 627
Per capita (million Btu) 365
By source of production (trillion Btu)
    Coal................................. 228
    Natural gas.......................... 124
    Petroleum............................ 218
    Nuclear electric power 91
    Hydroelectric power 11
By end-use sector (trillion Btu)
    Residential 152
    Commercial 130
    Industrial 182
    Transportation 163
Electric energy, 2003
    Production (billion kWh) 30.5
    Net summer capability (million kW) 6.7
Gas utilities, 2003
    Customers (x1,000)................... 457
    Sales (trillion Btu)................... 63
    Revenues ($mil)..................... $457
Nuclear plants, 2003 2

Transportation, 2004
Public Road & Street Mileage 93,245
    Urban............................. 5,922
    Rural 87,323
    Interstate.......................... 482
Vehicle miles of travel per capita........ 11,323.7
Total motor vehicle registrations...... 1,689,072
    Automobiles........................ 842,363
    Buses 6,489
    Trucks 840,220
    Motorcycles 28,671
Licensed drivers 1,315,819
    19 years & under 88,676
Deaths from motor vehicle accidents 254

State Summary

Capital City....................Carson City
Governor...................... Kenny Guinn
Capitol Building
Carson City, NV 89701
775-684-5670
Admitted as a state 1864
Area (square miles)................. 110,561
Population, 2004 (est.) 2,334,771
Largest City.......................Las Vegas
Population, 2004.................. 535,000
Personal income per capita, 2004
(in current dollars) $33,405
Gross state product ($ mil), 2004...... $100,317

Leading industries by payroll, 2003

Accommodation & Food services, Construction,
Health care/Social assistance

Leading agricultural commodities by receipts, 2003

Cattle, hay, dairy products, onions

Geography & Environment

Total area (sq. mi.)................... 110,561
land 109,826
water 735

Federally-owned land, 2004 (acres) .. 59,362,643
percent.............................84.5%

Highest point................. Boundary Peak
elevation (feet) 13,140

Lowest point ....Colorado River
elevation (feet) 470

General coastline (miles).................... 0

Tidal shoreline (miles)...................... 0

Capital City......................Carson City
Population 2000 52,457
Population 2004 55,974

Largest City........................Las Vegas
Population 2000 478,000
Population 2004 535,000

Number of cities with over 100,000 population

1990 3
2000 4
2004 4

State park and recreation areas, 2003

Area (acres x 1,000)..................... 133
Number of visitors (x 1,000) 3,288
Revenues (x 1,000).................... $2,357
percent of operating expenditures...... 26.9%

National forest system land, 2004

Acres 5,836,000

Demographics and Characteristics of the Population

Population

1980 800,493
1990 1,201,833
2000 1,998,257
2004 (estimate)................... 2,334,771
persons per sq. mile of land............21.3
2005 (projection).................. 2,352,086
Male.............................. 1,189,246
Female............................ 1,162,840
2010 (projection) 2,690,531
2020 (projection) 3,452,283
2030 (projection) 4,282,102
Male.............................. 2,075,434
Female............................ 2,206,668

Metropolitan and Non-Metro. area population

	Metro	Non-Metro
1980	657,000	144,000
1990	996,000	206,000
2000	1,748,000	251,000

Change in population, 2000-2004

Number............................. 336,514
percent............................16.8%
Natural increase (births minus deaths)... 64,292
Net internal migration................ 216,322
Net international migration 55,710

Persons by age, 2004

Under 5 years 169,018
18 years and over 1,731,175
65 years and over 262,079
85 years and over 24,000

Persons by age, 2010 (projected)

Total............................. 2,690,531
Under 5 years 196,094
5 to 17 years 468,991
18 and over 2,025,446
21 and over 1,919,022
65 and over 329,621
85 and over 33,455
Median age 37.8

Race, 2004 (estimate)

One Race
White.......................... 1,927,086
Black or African American 176,167
American Indian/Alaska Native....... 33,045
Pacific Islander 12,033
Asian Indian....................... 5,739
Chinese 17,988
Filipino 58,647
Japanese 12,220
Korean 12,115
Vietnamese...................... 10,067
Two or more races.................... 57,970

Persons of Hispanic origin, 2004

Total Hispanic or Latino 527,570
  Mexican........................... 410,010
  Puerto Rican 13,711
  Cuban 12,298
  Other Hispanic or Latino 36,187

Marital status, 2000

Population 15 years & over 1,563,580
  Never married 389,331
  Married........................... 834,952
  Separated 35,962
  Widowed.......................... 85,997
  Divorced 215,774

Language spoken at home, 2000

Population 5 years & over 1,853,720
  English only 1,425,748
  Spanish 299,947
  Other Indo-European languages 47,183
  Asian/Pacific Island languages........ 68,523

Households & families, 2000

Households........................... 751,165
  with persons under 18 years 264,800
  with persons over 65 years........... 159,831
  persons per household 2.62
Families............................. 498,333
  persons per family......................3.14
Married couples....................... 373,201
Female householder,
  no husband present................. 83,482
One-person households 186,745

Nativity, 2000

Number of persons born in state 425,626
  percent of population................. 21.3%

Immigration & Naturalization, 2004

Immigrants admitted................... 8,758
Persons naturalized 4,622
Asylums granted 54
Asylums denied 14

Vital Statistics and Health

Marriages

2002 146,468
2003 143,600
2004 145,763

Divorces

2002 15,478
2003 16,379
2004 14,828

Births

2003 33,647
  Birthrate (per 1,000)...................15.0
  Low birth weight (2,500g or less)........ 8.1%
  To unmarried mothers................ 39.1%

2003, continued
  White............................. 27,693
  Black 2,905
  Hispanic 12,207
  Asian/Pacific Islander 2,528
  Amer. Indian/Alaska Native........... 518
2004 (preliminary).................... 35,188
  Birthrate (per 1,000)..................15.1
  White............................. 29,032
  Black 2,958
  Hispanic 13,060
  Asian/Pacific Islander 2,666

Deaths

2002
All causes 16,927
  rate per 100,000................... 778.8
Heart disease 4,421
  rate per 100,000....................203.4
Malignant neoplasms 3,937
  rate per 100,000....................181.1
Cerebrovascular disease.................. 976
  rate per 100,000.....................44.9
Chronic lower respiratory disease 1,174
  rate per 100,000.....................54.0
2003 17,864
  rate per 100,000....................797.1
2004 (provisional) 17,735

Infant deaths

2003 (provisional) 203
  rate per 1,000 6
2004 (provisional) 223
  rate per 1,000 ....6.3

Abortions, 2000

Total................................ 14,000
  rate per 1,000 women age 15-44.........32.2

Physicians, 2003

Total................................. 4,152
  rate per 1,000 persons................... 185

Nurses, 2001

Total................................ 10,840
  rate per 1,000 persons.................. 517

Community Hospitals, 2003

Number................................. 25
Beds (x 1,000)..........................4.3
Patients admitted (x 1,000) 213
Average daily census (x 1,000) 3.0
Average cost per day $1,608
Outpatient visits (x mil)..................2.3

Disability status of population, 2004

5 to 20 years 4.6%
21 to 64 years 10.8%
65 years and over 33.3%

Education

Educational attainment, 2004

Population over 25 years	1,500,676
Less than 9th grade	105,776
High school graduates only.........	482,283
Bachelor's degree only	183,417
Graduate or professional degree......	105,686
Less than 9th grade percent	7.0%
High school graduate or more	86.3%
College graduate or more...........	24.5%
Graduate or professional degree........	7.0%

Public school enrollment, Fall 2002

Total..............................	369,498
Kindergarten through grade 8	270,941
Grades 9 through 12................	98,557
Enrollment, 2005 (projected)	410,600

Graduating public high school seniors

2004 (estimate)...................... 16,220

SAT scores, 2005

Average verbal score	508
Average math score	513
Percent of graduates taking test	39%

Public school teachers, 2004

Total (x 1,000)	20.0
Elementary (x 1,000)...................	11.8
Secondary (x 1,000)	8.2
Average salary	$42,300
Elementary......................	$41,900
Secondary.......................	$42,700

State receipts & expenditures for public schools, 2004

Revenue receipts ($mil)................	$3,025
Expenditures	
Total ($mil)........................	$3,399
Per capita	$1,516
Per pupil	$6,177

Institutions of higher education, 2004

Total..................................	17
Public.................................	7
Private...............................	10

Enrollment in institutions of higher education, Fall, 2003

Total...............................	101,804
Full-time men	19,194
Full-time women.....................	25,901
Part-time men	24,334
Part-time women.....................	32,375

Minority enrollment in institutions of higher education, Fall, 2003

Black, non-hispanic....................	6,666
Hispanic	11,244
Asian/Pacific Islander	8,907
American Indian/Alaska Native..........	1,353

Earned degrees conferred, 2003

Bachelor's	4,877
Master's..............................	1,527
First-professional.........................	178
Doctor's.................................	132

State & local financial support for higher education, 2003-2004

Full-time equivalent enrollment (x 1,000) ...	57.2
Appropriations per FTE................	$7,834
as a percent of tax revenue..............	5.6%

Social Insurance & Welfare Programs

Social Security benefits & beneficiaries, 2004

Beneficiaries

Total.............................	341,000
Retired & dependents..............	249,000
Survivors.........................	38,000
Disabled & dependents..............	54,000

Annual benefit payments ($ mil)

Total.............................	$3,594
Retired & dependents..............	$2,504
Survivors.........................	$512
Disabled & dependents..............	$578

Average Monthly Benefit

Retired & dependents..............	$962
Disabled & dependents..............	$960
Widowed..........................	$964

Medicare

Enrollment, 2001 (x 1,000)	251
Payments ($ mil, est.)	$1,300
Enrollment, 2003 (x 1,000)	274

Medicaid, 2002

Beneficiaries (x 1,000).....................	202
Payments ($ mil)	$724

State Children's Health Insurance, 2004

Enrollment (x 1,000)......................	38.5
Expenditures ($ mil).....................	$20.6

Persons without health insurance, 2003

Number (x 1,000)........................	426
percent...........................	18.9%
Number of children (x 1,000)	103
percent of children	17.4%

Federal public aid

Temporary Assistance for Needy Families, 2004

Recipients (x 1,000).......................	21
Families (x 1,000)	9

Supplemental Security Income, 2003

Recipients (x 1,000).......................	31
Payments ($ mil)	$144

Food Stamp Program, 2004

Participants (x 1,000)	120
Benefits ($ mil).........................	$120

Housing & Construction

Housing units

Total 2003 (estimate) 934,656
Total 2004 (estimate) 976,446
Seasonal or recreational use, 2003 23,000
Owner-occupied single-family, 2003.... 433,000
   Median value $170,333
Renter-occupied, 2003 317,000
   Median rent $771
Homeownership rate, 2003 ....64.8%
Homeownership rate, 2004 ....65.7%

New privately owned housing units, 2004

Number authorized (x 1,000) 44.6
Value ($ mil)........................ $5,461
Started 2005 (x 1,000, estimate) 36.1
Started 2006 (x 1,000, estimate) 35.0

Existing home sales

2002 (x 1,000)............................63.5
2003 (x 1,000)............................80.9
2004 (x 1,000)............................99.8

Government & Elections

State Officials 2006

Governor (name/party/term expires)
        Kenny Guinn
      Republican - 1/07
Lieutenant Governor........... Lorraine Hunt
Secretary of State................. Dean Heller
Attorney General............George J. Chanos
Chief Justice .... Nancy A. Becker

Governorship

Minimum age............................. 25
Length of term .... 4 years
Consecutive terms permitted 2
Who succeeds...................Lt. Governor

State Legislature

Name .... Legislature
Upper chamber ....Senate
   Number of members.................... 21
   Length of term.................... 4 years
   Party in majority, 2006 .... Republican
Lower chamber.................State Assembly
   Number of members.................... 42
   Length of term.................... 2 years
   Party in majority, 2006 ....Democratic

State Government Employees, 2004

Total................................. 25,279
Payroll $93,456,030

Local Government Employees, 2004

Total 71,097
Payroll $281,094,885

Local Governments by Type, 2002

Total................................... 210
   County............................... 16
   Municipal 19
   Township 0
   School District....................... 17
   Special District 158

Voting age population, November 2004

Total............................. 1,699,000
   Male............................ 856,000
   Female.......................... 842,000
   White.......................... 1,445,000
   Black 113,000
   Hispanic 301,000
   Asian 84,000

Presidential Election, 2004

Total Popular Vote 829,587
   Kerry 397,190
   Bush 418,690
Total Electoral Votes................... 5

Federal representation, 2006 (109th Congress)

Senator........................ John Ensign
   Party .... Republican
   Year term expires 2007
Senator........................ Harry Reid
   Party .... Democrat
   Year term expires 2011
Representatives, total 3
   Democrats............................. 1
   Republicans 2
   Other 0

Votes cast for US Senators

2002
Total vote (x 1,000) .... NA
Leading party........................... NA
Percent for leading party .... NA

2004
Total vote (x 1,000) 810,000
Leading party....................Democratic
Percent for leading party 61.1%

Votes cast for US Representatives

2002
Total vote (x 1,000) 502
   Democratic........................... 171
   Republican 301
Leading party.................... Republican
Percent for leading party 60.0%

2004
Total vote (x 1,000) 791
   Democratic........................... 334
   Republican 421
Leading party.................... Republican
Percent for leading party 53.2%

Women holding public office, 2006

US Congress 1
Statewide elected office..................... 2
State legislature 21

Black public officials, 2001

Total..................................... 14
   US and state legislatures 5
   City/county/regional offices 5
   Judicial/law enforcement.................. 2
   Education/school boards 2

Hispanic public officials, 2004

Total..................................... 7
   State executives & legislators 3
   City/county/regional offices 2
   Judicial/law enforcement.................. 1
   Education/school boards 1

Governmental Finance

State government revenues, 2004

Total revenue ($1,000) $10,136,127
   Revenue per capita 4,344.68

General Revenue ($ per capita) $3,136.84
   Intergovernmental 696.61
   Taxes 2,031.24
     general sales 970.75
     individual income tax.................. 0
     corporate income tax 0
   Current charges..................... 259.38
   Miscellaneous 149.61

State government expenditure, 2004

Total expenditure (x $1,000) $8,686,071
   Expenditure per capita............. 3,723.13
General Expenditure ($ per capita).... $3,238.62
   Education 1,290.84
   Public welfare...................... 553.85
   Health 90.42
   Hospitals.......................... .62.48
   Highways 382.99
   Police protection 26.59
   Correction 100.35
   Natural resources 50.69
   Parks & recreation..................... .8.25
   Governmental administration 86.26
   Interest on general debt 60.16

State debt & cash, 2004 ($ per capita)

Debt $1,546.20
Cash/security holdings.............. $9,151.81

Federal government grants to state & local government, 2004 (x $1,000)

Total $2,321,630
By Federal Agency
   Defense $22,297

By Federal Agency, continued
   Education 221,173
   Energy 48,151
   Environmental Protection Agency 27,720
   Health & Human Services. 976,594
   Homeland Security................... 8,094
   Housing & Urban Development...... 157,350
   Justice 83,292
   Labor 59,443
   Transportation 319,682
   Veterans Affairs.................... 5,241

Crime, Law Enforcement & Courts

Crime, 2004 (rates per 100,000 residents)

Property crimes 98,215
   Burglaries........................ 23,142
   Larcenies......................... 52,438
   Motor vehicle thefts 22,635
   Property crime rate................ 4,206.6
Violent crimes........................ 14,379
   Murders........................... 172
   Forcible rape...................... 954
   Robberies 4,905
   Aggravated assaults 8,348
   Violent crime rate.................. .615.9

Police Agencies, 2004

Total agencies............................ 36
Total employees 8,045
   Male officers...................... 4,292
   Female officers.................... 466
   Male civilians..................... 1,153
   Female civilians................... 2,134

Arrests, 2004

Total................................ 148,909
   Persons under 18 years of age 17,722

Prisoners under state & federal jurisdiction, 2004

Total prisoners....................... 11,365
   Percent change, 12/31/03 to 12/31/04 .... 7.8%
Sentenced to more than one year 11,280
   rate per 100,000...................... 474

Persons under sentence of death, 7/1/05

Total..................................... 85
   White............................. 42
   Black 34
   Hispanic 8

State's highest court

Name ....Supreme Court
Number of members........................ 5
Length of term .... 6 years
Intermediate appeals court? .... no

Labor & Income

Civilian labor force, 2004

Total.............................. 1,175,000
  Men 657,000
  Women 518,000
  Persons 16-19 years.................. 55,000
  White................................ 986,000
  Black 73,000
  Hispanic 220,000
  Asian 70,000

Civilian labor force as a percent of civilian non-institutional population, 2004

Total................................66.8%
  Men 74.2
  Women 59.3
  Persons 16-19 years....................45.8
  White................................66.5
  Black 64.9
  Hispanic 73.1
  Asian 70.8

Employment, 2004

Total.............................. 1,125,000
  Men 629,000
  Women 496,000
  Persons 16-19 years.................. 48,000
  White................................ 948,000
  Black 68,000
  Hispanic 211,000
  Asian 67,000

Full-time/part-time labor force, 2002

Full-time labor force, employed 927,000
Part-time labor force, employed........ 133,000
Unemployed, looking for
  Full-time work........................ 54,000
  Part-time work.......................... NA

Unemployment rate, 2004

Total.................................4.2%
  Men 4.2
  Women 4.2
  Persons 16-19 years.....................13.0
  White................................3.9
  Black 6.2
  Hispanic 3.8
  Asian 4.7

Unemployed by reason for unemployment (as a percent of total unemployment), 2002

Job losers or completed temp jobs 54.8%
Job leavers.............................. NA
Reentrants..............................24.2
New entrants .... NA

Labor unions, 2004

Membership 126,000
  percent of employed 12.5%

Experienced civilian labor force by private industry, first quarter 2004

Total.............................. 977,298
  Natural Resources & Mining 11,125
  Construction 107,646
  Manufacturing....................... 44,947
  Trade, transportation & utilities 198,766
  Information 14,541
  Finance 60,282
  Professional & business 128,195
  Education & Health 78,722
  Leisure & hospitality............... 306,463
  Other 24,779

Experienced civilian labor force by occupation, 2004

Management.......................... 45,520
Business & Financial................... 32,420
Legal................................. 6,890
Sales................................ 124,600
Office & Admin. Support.............. 189,610
Computers & Math 11,630
Architecture & Engineering 15,330
Arts & Entertainment................. 14,660
Education 43,710
Social Services 7,660
Healthcare Practitioner & Technical..... 37,300
Healthcare support 18,040
Maintenance & Repair 46,860
Construction 102,110
Transportation & moving 90,320
Production 41,580
Farming, fishing & forestry.............. 5,870

Hours and earnings of production workers on manufacturing payrolls, 2004

Average weekly hours 40.1
Average hourly earnings $14.60
Average weekly earnings $585.46

Average annual pay

2004 .... $37,106
  change from 2003 .... 5.2%

Household income

Median household income, three-year average,
  2002-2004........................ $46,984

Personal income, 2004 ($ per capita)

In current dollars..................... $33,405
In constant (2000) dollars $30,981

Poverty

Persons below poverty level, three-year average,
  2002-2004......................... 10.2%

Federal individual income tax returns, 2003

Returns filed...................... 1,044,025
Adjusted gross income ($1,000) $52,306,616
Total income tax paid ($1,000) $7,075,281

Economy, Business, Industry & Agriculture

Fortune 500 companies, 2005 3

Patents issued, 2004 476

Bankruptcy cases filed, 2004 19,400

Business firm ownership, 2002

Women-owned.	47,674
Sales ($ mil)	$8,639
Black-owned.	4,345
Sales ($ mil)	$446
Hispanic-owned.	9,745
Sales ($ mil)	$1,647
Asian-owned	8,884
Sales ($ mil)	$2,004
Amer. Indian/Alaska Native-owned	1,915
Sales ($ mil)	$218
Hawaiian/Pacific Isl.-owned	323
Sales ($ mil)	$54

Gross State Product, 2004 ($ mil)

Total Gross State Product	$100,317
Agriculture, forestry, fishing and hunting	203
Mining.	1,405
Utilities	2,031
Construction	10,313
Manufacturing, durable goods.	2,114
Manufacturing, non-durable goods	1,340
Wholesale trade.	3,981
Retail trade.	7,982
Transportation & warehousing	3,345
Information	2,269
Finance & insurance.	8,502
Real estate, rental, leasing	12,722
Professional and technical services	4,955
Educational services	201
Health care and social assistance	4,946
Accommodation/food services.	14,196
Other services, except government	1,742
Government	9,857

Establishments, by major industry group, 2003

Total.	53,335
Forestry, fishing & agriculture	65
Mining.	182
Construction	5,091
Manufacturing.	1,772
Wholesale trade.	2,702
Retail trade.	7,599
Transportation & warehousing	1,225
Information	1,028
Finance & insurance.	4,164
Professional/scientific/technical	6,623
Health care/social assistance	4,816
Accommodation/food services.	4,450

Annual payroll by major industry group, 2003

Total ($1,000)	$31,331,904
Forestry, fishing & agriculture	8,233
Mining.	497,784
Utilities	371,038
Construction	3,744,903
Manufacturing.	1,668,458
Wholesale trade.	1,410,287
Retail trade.	2,851,751
Transportation & warehousing	971,010
Information	708,195
Finance & insurance.	1,685,891
Professional/scientific/technical . . .	2,571,208
Health care/social assistance	3,017,939
Accommodation/food services.	6,551,986

Agriculture

Number of farms, 2004	3,000
Farm acreage, 2004	
Total.	6,000,000
Acres per farm, 2004	2,100
Farm income, 2003 ($mil)	
Net farm income	$111
Debt/asset ratio	8.5
Farm marketings, 2003 ($mil)	
Total.	$396
Crops	141
Livestock.	254

Principal commodities, in order by marketing receipts, 2003

Cattle, hay, dairy products, onions

Federal economic activity in state

Expenditures, 2003	
Total ($ mil)	$11,637
Per capita	$5,193
Defense ($ mil).	1,368
Non-defense ($ mil)	10,269
Defense department, 2003	
Payroll ($ mil)	$970
Contract awards ($ mil)	$457
Grants ($ mil).	$16
Homeland security grants ($1,000)	
2004	$37,196
2005	$28,386

FDIC insured financial institutions, 2004

Number	38
Assets ($bil)	$56.1
Deposits ($bil)	40.5

Fishing, 2004

Catch (x 1,000 lbs)	0
Value ($1,000).	0

8   Nevada

Mining, 2004 ($ mil)
Total non-fuel mineral production $3,250
Percent of U.S. 7.4%

Construction, 2003 ($ mil)
Total contracts (including non-building). $9,536
  residential........................... 5,519
  non-residential 2,225

Establishments, receipts, payroll & employees, by major industry group, 2002

Mining.................................. 44
  Receipts ($1,000).................... $61,093
  Annual payroll ($1,000)............. $15,424
  Paid employees 380

Utilities 109
  Receipts ($1,000)....................... NA
  Annual payroll ($1,000)........... $390,001
  Paid employees 5,731

Construction........................ 4,962
  Receipts ($1,000) $16,100,809
  Annual payroll ($1,000)......... $3,490,815
  Paid employees 95,253

Manufacturing 1,764
  Receipts ($1,000) $8,466,212
  Annual payroll ($1,000)......... $1,642,783
  Paid employees 42,503

Wholesale trade 2,612
  Receipts ($1,000) $16,513,814
  Annual payroll ($1,000)......... $1,278,651
  Paid employees 31,769

Retail trade 7,214
  Receipts ($1,000) $26,999,899
  Annual payroll ($1,000)......... $2,646,023
  Paid employees 112,339

Transportation...................... 1,141
  Receipts ($1,000) $1,842,072
  Annual payroll ($1,000)......... $707,214
  Paid employees 28,693

Information............................ 997
  Receipts ($1,000) .... NA
  Annual payroll ($1,000)............. $721,980
  Paid employees 17,845

Finance & insurance 4,126
  Receipts ($1,000) .... NA
  Annual payroll ($1,000)......... $1,703,560
  Paid employees 36,006

Professional, scientific & technical 6,332
  Receipts ($1,000) $5,665,309
  Annual payroll ($1,000)......... $2,209,669
  Paid employees 46,332

Health care & social assistance 4,596
  Receipts ($1,000) $7,553,145
  Annual payroll ($1,000)......... $2,741,900
  Paid employees 76,552

Accommodation & food service........... 4,252
  Receipts ($1,000) $19,537,592
  Annual payroll ($1,000)......... $6,016,270
  Paid employees 269,098

Communication, Energy & Transportation

Communication
Daily newspapers, 2004 8
Households with computers, 2003..........61%
Households with internet access, 2003 ......55%

Energy
Electricity Consumption, 2001
  Total (trillion Btu)........................ 629
  Per capita (million Btu) 301
By source of production (trillion Btu)
  Coal 189
  Natural gas............................ 181
  Petroleum............................. 250
  Nuclear electric power 0
  Hydroelectric power.................... 26
By end-use sector (trillion Btu)
  Residential 147
  Commercial 108
  Industrial 169
  Transportation 205
Electric energy, 2003
  Production (billion kWh) 33.2
  Net summer capability (million kW) 7.5
Gas utilities, 2003
  Customers (x1,000).................... 645
  Sales (trillion Btu)...................... 80
  Revenues ($mil)....................... $595
Nuclear plants, 2003 0

Transportation, 2004
Public Road & Street Mileage 33,977
  Urban................................. 5,727
  Rural 28,250
  Interstate.............................. 560
Vehicle miles of travel per capita....... 8,636.3
Total motor vehicle registrations...... 1,281,424
  Automobiles........................ 642,818
  Buses 1,901
  Trucks 636,705
  Motorcycles 44,823
Licensed drivers 1,548,097
  19 years & under 59,709
Deaths from motor vehicle accidents 395

State Summary

Capital City. . . . . .Concord
Governor. . . . . John Lynch
Office of the Governor
25 Capitol St
Room 212
Concord, NH 03301
603-271-7532
Admitted as a state 1788
Area (square miles) 9,350
Population, 2004 (est.) 1,299,500
Largest City. . . . . Manchester
Population, 2004. 109,000
Personal income per capita, 2004
(in current dollars) $37,040
Gross state product ($ mil), 2004 . . . . . . $51,871

Leading industries by payroll, 2003

Manufacturing, Health care/Social assistance,
Retail trade

Leading agricultural commodities by receipts, 2003

Greenhouse, dairy products, apples, cattle

Geography & Environment

Total area (sq. mi.) 9,350
land 8,968
water 382

Federally-owned land, 2004 (acres) 775,665
percent. 13.5%

Highest point. . . . . .Mt. Washington
elevation (feet) 6,288

Lowest point . . . . .Atlantic Ocean
elevation (feet) . . . . sea level

General coastline (miles). 13

Tidal shoreline (miles). 131

Capital City. . . . . .Concord
Population 2000 40,687
Population 2004 42,345

Largest City. . . . . Manchester
Population 2000 107,000
Population 2004 109,000

Number of cities with over 100,000 population

1990 0
2000 1
2004 1

State park and recreation areas, 2003

Area (acres x 1,000). 86
Number of visitors (x 1,000) 5,472
Revenues (x 1,000). $8,500
percent of operating expenditures. 100.0%

National forest system land, 2004

Acres 732,000

Demographics and Characteristics of the Population

Population

1980 920,610
1990 1,109,252
2000 1,235,786
2004 (estimate). 1,299,500
persons per sq. mile of land. 144.9
2005 (projection). 1,314,821
Male. 647,628
Female. 667,193
2010 (projection) 1,385,560
2020 (projection) 1,524,751
2030 (projection) 1,646,471
Male. 809,490
Female. 836,981

Metropolitan and Non-Metro. area population

	Metro	Non-Metro
1980	511,000	410,000
1990	622,000	487,000
2000	740,000	496,000

Change in population, 2000-2004

Number 63,714
percent. 5.2%
Natural increase (births minus deaths). . . 20,730
Net internal migration 33,774
Net international migration 9,624

Persons by age, 2004

Under 5 years 72,678
18 years and over 994,506
65 years and over 156,672
85 years and over 21,723

Persons by age, 2010 (projected)

Total. 1,385,560
Under 5 years 82,238
5 to 17 years 221,926
18 and over 1,081,396
21 and over 1,028,299
65 and over 178,823
85 and over 26,264
Median age 39.6

Race, 2004 (estimate)

One Race
White. 1,249,579
Black or African American 12,263
American Indian/Alaska Native. 3,214
Pacific Islander 520
Asian Indian. 5,268
Chinese 5,167
Filipino 2,799
Japanese 307
Korean. 2,604
Vietnamese. 2,364
Two or more races. 12,100

2   New Hampshire

Persons of Hispanic origin, 2004
Total Hispanic or Latino 26,108
  Mexican........................... 6,518
  Puerto Rican 7,261
  Cuban 1,291
  Other Hispanic or Latino 3,599

Marital status, 2000
Population 15 years & over 978,641
  Never married 243,682
  Married.......................... 560,761
  Separated 13,701
  Widowed.......................... 57,740
  Divorced 102,757

Language spoken at home, 2000
Population 5 years & over 1,160,340
  English only 1,064,252
  Spanish 18,647
  Other Indo-European languages 64,067
  Asian/Pacific Island languages........ 9,891

Households & families, 2000
Households.......................... 474,606
  with persons under 18 years 168,371
  with persons over 65 years.......... 101,849
  persons per household 2.53
Families............................. 323,651
  persons per family....................3.03
Married couples..................... 262,438
Female householder,
  no husband present................ 42,952
One-person households 116,014

Nativity, 2000
Number of persons born in state 534,558
  percent of population 43.3%

Immigration & Naturalization, 2004
Immigrants admitted.................. 2,198
Persons naturalized 958
Asylums granted 20
Asylums denied 7

Vital Statistics and Health

Marriages
2002 10,564
2003 10,327
2004 10,383

Divorces
2002 5,483
2003 5,219
2004 5,131

Births
2003 14,393
  Birthrate (per 1,000)..................11.2
  Low birth weight (2,500g or less)........ 6.2%
  To unmarried mothers............... 24.8%

2003, continued
  White........................ 13,646
  Black 244
  Hispanic 527
  Asian/Pacific Islander 468
  Amer. Indian/Alaska Native 35
2004 (preliminary).................... 14,566
  Birthrate (per 1,000)...................11.2
  White........................ 13,767
  Black 256
  Hispanic 461
  Asian/Pacific Islander 519

Deaths
2002
All causes 9,853
  rate per 100,000..................... 772.8
Heart disease 2,776
  rate per 100,000.....................217.7
Malignant neoplasms 2,529
  rate per 100,000.....................198.3
Cerebrovascular disease................. 627
  rate per 100,000.....................49.2
Chronic lower respiratory disease 577
  rate per 100,000.....................45.3
2003 9,691
  rate per 100,000.....................752.6
2004 (provisional) 10,051

Infant deaths
2003 (provisional) 52
  rate per 1,000 ....3.6
2004 (provisional) 89
  rate per 1,000 6

Abortions, 2000
Total................................. 3,000
  rate per 1,000 women age 15-44 ....11.2

Physicians, 2003
Total................................. 3,392
  rate per 1,000 persons.................. 263

Nurses, 2001
Total............................... 11,190
  rate per 1,000 persons.................. 889

Community Hospitals, 2003
Number................................. 28
Beds (x 1,000)..........................2.8
Patients admitted (x 1,000) 118
Average daily census (x 1,000) 1.7
Average cost per day $1,389
Outpatient visits (x mil)....................3.1

Disability status of population, 2004
5 to 20 years 9.4%
21 to 64 years 11.3%
65 years and over 36.1%

Education

Educational attainment, 2004

Population over 25 years	854,239
Less than 9th grade	29,010
High school graduates only	250,043
Bachelor's degree only	174,768
Graduate or professional degree	99,299
Less than 9th grade percent	3.4%
High school graduate or more	90.8%
College graduate or more	35.4%
Graduate or professional degree	11.6%

Public school enrollment, Fall 2002

Total	207,671
Kindergarten through grade 8	143,618
Grades 9 through 12	64,053
Enrollment, 2005 (projected)	201,100

Graduating public high school seniors

2004 (estimate)	13,250

SAT scores, 2005

Average verbal score	525
Average math score	525
Percent of graduates taking test	81%

Public school teachers, 2004

Total (x 1,000)	15.1
Elementary (x 1,000)	10.5
Secondary (x 1,000)	4.6
Average salary	$42,700
Elementary	$42,700
Secondary	$42,700

State receipts & expenditures for public schools, 2004

Revenue receipts ($mil)	$2,075
Expenditures	
Total ($mil)	$2,103
Per capita	$1,632
Per pupil	$9,902

Institutions of higher education, 2004

Total	25
Public	9
Private	16

Enrollment in institutions of higher education, Fall, 2003

Total	70,438
Full-time men	20,630
Full-time women	25,624
Part-time men	8,551
Part-time women	15,633

Minority enrollment in institutions of higher education, Fall, 2003

Black, non-hispanic	1,055
Hispanic	1,317
Asian/Pacific Islander	1,466
American Indian/Alaska Native	307

Earned degrees conferred, 2003

Bachelor's	7,563
Master's	2,387
First-professional	191
Doctor's	142

State & local financial support for higher education, 2003-2004

Full-time equivalent enrollment (x 1,000)	30.5
Appropriations per FTE	$3,316
as a percent of tax revenue	3.0%

Social Insurance & Welfare Programs

Social Security benefits & beneficiaries, 2004

Beneficiaries	
Total	219,000
Retired & dependents	154,000
Survivors	26,000
Disabled & dependents	40,000
Annual benefit payments ($ mil)	
Total	$2,327
Retired & dependents	$1,584
Survivors	$356
Disabled & dependents	$386
Average Monthly Benefit	
Retired & dependents	$978
Disabled & dependents	$897
Widowed	$976

Medicare

Enrollment, 2001 (x 1,000)	173
Payments ($ mil, est.)	$700
Enrollment, 2003 (x 1,000)	180

Medicaid, 2002

Beneficiaries (x 1,000)	104
Payments ($ mil)	$746

State Children's Health Insurance, 2004

Enrollment (x 1,000)	11.0
Expenditures ($ mil)	$7.3

Persons without health insurance, 2003

Number (x 1,000)	131
percent	10.3%
Number of children (x 1,000)	17
percent of children	5.5%

Federal public aid

Temporary Assistance for Needy Families, 2004

Recipients (x 1,000)	14
Families (x 1,000)	6

Supplemental Security Income, 2003

Recipients (x 1,000)	13
Payments ($ mil)	$58

Food Stamp Program, 2004

Participants (x 1,000)	48
Benefits ($ mil)	$44

Housing & Construction

Housing units

Total 2003 (estimate) 568,018
Total 2004 (estimate) 575,671
Seasonal or recreational use, 2003 53,000
Owner-occupied single-family, 2003.... 280,000
  Median value $208,403
Renter-occupied, 2003 132,000
  Median rent $780
Homeownership rate, 2003 .... 74.4%
Homeownership rate, 2004 .... 73.3%

New privately owned housing units, 2004

Number authorized (x 1,000) 8.7
Value ($ mil) $1,385
Started 2005 (x 1,000, estimate) 7.0
Started 2006 (x 1,000, estimate) 6.6

Existing home sales

2002 (x 1,000) 23.8
2003 (x 1,000) 25.4
2004 (x 1,000) 27.2

Government & Elections

State Officials 2006

Governor (name/party/term expires)
John Lynch
Democrat - 1/07
Lieutenant Governor..........(no Lt. Governor)
Secretary of State.......... William H. Gardner
Attorney General................. Kelly Ayotte
Chief Justice .... John T. Broderick Jr.

Governorship

Minimum age........................... 30
Length of term .... 2 years
Consecutive terms permitted ...... not specified
Who succeeds.................. Pres. of Senate

State Legislature

Name .... General Court
Upper chamber ....Senate
  Number of members.................... 24
  Length of term..................... 2 years
  Party in majority, 2006 .... Republican
Lower chamber........House of Representatives
  Number of members................... 400
  Length of term..................... 2 years
  Party in majority, 2006 .... Republican

State Government Employees, 2004

Total............................... 19,955
Payroll.......................... $64,718,470

Local Government Employees, 2004

Total............................... 48,529
Payroll......................... $148,655,499

Local Governments by Type, 2002

Total..................................... 559
  County.................................. 10
  Municipal 13
  Township 221
  School District........................ 167
  Special District 148

Voting age population, November 2004

Total................................. 982,000
  Male................................ 479,000
  Female.............................. 503,000
  White............................... 943,000
  Black 6,000
  Hispanic 11,000
  Asian 17,000

Presidential Election, 2004

Total Popular Vote 677,738
  Kerry 340,511
  Bush................................ 331,237
Total Electoral Votes...................... 4

Federal representation, 2006 (109th Congress)

Senator........................John Sununu
  Party .... Republican
  Year term expires 2009
Senator.......................... Judd Gregg
  Party .... Republican
  Year term expires 2011
Representatives, total 2
  Democrats............................. 0
  Republicans 2
  Other.................................. 0

Votes cast for US Senators

2002
Total vote (x 1,000) 447,000
Leading party.................... Republican
Percent for leading party 50.8%

2004
Total vote (x 1,000) 657,000
Leading party.................... Republican
Percent for leading party 66.2%

Votes cast for US Representatives

2002
Total vote (x 1,000) 443
  Democratic........................... 176
  Republican 255
Leading party.................... Republican
Percent for leading party 57.5%

2004
Total vote (x 1,000) 652
  Democratic........................... 244
  Republican 396
Leading party.................... Republican
Percent for leading party 60.8%

Women holding public office, 2006

US Congress 0
Statewide elected office...................... 0
State legislature 130

Black public officials, 2001

Total...................................... 5
   US and state legislatures 5
   City/county/regional offices 0
   Judicial/law enforcement.................. 0
   Education/school boards................... 0

Hispanic public officials, 2004

Total...................................... 2
   State executives & legislators 1
   City/county/regional offices 0
   Judicial/law enforcement.................. 0
   Education/school boards................... 1

Governmental Finance

State government revenues, 2004

Total revenue ($1,000) $6,174,660
   Revenue per capita 4,753.39

General Revenue ($ per capita) $3,867.68
   Intergovernmental 1,290.90
   Taxes 1,543.79
      general sales 0
      individual income tax...............42.16
      corporate income tax 313.78
   Current charges......................557.31
   Miscellaneous 475.68

State government expenditure, 2004

Total expenditure (x $1,000) $5,654,063
   Expenditure per capita............. 4,352.63
General Expenditure ($ per capita).... $3,804.65
   Education 1,283.92
   Public welfare..................... 1,110.03
   Health 105.98
   Hospitals............................ 38.64
   Highways 288.03
   Police protection 28.83
   Correction 72.69
   Natural resources 47.24
   Parks & recreation....................10.51
   Governmental administration 154.06
   Interest on general debt 232.36

State debt & cash, 2004 ($ per capita)

Debt $4,537.42
Cash/security holdings.............. $7,832.99

Federal government grants to state & local government, 2004 (x $1,000)

Total............................ $1,878,737
By Federal Agency
   Defense $38,136

By Federal Agency, continued
   Education 142,390
   Energy 6,390
   Environmental Protection Agency 28,113
   Health & Human Services. 983,258
   Homeland Security................... 7,615
   Housing & Urban Development...... 145,953
   Justice 69,358
   Labor 31,113
   Transportation 225,632
   Veterans Affairs.................... 4,943

Crime, Law Enforcement & Courts

Crime, 2004 (rates per 100,000 residents)

Property crimes 26,511
   Burglaries......................... 4,966
   Larcenies......................... 19,603
   Motor vehicle thefts 1,942
   Property crime rate................. 2,040.1
Violent crimes......................... 2,170
   Murders........................... 18
   Forcible rape....................... 459
   Robberies 500
   Aggravated assaults 1,193
   Violent crime rate 167.0

Police Agencies, 2004

Total agencies........................ 135
Total employees 2,644
   Male officers...................... 1,857
   Female officers..................... 148
   Male civilians...................... 179
   Female civilians.................... 460

Arrests, 2004

Total................................ 43,769
   Persons under 18 years of age 7,812

Prisoners under state & federal jurisdiction, 2004

Total prisoners........................ 2,448
   Percent change, 12/31/03 to 12/31/04 .... 0.6%
Sentenced to more than one year 2,448
   rate per 100,000...................... 187

Persons under sentence of death, 7/1/05

Total...................................... 0
   White...................................... 0
   Black 0
   Hispanic 0

State's highest court

Name ....Supreme Court
Number of members...................... 5
Length of term ....to age 70
Intermediate appeals court? .... no

Labor & Income

Civilian labor force, 2004

Total	724,000
Men	387,000
Women	337,000
Persons 16-19 years	40,000
White	695,000
Black	0
Hispanic	13,000
Asian	12,000

Civilian labor force as a percent of civilian non-institutional population, 2004

Total	71.1%
Men	77.9
Women	64.7
Persons 16-19 years	52.9
White	71.0
Black	0.0
Hispanic	81.8
Asian	67.6

Employment, 2004

Total	698,000
Men	372,000
Women	326,000
Persons 16-19 years	35,000
White	670,000
Black	0
Hispanic	13,000
Asian	11,000

Full-time/part-time labor force, 2002

Full-time labor force, employed	537,000
Part-time labor force, employed	135,000
Unemployed, looking for	
Full-time work	27,000
Part-time work	NA

Unemployment rate, 2004

Total	3.7%
Men	4.0
Women	3.3
Persons 16-19 years	12.3
White	3.6
Black	NA
Hispanic	5.3
Asian	3.0

Unemployed by reason for unemployment (as a percent of total unemployment), 2002

Job losers or completed temp jobs	63.6%
Job leavers	NA
Reentrants	NA
New entrants	NA

Labor unions, 2004

Membership	61,000
percent of employed	9.9%

Experienced civilian labor force by private industry, first quarter 2004

Total	514,259
Natural Resources & Mining	2,221
Construction	26,184
Manufacturing	79,653
Trade, transportation & utilities	136,117
Information	12,376
Finance	35,124
Professional & business	55,581
Education & Health	89,298
Leisure & hospitality	58,308
Other	18,901

Experienced civilian labor force by occupation, 2004

Management	33,460
Business & Financial	24,700
Legal	3,040
Sales	79,840
Office & Admin. Support	106,750
Computers & Math	14,360
Architecture & Engineering	13,230
Arts & Entertainment	5,930
Education	44,100
Social Services	8,240
Healthcare Practitioner & Technical	30,710
Healthcare support	13,850
Maintenance & Repair	24,570
Construction	26,310
Transportation & moving	35,860
Production	49,990
Farming, fishing & forestry	4,130

Hours and earnings of production workers on manufacturing payrolls, 2004

Average weekly hours	40.0
Average hourly earnings	$15.48
Average weekly earnings	$619.20

Average annual pay

2004	$39,176
change from 2003	4.9%

Household income

Median household income, three-year average, 2002-2004	$57,352

Personal income, 2004 ($ per capita)

In current dollars	$37,040
In constant (2000) dollars	$34,352

Poverty

Persons below poverty level, three-year average, 2002-2004	5.7%

Federal individual income tax returns, 2003

Returns filed	634,654
Adjusted gross income ($1,000)	$32,337,174
Total income tax paid ($1,000)	$4,264,307

Economy, Business, Industry & Agriculture

Fortune 500 companies, 2005 1

Patents issued, 2004 681

Bankruptcy cases filed, 2004 4,500

Business firm ownership, 2002

Women-owned 31,024
    Sales ($ mil) $4,665
Black-owned 470
    Sales ($ mil) $68
Hispanic-owned 929
    Sales ($ mil) $224
Asian-owned 1,528
    Sales ($ mil) $410
Amer. Indian/Alaska Native-owned 535
    Sales ($ mil) $59
Hawaiian/Pacific Isl.-owned 18
    Sales ($ mil) $3

Gross State Product, 2004 ($ mil)

Total Gross State Product $51,871
    Agriculture, forestry, fishing and
        hunting 214
    Mining 40
    Utilities 1,816
    Construction 2,850
    Manufacturing, durable goods 4,847
    Manufacturing, non-durable goods 1,623
    Wholesale trade 3,316
    Retail trade 4,605
    Transportation & warehousing 902
    Information 1,679
    Finance & insurance 4,366
    Real estate, rental, leasing 7,232
    Professional and technical services 3,195
    Educational services 849
    Health care and social assistance 4,195
    Accommodation/food services 1,560
    Other services, except government 1,250
    Government 4,718

Establishments, by major industry group, 2003

Total 38,294
    Forestry, fishing & agriculture 181
    Mining 42
    Construction 4,612
    Manufacturing 2,162
    Wholesale trade 2,012
    Retail trade 6,657
    Transportation & warehousing 831
    Information 770
    Finance & insurance 1,838
    Professional/scientific/technical 3,988
    Health care/social assistance 3,269
    Accommodation/food services 3,237

Annual payroll by major industry group, 2003

Total ($1,000) $18,846,455
    Forestry, fishing & agriculture 30,200
    Mining 20,244
    Utilities 216,139
    Construction 1,214,292
    Manufacturing 3,359,994
    Wholesale trade 1,259,461
    Retail trade 2,184,585
    Transportation & warehousing 370,463
    Information 739,762
    Finance & insurance 1,533,326
    Professional/scientific/technical . . . 1,355,623
    Health care/social assistance 2,592,124
    Accommodation/food services 698,952

Agriculture

Number of farms, 2004 3,000
Farm acreage, 2004
    Total . . . . < 500,000
    Acres per farm, 2004 132
Farm income, 2003 ($mil)
    Net farm income $17
    Debt/asset ratio 10.7
Farm marketings, 2003 ($mil)
Total $150
    Crops 88
    Livestock 62

Principal commodities, in order by marketing receipts, 2003

    Greenhouse, dairy products, apples, cattle

Federal economic activity in state

Expenditures, 2003
    Total ($ mil) $7,349
    Per capita $5,707
    Defense ($ mil) 827
    Non-defense ($ mil) 6,522
Defense department, 2003
    Payroll ($ mil) $285
    Contract awards ($ mil) $545
    Grants ($ mil) $17
    Homeland security grants ($1,000)
        2004 . . . . $24,110
        2005 . . . . $16,776

FDIC insured financial institutions, 2004

Number 30
    Assets ($bil) $31.2
    Deposits ($bil) 29.4

Fishing, 2004

Catch (x 1,000 lbs) 21,958
Value ($1,000) $8,805

Mining, 2004 ($ mil)

Total non-fuel mineral production $65
Percent of U.S. 0.2%

Construction, 2003 ($ mil)

Total contracts (including non-building). $2,170
  residential 1,222
  non-residential 691

Establishments, receipts, payroll & employees, by major industry group, 2002

Mining 110
  Receipts ($1,000) $379,558
  Annual payroll ($1,000) $82,671
  Paid employees 1,915
Utilities 98
  Receipts ($1,000) .... NA
  Annual payroll ($1,000) $197,608
  Paid employees 3,305
Construction 4,394
  Receipts ($1,000) $5,222,133
  Annual payroll ($1,000) $1,247,448
  Paid employees 33,541
Manufacturing 2,213
  Receipts ($1,000) $15,235,144
  Annual payroll ($1,000) $3,421,148
  Paid employees 83,545
Wholesale trade 2,004
  Receipts ($1,000) $13,741,876
  Annual payroll ($1,000) $1,138,656
  Paid employees 23,539
Retail trade 6,702
  Receipts ($1,000) $20,830,057
  Annual payroll ($1,000) $2,037,551
  Paid employees 93,804
Transportation 815
  Receipts ($1,000) $1,297,644
  Annual payroll ($1,000) $465,186
  Paid employees 15,400
Information 769
  Receipts ($1,000) .... NA
  Annual payroll ($1,000) $674,753
  Paid employees 14,614
Finance & insurance 1,764
  Receipts ($1,000) .... NA
  Annual payroll ($1,000) $1,281,347
  Paid employees 25,506
Professional, scientific & technical 3,990
  Receipts ($1,000) $2,866,611
  Annual payroll ($1,000) $1,306,787
  Paid employees 28,962

Health care & social assistance 3,221
  Receipts ($1,000) $5,518,477
  Annual payroll ($1,000) $2,425,409
  Paid employees 73,918
Accommodation & food service 3,160
  Receipts ($1,000) $2,082,145
  Annual payroll ($1,000) $632,846
  Paid employees 47,831

Communication, Energy & Transportation

Communication

Daily newspapers, 2004 11
Households with computers, 2003 .... 72%
Households with internet access, 2003 ...... 65%

Energy

Electricity Consumption, 2001
  Total (trillion Btu) 322
  Per capita (million Btu) 256
By source of production (trillion Btu)
  Coal 40
  Natural gas 25
  Petroleum 178
  Nuclear electric power 91
  Hydroelectric power 10
By end-use sector (trillion Btu)
  Residential 87
  Commercial 65
  Industrial 68
  Transportation 102
Electric energy, 2003
  Production (billion kWh) 21.6
  Net summer capability (million kW) 4.2
Gas utilities, 2003
  Customers (x1,000) 103
  Sales (trillion Btu) 17
  Revenues ($mil) $178
Nuclear plants, 2003 1

Transportation, 2004

Public Road & Street Mileage 15,630
  Urban 3,036
  Rural 12,594
  Interstate 235
Vehicle miles of travel per capita 10,658.1
Total motor vehicle registrations 1,178,312
  Automobiles 672,560
  Buses 1,894
  Trucks 503,858
  Motorcycles 66,319
Licensed drivers 985,775
  19 years & under 54,794
Deaths from motor vehicle accidents 171

New Jersey   1

State Summary

Capital City........................ Trenton
Governor........................Jon Corzine
The State House
PO Box 001
Trenton, NJ 08625
609-292-6000
Admitted as a state 1787
Area (square miles) 8,721
Population, 2004 (est.) 8,698,879
Largest City......................... Newark
Population, 2004 280,000
Personal income per capita, 2004
(in current dollars) $41,332
Gross state product ($ mil), 2004 ..... $416,053

Leading industries by payroll, 2003

Professional/Scientific/Technical, Health care/
Social assistance, Manufacturing

Leading agricultural commodities by receipts, 2003

Greenhouse, horses/mules, blueberries, chicken
eggs

Geography & Environment

Total area (sq. mi.)..................... 8,721
land 7,417
water 1,304
Federally-owned land, 2004 (acres) 148,441
percent............................. 3.1%
Highest point...................... High Point
elevation (feet) 1,803
Lowest point ....Atlantic Ocean
elevation (feet) .... sea level
General coastline (miles)................... 130
Tidal shoreline (miles)................... 1,792
Capital City......................... Trenton
Population 2000 85,403
Population 2004 85,379
Largest City......................... Newark
Population 2000 274,000
Population 2004 280,000

Number of cities with over 100,000 population

1990 4
2000 4
2004 4

State park and recreation areas, 2003

Area (acres x 1,000)..................... 380
Number of visitors (x 1,000) 14,943
Revenues (x 1,000)................... $2,324
percent of operating expenditures....... 6.4%

National forest system land, 2004

Acres .... NA

Demographics and Characteristics of the Population

Population

1980 7,364,823
1990 7,730,188
2000 8,414,350
2004 (estimate)................... 8,698,879
persons per sq. mile of land........... 1172.8
2005 (projection)................... 8,745,279
Male............................. 4,250,701
Female......................... 4,494,578
2010 (projection) 9,018,231
2020 (projection) 9,461,635
2030 (projection) 9,802,440
Male............................. 4,778,485
Female......................... 5,023,955

Metropolitan and Non-Metro. area population

	Metro	Non-Metro
1980	7,365,000	0
1990	7,730,000	0
2000	8,414,000	0

Change in population, 2000-2004

Number 284,532
percent............................. 3.4%
Natural increase (births minus deaths).. 179,434
Net internal migration .... -135,483
Net international migration 244,994

Persons by age, 2004

Under 5 years 581,467
18 years and over 6,542,820
65 years and over 1,126,141
85 years and over 162,808

Persons by age, 2010 (projected)

Total............................ 9,018,231
Under 5 years 587,220
5 to 17 years 1,501,004
18 and over 6,930,007
21 and over 6,596,213
65 and over 1,231,585
85 and over 198,835
Median age 38.9

Race, 2004 (estimate)

One Race
White............................ 6,690,290
Black or African American 1,259,839
American Indian/Alaska Native....... 26,625
Pacific Islander 6,734
Asian Indian...................... 229,994
Chinese 136,109
Filipino 92,009
Japanese 9,420
Korean 70,825
Vietnamese....................... 29,367
Two or more races.................... 108,283

2   New Jersey

Persons of Hispanic origin, 2004

Total Hispanic or Latino 1,274,500
  Mexican................. 116,479
  Puerto Rican 441,134
  Cuban 80,681
  Other Hispanic or Latino 117,526

Marital status, 2000

Population 15 years & over 6,655,333
  Never married 1,870,149
  Married........................ 3,640,467
  Separated 159,728
  Widowed........................ 492,495
  Divorced...................... 499,150

Language spoken at home, 2000

Population 5 years & over 7,856,268
  English only..................... 5,854,578
  Spanish 967,741
  Other Indo-European languages 659,248
  Asian/Pacific Island languages....... 275,832

Households & families, 2000

Households...................... 3,064,645
  with persons under 18 years 1,122,728
  with persons over 65 years........... 793,781
  persons per household 2.68
Families........................ 2,154,539
  persons per family.......................3.21
Married couples.................. 1,638,322
Female householder,
  no husband present................ 387,012
One-person households 751,287

Nativity, 2000

Number of persons born in state 4,490,524
  percent of population................. 53.4%

Immigration & Naturalization, 2004

Immigrants admitted.................. 50,303
Persons naturalized 30,291
Asylums granted 225
Asylums denied 48

Vital Statistics and Health

Marriages

2002 51,469
2003 50,228
2004 50,662

Divorces

2002 29,191
2003 27,417
2004 25,981

Births

2003 116,983
  Birthrate (per 1,000)....................13.5
  Low birth weight (2,500g or less)........ 8.1%
  To unmarried mothers................ 29.3%

2003, continued
  White............................. 85,278
  Black 20,120
  Hispanic 26,504
  Asian/Pacific Islander 10,685
  Amer. Indian/Alaska Native............ 186
2004 (preliminary).................... 114,916
  Birthrate (per 1,000).....................13.2
  White............................. 84,139
  Black 19,730
  Hispanic 27,312
  Asian/Pacific Islander 10,875

Deaths

2002
All causes 74,009
  rate per 100,000.....................861.5
Heart disease 22,510
  rate per 100,000.....................262.0
Malignant neoplasms 17,827
  rate per 100,000.....................207.5
Cerebrovascular disease................. 4,016
  rate per 100,000......................46.8
Chronic lower respiratory disease 2,885
  rate per 100,000......................33.6
2003 73,683
  rate per 100,000.....................853.0
2004 (provisional) 71,496

Infant deaths

2003 (provisional) 660
  rate per 1,000 ....5.6
2004 (provisional) 573
  rate per 1,000 5

Abortions, 2000

Total.............................. 66,000
  rate per 1,000 women age 15-44.........36.3

Physicians, 2003

Total.............................. 26,804
  rate per 1,000 persons.................. 310

Nurses, 2001

Total.............................. 71,500
  rate per 1,000 persons.................. 840

Community Hospitals, 2003

Number................................ 78
Beds (x 1,000)...........................22.8
Patients admitted (x 1,000) 1,108
Average daily census (x 1,000) 16.9
Average cost per day $1,411
Outpatient visits (x mil).................14.7

Disability status of population, 2004

5 to 20 years 6.4%
21 to 64 years 9.1%
65 years and over 35.5%

Education

Educational attainment, 2004

Population over 25 years 5,659,640
  Less than 9th grade 302,061
  High school graduates only. 1,724,176
  Bachelor's degree only 1,184,661
  Graduate or professional degree. 700,294
  Less than 9th grade percent 5.3%
  High school graduate or more 87.6%
  College graduate or more. 34.6%
  Graduate or professional degree. 12.4%

Public school enrollment, Fall 2002

Total. 1,367,438
  Kindergarten through grade 8 978,762
  Grades 9 through 12 388,676
Enrollment, 2005 (projected) 1,399,800

Graduating public high school seniors

2004 (estimate). 88,330

SAT scores, 2005

Average verbal score 503
Average math score 517
Percent of graduates taking test 86%

Public school teachers, 2004

Total (x 1,000) 107.5
  Elementary (x 1,000). 39.7
  Secondary (x 1,000) 67.8
Average salary $55,600
  Elementary. $54,400
  Secondary. $56,300

State receipts & expenditures for public schools, 2004

Revenue receipts ($mil). $18,143
Expenditures
Total ($mil). $16,449
  Per capita $1,903
  Per pupil $11,847

Institutions of higher education, 2004

Total. 58
  Public. 33
  Private 25

Enrollment in institutions of higher education, Fall, 2003

Total. 391,669
  Full-time men 106,515
  Full-time women. 128,861
  Part-time men 59,068
  Part-time women. 97,225

Minority enrollment in institutions of higher education, Fall, 2003

Black, non-hispanic. 46,591
Hispanic 42,827
Asian/Pacific Islander 28,002
American Indian/Alaska Native. 972

Earned degrees conferred, 2003

Bachelor's 29,604
Master's. 11,140
First-professional. 1,609
Doctor's. 1,052

State & local financial support for higher education, 2003-2004

Full-time equivalent enrollment (x 1,000) . .195.5
Appropriations per FTE. $8,326
  as a percent of tax revenue. 5.7%

Social Insurance & Welfare Programs

Social Security benefits & beneficiaries, 2004

Beneficiaries
  Total. 1,370,000
  Retired & dependents. 1,007,000
  Survivors. 173,000
  Disabled & dependents. 190,000
Annual benefit payments ($ mil)
  Total. $15,777
  Retired & dependents. $11,191
  Survivors. $2,529
  Disabled & dependents. $2,058
Average Monthly Benefit
  Retired & dependents. $1,054
  Disabled & dependents. $976
  Widowed. $1,014

Medicare

Enrollment, 2001 (x 1,000) 1,208
  Payments ($ mil, est.) $6,900
Enrollment, 2003 (x 1,000) 1,220

Medicaid, 2002

Beneficiaries (x 1,000). 954
Payments ($ mil) $5,497

State Children's Health Insurance, 2004

Enrollment (x 1,000). 127.2
Expenditures ($ mil). $221.9

Persons without health insurance, 2003

Number (x 1,000). 1,201
  percent. 14.0%
Number of children (x 1,000) 237
  percent of children 11.0%

Federal public aid

Temporary Assistance for Needy Families, 2004
Recipients (x 1,000). 108
Families (x 1,000) 45

Supplemental Security Income, 2003
Recipients (x 1,000). 150
Payments ($ mil) $732

Food Stamp Program, 2004

Participants (x 1,000) 369
Benefits ($ mil). $378

4   New Jersey

Housing & Construction

Housing units
Total 2003 (estimate) 3,389,525
Total 2004 (estimate) 3,414,739
Seasonal or recreational use, 2003 97,000
Owner-occupied single-family, 2003.. 1,795,000
 Median value $245,573
Renter-occupied, 2003 1,039,000
 Median rent $856
Homeownership rate, 2003 .... 66.9%
Homeownership rate, 2004 .... 68.8%

New privately owned housing units, 2004
Number authorized (x 1,000) 35.9
Value ($ mil) $4,294
Started 2005 (x 1,000, estimate) 26.5
Started 2006 (x 1,000, estimate) 26.1

Existing home sales
2002 (x 1,000) 166.8
2003 (x 1,000) 174.3
2004 (x 1,000) 188.7

Government & Elections

State Officials 2006
Governor (name/party/term expires)
Jon Corzine
Democrat - 1/10
Lieutenant Governor..........(no Lt. Governor)
Secretary of State............. Regena Thomas
Attorney General............. Peter C. Harvey
Chief Justice .... Deborah Poritz

Governorship
Minimum age........................... 30
Length of term .... 4 years
Consecutive terms permitted 2
Who succeeds................. Pres. of Senate

State Legislature
Name .... Legislature
Upper chamber ....Senate
 Number of members.................... 40
 Length of term..................... 4 years
 Party in majority, 2006 ....Democratic
Lower chamber.............. General Assembly
 Number of members.................... 80
 Length of term..................... 2 years
 Party in majority, 2006 ....Democratic

State Government Employees, 2004
Total............................... 149,374
Payroll $675,358,751

Local Government Employees, 2004
Total............................... 345,815
Payroll $1,504,509,327

Local Governments by Type, 2002
Total............................... 1,412
 County................................ 21
 Municipal 324
 Township 242
 School District....................... 549
 Special District 276

Voting age population, November 2004
Total............................... 6,413,000
 Male............................... 3,052,000
 Female............................. 3,361,000
 White.............................. 5,174,000
 Black 845,000
 Hispanic 906,000
 Asian 335,000

Presidential Election, 2004
Total Popular Vote 3,611,691
 Kerry 1,911,430
 Bush.............................. 1,670,003
Total Electoral Votes...................... 15

Federal representation, 2006 (109th Congress)
Senator.................... Robert Menendez
 Party .... Democrat
 Year term expires 2007
Senator.................... Frank Lautenberg
 Party .... Democrat
 Year term expires 2009
Representatives, total 13
 Democrats........................... 7
 Republicans 6
 Other 0

Votes cast for US Senators
2002
Total vote (x 1,000) 2,113,000
Leading party.....................Democratic
Percent for leading party 53.9%
2004
Total vote (x 1,000) .... NA
Leading party....................... NA
Percent for leading party .... NA

Votes cast for US Representatives
2002
Total vote (x 1,000) 2,006
 Democratic.......................... 1,030
 Republican 934
Leading party.....................Democratic
Percent for leading party 51.4%
2004
Total vote (x 1,000) 3,285
 Democratic.......................... 1,721
 Republican 1,515
Leading party.....................Democratic
Percent for leading party 52.4%

Women holding public office, 2006
US Congress 0
Statewide elected office 0
State legislature 19

Black public officials, 2001
Total 249
  US and state legislatures 16
  City/county/regional offices 139
  Judicial/law enforcement 1
  Education/school boards 93

Hispanic public officials, 2004
Total 100
  State executives & legislators 5
  City/county/regional offices 55
  Judicial/law enforcement 40
  Education/school boards 0

Governmental Finance

State government revenues, 2004
Total revenue ($1,000) $50,588,543
  Revenue per capita 5,824.82

General Revenue ($ per capita) $4,364.31
  Intergovernmental 1,103.06
  Taxes 2,415.82
    general sales 720.98
    individual income tax 852.13
    corporate income tax 218.42
  Current charges 497.06
  Miscellaneous 348.37

State government expenditure, 2004
Total expenditure (x $1,000) $46,455,897
  Expenditure per capita 5,348.98
General Expenditure ($ per capita) $4,152.50
  Education 1,395.84
  Public welfare 989.42
  Health 88.68
  Hospitals 186.11
  Highways 275.01
  Police protection 49.66
  Correction 158.36
  Natural resources 38.09
  Parks & recreation 45.97
  Governmental administration 161.75
  Interest on general debt 133.19

State debt & cash, 2004 ($ per capita)
Debt $4,118.62
Cash/security holdings $10,074.08

Federal government grants to state & local government, 2004 (x $1,000)
Total $11,333,180
By Federal Agency
  Defense $98,928

By Federal Agency, continued
  Education 927,276
  Energy 38,732
  Environmental Protection Agency 82,368
  Health & Human Services 6,381,963
  Homeland Security 71,943
  Housing & Urban Development 1,292,431
  Justice 188,682
  Labor 239,348
  Transportation 1,323,741
  Veterans Affairs 16,578

Crime, Law Enforcement & Courts

Crime, 2004 (rates per 100,000 residents)
Property crimes 211,313
  Burglaries 41,030
  Larcenies 139,977
  Motor vehicle thefts 30,306
  Property crime rate 2,429.2
Violent crimes 30,943
  Murders 392
  Forcible rape 1,331
  Robberies 13,076
  Aggravated assaults 16,144
  Violent crime rate 355.7

Police Agencies, 2004
Total agencies 533
Total employees 40,195
  Male officers 28,835
  Female officers 2,478
  Male civilians 3,245
  Female civilians 5,637

Arrests, 2004
Total 379,625
  Persons under 18 years of age 60,443

Prisoners under state & federal jurisdiction, 2004
Total prisoners 26,757
  Percent change, 12/31/03 to 12/31/04 ... -1.8%
Sentenced to more than one year 26,757
  rate per 100,000 306

Persons under sentence of death, 7/1/05
Total 14
  White 7
  Black 7
  Hispanic 0

State's highest court
Name .... Supreme Court
Number of members 7
Length of term .... 7 years
Intermediate appeals court? .... yes

Labor & Income

Civilian labor force, 2004

Total	4,388,000
Men	2,356,000
Women	2,032,000
Persons 16-19 years	178,000
White	3,489,000
Black	583,000
Hispanic	621,000
Asian	266,000

Civilian labor force as a percent of civilian non-institutional population, 2004

Total	65.8%
Men	74.0
Women	58.4
Persons 16-19 years	36.3
White	65.8
Black	65.2
Hispanic	72.2
Asian	66.5

Employment, 2004

Total	4,178,000
Men	2,245,000
Women	1,933,000
Persons 16-19 years	153,000
White	3,343,000
Black	530,000
Hispanic	592,000
Asian	257,000

Full-time/part-time labor force, 2002

Full-time labor force, employed	3,459,000
Part-time labor force, employed	653,000
Unemployed, looking for	
Full-time work	218,000
Part-time work	37,000

Unemployment rate, 2004

Total	4.8%
Men	4.7
Women	4.9
Persons 16-19 years	13.8
White	4.2
Black	9.1
Hispanic	4.6
Asian	3.3

Unemployed by reason for unemployment (as a percent of total unemployment), 2002

Job losers or completed temp jobs	63.1%
Job leavers	NA
Reentrants	23.9
New entrants	NA

Labor unions, 2004

Membership	745,000
percent of employed	19.8%

Experienced civilian labor force by private industry, first quarter 2004

Total	3,208,338
Natural Resources & Mining	8,178
Construction	153,439
Manufacturing	335,898
Trade, transportation & utilities	849,277
Information	98,770
Finance	256,955
Professional & business	567,798
Education & Health	494,104
Leisure & hospitality	300,385
Other	117,140

Experienced civilian labor force by occupation, 2004

Management	184,160
Business & Financial	178,950
Legal	33,360
Sales	424,940
Office & Admin. Support	766,960
Computers & Math	115,390
Architecture & Engineering	58,320
Arts & Entertainment	44,370
Education	252,000
Social Services	56,170
Healthcare Practitioner & Technical	192,560
Healthcare support	100,540
Maintenance & Repair	141,420
Construction	141,140
Transportation & moving	318,550
Production	219,250
Farming, fishing & forestry	10,190

Hours and earnings of production workers on manufacturing payrolls, 2004

Average weekly hours	42.1
Average hourly earnings	$15.67
Average weekly earnings	$659.71

Average annual pay

2004	$48,064
change from 2003	3.7%

Household income

Median household income, three-year average, 2002-2004	$56,772

Personal income, 2004 ($ per capita)

In current dollars	$41,332
In constant (2000) dollars	$38,333

Poverty

Persons below poverty level, three-year average, 2002-2004	8.2%

Federal individual income tax returns, 2003

Returns filed	4,082,108
Adjusted gross income ($1,000)	$247,077,300
Total income tax paid ($1,000)	$36,267,498

Economy, Business, Industry & Agriculture

Fortune 500 companies, 2005 24

Patents issued, 2004 3,352

Bankruptcy cases filed, 2004 42,500

Business firm ownership, 2002
Women-owned....................... 185,197
  Sales ($ mil) $35,583
Black-owned........................ 36,283
  Sales ($ mil) $3,216
Hispanic-owned.................... 49,846
  Sales ($ mil) $9,155
Asian-owned 51,974
  Sales ($ mil) $20,945
Amer. Indian/Alaska Native-owned 2,645
  Sales ($ mil) $284
Hawaiian/Pacific Isl.-owned.............. 555
  Sales ($ mil) $129

Gross State Product, 2004 ($ mil)
Total Gross State Product $416,053
  Agriculture, forestry, fishing and
    hunting 543
  Mining............................ 199
  Utilities 8,280
  Construction 17,768
  Manufacturing, durable goods........ 13,776
  Manufacturing, non-durable goods ... 31,581
  Wholesale trade.................... 33,273
  Retail trade...................... 27,156
  Transportation & warehousing 12,602
  Information 19,020
  Finance & insurance................ 35,109
  Real estate, rental, leasing 65,656
  Professional and technical services.... 33,652
  Educational services............... 3,218
  Health care and social assistance..... 28,411
  Accommodation/food services........ 10,013
  Other services, except government 8,453
  Government....................... 42,228

Establishments, by major industry group, 2003
Total............................... 237,842
  Forestry, fishing & agriculture 268
  Mining............................ 110
  Construction 23,981
  Manufacturing..................... 10,281
  Wholesale trade.................... 16,709
  Retail trade....................... 34,782
  Transportation & warehousing 7,133
  Information 4,087
  Finance & insurance................ 13,453
  Professional/scientific/technical 31,104
  Health care/social assistance 23,791
  Accommodation/food services........ 18,083

Annual payroll by major industry group, 2003
Total ($1,000).................... $154,521,098
  Forestry, fishing & agriculture........ 33,079
  Mining........................... 131,662
  Utilities....................... 1,601,918
  Construction 8,005,832
  Manufacturing.................... 16,851,246
  Wholesale trade................... 15,396,571
  Retail trade...................... 10,569,268
  Transportation & warehousing 6,086,090
  Information 8,310,442
  Finance & insurance.............. 16,581,568
  Professional/scientific/technical .. 17,499,599
  Health care/social assistance 17,359,587
  Accommodation/food services..... 4,700,761

Agriculture
Number of farms, 2004 10,000
Farm acreage, 2004
  Total.......................... 1,000,000
  Acres per farm, 2004 83
Farm income, 2003 ($mil)
  Net farm income $127
  Debt/asset ratio 7.4
Farm marketings, 2003 ($mil)
  Total................................ $846
    Crops.............................. 658
    Livestock.......................... 188

Principal commodities, in order by marketing receipts, 2003
Greenhouse, horses/mules, blueberries, chicken eggs

Federal economic activity in state
Expenditures, 2003
  Total ($ mil) $53,679
  Per capita $6,214
  Defense ($ mil)..................... 5,330
  Non-defense ($ mil) 48,349
Defense department, 2003
  Payroll ($ mil) $1,657
  Contract awards ($ mil)............. $3,793
  Grants ($ mil)........................ $66
  Homeland security grants ($1,000)
    2004 .... $95,795
    2005 .... $60,811

FDIC insured financial institutions, 2004
Number................................ 139
  Assets ($bil) $167.7
  Deposits ($bil) 211.3

Fishing, 2004
Catch (x 1,000 lbs)................. 185,615
Value ($1,000)..................... $139,427

Mining, 2004 ($ mil)
Total non-fuel mineral production $330
Percent of U.S. 0.8%

Construction, 2003 ($ mil)
Total contracts (including non-building) $11,739
   residential............................. 4,344
   non-residential 5,135

Establishments, receipts, payroll & employees, by major industry group, 2002

Mining 612
   Receipts ($1,000) $9,803,360
   Annual payroll ($1,000) $588,470
   Paid employees 13,289

Utilities 271
   Receipts ($1,000) .... NA
   Annual payroll ($1,000) $1,259,286
   Paid employees 21,241

Construction........................ 23,612
   Receipts ($1,000) $37,867,759
   Annual payroll ($1,000) $8,262,952
   Paid employees 210,620

Manufacturing 10,656
   Receipts ($1,000) $96,599,807
   Annual payroll ($1,000) $15,877,239
   Paid employees 369,811

Wholesale trade 16,803
   Receipts ($1,000) $256,925,492
   Annual payroll ($1,000) $14,428,836
   Paid employees 273,837

Retail trade 34,741
   Receipts ($1,000) $102,153,833
   Annual payroll ($1,000) $9,856,227
   Paid employees 434,574

Transportation........................ 7,187
   Receipts ($1,000) $16,421,043
   Annual payroll ($1,000) $5,742,202
   Paid employees 161,594

Information........................... 4,019
   Receipts ($1,000) .... NA
   Annual payroll ($1,000) $7,817,047
   Paid employees 127,980

Finance & insurance 11,921
   Receipts ($1,000) .... NA
   Annual payroll ($1,000) $13,633,456
   Paid employees 222,413

Professional, scientific & technical 31,531
   Receipts ($1,000) $36,005,523
   Annual payroll ($1,000) $16,826,945
   Paid employees 287,357

Health care & social assistance 23,504
   Receipts ($1,000) $38,708,974
   Annual payroll ($1,000)......... $16,245,011
   Paid employees 449,412

Accommodation & food service......... 17,537
   Receipts ($1,000) $15,715,595
   Annual payroll ($1,000).......... $4,335,892
   Paid employees 268,992

Communication, Energy & Transportation

Communication

Daily newspapers, 2004 17
Households with computers, 2003 .... 66%
Households with internet access, 2003 ...... 61%

Energy

Electricity Consumption, 2001
Total (trillion Btu).................... 2,500
Per capita (million Btu) 294
By source of production (trillion Btu)
   Coal 112
   Natural gas............................ 586
   Petroleum.......................... 1,246
   Nuclear electric power 318
   Hydroelectric power..................... 1
By end-use sector (trillion Btu)
   Residential 573
   Commercial 554
   Industrial 491
   Transportation 882
Electric energy, 2003
   Production (billion kWh) 57.4
   Net summer capability (million kW) 18.6
Gas utilities, 2003
   Customers (x1,000)................... 2,646
   Sales (trillion Btu)..................... 397
   Revenues ($mil)..................... $3,154
Nuclear plants, 2003 4

Transportation, 2004

Public Road & Street Mileage 38,122
   Urban............................. 31,151
   Rural 6,971
   Interstate............................ 431
Vehicle miles of travel per capita........ 8,373.8
Total motor vehicle registrations...... 6,224,256
   Automobiles...................... 4,016,485
   Buses 23,239
   Trucks 2,184,532
   Motorcycles 149,911
Licensed drivers 5,799,532
   19 years & under 229,517
Deaths from motor vehicle accidents 731

State Summary

Capital City........................Santa Fe
Governor.................... Bill Richardson
State Capitol
Fourth Floor
Santa Fe, NM 87300
505-827-3000
Admitted as a state 1912
Area (square miles) 121,590
Population, 2004 (est.) 1,903,289
Largest City.....................Albuquerque
Population, 2004.................... 484,000
Personal income per capita, 2004
(in current dollars) $26,191
Gross state product ($ mil), 2004 .... $61,012

Leading industries by payroll, 2003

Health care/Social assistance, Retail trade, Pro-
fessional/Scientific/Technical

Leading agricultural commodities by receipts, 2003

Dairy products, cattle, hay, pecans

Geography & Environment

Total area (sq. mi.).................... 121,590
land 121,356
water 234
Federally-owned land, 2004 (acres) .. 32,483,877
percent............................41.8%
Highest point.................... Wheeler Peak
elevation (feet) 13,161
Lowest point .... Red Bluff Reservoir
elevation (feet) 2,842
General coastline (miles)..................... 0
Tidal shoreline (miles)...................... 0
Capital City........................Santa Fe
Population 2000 62,203
Population 2004 68,041
Largest City.....................Albuquerque
Population 2000 449,000
Population 2004 484,000

Number of cities with over 100,000 population

1990 1
2000 1
2004 1

State park and recreation areas, 2003

Area (acres x 1,000)...................... 91
Number of visitors (x 1,000) 3,983
Revenues (x 1,000).................... $3,838
percent of operating expenditures...... 22.8%

National forest system land, 2004

Acres 9,419,000

Demographics and Characteristics of the Population

Population

1980 1,302,894
1990 1,515,069
2000 1,819,046
2004 (estimate)..................... 1,903,289
persons per sq. mile of land.............15.7
2005 (projection)................... 1,902,057
Male............................. 928,865
Female......................... 973,192
2010 (projection) 1,980,225
2020 (projection) 2,084,341
2030 (projection) 2,099,708
Male........................... 1,003,729
Female......................... 1,095,979

Metropolitan and Non-Metro. area population

	Metro	Non-Metro
1980	609,000	694,000
1990	733,000	782,000
2000	1,035,000	784,000

Change in population, 2000-2004

Number............................. 84,243
percent............................4.6%
Natural increase (births minus deaths)... 57,808
Net internal migration.................3,985
Net international migration 23,267

Persons by age, 2004

Under 5 years 133,366
18 years and over 1,411,002
65 years and over 229,474
85 years and over 26,817

Persons by age, 2010 (projected)

Total............................. 1,980,225
Under 5 years..................... 145,063
5 to 17 years 334,342
18 and over 1,500,820
21 and over 1,417,808
65 and over 278,967
85 and over 38,326
Median age 38.3

Race, 2004 (estimate)

One Race
White........................... 1,612,343
Black or African American 44,749
American Indian/Alaska Native...... 192,135
Pacific Islander 2,421
Asian Indian...................... 3,685
Chinese 4,775
Filipino 3,738
Japanese 3,150
Korean........................... 3,588
Vietnamese......................... 1,004
Two or more races...................... 27,616

Persons of Hispanic origin, 2004

Total Hispanic or Latino 808,693
  Mexican............................. 439,746
  Puerto Rican 5,868
  Cuban 2,998
  Other Hispanic or Latino 353,950

Marital status, 2000

Population 15 years & over 1,398,496
  Never married 384,586
  Married........................... 741,203
  Separated 25,173
  Widowed........................... 85,308
  Divorced 162,226

Language spoken at home, 2000

Population 5 years & over 1,689,911
  English only 1,072,947
  Spanish 485,681
  Other Indo-European languages 22,032
  Asian/Pacific Island languages........ 11,517

Households & families, 2000

Households........................... 677,971
  with persons under 18 years 261,684
  with persons over 65 years.......... 151,722
  persons per household 2.63
Families............................. 466,515
  persons per family.....................3.18
Married couples 341,818
Female householder,
  no husband present.................. 89,622
One-person households 172,181

Nativity, 2000

Number of persons born in state 937,212
  percent of population................. 51.5%

Immigration & Naturalization, 2004

Immigrants admitted.................... 3,024
Persons naturalized 1,449
Asylums granted 4
Asylums denied 3

Vital Statistics and Health

Marriages

2002 14,662
2003 12,865
2004 14,067

Divorces

2002 8,099
2003 9,740
2004 8,829

Births

2003 27,821
  Birthrate (per 1,000)....................14.8
  Low birth weight (2,500g or less)........8.5%
  To unmarried mothers................48.4%

2003, continued
  White............................... 23,306
  Black 533
  Hispanic 14,856
  Asian/Pacific Islander 402
  Amer. Indian/Alaska Native........... 3,603

2004 (preliminary)..................... 28,386
  Birthrate (per 1,000)..................14.9
  White................................ 23,856
  Black 502
  Hispanic 15,163
  Asian/Pacific Islander 410

Deaths

2002
All causes 14,344
  rate per 100,000....................773.2
Heart disease 3,360
  rate per 100,000....................181.1
Malignant neoplasms 3,067
  rate per 100,000....................165.3
Cerebrovascular disease.................... 715
  rate per 100,000....................38.5
Chronic lower respiratory disease 857
  rate per 100,000....................46.2
2003 14,877
  rate per 100,000....................793.6
2004 (provisional) 14,061

Infant deaths

2003 (provisional) 157
  rate per 1,000 ....5.7
2004 (provisional) 170
  rate per 1,000 6

Abortions, 2000

Total................................ 6,000
  rate per 1,000 women age 15-44..........14.7

Physicians, 2003

Total................................ 4,473
  rate per 1,000 persons................... 239

Nurses, 2001

Total................................ 11,630
  rate per 1,000 persons................... 635

Community Hospitals, 2003

Number 37
Beds (x 1,000).........................3.7
Patients admitted (x 1,000) 166
Average daily census (x 1,000) 2.1
Average cost per day $1,563
Outpatient visits (x mil)..................4.5

Disability status of population, 2004

5 to 20 years 6.4%
21 to 64 years 14.9%
65 years and over 44.5%

Education

Educational attainment, 2004

Population over 25 years 1,186,937
Less than 9th grade 105,733
High school graduates only......... 319,398
Bachelor's degree only 162,516
Graduate or professional degree...... 117,821
Less than 9th grade percent 8.9%
High school graduate or more 82.9%
College graduate or more.............. 25.1%
Graduate or professional degree........ 9.9%

Public school enrollment, Fall 2002

Total................................ 320,234
Kindergarten through grade 8 224,497
Grades 9 through 12................. 95,737
Enrollment, 2005 (projected) 316,400

Graduating public high school seniors

2004 (estimate)....................... 18,050

SAT scores, 2005

Average verbal score 558
Average math score 547
Percent of graduates taking test 13%

Public school teachers, 2004

Total (x 1,000) 21.5
Elementary (x 1,000)....................15.3
Secondary (x 1,000) 6.2
Average salary $38,100
Elementary $37,700
Secondary.......................... $38,900

State receipts & expenditures for public schools, 2004

Revenue receipts ($mil)................ $2,901
Expenditures
Total ($mil)........................... $3,022
Per capita $1,608
Per pupil $8,772

Institutions of higher education, 2004

Total................................... 42
Public.................................. 27
Private 15

Enrollment in institutions of higher education, Fall, 2003

Total................................ 127,768
Full-time men 29,038
Full-time women.................... 38,888
Part-time men 23,288
Part-time women.................... 36,554

Minority enrollment in institutions of higher education, Fall, 2003

Black, non-hispanic.................... 3,189
Hispanic 46,498
Asian/Pacific Islander 2,335
American Indian/Alaska Native........ 10,789

Earned degrees conferred, 2003

Bachelor's 7,027
Master's............................. 2,622
First-professional...................... 246
Doctor's............................... 244

State & local financial support for higher education, 2003-2004

Full-time equivalent enrollment (x 1,000) ...79.6
Appropriations per FTE................. $5,586
as a percent of tax revenue............. 14.5%

Social Insurance & Welfare Programs

Social Security benefits & beneficiaries, 2004

Beneficiaries
Total............................. 304,000
Retired & dependents............... 205,000
Survivors.......................... 44,000
Disabled & dependents.............. 55,000
Annual benefit payments ($ mil)
Total.............................. $2,871
Retired & dependents............... $1,858
Survivors........................... $506
Disabled & dependents.............. $507
Average Monthly Benefit
Retired & dependents................ $892
Disabled & dependents............... $861
Widowed............................. $850

Medicare

Enrollment, 2001 (x 1,000) 238
Payments ($ mil, est.) $900
Enrollment, 2003 (x 1,000) 250

Medicaid, 2002

Beneficiaries (x 1,000)................... 799
Payments ($ mil) $1,797

State Children's Health Insurance, 2004

Enrollment (x 1,000)....................20.8
Expenditures ($ mil)....................$21.4

Persons without health insurance, 2003

Number (x 1,000)........................ 414
percent.......................... 22.1%
Number of children (x 1,000) 65
percent of children 13.2%

Federal public aid

Temporary Assistance for Needy Families, 2004
Recipients (x 1,000)....................... 46
Families (x 1,000) 18

Supplemental Security Income, 2003
Recipients (x 1,000)....................... 50
Payments ($ mil) $223

Food Stamp Program, 2004

Participants (x 1,000) 223
Benefits ($ mil)........................ $217

Housing & Construction

Housing units

Total 2003 (estimate)	813,800
Total 2004 (estimate)	825,540
Seasonal or recreational use, 2003	35,000
Owner-occupied single-family, 2003	363,000
Median value	$118,764
Renter-occupied, 2003	211,000
Median rent	$523
Homeownership rate, 2003	70.3%
Homeownership rate, 2004	71.5%

New privately owned housing units, 2004

Number authorized (x 1,000)	12.6
Value ($ mil)	$1,747
Started 2005 (x 1,000, estimate)	10.3
Started 2006 (x 1,000, estimate)	10.1

Existing home sales

2002 (x 1,000)	38.9
2003 (x 1,000)	43.3
2004 (x 1,000)	50.6

Government & Elections

State Officials 2006

Governor (name/party/term expires)
Bill Richardson
Democrat - 1/07

Lieutenant Governor	Diane Denish
Secretary of State	Rebecca Vigil-Giron
Attorney General	Patricia Madrid
Chief Justice	Richard C. Bosson

Governorship

Minimum age	30
Length of term	4 years
Consecutive terms permitted	2
Who succeeds	Lt. Governor

State Legislature

Name	Legislature
Upper chamber	Senate
Number of members	42
Length of term	4 years
Party in majority, 2006	Democratic
Lower chamber	House of Representatives
Number of members	70
Length of term	2 years
Party in majority, 2006	Democratic

State Government Employees, 2004

Total	49,286
Payroll	$146,757,194

Local Government Employees, 2004

Total	75,356
Payroll	$202,031,453

Local Governments by Type, 2002

Total	858
County	33
Municipal	101
Township	0
School District	96
Special District	628

Voting age population, November 2004

Total	1,375,000
Male	658,000
Female	717,000
White	1,151,000
Black	34,000
Hispanic	544,000
Asian	11,000

Presidential Election, 2004

Total Popular Vote	756,304
Kerry	370,942
Bush	376,930
Total Electoral Votes	5

Federal representation, 2006 (109th Congress)

Senator	Jeff Bingaman
Party	Democrat
Year term expires	2007
Senator	Pete V. Domenici
Party	Republican
Year term expires	2009
Representatives, total	3
Democrats	1
Republicans	2
Other	0

Votes cast for US Senators

2002

Total vote (x 1,000)	483,000
Leading party	Republican
Percent for leading party	65.0%

2004

Total vote (x 1,000)	NA
Leading party	NA
Percent for leading party	NA

Votes cast for US Representatives

2002

Total vote (x 1,000)	437
Democratic	262
Republican	175
Leading party	Democratic
Percent for leading party	59.9%

2004

Total vote (x 1,000)	743
Democratic	385
Republican	358
Leading party	Democratic
Percent for leading party	51.8%

Women holding public office, 2006
US Congress 1
Statewide elected office...................... 3
State legislature 35

Black public officials, 2001
Total.. 4
    US and state legislatures 1
    City/county/regional offices 0
    Judicial/law enforcement................... 2
    Education/school boards 1

Hispanic public officials, 2004
Total.................................... 627
    State executives & legislators 50
    City/county/regional offices 326
    Judicial/law enforcement............... 100
    Education/school boards 151

Governmental Finance

State government revenues, 2004
Total revenue ($1,000) $11,809,742
    Revenue per capita 6,205.85

General Revenue ($ per capita)....... $5,148.94
    Intergovernmental 1,863.63
    Taxes 2,102.88
        general sales 758.43
        individual income tax.............529.29
        corporate income tax 72.62
    Current charges..................... 398.34
    Miscellaneous 784.08

State government expenditure, 2004
Total expenditure (x $1,000) $11,024,686
    Expenditure per capita............. 5,793.32
General Expenditure ($ per capita).... $5,261.89
    Education 2,003.79
    Public welfare..................... 1,309.81
    Health 126.49
    Hospitals.......................... 256.06
    Highways 332.88
    Police protection...................58.79
    Correction 133.81
    Natural resources 91.10
    Parks & recreation.................31.24
    Governmental administration 205.57
    Interest on general debt 86.29

State debt & cash, 2004 ($ per capita)
Debt $2,843.56
Cash/security holdings............. $17,826.29

Federal government grants to state & local government, 2004 (x $1,000)
Total............................. $4,662,536
By Federal Agency
    Defense $48,135

By Federal Agency, continued
    Education 532,553
    Energy........................ 62,227
    Environmental Protection Agency 47,761
    Health & Human Services. 2,540,713
    Homeland Security.................. 19,981
    Housing & Urban Development...... 167,670
    Justice 91,174
    Labor 61,602
    Transportation 305,088
    Veterans Affairs................... 3,127

Crime, Law Enforcement & Courts

Crime, 2004 (rates per 100,000 residents)
Property crimes 79,895
    Burglaries......................... 19,924
    Larcenies.......................... 52,069
    Motor vehicle thefts 7,902
    Property crime rate................. 4,197.7
Violent crimes........................ 13,081
    Murders........................... 169
    Forcible rape........................ 1,039
    Robberies 2,062
    Aggravated assaults 9,811
    Violent crime rate 687.3

Police Agencies, 2004
Total agencies............................ 94
Total employees 5,373
    Male officers....................... 3,573
    Female officers...................... 371
    Male civilians....................... 423
    Female civilians................... 1,006

Arrests, 2004
Total.................................. 92,672
    Persons under 18 years of age 10,994

Prisoners under state & federal jurisdiction, 2004
Total prisoners........................ 6,379
    Percent change, 12/31/03 to 12/31/04 ....2.5%
Sentenced to more than one year 6,111
    rate per 100,000...................... 318

Persons under sentence of death, 7/1/05
Total..................................... 2
    White..................................... 2
    Black 0
    Hispanic 0

State's highest court
Name ....Supreme Court
Number of members...................... 5
Length of term........................ 8 years
Intermediate appeals court? ....yes

Labor & Income

Civilian labor force, 2004

Total	911,000
Men	484,000
Women	427,000
Persons 16-19 years	44,000
White	783,000
Black	19,000
Hispanic	369,000
Asian	0

Civilian labor force as a percent of civilian non-institutional population, 2004

Total	63.5%
Men	69.9
Women	57.5
Persons 16-19 years	40.0
White	63.9
Black	62.6
Hispanic	63.9
Asian	0.0

Employment, 2004

Total	860,000
Men	457,000
Women	403,000
Persons 16-19 years	36,000
White	744,000
Black	17,000
Hispanic	341,000
Asian	0

Full-time/part-time labor force, 2002

Full-time labor force, employed	668,000
Part-time labor force, employed	162,000
Unemployed, looking for	
Full-time work	40,000
Part-time work	NA

Unemployment rate, 2004

Total	5.6%
Men	5.4
Women	5.8
Persons 16-19 years	18.9
White	5.0
Black	13.7
Hispanic	7.5
Asian	NA

Unemployed by reason for unemployment (as a percent of total unemployment), 2002

Job losers or completed temp jobs	47.9%
Job leavers	NA
Reentrants	35.4
New entrants	NA

Labor unions, 2004

Membership	49,000
percent of employed	6.7%

Experienced civilian labor force by private industry, first quarter 2004

Total	568,758
Natural Resources & Mining	23,526
Construction	47,595
Manufacturing	34,956
Trade, transportation & utilities	134,576
Information	14,951
Finance	32,754
Professional & business	88,380
Education & Health	90,073
Leisure & hospitality	80,872
Other	20,556

Experienced civilian labor force by occupation, 2004

Management	40,650
Business & Financial	22,210
Legal	5,650
Sales	77,390
Office & Admin. Support	120,510
Computers & Math	10,730
Architecture & Engineering	19,260
Arts & Entertainment	6,740
Education	NA
Social Services	12,640
Healthcare Practitioner & Technical	36,530
Healthcare support	20,310
Maintenance & Repair	32,270
Construction	55,170
Transportation & moving	45,050
Production	31,960
Farming, fishing & forestry	8,750

Hours and earnings of production workers on manufacturing payrolls, 2004

Average weekly hours	39.6
Average hourly earnings	$13.13
Average weekly earnings	$519.95

Average annual pay

2004	$31,411
change from 2003	4.0%

Household income

Median household income, three-year average, 2002-2004	$37,587

Personal income, 2004 ($ per capita)

In current dollars	$26,191
In constant (2000) dollars	$24,291

Poverty

Persons below poverty level, three-year average, 2002-2004	17.5%

Federal individual income tax returns, 2003

Returns filed	813,731
Adjusted gross income ($1,000)	$29,959,183
Total income tax paid ($1,000)	$3,243,294

Economy, Business, Industry & Agriculture

Fortune 500 companies, 2005 0

Patents issued, 2004 383

Bankruptcy cases filed, 2004 9,400

Business firm ownership, 2002

Women-owned. 42,252
   Sales ($ mil) $4,710
Black-owned. 1,541
   Sales ($ mil) $273
Hispanic-owned. 29,716
   Sales ($ mil) $5,109
Asian-owned 2,370
   Sales ($ mil) $683
Amer. Indian/Alaska Native-owned 6,819
   Sales ($ mil) $792
Hawaiian/Pacific Isl.-owned . . . . NA
   Sales ($ mil) $18

Gross State Product, 2004 ($ mil)

Total Gross State Product $61,012
   Agriculture, forestry, fishing and
      hunting 1,001
   Mining. 4,766
   Utilities 1,400
   Construction 2,763
   Manufacturing, durable goods. 4,318
   Manufacturing, non-durable goods 1,128
   Wholesale trade. 2,202
   Retail trade. 4,431
   Transportation & warehousing 1,657
   Information 1,716
   Finance & insurance. 2,284
   Real estate, rental, leasing 7,105
   Professional and technical services 4,026
   Educational services 280
   Health care and social assistance 4,107
   Accommodation/food services. 1,831
   Other services, except government 1,334
   Government 12,173

Establishments, by major industry group, 2003

Total. 43,568
   Forestry, fishing & agriculture 100
   Mining. 589
   Construction 5,005
   Manufacturing. 1,532
   Wholesale trade. 2,044
   Retail trade. 7,241
   Transportation & warehousing 1,239
   Information 852
   Finance & insurance. 2,718
   Professional/scientific/technical 4,424
   Health care/social assistance 4,142
   Accommodation/food services. 3,808

Annual payroll by major industry group, 2003

Total ($1,000) $15,848,550
   Forestry, fishing & agriculture 10,962
   Mining. 634,064
   Utilities 281,241
   Construction 1,411,044
   Manufacturing. 1,199,092
   Wholesale trade. 729,174
   Retail trade. 1,883,863
   Transportation & warehousing 470,943
   Information 483,195
   Finance & insurance. 932,546
   Professional/scientific/technical . . . 1,449,359
   Health care/social assistance 2,994,531
   Accommodation/food services. 846,404

Agriculture

Number of farms, 2004 18,000
Farm acreage, 2004
   Total. 45,000,000
   Acres per farm, 2004 2,554
Farm income, 2003 ($mil)
   Net farm income $716
   Debt/asset ratio .13.3
Farm marketings, 2003 ($mil)
Total. $2,140
   Crops 543
   Livestock 1,597

Principal commodities, in order by marketing receipts, 2003

     Dairy products, cattle, hay, pecans

Federal economic activity in state

Expenditures, 2003
   Total ($ mil) $18,736
   Per capita $9,995
   Defense ($ mil). 2,158
   Non-defense ($ mil) 16,578
Defense department, 2003
   Payroll ($ mil) $1,245
   Contract awards ($ mil) $973
   Grants ($ mil). $32
   Homeland security grants ($1,000)
      2004 . . . . $24,946
      2005 . . . . $18,499

FDIC insured financial institutions, 2004

Number 58
   Assets ($bil) $15.8
   Deposits ($bil) 18.2

Fishing, 2004

Catch (x 1,000 lbs) 0
Value ($1,000). 0

Mining, 2004 ($ mil)
Total non-fuel mineral production $811
Percent of U.S. 1.9%

Construction, 2003 ($ mil)
Total contracts (including non-building). $3,096
   residential......................... 1,514
   non-residential 1,124

**Establishments, receipts, payroll & employees,
by major industry group, 2002**

Mining 389
   Receipts ($1,000) $813,202
   Annual payroll ($1,000)........... $185,370
   Paid employees 4,278

Utilities 220
   Receipts ($1,000) .... NA
   Annual payroll ($1,000)........... $257,647
   Paid employees 5,042

Construction........................ 4,768
   Receipts ($1,000) $6,017,501
   Annual payroll ($1,000)......... $1,329,192
   Paid employees 45,282

Manufacturing 1,587
   Receipts ($1,000) $10,168,130
   Annual payroll ($1,000)......... $1,241,383
   Paid employees 33,085

Wholesale trade 2,046
   Receipts ($1,000) $8,993,729
   Annual payroll ($1,000)........... $708,115
   Paid employees 19,865

Retail trade 7,227
   Receipts ($1,000) $18,328,637
   Annual payroll ($1,000)......... $1,766,744
   Paid employees 89,413

Transportation 1,152
   Receipts ($1,000) $1,655,584
   Annual payroll ($1,000)......... $389,904
   Paid employees 13,466

Information.......................... 840
   Receipts ($1,000) .... NA
   Annual payroll ($1,000)........... $445,810
   Paid employees 15,138

Finance & insurance 2,649
   Receipts ($1,000) .... NA
   Annual payroll ($1,000)......... $1,146,519
   Paid employees 40,689

Professional, scientific & technical 4,401
   Receipts ($1,000) $3,272,378
   Annual payroll ($1,000)......... $1,307,158
   Paid employees 30,944

Health care & social assistance 4,049
   Receipts ($1,000) $6,103,864
   Annual payroll ($1,000)......... $2,548,044
   Paid employees 82,594

Accommodation & food service.......... 3,756
   Receipts ($1,000) $2,771,474
   Annual payroll ($1,000)........... $779,512
   Paid employees 69,986

Communication, Energy & Transportation

Communication
Daily newspapers, 2004 18
Households with computers, 2003..........54%
Households with internet access, 2003 ......45%

Energy
Electricity Consumption, 2001
Total (trillion Btu) 679
Per capita (million Btu) 371
By source of production (trillion Btu)
   Coal 297
   Natural gas.......................... 262
   Petroleum........................... 251
   Nuclear electric power 0
   Hydroelectric power................. 2
By end-use sector (trillion Btu)
   Residential 107
   Commercial 122
   Industrial 220
   Transportation 230
Electric energy, 2003
   Production (billion kWh) 32.7
   Net summer capability (million kW) 6.3
Gas utilities, 2003
   Customers (x1,000).................. 544
   Sales (trillion Btu)................. 53
   Revenues ($mil)..................... $398
Nuclear plants, 2003 0

Transportation, 2004
Public Road & Street Mileage 64,004
   Urban.............................. 7,958
   Rural 56,046
   Interstate......................... 1,000
Vehicle miles of travel per capita 12,328.5
Total motor vehicle registrations...... 1,542,964
   Automobiles........................ 695,825
   Buses 3,533
   Trucks 843,606
   Motorcycles 36,294
Licensed drivers 1,271,365
   19 years & under 51,050
Deaths from motor vehicle accidents 521

State Summary

Capital City..........................Albany
Governor......................George Pataki
State Capitol
Albany, NY 12224
518-474-7516

Admitted as a state 1788
Area (square miles) 54,556
Population, 2004 (est.) 19,227,088
Largest City........................New York
Population, 2004................. 8,104,000
Personal income per capita, 2004
(in current dollars) $38,228
Gross state product ($ mil), 2004 ..... $896,739

Leading industries by payroll, 2003

Finance & Insurance, Health care/Social assistance, Professional/Scientific/Technical

Leading agricultural commodities by receipts, 2003

Dairy products, greenhouse, hay, cattle

Geography & Environment

Total area (sq. mi.)..................... 54,556
land 47,214
water 7,342

Federally-owned land, 2004 (acres) 233,533
percent.............................. 0.8%

Highest point....................... Mt. Marcy
elevation (feet) 5,344

Lowest point .... Atlantic Ocean
elevation (feet) .... sea level

General coastline (miles)................... 127

Tidal shoreline (miles)................... 1,850

Capital City......................... Albany
Population 2000 95,658
Population 2004 94,226

Largest City........................New York
Population 2000 8,008,000
Population 2004 8,104,000

Number of cities with over 100,000 population

1990 5
2000 5
2004 5

State park and recreation areas, 2003

Area (acres x 1,000)................... 1,532
Number of visitors (x 1,000) 57,001
Revenues (x 1,000)................... $54,103
percent of operating expenditures...... 33.1%

National forest system land, 2004

Acres 16,000

Demographics and Characteristics of the Population

Population

1980 17,558,072
1990 17,990,455
2000 18,976,457
2004 (estimate)..................... 19,227,088
persons per sq. mile of land............ 407.2
2005 (projection)................... 19,258,082
Male...................... 9,292,818
Female...................... 9,965,264
2010 (projection)................... 19,443,672
2020 (projection)................... 19,576,920
2030 (projection)................... 19,477,429
Male...................... 9,382,817
Female...................... 10,094,612

Metropolitan and Non-Metro. area population

	Metro	Non-Metro
1980	15,869,000	1,689,000
1990	16,386,000	1,605,000
2000	17,473,000	1,503,000

Change in population, 2000-2004

Number 250,267
percent............................. 1.3%
Natural increase (births minus deaths).. 431,630
Net internal migration................ -771,944
Net international migration 562,265

Persons by age, 2004

Under 5 years 1,246,045
18 years and over 14,654,725
65 years and over 2,492,816
85 years and over 353,883

Persons by age, 2010 (projected)

Total........................... 19,443,672
Under 5 years 1,250,867
5 to 17 years 3,170,009
18 and over 15,022,796
21 and over 14,167,351
65 and over 2,651,655
85 and over 439,007
Median age 37.9

Race, 2004 (estimate)

One Race
White........................... 14,216,281
Black or African American 3,361,053
American Indian/Alaska Native...... 103,443
Pacific Islander 17,876
Asian Indian....................... 317,375
Chinese 506,839
Filipino 99,021
Japanese 34,060
Korean 128,256
Vietnamese........................ 25,563
Two or more races................... 279,269

Persons of Hispanic origin, 2004

Total Hispanic or Latino	3,003,572
Mexican	315,265
Puerto Rican	1,109,645
Cuban	74,457
Other Hispanic or Latino	207,309

Marital status, 2000

Population 15 years & over	15,055,876
Never married	4,772,713
Married	7,527,938
Separated	481,788
Widowed	1,084,023
Divorced	1,174,358

Language spoken at home, 2000

Population 5 years & over	17,749,110
English only	12,786,189
Spanish	2,416,126
Other Indo-European languages	1,654,540
Asian/Pacific Island languages	671,019

Households & families, 2000

Households	7,056,860
with persons under 18 years	2,466,483
with persons over 65 years	1,767,452
persons per household	2.61
Families	4,639,387
persons per family	3.22
Married couples	3,289,514
Female householder, no husband present	1,038,176
One-person households	1,982,742

Nativity, 2000

Number of persons born in state	12,384,940
percent of population	65.3%

Immigration & Naturalization, 2004

Immigrants admitted	102,390
Persons naturalized	66,234
Asylums granted	1,012
Asylums denied	224

Vital Statistics and Health

Marriages

2002	139,682
2003	130,900
2004	130,813

Divorces

2002	65,340
2003	61,011
2004	57,830

Births

2003	253,714
Birthrate (per 1,000)	13.2
Low birth weight (2,500g or less)	7.9%
To unmarried mothers	36.5%

2003, continued

White	184,059
Black	48,098
Hispanic	55,340
Asian/Pacific Islander	21,394
Amer. Indian/Alaska Native	636

2004 (preliminary)	250,894
Birthrate (per 1,000)	13.0
White	178,771
Black	49,765
Hispanic	57,081
Asian/Pacific Islander	21,662

Deaths

2002

All causes	158,118
rate per 100,000	825.4
Heart disease	56,672
rate per 100,000	295.8
Malignant neoplasms	36,661
rate per 100,000	191.4
Cerebrovascular disease	7,625
rate per 100,000	39.8
Chronic lower respiratory disease	6,966
rate per 100,000	36.4
2003	155,852
rate per 100,000	812.1
2004 (provisional)	151,656

Infant deaths

2003 (provisional)	1,642
rate per 1,000	6.3
2004 (provisional)	1,561
rate per 1,000	6

Abortions, 2000

Total	165,000
rate per 1,000 women age 15-44	39.1

Physicians, 2003

Total	75,048
rate per 1,000 persons	391

Nurses, 2001

Total	165,580
rate per 1,000 persons	868

Community Hospitals, 2003

Number	207
Beds (x 1,000)	64.7
Patients admitted (x 1,000)	2,499
Average daily census (x 1,000)	50.6
Average cost per day	$1,402
Outpatient visits (x mil)	48.0

Disability status of population, 2004

5 to 20 years	6.4%
21 to 64 years	10.8%
65 years and over	36.3%

Education

Educational attainment, 2004

Population over 25 years	12,503,217
Less than 9th grade	805,245
High school graduates only	3,743,798
Bachelor's degree only	2,169,212
Graduate or professional degree	1,645,542
Less than 9th grade percent	6.4%
High school graduate or more	85.4%
College graduate or more	30.6%
Graduate or professional degree	13.2%

Public school enrollment, Fall 2002

Total	2,888,233
Kindergarten through grade 8	2,016,810
Grades 9 through 12	871,423
Enrollment, 2005 (projected)	2,842,800

Graduating public high school seniors

2004 (estimate)	150,880

SAT scores, 2005

Average verbal score	497
Average math score	511
Percent of graduates taking test	92%

Public school teachers, 2004

Total (x 1,000)	224
Elementary (x 1,000)	111
Secondary (x 1,000)	113
Average salary	$55,200
Elementary	$54,700
Secondary	$55,800

State receipts & expenditures for public schools, 2004

Revenue receipts ($mil)	$38,500
Expenditures	
Total ($mil)	$39,309
Per capita	$2,046
Per pupil	$12,408

Institutions of higher education, 2004

Total	307
Public	78
Private	229

Enrollment in institutions of higher education, Fall, 2003

Total	1,157,256
Full-time men	358,096
Full-time women	451,960
Part-time men	126,906
Part-time women	220,294

Minority enrollment in institutions of higher education, Fall, 2003

Black, non-hispanic	145,359
Hispanic	114,267
Asian/Pacific Islander	76,987
American Indian/Alaska Native	3,550

Earned degrees conferred, 2003

Bachelor's	105,103
Master's	58,210
First-professional	8,117
Doctor's	3,741

State & local financial support for higher education, 2003-2004

Full-time equivalent enrollment (x 1,000)	487.3
Appropriations per FTE	$6,663
as a percent of tax revenue	5.1%

Social Insurance & Welfare Programs

Social Security benefits & beneficiaries, 2004

Beneficiaries	
Total	3,045,000
Retired & dependents	2,162,000
Survivors	387,000
Disabled & dependents	497,000
Annual benefit payments ($ mil)	
Total	$33,354
Retired & dependents	$22,849
Survivors	$5,364
Disabled & dependents	$5,141
Average Monthly Benefit	
Retired & dependents	$1,011
Disabled & dependents	$943
Widowed	$973

Medicare

Enrollment, 2001 (x 1,000)	2,729
Payments ($ mil, est.)	$20,400
Enrollment, 2003 (x 1,000)	2,763

Medicaid, 2002

Beneficiaries (x 1,000)	3,921
Payments ($ mil)	$31,489

State Children's Health Insurance, 2004

Enrollment (x 1,000)	826.6
Expenditures ($ mil)	$296.9

Persons without health insurance, 2003

Number (x 1,000)	2,866
percent	15.1%
Number of children (x 1,000)	432
percent of children	9.4%

Federal public aid

Temporary Assistance for Needy Families, 2004	
Recipients (x 1,000)	336
Families (x 1,000)	147
Supplemental Security Income, 2003	
Recipients (x 1,000)	625
Payments ($ mil)	$3,400

Food Stamp Program, 2004

Participants (x 1,000)	1,598
Benefits ($ mil)	$1,876

Housing & Construction

Housing units

Total 2003 (estimate)	7,789,237
Total 2004 (estimate)	7,819,359
Seasonal or recreational use, 2003	216,000
Owner-occupied single-family, 2003	2,804,000
Median value	$198,883
Renter-occupied, 2003	3,243,000
Median rent	$770
Homeownership rate, 2003	54.3%
Homeownership rate, 2004	54.8%

New privately owned housing units, 2004

Number authorized (x 1,000)	53.5
Value ($ mil)	$6,945
Started 2005 (x 1,000, estimate)	38.8
Started 2006 (x 1,000, estimate)	37.5

Existing home sales

2002 (x 1,000)	290.4
2003 (x 1,000)	282.6
2004 (x 1,000)	307.5

Government & Elections

State Officials 2006

Governor (name/party/term expires)
George Pataki
Republican - 1/07

Lieutenant Governor	Mary Donahue
Secretary of State	Frank Milano (Actg)
Attorney General	Eliott Spitzer
Chief Justice	Judith Kaye

Governorship

Minimum age	30
Length of term	4 years
Consecutive terms permitted	not specified
Who succeeds	Lt. Governor

State Legislature

Name	Legislature
Upper chamber	Senate
Number of members	62
Length of term	2 years
Party in majority, 2006	Republican
Lower chamber	Assembly
Number of members	150
Length of term	2 years
Party in majority, 2006	Democratic

State Government Employees, 2004

Total	246,385
Payroll	$1,080,559,036

Local Government Employees, 2004

Total	938,009
Payroll	$4,013,562,813

Local Governments by Type, 2002

Total	3,420
County	57
Municipal	616
Township	929
School District	683
Special District	1,135

Voting age population, November 2004

Total	14,492,000
Male	6,865,000
Female	7,627,000
White	11,055,000
Black	2,354,000
Hispanic	1,976,000
Asian	939,000

Presidential Election, 2004

Total Popular Vote	7,391,036
Kerry	4,314,280
Bush	2,962,567
Total Electoral Votes	31

Federal representation, 2006 (109th Congress)

Senator	Hillary Clinton
Party	Democrat
Year term expires	2007
Senator	Charles Schumer
Party	Democrat
Year term expires	2011
Representatives, total	29
Democrats	20
Republicans	9
Other	0

Votes cast for US Senators

2002

Total vote (x 1,000)	NA
Leading party	NA
Percent for leading party	NA

2004

Total vote (x 1,000)	7,448,000
Leading party	Democratic
Percent for leading party	58.9%

Votes cast for US Representatives

2002

Total vote (x 1,000)	4,701
Democratic	1,778
Republican	1,526
Leading party	Democratic
Percent for leading party	37.8%

2004

Total vote (x 1,000)	7,448
Democratic	3,457
Republican	2,209
Leading party	Democratic
Percent for leading party	46.4%

Women holding public office, 2006

US Congress 7
Statewide elected office...................... 1
State legislature 49

Black public officials, 2001

Total.................................... 325
    US and state legislatures 34
    City/county/regional offices 83
    Judicial/law enforcement................. 83
    Education/school boards 125

Hispanic public officials, 2004

Total.................................... 61
    State executives & legislators 15
    City/county/regional offices 26
    Judicial/law enforcement................. 15
    Education/school boards 5

Governmental Finance

State government revenues, 2004

Total revenue ($1,000) $136,520,762
    Revenue per capita 7,080.59

General Revenue ($ per capita) $5,513.21
    Intergovernmental 2,481.10
    Taxes 2,376.77
        general sales 521.25
        individual income tax............1,278.32
        corporate income tax 106.04
    Current charges......................339.06
    Miscellaneous 316.28

State government expenditure, 2004

Total expenditure (x $1,000) $132,883,277
    Expenditure per capita............. 6,891.93
General Expenditure ($ per capita).... $5,614.24
    Education 1,626.44
    Public welfare...................... 2,134.46
    Health 271.31
    Hospitals........................... 200.22
    Highways 190.49
    Police protection..................... 42.46
    Correction 134.16
    Natural resources 18.50
    Parks & recreation.................... 24.67
    Governmental administration 221.20
    Interest on general debt 156.65

State debt & cash, 2004 ($ per capita)

Debt $4,963.94
Cash/security holdings............. $13,607.96

Federal government grants to state & local government, 2004 (x $1,000)

Total........................... $50,008,574
By Federal Agency
    Defense $210,427

By Federal Agency, continued
    Education 2,754,077
    Energy 164,847
    Environmental Protection Agency ... 134,919
    Health & Human Services. 31,516,934
    Homeland Security.................. 155,616
    Housing & Urban Development.... 3,832,412
    Justice 509,419
    Labor 474,770
    Transportation 7,987,502
    Veterans Affairs.................... 21,785

Crime, Law Enforcement & Courts

Crime, 2004 (rates per 100,000 residents)

Property crimes 422,734
    Burglaries......................... 70,696
    Larcenies......................... 311,036
    Motor vehicle thefts 41,002
    Property crime rate................. 2,198.6
Violent crimes........................ 84,914
    Murders........................... 889
    Forcible rape....................... 3,608
    Robberies 33,506
    Aggravated assaults 46,911
    Violent crime rate.....................441.6

Police Agencies, 2004

Total agencies............................ 465
Total employees 86,481
    Male officers...................... 54,783
    Female officers..................... 8,325
    Male civilians...................... 7,631
    Female civilians.................... 15,742

Arrests, 2004

Total............................... 315,889
    Persons under 18 years of age 47,820

Prisoners under state & federal jurisdiction, 2004

Total prisoners....................... 63,751
    Percent change, 12/31/03 to 12/31/04 ... -2.2%
Sentenced to more than one year 63,751
    rate per 100,000....................... 331

Persons under sentence of death, 7/1/05

Total.................................... 2
    White............................. 1
    Black 1
    Hispanic 0

State's highest court

Name .... Court of Appeals
Number of members........................ 7
Length of term .... 14 years
Intermediate appeals court? ....yes

Labor & Income

Civilian labor force, 2004

Total	9,370,000
Men	4,965,000
Women	4,406,000
Persons 16-19 years	387,000
White	7,136,000
Black	1,481,000
Hispanic	1,354,000
Asian	621,000

Civilian labor force as a percent of civilian non-institutional population, 2004

Total	62.9%
Men	70.3
Women	56.2
Persons 16-19 years	36.5
White	63.5
Black	59.4
Hispanic	63.3
Asian	63.5

Employment, 2004

Total	8,823,000
Men	4,671,000
Women	4,151,000
Persons 16-19 years	324,000
White	6,774,000
Black	1,330,000
Hispanic	1,249,000
Asian	597,000

Full-time/part-time labor force, 2002

Full-time labor force, employed	7,273,000
Part-time labor force, employed	1,517,000
Unemployed, looking for	
Full-time work	491,000
Part-time work	81,000

Unemployment rate, 2004

Total	5.8%
Men	5.9
Women	5.8
Persons 16-19 years	16.3
White	5.1
Black	10.1
Hispanic	7.7
Asian	4.0

Unemployed by reason for unemployment (as a percent of total unemployment), 2002

Job losers or completed temp jobs	58.8%
Job leavers	8.0
Reentrants	25.7
New entrants	7.3

Labor unions, 2004

Membership	1,996,000
percent of employed	25.3%

Experienced civilian labor force by private industry, first quarter 2004

Total	6,723,516
Natural Resources & Mining	22,673
Construction	291,353
Manufacturing	594,740
Trade, transportation & utilities	1,436,082
Information	267,714
Finance	690,013
Professional & business	1,029,425
Education & Health	1,415,786
Leisure & hospitality	619,628
Other	307,451

Experienced civilian labor force by occupation, 2004

Management	384,400
Business & Financial	353,550
Legal	98,810
Sales	882,170
Office & Admin. Support	1,607,750
Computers & Math	181,050
Architecture & Engineering	104,970
Arts & Entertainment	173,380
Education	675,780
Social Services	151,060
Healthcare Practitioner & Technical	437,720
Healthcare support	278,490
Maintenance & Repair	303,400
Construction	310,200
Transportation & moving	462,520
Production	437,440
Farming, fishing & forestry	1,250

Hours and earnings of production workers on manufacturing payrolls, 2004

Average weekly hours	39.7
Average hourly earnings	$17.29
Average weekly earnings	$686.41

Average annual pay

2004	$49,941
change from 2003	5.6%

Household income

Median household income, three-year average, 2002-2004	$44,228

Personal income, 2004 ($ per capita)

In current dollars	$38,228
In constant (2000) dollars	$35,454

Poverty

Persons below poverty level, three-year average, 2002-2004	14.4%

Federal individual income tax returns, 2003

Returns filed	8,589,932
Adjusted gross income ($1,000)	$465,511,760
Total income tax paid ($1,000)	$67,837,781

Economy, Business, Industry & Agriculture

Fortune 500 companies, 2005 54

Patents issued, 2004 6,618

Bankruptcy cases filed, 2004 80,200

Business firm ownership, 2002

Women-owned 505,134
  Sales ($ mil) $71,414
Black-owned 129,339
  Sales ($ mil) $7,906
Hispanic-owned 163,659
  Sales ($ mil) $12,752
Asian-owned 145,626
  Sales ($ mil) $32,030
Amer. Indian/Alaska Native-owned 12,307
  Sales ($ mil) $897
Hawaiian/Pacific Isl.-owned 4,868
  Sales ($ mil) $201

Gross State Product, 2004 ($ mil)

Total Gross State Product $896,739
  Agriculture, forestry, fishing and
    hunting 1,670
  Mining 454
  Utilities 18,457
  Construction 28,773
  Manufacturing, durable goods 30,345
  Manufacturing, non-durable goods . . . 31,736
  Wholesale trade 47,242
  Retail trade 49,541
  Transportation & warehousing 16,557
  Information 62,071
  Finance & insurance 150,069
  Real estate, rental, leasing 114,056
  Professional and technical services 75,337
  Educational services 12,898
  Health care and social assistance 70,059
  Accommodation/food services 20,163
  Other services, except government 18,946
  Government 91,801

Establishments, by major industry group, 2003

Total 502,948
  Forestry, fishing & agriculture 667
  Mining 387
  Construction 43,357
  Manufacturing 20,328
  Wholesale trade 35,966
  Retail trade 76,777
  Transportation & warehousing 11,660
  Information 11,001
  Finance & insurance 28,568
  Professional/scientific/technical 55,834
  Health care/social assistance 51,167
  Accommodation/food services 40,394

Annual payroll by major industry group, 2003

Total ($1,000) $332,635,342
  Forestry, fishing & agriculture 148,164
  Mining 189,106
  Utilities 3,266,209
  Construction 14,798,998
  Manufacturing 25,388,963
  Wholesale trade 20,894,567
  Retail trade 19,294,985
  Transportation & warehousing 7,752,088
  Information 20,921,662
  Finance & insurance 68,294,052
  Professional/scientific/technical . . 34,872,153
  Health care/social assistance 45,581,431
  Accommodation/food services 8,765,622

Agriculture

Number of farms, 2004 36,000
Farm acreage, 2004
  Total 8,000,000
  Acres per farm, 2004 211
Farm income, 2003 ($mil)
  Net farm income $597
  Debt/asset ratio 17.9
Farm marketings, 2003 ($mil)
Total $3,139
  Crops 1,225
  Livestock 1,915

Principal commodities, in order by marketing receipts, 2003

  Dairy products, greenhouse, hay, cattle

Federal economic activity in state

Expenditures, 2003
  Total ($ mil) $137,898
  Per capita $7,186
  Defense ($ mil) 6,286
  Non-defense ($ mil) 131,612
Defense department, 2003
  Payroll ($ mil) $2,017
  Contract awards ($ mil) $4,320
  Grants ($ mil) $155
  Homeland security grants ($1,000)
    2004 . . . . $178,492
    2005 . . . . $298,351

FDIC insured financial institutions, 2004

Number 200
  Assets ($bil) $1,166.2
  Deposits ($bil) 637.6

Fishing, 2004

Catch (x 1,000 lbs) 33,722
Value ($1,000) $46,392

8   New York

Mining, 2004 ($ mil)
Total non-fuel mineral production $1,060
Percent of U.S. 2.4%

Construction, 2003 ($ mil)
Total contracts (including non-building) $20,556
   residential........................... 7,589
   non-residential 7,407

Establishments, receipts, payroll & employees, by major industry group, 2002

Mining 204
   Receipts ($1,000) $815,465
   Annual payroll ($1,000)........... $144,475
   Paid employees 3,752

Utilities 402
   Receipts ($1,000) .... NA
   Annual payroll ($1,000)......... $3,305,174
   Paid employees 46,199

Construction........................ 41,962
   Receipts ($1,000) $65,368,319
   Annual payroll ($1,000)......... $14,874,984
   Paid employees 370,149

Manufacturing 21,066
   Receipts ($1,000) $147,317,463
   Annual payroll ($1,000)......... $25,373,757
   Paid employees 641,434

Wholesale trade 35,845
   Receipts ($1,000) $343,663,041
   Annual payroll ($1,000)......... $19,771,869
   Paid employees 413,226

Retail trade 76,425
   Receipts ($1,000) $178,067,530
   Annual payroll ($1,000)......... $18,152,597
   Paid employees 837,806

Transportation....................... 11,440
   Receipts ($1,000) $18,845,179
   Annual payroll ($1,000)......... $6,201,957
   Paid employees 199,815

Information.......................... 10,916
   Receipts ($1,000) .... NA
   Annual payroll ($1,000)......... $18,443,187
   Paid employees 307,762

Finance & insurance 26,089
   Receipts ($1,000) .... NA
   Annual payroll ($1,000)......... $80,287,974
   Paid employees 781,833

Professional, scientific & technical 55,691
   Receipts ($1,000) $83,549,043
   Annual payroll ($1,000)......... $33,732,270
   Paid employees 563,081

Health care & social assistance 50,270
   Receipts ($1,000) $98,966,149
   Annual payroll ($1,000)......... $43,477,657
   Paid employees 1,234,153

Accommodation & food service.......... 39,428
   Receipts ($1,000) $27,835,952
   Annual payroll ($1,000)......... $7,972,279
   Paid employees 527,649

Communication, Energy & Transportation

Communication
Daily newspapers, 2004 59
Households with computers, 2003 .... 60%
Households with internet access, 2003 ..... 53%

Energy
Electricity Consumption, 2001
   Total (trillion Btu)..................... 4,135
   Per capita (million Btu) 217
By source of production (trillion Btu)
   Coal 315
   Natural gas 1,206
   Petroleum........................... 1,713
   Nuclear electric power 422
   Hydroelectric power 225
By end-use sector (trillion Btu)
   Residential 1,194
   Commercial 1,303
   Industrial 667
   Transportation 970
Electric energy, 2003
   Production (billion kWh) 137.6
   Net summer capability (million kW) 36.7
Gas utilities, 2003
   Customers (x1,000).................. 4,269
   Sales (trillion Btu)................... 550
   Revenues ($mil) $5,953
Nuclear plants, 2003 6

Transportation, 2004
Public Road & Street Mileage 113,341
   Urban.............................. 41,224
   Rural 72,117
   Interstate............................ 1,674
Vehicle miles of travel per capita......... 7,197.9
Total motor vehicle registrations..... 11,098,785
   Automobiles..................... 8,548,783
   Buses 64,151
   Trucks 2,485,851
   Motorcycles 170,148
Licensed drivers 11,246,675
   19 years & under 424,465
Deaths from motor vehicle accidents 1,493

State Summary

Capital City . . . . Raleigh
Governor . . . . Michael Easley
Office of the Governor
20301 Mail Service Center
Raleigh, NC 27699
919-733-4240
Admitted as a state 1789
Area (square miles) 53,819
Population, 2004 (est.) 8,541,221
Largest City . . . . Charlotte
Population, 2004 594,000
Personal income per capita, 2004
(in current dollars) $29,246
Gross state product ($ mil), 2004 . . . . . . $336,398

Leading industries by payroll, 2003

Manufacturing, Health care/Social assistance,
Finance & Insurance

Leading agricultural commodities by receipts, 2003

Hogs, broilers, greenhouse, tobacco

Geography & Environment

Total area (sq. mi.) 53,819
land 48,711
water 5,108

Federally-owned land, 2004 (acres) . . . 3,710,338
percent 11.8%

Highest point . . . . Mt. Mitchell
elevation (feet) 6,684

Lowest point . . . . Atlantic Ocean
elevation (feet) . . . . sea level

General coastline (miles) 301

Tidal shoreline (miles) 3,375

Capital City . . . . Raleigh
Population 2000 276,000
Population 2004 327,000

Largest City . . . . Charlotte
Population 2000 541,000
Population 2004 594,000

Number of cities with over 100,000 population

1990 5
2000 6
2004 7

State park and recreation areas, 2003

Area (acres x 1,000) 171
Number of visitors (x 1,000) 13,213
Revenues (x 1,000) $3,187
percent of operating expenditures 11.0%

National forest system land, 2004

Acres 1,255,000

Demographics and Characteristics of the Population

Population

1980 5,881,766
1990 6,628,637
2000 8,049,313
2004 (estimate) 8,541,221
persons per sq. mile of land 175.3
2005 (projection) 8,702,410
Male 4,277,829
Female 4,424,581
2010 (projection) 9,345,823
2020 (projection) 10,709,289
2030 (projection) 12,227,739
Male 6,065,373
Female 6,162,366

Metropolitan and Non-Metro. area population

	Metro	Non-Metro
1980	3,204,000	2,678,000
1990	3,758,000	2,871,000
2000	5,437,000	2,612,000

Change in population, 2000-2004

Number 494,730
percent 6.1%
Natural increase (births minus deaths) . . 195,788
Net internal migration 166,864
Net international migration 131,807

Persons by age, 2004

Under 5 years 600,113
18 years and over 6,422,729
65 years and over 1,032,249
85 years and over 120,640

Persons by age, 2010 (projected)

Total 9,345,823
Under 5 years 645,144
5 to 17 years 1,623,694
18 and over 7,076,985
21 and over 6,639,898
65 and over 1,161,164
85 and over 155,537
Median age 36.9

Race, 2004 (estimate)

One Race
White 6,332,037
Black or African American 1,861,416
American Indian/Alaska Native 110,198
Pacific Islander 5,784
Asian Indian 36,056
Chinese 24,919
Filipino 13,594
Japanese 3,046
Korean 23,195
Vietnamese 15,192
Two or more races 83,487

Persons of Hispanic origin, 2004

Total Hispanic or Latino	506,206
Mexican	358,648
Puerto Rican	33,624
Cuban	5,203
Other Hispanic or Latino	24,960

Marital status, 2000

Population 15 years & over	6,393,707
Never married	1,598,427
Married	3,599,657
Separated	191,811
Widowed	434,772
Divorced	575,434

Language spoken at home, 2000

Population 5 years & over	7,513,165
English only	6,909,648
Spanish	378,942
Other Indo-European languages	119,961
Asian/Pacific Island languages	78,246

Households & families, 2000

Households	3,132,013
with persons under 18 years	1,104,659
with persons over 65 years	682,982
persons per household	2.49
Families	2,158,869
persons per family	2.98
Married couples	1,645,346
Female householder, no husband present	389,997
One-person households	795,271

Nativity, 2000

Number of persons born in state	5,073,066
percent of population	63.0%

Immigration & Naturalization, 2004

Immigrants admitted	10,718
Persons naturalized	5,084
Asylums granted	178
Asylums denied	36

Vital Statistics and Health

Marriages

2002	63,730
2003	61,932
2004	62,235

Divorces

2002	37,049
2003	35,678
2004	35,926

Births

2003	118,323
Birthrate (per 1,000)	14.1
Low birth weight (2,500g or less)	9.0%
To unmarried mothers	35.3%

2003, continued

White	86,395
Black	27,140
Hispanic	16,084
Asian/Pacific Islander	3,106
Amer. Indian/Alaska Native	1,637
2004 (preliminary)	119,851
Birthrate (per 1,000)	14.0
White	87,414
Black	27,623
Hispanic	17,295
Asian/Pacific Islander	3,237

Deaths

2002	
All causes	72,027
rate per 100,000	865.7
Heart disease	18,524
rate per 100,000	222.6
Malignant neoplasms	16,210
rate per 100,000	194.8
Cerebrovascular disease	5,259
rate per 100,000	63.2
Chronic lower respiratory disease	3,674
rate per 100,000	44.2
2003	73,548
rate per 100,000	874.8
2004 (provisional)	72,437

Infant deaths

2003 (provisional)	931
rate per 1,000	7.9
2004 (provisional)	1,022
rate per 1,000	8.5

Abortions, 2000

Total	38,000
rate per 1,000 women age 15-44	21.0

Physicians, 2003

Total	21,287
rate per 1,000 persons	253

Nurses, 2001

Total	72,050
rate per 1,000 persons	878

Community Hospitals, 2003

Number	113
Beds (x 1,000)	23.3
Patients admitted (x 1,000)	987
Average daily census (x 1,000)	16.6
Average cost per day	$1,200
Outpatient visits (x mil)	14.5

Disability status of population, 2004

5 to 20 years	7.2%
21 to 64 years	13.1%
65 years and over	44.1%

Education

Educational attainment, 2004

Population over 25 years 5,469,848
  Less than 9th grade 382,779
  High school graduates only........ 1,595,642
  Bachelor's degree only 923,548
  Graduate or professional degree...... 421,610
  Less than 9th grade percent 7.0%
  High school graduate or more 80.9%
  College graduate or more.............. 23.4%
  Graduate or professional degree........ 7.7%

Public school enrollment, Fall 2002

Total............................. 1,335,954
  Kindergarten through grade 8 963,967
  Grades 9 through 12................ 371,987
Enrollment, 2005 (projected) 1,354,500

Graduating public high school seniors

2004 (estimate)........................ 71,380

SAT scores, 2005

Average verbal score 499
Average math score........................ 511
Percent of graduates taking test 74%

Public school teachers, 2004

Total (x 1,000) 87.9
  Elementary (x 1,000)....................61.7
  Secondary (x 1,000) 26.3
Average salary $43,200
  Elementary......................... $43,200
  Secondary.......................... $43,200

State receipts & expenditures for public schools, 2004

Revenue receipts ($mil)................. $9,422
Expenditures
Total ($mil)......................... $10,382
  Per capita $1,233
  Per pupil $7,511

Institutions of higher education, 2004

Total.................................. 130
  Public............................... 75
  Private.............................. 55

Enrollment in institutions of higher education, Fall, 2003

Total................................ 468,025
  Full-time men 127,779
  Full-time women................... 172,020
  Part-time men 61,269
  Part-time women................... 106,957

Minority enrollment in institutions of higher education, Fall, 2003

Black, non-hispanic.................. 108,190
Hispanic 9,649
Asian/Pacific Islander 10,539
American Indian/Alaska Native......... 5,657

Earned degrees conferred, 2003

Bachelor's 37,272
Master's.............................. 10,143
First-professional...................... 1,861
Doctor's.............................. 1,138

State & local financial support for higher education, 2003-2004

Full-time equivalent enrollment (x 1,000) ..315.2
Appropriations per FTE................ $6,699
  as a percent of tax revenue............ 11.4%

Social Insurance & Welfare Programs

Social Security benefits & beneficiaries, 2004

Beneficiaries
  Total........................... 1,467,000
  Retired & dependents............... 977,000
  Survivors......................... 192,000
  Disabled & dependents............. 299,000
Annual benefit payments ($ mil)
  Total........................... $14,779
  Retired & dependents............... $9,565
  Survivors......................... $2,302
  Disabled & dependents............. $2,912
Average Monthly Benefit
  Retired & dependents................. $934
  Disabled & dependents.............. $877
  Widowed............................ $860

Medicare

Enrollment, 2001 (x 1,000) 1,155
  Payments ($ mil, est.) $6,800
Enrollment, 2003 (x 1,000) 1,205

Medicaid, 2002

Beneficiaries (x 1,000).................. 1,355
Payments ($ mil) $6,041

State Children's Health Insurance, 2004

Enrollment (x 1,000)....................174.3
Expenditures ($ mil)...................$166.2

Persons without health insurance, 2003

Number (x 1,000)...................... 1,424
  percent............................ 17.3%
Number of children (x 1,000) 249
  percent of children 11.9%

Federal public aid

Temporary Assistance for Needy Families, 2004
Recipients (x 1,000) 77
Families (x 1,000) 38

Supplemental Security Income, 2003
Recipients (x 1,000)...................... 194
Payments ($ mil) $825

Food Stamp Program, 2004

Participants (x 1,000) 747
Benefits ($ mil)......................... $753

Housing & Construction

Housing units

Total 2003 (estimate)	3,790,028
Total 2004 (estimate)	3,860,078
Seasonal or recreational use, 2003	166,000
Owner-occupied single-family, 2003	1,678,000
Median value	$125,428
Renter-occupied, 2003	1,020,000
Median rent	$601
Homeownership rate, 2003	70.0%
Homeownership rate, 2004	69.8%

New privately owned housing units, 2004

Number authorized (x 1,000)	93.1
Value ($ mil)	$12,845
Started 2005 (x 1,000, estimate)	71.1
Started 2006 (x 1,000, estimate)	70.2

Existing home sales

2002 (x 1,000)	142.1
2003 (x 1,000)	156.3
2004 (x 1,000)	192.6

Government & Elections

State Officials 2006

Governor (name/party/term expires)
Michael Easley
Democrat - 1/09

Lieutenant Governor	Beverly Perdue
Secretary of State	Elaine Marshall
Attorney General	Roy Cooper
Chief Justice	I. Beverly Lake Jr.

Governorship

Minimum age	30
Length of term	4 years
Consecutive terms permitted	2
Who succeeds	Lt. Governor

State Legislature

Name	General Assembly
Upper chamber	Senate
Number of members	50
Length of term	2 years
Party in majority, 2006	Democratic
Lower chamber	House of Representatives
Number of members	120
Length of term	2 years
Party in majority, 2006	Democratic

State Government Employees, 2004

Total	132,110
Payroll	$430,230,754

Local Government Employees, 2004

Total	321,830
Payroll	$982,113,650

Local Governments by Type, 2002

Total	960
County	100
Municipal	541
Township	0
School District	0
Special District	319

Voting age population, November 2004

Total	6,250,000
Male	2,979,000
Female	3,271,000
White	4,709,000
Black	1,241,000
Hispanic	327,000
Asian	125,000

Presidential Election, 2004

Total Popular Vote	3,501,007
Kerry	1,525,849
Bush	1,961,166
Total Electoral Votes	15

Federal representation, 2006 (109th Congress)

Senator	Elizabeth Dole
Party	Republican
Year term expires	2009
Senator	Richard Burr
Party	Republican
Year term expires	2011
Representatives, total	13
Democrats	6
Republicans	7
Other	0

Votes cast for US Senators

2002

Total vote (x 1,000)	2,331,000
Leading party	Republican
Percent for leading party	53.6%

2004

Total vote (x 1,000)	3,472,000
Leading party	Republican
Percent for leading party	51.6%

Votes cast for US Representatives

2002

Total vote (x 1,000)	2,244
Democratic	971
Republican	1,209
Leading party	Republican
Percent for leading party	53.9%

2004

Total vote (x 1,000)	3,413
Democratic	1,670
Republican	1,743
Leading party	Republican
Percent for leading party	51.1%

Women holding public office, 2006
US Congress 3
Statewide elected office...................... 4
State legislature 39

Black public officials, 2001
Total..................................... 491
   US and state legislatures 28
   City/county/regional offices 349
   Judicial/law enforcement.................. 29
   Education/school boards 85

Hispanic public officials, 2004
Total...................................... 4
   State executives & legislators 2
   City/county/regional offices 2
   Judicial/law enforcement.................. 0
   Education/school boards 0

Governmental Finance

State government revenues, 2004
Total revenue ($1,000) $44,371,161
   Revenue per capita 5,195.69

General Revenue ($ per capita) $3,858.45
   Intergovernmental 1,359.34
   Taxes 1,971.48
      general sales 509.58
      individual income tax.............879.51
      corporate income tax 98.02
   Current charges......................327.18
   Miscellaneous 200.45

State government expenditure, 2004
Total expenditure (x $1,000) $37,050,568
   Expenditure per capita............. 4,338.47
General Expenditure ($ per capita).... $3,865.23
   Education 1,556.31
   Public welfare..................... 1,025.26
   Health 149.23
   Hospitals...........................129.63
   Highways 374.48
   Police protection 44.29
   Correction 121.91
   Natural resources 60.53
   Parks & recreation...................17.68
   Governmental administration 89.51
   Interest on general debt 51.60

State debt & cash, 2004 ($ per capita)
Debt $1,651.39
Cash/security holdings.............. $8,630.37

Federal government grants to state & local government, 2004 (x $1,000)
Total............................ $12,574,492
By Federal Agency
   Defense $116,236

By Federal Agency, continued
   Education 975,830
   Energy 25,739
   Environmental Protection Agency 83,557
   Health & Human Services. 8,022,570
   Homeland Security.................. 114,607
   Housing & Urban Development...... 680,069
   Justice 153,191
   Labor 315,411
   Transportation 1,014,418
   Veterans Affairs..................... 4,238

Crime, Law Enforcement & Courts

Crime, 2004 (rates per 100,000 residents)
Property crimes 355,328
   Burglaries........................ 101,193
   Larcenies......................... 227,147
   Motor vehicle thefts 26,988
   Property crime rate............... 4,160.2
Violent crimes......................... 38,244
   Murders........................... 532
   Forcible rape....................... 2,339
   Robberies 11,782
   Aggravated assaults 23,591
   Violent crime rate....................447.8

Police Agencies, 2004
Total agencies........................... 509
Total employees 29,571
   Male officers...................... 18,414
   Female officers..................... 2,355
   Male civilians...................... 3,764
   Female civilians.................... 5,038

Arrests, 2004
Total................................ 393,819
   Persons under 18 years of age 37,870

Prisoners under state & federal jurisdiction, 2004
Total prisoners........................ 35,434
   Percent change, 12/31/03 to 12/31/04 .... 5.6%
   Sentenced to more than one year 30,683
   rate per 100,000....................... 357

Persons under sentence of death, 7/1/05
Total.................................. 192
   White............................. 71
   Black 105
   Hispanic 4

State's highest court
Name ....Supreme Court
Number of members...................... 7
Length of term .... 8 years
Intermediate appeals court? ....yes

Labor & Income

Civilian labor force, 2004

Total	4,243,000
Men	2,270,000
Women	1,973,000
Persons 16-19 years	185,000
White	3,216,000
Black	837,000
Hispanic	319,000
Asian	84,000

Civilian labor force as a percent of civilian non-institutional population, 2004

Total	65.9%
Men	73.6
Women	58.8
Persons 16-19 years	42.8
White	66.5
Black	64.0
Hispanic	74.5
Asian	65.4

Employment, 2004

Total	4,016,000
Men	2,154,000
Women	1,862,000
Persons 16-19 years	150,000
White	3,089,000
Black	749,000
Hispanic	303,000
Asian	82,000

Full-time/part-time labor force, 2002

Full-time labor force, employed	3,262,000
Part-time labor force, employed	628,000
Unemployed, looking for	
Full-time work	243,000
Part-time work	NA

Unemployment rate, 2004

Total	5.4%
Men	5.1
Women	5.6
Persons 16-19 years	19.2
White	3.9
Black	10.5
Hispanic	5.1
Asian	2.0

Unemployed by reason for unemployment (as a percent of total unemployment), 2002

Job losers or completed temp jobs	55.5%
Job leavers	NA
Reentrants	28.5
New entrants	NA

Labor unions, 2004

Membership	97,000
percent of employed	2.7%

Experienced civilian labor force by private industry, first quarter 2004

Total	3,077,909
Natural Resources & Mining	30,375
Construction	211,720
Manufacturing	578,521
Trade, transportation & utilities	715,082
Information	72,625
Finance	185,372
Professional & business	424,769
Education & Health	422,164
Leisure & hospitality	334,021
Other	95,884

Experienced civilian labor force by occupation, 2004

Management	175,000
Business & Financial	121,290
Legal	19,630
Sales	401,430
Office & Admin. Support	596,980
Computers & Math	79,880
Architecture & Engineering	52,680
Arts & Entertainment	32,770
Education	243,460
Social Services	47,690
Healthcare Practitioner & Technical	189,210
Healthcare support	112,830
Maintenance & Repair	171,620
Construction	170,250
Transportation & moving	302,440
Production	424,050
Farming, fishing & forestry	6,470

Hours and earnings of production workers on manufacturing payrolls, 2004

Average weekly hours	40.3
Average hourly earnings	$14.25
Average weekly earnings	$574.28

Average annual pay

2004	$34,791
change from 2003	3.7%

Household income

Median household income, three-year average, 2002-2004 .... $39,000

Personal income, 2004 ($ per capita)

In current dollars	$29,246
In constant (2000) dollars	$27,124

Poverty

Persons below poverty level, three-year average, 2002-2004 .... 14.8%

Federal individual income tax returns, 2003

Returns filed	3,680,813
Adjusted gross income ($1,000)	$157,402,225
Total income tax paid ($1,000)	$17,744,660

Economy, Business, Industry & Agriculture

Fortune 500 companies, 2005 14

Patents issued, 2004 2,075

Bankruptcy cases filed, 2004 37,700

Business firm ownership, 2002

Women-owned....................... 173,874
   Sales ($ mil) $26,743
Black-owned......................... 52,134
   Sales ($ mil) $3,680
Hispanic-owned....................... 9,047
   Sales ($ mil) $1,790
Asian-owned 13,711
   Sales ($ mil) $4,006
Amer. Indian/Alaska Native-owned 5,973
   Sales ($ mil) $592
Hawaiian/Pacific Isl.-owned............. 194
   Sales ($ mil) $17

Gross State Product, 2004 ($ mil)

Total Gross State Product $336,398
   Agriculture, forestry, fishing and
      hunting 3,546
   Mining.............................. 545
   Utilities........................... 6,354
   Construction 14,629
   Manufacturing, durable goods....... 25,312
   Manufacturing, non-durable goods ... 46,983
   Wholesale trade.................... 18,717
   Retail trade....................... 22,017
   Transportation & warehousing 8,132
   Information 10,707
   Finance & insurance................ 34,542
   Real estate, rental, leasing........ 32,848
   Professional and technical services.... 15,627
   Educational services................ 2,167
   Health care and social assistance..... 19,862
   Accommodation/food services........ 7,535
   Other services, except government 6,960
   Government....................... 42,924

Establishments, by major industry group, 2003

Total............................... 208,387
   Forestry, fishing & agriculture........... 985
   Mining.............................. 197
   Construction 25,460
   Manufacturing...................... 10,527
   Wholesale trade.................... 11,724
   Retail trade....................... 35,744
   Transportation & warehousing 5,579
   Information 3,232
   Finance & insurance................ 12,759
   Professional/scientific/technical 19,453
   Health care/social assistance 18,448
   Accommodation/food services........ 16,097

Annual payroll by major industry group, 2003

Total ($1,000) $104,552,297
   Forestry, fishing & agriculture....... 133,043
   Mining........................... 143,176
   Utilities........................ 1,276,559
   Construction 6,635,417
   Manufacturing.................. 20,024,261
   Wholesale trade.................. 7,130,353
   Retail trade..................... 8,781,179
   Transportation & warehousing 3,788,251
   Information 3,780,593
   Finance & insurance............. 9,849,937
   Professional/scientific/technical ... 8,219,268
   Health care/social assistance 14,440,303
   Accommodation/food services..... 3,476,467

Agriculture

Number of farms, 2004 52,000
Farm acreage, 2004
   Total......................... 9,000,000
   Acres per farm, 2004 173
Farm income, 2003 ($mil)
   Net farm income $1,629
   Debt/asset ratio 13.8
Farm marketings, 2003 ($mil)
Total................................ $6,916
   Crops............................. 2,759
   Livestock........................... 4,158

Principal commodities, in order by marketing receipts, 2003

      Hogs, broilers, greenhouse, tobacco

Federal economic activity in state

Expenditures, 2003
   Total ($ mil) $51,766
   Per capita $6,157
   Defense ($ mil)..................... 7,508
   Non-defense ($ mil) 44,259
Defense department, 2003
   Payroll ($ mil) $5,632
   Contract awards ($ mil).............. $2,091
   Grants ($ mil)......................... $68
   Homeland security grants ($1,000)
      2004 .... $65,392
      2005 .... $46,609

FDIC insured financial institutions, 2004

Number............................... 108
   Assets ($bil) $1,302.3
   Deposits ($bil) 163.9

Fishing, 2004

Catch (x 1,000 lbs)................... 136,444
Value ($1,000)...................... $77,138

Mining, 2004 ($ mil)

Total non-fuel mineral production $822
Percent of U.S. 1.9%

Construction, 2003 ($ mil)

Total contracts (including non-building) $18,853
  residential. 11,676
  non-residential 4,891

Establishments, receipts, payroll & employees, by major industry group, 2002

Mining 175
  Receipts ($1,000) $1,250,027
  Annual payroll ($1,000). $199,204
  Paid employees 4,152

Utilities 375
  Receipts ($1,000) . . . . NA
  Annual payroll ($1,000). $1,216,131
  Paid employees 20,515

Construction. 25,275
  Receipts ($1,000) $34,385,593
  Annual payroll ($1,000). $6,715,454
  Paid employees 225,444

Manufacturing 10,762
  Receipts ($1,000) $156,821,943
  Annual payroll ($1,000). $20,647,572
  Paid employees 623,333

Wholesale trade 11,913
  Receipts ($1,000) $104,331,152
  Annual payroll ($1,000). $7,245,997
  Paid employees 162,230

Retail trade 35,851
  Receipts ($1,000) $88,821,486
  Annual payroll ($1,000). $8,453,694
  Paid employees 435,421

Transportation 5,507
  Receipts ($1,000) $7,895,233
  Annual payroll ($1,000). $2,927,986
  Paid employees 96,013

Information. 3,150
  Receipts ($1,000) . . . . NA
  Annual payroll ($1,000). $3,436,808
  Paid employees 77,554

Finance & insurance 12,233
  Receipts ($1,000) . . . . NA
  Annual payroll ($1,000). $9,140,171
  Paid employees 176,945

Professional, scientific & technical 19,140
  Receipts ($1,000) $17,622,547
  Annual payroll ($1,000). $7,243,876
  Paid employees 157,745

Health care & social assistance 17,962
  Receipts ($1,000) $32,026,359
  Annual payroll ($1,000). $13,550,696
  Paid employees 421,111

Accommodation & food service 15,747
  Receipts ($1,000) $11,237,386
  Annual payroll ($1,000). $3,184,887
  Paid employees 281,788

Communication, Energy & Transportation

Communication

Daily newspapers, 2004 47
Households with computers, 2003 . . . . .58%
Households with internet access, 2003 . . . . . .51%

Energy

Electricity Consumption, 2001
  Total (trillion Btu) 2,591
  Per capita (million Btu) 316
By source of production (trillion Btu)
  Coal 757
  Natural gas 216
  Petroleum 950
  Nuclear electric power 395
  Hydroelectric power. 26
By end-use sector (trillion Btu)
  Residential 641
  Commercial 513
  Industrial 743
  Transportation 694
Electric energy, 2003
  Production (billion kWh) 127.6
  Net summer capability (million kW) 27.3
Gas utilities, 2003
  Customers (x1,000). 1,064
  Sales (trillion Btu). 145
  Revenues ($mil). $1,357
Nuclear plants, 2003 5

Transportation, 2004

Public Road & Street Mileage 102,666
  Urban. 24,680
  Rural 77,986
  Interstate. 1,046
Vehicle miles of travel per capita 11,222.0
Total motor vehicle registrations 6,198,470
  Automobiles. 3,657,863
  Buses 32,815
  Trucks 2,507,792
  Motorcycles 100,366
Licensed drivers 6,122,137
  19 years & under 208,101
Deaths from motor vehicle accidents 1,557

State Summary

Capital City. . . . . Bismarck
Governor. . . . . .John Hoeven
Dept 101
600 E Boulevard Ave
Bismarck, ND 58505
701-328-2200
Admitted as a state 1889
Area (square miles) 70,700
Population, 2004 (est.) 634,366
Largest City. . . . . Fargo
Population, 2004. 91,048
Personal income per capita, 2004
(in current dollars) $31,398
Gross state product ($ mil), 2004 . . . . . . $22,687

Leading industries by payroll, 2003

Health care/Social assistance, Retail trade,
Manufacturing

**Leading agricultural commodities by receipts,
2003**

Wheat, cattle, soybeans, barley

Geography & Environment

Total area (sq. mi.). 70,700
land 68,976
water 1,724

Federally-owned land, 2004 (acres) . . . 1,185,777
percent. 2.7%

Highest point. . . . . . . White Butte (Slope County)
elevation (feet) 3,506

Lowest point . . . . .Red River
elevation (feet) 750

General coastline (miles). 0

Tidal shoreline (miles). 0

Capital City. . . . . .Bismarck
Population 2000 55,532
Population 2004 56,619

Largest City. . . . . Fargo
Population 2000 90,599
Population 2004 91,048

Number of cities with over 100,000 population

1990 0
2000 0
2004 0

State park and recreation areas, 2003

Area (acres x 1,000). 17
Number of visitors (x 1,000) 1,134
Revenues (x 1,000). $776
percent of operating expenditures. 29.0%

National forest system land, 2004

Acres 1,106,000

Demographics and Characteristics of the Population

Population

1980 652,717
1990 638,800
2000 642,200
2004 (estimate). 634,366
persons per sq. mile of land. 9.2
2005 (projection). 635,468
Male 318,422
Female 317,046
2010 (projection) 636,623
2020 (projection) 630,112
2030 (projection) 606,566
Male. 306,858
Female. 299,708

Metropolitan and Non-Metro. area population

	Metro	Non-Metro
1980	234,000	418,000
1990	257,000	381,000
2000	284,000	358,000

Change in population, 2000-2004

Number . . . . -7,838
percent. . . . . -1.2%
Natural increase (births minus deaths). . . . 7,182
Net internal migration . . . . -17,742
Net international migration 3,023

Persons by age, 2004

Under 5 years 35,754
18 years and over 495,411
65 years and over 93,171
85 years and over 16,413

Persons by age, 2010 (projected)

Total. 636,623
Under 5 years 38,869
5 to 17 years 103,095
18 and over 494,659
21 and over 463,226
65 and over 97,108
85 and over 18,232
Median age 38.4

Race, 2004 (estimate)

One Race

White. 586,336
Black or African American 4,583
American Indian/Alaska Native. 33,032
Pacific Islander 245
Asian Indian. 1,158
Chinese 592
Filipino 947
Japanese 153
Korean 286
Vietnamese. 514
Two or more races. 6,020

Persons of Hispanic origin, 2004

Total Hispanic or Latino 6,936
Mexican............................. 5,159
Puerto Rican 218
Cuban 200
Other Hispanic or Latino 479

Marital status, 2000

Population 15 years & over 512,281
Never married 141,390
Married.......................... 290,976
Separated 3,586
Widowed.......................... 36,884
Divorced.......................... 39,958

Language spoken at home, 2000

Population 5 years & over 603,106
English only 565,130
Spanish 8,263
Other Indo-European languages 24,191
Asian/Pacific Island languages........ 1,933

Households & families, 2000

Households.......................... 257,152
with persons under 18 years 83,975
with persons over 65 years........... 63,607
persons per household 2.41
Families............................ 166,150
persons per family...................... 3
Married couples 137,433
Female householder,
no husband present................. 20,148
One-person households 75,420

Nativity, 2000

Number of persons born in state 465,667
percent of population 72.5%

Immigration & Naturalization, 2004

Immigrants admitted 578
Persons naturalized 267
Asylums granted .... NA
Asylums denied 0

Vital Statistics and Health

Marriages

2002 4,316
2003 4,562
2004 4,424

Divorces

2002 1,873
2003 1,860
2004 1,979

Births

2003 7,972
Birthrate (per 1,000)................... 12.6
Low birth weight (2,500g or less)........ 6.5%
To unmarried mothers................ 28.5%

2003, continued
White.............................. 6,893
Black.............................. 109
Hispanic 168
Asian/Pacific Islander 115
Amer. Indian/Alaska Native 858
2004 (preliminary).................... 8,189
Birthrate (per 1,000)................... 12.9
White.............................. 7,017
Black 96
Hispanic 167
Asian/Pacific Islander 101

Deaths

2002
All causes 5,892
rate per 100,000.................... 929.2
Heart disease 1,623
rate per 100,000.................... 255.9
Malignant neoplasms 1,293
rate per 100,000.................... 203.9
Cerebrovascular disease................. 469
rate per 100,000..................... 74.0
Chronic lower respiratory disease 322
rate per 100,000..................... 50.8
2003 6,095
rate per 100,000.................... 961.6
2004 (provisional) 5,603

Infant deaths

2003 (provisional) 57
rate per 1,000 .... 7.2
2004 (provisional) 40
rate per 1,000 .... 4.9

Abortions, 2000

Total................................ 1,000
rate per 1,000 women age 15-44.......... 9.9

Physicians, 2003

Total................................ 1,529
rate per 1,000 persons.................. 241

Nurses, 2001

Total................................ 6,460
rate per 1,000 persons................ 1,014

Community Hospitals, 2003

Number.............................. 40
Beds (x 1,000)......................... 3.6
Patients admitted (x 1,000) 88
Average daily census (x 1,000) 2.1
Average cost per day $859
Outpatient visits (x mil) 1.8

Disability status of population, 2004

5 to 20 years 7.3%
21 to 64 years 10.9%
65 years and over...................... 36.5%

Education

Educational attainment, 2004

Population over 25 years 409,258
    Less than 9th grade 22,426
    High school graduates only......... 118,306
    Bachelor's degree only 72,714
    Graduate or professional degree....... 25,469
    Less than 9th grade percent 5.5%
    High school graduate or more 89.5%
    College graduate or more.............. 25.2%
    Graduate or professional degree........ 6.2%

Public school enrollment, Fall 2002

Total................................. 104,225
    Kindergarten through grade 8 69,089
    Grades 9 through 12................. 35,136
Enrollment, 2005 (projected) 97,600

Graduating public high school seniors

2004 (estimate)....................... 7,790

SAT scores, 2005

Average verbal score 590
Average math score 605
Percent of graduates taking test 4%

Public school teachers, 2004

Total (x 1,000) 7.7
    Elementary (x 1,000)................. 5.2
    Secondary (x 1,000) 2.5
Average salary $35,400
    Elementary $35,800
    Secondary......................... $34,800

State receipts & expenditures for public schools, 2004

Revenue receipts ($mil).................. $847
Expenditures
Total ($mil).......................... $833
    Per capita $1,316
    Per pupil $7,112

Institutions of higher education, 2004

Total.................................. 21
    Public............................... 15
    Private 6

Enrollment in institutions of higher education, Fall, 2003

Total................................ 48,641
    Full-time men 18,856
    Full-time women.................... 18,477
    Part-time men 4,735
    Part-time women.................... 6,573

Minority enrollment in institutions of higher education, Fall, 2003

Black, non-hispanic...................... 661
Hispanic 444
Asian/Pacific Islander 451
American Indian/Alaska Native.......... 3,254

Earned degrees conferred, 2003

Bachelor's 4,882
Master's 928
First-professional...................... 180
Doctor's.............................. 90

State & local financial support for higher education, 2003-2004

Full-time equivalent enrollment (x 1,000) ...36.2
Appropriations per FTE................. $4,345
    as a percent of tax revenue............ 11.8%

Social Insurance & Welfare Programs

Social Security benefits & beneficiaries, 2004

Beneficiaries
    Total............................. 115,000
    Retired & dependents............... 82,000
    Survivors.......................... 19,000
    Disabled & dependents.............. 14,000
Annual benefit payments ($ mil)
    Total.............................. $1,125
    Retired & dependents............... $746
    Survivors........................... $251
    Disabled & dependents.............. $128
Average Monthly Benefit
    Retired & dependents............... $891
    Disabled & dependents.............. $840
    Widowed........................... $879

Medicare

Enrollment, 2001 (x 1,000) 103
    Payments ($ mil, est.) $600
Enrollment, 2003 (x 1,000) 103

Medicaid, 2002

Beneficiaries (x 1,000)..................... 70
Payments ($ mil) $423

State Children's Health Insurance, 2004

Enrollment (x 1,000)...................... 5.1
Expenditures ($ mil).................... $6.9

Persons without health insurance, 2003

Number (x 1,000)......................... 69
    percent........................... 10.9%
Number of children (x 1,000) 11
    percent of children 7.5%

Federal public aid

Temporary Assistance for Needy Families, 2004
Recipients (x 1,000)....................... 8
Families (x 1,000) 3

Supplemental Security Income, 2003
Recipients (x 1,000)....................... 8
Payments ($ mil) $32

Food Stamp Program, 2004

Participants (x 1,000) 41
Benefits ($ mil)........................... $40

Housing & Construction

Housing units

Total 2003 (estimate)	297,525
Total 2004 (estimate)	300,815
Seasonal or recreational use, 2003	16,000
Owner-occupied single-family, 2003	129,000
Median value	$81,796
Renter-occupied, 2003	80,000
Median rent	$456
Homeownership rate, 2003	68.7%
Homeownership rate, 2004	70.0%

New privately owned housing units, 2004

Number authorized (x 1,000)	4.0
Value ($ mil)	$434
Started 2005 (x 1,000, estimate)	3.4
Started 2006 (x 1,000, estimate)	3.3

Existing home sales

2002 (x 1,000)	12.3
2003 (x 1,000)	12.9
2004 (x 1,000)	14.5

Government & Elections

State Officials 2006

Governor (name/party/term expires)
John Hoeven
Republican - 12/08

Lieutenant Governor	Jack Dalrymple
Secretary of State	Al Jaeger
Attorney General	Wayne Stenehjem
Chief Justice	Gerald VandeWalle

Governorship

Minimum age	30
Length of term	4 years
Consecutive terms permitted	not specified
Who succeeds	Lt. Governor

State Legislature

Name	Legislative Assembly
Upper chamber	Senate
Number of members	47
Length of term	4 years
Party in majority, 2006	Republican
Lower chamber	House of Representatives
Number of members	94
Length of term	2 years
Party in majority, 2006	Republican

State Government Employees, 2004

Total	17,754
Payroll	$51,915,712

Local Government Employees, 2004

Total	23,130
Payroll	$71,091,984

Local Governments by Type, 2002

Total	2,735
County	53
Municipal	360
Township	1,332
School District	226
Special District	764

Voting age population, November 2004

Total	466,000
Male	228,000
Female	238,000
White	443,000
Black	3,000
Hispanic	6,000
Asian	

Presidential Election, 2004

Total Popular Vote	312,833
Kerry	111,052
Bush	196,651
Total Electoral Votes	3

Federal representation, 2006 (109th Congress)

Senator	Kent Conrad
Party	Democrat
Year term expires	2007
Senator	Byron Dorgan
Party	Democrat
Year term expires	2011
Representatives, total	1
Democrats	1
Republicans	0
Other	0

Votes cast for US Senators

2002

Total vote (x 1,000)	NA
Leading party	NA
Percent for leading party	NA

2004

Total vote (x 1,000)	311,000
Leading party	Democratic
Percent for leading party	68.3%

Votes cast for US Representatives

2002

Total vote (x 1,000)	231
Democratic	121
Republican	110
Leading party	Democratic
Percent for leading party	52.4%

2004

Total vote (x 1,000)	311
Democratic	185
Republican	126
Leading party	Democratic
Percent for leading party	59.6%

Women holding public office, 2006

US Congress 0
Statewide elected office. 2
State legislature 23

Black public officials, 2001

Total....................................... 0
   US and state legislatures 0
   City/county/regional offices 0
   Judicial/law enforcement.................. 0
   Education/school boards 0

Hispanic public officials, 2004

Total....................................... 1
   State executives & legislators 0
   City/county/regional offices 1
   Judicial/law enforcement.................. 0
   Education/school boards 0

Governmental Finance

State government revenues, 2004

Total revenue ($1,000) $5,228,053
   Revenue per capita 8,220.21

General Revenue ($ per capita) $4,987.47
   Intergovernmental 1,919.10
   Taxes 1,932.22
      general sales 577.52
      individual income tax............. 336.45
      corporate income tax 78.31
   Current charges..................... 811.74
   Miscellaneous 324.42

State government expenditure, 2004

Total expenditure (x $1,000) $3,197,884
   Expenditure per capita............. 5,028.12
General Expenditure ($ per capita).... $4,677.20
   Education 1,662.04
   Public welfare...................... 1,073.95
   Health 89.75
   Hospitals........................... 69.19
   Highways 605.59
   Police protection 21.80
   Correction 71.47
   Natural resources 210.52
   Parks & recreation................... 21.91
   Governmental administration 193.47
   Interest on general debt 120.30

State debt & cash, 2004 ($ per capita)

Debt $2,613.82
Cash/security holdings............. $11,480.72

Federal government grants to state & local government, 2004 (x $1,000)

Total.......................... $1,515,253

By Federal Agency
   Defense $38,007

By Federal Agency, continued
   Education 155,718
   Energy 15,731
   Environmental Protection Agency 28,740
   Health & Human Services. 555,679
   Homeland Security.................. 17,121
   Housing & Urban Development...... 104,802
   Justice 42,909
   Labor 24,315
   Transportation 241,130
   Veterans Affairs.................... 1,695

Crime, Law Enforcement & Courts

Crime, 2004 (rates per 100,000 residents)

Property crimes 12,158
   Burglaries........................... 1,910
   Larcenies........................... 9,342
   Motor vehicle thefts 906
   Property crime rate.................. 1,916.6
Violent crimes......................... 504
   Murders........................... 9
   Forcible rape....................... 159
   Robberies 39
   Aggravated assaults 297
   Violent crime rate 79.4

Police Agencies, 2004

Total agencies........................... 96
Total employees 1,614
   Male officers....................... 1,097
   Female officers 85
   Male civilians....................... 138
   Female civilians...................... 294

Arrests, 2004

Total............................... 26,010
   Persons under 18 years of age 6,396

Prisoners under state & federal jurisdiction, 2004

Total prisoners....................... 1,327
   Percent change, 12/31/03 to 12/31/04 .... 7.1%
Sentenced to more than one year 1,238
   rate per 100,000....................... 195

Persons under sentence of death, 7/1/05

Total.................................. 0
   White................................ 0
   Black 0
   Hispanic 0

State's highest court

Name ....Supreme Court
Number of members........................ 5
Length of term .... 10 years
Intermediate appeals court? .... no

Labor & Income

Civilian labor force, 2004

Total 359,000
  Men 189,000
  Women 170,000
  Persons 16-19 years................ 22,000
  White............................ 339,000
  Black 0
  Hispanic 0
  Asian 0

Civilian labor force as a percent of civilian non-institutional population, 2004

Total................................72.3%
  Men 77.1
  Women 67.6
  Persons 16-19 years................56.0
  White............................73.0
  Black 0.0
  Hispanic 0.0
  Asian 0.0

Employment, 2004

Total 347,000
  Men 181,000
  Women 166,000
  Persons 16-19 years................ 20,000
  White............................ 330,000
  Black 0
  Hispanic 0
  Asian 0

Full-time/part-time labor force, 2002

Full-time labor force, employed 266,000
Part-time labor force, employed 66,000
Unemployed, looking for
  Full-time work...................... 11,000
  Part-time work......................... NA

Unemployment rate, 2004

Total 3.4%
  Men 4.2
  Women 2.5
  Persons 16-19 years....................10.9
  White................................2.9
  Black .... NA
  Hispanic .... NA
  Asian .... NA

Unemployed by reason for unemployment (as a percent of total unemployment), 2002

Job losers or completed temp jobs .... NA
Job leavers............................... NA
Reentrants................................ NA
New entrants .... NA

Labor unions, 2004

Membership 22,000
  percent of employed 7.7%

Experienced civilian labor force by private industry, first quarter 2004

Total 247,669
  Natural Resources & Mining 5,550
  Construction 13,452
  Manufacturing...................... 23,526
  Trade, transportation & utilities 69,722
  Information 7,551
  Finance 18,139
  Professional & business 23,423
  Education & Health 45,909
  Leisure & hospitality................. 29,156
  Other............................. 11,241

Experienced civilian labor force by occupation, 2004

Management........................... 14,660
Business & Financial.................... 9,250
Legal................................. 1,560
Sales 35,500
Office & Admin. Support 54,080
Computers & Math 4,610
Architecture & Engineering 4,170
Arts & Entertainment................... 3,480
Education 20,940
Social Services 4,830
Healthcare Practitioner & Technical..... 18,170
Healthcare support 10,920
Maintenance & Repair 15,160
Construction 18,600
Transportation & moving 26,280
Production 20,230
Farming, fishing & forestry............. 4,510

Hours and earnings of production workers on manufacturing payrolls, 2004

Average weekly hours 39.3
Average hourly earnings $14.35
Average weekly earnings $563.96

Average annual pay

2004 .... $28,987
  change from 2003 .... 4.9%

Household income

Median household income, three-year average,
  2002-2004........................ $39,594

Personal income, 2004 ($ per capita)

In current dollars..................... $31,398
In constant (2000) dollars $29,120

Poverty

Persons below poverty level, three-year average,
  2002-2004......................... 10.3%

Federal individual income tax returns, 2003

Returns filed........................ 302,426
Adjusted gross income ($1,000) $11,284,748
Total income tax paid ($1,000) $1,257,603

Economy, Business, Industry & Agriculture

Fortune 500 companies, 2005 0

Patents issued, 2004 66

Bankruptcy cases filed, 2004 2,300

Business firm ownership, 2002

Women-owned. 13,203
  Sales ($ mil) $1,318
Black-owned. 78
  Sales ($ mil) $14
Hispanic-owned. 230
  Sales ($ mil) . . . . NA
Asian-owned 278
  Sales ($ mil) $176
Amer. Indian/Alaska Native-owned 853
  Sales ($ mil) $121
Hawaiian/Pacific Isl.-owned. . . . . NA
  Sales ($ mil) . . . . NA

Gross State Product, 2004 ($ mil)

Total Gross State Product $22,687
  Agriculture, forestry, fishing and
    hunting 1,112
  Mining. 512
  Utilities 644
  Construction 1,048
  Manufacturing, durable goods. 1,711
  Manufacturing, non-durable goods 655
  Wholesale trade. 1,813
  Retail trade. 1,728
  Transportation & warehousing 897
  Information 810
  Finance & insurance. 1,500
  Real estate, rental, leasing 1,840
  Professional and technical services 855
  Educational services 93
  Health care and social assistance 2,069
  Accommodation/food services. 565
  Other services, except government 535
  Government 3,626

Establishments, by major industry group, 2003

Total. 20,459
  Forestry, fishing & agriculture 155
  Mining. 167
  Construction 2,191
  Manufacturing. 714
  Wholesale trade. 1,445
  Retail trade. 3,460
  Transportation & warehousing 997
  Information 393
  Finance & insurance. 1,543
  Professional/scientific/technical 1,322
  Health care/social assistance 1,612
  Accommodation/food services. 1,759

Annual payroll by major industry group, 2003

Total ($1,000) $6,903,847
  Forestry, fishing & agriculture . . . . NA
  Mining. 221,847
  Utilities 205,965
  Construction 542,574
  Manufacturing. 725,889
  Wholesale trade. 551,196
  Retail trade. 789,161
  Transportation & warehousing 254,296
  Information 274,293
  Finance & insurance. 484,703
  Professional/scientific/technical 370,925
  Health care/social assistance 1,447,402
  Accommodation/food services. 259,481

Agriculture

Number of farms, 2004 30,000
Farm acreage, 2004
  Total. 39,000,000
  Acres per farm, 2004 1,300
Farm income, 2003 ($mil)
  Net farm income $1,315
  Debt/asset ratio .16.8
Farm marketings, 2003 ($mil)
  Total. $3,778
  Crops 2,907
  Livestock 870

Principal commodities, in order by marketing receipts, 2003

Wheat, cattle, soybeans, barley

Federal economic activity in state

Expenditures, 2003
  Total ($ mil) $5,726
  Per capita $9,033
  Defense ($ mil). 712
  Non-defense ($ mil) 5,014
Defense department, 2003
  Payroll ($ mil) $435
  Contract awards ($ mil) $280
  Grants ($ mil). $27
  Homeland security grants ($1,000)
    2004 . . . . $19,421
    2005 . . . . $14,376

FDIC insured financial institutions, 2004

Number 103
  Assets ($bil) $15.4
  Deposits ($bil) .11.4

Fishing, 2004

Catch (x 1,000 lbs) 0
Value ($1,000). 0

8　North Dakota

Mining, 2004 ($ mil)
Total non-fuel mineral production $52
Percent of U.S. 0.1%

Construction, 2003 ($ mil)
Total contracts (including non-building).　$1,102
　　residential............................ 413
　　non-residential 246

Establishments, receipts, payroll & employees,
**　by major industry group, 2002**

Mining................................. 777
　　Receipts ($1,000) $2,421,333
　　Annual payroll ($1,000)........... $435,731
　　Paid employees 10,825
Utilities 118
　　Receipts ($1,000) .... NA
　　Annual payroll ($1,000)........... $190,949
　　Paid employees 3,316
Construction......................... 2,021
　　Receipts ($1,000) $2,338,220
　　Annual payroll ($1,000)........... $516,797
　　Paid employees 16,864
Manufacturing 724
　　Receipts ($1,000) $6,856,653
　　Annual payroll ($1,000)........... $757,012
　　Paid employees 23,370
Wholesale trade 1,485
　　Receipts ($1,000) $8,806,340
　　Annual payroll ($1,000)........... $523,198
　　Paid employees 15,958
Retail trade........................... 3,433
　　Receipts ($1,000) $7,723,945
　　Annual payroll ($1,000)........... $729,605
　　Paid employees 41,342
Transportation 999
　　Receipts ($1,000) $1,021,195
　　Annual payroll ($1,000)........... $231,523
　　Paid employees 8,103
Information............................ 389
　　Receipts ($1,000) .... NA
　　Annual payroll ($1,000)........... $254,729
　　Paid employees 7,703
Finance & insurance 1,520
　　Receipts ($1,000) .... NA
　　Annual payroll ($1,000)........... $466,989
　　Paid employees 13,085
Professional, scientific & technical 1,309
　　Receipts ($1,000) $871,152
　　Annual payroll ($1,000)........... $353,641
　　Paid employees 10,972

Health care & social assistance 1,584
　　Receipts ($1,000) $3,027,796
　　Annual payroll ($1,000)......... $1,348,233
　　Paid employees 47,960
Accommodation & food service.......... 1,765
　　Receipts ($1,000) $854,656
　　Annual payroll ($1,000)........... $244,609
　　Paid employees 26,166

Communication, Energy & Transportation

Communication
Daily newspapers, 2004 10
Households with computers, 2003 ....61%
Households with internet access, 2003 ......53%

Energy
Electricity Consumption, 2001
Total (trillion Btu)...................... 407
Per capita (million Btu) 640
By source of production (trillion Btu)
　　Coal 420
　　Natural gas......................... 63
　　Petroleum........................... 138
　　Nuclear electric power 0
　　Hydroelectric power.................. 14
By end-use sector (trillion Btu)
　　Residential 61
　　Commercial 56
　　Industrial 203
　　Transportation 88
Electric energy, 2003
　　Production (billion kWh) 31.3
　　Net summer capability (million kW) 4.7
Gas utilities, 2003
　　Customers (x1,000)................... 126
　　Sales (trillion Btu)................... 24
　　Revenues ($mil)..................... $168
Nuclear plants, 2003 0

Transportation, 2004
Public Road & Street Mileage 86,782
　　Urban.............................. 1,846
　　Rural 84,936
　　Interstate 571
Vehicle miles of travel per capita........ 11,977.9
Total motor vehicle registrations........ 700,882
　　Automobiles........................ 347,009
　　Buses 2,645
　　Trucks 351,228
　　Motorcycles 20,953
Licensed drivers 461,780
　　19 years & under 35,384
Deaths from motor vehicle accidents 100

State Summary

Capital City. . . . . Columbus
Governor. . . . . .Bob Taft
30th Floor
77 South High St
Columbus, OH 43215
614-466-3555
Admitted as a state 1803
Area (square miles). 44,825
Population, 2004 (est.) 11,459,011
Largest City. . . . . Columbus
Population, 2004. 730,000
Personal income per capita, 2004
(in current dollars) $31,322
Gross state product ($ mil), 2004 . . . . . $419,866

Leading industries by payroll, 2003

Manufacturing, Health care/Social assistance,
Finance & Insurance

Leading agricultural commodities by receipts, 2003

Soybeans, corn, dairy products, greenhouse

Geography & Environment

Total area (sq. mi.). 44,825
land 40,948
water 3,877

Federally-owned land, 2004 (acres) 448,381
percent. 1.7%

Highest point. . . . . Campbell Hill
elevation (feet) 1,549

Lowest point . . . . Ohio River
elevation (feet) 455

General coastline (miles). 0

Tidal shoreline (miles). 0

Capital City. . . . . Columbus
Population 2000 711,000
Population 2004 730,000

Largest City. . . . . Columbus
Population 2000 711,000
Population 2004 730,000

Number of cities with over 100,000 population

1990 6
2000 6
2004 6

State park and recreation areas, 2003

Area (acres x 1,000). 164
Number of visitors (x 1,000) 57,238
Revenues (x 1,000). $29,501
percent of operating expenditures. 45.2%

National forest system land, 2004

Acres 237,000

Demographics and Characteristics of the Population

Population

1980 10,797,630
1990 10,847,115
2000 11,353,140
2004 (estimate). 11,459,011
persons per sq. mile of land. 279.8
2005 (projection) 11,477,557
Male. 5,590,659
Female. 5,886,898
2010 (projection) 11,576,181
2020 (projection) 11,644,058
2030 (projection) 11,550,528
Male. 5,669,284
Female. 5,881,244

Metropolitan and Non-Metro. area population

	Metro	Non-Metro
1980	8,521,000	2,277,000
1990	8,567,000	2,280,000
2000	9,214,000	2,139,000

Change in population, 2000-2004

Number. 105,866
percent. 0.9%
Natural increase (births minus deaths). . 172,340
Net internal migration . . . . -133,416
Net international migration 63,691

Persons by age, 2004

Under 5 years 730,035
18 years and over 8,679,799
65 years and over 1,524,916
85 years and over 208,433

Persons by age, 2010 (projected)

Total. 11,576,181
Under 5 years 760,100
5 to 17 years 1,984,331
18 and over 8,831,750
21 and over 8,350,612
65 and over 1,586,981
85 and over 247,148
Median age 38.1

Race, 2004 (estimate)

One Race
White. 9,768,243
Black or African American 1,362,446
American Indian/Alaska Native. 26,025
Pacific Islander 3,556
Asian Indian. 45,787
Chinese 37,687
Filipino 18,299
Japanese 9,537
Korean. 16,433
Vietnamese. 13,975
Two or more races. 139,647

2　Ohio

Persons of Hispanic origin, 2004

Total Hispanic or Latino 242,100
　Mexican........................... 106,858
　Puerto Rican 81,834
　Cuban 2,947
　Other Hispanic or Latino 26,940

Marital status, 2000

Population 15 years & over 8,952,721
　Never married 2,345,613
　Married......................... 4,870,280
　Separated 143,244
　Widowed........................... 635,643
　Divorced 948,988

Language spoken at home, 2000

Population 5 years & over 10,599,968
　English only 9,951,475
　Spanish 213,147
　Other Indo-European languages 296,816
　Asian/Pacific Island languages....... 84,658

Households & families, 2000

Households......................... 4,445,773
　with persons under 18 years 1,534,008
　with persons over 65 years........ 1,058,224
　persons per household 2.49
Families........................... 2,993,023
　persons per family.....................3.04
Married couples................... 2,285,798
Female householder,
　no husband present................ 536,878
One-person households 1,215,614

Nativity, 2000

Number of persons born in state 8,485,725
　percent of population................ 74.7%

Immigration & Naturalization, 2004

Immigrants admitted.................. 11,599
Persons naturalized 8,590
Asylums granted 192
Asylums denied 34

Vital Statistics and Health

Marriages

2002............................... 80,373
2003............................... 76,808
2004............................... 75,287

Divorces

2002............................... 45,955
2003............................... 42,626
2004............................... 40,770

Births

2003 149,679
　Birthrate (per 1,000)...................13.1
　Low birth weight (2,500g or less)........ 8.3%
　To unmarried mothers................ 36.2%

2003, continued
　White............................. 125,476
　Black 23,059
　Hispanic 5,444
　Asian/Pacific Islander 3,144
　Amer. Indian/Alaska Native............. 304

2004 (preliminary)................... 149,154
　Birthrate (per 1,000)....................13.0
　White............................. 121,516
　Black 23,910
　Hispanic 5,737
　Asian/Pacific Islander 3,418

Deaths

2002
All causes 109,766
　rate per 100,000...................... 961.1
Heart disease 31,388
　rate per 100,000......................274.8
Malignant neoplasms 25,173
　rate per 100,000......................220.4
Cerebrovascular disease................ 7,252
　rate per 100,000.......................63.5
Chronic lower respiratory disease 6,063
　rate per 100,000.......................53.1
2003 108,660
　rate per 100,000...................... 950.2
2004 (provisional) 105,776

Infant deaths

2003 (provisional) 1,162
　rate per 1,000 .... 7.8
2004 (provisional) 1,120
　rate per 1,000 .... 7.5

Abortions, 2000

Total............................... 40,000
　rate per 1,000 women age 15-44..........16.5

Physicians, 2003

Total............................... 29,153
　rate per 1,000 persons................... 255

Nurses, 2001

Total.............................. 103,870
　rate per 1,000 persons................. 912

Community Hospitals, 2003

Number.............................. 163
Beds (x 1,000)...........................33.0
Patients admitted (x 1,000) 1,458
Average daily census (x 1,000) 20.6
Average cost per day $1,504
Outpatient visits (x mil)..................30.0

Disability status of population, 2004

5 to 20 years 7.5%
21 to 64 years 13%
65 years and over 39.3%

Education

Educational attainment, 2004

Population over 25 years	7,381,159
Less than 9th grade	232,970
High school graduates only	2,762,098
Bachelor's degree only	1,105,969
Graduate or professional degree	617,310
Less than 9th grade percent	3.2%
High school graduate or more	88.1%
College graduate or more	24.6%
Graduate or professional degree	8.4%

Public school enrollment, Fall 2002

Total	1,838,285
Kindergarten through grade 8	1,283,795
Grades 9 through 12	554,490
Enrollment, 2005 (projected)	1,804,300

Graduating public high school seniors

2004 (estimate)	116,270

SAT scores, 2005

Average verbal score	539
Average math score	543
Percent of graduates taking test	29%

Public school teachers, 2004

Total (x 1,000)	117.8
Elementary (x 1,000)	80.6
Secondary (x 1,000)	37.2
Average salary	$47,500
Elementary	$47,500
Secondary	$47,400

State receipts & expenditures for public schools, 2004

Revenue receipts ($mil)	$18,546
Expenditures	
Total ($mil)	$19,065
Per capita	$1,667
Per pupil	$10,102

Institutions of higher education, 2004

Total	187
Public	61
Private	126

Enrollment in institutions of higher education, Fall, 2003

Total	620,351
Full-time men	186,389
Full-time women	229,357
Part-time men	79,454
Part-time women	125,151

Minority enrollment in institutions of higher education, Fall, 2003

Black, non-hispanic	63,569
Hispanic	10,801
Asian/Pacific Islander	11,981
American Indian/Alaska Native	3,523

Earned degrees conferred, 2003

Bachelor's	54,852
Master's	18,824
First-professional	3,089
Doctor's	1,858

State & local financial support for higher education, 2003-2004

Full-time equivalent enrollment (x 1,000)	378.7
Appropriations per FTE	$4,680
as a percent of tax revenue	6.0%

Social Insurance & Welfare Programs

Social Security benefits & beneficiaries, 2004

Beneficiaries	
Total	1,951,000
Retired & dependents	1,346,000
Survivors	311,000
Disabled & dependents	293,000
Annual benefit payments ($ mil)	
Total	$20,609
Retired & dependents	$13,480
Survivors	$4,275
Disabled & dependents	$2,854
Average Monthly Benefit	
Retired & dependents	$970
Disabled & dependents	$876
Widowed	$952

Medicare

Enrollment, 2001 (x 1,000)	1,705
Payments ($ mil, est.)	$10,700
Enrollment, 2003 (x 1,000)	1,727

Medicaid, 2002

Beneficiaries (x 1,000)	1,656
Payments ($ mil)	$9,186

State Children's Health Insurance, 2004

Enrollment (x 1,000)	220.2
Expenditures ($ mil)	$167.1

Persons without health insurance, 2003

Number (x 1,000)	1,362
percent	12.1%
Number of children (x 1,000)	236
percent of children	8.3%

Federal public aid

Temporary Assistance for Needy Families, 2004

Recipients (x 1,000)	186
Families (x 1,000)	85

Supplemental Security Income, 2003

Recipients (x 1,000)	244
Payments ($ mil)	$1,204

Food Stamp Program, 2004

Participants (x 1,000)	945
Benefits ($ mil)	$1,009

Housing & Construction

Housing units

Total 2003 (estimate)	4,923,098
Total 2004 (estimate)	4,966,746
Seasonal or recreational use, 2003	47,000
Owner-occupied single-family, 2003	2,727,000
Median value	$118,956
Renter-occupied, 2003	1,314,000
Median rent	$575
Homeownership rate, 2003	72.8%
Homeownership rate, 2004	73.1%

New privately owned housing units, 2004

Number authorized (x 1,000)	51.7
Value ($ mil)	$7,974
Started 2005 (x 1,000, estimate)	49.7
Started 2006 (x 1,000, estimate)	48.8

Existing home sales

2002 (x 1,000)	237.0
2003 (x 1,000)	253.1
2004 (x 1,000)	275.7

Government & Elections

State Officials 2006

Governor (name/party/term expires)
Bob Taft
Republican - 1/07

Lieutenant Governor	Bruce Johnson
Secretary of State	Kenneth Blackwell
Attorney General	Jim Petro
Chief Justice	Thomas Moyer

Governorship

Minimum age	not specified
Length of term	4 years
Consecutive terms permitted	2
Who succeeds	Lt. Governor

State Legislature

Name	General Assembly
Upper chamber	Senate
Number of members	33
Length of term	4 years
Party in majority, 2006	Republican
Lower chamber	House of Representatives
Number of members	99
Length of term	2 years
Party in majority, 2006	Republican

State Government Employees, 2004

Total	136,041
Payroll	$495,366,772

Local Government Employees, 2004

Total	487,185
Payroll	$1,618,514,587

Local Governments by Type, 2002

Total	3,636
County	88
Municipal	942
Township	1,308
School District	667
Special District	631

Voting age population, November 2004

Total	8,469,000
Male	4,037,000
Female	4,432,000
White	7,381,000
Black	895,000
Hispanic	209,000
Asian	73,000

Presidential Election, 2004

Total Popular Vote	5,627,908
Kerry	2,741,167
Bush	2,859,768
Total Electoral Votes	20

Federal representation, 2006 (109th Congress)

Senator	Mike DeWine
Party	Republican
Year term expires	2007
Senator	George Voinovich
Party	Republican
Year term expires	2011
Representatives, total	18
Democrats	6
Republicans	12
Other	0

Votes cast for US Senators

2002

Total vote (x 1,000)	NA
Leading party	NA
Percent for leading party	NA

2004

Total vote (x 1,000)	5,426,000
Leading party	Republican
Percent for leading party	63.8%

Votes cast for US Representatives

2002

Total vote (x 1,000)	3,158
Democratic	1,332
Republican	1,776
Leading party	Republican
Percent for leading party	56.2%

2004

Total vote (x 1,000)	5,184
Democratic	2,515
Republican	2,650
Leading party	Republican
Percent for leading party	51.1%

Women holding public office, 2006
US Congress 4
Statewide elected office 2
State legislature 26

Black public officials, 2001
Total 313
  US and state legislatures 20
  City/county/regional offices 217
  Judicial/law enforcement 28
  Education/school boards 48

Hispanic public officials, 2004
Total 5
  State executives & legislators 0
  City/county/regional offices 4
  Judicial/law enforcement 1
  Education/school boards 0

Governmental Finance

State government revenues, 2004
Total revenue ($1,000) $76,443,362
  Revenue per capita 6,676.28

General Revenue ($ per capita) $3,994.09
  Intergovernmental 1,298.73
  Taxes 1,962.93
    general sales 688.34
    individual income tax............. 760.28
    corporate income tax 92.63
  Current charges.................... 445.73
  Miscellaneous 286.71

State government expenditure, 2004
Total expenditure (x $1,000) $58,874,466
  Expenditure per capita.............. 5,141.87
General Expenditure ($ per capita).... $4,063.24
  Education 1,485.30
  Public welfare.................... 1,184.16
  Health 169.13
  Hospitals.........................137.96
  Highways 264.83
  Police protection 22.22
  Correction 136.08
  Natural resources 36.35
  Parks & recreation.......................9.88
  Governmental administration 169.64
  Interest on general debt 104.16

State debt & cash, 2004 ($ per capita)
Debt $1,937.41
Cash/security holdings............. $14,562.32

Federal government grants to state & local government, 2004 (x $1,000)
Total $16,513,740
By Federal Agency
  Defense $114,915

By Federal Agency, continued
  Education 1,267,074
  Energy........................ 40,443
  Environmental Protection Agency ... 157,598
  Health & Human Services. 10,696,462
  Homeland Security.................. 87,879
  Housing & Urban Development.... 1,348,263
  Justice 199,047
  Labor 315,626
  Transportation 1,224,484
  Veterans Affairs................... 16,732

Crime, Law Enforcement & Courts

Crime, 2004 (rates per 100,000 residents)
Property crimes 420,910
  Burglaries......................... 96,954
  Larcenies........................ 283,103
  Motor vehicle thefts 40,853
  Property crime rate................ 3,673.2
Violent crimes......................... 39,163
  Murders........................ 517
  Forcible rape..................... 4,646
  Robberies 17,543
  Aggravated assaults 16,457
  Violent crime rate....................341.8

Police Agencies, 2004
Total agencies............................ 536
Total employees 28,024
  Male officers..................... 17,636
  Female officers.................... 1,953
  Male civilians..................... 3,427
  Female civilians................... 5,008

Arrests, 2004
Total 271,838
  Persons under 18 years of age 47,954

Prisoners under state & federal jurisdiction, 2004
Total prisoners....................... 44,806
  Percent change, 12/31/03 to 12/31/04 .... 0.1%
Sentenced to more than one year 44,806
  rate per 100,000........................ 391

Persons under sentence of death, 7/1/05
Total 196
  White............................. 92
  Black 98
  Hispanic 2

State's highest court
Name ....Supreme Court
Number of members....................... 7
Length of term .... 6 years
Intermediate appeals court? ....yes

Labor & Income

Civilian labor force, 2004

Total	5,884,000
Men	3,105,000
Women	2,778,000
Persons 16-19 years	344,000
White	5,110,000
Black	599,000
Hispanic	156,000
Asian	95,000

Civilian labor force as a percent of civilian non-institutional population, 2004

Total	66.6%
Men	73.5
Women	60.4
Persons 16-19 years	52.4
White	66.7
Black	64.8
Hispanic	75.7
Asian	72.8

Employment, 2004

Total	5,514,000
Men	2,900,000
Women	2,613,000
Persons 16-19 years	287,000
White	4,833,000
Black	521,000
Hispanic	147,000
Asian	90,000

Full-time/part-time labor force, 2002

Full-time labor force, employed	4,387,000
Part-time labor force, employed	1,111,000
Unemployed, looking for	
Full-time work	272,000
Part-time work	59,000

Unemployment rate, 2004

Total	6.3%
Men	6.6
Women	5.9
Persons 16-19 years	16.3
White	5.4
Black	13.0
Hispanic	5.7
Asian	5.1

Unemployed by reason for unemployment (as a percent of total unemployment), 2002

Job losers or completed temp jobs	52.6%
Job leavers	NA
Reentrants	29.3
New entrants	NA

Labor unions, 2004

Membership	759,000
percent of employed	15.2%

Experienced civilian labor force by private industry, first quarter 2004

Total	4,441,062
Natural Resources & Mining	23,666
Construction	215,836
Manufacturing	820,361
Trade, transportation & utilities	1,013,000
Information	92,917
Finance	300,595
Professional & business	607,662
Education & Health	727,058
Leisure & hospitality	470,045
Other	167,907

Experienced civilian labor force by occupation, 2004

Management	208,880
Business & Financial	219,500
Legal	32,010
Sales	545,210
Office & Admin. Support	893,820
Computers & Math	98,440
Architecture & Engineering	93,780
Arts & Entertainment	54,560
Education	285,140
Social Services	62,690
Healthcare Practitioner & Technical	292,870
Healthcare support	164,290
Maintenance & Repair	220,940
Construction	NA
Transportation & moving	438,340
Production	572,870
Farming, fishing & forestry	11,190

Hours and earnings of production workers on manufacturing payrolls, 2004

Average weekly hours	41.7
Average hourly earnings	$18.47
Average weekly earnings	$770.20

Average annual pay

2004	$36,441
change from 2003	3.7%

Household income

Median household income, three-year average, 2002-2004	$44,160

Personal income, 2004 ($ per capita)

In current dollars	$31,322
In constant (2000) dollars	$29,049

Poverty

Persons below poverty level, three-year average, 2002-2004	10.8%

Federal individual income tax returns, 2003

Returns filed	5,444,137
Adjusted gross income ($1,000)	$227,753,519
Total income tax paid ($1,000)	$26,153,931

Economy, Business, Industry & Agriculture

Fortune 500 companies, 2005 30

Patents issued, 2004 3,417

Bankruptcy cases filed, 2004 90,900

Business firm ownership, 2002

Women-owned. 229,973
   Sales ($ mil) $32,324
Black-owned. 35,661
   Sales ($ mil) $3,618
Hispanic-owned. 7,107
   Sales ($ mil) $1,397
Asian-owned 13,750
   Sales ($ mil) $5,167
Amer. Indian/Alaska Native-owned 3,123
   Sales ($ mil) $500
Hawaiian/Pacific Isl.-owned . . . . NA
   Sales ($ mil) $32

Gross State Product, 2004 ($ mil)

Total Gross State Product $419,866
   Agriculture, forestry, fishing and
      hunting 1,930
   Mining. 1,322
   Utilities 9,009
   Construction 16,970
   Manufacturing, durable goods 56,984
   Manufacturing, non-durable goods . . . 27,649
   Wholesale trade. 25,288
   Retail trade. 29,639
   Transportation & warehousing 12,477
   Information 12,284
   Finance & insurance. 32,518
   Real estate, rental, leasing 44,588
   Professional and technical services 22,368
   Educational services 2,902
   Health care and social assistance 33,201
   Accommodation/food services. 9,173
   Other services, except government 10,207
   Government 46,370

Establishments, by major industry group, 2003

Total. 270,255
   Forestry, fishing & agriculture 363
   Mining. 746
   Construction 26,595
   Manufacturing. 17,082
   Wholesale trade. 15,629
   Retail trade. 41,702
   Transportation & warehousing 7,412
   Information 4,240
   Finance & insurance. 18,129
   Professional/scientific/technical 25,038
   Health care/social assistance 26,526
   Accommodation/food services. 22,800

Annual payroll by major industry group, 2003

Total ($1,000) $157,464,859
   Forestry, fishing & agriculture 42,265
   Mining. 416,792
   Utilities 2,024,259
   Construction 8,803,707
   Manufacturing. 34,972,296
   Wholesale trade. 9,926,732
   Retail trade. 12,060,771
   Transportation & warehousing 5,621,387
   Information 5,488,721
   Finance & insurance. 12,280,964
   Professional/scientific/technical . . 11,384,272
   Health care/social assistance 22,746,471
   Accommodation/food services. 4,582,605

Agriculture

Number of farms, 2004 77,000
Farm acreage, 2004
   Total. 15,000,000
   Acres per farm, 2004 189
Farm income, 2003 ($mil)
   Net farm income $1,470
   Debt/asset ratio 11
Farm marketings, 2003 ($mil)
Total. $4,662
   Crops 2,853
   Livestock 1,809

Principal commodities, in order by marketing receipts, 2003

Soybeans, corn, dairy products, greenhouse

Federal economic activity in state

Expenditures, 2003
   Total ($ mil) $69,902
   Per capita $6,113
   Defense ($ mil). 6,777
   Non-defense ($ mil) 63,124
Defense department, 2003
   Payroll ($ mil) $2,523
   Contract awards ($ mil) $4,326
   Grants ($ mil). $76
   Homeland security grants ($1,000)
      2004 . . . . $103,582
      2005 . . . . $77,823

FDIC insured financial institutions, 2004

Number 290
   Assets ($bil) $1,579.7
   Deposits ($bil) 200.2

Fishing, 2004

Catch (x 1,000 lbs) 3,877
Value ($1,000). $2,851

Mining, 2004 ($ mil)

Total non-fuel mineral production $1,090
Percent of U.S. 2.5%

Construction, 2003 ($ mil)

Total contracts (including non-building) $16,792
residential 8,193
non-residential 5,521

Establishments, receipts, payroll & employees, by major industry group, 2002

Mining 2,171
Receipts ($1,000) $9,123,846
Annual payroll ($1,000) $1,053,328
Paid employees 26,457

Utilities 602
Receipts ($1,000) . . . . NA
Annual payroll ($1,000) $1,892,953
Paid employees 25,055

Construction 26,855
Receipts ($1,000) $40,273,765
Annual payroll ($1,000) $9,171,095
Paid employees 257,396

Manufacturing 17,494
Receipts ($1,000) $243,903,865
Annual payroll ($1,000) $35,301,070
Paid employees 868,732

Wholesale trade 16,000
Receipts ($1,000) $166,446,529
Annual payroll ($1,000) $9,635,439
Paid employees 234,663

Retail trade 42,280
Receipts ($1,000) $119,778,409
Annual payroll ($1,000) $11,545,773
Paid employees 611,814

Transportation 7,459
Receipts ($1,000) $15,546,563
Annual payroll ($1,000) $5,381,792
Paid employees 160,945

Information 4,205
Receipts ($1,000) . . . . NA
Annual payroll ($1,000) $5,092,867
Paid employees 112,938

Finance & insurance 17,591
Receipts ($1,000) . . . . NA
Annual payroll ($1,000) $11,280,117
Paid employees 260,062

Professional, scientific & technical 24,960
Receipts ($1,000) $24,241,958
Annual payroll ($1,000) $11,189,346
Paid employees 239,849

Health care & social assistance 26,415
Receipts ($1,000) $50,262,849
Annual payroll ($1,000) $21,597,000
Paid employees 683,742

Accommodation & food service 22,663
Receipts ($1,000) $14,875,890
Annual payroll ($1,000) $4,259,470
Paid employees 418,855

Communication, Energy & Transportation

Communication

Daily newspapers, 2004 84
Households with computers, 2003 . . . . .59%
Households with internet access, 2003 . . . . . .53%

Energy

Electricity Consumption, 2001
Total (trillion Btu) 3,982
Per capita (million Btu) 350
By source of production (trillion Btu)
Coal 1,343
Natural gas 836
Petroleum 1,305
Nuclear electric power 162
Hydroelectric power 5
By end-use sector (trillion Btu)
Residential 892
Commercial 682
Industrial 1,429
Transportation 979
Electric energy, 2003
Production (billion kWh) 146.6
Net summer capability (million kW) 34.1
Gas utilities, 2003
Customers (x1,000) 2,225
Sales (trillion Btu) 299
Revenues ($mil) $2,723
Nuclear plants, 2003 2

Transportation, 2004

Public Road & Street Mileage 124,752
Urban 44,479
Rural 80,273
Interstate 1,574
Vehicle miles of travel per capita 9,743.8
Total motor vehicle registrations 10,636,290
Automobiles 6,452,386
Buses 41,936
Trucks 4,141,968
Motorcycles 298,652
Licensed drivers 7,675,007
19 years & under 387,606
Deaths from motor vehicle accidents 1,286

State Summary

Capital City...................Oklahoma City
Governor........................Brad Henry
Cap Building
2300 N Lincoln Blvd
Room 212
Oklahoma City, OK 73105
405-521-2342
Admitted as a state 1907
Area (square miles)................... 69,898
Population, 2004 (est.) 3,523,553
Largest City...................Oklahoma City
Population, 2004................... 528,000
Personal income per capita, 2004
(in current dollars) $28,089
Gross state product ($ mil), 2004 ..... $107,600

Leading industries by payroll, 2003

Manufacturing, Health care/Social assistance,
Retail trade

Leading agricultural commodities by receipts, 2003

Cattle, wheat, hogs, broilers

Geography & Environment

Total area (sq. mi.).................... 69,898
land 68,667
water 1,231
Federally-owned land, 2004 (acres) ... 1,586,148
percent............................. 3.6%
Highest point...................... Black Mesa
elevation (feet) 4,973
Lowest point .... Little River
elevation (feet) 289
General coastline (miles)..................... 0
Tidal shoreline (miles)........................ 0
Capital City...................Oklahoma City
Population 2000 506,000
Population 2004 528,000
Largest City...................Oklahoma City
Population 2000 506,000
Population 2004 528,000

Number of cities with over 100,000 population

1990 2
2000 2
2004 3

State park and recreation areas, 2003

Area (acres x 1,000)...................... 72
Number of visitors (x 1,000) 14,247
Revenues (x 1,000).................... $22,989
percent of operating expenditures...... 55.0%

National forest system land, 2004

Acres 400,000

Demographics and Characteristics of the Population

Population

1980 3,025,290
1990 3,145,585
2000 3,450,654
2004 (estimate)...................... 3,523,553
persons per sq. mile of land............51.3
2005 (projection)................... 3,521,379
Male........................... 1,734,960
Female.......................... 1,786,419
2010 (projection) 3,591,516
2020 (projection) 3,735,690
2030 (projection) 3,913,251
Male........................... 1,943,355
Female.......................... 1,969,896

Metropolitan and Non-Metro. area population

	Metro	Non-Metro
1980	1,724,000	1,301,000
1990	1,870,000	1,276,000
2000	2,098,000	1,352,000

Change in population, 2000-2004

Number............................. 72,899
percent............................. 2.1%
Natural increase (births minus deaths)... 62,216
Net internal migration .... -18,211
Net international migration 30,484

Persons by age, 2004

Under 5 years 242,240
18 years and over 2,663,683
65 years and over 464,440
85 years and over 54,305

Persons by age, 2010 (projected)

Total.......................... 3,591,516
Under 5 years 254,682
5 to 17 years 640,391
18 and over 2,696,443
21 and over 2,539,585
65 and over 494,966
85 and over 70,555
Median age 36.8

Race, 2004 (estimate)

One Race
White......................... 2,770,299
Black or African American 272,224
American Indian/Alaska Native...... 283,844
Pacific Islander 2,934
Asian Indian....................... 11,491
Chinese 5,299
Filipino 6,168
Japanese 4,686
Korean........................... 5,582
Vietnamese........................ 14,318
Two or more races.................... 140,406

Persons of Hispanic origin, 2004

Total Hispanic or Latino	218,775
Mexican	174,865
Puerto Rican	7,042
Cuban	241
Other Hispanic or Latino	22,302

Marital status, 2000

Population 15 years & over	2,717,552
Never married	608,732
Married	1,557,157
Separated	46,198
Widowed	190,229
Divorced	315,236

Language spoken at home, 2000

Population 5 years & over	3,215,719
English only	2,977,187
Spanish	141,060
Other Indo-European languages	36,892
Asian/Pacific Island languages	34,517

Households & families, 2000

Households	1,342,293
with persons under 18 years	479,275
with persons over 65 years	319,395
persons per household	2.49
Families	921,750
persons per family	3.02
Married couples	717,611
Female householder, no husband present	152,575
One-person households	358,560

Nativity, 2000

Number of persons born in state	2,158,827
percent of population	62.6%

Immigration & Naturalization, 2004

Immigrants admitted	3,506
Persons naturalized	1,765
Asylums granted	17
Asylums denied	8

Vital Statistics and Health

Marriages

2002	17,373
2003	19,613
2004	22,812

Divorces

2002	NA
2003	NA
2004	17,146

Births

2003	50,981
Birthrate (per 1,000)	14.5
Low birth weight (2,500g or less)	7.8%
To unmarried mothers	37.1%

2003, continued

White	39,578
Black	4,568
Hispanic	5,654
Asian/Pacific Islander	1,076
Amer. Indian/Alaska Native	5,263
2004 (preliminary)	51,283
Birthrate (per 1,000)	14.6
White	40,042
Black	4,705
Hispanic	6,007
Asian/Pacific Islander	1,134

Deaths

2002

All causes	35,502
rate per 100,000	1,016.2
Heart disease	11,230
rate per 100,000	321.4
Malignant neoplasms	7,474
rate per 100,000	213.9
Cerebrovascular disease	2,427
rate per 100,000	69.5
Chronic lower respiratory disease	1,988
rate per 100,000	56.9
2003	35,733
rate per 100,000	1,017.6
2004 (provisional)	34,648

Infant deaths

2003 (provisional)	378
rate per 1,000	7.4
2004 (provisional)	422
rate per 1,000	8.2

Abortions, 2000

Total	7,000
rate per 1,000 women age 15-44	10.1

Physicians, 2003

Total	6,034
rate per 1,000 persons	172

Nurses, 2001

Total	22,890
rate per 1,000 persons	660

Community Hospitals, 2003

Number	108
Beds (x 1,000)	11.0
Patients admitted (x 1,000)	450
Average daily census (x 1,000)	6.5
Average cost per day	$1,177
Outpatient visits (x mil)	5.5

Disability status of population, 2004

5 to 20 years	7.4%
21 to 64 years	17%
65 years and over	44.1%

Education

Educational attainment, 2004

Population over 25 years 2,225,209
  Less than 9th grade 118,629
  High school graduates only 712,476
  Bachelor's degree only 339,024
  Graduate or professional degree 155,975
  Less than 9th grade percent 5.3%
  High school graduate or more 85.2%
  College graduate or more 22.9%
  Graduate or professional degree 7.0%

Public school enrollment, Fall 2002

Total 624,548
  Kindergarten through grade 8 449,039
  Grades 9 through 12 175,509
Enrollment, 2005 (projected) 608,500

Graduating public high school seniors

2004 (estimate) 36,670

SAT scores, 2005

Average verbal score 570
Average math score 563
Percent of graduates taking test 7%

Public school teachers, 2004

Total (x 1,000) 39.2
  Elementary (x 1,000) 20.4
  Secondary (x 1,000) 18.8
Average salary $35,100
  Elementary $34,800
  Secondary $35,300

State receipts & expenditures for public schools, 2004

Revenue receipts ($mil) $4,343
Expenditures
Total ($mil) $4,078
  Per capita $1,163
  Per pupil $6,405

Institutions of higher education, 2004

Total 53
  Public 29
  Private 24

Enrollment in institutions of higher education, Fall, 2003

Total 221,797
  Full-time men 65,180
  Full-time women 78,399
  Part-time men 31,712
  Part-time women 46,506

Minority enrollment in institutions of higher education, Fall, 2003

Black, non-hispanic 18,345
Hispanic 6,927
Asian/Pacific Islander 4,493
American Indian/Alaska Native 20,081

Earned degrees conferred, 2003

Bachelor's 16,348
Master's 5,389
First-professional 1,082
Doctor's 416

State & local financial support for higher education, 2003-2004

Full-time equivalent enrollment (x 1,000) . . 133.4
Appropriations per FTE $4,872
  as a percent of tax revenue 9.9%

Social Insurance & Welfare Programs

Social Security benefits & beneficiaries, 2004

Beneficiaries
  Total 623,000
  Retired & dependents 420,000
  Survivors 96,000
  Disabled & dependents 107,000
Annual benefit payments ($ mil)
  Total $6,234
  Retired & dependents $3,993
  Survivors $1,198
  Disabled & dependents $1,043
Average Monthly Benefit
  Retired & dependents $916
  Disabled & dependents $880
  Widowed $894

Medicare

Enrollment, 2001 (x 1,000) 511
  Payments ($ mil, est.) $2,300
Enrollment, 2003 (x 1,000) 521

Medicaid, 2002

Beneficiaries (x 1,000) 631
Payments ($ mil) $2,238

State Children's Health Insurance, 2004

Enrollment (x 1,000) 100.8
Expenditures ($ mil) $46.1

Persons without health insurance, 2003

Number (x 1,000) 701
  percent 20.4%
Number of children (x 1,000) 154
  percent of children 17.9%

Federal public aid

Temporary Assistance for Needy Families, 2004
Recipients (x 1,000) 34
Families (x 1,000) 14

Supplemental Security Income, 2003
Recipients (x 1,000) 75
Payments ($ mil) $339

Food Stamp Program, 2004

Participants (x 1,000) 412
Benefits ($ mil) $398

4   Oklahoma

Housing & Construction

Housing units

Total 2003 (estimate)	1,557,993
Total 2004 (estimate)	1,572,756
Seasonal or recreational use, 2003	39,000
Owner-occupied single-family, 2003	749,000
Median value	$85,502
Renter-occupied, 2003	421,000
Median rent	$519
Homeownership rate, 2003	69.1%
Homeownership rate, 2004	71.1%

New privately owned housing units, 2004

Number authorized (x 1,000)	17.1
Value ($ mil)	$2,184
Started 2005 (x 1,000, estimate)	14.3
Started 2006 (x 1,000, estimate)	14.2

Existing home sales

2002 (x 1,000)	79.5
2003 (x 1,000)	85.1
2004 (x 1,000)	93.6

Government & Elections

State Officials 2006

Governor (name/party/term expires)
Brad Henry
Democrat - 1/07

Lieutenant Governor	Mary Fallin
Secretary of State	Susan Savage
Attorney General	Drew Edmondson
Chief Justice	Joseph Watt

Governorship

Minimum age	31
Length of term	4 years
Consecutive terms permitted	2
Who succeeds	Lt. Governor

State Legislature

Name	Legislature
Upper chamber	Senate
Number of members	48
Length of term	4 years
Party in majority, 2006	Democratic
Lower chamber	House of Representatives
Number of members	101
Length of term	2 years
Party in majority, 2006	Republican

State Government Employees, 2004

Total	64,094
Payroll	$193,697,423

Local Government Employees, 2004

Total	136,845
Payroll	$337,707,406

Local Governments by Type, 2002

Total	1,798
County	77
Municipal	590
Township	0
School District	571
Special District	560

Voting age population, November 2004

Total	2,602,000
Male	1,247,000
Female	1,355,000
White	2,031,000
Black	190,000
Hispanic	135,000
Asian	34,000

Presidential Election, 2004

Total Popular Vote	1,463,758
Kerry	503,966
Bush	959,792
Total Electoral Votes	7

Federal representation, 2006 (109th Congress)

Senator	James Inhofe
Party	Republican
Year term expires	2009
Senator	Tom Coburn
Party	Republican
Year term expires	2011
Representatives, total	5
Democrats	1
Republicans	4
Other	0

Votes cast for US Senators

2002

Total vote (x 1,000)	1,018,000
Leading party	Republican
Percent for leading party	57.3%

2004

Total vote (x 1,000)	1,447,000
Leading party	Republican
Percent for leading party	52.8%

Votes cast for US Representatives

2002

Total vote (x 1,000)	1,002
Democratic	392
Republican	547
Leading party	Republican
Percent for leading party	54.6%

2004

Total vote (x 1,000)	1,375
Democratic	389
Republican	875
Leading party	Republican
Percent for leading party	63.7%

Women holding public office, 2006

US Congress 0
Statewide elected office 4
State legislature 22

Black public officials, 2001

Total 105
　US and state legislatures 6
　City/county/regional offices 75
　Judicial/law enforcement 3
　Education/school boards 21

Hispanic public officials, 2004

Total 1
　State executives & legislators 0
　City/county/regional offices 0
　Judicial/law enforcement 0
　Education/school boards 1

Governmental Finance

State government revenues, 2004

Total revenue ($1,000) $17,520,326
　Revenue per capita 4,971.72

General Revenue ($ per capita) $3,887.66
　Intergovernmental 1,295.58
　Taxes 1,823.70
　　general sales 452.40
　　individual income tax 658.09
　　corporate income tax 37.83
　Current charges 478.46
　Miscellaneous 289.91

State government expenditure, 2004

Total expenditure (x $1,000) $14,914,919
　Expenditure per capita 4,232.38
General Expenditure ($ per capita) $3,711.20
　Education 1,587.42
　Public welfare 1,003.17
　Health 140.58
　Hospitals 43.80
　Highways 298.13
　Police protection 29.17
　Correction 142.17
　Natural resources 58.22
　Parks & recreation 21.92
　Governmental administration 162.25
　Interest on general debt 81.33

State debt & cash, 2004 ($ per capita)

Debt $1,966.54
Cash/security holdings $8,023.11

Federal government grants to state & local government, 2004 (x $1,000)

Total $5,270,581
By Federal Agency
　Defense $19,271

By Federal Agency, continued

Education 556,138
Energy 9,681
Environmental Protection Agency 65,391
Health & Human Services 2,906,542
Homeland Security 35,493
Housing & Urban Development 429,291
Justice 82,389
Labor 78,151
Transportation 567,799
Veterans Affairs 26,379

Crime, Law Enforcement & Courts

Crime, 2004 (rates per 100,000 residents)

Property crimes 149,472
　Burglaries 35,244
　Larcenies 101,271
　Motor vehicle thefts 12,957
　Property crime rate 4,242.1
Violent crimes 17,635
　Murders 186
　Forcible rape 1,557
　Robberies 3,090
　Aggravated assaults 12,802
　Violent crime rate 500.5

Police Agencies, 2004

Total agencies 298
Total employees 10,446
　Male officers 6,478
　Female officers 519
　Male civilians 1,387
　Female civilians 2,062

Arrests, 2004

Total 158,957
　Persons under 18 years of age 23,128

Prisoners under state & federal jurisdiction, 2004

Total prisoners 23,319
　Percent change, 12/31/03 to 12/31/04 .... 2.2%
Sentenced to more than one year 22,913
　rate per 100,000 649

Persons under sentence of death, 7/1/05

Total 97
　White 51
　Black 38
　Hispanic 2

State's highest court

Name .... Supreme Court*
Number of members 9
Length of term .... 6 years
Intermediate appeals court? .... yes

6   Oklahoma

Labor & Income

Civilian labor force, 2004

Total	1,714,000
Men	915,000
Women	798,000
Persons 16-19 years	89,000
White	1,358,000
Black	125,000
Hispanic	70,000
Asian	0

Civilian labor force as a percent of civilian non-institutional population, 2004

Total	64.2%
Men	71.3
Women	57.6
Persons 16-19 years	47.3
White	64.4
Black	63.2
Hispanic	72.5
Asian	0.0

Employment, 2004

Total	1,630,000
Men	874,000
Women	756,000
Persons 16-19 years	79,000
White	1,302,000
Black	116,000
Hispanic	67,000
Asian	0

Full-time/part-time labor force, 2002

Full-time labor force, employed	1,338,000
Part-time labor force, employed	279,000
Unemployed, looking for	
Full-time work	64,000
Part-time work	NA

Unemployment rate, 2004

Total	4.9%
Men	4.5
Women	5.3
Persons 16-19 years	12.2
White	4.1
Black	7.2
Hispanic	4.6
Asian	NA

Unemployed by reason for unemployment (as a percent of total unemployment), 2002

Job losers or completed temp jobs	52.6%
Job leavers	NA
Reentrants	NA
New entrants	NA

Labor unions, 2004

Membership	86,000
percent of employed	6.1%

Experienced civilian labor force by private industry, first quarter 2004

Total	1,115,747
Natural Resources & Mining	36,972
Construction	61,267
Manufacturing	141,011
Trade, transportation & utilities	274,114
Information	31,641
Finance	78,816
Professional & business	156,478
Education & Health	171,765
Leisure & hospitality	126,371
Other	36,513

Experienced civilian labor force by occupation, 2004

Management	76,460
Business & Financial	51,620
Legal	10,610
Sales	144,390
Office & Admin. Support	257,420
Computers & Math	23,020
Architecture & Engineering	22,600
Arts & Entertainment	13,660
Education	95,010
Social Services	19,430
Healthcare Practitioner & Technical	77,500
Healthcare support	44,530
Maintenance & Repair	69,090
Construction	70,700
Transportation & moving	100,250
Production	119,650
Farming, fishing & forestry	6,430

Hours and earnings of production workers on manufacturing payrolls, 2004

Average weekly hours	40.4
Average hourly earnings	$14.25
Average weekly earnings	$575.70

Average annual pay

2004	$30,743
change from 2003	3.5%

Household income

Median household income, three-year average, 2002-2004	$38,281

Personal income, 2004 ($ per capita)

In current dollars	$28,089
In constant (2000) dollars	$26,051

Poverty

Persons below poverty level, three-year average, 2002-2004	12.6%

Federal individual income tax returns, 2003

Returns filed	1,460,943
Adjusted gross income ($1,000)	$56,019,101
Total income tax paid ($1,000)	$6,264,064

Economy, Business, Industry & Agriculture

Fortune 500 companies, 2005 5

Patents issued, 2004 490

Bankruptcy cases filed, 2004 27,200

Business firm ownership, 2002

Women-owned. 75,029
   Sales ($ mil) $9,255
Black-owned. 7,443
   Sales ($ mil) $481
Hispanic-owned. 5,442
   Sales ($ mil) $1,140
Asian-owned 4,610
   Sales ($ mil) $946
Amer. Indian/Alaska Native-owned 17,112
   Sales ($ mil) $2,531
Hawaiian/Pacific Isl.-owned. 304
   Sales ($ mil) $10

Gross State Product, 2004 ($ mil)

Total Gross State Product $107,600
   Agriculture, forestry, fishing and
      hunting 1,842
   Mining. 6,876
   Utilities 2,710
   Construction 4,429
   Manufacturing, durable goods. 7,337
   Manufacturing, non-durable goods 4,644
   Wholesale trade. 5,586
   Retail trade. 8,405
   Transportation & warehousing 3,448
   Information 4,423
   Finance & insurance. 5,739
   Real estate, rental, leasing 10,494
   Professional and technical services. 4,878
   Educational services. 559
   Health care and social assistance. 7,518
   Accommodation/food services. 2,499
   Other services, except government 2,776
   Government. 18,229

Establishments, by major industry group, 2003

Total. 86,014
   Forestry, fishing & agriculture 199
   Mining. 2,175
   Construction 7,886
   Manufacturing. 3,946
   Wholesale trade. 4,673
   Retail trade. 13,856
   Transportation & warehousing 2,455
   Information 1,545
   Finance & insurance. 5,990
   Professional/scientific/technical 8,504
   Health care/social assistance 9,129
   Accommodation/food services. 6,464

Annual payroll by major industry group, 2003

Total ($1,000) $33,555,356
   Forestry, fishing & agriculture 30,383
   Mining. 1,341,037
   Utilities 542,067
   Construction 1,746,609
   Manufacturing. 5,168,240
   Wholesale trade. 1,966,004
   Retail trade. 3,165,497
   Transportation & warehousing 1,458,700
   Information 1,452,136
   Finance & insurance. 2,212,464
   Professional/scientific/technical . . . 2,522,147
   Health care/social assistance 5,111,824
   Accommodation/food services. 1,160,851

Agriculture

Number of farms, 2004 84,000
Farm acreage, 2004
   Total. 34,000,000
   Acres per farm, 2004 404
Farm income, 2003 ($mil)
   Net farm income $2,037
   Debt/asset ratio 15.6
Farm marketings, 2003 ($mil)
   Total. $4,526
   Crops 1,022
   Livestock. 3,504

Principal commodities, in order by marketing receipts, 2003

Cattle, wheat, hogs, broilers

Federal economic activity in state

Expenditures, 2003
   Total ($ mil) $25,254
   Per capita $7,192
   Defense ($ mil). 3,986
   Non-defense ($ mil) 21,268
Defense department, 2003
   Payroll ($ mil) $2,671
   Contract awards ($ mil) $1,515
   Grants ($ mil). $11
   Homeland security grants ($1,000)
      2004 . . . . $32,824
      2005 . . . . $29,974

FDIC insured financial institutions, 2004

Number. 274
   Assets ($bil) $56.4
   Deposits ($bil) 46.3

Fishing, 2004

Catch (x 1,000 lbs). 0
Value ($1,000). 0

8   Oklahoma

Mining, 2004 ($ mil)
Total non-fuel mineral production $498
Percent of U.S. 1.1%

Construction, 2003 ($ mil)
Total contracts (including non-building). $5,099
    residential............................ 2,537
    non-residential 1,675

Establishments, receipts, payroll & employees, by major industry group, 2002

Mining 152
    Receipts ($1,000) $270,239
    Annual payroll ($1,000)............. $61,768
    Paid employees 1,616

Utilities 413
    Receipts ($1,000) .... NA
    Annual payroll ($1,000)........... $506,937
    Paid employees 9,677

Construction.......................... 7,797
    Receipts ($1,000) $9,590,154
    Annual payroll ($1,000)......... $1,836,310
    Paid employees 62,684

Manufacturing 4,027
    Receipts ($1,000)............... $39,924,050
    Annual payroll ($1,000)......... $5,355,937
    Paid employees 149,983

Wholesale trade 4,770
    Receipts ($1,000) $30,799,789
    Annual payroll ($1,000)......... $1,886,831
    Paid employees 54,701

Retail trade 13,922
    Receipts ($1,000) $32,112,960
    Annual payroll ($1,000)......... $2,997,665
    Paid employees 167,949

Transportation....................... 2,398
    Receipts ($1,000) $4,649,332
    Annual payroll ($1,000)......... $1,100,325
    Paid employees 35,473

Information.......................... 1,489
    Receipts ($1,000) .... NA
    Annual payroll ($1,000).......... $1,477,701
    Paid employees 36,415

Finance & insurance 5,792
    Receipts ($1,000) .... NA
    Annual payroll ($1,000)......... $2,031,403
    Paid employees 55,768

Professional, scientific & technical 8,376
    Receipts ($1,000) $5,833,528
    Annual payroll ($1,000)......... $2,252,265
    Paid employees 58,630

Health care & social assistance 9,016
    Receipts ($1,000) $12,432,870
    Annual payroll ($1,000).......... $4,935,757
    Paid employees 177,152

Accommodation & food service........... 6,506
    Receipts ($1,000) $3,901,754
    Annual payroll ($1,000).......... $1,113,389
    Paid employees 111,156

Communication, Energy & Transportation

Communication
Daily newspapers, 2004 42
Households with computers, 2003 .... 55%
Households with internet access, 2003 ..... 48%

Energy
Electricity Consumption, 2001
Total (trillion Btu)...................... 1,540
Per capita (million Btu) 444
By source of production (trillion Btu)
    Coal 377
    Natural gas 548
    Petroleum............................ 588
    Nuclear electric power 0
    Hydroelectric power 23
By end-use sector (trillion Btu)
    Residential 298
    Commercial 233
    Industrial 544
    Transportation 466
Electric energy, 2003
    Production (billion kWh) 60.6
    Net summer capability (million kW) 18.2
Gas utilities, 2003
    Customers (x1,000).................... 953
    Sales (trillion Btu).................. 109
    Revenues ($mil)...................... $882
Nuclear plants, 2003 0

Transportation, 2004
Public Road & Street Mileage 112,713
    Urban............................... 15,113
    Rural 97,600
    Interstate.......................... 931
Vehicle miles of travel per capita....... 13,450.0
Total motor vehicle registrations...... 3,150,989
    Automobiles........................ 1,634,376
    Buses 17,958
    Trucks 1,498,655
    Motorcycles 84,651
Licensed drivers 2,369,621
    19 years & under 153,821
Deaths from motor vehicle accidents 774

State Summary

Capital City............................Salem
Governor.....................Ted Kulongoski

State Capitol
Room 160
900 Court St N
Salem, OR 97301
503-378-4582

Admitted as a state 1859
Area (square miles)................... 98,381
Population, 2004 (est.) 3,594,586
Largest City...................... Portland
  Population, 2004 533,000
Personal income per capita, 2004
  (in current dollars) $29,971
Gross state product ($ mil), 2004...... $128,103

Leading industries by payroll, 2003

Manufacturing, Health care/Social assistance,
Retail trade

Leading agricultural commodities by receipts, 2003

Greenhouse, cattle, dairy products, hay

Geography & Environment

Total area (sq. mi.).................... 98,381
  land 95,997
  water 2,384
Federally-owned land, 2004 (acres) .. 32,715,514
  percent............................ 53.1%
Highest point.......................Mt. Hood
  elevation (feet) 11,239
Lowest point .... Pacific Ocean
  elevation (feet) .... sea level
General coastline (miles).................... 26
Tidal shoreline (miles).................... 1,410
Capital City...........................Salem
  Population 2000 137,000
  Population 2004 146,000
Largest City........................ Portland
  Population 2000 529,000
  Population 2004 533,000

Number of cities with over 100,000 population

1990 3
2000 3
2004 3

State park and recreation areas, 2003

Area (acres x 1,000)....................... 95
Number of visitors (x 1,000) 39,244
Revenues (x 1,000).................... $15,414
  percent of operating expenditures...... 37.2%

National forest system land, 2004

Acres 15,667,000

Demographics and Characteristics of the Population

Population

1980 2,633,105
1990 2,842,321
2000 3,421,399
2004 (estimate)..................... 3,594,586
  persons per sq. mile of land.............37.4
2005 (projection)................... 3,596,083
  Male....................... 1,785,805
  Female....................... 1,810,278
2010 (projection) 3,790,996
2020 (projection) 4,260,393
2030 (projection) 4,833,918
  Male....................... 2,390,316
  Female....................... 2,443,602

Metropolitan and Non-Metro. area population

	Metro	Non-Metro
1980	1,763,000	870,000
1990	1,947,000	895,000
2000	2,502,000	919,000

Change in population, 2000-2004

Number 173,150
  percent............................. 5.1%
Natural increase (births minus deaths)... 60,566
Net internal migration 52,944
Net international migration 61,482

Persons by age, 2004

Under 5 years 226,069
18 years and over 2,742,229
65 years and over 459,821
85 years and over 69,898

Persons by age, 2010 (projected)

Total............................. 3,790,996
  Under 5 years 249,899
  5 to 17 years 613,267
  18 and over 2,927,830
  21 and over 2,780,260
  65 and over 494,328
  85 and over 80,959
  Median age 37.6

Race, 2004 (estimate)

One Race
  White........................... 3,266,596
  Black or African American 64,117
  American Indian/Alaska Native....... 49,138
  Pacific Islander 9,630
  Asian Indian....................... 8,795
  Chinese 23,958
  Filipino 15,426
  Japanese 12,531
  Korean......................... 12,424
  Vietnamese....................... 28,426
Two or more races..................... 83,225

2   Oregon

Persons of Hispanic origin, 2004

Total Hispanic or Latino	336,925
Mexican	271,916
Puerto Rican	7,614
Cuban	3,491
Other Hispanic or Latino	33,047

Marital status, 2000

Population 15 years & over	2,722,134
Never married	683,256
Married	1,510,784
Separated	46,276
Widowed	166,050
Divorced	315,768

Language spoken at home, 2000

Population 5 years & over	3,199,323
English only	2,810,654
Spanish	217,614
Other Indo-European languages	82,828
Asian/Pacific Island languages	75,279

Households & families, 2000

Households	1,333,723
with persons under 18 years	445,764
with persons over 65 years	305,475
persons per household	2.51
Families	877,671
persons per family	3.02
Married couples	692,532
Female householder, no husband present	130,782
One-person households	347,624

Nativity, 2000

Number of persons born in state	1,549,044
percent of population	45.3%

Immigration & Naturalization, 2004

Immigrants admitted	8,389
Persons naturalized	3,612
Asylums granted	77
Asylums denied	11

Vital Statistics and Health

Marriages

2002	24,979
2003	25,565
2004	29,040

Divorces

2002	16,146
2003	15,359
2004	14,774

Births

2003	45,953
Birthrate (per 1,000)	12.9
Low birth weight (2,500g or less)	6.1%
To unmarried mothers	31.7%

2003, continued

White	41,590
Black	1,024
Hispanic	8,440
Asian/Pacific Islander	2,493
Amer. Indian/Alaska Native	868
2004 (preliminary)	45,693
Birthrate (per 1,000)	12.7
White	41,251
Black	1,057
Hispanic	8,836
Asian/Pacific Islander	2,510

Deaths

2002

All causes	31,119
rate per 100,000	883.7
Heart disease	7,262
rate per 100,000	206.2
Malignant neoplasms	7,249
rate per 100,000	205.8
Cerebrovascular disease	2,645
rate per 100,000	75.1
Chronic lower respiratory disease	1,845
rate per 100,000	52.4
2003	30,934
rate per 100,000	869.0
2004 (provisional)	30,306

Infant deaths

2003 (provisional)	270
rate per 1,000	5.9
2004 (provisional)	250
rate per 1,000	5.5

Abortions, 2000

Total	17,000
rate per 1,000 women age 15-44	23.5

Physicians, 2003

Total	9,342
rate per 1,000 persons	262

Nurses, 2001

Total	26,040
rate per 1,000 persons	750

Community Hospitals, 2003

Number	58
Beds (x 1,000)	6.8
Patients admitted (x 1,000)	342
Average daily census (x 1,000)	4.0
Average cost per day	$1,842
Outpatient visits (x mil)	8.2

Disability status of population, 2004

5 to 20 years	7.3%
21 to 64 years	14%
65 years and over	41.1%

Education

Educational attainment, 2004

Population over 25 years	2,340,584
Less than 9th grade	105,751
High school graduates only	616,024
Bachelor's degree only	414,699
Graduate or professional degree	233,456
Less than 9th grade percent	4.5%
High school graduate or more	87.4%
College graduate or more	25.9%
Graduate or professional degree	10.0%

Public school enrollment, Fall 2002

Total	554,071
Kindergarten through grade 8	382,005
Grades 9 through 12	172,066
Enrollment, 2005 (projected)	555,700

Graduating public high school seniors

2004 (estimate)	32,530

SAT scores, 2005

Average verbal score	526
Average math score	528
Percent of graduates taking test	59%

Public school teachers, 2004

Total (x 1,000)	27.7
Elementary (x 1,000)	17.8
Secondary (x 1,000)	9.9
Average salary	$49,200
Elementary	$49,200
Secondary	$49,200

State receipts & expenditures for public schools, 2004

Revenue receipts ($mil)	$4,402
Expenditures	
Total ($mil)	$4,934
Per capita	$1,384
Per pupil	$8,575

Institutions of higher education, 2004

Total	59
Public	26
Private	33

Enrollment in institutions of higher education, Fall, 2003

Total	202,346
Full-time men	55,975
Full-time women	67,326
Part-time men	33,849
Part-time women	45,196

Minority enrollment in institutions of higher education, Fall, 2003

Black, non-hispanic	3,794
Hispanic	8,692
Asian/Pacific Islander	11,164
American Indian/Alaska Native	2,838

Earned degrees conferred, 2003

Bachelor's	15,601
Master's	5,622
First-professional	1,074
Doctor's	499

State & local financial support for higher education, 2003-2004

Full-time equivalent enrollment (x 1,000)	124.4
Appropriations per FTE	$4,772
as a percent of tax revenue	6.8%

Social Insurance & Welfare Programs

Social Security benefits & beneficiaries, 2004

Beneficiaries	
Total	611,000
Retired & dependents	445,000
Survivors	77,000
Disabled & dependents	90,000
Annual benefit payments ($ mil)	
Total	$6,437
Retired & dependents	$4,458
Survivors	$1,063
Disabled & dependents	$916
Average Monthly Benefit	
Retired & dependents	$964
Disabled & dependents	$894
Widowed	$967

Medicare

Enrollment, 2001 (x 1,000)	496
Payments ($ mil, est.)	$2,200
Enrollment, 2003 (x 1,000)	513

Medicaid, 2002

Beneficiaries (x 1,000)	621
Payments ($ mil)	$2,136

State Children's Health Insurance, 2004

Enrollment (x 1,000)	46.7
Expenditures ($ mil)	$25.3

Persons without health insurance, 2003

Number (x 1,000)	613
percent	17.2%
Number of children (x 1,000)	113
percent of children	13.5%

Federal public aid

Temporary Assistance for Needy Families, 2004	
Recipients (x 1,000)	42
Families (x 1,000)	19
Supplemental Security Income, 2003	
Recipients (x 1,000)	57
Payments ($ mil)	$271

Food Stamp Program, 2004

Participants (x 1,000)	420
Benefits ($ mil)	$415

Housing & Construction

Housing units

Total 2003 (estimate)	1,514,493
Total 2004 (estimate)	1,535,381
Seasonal or recreational use, 2003	18,000
Owner-occupied single-family, 2003	709,000
Median value	$171,039
Renter-occupied, 2003	509,000
Median rent	$657
Homeownership rate, 2003	68.0%
Homeownership rate, 2004	69.0%

New privately owned housing units, 2004

Number authorized (x 1,000)	27.3
Value ($ mil)	$4,458
Started 2005 (x 1,000, estimate)	19.6
Started 2006 (x 1,000, estimate)	20.0

Existing home sales

2002 (x 1,000)	72.1
2003 (x 1,000)	78.3
2004 (x 1,000)	90.7

Government & Elections

State Officials 2006

Governor (name/party/term expires)
Ted Kulongoski
Democrat - 1/07

Lieutenant Governor	(no Lt. Governor)
Secretary of State	Bill Bradbury
Attorney General	Hardy Meyers
Chief Justice	Wallace Carson

Governorship

Minimum age	30
Length of term	4 years
Consecutive terms permitted	8 out of any 12 yrs
Who succeeds	Sec. of State

State Legislature

Name	Legislature Assembly
Upper chamber	Senate
Number of members	30
Length of term	4 years
Party in majority, 2006	Democratic
Lower chamber	House of Representatives
Number of members	60
Length of term	2 years
Party in majority, 2006	Republican

State Government Employees, 2004

Total	57,423
Payroll	$208,383,937

Local Government Employees, 2004

Total	122,394
Payroll	$429,467,326

Local Governments by Type, 2002

Total	1,439
County	36
Municipal	240
Township	0
School District	236
Special District	927

Voting age population, November 2004

Total	2,727,000
Male	1,340,000
Female	1,387,000
White	2,498,000
Black	48,000
Hispanic	165,000
Asian	103,000

Presidential Election, 2004

Total Popular Vote	1,836,782
Kerry	943,163
Bush	866,831
Total Electoral Votes	7

Federal representation, 2006 (109th Congress)

Senator	Ron Wyden
Party	Democrat
Year term expires	2011
Senator	Gordon Smith
Party	Republican
Year term expires	2009
Representatives, total	5
Democrats	4
Republicans	1
Other	0

Votes cast for US Senators

2002

Total vote (x 1,000)	1,267,000
Leading party	Republican
Percent for leading party	56.2%

2004

Total vote (x 1,000)	1,781,000
Leading party	Democratic
Percent for leading party	63.4%

Votes cast for US Representatives

2002

Total vote (x 1,000)	1,240
Democratic	677
Republican	529
Leading party	Democratic
Percent for leading party	54.6%

2004

Total vote (x 1,000)	1,772
Democratic	952
Republican	762
Leading party	Democratic
Percent for leading party	53.7%

Women holding public office, 2006

US Congress 1
Statewide elected office..................... 1
State legislature 25

Black public officials, 2001

Total...................................... 6
   US and state legislatures 3
   City/county/regional offices 1
   Judicial/law enforcement.................. 2
   Education/school boards.................. 0

Hispanic public officials, 2004

Total..................................... 14
   State executives & legislators 3
   City/county/regional offices 5
   Judicial/law enforcement.................. 5
   Education/school boards................. 1

Governmental Finance

State government revenues, 2004

Total revenue ($1,000) $24,488,705
   Revenue per capita 6,819.47

General Revenue ($ per capita) $3,833.51
   Intergovernmental 1,158.71
   Taxes 1,699.55
      general sales 0
      individual income tax............. 1,189.29
      corporate income tax 89.13
   Current charges..................... 596.96
   Miscellaneous 378.30

State government expenditure, 2004

Total expenditure (x $1,000) $18,788,196
   Expenditure per capita............. 5,232.02
General Expenditure ($ per capita).... $4,054.65
   Education 1,521.93
   Public welfare.......................979.52
   Health 79.50
   Hospitals...........................188.75
   Highways 343.26
   Police protection 54.63
   Correction 137.61
   Natural resources 105.89
   Parks & recreation.................. 20.53
   Governmental administration 263.66
   Interest on general debt 104.72

State debt & cash, 2004 ($ per capita)

Debt $2,922.77
Cash/security holdings............ $16,456.35

Federal government grants to state & local government, 2004 (x $1,000)

Total........................... $5,184,929
By Federal Agency
   Defense $38,120

By Federal Agency, continued
   Education 456,573
   Energy........................... 16,176
   Environmental Protection Agency 75,372
   Health & Human Services. 2,808,885
   Homeland Security................. 44,178
   Housing & Urban Development...... 349,489
   Justice 81,110
   Labor 165,473
   Transportation 536,715
   Veterans Affairs..................... 2,915

Crime, Law Enforcement & Courts

Crime, 2004 (rates per 100,000 residents)

Property crimes 166,475
   Burglaries......................... 30,072
   Larcenies........................ 117,868
   Motor vehicle thefts 18,535
   Property crime rate................ 4,631.3
Violent crimes....................... 10,724
   Murders............................ 90
   Forcible rape....................... 1,283
   Robberies 2,751
   Aggravated assaults 6,600
   Violent crime rate 298.3

Police Agencies, 2004

Total agencies........................ 145
Total employees 6,924
   Male officers....................... 4,423
   Female officers 497
   Male civilians....................... 478
   Female civilians.................... 1,526

Arrests, 2004

Total............................. 155,202
   Persons under 18 years of age 30,109

Prisoners under state & federal jurisdiction, 2004

Total prisoners....................... 13,183
   Percent change, 12/31/03 to 12/31/04 .... 3.7%
Sentenced to more than one year 13,167
   rate per 100,000....................... 365

Persons under sentence of death, 7/1/05

Total................................. 32
   White.............................. 26
   Black 2
   Hispanic 2

State's highest court

Name .... Supreme Court
Number of members...................... 7
Length of term .... 6 years
Intermediate appeals court? ....yes

6   Oregon

Labor & Income

Civilian labor force, 2004
Total............................ 1,850,000
  Men 1,010,000
  Women 840,000
  Persons 16-19 years................. 78,000
  White.......................... 1,678,000
  Black 32,000
  Hispanic 176,000
  Asian 65,000

Civilian labor force as a percent of civilian non-institutional population, 2004
Total................................ 66.1%
  Men 73.5
  Women 59.0
  Persons 16-19 years................ 44.1
  White.............................. 65.9
  Black 69.1
  Hispanic 78.6
  Asian 70.2

Employment, 2004
Total............................ 1,710,000
  Men 930,000
  Women 780,000
  Persons 16-19 years.............. 60,000
  White.......................... 1,554,000
  Black 28,000
  Hispanic 158,000
  Asian 60,000

Full-time/part-time labor force, 2002
Full-time labor force, employed 1,360,000
Part-time labor force, employed....... 335,000
Unemployed, looking for
  Full-time work..................... 116,000
  Part-time work...................... 22,000

Unemployment rate, 2004
Total................................. 7.6%
  Men 8.0
  Women 7.1
  Persons 16-19 years................ 22.3
  White............................... 7.4
  Black 11.6
  Hispanic 9.8
  Asian 7.4

Unemployed by reason for unemployment (as a percent of total unemployment), 2002
Job losers or completed temp jobs 59.4%
Job leavers............................... NA
Reentrants.............................. 24.6
New entrants .... NA

Labor unions, 2004
Membership 224,000
  percent of employed 15.2%

Experienced civilian labor force by private industry, first quarter 2004
Total............................ 1,300,016
  Natural Resources & Mining 42,074
  Construction 75,614
  Manufacturing..................... 192,747
  Trade, transportation & utilities 307,883
  Information 32,343
  Finance 84,390
  Professional & business 170,686
  Education & Health 186,203
  Leisure & hospitality............... 148,658
  Other.............................. 58,911

Experienced civilian labor force by occupation, 2004
Management......................... 72,830
Business & Financial................... 64,350
Legal................................. 9,880
Sales............................... 170,420
Office & Admin. Support.............. 268,640
Computers & Math 34,570
Architecture & Engineering 33,830
Arts & Entertainment................. 19,930
Education 100,360
Social Services 30,870
Healthcare Practitioner & Technical..... 69,500
Healthcare support................... 36,810
Maintenance & Repair 63,080
Construction 72,950
Transportation & moving 127,330
Production 127,780
Farming, fishing & forestry............. 1,820

Hours and earnings of production workers on manufacturing payrolls, 2004
Average weekly hours 39.1
Average hourly earnings $15.34
Average weekly earnings $599.79

Average annual pay
2004 .... $35,630
  change from 2003 .... 3.3%

Household income
Median household income, three-year average,
  2002-2004........................ $42,617

Personal income, 2004 ($ per capita)
In current dollars.................... $29,971
In constant (2000) dollars $27,796

Poverty
Persons below poverty level, three-year average,
  2002-2004.......................... 11.7%

Federal individual income tax returns, 2003
Returns filed...................... 1,571,871
Adjusted gross income ($1,000) $67,955,934
Total income tax paid ($1,000) $7,636,034

Economy, Business, Industry & Agriculture

Fortune 500 companies, 2005 1

Patents issued, 2004 1,967

Bankruptcy cases filed, 2004 24,900

Business firm ownership, 2002

Women-owned.	88,318
Sales ($ mil)	$10,618
Black-owned.	2,207
Sales ($ mil)	$375
Hispanic-owned.	6,399
Sales ($ mil)	$1,449
Asian-owned	9,068
Sales ($ mil)	$2,207
Amer. Indian/Alaska Native-owned	3,070
Sales ($ mil)	$302
Hawaiian/Pacific Isl.-owned	372
Sales ($ mil)	$61

Gross State Product, 2004 ($ mil)

Total Gross State Product	$128,103
Agriculture, forestry, fishing and hunting	3,379
Mining.	133
Utilities	2,239
Construction	6,175
Manufacturing, durable goods	15,308
Manufacturing, non-durable goods	4,273
Wholesale trade.	9,032
Retail trade.	8,063
Transportation & warehousing	3,752
Information	4,434
Finance & insurance.	7,010
Real estate, rental, leasing	17,937
Professional and technical services	6,397
Educational services	808
Health care and social assistance	9,770
Accommodation/food services.	3,245
Other services, except government	2,947
Government	16,386

Establishments, by major industry group, 2003

Total.	103,064
Forestry, fishing & agriculture	1,519
Mining.	152
Construction	12,474
Manufacturing.	5,482
Wholesale trade.	5,650
Retail trade.	14,308
Transportation & warehousing	2,948
Information	1,906
Finance & insurance	6,064
Professional/scientific/technical	10,297
Health care/social assistance	10,144
Accommodation/food services.	9,039

Annual payroll by major industry group, 2003

Total ($1,000)	$44,347,211
Forestry, fishing & agriculture	421,929
Mining.	62,318
Utilities	552,601
Construction	2,892,155
Manufacturing.	7,250,037
Wholesale trade.	3,357,062
Retail trade.	4,141,486
Transportation & warehousing	1,858,986
Information	1,780,597
Finance & insurance.	3,200,135
Professional/scientific/technical . . .	3,307,331
Health care/social assistance	5,981,928
Accommodation/food services.	1,716,282

Agriculture

Number of farms, 2004	40,000
Farm acreage, 2004	
Total.	17,000,000
Acres per farm, 2004	430
Farm income, 2003 ($mil)	
Net farm income	$493
Debt/asset ratio	13.1
Farm marketings, 2003 ($mil)	
Total.	$3,284
Crops	2,479
Livestock.	805

Principal commodities, in order by marketing receipts, 2003

Greenhouse, cattle, dairy products, hay

Federal economic activity in state

Expenditures, 2003	
Total ($ mil)	$21,253
Per capita	$5,971
Defense ($ mil).	1,097
Non-defense ($ mil)	20,156
Defense department, 2003	
Payroll ($ mil)	$660
Contract awards ($ mil)	$491
Grants ($ mil).	$14
Homeland security grants ($1,000)	
2004	$41,665
2005	$34,820

FDIC insured financial institutions, 2004

Number	40
Assets ($bil)	$23.6
Deposits ($bil)	39.2

Fishing, 2004

Catch (x 1,000 lbs)	294,752
Value ($1,000).	$101,081

Mining, 2004 ($ mil)
Total non-fuel mineral production $356
Percent of U.S. 0.8%

Construction, 2003 ($ mil)
Total contracts (including non-building). $7,356
residential. 4,309
non-residential 1,890

Establishments, receipts, payroll & employees, by major industry group, 2002

Mining 886
  Receipts ($1,000) $3,408,913
  Annual payroll ($1,000). $710,567
  Paid employees 16,059

Utilities 219
  Receipts ($1,000) . . . . NA
  Annual payroll ($1,000). $543,500
  Paid employees 8,381

Construction 11,854
  Receipts ($1,000) $13,772,785
  Annual payroll ($1,000). $3,103,299
  Paid employees 87,977

Manufacturing 5,597
  Receipts ($1,000) $45,864,552
  Annual payroll ($1,000). $7,173,223
  Paid employees 184,151

Wholesale trade 5,770
  Receipts ($1,000) $56,855,958
  Annual payroll ($1,000). $3,078,800
  Paid employees 74,594

Retail trade 14,277
  Receipts ($1,000) $37,896,022
  Annual payroll ($1,000). $3,983,810
  Paid employees 183,706

Transportation 2,846
  Receipts ($1,000) $4,892,472
  Annual payroll ($1,000). $1,651,722
  Paid employees 48,943

Information 1,869
  Receipts ($1,000) . . . . NA
  Annual payroll ($1,000). $1,793,405
  Paid employees 39,918

Finance & insurance 5,914
  Receipts ($1,000) . . . . NA
  Annual payroll ($1,000). $2,999,900
  Paid employees 64,366

Professional, scientific & technical 10,141
  Receipts ($1,000) $6,956,805
  Annual payroll ($1,000). $3,594,757
  Paid employees 77,515

Health care & social assistance 9,975
  Receipts ($1,000) $13,860,847
  Annual payroll ($1,000). $5,561,201
  Paid employees 165,787

Accommodation & food service 8,816
  Receipts ($1,000) $5,527,223
  Annual payroll ($1,000). $1,589,959
  Paid employees 130,010

Communication, Energy & Transportation

Communication
Daily newspapers, 2004 19
Households with computers, 2003 . . . . 67%
Households with internet access, 2003 . . . . . 61%

Energy
Electricity Consumption, 2001
  Total (trillion Btu) 1,064
  Per capita (million Btu) 307
By source of production (trillion Btu)
  Coal 43
  Natural gas 236
  Petroleum 368
  Nuclear electric power 0
  Hydroelectric power 291
By end-use sector (trillion Btu)
  Residential 252
  Commercial 208
  Industrial 298
  Transportation 307
Electric energy, 2003
  Production (billion kWh) 49
  Net summer capability (million kW) 12.9
Gas utilities, 2003
  Customers (x1,000) 701
  Sales (trillion Btu) 75
  Revenues ($mil) $640
Nuclear plants, 2003 0

Transportation, 2004
Public Road & Street Mileage 65,861
  Urban. 12,358
  Rural 53,503
  Interstate. 728
Vehicle miles of travel per capita 9,904.8
Total motor vehicle registrations 3,003,227
  Automobiles. 1,475,253
  Buses 15,582
  Trucks 1,512,392
  Motorcycles 75,453
Licensed drivers 2,625,856
  19 years & under 109,624
Deaths from motor vehicle accidents 456

Pennsylvania　　**1**

State Summary

Capital City...................... Harrisburg
Governor..........................Ed Rendell
Room 225
Main Capitol Building
Harrisburg, PA 17120
717-787-2500
Admitted as a state 1787
Area (square miles).................... 46,055
Population, 2004 (est.) 12,406,292
Largest City..................... Philadelphia
Population, 2004................. 1,470,000
Personal income per capita, 2004
(in current dollars) $33,348
Gross state product ($ mil), 2004 ..... $468,089

Leading industries by payroll, 2003

Manufacturing, Health care/Social assistance,
Professional/Scientific/Technical

Leading agricultural commodities by receipts, 2003

Dairy products, cattle, greenhouse, chicken eggs

Geography & Environment

Total area (sq. mi.).................... 46,055
land 44,817
water 1,239
Federally-owned land, 2004 (acres) 719,864
percent............................. 2.5%
Highest point.......................Mt. Davis
elevation (feet) 3,213
Lowest point ....Delaware River
elevation (feet) .... sea level
General coastline (miles)..................... 0
Tidal shoreline (miles)...................... 83
Capital City..................... Harrisburg
Population 2000 48,950
Population 2004 47,635
Largest City..................... Philadelphia
Population 2000 1,518,000
Population 2004 1,470,000

Number of cities with over 100,000 population

1990 4
2000 4
2004 4

State park and recreation areas, 2003

Area (acres x 1,000)........................ 290
Number of visitors (x 1,000) 36,031
Revenues (x 1,000).................... $16,925
percent of operating expenditures...... 21.4%

National forest system land, 2004

Acres 513,000

Demographics and Characteristics of the Population

Population

1980 11,863,895
1990 11,881,643
2000 12,281,054
2004 (estimate)................... 12,406,292
persons per sq. mile of land............276.8
2005 (projection).................. 12,426,603
Male....................... 6,006,371
Female....................... 6,420,232
2010 (projection) 12,584,487
2020 (projection)................. 12,787,354
2030 (projection)................. 12,768,184
Male....................... 6,139,811
Female....................... 6,628,373

Metropolitan and Non-Metro. area population

	Metro	Non-Metro
1980	10,038,000	1,826,000
1990	10,077,000	1,805,000
2000	10,392,000	1,890,000

Change in population, 2000-2004

Number............................ 125,238
percent............................. 1.0%
Natural increase (births minus deaths)... 61,192
Net internal migration .... -19,365
Net international migration 86,811

Persons by age, 2004

Under 5 years 719,125
18 years and over 9,569,283
65 years and over 1,896,503
85 years and over 290,886

Persons by age, 2010 (projected)

Total............................ 12,584,487
Under 5 years 746,518
5 to 17 years 2,001,077
18 and over 9,836,892
21 and over 9,310,043
65 and over 1,956,235
85 and over 338,052
Median age 40

Race, 2004 (estimate)

One Race
White........................ 10,693,313
Black or African American 1,304,439
American Indian/Alaska Native....... 21,900
Pacific Islander 5,203
Asian Indian....................... 77,172
Chinese 69,733
Filipino 15,062
Japanese 6,178
Korean 21,129
Vietnamese....................... 41,107
Two or more races.................... 114,680

Persons of Hispanic origin, 2004

Total Hispanic or Latino 447,846
  Mexican............................. 70,176
  Puerto Rican 256,620
  Cuban 9,878
  Other Hispanic or Latino 36,215

Marital status, 2000

Population 15 years & over 9,861,713
  Never married 2,682,386
  Married.......................... 5,354,910
  Separated 216,958
  Widowed........................... 808,660
  Divorced 798,799

Language spoken at home, 2000

Population 5 years & over 11,555,538
  English only 10,583,054
  Spanish 356,754
  Other Indo-European languages 428,122
  Asian/Pacific Island languages....... 143,955

Households & families, 2000

Households......................... 4,777,003
  with persons under 18 years 1,559,281
  with persons over 65 years......... 1,328,237
  persons per household 2.48
Families.......................... 3,208,388
  persons per family......................3.04
Married couples 2,467,673
Female householder,
  no husband present................ 554,693
One-person households 1,320,941

Nativity, 2000

Number of persons born in state 9,544,251
  percent of population................. 77.7%

Immigration & Naturalization, 2004

Immigrants admitted.................. 18,232
Persons naturalized 10,205
Asylums granted 199
Asylums denied 66

Vital Statistics and Health

Marriages

2002 70,269
2003 72,635
2004 73,599

Divorces

2002 38,016
2003 37,765
2004 36,692

Births

2003 145,959
  Birthrate (per 1,000).....................11.8
  Low birth weight (2,500g or less)........ 8.1%
  To unmarried mothers................. 33.9%

2003, continued
  White............................. 114,043
  Black............................. 21,333
  Hispanic 10,494
  Asian/Pacific Islander 4,975
  Amer. Indian/Alaska Native............ 311
2004 (preliminary)................... 145,768
  Birthrate (per 1,000)................... 11.7
  White............................. 117,754
  Black 22,081
  Hispanic 11,686
  Asian/Pacific Islander 5,597

Deaths

2002
All causes 130,223
  rate per 100,000.................. 1,055.7
Heart disease 38,852
  rate per 100,000.....................315.0
Malignant neoplasms 29,849
  rate per 100,000................... 242.0
Cerebrovascular disease................. 8,579
  rate per 100,000......................69.5
Chronic lower respiratory disease 6,017
  rate per 100,000......................48.8
2003 129,767
  rate per 100,000.................. 1,049.4
2004 (provisional) 125,654

Infant deaths

2003 (provisional) 981
  rate per 1,000 ....6.9
2004 (provisional) 1,002
  rate per 1,000 ....6.9

Abortions, 2000

Total...............................37,000
  rate per 1,000 women age 15-44..........14.3

Physicians, 2003

Total............................... 36,421
  rate per 1,000 persons.................. 295

Nurses, 2001

Total............................... 132,120
  rate per 1,000 persons............... 1,074

Community Hospitals, 2003

Number 201
Beds (x 1,000)...........................40.9
Patients admitted (x 1,000) 1,824
Average daily census (x 1,000) 28.2
Average cost per day $1,326
Outpatient visits (x mil).................33.0

Disability status of population, 2004

5 to 20 years 7.2%
21 to 64 years 13.2%
65 years and over 38.6%

Education

Educational attainment, 2004

Population over 25 years	8,137,533
Less than 9th grade	327,176
High school graduates only	3,166,634
Bachelor's degree only	1,266,681
Graduate or professional degree	744,136
Less than 9th grade percent	4.0%
High school graduate or more	86.5%
College graduate or more	25.3%
Graduate or professional degree	9.1%

Public school enrollment, Fall 2002

Total	1,816,747
Kindergarten through grade 8	1,241,636
Grades 9 through 12	575,111
Enrollment, 2005 (projected)	1,785,000

Graduating public high school seniors

2004 (estimate)	121,550

SAT scores, 2005

Average verbal score	501
Average math score	503
Percent of graduates taking test	75%

Public school teachers, 2004

Total (x 1,000)	118.3
Elementary (x 1,000)	61.9
Secondary (x 1,000)	56.5
Average salary	$51,800
Elementary	$51,900
Secondary	$51,800

State receipts & expenditures for public schools, 2004

Revenue receipts ($mil)	$19,374
Expenditures	
Total ($mil)	$20,008
Per capita	$1,617
Per pupil	$9,949

Institutions of higher education, 2004

Total	262
Public	65
Private	197

Enrollment in institutions of higher education, Fall, 2003

Total	696,770
Full-time men	229,847
Full-time women	270,142
Part-time men	72,386
Part-time women	124,395

Minority enrollment in institutions of higher education, Fall, 2003

Black, non-hispanic	62,119
Hispanic	16,738
Asian/Pacific Islander	25,480
American Indian/Alaska Native	1,791

Earned degrees conferred, 2003

Bachelor's	72,351
Master's	24,038
First-professional	4,442
Doctor's	2,431

State & local financial support for higher education, 2003-2004

Full-time equivalent enrollment (x 1,000)	322.7
Appropriations per FTE	$5,355
as a percent of tax revenue	5.6%

Social Insurance & Welfare Programs

Social Security benefits & beneficiaries, 2004

Beneficiaries	
Total	2,405,000
Retired & dependents	1,703,000
Survivors	349,000
Disabled & dependents	354,000
Annual benefit payments ($ mil)	
Total	$25,893
Retired & dependents	$17,477
Survivors	$4,884
Disabled & dependents	$3,533
Average Monthly Benefit	
Retired & dependents	$982
Disabled & dependents	$910
Widowed	$966

Medicare

Enrollment, 2001 (x 1,000)	2,095
Payments ($ mil, est.)	$15,100
Enrollment, 2003 (x 1,000)	2,110

Medicaid, 2002

Beneficiaries (x 1,000)	1,627
Payments ($ mil)	$8,524

State Children's Health Insurance, 2004

Enrollment (x 1,000)	177.4
Expenditures ($ mil)	$126.6

Persons without health insurance, 2003

Number (x 1,000)	1,384
percent	11.4%
Number of children (x 1,000)	239
percent of children	8.4%

Federal public aid

Temporary Assistance for Needy Families, 2004

Recipients (x 1,000)	231
Families (x 1,000)	88

Supplemental Security Income, 2003

Recipients (x 1,000)	311
Payments ($ mil)	$1,599

Food Stamp Program, 2004

Participants (x 1,000)	961
Benefits ($ mil)	$933

4   Pennsylvania

Housing & Construction

Housing units
Total 2003 (estimate) 5,350,791
Total 2004 (estimate) 5,385,729
Seasonal or recreational use, 2003 179,000
Owner-occupied single-family, 2003.. 3,002,000
   Median value $110,020
Renter-occupied, 2003 1,334,000
   Median rent $602
Homeownership rate, 2003 .... 73.7%
Homeownership rate, 2004 .... 74.9%

New privately owned housing units, 2004
Number authorized (x 1,000) 49.7
Value ($ mil)......................... $6,767
Started 2005 (x 1,000, estimate)...........39.4
Started 2006 (x 1,000, estimate)...........39.0

Existing home sales
2002 (x 1,000)...................... 204.7
2003 (x 1,000)......................219.6
2004 (x 1,000)...................... 244.6

Government & Elections

State Officials 2006
Governor (name/party/term expires)
Ed Rendell
Democrat - 1/07
Lieutenant Governor..... Catherine Baker Knoll
Secretary of State.................Pedro Cortes
Attorney General.................Tom Corbett
Chief Justice ....Ralph Cappy

Governorship
Minimum age........................... 30
Length of term .... 4 years
Consecutive terms permitted 2
Who succeeds...................Lt. Governor

State Legislature
Name .... General Assembly
Upper chamber ....Senate
   Number of members.................... 50
   Length of term..................... 4 years
   Party in majority, 2006 .... Republican
Lower chamber.......House of Representatives
   Number of members................... 203
   Length of term................... 2 years
   Party in majority, 2006 .... Republican

State Government Employees, 2004
Total.............................. 161,089
Payroll $608,192,529

Local Government Employees, 2004
Total.............................. 409,290
Payroll $1,473,786,258

Local Governments by Type, 2002
Total................................. 5,031
   County................................. 66
   Municipal........................... 1,018
   Township 1,546
   School District....................... 516
   Special District 1,885

Voting age population, November 2004
Total............................. 9,356,000
   Male....................... 4,467,000
   Female...................... 4,889,000
   White....................... 8,218,000
   Black......................... 853,000
   Hispanic 255,000
   Asian 210,000

Presidential Election, 2004
Total Popular Vote 5,769,590
   Kerry 2,938,095
   Bush.......................... 2,793,847
Total Electoral Votes........................ 21

Federal representation, 2006 (109th Congress)
Senator.......................Rick Santorum
   Party .... Republican
   Year term expires 2007
Senator....................... Arlen Specter
   Party .... Republican
   Year term expires 2011
Representatives, total 19
   Democrats......................... 7
   Republicans 12
   Other................................. 0

Votes cast for US Senators
2002
Total vote (x 1,000) .... NA
Leading party............................ NA
Percent for leading party .... NA

2004
Total vote (x 1,000) 5,559,000
Leading party................... Republican
Percent for leading party 52.6%

Votes cast for US Representatives
2002
Total vote (x 1,000) 3,310
   Democratic......................... 1,349
   Republican 1,859
Leading party................... Republican
Percent for leading party 56.2%

2004
Total vote (x 1,000) 5,151
   Democratic......................... 2,478
   Republican 2,565
Leading party.................. Republican
Percent for leading party 49.8%

Women holding public office, 2006

US Congress 2
Statewide elected office 1
State legislature 32

Black public officials, 2001

Total 185
    US and state legislatures 19
    City/county/regional offices 74
    Judicial/law enforcement 65
    Education/school boards 27

Hispanic public officials, 2004

Total 17
    State executives & legislators 1
    City/county/regional offices 10
    Judicial/law enforcement 3
    Education/school boards 3

Governmental Finance

State government revenues, 2004

Total revenue ($1,000) $69,212,674
    Revenue per capita 5,584.37

General Revenue ($ per capita) $4,036.53
    Intergovernmental 1,234.32
    Taxes 2,045.09
        general sales 627.17
        individual income tax 590.88
        corporate income tax 135.39
    Current charges 460.45
    Miscellaneous 296.67

State government expenditure, 2004

Total expenditure (x $1,000) $57,353,773
    Expenditure per capita 4,627.54
General Expenditure ($ per capita) $3,892.44
    Education 1,241.84
    Public welfare 1,353.27
    Health 118.69
    Hospitals 177.63
    Highways 324.87
    Police protection 48.74
    Correction 120.09
    Natural resources 50.94
    Parks & recreation 13.58
    Governmental administration 166.87
    Interest on general debt 90.64

State debt & cash, 2004 ($ per capita)

Debt $2,097.45
Cash/security holdings $8,434.11

Federal government grants to state & local government, 2004 (x $1,000)

Total $19,915,826

By Federal Agency
    Defense $232,139

By Federal Agency, continued
    Education 1,349,422
    Energy 98,062
    Environmental Protection Agency ... 164,126
    Health & Human Services 12,493,067
    Homeland Security 114,766
    Housing & Urban Development 1,543,558
    Justice 225,797
    Labor 430,203
    Transportation 2,028,265
    Veterans Affairs 31,198

Crime, Law Enforcement & Courts

Crime, 2004 (rates per 100,000 residents)

Property crimes 299,611
    Burglaries 54,443
    Larcenies 214,199
    Motor vehicle thefts 30,969
    Property crime rate 2,415.0
Violent crimes 50,998
    Murders 650
    Forcible rape 3,535
    Robberies 18,474
    Aggravated assaults 28,339
    Violent crime rate 411.1

Police Agencies, 2004

Total agencies 715
Total employees 27,006
    Male officers 20,109
    Female officers 2,647
    Male civilians 1,612
    Female civilians 2,638

Arrests, 2004

Total 441,127
    Persons under 18 years of age 104,140

Prisoners under state & federal jurisdiction, 2004

Total prisoners 40,963
    Percent change, 12/31/03 to 12/31/04 .... 0.2%
Sentenced to more than one year 40,931
    rate per 100,000 329

Persons under sentence of death, 7/1/05

Total 233
    White 70
    Black 143
    Hispanic 18

State's highest court

Name .... Supreme Court
Number of members 7
Length of term .... 10 years
Intermediate appeals court? .... yes

Labor & Income

Civilian labor force, 2004

Total 6,260,000
  Men 3,310,000
  Women 2,950,000
  Persons 16-19 years 337,000
  White 5,552,000
  Black 540,000
  Hispanic 216,000
  Asian 119,000

Civilian labor force as a percent of civilian non-institutional population, 2004

Total 64.5%
  Men 71.6
  Women 58.1
  Persons 16-19 years 48.8
  White 64.9
  Black 60.5
  Hispanic 67.5
  Asian 69.7

Employment, 2004

Total 5,911,000
  Men 3,103,000
  Women 2,808,000
  Persons 16-19 years 275,000
  White 5,279,000
  Black 476,000
  Hispanic 199,000
  Asian 110,000

Full-time/part-time labor force, 2002

Full-time labor force, employed 4,755,000
Part-time labor force, employed 1,179,000
Unemployed, looking for
  Full-time work 293,000
  Part-time work 63,000

Unemployment rate, 2004

Total 5.6%
  Men 6.3
  Women 4.8
  Persons 16-19 years 18.4
  White 4.9
  Black 11.8
  Hispanic 8.0
  Asian 7.1

Unemployed by reason for unemployment (as a percent of total unemployment), 2002

Job losers or completed temp jobs 57.0%
Job leavers . . . . NA
Reentrants 28.9
New entrants . . . . NA

Labor unions, 2004

Membership 793,000
  percent of employed 15.0%

Experienced civilian labor force by private industry, first quarter 2004

Total 4,690,594
  Natural Resources & Mining 38,919
  Construction 230,791
  Manufacturing 687,282
  Trade, transportation & utilities . . . 1,095,302
  Information 113,975
  Finance 335,382
  Professional & business 617,199
  Education & Health 934,803
  Leisure & hospitality 446,901
  Other 189,405

Experienced civilian labor force by occupation, 2004

Management 249,570
Business & Financial 218,130
Legal 42,770
Sales 590,570
Office & Admin. Support 978,640
Computers & Math 105,020
Architecture & Engineering 90,780
Arts & Entertainment 53,430
Education 325,200
Social Services 99,820
Healthcare Practitioner & Technical 330,010
Healthcare support 160,900
Maintenance & Repair 235,010
Construction 233,090
Transportation & moving 424,210
Production 474,740
Farming, fishing & forestry 430

Hours and earnings of production workers on manufacturing payrolls, 2004

Average weekly hours 40.3
Average hourly earnings $15.15
Average weekly earnings $610.55

Average annual pay

2004 . . . . $38,555
  change from 2003 . . . . 4.2%

Household income

Median household income, three-year average, 2002-2004 . . . . $44,286

Personal income, 2004 ($ per capita)

In current dollars $33,348
In constant (2000) dollars $30,928

Poverty

Persons below poverty level, three-year average, 2002-2004 . . . . 10.4%

Federal individual income tax returns, 2003

Returns filed 5,771,764
Adjusted gross income ($1,000) . . . $261,845,583
Total income tax paid ($1,000) $32,646,720

Economy, Business, Industry & Agriculture

Fortune 500 companies, 2005 27

Patents issued, 2004 3,223

Bankruptcy cases filed, 2004 59,100

Business firm ownership, 2002

Women-owned. 227,119
   Sales ($ mil) $39,085
Black-owned. 24,770
   Sales ($ mil) $2,166
Hispanic-owned. 11,027
   Sales ($ mil) $1,847
Asian-owned 22,655
   Sales ($ mil) $6,817
Amer. Indian/Alaska Native-owned 2,362
   Sales ($ mil) . . . . NA
Hawaiian/Pacific Isl.-owned. 299
   Sales ($ mil) $42

Gross State Product, 2004 ($ mil)

Total Gross State Product $468,089
   Agriculture, forestry, fishing and
      hunting 2,468
   Mining. 2,695
   Utilities 12,326
   Construction 20,398
   Manufacturing, durable goods. 34,370
   Manufacturing, non-durable goods . . . 40,911
   Wholesale trade. 26,814
   Retail trade. 31,608
   Transportation & warehousing 14,695
   Information 17,955
   Finance & insurance. 35,707
   Real estate, rental, leasing 55,986
   Professional and technical services 31,819
   Educational services 8,264
   Health care and social assistance. 42,035
   Accommodation/food services. 9,915
   Other services, except government 12,068
   Government 44,936

Establishments, by major industry group, 2003

Total. 298,081
   Forestry, fishing & agriculture 619
   Mining. 900
   Construction 28,648
   Manufacturing. 16,185
   Wholesale trade. 15,848
   Retail trade. 47,589
   Transportation & warehousing 7,503
   Information 5,244
   Finance & insurance. 18,852
   Professional/scientific/technical 28,741
   Health care/social assistance 32,864
   Accommodation/food services. 25,343

Annual payroll by major industry group, 2003

Total ($1,000) $174,513,098
   Forestry, fishing & agriculture 77,968
   Mining. 924,663
   Utilities 2,548,468
   Construction 9,985,069
   Manufacturing. 27,205,038
   Wholesale trade. 11,281,914
   Retail trade. 13,376,874
   Transportation & warehousing 5,974,645
   Information 6,862,246
   Finance & insurance. 15,948,942
   Professional/scientific/technical . . . 17,169,141
   Health care/social assistance 26,368,057
   Accommodation/food services. 4,700,045

Agriculture

Number of farms, 2004 58,000
Farm acreage, 2004
   Total. 8,000,000
   Acres per farm, 2004 132
Farm income, 2003 ($mil)
   Net farm income $1,107
   Debt/asset ratio 12.1
Farm marketings, 2003 ($mil)
   Total. $4,266
     Crops 1,407
     Livestock 2,859

Principal commodities, in order by marketing receipts, 2003

Dairy products, cattle, greenhouse, chicken eggs

Federal economic activity in state

Expenditures, 2003
   Total ($ mil) $90,350
   Per capita $7,307
   Defense ($ mil). 8,054
   Non-defense ($ mil) 82,296
Defense department, 2003
   Payroll ($ mil) $2,521
   Contract awards ($ mil) $5,491
   Grants ($ mil). $176
   Homeland security grants ($1,000)
     2004 . . . . $109,866
     2005 . . . . $87,671

FDIC insured financial institutions, 2004

Number 262
   Assets ($bil) $331.0
   Deposits ($bil) 210.7

Fishing, 2004

Catch (x 1,000 lbs) 45
Value ($1,000). $65

Mining, 2004 ($ mil)

Total non-fuel mineral production $1,400
Percent of U.S. 3.2%

Construction, 2003 ($ mil)

Total contracts (including non-building) $14,655
   residential 6,216
   non-residential 5,793

Establishments, receipts, payroll & employees, by major industry group, 2002

Mining 21
   Receipts ($1,000) $34,173
   Annual payroll ($1,000) $8,408
   Paid employees 195

Utilities 672
   Receipts ($1,000) .... NA
   Annual payroll ($1,000) $2,395,327
   Paid employees 33,853

Construction 27,589
   Receipts ($1,000) $46,642,336
   Annual payroll ($1,000) $10,143,071
   Paid employees 277,400

Manufacturing 16,665
   Receipts ($1,000) $181,462,443
   Annual payroll ($1,000) $27,520,049
   Paid employees 715,453

Wholesale trade 15,991
   Receipts ($1,000) $183,741,873
   Annual payroll ($1,000) $10,092,050
   Paid employees 233,934

Retail trade 48,041
   Receipts ($1,000) $130,713,197
   Annual payroll ($1,000) $12,669,071
   Paid employees 661,993

Transportation 7,461
   Receipts ($1,000) $13,774,754
   Annual payroll ($1,000) $4,917,291
   Paid employees 172,280

Information 5,098
   Receipts ($1,000) .... NA
   Annual payroll ($1,000) $6,436,919
   Paid employees 143,923

Finance & insurance 18,207
   Receipts ($1,000) .... NA
   Annual payroll ($1,000) $15,246,666
   Paid employees 310,536

Professional, scientific & technical 28,412
   Receipts ($1,000) $36,708,036
   Annual payroll ($1,000) $16,479,390
   Paid employees 306,008

Health care & social assistance 32,651
   Receipts ($1,000) $59,086,822
   Annual payroll ($1,000) $25,054,392
   Paid employees 785,509

Accommodation & food service 24,778
   Receipts ($1,000) $15,305,402
   Annual payroll ($1,000) $4,262,263
   Paid employees 382,019

Communication, Energy & Transportation

Communication

Daily newspapers, 2004 81
Households with computers, 2003 .... .60%
Households with internet access, 2003 ..... .55%

Energy

Electricity Consumption, 2001
Total (trillion Btu) 3,923
Per capita (million Btu) 319
By source of production (trillion Btu)
   Coal 1,379
   Natural gas 669
   Petroleum 1,454
   Nuclear electric power 770
   Hydroelectric power 11
By end-use sector (trillion Btu)
   Residential 931
   Commercial 709
   Industrial 1,286
   Transportation 997
Electric energy, 2003
   Production (billion kWh) 206.3
   Net summer capability (million kW) 42.4
Gas utilities, 2003
   Customers (x1,000) 2,558
   Sales (trillion Btu) 357
   Revenues ($mil) $3,657
Nuclear plants, 2003 9

Transportation, 2004

Public Road & Street Mileage 120,623
   Urban 44,416
   Rural 76,207
   Interstate 1,757
Vehicle miles of travel per capita 8,711.1
Total motor vehicle registrations 9,821,267
   Automobiles 6,000,676
   Buses 37,396
   Trucks 3,783,195
   Motorcycles 292,196
Licensed drivers 8,430,142
   19 years & under 361,010
Deaths from motor vehicle accidents 1,490

State Summary

Capital City. . . . . Providence
Governor. . . . . .Don Carcieri
State House
Providence, RI 02903
401-222-2080
Admitted as a state 1790
Area (square miles) 1,545
Population, 2004 (est.) 1,080,632
Largest City. . . . . Providence
Population, 2004. 178,000
Personal income per capita, 2004
(in current dollars) $33,733
Gross state product ($ mil), 2004 . . . . . . $41,679

Leading industries by payroll, 2003

Health care/Social assistance, Manufacturing,
Finance & Insurance

Leading agricultural commodities by receipts, 2003

Greenhouse, dairy products, sweet corn, cattle

Geography & Environment

Total area (sq. mi.). 1,545
land 1,045
water 500

Federally-owned land, 2004 (acres) 2,923
percent. 0.4%

Highest point. . . . . Jerimoth Hill
elevation (feet) 812

Lowest point . . . . .Atlantic Ocean
elevation (feet) . . . . sea level

General coastline (miles). 40

Tidal shoreline (miles). 384

Capital City. . . . . Providence
Population 2000 174,000
Population 2004 178,000

Largest City. . . . . Providence
Population 2000 174,000
Population 2004 178,000

Number of cities with over 100,000 population

1990 1
2000 1
2004 1

State park and recreation areas, 2003

Area (acres x 1,000). 9
Number of visitors (x 1,000) 6,572
Revenues (x 1,000). . . . .
percent of operating expenditures. . . . . . . NA

National forest system land, 2004

Acres . . . . NA

Demographics and Characteristics of the Population

Population

1980 947,154
1990 1,003,464
2000 1,048,319
2004 (estimate). 1,080,632
persons per sq. mile of land. 1034.1
2005 (projection). 1,086,575
Male. 522,400
Female. 564,175
2010 (projection) 1,116,652
2020 (projection) 1,154,230
2030 (projection) 1,152,941
Male. 554,029
Female. 598,912

Metropolitan and Non-Metro. area population

	Metro	Non-Metro
1980	878,000	69,000
1990	928,000	75,000
2000	986,000	62,000

Change in population, 2000-2004

Number 32,313
percent. 3.1%
Natural increase (births minus deaths). . . 10,964
Net internal migration 5,826
Net international migration 15,990

Persons by age, 2004

Under 5 years 61,538
18 years and over 836,819
65 years and over 150,587
85 years and over 26,290

Persons by age, 2010 (projected)

Total. 1,116,652
Under 5 years 66,193
5 to 17 years 183,080
18 and over 867,379
21 and over 811,581
65 and over 157,358
85 and over 29,893
Median age 38.2

Race, 2004 (estimate)

One Race
White. 962,437
Black or African American 65,958
American Indian/Alaska Native. 6,366
Pacific Islander 1,275
Asian Indian. 5,267
Chinese 3,923
Filipino 2,130
Japanese 691
Korean. 1,517
Vietnamese. 2,512
Two or more races. 15,833

Persons of Hispanic origin, 2004

Total Hispanic or Latino 109,192
Mexican............................. 6,932
Puerto Rican 39,082
Cuban 939
Other Hispanic or Latino 6,138

Marital status, 2000

Population 15 years & over 841,503
Never married 249,926
Married........................... 433,374
Separated 15,989
Widowed............................ 63,113
Divorced 79,101

Language spoken at home, 2000

Population 5 years & over 985,184
English only 788,560
Spanish 79,443
Other Indo-European languages 91,449
Asian/Pacific Island languages........ 19,926

Households & families, 2000

Households.......................... 408,424
with persons under 18 years 134,399
with persons over 65 years.......... 107,335
persons per household 2.47
Families............................ 265,398
persons per family....................3.07
Married couples..................... 196,757
Female householder,
no husband present................. 52,609
One-person households 116,678

Nativity, 2000

Number of persons born in state 643,912
percent of population................ 61.4%

Immigration & Naturalization, 2004

Immigrants admitted.................. 3,689
Persons naturalized 2,185
Asylums granted 44
Asylums denied 5

Vital Statistics and Health

Marriages

2002................................. 8,278
2003................................. 8,349
2004................................. 8,243

Divorces

2002................................. 3,388
2003................................. 3,356
2004................................. 3,287

Births

2003................................. 13,209
Birthrate (per 1,000)...................12.3
Low birth weight (2,500g or less)........ 8.5%
To unmarried mothers................. 35.8%

2003, continued
White......................... 11,208
Black 1,260
Hispanic 2,514
Asian/Pacific Islander 562
Amer. Indian/Alaska Native......... 161

2004 (preliminary)..................... 12,778
Birthrate (per 1,000)................11.8
White......................... 10,874
Black 1,196
Hispanic 2,429
Asian/Pacific Islander 544

Deaths

2002
All causes 10,246
rate per 100,000.......................957.8
Heart disease 3,109
rate per 100,000................... 290.6
Malignant neoplasms 2,404
rate per 100,000................... 224.7
Cerebrovascular disease.................... 605
rate per 100,000......................56.6
Chronic lower respiratory disease 521
rate per 100,000......................48.7
2003 10,038
rate per 100,000......................932.8
2004 (provisional) 9,804

Infant deaths

2003 (provisional) 76
rate per 1,000 ....5.8
2004 (provisional) 59
rate per 1,000 ....4.6

Abortions, 2000

Total................................. 6,000
rate per 1,000 women age 15-44.........24.1

Physicians, 2003

Total................................. 3,770
rate per 1,000 persons.................. 350

Nurses, 2001

Total................................ 11,160
rate per 1,000 persons................ 1,053

Community Hospitals, 2003

Number................................... 11
Beds (x 1,000)...........................2.4
Patients admitted (x 1,000) 122
Average daily census (x 1,000) 1.8
Average cost per day $1,591
Outpatient visits (x mil)....................2.0

Disability status of population, 2004

5 to 20 years 8.8%
21 to 64 years 12.6%
65 years and over..................... 38.1%

Education

Educational attainment, 2004

Population over 25 years 705,453
Less than 9th grade 43,296
High school graduates only......... 209,322
Bachelor's degree only 119,338
Graduate or professional degree....... 79,107
Less than 9th grade percent 6.1%
High school graduate or more 81.1%
College graduate or more.............. 27.2%
Graduate or professional degree....... 11.2%

Public school enrollment, Fall 2002

Total................................. 159,205
Kindergarten through grade 8 112,544
Grades 9 through 12 46,661
Enrollment, 2005 (projected) 159,600

Graduating public high school seniors

2004 (estimate)........................ 9,280

SAT scores, 2005

Average verbal score 503
Average math score 505
Percent of graduates taking test 72%

Public school teachers, 2004

Total (x 1,000) 13.7
Elementary (x 1,000)..................... 8.3
Secondary (x 1,000) 5.3
Average salary $52,300
Elementary............................ $52,300
Secondary............................. $52,300

State receipts & expenditures for public schools, 2004

Revenue receipts ($mil)................. $1,496
Expenditures
Total ($mil)........................... $1,715
Per capita $1,594
Per pupil $10,976

Institutions of higher education, 2004

Total.................................... 13
Public.................................. 3
Private 10

Enrollment in institutions of higher education, Fall, 2003

Total.................................. 81,415
Full-time men 25,934
Full-time women.................... 31,720
Part-time men 8,506
Part-time women.................... 15,255

Minority enrollment in institutions of higher education, Fall, 2003

Black, non-hispanic.................... 3,921
Hispanic 4,111
Asian/Pacific Islander 2,805
American Indian/Alaska Native........... 272

Earned degrees conferred, 2003

Bachelor's 9,108
Master's.............................. 2,056
First-professional...................... 250
Doctor's................................ 246

State & local financial support for higher education, 2003-2004

Full-time equivalent enrollment (x 1,000) ...27.8
Appropriations per FTE................ $6,180
as a percent of tax revenue............. 4.7%

Social Insurance & Welfare Programs

Social Security benefits & beneficiaries, 2004

Beneficiaries
Total............................. 192,000
Retired & dependents.............. 135,000
Survivors......................... 22,000
Disabled & dependents............. 35,000
Annual benefit payments ($ mil)
Total............................. $2,007
Retired & dependents.............. $1,371
Survivors......................... $294
Disabled & dependents............. $342
Average Monthly Benefit
Retired & dependents.............. $955
Disabled & dependents............. $877
Widowed........................... $962

Medicare

Enrollment, 2001 (x 1,000) 172
Payments ($ mil, est.) $1,100
Enrollment, 2003 (x 1,000) 172

Medicaid, 2002

Beneficiaries (x 1,000)................. 199
Payments ($ mil) $1,251

State Children's Health Insurance, 2004

Enrollment (x 1,000)....................25.6
Expenditures ($ mil)....................$25.2

Persons without health insurance, 2003

Number (x 1,000)........................ 108
percent........................... 10.2%
Number of children (x 1,000) 13
percent of children 5.2%

Federal public aid

Temporary Assistance for Needy Families, 2004
Recipients (x 1,000)....................... 32
Families (x 1,000) 12

Supplemental Security Income, 2003
Recipients (x 1,000)....................... 29
Payments ($ mil) $150

Food Stamp Program, 2004

Participants (x 1,000) 78
Benefits ($ mil)............................ $74

Housing & Construction

Housing units

Total 2003 (estimate)	445,061
Total 2004 (estimate)	446,305
Seasonal or recreational use, 2003	12,000
Owner-occupied single-family, 2003	212,000
Median value	$205,244
Renter-occupied, 2003	151,000
Median rent	$686
Homeownership rate, 2003	59.9%
Homeownership rate, 2004	61.5%

New privately owned housing units, 2004

Number authorized (x 1,000)	2.5
Value ($ mil)	$362
Started 2005 (x 1,000, estimate)	2.4
Started 2006 (x 1,000, estimate)	2.4

Existing home sales

2002 (x 1,000)	17.1
2003 (x 1,000)	16.9
2004 (x 1,000)	19.2

Government & Elections

State Officials 2006

Governor (name/party/term expires)
Don Carcieri
Republican - 1/07

Lieutenant Governor	Charles Fogarty
Secretary of State	Matt Brown
Attorney General	Patrick Lynch
Chief Justice	Frank Williams

Governorship

Minimum age	not specified
Length of term	4 years
Consecutive terms permitted	2
Who succeeds	Lt. Governor

State Legislature

Name	General Assembly
Upper chamber	Senate
Number of members	38
Length of term	2 years
Party in majority, 2006	Democratic
Lower chamber	House of Representatives
Number of members	75
Length of term	2 years
Party in majority, 2006	Democratic

State Government Employees, 2004

Total	20,158
Payroll	$81,779,716

Local Government Employees, 2004

Total	30,363
Payroll	$123,809,174

Local Governments by Type, 2002

Total	118
County	0
Municipal	8
Township	31
School District	4
Special District	75

Voting age population, November 2004

Total	813,000
Male	385,000
Female	428,000
White	732,000
Black	46,000
Hispanic	58,000
Asian	27,000

Presidential Election, 2004

Total Popular Vote	437,134
Kerry	259,765
Bush	169,046
Total Electoral Votes	4

Federal representation, 2006 (109th Congress)

Senator	Lincoln Chafee
Party	Republican
Year term expires	2007
Senator	John Reed
Party	Democrat
Year term expires	2009
Representatives, total	2
Democrats	2
Republicans	0
Other	0

Votes cast for US Senators

2002

Total vote (x 1,000)	324,000
Leading party	Democratic
Percent for leading party	78.4%

2004

Total vote (x 1,000)	NA
Leading party	NA
Percent for leading party	NA

Votes cast for US Representatives

2002

Total vote (x 1,000)	329
Democratic	225
Republican	97
Leading party	Democratic
Percent for leading party	68.3%

2004

Total vote (x 1,000)	402
Democratic	279
Republican	113
Leading party	Democratic
Percent for leading party	69.5%

Women holding public office, 2006

US Congress 0
Statewide elected office...................... 0
State legislature 19

Black public officials, 2001

Total...................................... 8
   US and state legislatures 7
   City/county/regional offices 1
   Judicial/law enforcement................... 0
   Education/school boards................... 0

Hispanic public officials, 2004

Total...................................... 6
   State executives & legislators 3
   City/county/regional offices 3
   Judicial/law enforcement.................. 0
   Education/school boards.................. 0

Governmental Finance

State government revenues, 2004

Total revenue ($1,000) $7,266,196
   Revenue per capita 6,727.96

General Revenue ($ per capita) $5,202.85
   Intergovernmental 1,940.62
   Taxes 2,230.43
      general sales 745.04
      individual income tax............. 833.28
      corporate income tax 64.33
   Current charges...................... 414.47
   Miscellaneous 617.33

State government expenditure, 2004

Total expenditure (x $1,000) $6,386,602
   Expenditure per capita............. 5,913.52
General Expenditure ($ per capita).... $4,973.22
   Education 1,359.66
   Public welfare..................... 1,816.49
   Health 190.48
   Hospitals.......................... 100.04
   Highways 237.36
   Police protection 46.03
   Correction 150.22
   Natural resources 34.62
   Parks & recreation..................... 8.27
   Governmental administration 275.77
   Interest on general debt 216.85

State debt & cash, 2004 ($ per capita)

Debt $6,009.91
Cash/security holdings............. $11,810.63

Federal government grants to state & local government, 2004 (x $1,000)

Total $2,329,088
By Federal Agency
   Defense $25,310

By Federal Agency, continued

   Education 157,668
   Energy 4,590
   Environmental Protection Agency 36,894
   Health & Human Services. 1,448,237
   Homeland Security.................. 3,118
   Housing & Urban Development...... 228,872
   Justice 40,431
   Labor 33,822
   Transportation 207,327
   Veterans Affairs................... 5,174

Crime, Law Enforcement & Courts

Crime, 2004 (rates per 100,000 residents)

Property crimes 31,166
   Burglaries......................... 5,465
   Larcenies.......................... 21,623
   Motor vehicle thefts 4,078
   Property crime rate................. 2,884.1
Violent crimes........................ 2,673
   Murders 26
   Forcible rape...................... 320
   Robberies 731
   Aggravated assaults 1,596
   Violent crime rate 247.4

Police Agencies, 2004

Total agencies............................. 43
Total employees 3,094
   Male officers 2,308
   Female officers 165
   Male civilians..................... 285
   Female civilians................... 336

Arrests, 2004

Total.................................. 43,576
   Persons under 18 years of age 7,195

Prisoners under state & federal jurisdiction, 2004

Total prisoners........................ 3,430
   Percent change, 12/31/03 to 12/31/04 ... -2.8%
Sentenced to more than one year 1,894
   rate per 100,000...................... 175

Persons under sentence of death, 7/1/05

Total.................................. 0
   White............................. 0
   Black 0
   Hispanic 0

State's highest court

Name .... .Supreme Court
Number of members 5
Length of term .... .life
Intermediate appeals court? .... no

Labor & Income

Civilian labor force, 2004

Total................................. 562,000
  Men 288,000
  Women 275,000
  Persons 16-19 years................. 35,000
  White............................. 506,000
  Black 32,000
  Hispanic 47,000
  Asian 16,000

Civilian labor force as a percent of civilian non-institutional population, 2004

Total.................................66.4%
  Men 71.5
  Women 61.7
  Persons 16-19 years................51.7
  White.............................66.2
  Black 68.7
  Hispanic 66.6
  Asian 69.0

Employment, 2004

Total................................. 532,000
  Men 272,000
  Women 261,000
  Persons 16-19 years................. 30,000
  White............................. 481,000
  Black 29,000
  Hispanic 44,000
  Asian 14,000

Full-time/part-time labor force, 2002

Full-time labor force, employed 415,000
Part-time labor force, employed 113,000
Unemployed, looking for
  Full-time work...................... 22,000
  Part-time work......................... NA

Unemployment rate, 2004

Total................................. 5.4%
  Men 5.5
  Women 5.2
  Persons 16-19 years................14.5
  White.............................4.9
  Black 11.0
  Hispanic 7.7
  Asian 8.6

Unemployed by reason for unemployment (as a percent of total unemployment), 2002

Job losers or completed temp jobs 53.6%
Job leavers.............................. NA
Reentrants..............................32.1
New entrants .... NA

Labor unions, 2004

Membership 79,000
  percent of employed 16.3%

Experienced civilian labor force by private industry, first quarter 2004

Total................................. 398,781
  Natural Resources & Mining 705
  Construction 18,464
  Manufacturing...................... 56,811
  Trade, transportation & utilities 78,333
  Information 11,122
  Finance 31,860
  Professional & business.............. 50,945
  Education & Health 87,938
  Leisure & hospitality................ 44,189
  Other............................. 17,813

Experienced civilian labor force by occupation, 2004

Management.......................... 22,690
Business & Financial.................... 19,590
Legal.................................. 3,280
Sales................................. 44,550
Office & Admin. Support............... 82,420
Computers & Math 10,360
Architecture & Engineering 8,150
Arts & Entertainment................... 6,660
Education 33,970
Social Services 10,070
Healthcare Practitioner & Technical..... 27,940
Healthcare support.................... 16,440
Maintenance & Repair 16,190
Construction 21,380
Transportation & moving 28,900
Production 39,960
Farming, fishing & forestry............. 1,730

Hours and earnings of production workers on manufacturing payrolls, 2004

Average weekly hours 39.2
Average hourly earnings $13.03
Average weekly earnings $510.78

Average annual pay

2004 .... $37,651
  change from 2003 .... 3.4%

Household income

Median household income, three-year average,
  2002-2004......................... $46,199

Personal income, 2004 ($ per capita)

In current dollars..................... $33,733
In constant (2000) dollars $31,285

Poverty

Persons below poverty level, three-year average,
  2002-2004.......................... 11.3%

Federal individual income tax returns, 2003

Returns filed......................... 498,063
Adjusted gross income ($1,000) $23,700,505
Total income tax paid ($1,000) $2,970,458

Economy, Business, Industry & Agriculture

Fortune 500 companies, 2005 2

Patents issued, 2004 368

Bankruptcy cases filed, 2004 4,300

Business firm ownership, 2002

Women-owned. 23,195
   Sales ($ mil) $3,641
Black-owned. 1,766
   Sales ($ mil) . . . . NA
Hispanic-owned. 3,415
   Sales ($ mil) $214
Asian-owned 1,552
   Sales ($ mil) $331
Amer. Indian/Alaska Native-owned 446
   Sales ($ mil) $27
Hawaiian/Pacific Isl.-owned . . . . NA
   Sales ($ mil) $7

Gross State Product, 2004 ($ mil)

Total Gross State Product $41,679
   Agriculture, forestry, fishing and
      hunting 96
   Mining. 12
   Utilities 735
   Construction 2,459
   Manufacturing, durable goods. . . . . NA
   Manufacturing, non-durable goods . . . . . . NA
   Wholesale trade. 2,062
   Retail trade. 2,746
   Transportation & warehousing 644
   Information 1,720
   Finance & insurance. 5,795
   Real estate, rental, leasing 5,421
   Professional and technical services 2,198
   Educational services 848
   Health care and social assistance 3,798
   Accommodation/food services. 1,161
   Other services, except government 893
   Government 4,945

Establishments, by major industry group, 2003

Total. 29,333
   Forestry, fishing & agriculture 54
   Mining. 23
   Construction 3,358
   Manufacturing. 2,048
   Wholesale trade. 1,464
   Retail trade. 4,204
   Transportation & warehousing 658
   Information 382
   Finance & insurance. 1,477
   Professional/scientific/technical 3,045
   Health care/social assistance 3,014
   Accommodation/food services. 2,774

Annual payroll by major industry group, 2003

Total ($1,000) $14,538,391
   Forestry, fishing & agriculture . . . . NA
   Mining. . . . . NA
   Utilities 94,321
   Construction 931,569
   Manufacturing. 2,362,793
   Wholesale trade. 752,326
   Retail trade. 1,208,873
   Transportation & warehousing 304,650
   Information 363,970
   Finance & insurance. 1,831,391
   Professional/scientific/technical 971,922
   Health care/social assistance 2,524,318
   Accommodation/food services. 550,584

Agriculture

Number of farms, 2004 1,000
Farm acreage, 2004
   Total. . . . . < 500,000
   Acres per farm, 2004 71
Farm income, 2003 ($mil)
   Net farm income $10
   Debt/asset ratio 10.1
Farm marketings, 2003 ($mil)
Total. $57
   Crops 49
   Livestock 9

Principal commodities, in order by marketing receipts, 2003

   Greenhouse, dairy products, sweet corn, cattle

Federal economic activity in state

Expenditures, 2003
   Total ($ mil) $8,036
   Per capita $7,467
   Defense ($ mil). 1,080
   Non-defense ($ mil) 6,956
Defense department, 2003
   Payroll ($ mil) $608
   Contract awards ($ mil) $489
   Grants ($ mil). $18
   Homeland security grants ($1,000)
      2004 . . . . $23,485
      2005 . . . . $16,074

FDIC insured financial institutions, 2004

Number 15
   Assets ($bil) $246.1
   Deposits ($bil) 19.9

Fishing, 2004

Catch (x 1,000 lbs) 97,412
Value ($1,000). $71,141

Mining, 2004 ($ mil)

Total non-fuel mineral production $37
Percent of U.S. 0.1%

Construction, 2003 ($ mil)

Total contracts (including non-building). $1,183
    residential............................ 558
    non-residential 323

**Establishments, receipts, payroll & employees,
by major industry group, 2002**

Mining................................ 84
    Receipts ($1,000) $266,806
    Annual payroll ($1,000)............. $48,510
    Paid employees 1,395

Utilities 29
    Receipts ($1,000) .... NA
    Annual payroll ($1,000)............. $98,626
    Paid employees 1,552

Construction........................ 3,192
    Receipts ($1,000) $4,356,409
    Annual payroll ($1,000)........... $885,539
    Paid employees 27,289

Manufacturing 2,131
    Receipts ($1,000) $10,818,058
    Annual payroll ($1,000)........... $2,294,561
    Paid employees 62,285

Wholesale trade 1,479
    Receipts ($1,000) $8,566,430
    Annual payroll ($1,000)........... $699,457
    Paid employees 17,688

Retail trade........................... 4,134
    Receipts ($1,000) $10,342,351
    Annual payroll ($1,000)......... $1,045,721
    Paid employees 50,665

Transportation........................ 632
    Receipts ($1,000) $723,864
    Annual payroll ($1,000)........... $227,785
    Paid employees 9,360

Information........................... 365
    Receipts ($1,000) .... NA
    Annual payroll ($1,000)........... $343,554
    Paid employees 8,800

Finance & insurance 1,388
    Receipts ($1,000) .... NA
    Annual payroll ($1,000)......... $1,325,427
    Paid employees 26,251

Professional, scientific & technical 2,946
    Receipts ($1,000) $2,158,832
    Annual payroll ($1,000)........... $857,506
    Paid employees 19,576

Health care & social assistance 2,981
    Receipts ($1,000) $5,186,163
    Annual payroll ($1,000)......... $2,309,529
    Paid employees 73,276

Accommodation & food service.......... 2,701
    Receipts ($1,000) $1,731,799
    Annual payroll ($1,000)........... $502,394
    Paid employees 38,573

Communication, Energy & Transportation

Communication

Daily newspapers, 2004 6
Households with computers, 2003 .... .62%
Households with internet access, 2003 ..... .56%

Energy

Electricity Consumption, 2001
Total (trillion Btu)..................... 227
Per capita (million Btu) 215
By source of production (trillion Btu)
    Coal .... < 0.5
    Natural gas........................... 99
    Petroleum........................... 100
    Nuclear electric power 0
    Hydroelectric power.................. < 0.5
By end-use sector (trillion Btu)
    Residential 73
    Commercial 63
    Industrial 26
    Transportation 66
Electric energy, 2003
    Production (billion kWh) 5.6
    Net summer capability (million kW) 1.7
Gas utilities, 2003
    Customers (x1,000).................... 244
    Sales (trillion Btu)..................... 30
    Revenues ($mil)...................... $331
Nuclear plants, 2003 0

Transportation, 2004

Public Road & Street Mileage 6,419
    Urban.............................. 5,193
    Rural 1,226
    Interstate............................ 71
Vehicle miles of travel per capita 7,845.4
Total motor vehicle registrations 807,995
    Automobiles........................ 531,872
    Buses 1,726
    Trucks 274,397
    Motorcycles 26,506
Licensed drivers 741,841
    19 years & under 26,358
Deaths from motor vehicle accidents 83

South Carolina 1

State Summary

Capital City. . . . . Columbia
Governor. . . . . .Mark Sanford
PO Box 11829
Columbia, SC 29211
803-734-9400
Admitted as a state 1788
Area (square miles). 32,020
Population, 2004 (est.) 4,198,068
Largest City. . . . . Columbia
Population, 2004. 116,000
Personal income per capita, 2004
(in current dollars) $27,172
Gross state product ($ mil), 2004 . . . . . . $136,125

Leading industries by payroll, 2003

Manufacturing, Health care/Social assistance,
Retail trade

Leading agricultural commodities by receipts, 2003

Broilers, greenhouse, turkeys, tobacco

Geography & Environment

Total area (sq. mi.). 32,020
land 30,110
water 1,911

Federally-owned land, 2004 (acres) 560,956
percent. 2.9%

Highest point. . . . . .Sassafras Mountain
elevation (feet) 3,560

Lowest point . . . . .Atlantic Ocean
elevation (feet) . . . . sea level

General coastline (miles). 187

Tidal shoreline (miles). 2,876

Capital City. . . . . Columbia
Population 2000 116,000
Population 2004 116,000

Largest City. . . . . Columbia
Population 2000 116,000
Population 2004 116,000

Number of cities with over 100,000 population

1990 0
2000 1
2004 2

State park and recreation areas, 2003

Area (acres x 1,000). 80
Number of visitors (x 1,000) 7,544
Revenues (x 1,000). $13,769
percent of operating expenditures. 58.0%

National forest system land, 2004

Acres 624,000

Demographics and Characteristics of the Population

Population

1980 3,121,820
1990 3,486,703
2000 4,012,012
2004 (estimate). 4,198,068
persons per sq. mile of land. 139.4
2005 (projection). 4,239,310
Male. 2,062,588
Female. 2,176,722
2010 (projection) 4,446,704
2020 (projection) 4,822,577
2030 (projection) 5,148,569
Male. 2,501,280
Female. 2,647,289

Metropolitan and Non-Metro. area population

	Metro	Non-Metro
1980	1,865,000	1,256,000
1990	2,113,000	1,374,000
2000	2,807,000	1,205,000

Change in population, 2000-2004

Number 186,252
percent. 4.6%
Natural increase (births minus deaths). . . 78,544
Net internal migration 79,476
Net international migration 30,218

Persons by age, 2004

Under 5 years 280,272
18 years and over 3,173,368
65 years and over 520,392
85 years and over 59,451

Persons by age, 2010 (projected)

Total. 4,446,704
Under 5 years 287,544
5 to 17 years 748,805
18 and over 3,410,355
21 and over 3,210,714
65 and over 605,660
85 and over 78,253
Median age 38.4

Race, 2004 (estimate)

One Race
White. 2,868,094
Black or African American 1,232,732
American Indian/Alaska Native. 15,677
Pacific Islander 2,283
Asian Indian. 8,052
Chinese 7,526
Filipino 8,451
Japanese 2,011
Korean 6,099
Vietnamese. 5,116
Two or more races. 34,897

Persons of Hispanic origin, 2004

Total Hispanic or Latino	120,681
Mexican	73,485
Puerto Rican	9,483
Cuban	2,530
Other Hispanic or Latino	9,972

Marital status, 2000

Population 15 years & over	3,168,918
Never married	823,919
Married	1,717,554
Separated	104,574
Widowed	231,331
Divorced	291,540

Language spoken at home, 2000

Population 5 years & over	3,748,669
English only	3,552,240
Spanish	110,030
Other Indo-European languages	55,116
Asian/Pacific Island languages	25,534

Households & families, 2000

Households	1,533,854
with persons under 18 years	560,160
with persons over 65 years	346,175
persons per household	2.53
Families	1,072,822
persons per family	3.02
Married couples	783,142
Female householder, no husband present	226,958
One-person households	383,142

Nativity, 2000

Number of persons born in state	2,568,954
percent of population	64.0%

Immigration & Naturalization, 2004

Immigrants admitted	2,496
Persons naturalized	1,748
Asylums granted	23
Asylums denied	3

Vital Statistics and Health

Marriages

2002	38,207
2003	37,183
2004	34,546

Divorces

2002	13,956
2003	13,602
2004	13,448

Births

2003	55,649
Birthrate (per 1,000)	13.4
Low birth weight (2,500g or less)	10.1%
To unmarried mothers	41.1%

2003, continued

White	36,266
Black	18,345
Hispanic	3,587
Asian/Pacific Islander	893
Amer. Indian/Alaska Native	154
2004 (preliminary)	56,592
Birthrate (per 1,000)	13.5
White	35,789
Black	19,613
Hispanic	4,334
Asian/Pacific Islander	970

Deaths

2002

All causes	37,736
rate per 100,000	918.8
Heart disease	9,659
rate per 100,000	235.2
Malignant neoplasms	8,333
rate per 100,000	202.9
Cerebrovascular disease	2,822
rate per 100,000	68.7
Chronic lower respiratory disease	1,889
rate per 100,000	46.0
2003	38,111
rate per 100,000	919.0
2004 (provisional)	36,055

Infant deaths

2003 (provisional)	451
rate per 1,000	8.1
2004 (provisional)	476
rate per 1,000	8.4

Abortions, 2000

Total	8,000
rate per 1,000 women age 15-44	9.3

Physicians, 2003

Total	9,521
rate per 1,000 persons	230

Nurses, 2001

Total	28,130
rate per 1,000 persons	693

Community Hospitals, 2003

Number	61
Beds (x 1,000)	11.1
Patients admitted (x 1,000)	506
Average daily census (x 1,000)	8.1
Average cost per day	$1,355
Outpatient visits (x mil)	7.4

Disability status of population, 2004

5 to 20 years	8.1%
21 to 64 years	14.6%
65 years and over	42.8%

Education

Educational attainment, 2004

Population over 25 years 2,675,694
   Less than 9th grade 172,988
   High school graduates only.......... 812,075
   Bachelor's degree only 446,462
   Graduate or professional degree...... 210,890
   Less than 9th grade percent 6.5%
   High school graduate or more 83.6%
   College graduate or more.............. 24.9%
   Graduate or professional degree........ 7.9%

Public school enrollment, Fall 2002

Total.............................. 694,584
   Kindergarten through grade 8 500,557
   Grades 9 through 12................ 194,027
Enrollment, 2005 (projected) 688,800

Graduating public high school seniors

2004 (estimate)....................... 32,110

SAT scores, 2005

Average verbal score 494
Average math score 499
Percent of graduates taking test 64%

Public school teachers, 2004

Total (x 1,000) 45.2
   Elementary (x 1,000)...................31.8
   Secondary (x 1,000) 13.3
Average salary $41,200
   Elementary $39,300
   Secondary.......................... $40,000

State receipts & expenditures for public schools, 2004

Revenue receipts ($mil)................. $6,004
Expenditures
Total ($mil).......................... $5,899
   Per capita $1,422
   Per pupil $7,395

Institutions of higher education, 2004

Total................................. 63
   Public................................ 33
   Private............................... 30

Enrollment in institutions of higher education, Fall, 2003

Total............................... 209,080
   Full-time men 58,887
   Full-time women.................... 80,526
   Part-time men 22,743
   Part-time women................... 46,924

Minority enrollment in institutions of higher education, Fall, 2003

Black, non-hispanic................... 56,447
Hispanic 2,789
Asian/Pacific Islander 2,837
American Indian/Alaska Native........... 825

Earned degrees conferred, 2003

Bachelor's 17,817
Master's 4,496
First-professional....................... 738
Doctor's............................... 428

State & local financial support for higher education, 2003-2004

Full-time equivalent enrollment (x 1,000) . .137.1
Appropriations per FTE................ $5,053
   as a percent of tax revenue.............. 7.0%

Social Insurance & Welfare Programs

Social Security benefits & beneficiaries, 2004

Beneficiaries
   Total............................ 751,000
   Retired & dependents.............. 489,000
   Survivors......................... 104,000
   Disabled & dependents............. 157,000
Annual benefit payments ($ mil)
   Total............................. $7,538
   Retired & dependents.............. $4,761
   Survivors.......................... $1,231
   Disabled & dependents.............. $1,546
Average Monthly Benefit
   Retired & dependents............... $931
   Disabled & dependents.............. $884
   Widowed........................... $854

Medicare

Enrollment, 2001 (x 1,000) 580
   Payments ($ mil, est.) $3,400
Enrollment, 2003 (x 1,000) 606

Medicaid, 2002

Beneficiaries (x 1,000)................... 809
Payments ($ mil) $3,383

State Children's Health Insurance, 2004

Enrollment (x 1,000).....................75.6
Expenditures ($ mil)................... $50.8

Persons without health insurance, 2003

Number (x 1,000)....................... 584
   percent........................... 14.4%
Number of children (x 1,000) 92
   percent of children 8.9%

Federal public aid

Temporary Assistance for Needy Families, 2004
Recipients (x 1,000)...................... 39
Families (x 1,000) 17

Supplemental Security Income, 2003
Recipients (x 1,000)...................... 106
Payments ($ mil) $461

Food Stamp Program, 2004

Participants (x 1,000) 497
Benefits ($ mil)......................... $501

Housing & Construction

Housing units

Total 2003 (estimate) 1,858,004
Total 2004 (estimate) 1,890,682
Seasonal or recreational use, 2003 96,000
Owner-occupied single-family, 2003.... 818,000
  Median value $121,290
Renter-occupied, 2003 466,000
  Median rent $586
Homeownership rate, 2003 .... 75.0%
Homeownership rate, 2004 .... 76.2%

New privately owned housing units, 2004

Number authorized (x 1,000) 43.2
Value ($ mil) $5,641
Started 2005 (x 1,000, estimate) 33.4
Started 2006 (x 1,000, estimate) 32.3

Existing home sales

2002 (x 1,000) 72.7
2003 (x 1,000) 83.0
2004 (x 1,000) 99.3

Government & Elections

State Officials 2006

Governor (name/party/term expires)
Mark Sanford
Republican - 1/07
Lieutenant Governor .... R. Andre Bauer
Secretary of State .... Mark Hammond
Attorney General .... Henry McMaster
Chief Justice .... Jean Toal

Governorship

Minimum age 30
Length of term .... 4 years
Consecutive terms permitted 2
Who succeeds .... Lt. Governor

State Legislature

Name .... General Assembly
Upper chamber .... Senate
  Number of members 46
  Length of term .... 4 years
  Party in majority, 2006 .... Republican
Lower chamber .... House of Representatives
  Number of members 124
  Length of term .... 2 years
  Party in majority, 2006 .... Republican

State Government Employees, 2004

Total 75,603
Payroll $226,910,112

Local Government Employees, 2004

Total 167,401
Payroll $470,166,800

Local Governments by Type, 2002

Total 701
  County 46
  Municipal 269
  Township 0
  School District 85
  Special District 301

Voting age population, November 2004

Total 3,061,000
  Male 1,441,000
  Female 1,620,000
  White 2,188,000
  Black 837,000
  Hispanic 52,000
  Asian 4,000

Presidential Election, 2004

Total Popular Vote 1,617,730
  Kerry 661,699
  Bush 937,974
Total Electoral Votes 8

Federal representation, 2006 (109th Congress)

Senator .... Lindsey Graham
  Party .... Republican
  Year term expires 2009
Senator .... Jim Demint
  Party .... Republican
  Year term expires 2011
Representatives, total 6
  Democrats 2
  Republicans 4
  Other 0

Votes cast for US Senators

2002

Total vote (x 1,000) 1,103,000
Leading party .... Republican
Percent for leading party 54.4%

2004

Total vote (x 1,000) 1,597,000
Leading party .... Republican
Percent for leading party 53.7%

Votes cast for US Representatives

2002

Total vote (x 1,000) 984
  Democratic 345
  Republican 569
Leading party .... Republican
Percent for leading party 57.8%

2004

Total vote (x 1,000) 1,439
  Democratic 486
  Republican 913
Leading party .... Republican
Percent for leading party 63.5%

Women holding public office, 2006

US Congress 0
Statewide elected office..................... 1
State legislature 15

Black public officials, 2001

Total................................... 534
  US and state legislatures 32
  City/county/regional offices 335
  Judicial/law enforcement................. 9
  Education/school boards................ 158

Hispanic public officials, 2004

Total..................................... 1
  State executives & legislators 1
  City/county/regional offices 0
  Judicial/law enforcement................. 0
  Education/school boards................. 0

Governmental Finance

State government revenues, 2004

Total revenue ($1,000) $21,241,956
  Revenue per capita 5,060.02

General Revenue ($ per capita) $4,010.54
  Intergovernmental 1,483.81
  Taxes 1,620.67
    general sales 649.51
    individual income tax............. 580.92
    corporate income tax 46.81
  Current charges..................... 617.85
  Miscellaneous 288.20

State government expenditure, 2004

Total expenditure (x $1,000) $21,427,748
  Expenditure per capita............. 5,104.28
General Expenditure ($ per capita).... $4,278.35
  Education 1,451.01
  Public welfare..................... 1,175.88
  Health 161.41
  Hospitals.......................... 233.10
  Highways 336.52
  Police protection 43.53
  Correction 99.99
  Natural resources 47.89
  Parks & recreation.................... 16.27
  Governmental administration 180.89
  Interest on general debt 107.95

State debt & cash, 2004 ($ per capita)

Debt $2,659.09
Cash/security holdings.............. $7,250.19

Federal government grants to state & local government, 2004 (x $1,000)

Total........................... $6,145,106
By Federal Agency
  Defense $76,770

By Federal Agency, continued
  Education 548,713
  Energy........................... 22,495
  Environmental Protection Agency 34,888
  Health & Human Services. 3,740,808
  Homeland Security.................. 24,887
  Housing & Urban Development...... 329,424
  Justice 111,901
  Labor 114,521
  Transportation 600,894
  Veterans Affairs 6,611

Crime, Law Enforcement & Courts

Crime, 2004 (rates per 100,000 residents)

Property crimes 189,113
  Burglaries......................... 43,425
  Larcenies......................... 130,051
  Motor vehicle thefts 15,637
  Property crime rate................. 4,504.8
Violent crimes....................... 32,922
  Murders 288
  Forcible rape....................... 1,718
  Robberies 5,446
  Aggravated assaults 25,470
  Violent crime rate.................... 784.2

Police Agencies, 2004

Total agencies........................... 358
Total employees 14,592
  Male officers...................... 9,411
  Female officers..................... 1,156
  Male civilians...................... 1,455
  Female civilians.................... 2,570

Arrests, 2004

Total................................ 26,540
  Persons under 18 years of age 2,866

Prisoners under state & federal jurisdiction, 2004

Total prisoners...................... 23,428
  Percent change, 12/31/03 to 12/31/04 ... -1.2%
  Sentenced to more than one year 22,730
  rate per 100,000...................... 539

Persons under sentence of death, 7/1/05

Total.................................. 77
  White............................... 37
  Black 40
  Hispanic 0

State's highest court

Name ....Supreme Court
Number of members....................... 5
Length of term...................... 10 years
Intermediate appeals court? ....yes

Labor & Income

Civilian labor force, 2004

Total	2,077,000
Men	1,075,000
Women	1,002,000
Persons 16-19 years	92,000
White	1,469,000
Black	573,000
Hispanic	46,000
Asian	0

Civilian labor force as a percent of civilian non-institutional population, 2004

Total	65.1%
Men	71.2
Women	59.5
Persons 16-19 years	37.3
White	65.2
Black	64.2
Hispanic	77.8
Asian	0.0

Employment, 2004

Total	1,935,000
Men	1,004,000
Women	931,000
Persons 16-19 years	77,000
White	1,387,000
Black	514,000
Hispanic	44,000
Asian	0

Full-time/part-time labor force, 2002

Full-time labor force, employed	1,568,000
Part-time labor force, employed	283,000
Unemployed, looking for	
Full-time work	102,000
Part-time work	NA

Unemployment rate, 2004

Total	6.9%
Men	6.7
Women	7.1
Persons 16-19 years	16.8
White	5.6
Black	10.2
Hispanic	4.6
Asian	NA

Unemployed by reason for unemployment (as a percent of total unemployment), 2002

Job losers or completed temp jobs	54.7%
Job leavers	NA
Reentrants	28.2
New entrants	NA

Labor unions, 2004

Membership	54,000
percent of employed	3.0%

Experienced civilian labor force by private industry, first quarter 2004

Total	1,456,158
Natural Resources & Mining	13,115
Construction	113,340
Manufacturing	268,204
Trade, transportation & utilities	348,111
Information	26,498
Finance	89,648
Professional & business	191,740
Education & Health	158,814
Leisure & hospitality	193,512
Other	47,266

Experienced civilian labor force by occupation, 2004

Management	94,430
Business & Financial	51,480
Legal	11,430
Sales	184,090
Office & Admin. Support	276,820
Computers & Math	21,900
Architecture & Engineering	35,570
Arts & Entertainment	15,080
Education	100,560
Social Services	22,070
Healthcare Practitioner & Technical	90,660
Healthcare support	41,760
Maintenance & Repair	87,220
Construction	83,120
Transportation & moving	145,190
Production	207,340
Farming, fishing & forestry	3,350

Hours and earnings of production workers on manufacturing payrolls, 2004

Average weekly hours	39.5
Average hourly earnings	$14.73
Average weekly earnings	$581.84

Average annual pay

2004	$31,839
change from 2003	3.6%

Household income

Median household income, three-year average, 2002-2004	$39,326

Personal income, 2004 ($ per capita)

In current dollars	$27,172
In constant (2000) dollars	$25,200

Poverty

Persons below poverty level, three-year average, 2002-2004	14.0%

Federal individual income tax returns, 2003

Returns filed	1,804,803
Adjusted gross income ($1,000)	$70,930,507
Total income tax paid ($1,000)	$7,519,969

Economy, Business, Industry & Agriculture

Fortune 500 companies, 2005 1

Patents issued, 2004 581

Bankruptcy cases filed, 2004 15,900

Business firm ownership, 2002

Women-owned. 76,831
　Sales ($ mil) $10,891
Black-owned. 28,620
　Sales ($ mil) $1,692
Hispanic-owned. 3,019
　Sales ($ mil) $694
Asian-owned 4,416
　Sales ($ mil) $2,554
Amer. Indian/Alaska Native-owned 1,445
　Sales ($ mil) $157
Hawaiian/Pacific Isl.-owned 58
　Sales ($ mil) $11

Gross State Product, 2004 ($ mil)

Total Gross State Product $136,125
　Agriculture, forestry, fishing and
　　hunting 1,198
　Mining. 158
　Utilities 3,944
　Construction 7,670
　Manufacturing, durable goods. 13,953
　Manufacturing, non-durable goods . . . 12,312
　Wholesale trade. 7,643
　Retail trade. 10,903
　Transportation & warehousing 3,170
　Information 3,608
　Finance & insurance. 6,665
　Real estate, rental, leasing 15,185
　Professional and technical services 5,830
　Educational services. 650
　Health care and social assistance. 7,668
　Accommodation/food services. 4,417
　Other services, except government 3,263
　Government 21,094

Establishments, by major industry group, 2003

Total. 99,128
　Forestry, fishing & agriculture 660
　Mining. 84
　Construction 11,387
　Manufacturing. 4,321
　Wholesale trade. 4,830
　Retail trade. 18,379
　Transportation & warehousing 2,483
　Information 1,253
　Finance & insurance. 6,690
　Professional/scientific/technical 8,567
　Health care/social assistance 8,654
　Accommodation/food services. 8,351

Annual payroll by major industry group, 2003

Total ($1,000) $44,593,582
　Forestry, fishing & agriculture 176,397
　Mining. 52,215
　Utilities 615,268
　Construction 3,106,873
　Manufacturing. 10,520,747
　Wholesale trade. 2,499,890
　Retail trade. 4,111,894
　Transportation & warehousing 1,519,727
　Information 1,141,237
　Finance & insurance. 2,687,788
　Professional/scientific/technical . . . 2,947,233
　Health care/social assistance 6,211,542
　Accommodation/food services. 1,921,895

Agriculture

Number of farms, 2004 24,000
Farm acreage, 2004
　Total. 5,000,000
　Acres per farm, 2004 199
Farm income, 2003 ($mil)
　Net farm income $681
　Debt/asset ratio 13.7
Farm marketings, 2003 ($mil)
　Total. $1,644
　Crops 754
　Livestock 890

Principal commodities, in order by marketing receipts, 2003

　　Broilers, greenhouse, turkeys, tobacco

Federal economic activity in state

Expenditures, 2003
　Total ($ mil) $28,038
　Per capita $6,761
　Defense ($ mil). 4,257
　Non-defense ($ mil) 23,781
Defense department, 2003
　Payroll ($ mil) $2,807
　Contract awards ($ mil) $1,540
　Grants ($ mil). $51
　Homeland security grants ($1,000)
　　2004 . . . . $40,643
　　2005 . . . . $26,284

FDIC insured financial institutions, 2004

Number 96
　Assets ($bil) $44.5
　Deposits ($bil) 48.1

Fishing, 2004

Catch (x 1,000 lbs) 12,439
Value ($1,000). $18,541

Mining, 2004 ($ mil)

Total non-fuel mineral production $586
Percent of U.S. 1.3%

Construction, 2003 ($ mil)

Total contracts (including non-building). $9,707
   residential........................... 5,621
   non-residential 2,419

Establishments, receipts, payroll & employees, by major industry group, 2002

Mining 62
   Receipts ($1,000) $206,689
   Annual payroll ($1,000) $50,188
   Paid employees 1,208

Utilities 298
   Receipts ($1,000) .... NA
   Annual payroll ($1,000) $540,018
   Paid employees 10,008

Construction 11,341
   Receipts ($1,000) $15,285,860
   Annual payroll ($1,000) $3,397,754
   Paid employees 110,818

Manufacturing 4,457
   Receipts ($1,000) $81,132,781
   Annual payroll ($1,000) $10,602,614
   Paid employees 289,933

Wholesale trade 4,917
   Receipts ($1,000) $32,988,974
   Annual payroll ($1,000) $2,402,811
   Paid employees 60,376

Retail trade 18,416
   Receipts ($1,000) $40,629,089
   Annual payroll ($1,000) $3,915,453
   Paid employees 212,926

Transportation 2,419
   Receipts ($1,000) $4,296,475
   Annual payroll ($1,000) $1,409,426
   Paid employees 46,772

Information 1,221
   Receipts ($1,000) .... NA
   Annual payroll ($1,000) $1,097,121
   Paid employees 29,696

Finance & insurance 6,366
   Receipts ($1,000) .... NA
   Annual payroll ($1,000) $2,514,135
   Paid employees 65,370

Professional, scientific & technical 8,395
   Receipts ($1,000) $7,494,425
   Annual payroll ($1,000) $2,726,858
   Paid employees 63,924

Health care & social assistance 8,532
   Receipts ($1,000) $14,823,456
   Annual payroll ($1,000) $5,901,018
   Paid employees 179,660

Accommodation & food service 8,135
   Receipts ($1,000) $6,104,316
   Annual payroll ($1,000) $1,728,556
   Paid employees 152,822

Communication, Energy & Transportation

Communication

Daily newspapers, 2004 16
Households with computers, 2003 .... 55%
Households with internet access, 2003 ..... 46%

Energy

Electricity Consumption, 2001
Total (trillion Btu) 1,549
Per capita (million Btu) 382
By source of production (trillion Btu)
   Coal 414
   Natural gas 147
   Petroleum 470
   Nuclear electric power 521
   Hydroelectric power 2
By end-use sector (trillion Btu)
   Residential 322
   Commercial 235
   Industrial 609
   Transportation 383
Electric energy, 2003
   Production (billion kWh) 93.8
   Net summer capability (million kW) ... 20.7
Gas utilities, 2003
   Customers (x1,000) 574
   Sales (trillion Btu) 122
   Revenues ($mil) $981
Nuclear plants, 2003 7

Transportation, 2004

Public Road & Street Mileage 66,250
   Urban 10,688
   Rural 55,562
   Interstate 844
Vehicle miles of travel per capita 11,806.3
Total motor vehicle registrations 3,257,072
   Automobiles 1,922,964
   Buses 17,100
   Trucks 1,317,008
   Motorcycles 60,029
Licensed drivers 2,972,369
   19 years & under 177,298
Deaths from motor vehicle accidents 1,046

State Summary

Capital City............................Pierre
Governor.....................Michael Rounds
500 East Capitol St
Pierre, SD 57501
605-773-3212
Admitted as a state 1889
Area (square miles) 77,117
Population, 2004 (est.) 770,883
Largest City........................Sioux Falls
Population, 2004....................137,000
Personal income per capita, 2004
(in current dollars) $30,856
Gross state product ($ mil), 2004.......$29,386

Leading industries by payroll, 2003

Health care/Social assistance, Manufacturing,
Retail trade

Leading agricultural commodities by receipts, 2003

Cattle, soybeans, corn, wheat

Geography & Environment

Total area (sq. mi.).....................77,117
land 75,885
water 1,232

Federally-owned land, 2004 (acres) ...3,028,003
percent..............................6.2%

Highest point.....................Harney Peak
elevation (feet) 7,242

Lowest point ....Big Stone Lake
elevation (feet) 966

General coastline (miles)......................0

Tidal shoreline (miles).......................0

Capital City............................Pierre
Population 2000 13,876
Population 2004 13,983

Largest City........................Sioux Falls
Population 2000 124,000
Population 2004 137,000

Number of cities with over 100,000 population

1990 0
2000 1
2004 1

State park and recreation areas, 2003

Area (acres x 1,000)......................105
Number of visitors (x 1,000) 9,081
Revenues (x 1,000)....................$7,541
percent of operating expenditures......60.4%

National forest system land, 2004

Acres 2,014,000

Demographics and Characteristics of the Population

Population

1980 690,768
1990 696,004
2000 754,844
2004 (estimate)......................770,883
persons per sq. mile of land.............10.2
2005 (projection)....................771,803
Male..............................385,095
Female............................386,708
2010 (projection) 786,399
2020 (projection) 801,939
2030 (projection)....................800,462
Male..............................400,475
Female............................399,987

Metropolitan and Non-Metro. area population

	Metro	Non-Metro
1980	180,000	511,000
1990	205,000	491,000
2000	261,000	494,000

Change in population, 2000-2004

Number.............................16,043
percent..............................2.1%
Natural increase (births minus deaths)...15,226
Net internal migration ....-1,973
Net international migration 3,259

Persons by age, 2004

Under 5 years 51,720
18 years and over 580,009
65 years and over 109,493
85 years and over 17,658

Persons by age, 2010 (projected)

Total...............................786,399
Under 5 years......................54,618
5 to 17 years 139,534
18 and over 592,247
21 and over 560,170
65 and over 114,459
85 and over 21,025
Median age 37.5

Race, 2004 (estimate)

One Race
White...............................683,768
Black or African American............6,006
American Indian/Alaska Native.......66,535
Pacific Islander 280
Asian Indian.........................755
Chinese 817
Filipino 1,183
Japanese 367
Korean 367
Vietnamese..........................1,408
Two or more races.....................9,086

Persons of Hispanic origin, 2004

Total Hispanic or Latino	12,773
Mexican..............................	8,946
Puerto Rican	448
Cuban	0
Other Hispanic or Latino	1,617

Marital status, 2000

Population 15 years & over	589,612
Never married	153,889
Married............................	336,668
Separated	5,896
Widowed...........................	41,273
Divorced	51,886

Language spoken at home, 2000

Population 5 years & over	703,820
English only	658,245
Spanish	10,052
Other Indo-European languages	19,510
Asian/Pacific Island languages........	3,053

Households & families, 2000

Households..........................	290,245
with persons under 18 years	100,977
with persons over 65 years...........	72,515
persons per household	2.5
Families.............................	194,330
persons per family.....................	3.07
Married couples......................	157,391
Female householder,	
no husband present.................	26,205
One-person households	80,040

Nativity, 2000

Number of persons born in state	513,867
percent of population	68.1%

Immigration & Naturalization, 2004

Immigrants admitted....................	727
Persons naturalized	257
Asylums granted	7
Asylums denied	3

Vital Statistics and Health

Marriages

2002	6,687
2003	6,428
2004	6,485

Divorces

2002	2,545
2003	2,289
2004	2,364

Births

2003	11,027
Birthrate (per 1,000)..................14.4	
Low birth weight (2,500g or less)........ 6.6%	
To unmarried mothers................34.2%	

2003, continued

White.............................	8,910
Black	122
Hispanic	340
Asian/Pacific Islander	127
Amer. Indian/Alaska Native...........	1,876
2004 (preliminary)...................	11,340
Birthrate (per 1,000)..................14.7	
White.............................	9,199
Black	147
Hispanic	395
Asian/Pacific Islander	120

Deaths

2002

All causes	6,898
rate per 100,000....................	906.4
Heart disease	1,937
rate per 100,000....................	254.5
Malignant neoplasms	1,562
rate per 100,000....................	205.2
Cerebrovascular disease................	518
rate per 100,000.....................68.1	
Chronic lower respiratory disease	383
rate per 100,000.....................50.3	
2003	7,133
rate per 100,000.....................933.3	
2004 (provisional)	6,836

Infant deaths

2003 (provisional)	80
rate per 1,000 ....7.1	
2004 (provisional)	89
rate per 1,000 ....7.7	

Abortions, 2000

Total................................	1,000
rate per 1,000 women age 15-44...........5.5	

Physicians, 2003

Total................................	1,640
rate per 1,000 persons..................	215

Nurses, 2001

Total................................	8,440
rate per 1,000 persons...............	1,114

Community Hospitals, 2003

Number..............................	50
Beds (x 1,000)........................	4.4
Patients admitted (x 1,000)	103
Average daily census (x 1,000)	2.7
Average cost per day	$747
Outpatient visits (x mil)....................	1.5

Disability status of population, 2004

5 to 20 years	5.6%
21 to 64 years	10.5%
65 years and over	36.9%

Education

Educational attainment, 2004

Population over 25 years	479,068
Less than 9th grade	22,879
High school graduates only	160,952
Bachelor's degree only	82,997
Graduate or professional degree	28,225
Less than 9th grade percent	4.8%
High school graduate or more	87.5%
College graduate or more	25.5%
Graduate or professional degree	5.9%

Public school enrollment, Fall 2002

Total	128,039
Kindergarten through grade 8	87,441
Grades 9 through 12	40,598
Enrollment, 2005 (projected)	122,700

Graduating public high school seniors

2004 (estimate)	9,090

SAT scores, 2005

Average verbal score	589
Average math score	589
Percent of graduates taking test	5%

Public school teachers, 2004

Total (x 1,000)	9.0
Elementary (x 1,000)	6.3
Secondary (x 1,000)	2.7
Average salary	$33,200
Elementary	$33,300
Secondary	$33,100

State receipts & expenditures for public schools, 2004

Revenue receipts ($mil)	$1,006
Expenditures	
Total ($mil)	$1,017
Per capita	$1,329
Per pupil	$7,611

Institutions of higher education, 2004

Total	26
Public	14
Private	12

Enrollment in institutions of higher education, Fall, 2003

Total	49,157
Full-time men	15,467
Full-time women	17,438
Part-time men	5,818
Part-time women	10,434

Minority enrollment in institutions of higher education, Fall, 2003

Black, non-hispanic	599
Hispanic	464
Asian/Pacific Islander	340
American Indian/Alaska Native	3,504

Earned degrees conferred, 2003

Bachelor's	4,344
Master's	1,070
First-professional	166
Doctor's	75

State & local financial support for higher education, 2003-2004

Full-time equivalent enrollment (x 1,000)	28.1
Appropriations per FTE	$4,408
as a percent of tax revenue	8.2%

Social Insurance & Welfare Programs

Social Security benefits & beneficiaries, 2004

Beneficiaries	
Total	140,000
Retired & dependents	101,000
Survivors	21,000
Disabled & dependents	18,000
Annual benefit payments ($ mil)	
Total	$1,340
Retired & dependents	$913
Survivors	$264
Disabled & dependents	$163
Average Monthly Benefit	
Retired & dependents	$878
Disabled & dependents	$835
Widowed	$873

Medicare

Enrollment, 2001 (x 1,000)	120
Payments ($ mil, est.)	$600
Enrollment, 2003 (x 1,000)	122

Medicaid, 2002

Beneficiaries (x 1,000)	118
Payments ($ mil)	$504

State Children's Health Insurance, 2004

Enrollment (x 1,000)	13.4
Expenditures ($ mil)	$10.9

Persons without health insurance, 2003

Number (x 1,000)	91
percent	12.2%
Number of children (x 1,000)	16
percent of children	8.4%

Federal public aid

Temporary Assistance for Needy Families, 2004

Recipients (x 1,000)	6
Families (x 1,000)	3

Supplemental Security Income, 2003

Recipients (x 1,000)	13
Payments ($ mil)	$52

Food Stamp Program, 2004

Participants (x 1,000)	53
Benefits ($ mil)	$54

Housing & Construction

Housing units

Total 2003 (estimate) 337,931
Total 2004 (estimate) 342,620
Seasonal or recreational use, 2003 12,000
Owner-occupied single-family, 2003.... 146,000
　　Median value $96,977
Renter-occupied, 2003 87,000
　　Median rent $490
Homeownership rate, 2003 .... 70.9%
Homeownership rate, 2004 .... 68.5%

New privately owned housing units, 2004

Number authorized (x 1,000) 5.8
Value ($ mil) $656
Started 2005 (x 1,000, estimate) 4.9
Started 2006 (x 1,000, estimate) 4.8

Existing home sales

2002 (x 1,000) 14.9
2003 (x 1,000) 15.6
2004 (x 1,000) 17.3

Government & Elections

State Officials 2006

Governor (name/party/term expires)
　　　　Michael Rounds
　　　　Republican - 1/07
Lieutenant Governor .... Dennis Daugaard
Secretary of State .... Chris Nelson
Attorney General .... Larry Long
Chief Justice .... Dave Gilbertson

Governorship

Minimum age .... not specified
Length of term .... 4 years
Consecutive terms permitted 2
Who succeeds .... Lt. Governor

State Legislature

Name .... Legislature
Upper chamber .... Senate
　　Number of members 35
　　Length of term .... 2 years
　　Party in majority, 2006 .... Republican
Lower chamber .... House of Representatives
　　Number of members 70
　　Length of term .... 2 years
　　Party in majority, 2006 .... Republican

State Government Employees, 2004

Total 13,201
Payroll $40,050,357

Local Government Employees, 2004

Total 30,348
Payroll $80,998,252

Local Governments by Type, 2002

Total 1,866
　　County 66
　　Municipal 308
　　Township 940
　　School District 176
　　Special District 376

Voting age population, November 2004

Total 564,000
　　Male 275,000
　　Female 289,000
　　White 530,000
　　Black 2,000
　　Hispanic 10,000
　　Asian 7,000

Presidential Election, 2004

Total Popular Vote 388,215
　　Kerry 149,244
　　Bush 232,584
Total Electoral Votes 3

Federal representation, 2006 (109th Congress)

Senator .... Tim Johnson
　　Party .... Democrat
　　Year term expires 2009
Senator .... John Thune
　　Party .... Republican
　　Year term expires 2011
Representatives, total 1
　　Democrats 0
　　Republicans 0
　　Other 0

Votes cast for US Senators

2002
Total vote (x 1,000) 338,000
Leading party .... Democratic
Percent for leading party 49.6%

2004
Total vote (x 1,000) 391,000
Leading party .... Republican
Percent for leading party 50.6%

Votes cast for US Representatives

2002
Total vote (x 1,000) 337
　　Democratic 154
　　Republican 180
Leading party .... Republican
Percent for leading party 53.5%

2004
Total vote (x 1,000) 389
　　Democratic 208
　　Republican 179
Leading party .... Democratic
Percent for leading party 53.4%

Women holding public office, 2006
US Congress............................... 1
Statewide elected office...................... 0
State legislature 17

Black public officials, 2001
Total...................................... 0
  US and state legislatures 0
  City/county/regional offices 0
  Judicial/law enforcement................... 0
  Education/school boards................... 0

Hispanic public officials, 2004
Total...................................... 0
  State executives & legislators 0
  City/county/regional offices 0
  Judicial/law enforcement................... 0
  Education/school boards................... 0

Governmental Finance

State government revenues, 2004
Total revenue ($1,000) $3,863,621
  Revenue per capita 5,011.18

General Revenue ($ per capita)....... $3,770.33
  Intergovernmental 1,607.42
  Taxes 1,378.37
    general sales 760.56
    individual income tax.................. 0
    corporate income tax 61.10
  Current charges......................271.76
  Miscellaneous 512.78

State government expenditure, 2004
Total expenditure (x $1,000) $2,989,366
  Expenditure per capita............. 3,877.26
General Expenditure ($ per capita).... $3,543.01
  Education 1,135.20
  Public welfare........................ 900.33
  Health 121.42
  Hospitals............................55.32
  Highways 541.46
  Police protection 31.66
  Correction 79.99
  Natural resources 128.02
  Parks & recreation......................35.12
  Governmental administration 143.18
  Interest on general debt 127.94

State debt & cash, 2004 ($ per capita)
Debt $3,389.19
Cash/security holdings............. $12,279.68

Federal government grants to state & local government, 2004 (x $1,000)
Total............................ $1,620,407
By Federal Agency
  Defense $34,508

By Federal Agency, continued
  Education 182,710
  Energy 4,863
  Environmental Protection Agency 34,155
  Health & Human Services. 633,066
  Homeland Security................... 5,615
  Housing & Urban Development...... 117,246
  Justice 45,238
  Labor 32,524
  Transportation 258,000
  Veterans Affairs.................... 2,867

Crime, Law Enforcement & Courts

Crime, 2004 (rates per 100,000 residents)
Property crimes 14,905
  Burglaries........................... 3,149
  Larcenies.......................... 10,910
  Motor vehicle thefts 846
  Property crime rate................. 1,933.5
Violent crimes......................... 1,322
  Murders............................. 18
  Forcible rape........................ 338
  Robberies 114
  Aggravated assaults 852
  Violent crime rate 171.5

Police Agencies, 2004
Total agencies......................... 151
Total employees 2,234
  Male officers........................ 1,278
  Female officers....................... 84
  Male civilians....................... 408
  Female civilians..................... 464

Arrests, 2004
Total............................... 24,475
  Persons under 18 years of age 4,734

Prisoners under state & federal jurisdiction, 2004
Total prisoners........................ 3,095
  Percent change, 12/31/03 to 12/31/04 .... 2.3%
Sentenced to more than one year 3,088
  rate per 100,000....................... 399

Persons under sentence of death, 7/1/05
Total...................................... 4
  White................................. 4
  Black 0
  Hispanic 0

State's highest court
Name ....Supreme Court
Number of members...................... 5
Length of term .... 8 years
Intermediate appeals court? .... no

Labor & Income

Civilian labor force, 2004

Total.............................. 431,000
  Men 224,000
  Women 207,000
  Persons 16-19 years................. 30,000
  White........................... 403,000
  Black 0
  Hispanic 0
  Asian 0

Civilian labor force as a percent of civilian non-institutional population, 2004

Total............................... 73.7%
  Men 78.1
  Women 69.4
  Persons 16-19 years................. 64.7
  White.............................. 74.6
  Black 0.0
  Hispanic 0.0
  Asian 0.0

Employment, 2004

Total.............................. 416,000
  Men 216,000
  Women 200,000
  Persons 16-19 years............... 27,000
  White........................... 391,000
  Black 0
  Hispanic 0
  Asian 0

Full-time/part-time labor force, 2002

Full-time labor force, employed 325,000
Part-time labor force, employed........ 83,000
Unemployed, looking for
  Full-time work..................... 10,000
  Part-time work....................... NA

Unemployment rate, 2004

Total................................ 3.7%
  Men 3.5
  Women 3.8
  Persons 16-19 years................. 10.3
  White............................... 2.9
  Black .... NA
  Hispanic .... NA
  Asian .... NA

Unemployed by reason for unemployment (as a percent of total unemployment), 2002

Job losers or completed temp jobs .... NA
Job leavers............................... NA
Reentrants................................ NA
New entrants .... NA

Labor unions, 2004

Membership 21,000
  percent of employed 6.0%

Experienced civilian labor force by private industry, first quarter 2004

Total............................... 288,610
  Natural Resources & Mining 3,466
  Construction 16,665
  Manufacturing...................... 37,926
  Trade, transportation & utilities 74,071
  Information 6,789
  Finance 27,308
  Professional & business.............. 23,126
  Education & Health 51,907
  Leisure & hospitality................ 36,993
  Other............................. 10,359

Experienced civilian labor force by occupation, 2004

Management......................... 12,800
Business & Financial.................. 12,000
Legal................................ 1,550
Sales............................... 39,780
Office & Admin. Support.............. 65,980
Computers & Math 5,130
Architecture & Engineering 3,930
Arts & Entertainment................. 4,600
Education 21,980
Social Services 4,530
Healthcare Practitioner & Technical..... 22,150
Healthcare support 10,480
Maintenance & Repair 15,330
Construction 19,870
Transportation & moving 28,290
Production 28,720
Farming, fishing & forestry............ 18,840

Hours and earnings of production workers on manufacturing payrolls, 2004

Average weekly hours 42.0
Average hourly earnings $13.36
Average weekly earnings $561.12

Average annual pay

2004 .... $28,281
  change from 2003 .... 4.0%

Household income

Median household income, three-year average,
  2002-2004......................... $40,518

Personal income, 2004 ($ per capita)

In current dollars..................... $30,856
In constant (2000) dollars $28,617

Poverty

Persons below poverty level, three-year average,
  2002-2004.......................... 12.5%

Federal individual income tax returns, 2003

Returns filed........................ 357,449
Adjusted gross income ($1,000) $13,475,212
Total income tax paid ($1,000) $1,587,066

Economy, Business, Industry & Agriculture

Fortune 500 companies, 2005 0

Patents issued, 2004 88

Bankruptcy cases filed, 2004 2,900

Business firm ownership, 2002

Women-owned.	15,573
Sales ($ mil)	$1,547
Black-owned.	122
Sales ($ mil)	$61
Hispanic-owned.	355
Sales ($ mil)	$122
Asian-owned	301
Sales ($ mil)	$96
Amer. Indian/Alaska Native-owned	1,304
Sales ($ mil)	$137
Hawaiian/Pacific Isl.-owned.	NA
Sales ($ mil)	NA

Gross State Product, 2004 ($ mil)

Total Gross State Product	$29,386
Agriculture, forestry, fishing and hunting	1,931
Mining.	74
Utilities	501
Construction	1,219
Manufacturing, durable goods.	2,490
Manufacturing, non-durable goods	691
Wholesale trade.	1,584
Retail trade.	2,315
Transportation & warehousing	744
Information	785
Finance & insurance.	5,244
Real estate, rental, leasing	2,237
Professional and technical services	709
Educational services.	185
Health care and social assistance.	2,501
Accommodation/food services.	778
Other services, except government	677
Government	3,712

Establishments, by major industry group, 2003

Total.	24,468
Forestry, fishing & agriculture	131
Mining.	65
Construction	2,996
Manufacturing.	938
Wholesale trade.	1,295
Retail trade.	4,240
Transportation & warehousing	1,033
Information	453
Finance & insurance.	1,845
Professional/scientific/technical	1,583
Health care/social assistance	2,093
Accommodation/food services.	2,160

Annual payroll by major industry group, 2003

Total ($1,000)	$7,961,531
Forestry, fishing & agriculture	NA
Mining.	42,662
Utilities	111,336
Construction	552,123
Manufacturing.	1,134,936
Wholesale trade.	484,115
Retail trade.	907,721
Transportation & warehousing	228,600
Information	244,719
Finance & insurance.	844,050
Professional/scientific/technical	308,878
Health care/social assistance	1,779,750
Accommodation/food services.	343,184

Agriculture

Number of farms, 2004 32,000
Farm acreage, 2004

Total.	44,000,000
Acres per farm, 2004	1,386

Farm income, 2003 ($mil)

Net farm income	$1,321
Debt/asset ratio	15.6

Farm marketings, 2003 ($mil)

Total.	$4,018
Crops	1,899
Livestock	2,119

Principal commodities, in order by marketing receipts, 2003

Cattle, soybeans, corn, wheat

Federal economic activity in state

Expenditures, 2003

Total ($ mil)	$6,202
Per capita	$8,114
Defense ($ mil).	501
Non-defense ($ mil)	5,700

Defense department, 2003

Payroll ($ mil)	$292
Contract awards ($ mil)	$208
Grants ($ mil).	$38
Homeland security grants ($1,000)	
2004	$19,996
2005	$14,809

FDIC insured financial institutions, 2004

Number	91
Assets ($bil)	$442.5
Deposits ($bil)	53.3

Fishing, 2004

Catch (x 1,000 lbs)	0
Value ($1,000).	0

Mining, 2004 ($ mil)
Total non-fuel mineral production $210
Percent of U.S. 0.5%

Construction, 2003 ($ mil)
Total contracts (including non-building). $1,188
   residential.............................. 564
   non-residential 221

Establishments, receipts, payroll & employees, by major industry group, 2002

Mining 222
   Receipts ($1,000) $684,682
   Annual payroll ($1,000)............ $118,984
   Paid employees 3,327

Utilities 151
   Receipts ($1,000) .... NA
   Annual payroll ($1,000)............ $100,704
   Paid employees 2,065

Construction......................... 2,846
   Receipts ($1,000) $2,643,417
   Annual payroll ($1,000)............ $534,046
   Paid employees 19,040

Manufacturing 926
   Receipts ($1,000) $10,710,187
   Annual payroll ($1,000)........... $1,096,775
   Paid employees 37,019

Wholesale trade 1,329
   Receipts ($1,000) $7,845,096
   Annual payroll ($1,000)............ $445,439
   Paid employees 14,973

Retail trade........................... 4,249
   Receipts ($1,000) $9,601,175
   Annual payroll ($1,000)............ $903,550
   Paid employees 49,152

Transportation......................... 997
   Receipts ($1,000) $904,994
   Annual payroll ($1,000)............ $195,726
   Paid employees 7,529

Information............................. 460
   Receipts ($1,000) .... NA
   Annual payroll ($1,000)............ $236,547
   Paid employees 8,003

Finance & insurance 1,849
   Receipts ($1,000) .... NA
   Annual payroll ($1,000)............ $775,719
   Paid employees 23,413

Professional, scientific & technical 1,568
   Receipts ($1,000) $934,637
   Annual payroll ($1,000)............ $321,032
   Paid employees 10,426

Health care & social assistance 2,085
   Receipts ($1,000) $3,467,289
   Annual payroll ($1,000).......... $1,607,630
   Paid employees 53,868

Accommodation & food service........... 2,203
   Receipts ($1,000) $1,226,459
   Annual payroll ($1,000)............ $326,341
   Paid employees 32,226

Communication, Energy & Transportation

Communication
Daily newspapers, 2004 11
Households with computers, 2003 ....62%
Households with internet access, 2003 .....54%

Energy
Electricity Consumption, 2001
Total (trillion Btu)....................... 248
Per capita (million Btu) 327
By source of production (trillion Btu)
   Coal 44
   Natural gas 37
   Petroleum............................. 112
   Nuclear electric power 0
   Hydroelectric power 35
By end-use sector (trillion Btu)
   Residential 60
   Commercial 50
   Industrial 54
   Transportation 83
Electric energy, 2003
   Production (billion kWh) 7.9
   Net summer capability (million kW) 2.7
Gas utilities, 2003
   Customers (x1,000)..................... 171
   Sales (trillion Btu)...................... 25
   Revenues ($mil)....................... $189
Nuclear plants, 2003 0

Transportation, 2004
Public Road & Street Mileage 83,547
   Urban................................ 2,443
   Rural 81,104
   Interstate............................. 678
Vehicle miles of travel per capita........ 11,497.4
Total motor vehicle registrations........ 841,167
   Automobiles.......................... 395,975
   Buses 2,757
   Trucks 442,435
   Motorcycles 41,602
Licensed drivers 563,298
   19 years & under 38,325
Deaths from motor vehicle accidents 197

State Summary

Capital City......................Nashville
Governor.....................Phil Bredesen
Tennessee State Capitol
Nashville, TN 37243
615-741-2001
Admitted as a state 1796
Area (square miles).................. 42,143
Population, 2004 (est.) 5,900,962
Largest City.......................Memphis
Population, 2004.................. 672,000
Personal income per capita, 2004
(in current dollars) $30,005
Gross state product ($ mil), 2004 ..... $217,626

Leading industries by payroll, 2003

Manufacturing, Health care/Social assistance,
Retail trade

Leading agricultural commodities by receipts, 2003

Cattle, broilers, greenhouse, soybeans

Geography & Environment

Total area (sq. mi.).................... 42,143
land 41,217
water 926

Federally-owned land, 2004 (acres) 865,837
percent............................. 3.2%

Highest point............... Clingmans Dome
elevation (feet) 6,643

Lowest point .... Mississippi River
elevation (feet) 178

General coastline (miles).................... 0

Tidal shoreline (miles)...................... 0

Capital City.......................Nashville
Population 2000 545,000
Population 2004 547,000

Largest City.......................Memphis
Population 2000 650,000
Population 2004 672,000

Number of cities with over 100,000 population

1990 4
2000 5
2004 5

State park and recreation areas, 2003

Area (acres x 1,000)...................... 154
Number of visitors (x 1,000) 27,020
Revenues (x 1,000)................... $32,516
percent of operating expenditures...... 50.7%

National forest system land, 2004

Acres 701,000

Demographics and Characteristics of the Population

Population

1980 4,591,120
1990 4,877,185
2000 5,689,283
2004 (estimate)................... 5,900,962
persons per sq. mile of land........... 143.2
2005 (projection).................. 5,965,317
Male.......................... 2,905,863
Female......................... 3,059,454
2010 (projection) 6,230,852
2020 (projection) 6,780,670
2030 (projection) 7,380,634
Male.......................... 3,557,315
Female......................... 3,823,319

Metropolitan and Non-Metro. area population

	Metro	Non-Metro
1980	3,048,000	1,543,000
1990	3,300,000	1,577,000
2000	3,862,000	1,827,000

Change in population, 2000-2004

Number............................ 211,700
percent............................. 3.7%
Natural increase (births minus deaths)... 96,450
Net internal migration................ 71,204
Net international migration 42,226

Persons by age, 2004

Under 5 years 384,704
18 years and over 4,509,673
65 years and over 738,053
85 years and over 83,725

Persons by age, 2010 (projected)

Total............................ 6,230,852
Under 5 years 412,075
5 to 17 years 1,066,840
18 and over 4,751,937
21 and over 4,487,827
65 and over 829,023
85 and over 110,070
Median age 37.9

Race, 2004 (estimate)

One Race
White......................... 4,762,789
Black or African American 991,435
American Indian/Alaska Native....... 17,005
Pacific Islander 2,929
Asian Indian...................... 17,280
Chinese 10,763
Filipino 7,301
Japanese 3,331
Korean........................... 9,168
Vietnamese......................... 8,204
Two or more races..................... 55,689

Persons of Hispanic origin, 2004

Total Hispanic or Latino 165,155
   Mexican............................ 115,319
   Puerto Rican 8,414
   Cuban 7,317
   Other Hispanic or Latino 11,765

Marital status, 2000

Population 15 years & over 4,522,630
   Never married 1,062,818
   Married....................... 2,537,195
   Separated 90,453
   Widowed........................ 316,584
   Divorced 511,057

Language spoken at home, 2000

Population 5 years & over 5,315,920
   English only 5,059,404
   Spanish 133,931
   Other Indo-European languages 68,879
   Asian/Pacific Island languages........ 39,701

Households & families, 2000

Households........................ 2,232,905
   with persons under 18 years 785,816
   with persons over 65 years........... 502,332
   persons per household 2.48
Families............................ 1,547,835
   persons per family......................2.99
Married couples.................... 1,173,960
Female householder,
   no husband present................. 287,899
One-person households 576,401

Nativity, 2000

Number of persons born in state 3,679,056
   percent of population................. 64.7%

Immigration & Naturalization, 2004

Immigrants admitted.................. 5,620
Persons naturalized 2,613
Asylums granted 54
Asylums denied 23

Vital Statistics and Health

Marriages

2002 75,909
2003 69,335
2004 67,104

Divorces

2002 29,792
2003 29,155
2004 28,858

Births

2003 78,890
   Birthrate (per 1,000)....................13.5
   Low birth weight (2,500g or less)........ 9.4%
   To unmarried mothers................ 37.2%

2003, continued
   White............................. 60,982
   Black 16,250
   Hispanic 4,934
   Asian/Pacific Islander 1,489
   Amer. Indian/Alaska Native............ 180

2004 (preliminary)..................... 79,641
   Birthrate (per 1,000)....................13.5
   White............................. 60,406
   Black 17,401
   Hispanic 5,838
   Asian/Pacific Islander 1,671

Deaths

2002
All causes 56,606
   rate per 100,000.....................976.4
Heart disease 16,226
   rate per 100,000.....................279.9
Malignant neoplasms 12,518
   rate per 100,000.....................215.9
Cerebrovascular disease............... 3,980
   rate per 100,000......................68.7
Chronic lower respiratory disease 3,011
   rate per 100,000......................51.9
2003 57,306
   rate per 100,000.....................981.0
2004 (provisional) 55,555

Infant deaths

2003 (provisional) 717
   rate per 1,000 ....9.1
2004 (provisional) 675
   rate per 1,000 ....8.5

Abortions, 2000

Total................................ 19,000
   rate per 1,000 women age 15-44..........15.2

Physicians, 2003

Total................................ 15,178
   rate per 1,000 persons................... 260

Nurses, 2001

Total................................ 48,880
   rate per 1,000 persons.................. 850

Community Hospitals, 2003

Number 125
Beds (x 1,000)...........................20.3
Patients admitted (x 1,000) 813
Average daily census (x 1,000) 12.4
Average cost per day $1,187
Outpatient visits (x mil)...................10.0

Disability status of population, 2004

5 to 20 years 7.1%
21 to 64 years 15.4%
65 years and over..................... 44.1%

Education

Educational attainment, 2004

Population over 25 years	3,848,775
Less than 9th grade	285,274
High school graduates only	1,267,276
Bachelor's degree only	552,606
Graduate or professional degree	302,309
Less than 9th grade percent	7.4%
High school graduate or more	82.9%
College graduate or more	24.3%
Graduate or professional degree	7.9%

Public school enrollment, Fall 2002

Total	928,000
Kindergarten through grade 8	673,729
Grades 9 through 12	254,271
Enrollment, 2005 (projected)	923,900

Graduating public high school seniors

2004 (estimate)	43,620

SAT scores, 2005

Average verbal score	572
Average math score	563
Percent of graduates taking test	16%

Public school teachers, 2004

Total (x 1,000)	58.6
Elementary (x 1,000)	42.4
Secondary (x 1,000)	16.2
Average salary	$40,300
Elementary	$40,000
Secondary	$41,100

State receipts & expenditures for public schools, 2004

Revenue receipts ($mil)	$6,191
Expenditures	
Total ($mil)	$6,309
Per capita	$1,079
Per pupil	$6,983

Institutions of higher education, 2004

Total	95
Public	22
Private	73

Enrollment in institutions of higher education, Fall, 2003

Total	281,080
Full-time men	87,113
Full-time women	113,840
Part-time men	30,497
Part-time women	49,630

Minority enrollment in institutions of higher education, Fall, 2003

Black, non-hispanic	48,641
Hispanic	4,044
Asian/Pacific Islander	4,710
American Indian/Alaska Native	1,013

Earned degrees conferred, 2003

Bachelor's	24,369
Master's	8,136
First-professional	1,411
Doctor's	731

State & local financial support for higher education, 2003-2004

Full-time equivalent enrollment (x 1,000)	169.4
Appropriations per FTE	$5,053
as a percent of tax revenue	8.9%

Social Insurance & Welfare Programs

Social Security benefits & beneficiaries, 2004

Beneficiaries	
Total	1,070,000
Retired & dependents	688,000
Survivors	161,000
Disabled & dependents	221,000
Annual benefit payments ($ mil)	
Total	$10,679
Retired & dependents	$6,635
Survivors	$1,954
Disabled & dependents	$2,089
Average Monthly Benefit	
Retired & dependents	$929
Disabled & dependents	$862
Widowed	$874

Medicare

Enrollment, 2001 (x 1,000)	842
Payments ($ mil, est.)	$5,500
Enrollment, 2003 (x 1,000)	872

Medicaid, 2002

Beneficiaries (x 1,000)	1,732
Payments ($ mil)	$4,748

State Children's Health Insurance, 2004

Enrollment (x 1,000)	NA
Expenditures ($ mil)	$4.5

Persons without health insurance, 2003

Number (x 1,000)	778
percent	13.2%
Number of children (x 1,000)	150
percent of children	10.8%

Federal public aid

Temporary Assistance for Needy Families, 2004

Recipients (x 1,000)	190
Families (x 1,000)	72

Supplemental Security Income, 2003

Recipients (x 1,000)	161
Payments ($ mil)	$719

Food Stamp Program, 2004

Participants (x 1,000)	806
Benefits ($ mil)	$812

Housing & Construction

Housing units

Total 2003 (estimate)	2,557,471
Total 2004 (estimate)	2,595,060
Seasonal or recreational use, 2003	48,000
Owner-occupied single-family, 2003	1,281,000
Median value	$110,000
Renter-occupied, 2003	688,000
Median rent	$548
Homeownership rate, 2003	70.8%
Homeownership rate, 2004	71.6%

New privately owned housing units, 2004

Number authorized (x 1,000)	44.8
Value ($ mil)	$5,863
Started 2005 (x 1,000, estimate)	34.2
Started 2006 (x 1,000, estimate)	34.3

Existing home sales

2002 (x 1,000)	112.0
2003 (x 1,000)	128.8
2004 (x 1,000)	156.1

Government & Elections

State Officials 2006

Governor (name/party/term expires)
Phil Bredesen
Democrat - 1/07

Lieutenant Governor	John S. Wilder
Secretary of State	Riley Darnell
Attorney General	Paul Summers
Chief Justice	Mickey Barker

Governorship

Minimum age	30
Length of term	4 years
Consecutive terms permitted	2
Who succeeds	Speaker of Senate

State Legislature

Name	General Assembly
Upper chamber	Senate
Number of members	33
Length of term	4 years
Party in majority, 2006	Republican
Lower chamber	House of Representatives
Number of members	99
Length of term	2 years
Party in majority, 2006	Democratic

State Government Employees, 2004

Total	81,905
Payroll	$245,995,811

Local Government Employees, 2004

Total	235,609
Payroll	$666,040,350

Local Governments by Type, 2002

Total	930
County	92
Municipal	349
Township	0
School District	14
Special District	475

Voting age population, November 2004

Total	4,402,000
Male	2,118,000
Female	2,283,000
White	3,655,000
Black	651,000
Hispanic	128,000
Asian	29,000

Presidential Election, 2004

Total Popular Vote	2,437,319
Kerry	1,036,477
Bush	1,384,375
Total Electoral Votes	11

Federal representation, 2006 (109th Congress)

Senator	Bill Frist
Party	Republican
Year term expires	2007
Senator	Lamar Alexander
Party	Republican
Year term expires	2009
Representatives, total	9
Democrats	5
Republicans	4
Other	0

Votes cast for US Senators

2002

Total vote (x 1,000)	1,642,000
Leading party	Republican
Percent for leading party	54.3%

2004

Total vote (x 1,000)	NA
Leading party	NA
Percent for leading party	NA

Votes cast for US Representatives

2002

Total vote (x 1,000)	1,529
Democratic	708
Republican	771
Leading party	Republican
Percent for leading party	50.4%

2004

Total vote (x 1,000)	2,219
Democratic	1,032
Republican	1,161
Leading party	Republican
Percent for leading party	52.3%

Women holding public office, 2006

US Congress 1
Statewide elected office. 0
State legislature 23

Black public officials, 2001

Total. 180
US and state legislatures 18
City/county/regional offices 108
Judicial/law enforcement. 27
Education/school boards 27

Hispanic public officials, 2004

Total. 2
State executives & legislators 1
City/county/regional offices 1
Judicial/law enforcement. 0
Education/school boards 0

Governmental Finance

State government revenues, 2004

Total revenue ($1,000) $23,920,818
Revenue per capita 4,059.19

General Revenue ($ per capita) $3,546.80
Intergovernmental 1,530.07
Taxes 1,617.03
general sales 991.89
individual income tax. 23.76
corporate income tax 117.90
Current charges. 260.91
Miscellaneous 138.79

State government expenditure, 2004

Total expenditure (x $1,000) $22,164,577
Expenditure per capita 3,761.17
General Expenditure ($ per capita). . . . $3,494.59
Education 1,099.23
Public welfare. 1,418.16
Health 163.30
Hospitals. 58.20
Highways 262.26
Police protection .24.12
Correction 101.15
Natural resources 38.12
Parks & recreation. 20.33
Governmental administration 84.07
Interest on general debt 30.92

State debt & cash, 2004 ($ per capita)

Debt $607.66
Cash/security holdings. $5,261.02

Federal government grants to state & local government, 2004 (x $1,000)

Total. $9,863,362
By Federal Agency
Defense $54,845

By Federal Agency, continued
Education 712,885
Energy 22,505
Environmental Protection Agency 49,110
Health & Human Services. 6,618,062
Homeland Security. 70,561
Housing & Urban Development. 493,475
Justice 114,582
Labor 164,220
Transportation 742,258
Veterans Affairs. 21,005

Crime, Law Enforcement & Courts

Crime, 2004 (rates per 100,000 residents)

Property crimes 254,123
Burglaries. 60,205
Larcenies. 169,169
Motor vehicle thefts 24,749
Property crime rate. 4,306.5
Violent crimes. 41,024
Murders. 351
Forcible rape. 2,220
Robberies 8,840
Aggravated assaults 29,613
Violent crime rate 695.2

Police Agencies, 2004

Total agencies. 443
Total employees 24,189
Male officers. 13,946
Female officers. 1,639
Male civilians. 3,470
Female civilians. 5,134

Arrests, 2004

Total. 269,127
Persons under 18 years of age 34,434

Prisoners under state & federal jurisdiction, 2004

Total prisoners. 25,884
Percent change, 12/31/03 to 12/31/04 . . . . 1.9%
Sentenced to more than one year 25,884
rate per 100,000. 437

Persons under sentence of death, 7/1/05

Total. 108
White. 60
Black 43
Hispanic 1

State's highest court

Name . . . . .Supreme Court
Number of members 5
Length of term . . . . 8 years
Intermediate appeals court? . . . . .yes

Labor & Income

Civilian labor force, 2004

Total	2,894,000
Men	1,529,000
Women	1,365,000
Persons 16-19 years	144,000
White	2,361,000
Black	458,000
Hispanic	83,000
Asian	0

Civilian labor force as a percent of civilian non-institutional population, 2004

Total	63.4%
Men	69.9
Women	57.4
Persons 16-19 years	45.0
White	62.8
Black	66.1
Hispanic	74.3
Asian	0.0

Employment, 2004

Total	2,747,000
Men	1,452,000
Women	1,295,000
Persons 16-19 years	123,000
White	2,263,000
Black	411,000
Hispanic	80,000
Asian	0

Full-time/part-time labor force, 2002

Full-time labor force, employed	2,343,000
Part-time labor force, employed	433,000
Unemployed, looking for	
Full-time work	129,000
Part-time work	NA

Unemployment rate, 2004

Total	5.1%
Men	5.1
Women	5.1
Persons 16-19 years	14.4
White	4.1
Black	10.2
Hispanic	4.3
Asian	NA

Unemployed by reason for unemployment (as a percent of total unemployment), 2002

Job losers or completed temp jobs	54.7%
Job leavers	NA
Reentrants	NA
New entrants	NA

Labor unions, 2004

Membership	164,000
percent of employed	6.7%

Experienced civilian labor force by private industry, first quarter 2004

Total	2,211,203
Natural Resources & Mining	9,299
Construction	113,710
Manufacturing	407,523
Trade, transportation & utilities	575,566
Information	48,811
Finance	138,206
Professional & business	295,059
Education & Health	305,625
Leisure & hospitality	244,751
Other	70,382

Experienced civilian labor force by occupation, 2004

Management	153,460
Business & Financial	77,810
Legal	13,510
Sales	258,100
Office & Admin. Support	454,310
Computers & Math	38,200
Architecture & Engineering	36,700
Arts & Entertainment	26,770
Education	138,840
Social Services	28,780
Healthcare Practitioner & Technical	149,670
Healthcare support	61,840
Maintenance & Repair	117,450
Construction	105,240
Transportation & moving	262,020
Production	321,480
Farming, fishing & forestry	1,230

Hours and earnings of production workers on manufacturing payrolls, 2004

Average weekly hours	40.0
Average hourly earnings	$13.85
Average weekly earnings	$554.00

Average annual pay

2004	$34,925
change from 2003	4.0%

Household income

Median household income, three-year average, 2002-2004	$38,550

Personal income, 2004 ($ per capita)

In current dollars	$30,005
In constant (2000) dollars	$27,828

Poverty

Persons below poverty level, three-year average, 2002-2004	14.9%

Federal individual income tax returns, 2003

Returns filed	2,565,045
Adjusted gross income ($1,000)	$105,526,051
Total income tax paid ($1,000)	$13,092,645

Economy, Business, Industry & Agriculture

Fortune 500 companies, 2005 7

Patents issued, 2004 874

Bankruptcy cases filed, 2004 62,900

Business firm ownership, 2002

Women-owned	117,934
Sales ($ mil)	$17,640
Black-owned	26,816
Sales ($ mil)	$1,766
Hispanic-owned	4,301
Sales ($ mil)	$1,007
Asian-owned	7,245
Sales ($ mil)	$2,231
Amer. Indian/Alaska Native-owned	3,567
Sales ($ mil)	$619
Hawaiian/Pacific Isl.-owned	NA
Sales ($ mil)	NA

Gross State Product, 2004 ($ mil)

Total Gross State Product	$217,626
Agriculture, forestry, fishing and hunting	1,164
Mining	387
Utilities	886
Construction	8,518
Manufacturing, durable goods	22,026
Manufacturing, non-durable goods . . .	16,116
Wholesale trade	14,555
Retail trade	18,408
Transportation & warehousing	10,595
Information	6,630
Finance & insurance	13,804
Real estate, rental, leasing	23,219
Professional and technical services	10,256
Educational services	1,864
Health care and social assistance	17,985
Accommodation/food services	6,611
Other services, except government	5,735
Government	26,268

Establishments, by major industry group, 2003

Total	130,057
Forestry, fishing & agriculture	292
Mining	219
Construction	10,725
Manufacturing	6,824
Wholesale trade	7,439
Retail trade	23,729
Transportation & warehousing	4,330
Information	2,504
Finance & insurance	9,141
Professional/scientific/technical	10,715
Health care/social assistance	13,268
Accommodation/food services	10,285

Annual payroll by major industry group, 2003

Total ($1,000)	$73,203,638
Forestry, fishing & agriculture	36,056
Mining	113,032
Utilities	159,662
Construction	4,027,865
Manufacturing	14,763,513
Wholesale trade	5,055,058
Retail trade	6,244,337
Transportation & warehousing	3,925,136
Information	2,372,435
Finance & insurance	5,346,429
Professional/scientific/technical . . .	4,607,489
Health care/social assistance	10,583,296
Accommodation/food services	2,499,382

Agriculture

Number of farms, 2004 85,000
Farm acreage, 2004

Total	12,000,000
Acres per farm, 2004	136

Farm income, 2003 ($mil)

Net farm income	$480
Debt/asset ratio	9.8

Farm marketings, 2003 ($mil)

Total	$2,339
Crops	1,268
Livestock	1,071

Principal commodities, in order by marketing receipts, 2003

Cattle, broilers, greenhouse, soybeans

Federal economic activity in state

Expenditures, 2003

Total ($ mil)	$42,602
Per capita	$7,293
Defense ($ mil)	3,493
Non-defense ($ mil)	39,109

Defense department, 2003

Payroll ($ mil)	$1,297
Contract awards ($ mil)	$2,190
Grants ($ mil)	$33
Homeland security grants ($1,000)	
2004	$54,157
2005	$32,605

FDIC insured financial institutions, 2004

Number	208
Assets ($bil)	$133.5
Deposits ($bil)	90.2

Fishing, 2004

Catch (x 1,000 lbs)	0
Value ($1,000)	0

Mining, 2004 ($ mil)

Total non-fuel mineral production $660
Percent of U.S. 1.5%

Construction, 2003 ($ mil)

Total contracts (including non-building) $10,127
  residential........................... 5,882
  non-residential 2,878

Establishments, receipts, payroll & employees, by major industry group, 2002

Mining............................... 5,978
  Receipts ($1,000)............... $50,406,285
  Annual payroll ($1,000)......... $4,996,691
  Paid employees 113,494

Utilities 158
  Receipts ($1,000)...................... NA
  Annual payroll ($1,000)........... $154,611
  Paid employees 3,493

Construction........................ 10,570
  Receipts ($1,000)............... $19,761,128
  Annual payroll ($1,000)......... $4,192,945
  Paid employees 123,972

Manufacturing 6,948
  Receipts ($1,000)............. $109,293,454
  Annual payroll ($1,000)......... $14,824,828
  Paid employees 411,495

Wholesale trade 7,566
  Receipts ($1,000)............... $97,792,030
  Annual payroll ($1,000)......... $4,895,194
  Paid employees 121,961

Retail trade 24,029
  Receipts ($1,000)............... $60,136,403
  Annual payroll ($1,000).......... $5,881,592
  Paid employees 304,652

Transportation........................ 4,395
  Receipts ($1,000)............... $11,650,494
  Annual payroll ($1,000)......... $3,825,895
  Paid employees 118,267

Information........................... 2,386
  Receipts ($1,000)...................... NA
  Annual payroll ($1,000)......... $2,070,347
  Paid employees 54,188

Finance & insurance 8,835
  Receipts ($1,000)...................... NA
  Annual payroll ($1,000)......... $5,078,547
  Paid employees 114,767

Professional, scientific & technical 10,553
  Receipts ($1,000).............. $11,022,883
  Annual payroll ($1,000)......... $4,110,022
  Paid employees 96,346

Health care & social assistance 13,093
  Receipts ($1,000)............... $24,475,539
  Annual payroll ($1,000)......... $9,715,094
  Paid employees 295,313

Accommodation & food service.......... 10,070
  Receipts ($1,000)............... $8,024,900
  Annual payroll ($1,000)......... $2,277,488
  Paid employees 202,641

Communication, Energy & Transportation

Communication

Daily newspapers, 2004 26
Households with computers, 2003.........57%
Households with internet access, 2003 .....49%

Energy

Electricity Consumption, 2001
Total (trillion Btu) 2,195
Per capita (million Btu) 382
By source of production (trillion Btu)
  Coal 688
  Natural gas 265
  Petroleum........................... 708
  Nuclear electric power 299
  Hydroelectric power 63
By end-use sector (trillion Btu)
  Residential 500
  Commercial 369
  Industrial 746
  Transportation 581
Electric energy, 2003
  Production (billion kWh) 92.2
  Net summer capability (million kW) 20.9
Gas utilities, 2003
  Customers (x1,000)................. 1,158
  Sales (trillion Btu)................. 173
  Revenues ($mil)..................... $1,425
Nuclear plants, 2003 3

Transportation, 2004

Public Road & Street Mileage 88,988
  Urban............................. 21,060
  Rural 67,928
  Interstate.......................... 1,105
Vehicle miles of travel per capita....... 12,024.2
Total motor vehicle registrations...... 5,034,662
  Automobiles...................... 2,889,051
  Buses 18,431
  Trucks 2,127,180
  Motorcycles 108,659
Licensed drivers 4,247,884
  19 years & under 224,121
Deaths from motor vehicle accidents 1,288

State Summary

Capital City. . . . . Austin
Governor. . . . . .Rick Perry
           PO Box 12428
           Austin, TX 78711
           512-463-2000
Admitted as a state 1845
Area (square miles) 268,581
Population, 2004 (est.) 22,490,022
Largest City. . . . . .Houston
    Population, 2004. 2,013,000
Personal income per capita, 2004
    (in current dollars) $30,222
Gross state product ($ mil), 2004 . . . . . $884,136

Leading industries by payroll, 2003

Manufacturing, Health care/Social assistance,
    Professional/Scientific/Technical

Leading agricultural commodities by receipts, 2003

Cattle, cotton, greenhouse, broilers

Geography & Environment

Total area (sq. mi.). 268,581
    land 261,797
    water 6,784
Federally-owned land, 2004 (acres) . . . 3,130,345
    percent. 1.9%
Highest point. . . . . .Gaudalupe Peak
    elevation (feet) 8,749
Lowest point . . . . Gulf of Mexico
    elevation (feet) . . . . sea level
General coastline (miles). 367
Tidal shoreline (miles). 3,359
Capital City. . . . . Austin
    Population 2000 657,000
    Population 2004 682,000
Largest City. . . . . .Houston
    Population 2000 1,954,000
    Population 2004 2,013,000

Number of cities with over 100,000 population

1990 17
2000 24
2004 24

State park and recreation areas, 2003

Area (acres x 1,000). 668
Number of visitors (x 1,000) 17,620
Revenues (x 1,000). $13,385
    percent of operating expenditures. 26.4%

National forest system land, 2004

Acres 755,000

Demographics and Characteristics of the Population

Population

1980 14,229,191
1990 16,986,510
2000 20,851,820
2004 (estimate). 22,490,022
    persons per sq. mile of land. 85.9
2005 (projection) 22,775,044
    Male. 11,297,620
    Female. 11,477,424
2010 (projection) 24,648,888
2020 (projection) 28,634,896
2030 (projection) 33,317,744
    Male. 16,505,982
    Female. 16,811,762

Metropolitan and Non-Metro. area population

	Metro	Non-Metro
1980	11,307,000	2,922,000
1990	13,867,000	3,119,000
2000	17,692,000	3,160,000

Change in population, 2000-2004

Number. 1,638,232
    percent. 7.9%
Natural increase (births minus deaths). . 930,519
Net internal migration 157,893
Net international migration 558,004

Persons by age, 2004

Under 5 years 1,842,808
18 years and over 16,223,243
65 years and over 2,216,610
85 years and over 245,992

Persons by age, 2010 (projected)

Total. 24,648,888
    Under 5 years 2,077,328
    5 to 17 years 4,708,080
    18 and over 17,863,480
    21 and over 16,797,215
    65 and over 2,587,383
    85 and over 346,800
    Median age. 33.4

Race, 2004 (estimate)

One Race
    White. 18,725,559
    Black or African American 2,633,219
    American Indian/Alaska Native. 153,353
    Pacific Islander 24,494
    Asian Indian. 182,361
    Chinese 129,541
    Filipino 72,179
    Japanese 19,377
    Korean. 54,025
    Vietnamese. 153,691
Two or more races. 235,411

2   Texas

Persons of Hispanic origin, 2004
Total Hispanic or Latino	7,656,151
Mexican	6,546,502
Puerto Rican	78,188
Cuban	32,794
Other Hispanic or Latino	629,282

Marital status, 2000
Population 15 years & over	15,937,643
Never married	4,080,037
Married	9,004,768
Separated	398,441
Widowed	908,446
Divorced	1,561,889

Language spoken at home, 2000
Population 5 years & over	19,241,518
English only	13,230,765
Spanish	5,195,182
Other Indo-European languages	358,019
Asian/Pacific Island languages	374,330

Households & families, 2000
Households	7,393,354
with persons under 18 years	3,027,570
with persons over 65 years	1,469,876
persons per household	2.74
Families	5,247,794
persons per family	3.28
Married couples	3,989,741
Female householder, no husband present	937,589
One-person households	1,752,141

Nativity, 2000
Number of persons born in state	12,970,203
percent of population	62.2%

Immigration & Naturalization, 2004
Immigrants admitted	91,799
Persons naturalized	35,417
Asylums granted	171
Asylums denied	185

Vital Statistics and Health

Marriages
2002	181,989
2003	178,751
2004	178,512

Divorces
2002	85,395
2003	84,316
2004	81,324

Births
2003	377,476
Birthrate (per 1,000)	17.1
Low birth weight (2,500g or less)	7.9%
To unmarried mothers	34.3%

2003, continued
White	324,790
Black	42,245
Hispanic	184,912
Asian/Pacific Islander	13,292
Amer. Indian/Alaska Native	911
2004 (preliminary)	384,389
Birthrate (per 1,000)	17.1
White	327,511
Black	42,422
Hispanic	189,586
Asian/Pacific Islander	13,587

Deaths
2002
All causes	155,524
rate per 100,000	714.1
Heart disease	43,452
rate per 100,000	199.5
Malignant neoplasms	34,164
rate per 100,000	156.9
Cerebrovascular disease	10,548
rate per 100,000	48.4
Chronic lower respiratory disease	7,720
rate per 100,000	35.4
2003	155,171
rate per 100,000	701.5
2004 (provisional)	151,123

Infant deaths
2003 (provisional)	2,400
rate per 1,000	6.4
2004 (provisional)	2,334
rate per 1,000	6.1

Abortions, 2000
Total	89,000
rate per 1,000 women age 15-44	18.8

Physicians, 2003
Total	46,802
rate per 1,000 persons	212

Nurses, 2001
Total	129,710
rate per 1,000 persons	607

Community Hospitals, 2003
Number	414
Beds (x 1,000)	57.3
Patients admitted (x 1,000)	2,550
Average daily census (x 1,000)	36.4
Average cost per day	$1,482
Outpatient visits (x mil)	32.3

Disability status of population, 2004
5 to 20 years	6.1%
21 to 64 years	11.2%
65 years and over	42.7%

Texas 3

Education

Educational attainment, 2004

Population over 25 years 13,479,849
- Less than 9th grade 1,381,348
- High school graduates only....... 3,485,844
- Bachelor's degree only 2,342,088
- Graduate or professional degree..... 1,111,832
- Less than 9th grade percent 10.2%
- High school graduate or more 78.3%
- College graduate or more............. 24.5%
- Graduate or professional degree........ 8.2%

Public school enrollment, Fall 2002

Total............................. 4,259,823
- Kindergarten through grade 8 3,079,665
- Grades 9 through 12.............. 1,180,158
Enrollment, 2005 (projected) 4,365,200

Graduating public high school seniors

2004 (estimate)...................... 236,670

SAT scores, 2005

Average verbal score 493
Average math score 502
Percent of graduates taking test 54%

Public school teachers, 2004

Total (x 1,000) 289.5
- Elementary (x 1,000)..................148.9
- Secondary (x 1,000) 140.6
Average salary $40,500
- Elementary....................... $40,000
- Secondary....................... $40,900

State receipts & expenditures for public schools, 2004

Revenue receipts ($mil)................ $35,387
Expenditures
Total ($mil)......................... $37,498
- Per capita $1,696
- Per pupil $7,698

Institutions of higher education, 2004

Total.................................... 208
- Public.............................. 111
- Private.............................. 97

Enrollment in institutions of higher education, Fall 2003

Total............................. 1,225,807
- Full-time men 314,894
- Full-time women.................. 387,047
- Part-time men 213,834
- Part-time women.................. 310,032

Minority enrollment in institutions of higher education, Fall 2003

Black, non-hispanic.................. 138,894
Hispanic 291,669
Asian/Pacific Islander 57,437
American Indian/Alaska Native.......... 6,095

Earned degrees conferred, 2003

Bachelor's 82,649
Master's 27,879
First-professional..................... 4,899
Doctor's.............................. 2,626

State & local financial support for higher education, 2003-2004

Full-time equivalent enrollment (x 1,000) ..812.9
Appropriations per FTE................. $5,282
- as a percent of tax revenue............. 9.5%

Social Insurance & Welfare Programs

Social Security benefits & beneficiaries, 2004

Beneficiaries
- Total........................... 2,865,000
- Retired & dependents............. 1,939,000
- Survivors......................... 474,000
- Disabled & dependents............. 452,000
Annual benefit payments ($ mil)
- Total............................. $28,664
- Retired & dependents............. $18,429
- Survivors......................... $5,923
- Disabled & dependents............. $4,312
Average Monthly Benefit
- Retired & dependents $930
- Disabled & dependents............. $884
- Widowed........................... $895

Medicare

Enrollment, 2001 (x 1,000) 2,300
- Payments ($ mil, est.) $16,300
Enrollment, 2003 (x 1,000) 2,390

Medicaid, 2002

Beneficiaries (x 1,000)................. 2,953
Payments ($ mil) $11,121

State Children's Health Insurance, 2004

Enrollment (x 1,000)...................650.9
Expenditures ($ mil)................. $282.5

Persons without health insurance, 2003

Number (x 1,000)...................... 5,374
- percent............................ 24.6%
Number of children (x 1,000) 1,264
- percent of children 20.0%

Federal public aid

Temporary Assistance for Needy Families, 2004
Recipients (x 1,000)...................... 250
Families (x 1,000) 105

Supplemental Security Income, 2003
Recipients (x 1,000)...................... 455
Payments ($ mil) $1,901

Food Stamp Program, 2004

Participants (x 1,000) 2,259
Benefits ($ mil)...................... $2,307

Housing & Construction

Housing units

Total 2003 (estimate)	8,673,856
Total 2004 (estimate)	8,846,728
Seasonal or recreational use, 2003	202,000
Owner-occupied single-family, 2003	4,179,000
Median value	$99,139
Renter-occupied, 2003	2,695,000
Median rent	$639
Homeownership rate, 2003	64.5%
Homeownership rate, 2004	65.6%

New privately owned housing units, 2004

Number authorized (x 1,000)	188.8
Value ($ mil)	$22,487
Started 2005 (x 1,000, estimate)	154.9
Started 2006 (x 1,000, estimate)	149.1

Existing home sales

2002 (x 1,000)	412.4
2003 (x 1,000)	425.4
2004 (x 1,000)	485.5

Government & Elections

State Officials 2006

Governor (name/party/term expires)
Rick Perry
Republican - 1/07

Lieutenant Governor	David Dewhurst
Secretary of State	Roger Williams
Attorney General	Greg Abbott
Chief Justice	Wallace B. Jefferson

Governorship

Minimum age	30
Length of term	4 years
Consecutive terms permitted	not specified
Who succeeds	Lt. Governor

State Legislature

Name	Legislature
Upper chamber	Senate
Number of members	31
Length of term	4 years
Party in majority, 2006	Republican
Lower chamber	House of Representatives
Number of members	150
Length of term	2 years
Party in majority, 2006	Republican

State Government Employees, 2004

Total	268,172
Payroll	$919,721,092

Local Government Employees, 2004

Total	1,002,992
Payroll	$2,922,215,247

Local Governments by Type, 2002

Total	4,784
County	254
Municipal	1,196
Township	0
School District	1,089
Special District	2,245

Voting age population, November 2004

Total	15,813,000
Male	7,667,000
Female	8,146,000
White	13,246,000
Black	1,669,000
Hispanic	5,232,000
Asian	508,000

Presidential Election, 2004

Total Popular Vote	7,410,765
Kerry	2,832,704
Bush	4,526,917
Total Electoral Votes	34

Federal representation, 2006 (109th Congress)

Senator	Kay Bailey Hutchison
Party	Republican
Year term expires	2007
Senator	John Cornyn
Party	Republican
Year term expires	2009
Representatives, total	32
Democrats	11
Republicans	21
Other	0

Votes cast for US Senators

2002

Total vote (x 1,000)	4,514,000
Leading party	Republican
Percent for leading party	55.3%

2004

Total vote (x 1,000)	NA
Leading party	NA
Percent for leading party	NA

Votes cast for US Representatives

2002

Total vote (x 1,000)	4,295
Democratic	1,885
Republican	2,291
Leading party	Republican
Percent for leading party	53.3%

2004

Total vote (x 1,000)	6,959
Democratic	2,714
Republican	4,013
Leading party	Republican
Percent for leading party	57.7%

Women holding public office, 2006

US Congress 4
Statewide elected office...................... 3
State legislature 36

Black public officials, 2001

Total................................... 460
   US and state legislatures 19
   City/county/regional offices 302
   Judicial/law enforcement................. 44
   Education/school boards................. 95

Hispanic public officials, 2004

Total................................. 2,013
   State executives & legislators 38
   City/county/regional offices 841
   Judicial/law enforcement................ 375
   Education/school boards............... 759

Governmental Finance

State government revenues, 2004

Total revenue ($1,000) $90,570,423
   Revenue per capita 4,030.37

General Revenue ($ per capita) $3,184.76
   Intergovernmental 1,140.96
   Taxes 1,368.45
      general sales 687.98
      individual income tax.................. 0
      corporate income tax 0
   Current charges.....................312.72
   Miscellaneous 362.63

State government expenditure, 2004

Total expenditure (x $1,000) $77,338,118
   Expenditure per capita............. 3,441.53
General Expenditure ($ per capita).... $3,010.88
   Education 1,215.40
   Public welfare..................... 828.28
   Health 57.96
   Hospitals......................... 130.38
   Highways 259.38
   Police protection 20.70
   Correction 132.28
   Natural resources 39.76
   Parks & recreation....................5.37
   Governmental administration 69.98
   Interest on general debt 46.33

State debt & cash, 2004 ($ per capita)

Debt $1,020.18
Cash/security holdings.............. $8,803.35

Federal government grants to state & local government, 2004 (x $1,000)

Total........................... $27,792,386
By Federal Agency
   Defense $192,055

By Federal Agency, continued
   Education 3,177,815
   Energy........................ 64,259
   Environmental Protection Agency ... 258,167
   Health & Human Services. 15,294,303
   Homeland Security................. 239,697
   Housing & Urban Development.... 1,726,627
   Justice 408,316
   Labor 584,069
   Transportation 3,002,069
   Veterans Affairs................... 33,133

Crime, Law Enforcement & Courts

Crime, 2004 (rates per 100,000 residents)

Property crimes 1,010,702
   Burglaries......................... 220,118
   Larcenies......................... 696,507
   Motor vehicle thefts 94,077
   Property crime rate................. 4,494.0
Violent crimes...................... 121,554
   Murders.......................... 1,364
   Forcible rape...................... 8,388
   Robberies 35,817
   Aggravated assaults 75,985
   Violent crime rate 540.5

Police Agencies, 2004

Total agencies........................... 996
Total employees 79,415
   Male officers 44,001
   Female officers 5,118
   Male civilians..................... 13,363
   Female civilians................... 16,933

Arrests, 2004

Total............................. 1,116,524
   Persons under 18 years of age 194,033

Prisoners under state & federal jurisdiction, 2004

Total prisoners...................... 168,105
   Percent change, 12/31/03 to 12/31/04 .... 0.7%
Sentenced to more than one year 157,617
   rate per 100,000...................... 694

Persons under sentence of death, 7/1/05

Total................................... 414
   White........................... 128
   Black 172
   Hispanic 110

State's highest court

Name ....Supreme Court
Number of members....................... 9
Length of term....................... 6 years
Intermediate appeals court? ....yes

Labor & Income

Civilian labor force, 2004

Total	10,989,000
Men	6,087,000
Women	4,901,000
Persons 16-19 years	477,000
White	9,211,000
Black	1,172,000
Hispanic	3,715,000
Asian	356,000

Civilian labor force as a percent of civilian non-institutional population, 2004

Total	67.1%
Men	76.4
Women	58.2
Persons 16-19 years	37.4
White	67.0
Black	66.4
Hispanic	66.4
Asian	68.5

Employment, 2004

Total	10,332,000
Men	5,718,000
Women	4,614,000
Persons 16-19 years	389,000
White	8,728,000
Black	1,034,000
Hispanic	3,474,000
Asian	342,000

Full-time/part-time labor force, 2002

Full-time labor force, employed	8,581,000
Part-time labor force, employed	1,489,000
Unemployed, looking for	
Full-time work	589,000
Part-time work	92,000

Unemployment rate, 2004

Total	6.0%
Men	6.1
Women	5.9
Persons 16-19 years	18.5
White	5.2
Black	11.7
Hispanic	6.5
Asian	3.9

Unemployed by reason for unemployment (as a percent of total unemployment), 2002

Job losers or completed temp jobs	51.1%
Job leavers	11.7
Reentrants	30.1
New entrants	7.0

Labor unions, 2004

Membership	457,000
percent of employed	5.0%

Experienced civilian labor force by private industry, first quarter 2004

Total	7,606,934
Natural Resources & Mining	209,137
Construction	542,173
Manufacturing	884,596
Trade, transportation & utilities	1,905,219
Information	227,845
Finance	577,677
Professional & business	1,068,535
Education & Health	1,038,886
Leisure & hospitality	871,148
Other	272,946

Experienced civilian labor force by occupation, 2004

Management	446,950
Business & Financial	361,140
Legal	67,570
Sales	1,040,620
Office & Admin. Support	1,631,130
Computers & Math	210,820
Architecture & Engineering	200,690
Arts & Entertainment	91,980
Education	635,920
Social Services	86,150
Healthcare Practitioner & Technical	439,330
Healthcare support	224,150
Maintenance & Repair	411,210
Construction	476,220
Transportation & moving	676,040
Production	661,980
Farming, fishing & forestry	910

Hours and earnings of production workers on manufacturing payrolls, 2004

Average weekly hours	39.8
Average hourly earnings	$13.98
Average weekly earnings	$556.40

Average annual pay

2004	$38,511
change from 2003	4.2%

Household income

Median household income, three-year average, 2002-2004	$41,275

Personal income, 2004 ($ per capita)

In current dollars	$30,222
In constant (2000) dollars	$28,029

Poverty

Persons below poverty level, three-year average, 2002-2004	16.4%

Federal individual income tax returns, 2003

Returns filed	9,298,799
Adjusted gross income ($1,000)	$415,647,089
Total income tax paid ($1,000)	$55,187,401

Economy, Business, Industry & Agriculture

Fortune 500 companies, 2005 48

Patents issued, 2004 6,239

Bankruptcy cases filed, 2004 92,200

Business firm ownership, 2002

Women-owned. 468,705
   Sales ($ mil) $65,819
Black-owned. 88,777
   Sales ($ mil) $6,689
Hispanic-owned. 319,460
   Sales ($ mil) $42,250
Asian-owned 78,018
   Sales ($ mil) $22,627
Amer. Indian/Alaska Native-owned 16,863
   Sales ($ mil) $3,321
Hawaiian/Pacific Isl.-owned 1,543
   Sales ($ mil) $277

Gross State Product, 2004 ($ mil)

Total Gross State Product $884,136
   Agriculture, forestry, fishing and
      hunting 7,907
   Mining. 56,971
   Utilities 26,485
   Construction 39,700
   Manufacturing, durable goods. 59,070
   Manufacturing, non-durable goods . . . 47,679
   Wholesale trade. 59,523
   Retail trade. 61,304
   Transportation & warehousing 31,627
   Information 40,500
   Finance & insurance. 58,595
   Real estate, rental, leasing 90,670
   Professional and technical services 56,077
   Educational services. 4,450
   Health care and social assistance 53,645
   Accommodation/food services. 22,218
   Other services, except government 20,366
   Government 101,864

Establishments, by major industry group, 2003

Total. 483,945
   Forestry, fishing & agriculture 1,283
   Mining. 5,909
   Construction 38,813
   Manufacturing. 20,881
   Wholesale trade. 31,460
   Retail trade. 75,745
   Transportation & warehousing 14,702
   Information 9,712
   Finance & insurance. 33,266
   Professional/scientific/technical 53,024
   Health care/social assistance 48,407
   Accommodation/food services. 37,318

Annual payroll by major industry group, 2003

Total ($1,000) $281,636,318
   Forestry, fishing & agriculture 245,775
   Mining. 7,023,231
   Utilities 3,294,588
   Construction 17,481,822
   Manufacturing. 34,782,351
   Wholesale trade. 19,568,190
   Retail trade. 21,877,532
   Transportation & warehousing . . . 12,705,371
   Information 16,027,339
   Finance & insurance. 21,970,511
   Professional/scientific/technical . . 27,719,400
   Health care/social assistance 33,126,200
   Accommodation/food services. 9,047,239

Agriculture

Number of farms, 2004 229,000
Farm acreage, 2004
   Total. 130,000,000
   Acres per farm, 2004 568
Farm income, 2003 ($mil)
   Net farm income $5,939
   Debt/asset ratio 11.8
Farm marketings, 2003 ($mil)
Total. $15,342
   Crops 5,031
   Livestock 10,311

Principal commodities, in order by marketing receipts, 2003

Cattle, cotton, greenhouse, broilers

Federal economic activity in state

Expenditures, 2003
   Total ($ mil) $140,451
   Per capita $6,350
   Defense ($ mil). 30,354
   Non-defense ($ mil) 110,097
Defense department, 2003
   Payroll ($ mil) $9,799
   Contract awards ($ mil) $22,868
   Grants ($ mil). $128
   Homeland security grants ($1,000)
      2004 . . . . $195,671
      2005 . . . . $138,570

FDIC insured financial institutions, 2004

Number 681
   Assets ($bil) $215.4
   Deposits ($bil) 310.3

Fishing, 2004

Catch (x 1,000 lbs) 85,557
Value ($1,000). $166,208

Mining, 2004 ($ mil)
Total non-fuel mineral production $2,400
Percent of U.S. 5.5%

Construction, 2003 ($ mil)
Total contracts (including non-building) $44,683
   residential........................... 23,583
   non-residential 12,942

Establishments, receipts, payroll & employees, by major industry group, 2002

Mining 24,087
   Receipts ($1,000) $182,911,093
   Annual payroll ($1,000)........ $21,173,895
   Paid employees 477,840

Utilities 2,222
   Receipts ($1,000) .... NA
   Annual payroll ($1,000)....... $3,123,223
   Paid employees 51,972

Construction...................... 37,444
   Receipts ($1,000) $94,067,369
   Annual payroll ($1,000)........ $18,723,430
   Paid employees 555,061

Manufacturing 21,450
   Receipts ($1,000) $310,815,965
   Annual payroll ($1,000)........ $34,105,193
   Paid employees 855,658

Wholesale trade 31,832
   Receipts ($1,000) $397,405,111
   Annual payroll ($1,000)........ $18,808,604
   Paid employees 439,755

Retail trade 75,703
   Receipts ($1,000) $228,694,755
   Annual payroll ($1,000)........ $21,104,589
   Paid employees 1,026,326

Transportation...................... 14,449
   Receipts ($1,000) $32,254,393
   Annual payroll ($1,000)......... $9,037,291
   Paid employees 271,881

Information......................... 9,671
   Receipts ($1,000) .... NA
   Annual payroll ($1,000)........ $15,682,756
   Paid employees 282,757

Finance & insurance 32,166
   Receipts ($1,000) .... NA
   Annual payroll ($1,000)........ $19,703,380
   Paid employees 416,898

Professional, scientific & technical 52,414
   Receipts ($1,000) $62,549,237
   Annual payroll ($1,000)........ $26,003,813
   Paid employees 495,406

Health care & social assistance 47,402
   Receipts ($1,000) $81,493,532
   Annual payroll ($1,000)........ $31,439,528
   Paid employees 996,891

Accommodation & food service.......... 36,591
   Receipts ($1,000) $29,914,774
   Annual payroll ($1,000).......... $8,432,938
   Paid employees 715,844

Communication, Energy & Transportation

Communication
Daily newspapers, 2004 85
Households with computers, 2003.......... 59%
Households with internet access, 2003 ..... 52%

Energy
Electricity Consumption, 2001
Total (trillion Btu)..................... 12,029
Per capita (million Btu) 564
By source of production (trillion Btu)
   Coal 1,493
   Natural gas............................ 4,435
   Petroleum.............................. 5,521
   Nuclear electric power 399
   Hydroelectric power 12
By end-use sector (trillion Btu)
   Residential 1,570
   Commercial 1,356
   Industrial 6,426
   Transportation 2,677
Electric energy, 2003
   Production (billion kWh) 379.2
   Net summer capability (million kW) 99.6
Gas utilities, 2003
   Customers (x1,000)..................... 4,186
   Sales (trillion Btu).................... 1,417
   Revenues ($mil)...................... $8,547
Nuclear plants, 2003 4

Transportation, 2004
Public Road & Street Mileage 303,176
   Urban............................. 83,447
   Rural 219,729
   Interstate........................ 3,233
Vehicle miles of travel per capita....... 10,271.1
Total motor vehicle registrations..... 16,906,714
   Automobiles...................... 8,735,544
   Buses 86,753
   Trucks 8,084,417
   Motorcycles 286,992
Licensed drivers 14,543,528
   19 years & under 689,718
Deaths from motor vehicle accidents 3,583

State Summary

Capital City..................Salt Lake City
Governor.................... Michael Leavitt
210 State Capitol
Salt Lake City, UT 84114
801-538-1000
Admitted as a state 1896
Area (square miles).................. 84,899
Population, 2004 (est.) 2,389,039
Largest City....................Salt Lake City
Population, 2004.................. 179,000
Personal income per capita, 2004
(in current dollars) $26,606
Gross state product ($ mil), 2004 ...... $82,611

Leading industries by payroll, 2003

Manufacturing, Health care/Social assistance, Retail trade

Leading agricultural commodities by receipts, 2003

Cattle, dairy products, hogs, hay

Geography & Environment

Total area (sq. mi.).................... 84,899
  land 82,144
  water 2,755

Federally-owned land, 2004 (acres) .. 30,271,905
  percent............................ 57.5%

Highest point.................... Kings Peak
  elevation (feet) 13,528

Lowest point .... Beaverdam Creek
  elevation (feet) 2,000

General coastline (miles)..................... 0

Tidal shoreline (miles)....................... 0

Capital City....................Salt Lake City
  Population 2000 182,000
  Population 2004 179,000

Largest City....................Salt Lake City
  Population 2000 182,000
  Population 2004 179,000

Number of cities with over 100,000 population

1990 1
2000 3
2004 2

State park and recreation areas, 2003

Area (acres x 1,000)...................... 122
Number of visitors (x 1,000) 5,806
Revenues (x 1,000)..................... $7,991
  percent of operating expenditures...... 46.6%

National forest system land, 2004

Acres 8,194,000

Demographics and Characteristics of the Population

Population

1980 1,461,037
1990 1,722,850
2000 2,233,169
2004 (estimate)..................... 2,389,039
  persons per sq. mile of land.............29.1
2005 (projection)................... 2,417,998
  Male....................... 1,211,646
  Female....................... 1,206,352
2010 (projection) 2,595,013
2020 (projection)................... 2,990,094
2030 (projection)................... 3,485,367
  Male....................... 1,752,459
  Female....................... 1,732,908

Metropolitan and Non-Metro. area population

	Metro	Non-Metro
1980	1,128,000	333,000
1990	1,336,000	387,000
2000	1,708,000	525,000

Change in population, 2000-2004

Number............................. 155,841
  percent............................. 7.0%
Natural increase (births minus deaths).. 148,864
Net internal migration..................-39,856
Net international migration 42,176

Persons by age, 2004

Under 5 years 232,793
18 years and over 1,648,925
65 years and over 207,711
85 years and over 25,700

Persons by age, 2010 (projected)

Total............................. 2,595,013
  Under 5 years..................... 240,868
  5 to 17 years 578,117
  18 and over 1,776,028
  21 and over 1,634,512
  65 and over 234,798
  85 and over 32,829
  Median age........................29.5

Race, 2004 (estimate)

One Race
  White........................... 2,241,072
  Black or African American........... 22,534
  American Indian/Alaska Native....... 32,191
  Pacific Islander 17,368
  Asian Indian...................... 9,936
  Chinese 8,710
  Filipino 4,987
  Japanese 4,051
  Korean 2,418
  Vietnamese........................ 5,171
Two or more races..................... 31,266

2   Utah

Persons of Hispanic origin, 2004
Total Hispanic or Latino 249,091
   Mexican.......................... 188,430
   Puerto Rican 2,027
   Cuban 3,138
   Other Hispanic or Latino 34,510

Marital status, 2000
Population 15 years & over 1,639,688
   Never married 457,473
   Married........................... 962,497
   Separated 19,676
   Widowed........................... 67,227
   Divorced 132,815

Language spoken at home, 2000
Population 5 years & over 2,023,875
   English only 1,770,626
   Spanish 150,244
   Other Indo-European languages..... 49,865
   Asian/Pacific Island languages....... 37,805

Households & families, 2000
Households........................... 701,281
   with persons under 18 years 321,108
   with persons over 65 years.......... 130,469
   persons per household 3.13
Families............................. 535,294
   persons per family....................3.57
Married couples...................... 442,931
Female householder,
   no husband present................. 65,941
One-person households 124,756

Nativity, 2000
Number of persons born in state 1,405,177
   percent of population................. 62.9%

Immigration & Naturalization, 2004
Immigrants admitted.................. 4,255
Persons naturalized 3,110
Asylums granted 17
Asylums denied 11

Vital Statistics and Health

Marriages
2002 24,073
2003 24,087
2004 23,796

Divorces
2002 9,494
2003 9,517
2004 9,811

Births
2003 49,860
   Birthrate (per 1,000)..................21.2
   Low birth weight (2,500g or less)....... 6.5%
   To unmarried mothers............... 17.2%

2003, continued
   White............................. 47,338
   Black 384
   Hispanic 7,072
   Asian/Pacific Islander 1,532
   Amer. Indian/Alaska Native............ 616

2004 (preliminary)................... 50,669
   Birthrate (per 1,000).................21.2
   White............................. 48,256
   Black 299
   Hispanic 7,180
   Asian/Pacific Islander 1,454

Deaths
2002
All causes 13,116
   rate per 100,000..................... 566.3
Heart disease 2,977
   rate per 100,000..................... 128.5
Malignant neoplasms................... 2,376
   rate per 100,000.....................102.6
Cerebrovascular disease.................. 903
   rate per 100,000.....................39.0
Chronic lower respiratory disease 603
   rate per 100,000.....................26.0
2003 13,408
   rate per 100,000.....................570.2
2004 (provisional) 13,331

Infant deaths
2003 (provisional) 252
   rate per 1,000 5
2004 (provisional) 257
   rate per 1,000 ....5.1

Abortions, 2000
Total................................. 4,000
   rate per 1,000 women age 15-44...........6.6

Physicians, 2003
Total................................. 4,987
   rate per 1,000 persons.................. 212

Nurses, 2001
Total................................ 13,830
   rate per 1,000 persons................. 607

Community Hospitals, 2003
Number................................. 42
Beds (x 1,000)..........................4.4
Patients admitted (x 1,000) 215
Average daily census (x 1,000) 2.5
Average cost per day $1,654
Outpatient visits (x mil)..................4.5

Disability status of population, 2004
5 to 20 years 5.4%
21 to 64 years 10.2%
65 years and over 37.6%

Education

Educational attainment, 2004

Population over 25 years 1,313,608
   Less than 9th grade 40,984
   High school graduates only......... 336,856
   Bachelor's degree only 255,298
   Graduate or professional degree..... 112,324
   Less than 9th grade percent 3.1%
   High school graduate or more 91.0%
   College graduate or more............. 30.8%
   Graduate or professional degree........ 8.6%

Public school enrollment, Fall 2002

Total.............................. 489,072
   Kindergarten through grade 8 342,570
   Grades 9 through 12................ 146,502
Enrollment, 2005 (projected) 498,200

Graduating public high school seniors

2004 (estimate)...................... 29,920

SAT scores, 2005

Average verbal score 566
Average math score 557
Percent of graduates taking test 7%

Public school teachers, 2004

Total (x 1,000) 21.7
   Elementary (x 1,000)..................... 11.7
   Secondary (x 1,000) 9.9
Average salary $39,000
   Elementary........................ $39,000
   Secondary........................ $39,000

State receipts & expenditures for public schools, 2004

Revenue receipts ($mil)................ $3,022
Expenditures
Total ($mil)......................... $3,103
   Per capita $1,319
   Per pupil $5,556

Institutions of higher education, 2004

Total.................................. 28
   Public............................... 13
   Private.............................. 15

Enrollment in institutions of higher education, Fall, 2003

Total............................. 191,218
   Full-time men 62,096
   Full-time women.................... 58,033
   Part-time men 34,289
   Part-time women.................... 36,800

Minority enrollment in institutions of higher education, Fall, 2003

Black, non-hispanic..................... 1,403
Hispanic 6,494
Asian/Pacific Islander 4,884
American Indian/Alaska Native.......... 1,995

Earned degrees conferred, 2003

Bachelor's 19,086
Master's............................. 3,827
First-professional........................ 410
Doctor's.............................. 336

State & local financial support for higher education, 2003-2004

Full-time equivalent enrollment (x 1,000) ..108.6
Appropriations per FTE................ $5,048
   as a percent of tax revenue............. 10.2%

Social Insurance & Welfare Programs

Social Security benefits & beneficiaries, 2004

Beneficiaries
   Total............................. 262,000
   Retired & dependents............... 191,000
   Survivors.......................... 36,000
   Disabled & dependents............... 36,000
Annual benefit payments ($ mil)
   Total............................. $2,710
   Retired & dependents............... $1,892
   Survivors.......................... $476
   Disabled & dependents............... $342
Average Monthly Benefit
   Retired & dependents................ $959
   Disabled & dependents............... $886
   Widowed........................... $982

Medicare

Enrollment, 2001 (x 1,000) 210
   Payments ($ mil, est.) $1,100
Enrollment, 2003 (x 1,000) 220

Medicaid, 2002

Beneficiaries (x 1,000).................... 275
Payments ($ mil) $1,216

State Children's Health Insurance, 2004

Enrollment (x 1,000).................... 38.7
Expenditures ($ mil).................. $28.0

Persons without health insurance, 2003

Number (x 1,000)....................... 298
   percent........................... 12.7%
Number of children (x 1,000) 69
   percent of children 9.0%

Federal public aid

Temporary Assistance for Needy Families, 2004
Recipients (x 1,000)....................... 23
Families (x 1,000) 9

Supplemental Security Income, 2003
Recipients (x 1,000)....................... 21
Payments ($ mil) $99

Food Stamp Program, 2004

Participants (x 1,000) 123
Benefits ($ mil)........................ $123

4   Utah

Housing & Construction

Housing units
Total 2003 (estimate) 826,953
Total 2004 (estimate) 848,737
Seasonal or recreational use, 2003 23,000
Owner-occupied single-family, 2003 488,000
   Median value $156,657
Renter-occupied, 2003 201,000
   Median rent $632
Homeownership rate, 2003 .... 73.4%
Homeownership rate, 2004 .... 74.9%

New privately owned housing units, 2004
Number authorized (x 1,000) 24.3
Value ($ mil) $3,633
Started 2005 (x 1,000, estimate) 19.9
Started 2006 (x 1,000, estimate) 19.8

Existing home sales
2002 (x 1,000) 40.9
2003 (x 1,000) 43.9
2004 (x 1,000) 43.6

Government & Elections

State Officials 2006
Governor (name/party/term expires)
     Michael Leavitt
     Republican - 1/09
Lieutenant Governor ....Gayle Herbert
Secretary of State ....(no Secty. of State)
Attorney General .... Mike Shurtleff
Chief Justice ....Christine Durham

Governorship
Minimum age 30
Length of term .... 4 years
Consecutive terms permitted ...... not specified
Who succeeds ....Lt. Governor

State Legislature
Name .... Legislature
Upper chamber ....Senate
   Number of members 29
   Length of term .... 4 years
   Party in majority, 2006 .... Republican
Lower chamber ....House of Representatives
   Number of members 75
   Length of term .... 2 years
   Party in majority, 2006 .... Republican

State Government Employees, 2004
Total 48,900
Payroll $158,969,037

Local Government Employees, 2004
Total 78,695
Payroll $229,240,869

Local Governments by Type, 2002
Total 605
   County 29
   Municipal 236
   Township 0
   School District 40
   Special District 300

Voting age population, November 2004
Total 1,629,000
   Male 811,000
   Female 818,000
   White 1,561,000
   Black 10,000
   Hispanic 104,000
   Asian 32,000

Presidential Election, 2004
Total Popular Vote 927,844
   Kerry 241,199
   Bush 663,742
Total Electoral Votes 5

Federal representation, 2006 (109th Congress)
Senator ....Orrin G. Hatch
   Party .... Republican
   Year term expires 2007
Senator ....Robert Bennett
   Party .... Republican
   Year term expires 2011
Representatives, total 3
   Democrats 1
   Republicans 2
   Other 0

Votes cast for US Senators
2002
Total vote (x 1,000) .... NA
Leading party .... NA
Percent for leading party .... NA
2004
Total vote (x 1,000) 912,000
Leading party .... Republican
Percent for leading party 68.7%

Votes cast for US Representatives
2002
Total vote (x 1,000) 557
   Democratic 221
   Republican 322
Leading party .... Republican
Percent for leading party 57.8%
2004
Total vote (x 1,000) 909
   Democratic 362
   Republican 520
Leading party .... Republican
Percent for leading party 57.3%

Women holding public office, 2006
US Congress 0
Statewide elected office. 0
State legislature 20

Black public officials, 2001
Total. 5
    US and state legislatures 1
    City/county/regional offices 3
    Judicial/law enforcement. 1
    Education/school boards. 0

Hispanic public officials, 2004
Total. 3
    State executives & legislators 0
    City/county/regional offices 3
    Judicial/law enforcement. 0
    Education/school boards. 0

Governmental Finance

State government revenues, 2004
Total revenue ($1,000) $13,167,850
    Revenue per capita 5,439.01

General Revenue ($ per capita) $3,948.80
    Intergovernmental 1,188.70
    Taxes 1,733.15
        general sales 644.73
        individual income tax. 698.90
        corporate income tax 59.89
    Current charges. 765.60
    Miscellaneous 261.34

State government expenditure, 2004
Total expenditure (x $1,000) $10,794,264
    Expenditure per capita. 4,458.60
General Expenditure ($ per capita). . . . $4,028.45
    Education 1,790.98
    Public welfare. .823.21
    Health 125.67
    Hospitals. 208.99
    Highways 337.51
    Police protection 47.34
    Correction 113.97
    Natural resources 71.36
    Parks & recreation. 17.24
    Governmental administration 236.23
    Interest on general debt 76.95

State debt & cash, 2004 ($ per capita)
Debt $2,049.62
Cash/security holdings. $8,043.22

Federal government grants to state & local government, 2004 (x $1,000)
Total. $2,947,857
By Federal Agency
    Defense $45,656

By Federal Agency, continued
    Education 296,455
    Energy 17,257
    Environmental Protection Agency 33,761
    Health & Human Services. 1,539,310
    Homeland Security 12,436
    Housing & Urban Development. 148,048
    Justice 54,610
    Labor 71,650
    Transportation 328,782
    Veterans Affairs. 3,246

Crime, Law Enforcement & Courts

Crime, 2004 (rates per 100,000 residents)
Property crimes 97,607
    Burglaries. 15,221
    Larcenies. 74,735
    Motor vehicle thefts 7,651
    Property crime rate. 4,085.6
Violent crimes. 5,639
    Murders. 46
    Forcible rape. 933
    Robberies 1,236
    Aggravated assaults 3,424
    Violent crime rate 236.0

Police Agencies, 2004
Total agencies. 123
Total employees 7,062
    Male officers. 4,193
    Female officers. 332
    Male civilians. 1,154
    Female civilians. 1,383

Arrests, 2004
Total. 90,811
    Persons under 18 years of age 21,687

Prisoners under state & federal jurisdiction, 2004
Total prisoners. 5,989
    Percent change, 12/31/03 to 12/31/04 . . . . 3.9%
Sentenced to more than one year 5,916
    rate per 100,000. 246

Persons under sentence of death, 7/1/05
Total. 10
    White. 6
    Black 2
    Hispanic 1

State's highest court
Name . . . . .Supreme Court
Number of members. 5
Length of term . . . . 10 years
Intermediate appeals court? . . . . no

Labor & Income

Civilian labor force, 2004

Total	1,206,000
Men	668,000
Women	538,000
Persons 16-19 years	99,000
White	1,147,000
Black	0
Hispanic	111,000
Asian	0

Civilian labor force as a percent of civilian non-institutional population, 2004

Total	71.0%
Men	79.5
Women	62.7
Persons 16-19 years	59.4
White	71.0
Black	0.0
Hispanic	74.8
Asian	0.0

Employment, 2004

Total	1,142,000
Men	633,000
Women	509,000
Persons 16-19 years	82,000
White	1,088,000
Black	0
Hispanic	100,000
Asian	0

Full-time/part-time labor force, 2002

Full-time labor force, employed	830,000
Part-time labor force, employed	278,000
Unemployed, looking for	
Full-time work	52,000
Part-time work	20,000

Unemployment rate, 2004

Total	5.3%
Men	5.2
Women	5.4
Persons 16-19 years	17.0
White	5.1
Black	NA
Hispanic	10.0
Asian	NA

Unemployed by reason for unemployment (as a percent of total unemployment), 2002

Job losers or completed temp jobs	45.8%
Job leavers	NA
Reentrants	37.5
New entrants	NA

Labor unions, 2004

Membership	58,000
percent of employed	5.8%

Experienced civilian labor force by private industry, first quarter 2004

Total	863,081
Natural Resources & Mining	10,558
Construction	66,052
Manufacturing	111,826
Trade, transportation & utilities	211,327
Information	28,689
Finance	64,280
Professional & business	132,624
Education & Health	108,815
Leisure & hospitality	100,895
Other	27,891

Experienced civilian labor force by occupation, 2004

Management	51,830
Business & Financial	41,000
Legal	7,740
Sales	119,670
Office & Admin. Support	192,170
Computers & Math	27,790
Architecture & Engineering	19,890
Arts & Entertainment	14,400
Education	61,350
Social Services	16,240
Healthcare Practitioner & Technical	49,060
Healthcare support	23,240
Maintenance & Repair	46,180
Construction	72,580
Transportation & moving	73,630
Production	87,310
Farming, fishing & forestry	5,540

Hours and earnings of production workers on manufacturing payrolls, 2004

Average weekly hours	38.1
Average hourly earnings	$15.38
Average weekly earnings	$585.98

Average annual pay

2004	$32,171
change from 2003	3.5%

Household income

Median household income, three-year average, 2002-2004	$50,614

Personal income, 2004 ($ per capita)

In current dollars	$26,606
In constant (2000) dollars	$24,675

Poverty

Persons below poverty level, three-year average, 2002-2004	9.6%

Federal individual income tax returns, 2003

Returns filed	969,812
Adjusted gross income ($1,000)	$41,014,757
Total income tax paid ($1,000)	$4,191,292

Economy, Business, Industry & Agriculture

Fortune 500 companies, 2005 1

Patents issued, 2004 784

Bankruptcy cases filed, 2004 21,300

Business firm ownership, 2002

Women-owned. 48,474
  Sales ($ mil) $5,920
Black-owned. 649
  Sales ($ mil) $193
Hispanic-owned. 5,178
  Sales ($ mil) $558
Asian-owned 2,824
  Sales ($ mil) $833
Amer. Indian/Alaska Native-owned 1,148
  Sales ($ mil) $83
Hawaiian/Pacific Isl.-owned 429
  Sales ($ mil) $152

Gross State Product, 2004 ($ mil)

Total Gross State Product $82,611
  Agriculture, forestry, fishing and
    hunting 493
  Mining. 1,036
  Utilities 1,206
  Construction 4,771
  Manufacturing, durable goods 5,510
  Manufacturing, non-durable goods 3,057
  Wholesale trade. 4,266
  Retail trade. 6,563
  Transportation & warehousing 3,071
  Information 3,333
  Finance & insurance. 7,633
  Real estate, rental, leasing 10,101
  Professional and technical services 4,917
  Educational services 776
  Health care and social assistance 4,646
  Accommodation/food services 2,083
  Other services, except government 2,758
  Government 11,781

Establishments, by major industry group, 2003

Total. 60,324
  Forestry, fishing & agriculture 64
  Mining. 308
  Construction 8,883
  Manufacturing. 3,046
  Wholesale trade. 3,382
  Retail trade. 8,280
  Transportation & warehousing 1,640
  Information 1,296
  Finance & insurance. 4,638
  Professional/scientific/technical 6,563
  Health care/social assistance 5,493
  Accommodation/food services 4,127

Annual payroll by major industry group, 2003

Total ($1,000) $26,788,628
  Forestry, fishing & agriculture 4,230
  Mining. 342,623
  Utilities 302,151
  Construction 1,939,296
  Manufacturing. 4,017,699
  Wholesale trade. 1,726,480
  Retail trade. 2,458,209
  Transportation & warehousing 1,401,905
  Information 1,205,930
  Finance & insurance. 2,051,229
  Professional/scientific/technical . . . 2,312,313
  Health care/social assistance 3,066,267
  Accommodation/food services. 875,804

Agriculture

Number of farms, 2004 15,000
Farm acreage, 2004
  Total. 12,000,000
  Acres per farm, 2004 758
Farm income, 2003 ($mil)
  Net farm income $368
  Debt/asset ratio 7.2
Farm marketings, 2003 ($mil)
  Total. $1,138
  Crops 258
  Livestock. 880

Principal commodities, in order by marketing receipts, 2003

Cattle, dairy products, hogs, hay

Federal economic activity in state

Expenditures, 2003
  Total ($ mil) $13,500
  Per capita $5,741
  Defense ($ mil). 3,102
  Non-defense ($ mil) 10,398
Defense department, 2003
  Payroll ($ mil) $1,343
  Contract awards ($ mil) $1,899
  Grants ($ mil). $23
  Homeland security grants ($1,000)
    2004 . . . . $27,033
    2005 . . . . $20,308

FDIC insured financial institutions, 2004

Number 67
  Assets ($bil) $193.3
  Deposits ($bil) 102.0

Fishing, 2004

Catch (x 1,000 lbs) 7,013
Value ($1,000). $18,234

8   Utah

Mining, 2004 ($ mil)

Total non-fuel mineral production $1,740
Percent of U.S. 4.0%

Construction, 2003 ($ mil)

Total contracts (including non-building). $4,950
   residential............................ 3,276
   non-residential 1,146

Establishments, receipts, payroll & employees, by major industry group, 2002

Mining 54
   Receipts ($1,000) $44,884
   Annual payroll ($1,000)............. $12,662
   Paid employees 381

Utilities 146
   Receipts ($1,000) .... NA
   Annual payroll ($1,000)........... $302,789
   Paid employees 4,223

Construction........................... 8,387
   Receipts ($1,000) $10,792,051
   Annual payroll ($1,000).......... $2,059,700
   Paid employees 67,569

Manufacturing 3,061
   Receipts ($1,000) $25,104,045
   Annual payroll ($1,000).......... $4,001,272
   Paid employees 109,944

Wholesale trade...................... 3,369
   Receipts ($1,000) $22,905,100
   Annual payroll ($1,000).......... $1,700,487
   Paid employees 44,061

Retail trade 8,135
   Receipts ($1,000) $23,675,432
   Annual payroll ($1,000).......... $2,331,772
   Paid employees 121,745

Transportation....................... 1,570
   Receipts ($1,000) $4,053,466
   Annual payroll ($1,000).......... $1,201,951
   Paid employees 37,931

Information........................... 1,273
   Receipts ($1,000) .... NA
   Annual payroll ($1,000).......... $1,374,213
   Paid employees 34,978

Finance & insurance 4,245
   Receipts ($1,000) .... NA
   Annual payroll ($1,000).......... $1,753,452
   Paid employees 42,233

Professional, scientific & technical 6,249
   Receipts ($1,000) $4,878,861
   Annual payroll ($1,000).......... $2,039,134
   Paid employees 52,051

Health care & social assistance 5,206
   Receipts ($1,000) $7,237,756
   Annual payroll ($1,000).......... $2,851,523
   Paid employees 97,346

Accommodation & food service........... 4,106
   Receipts ($1,000) $2,984,632
   Annual payroll ($1,000)............ $846,626
   Paid employees 80,759

Communication, Energy & Transportation

Communication

Daily newspapers, 2004 6
Households with computers, 2003 ....74%
Households with internet access, 2003 ......63%

Energy

Electricity Consumption, 2001
   Total (trillion Btu)........................ 725
   Per capita (million Btu) 318
By source of production (trillion Btu)
   Coal 390
   Natural gas............................. 168
   Petroleum.............................. 261
   Nuclear electric power 0
   Hydroelectric power..................... 5
By end-use sector (trillion Btu)
   Residential 140
   Commercial 140
   Industrial 233
   Transportation 213
Electric energy, 2003
   Production (billion kWh) 38
   Net summer capability (million kW) 5.8
Gas utilities, 2003
   Customers (x1,000).................... 731
   Sales (trillion Btu)...................... 90
   Revenues ($mil)....................... $575
Nuclear plants, 2003 0

Transportation, 2004

Public Road & Street Mileage 42,710
   Urban............................... 10,416
   Rural 32,294
   Interstate............................. 940
Vehicle miles of travel per capita....... 10,247.3
Total motor vehicle registrations...... 2,084,424
   Automobiles..................... 1,036,674
   Buses 1,289
   Trucks 1,046,461
   Motorcycles 44,386
Licensed drivers 1,582,599
   19 years & under 123,460
Deaths from motor vehicle accidents 296

State Summary

Capital City...................... Montpelier
Governor........................ Jim Douglas
109 State St
Pavilion Office Building
Montpelier, VT 05609
802-828-3333
Admitted as a state 1791
Area (square miles)..................... 9,614
Population, 2004 (est.) 621,394
Largest City.................... Burlington
Population, 2004.................... 38,934
Personal income per capita, 2004
(in current dollars) $32,770
Gross state product ($ mil), 2004 .... $21,921

Leading industries by payroll, 2003

Manufacturing, Health care/Social assistance,
Retail trade

**Leading agricultural commodities by receipts,
2003**

Dairy products, cattle, greenhouse, hay

Geography & Environment

Total area (sq. mi.)..................... 9,614
land 9,250
water 365

Federally-owned land, 2004 (acres) 443,249
percent............................. 7.5%

Highest point.................... Mt. Mansfield
elevation (feet) 4,393

Lowest point .... Lake Champlain
elevation (feet) 95

General coastline (miles)..................... 0

Tidal shoreline (miles)....................... 0

Capital City..................... Montpelier
Population 2000 8,035
Population 2004 8,013

Largest City..................... Burlington
Population 2000 38,889
Population 2004 38,934

Number of cities with over 100,000 population

1990 0
2000 0
2004 0

State park and recreation areas, 2003

Area (acres x 1,000)..................... 69
Number of visitors (x 1,000) 674
Revenues (x 1,000).................... $5,827
percent of operating expenditures...... 93.1%

National forest system land, 2004

Acres 394,000

Demographics and Characteristics of the Population

Population

1980 511,456
1990 562,758
2000 608,827
2004 (estimate)..................... 621,394
persons per sq. mile of land.............67.2
2005 (projection)..................... 630,979
Male............................. 310,420
Female......................... 320,559
2010 (projection) 652,512
2020 (projection) 690,686
2030 (projection) 711,867
Male............................. 352,460
Female......................... 359,407

Metropolitan and Non-Metro. area population

	Metro	Non-Metro
1980	115,000	396,000
1990	131,000	431,000
2000	169,000	439,000

Change in population, 2000-2004

Number............................. 12,567
percent............................. 2.1%
Natural increase (births minus deaths).... 4,999
Net internal migration 4,118
Net international migration 3,722

Persons by age, 2004

Under 5 years 31,181
18 years and over 486,500
65 years and over 80,762
85 years and over 11,478

Persons by age, 2010 (projected)

Total............................. 652,512
Under 5 years 34,303
5 to 17 years 98,069
18 and over 520,140
21 and over 490,832
65 and over 93,442
85 and over 14,066
Median age.........................40.6

Race, 2004 (estimate)

One Race
White............................. 602,311
Black or African American 3,704
American Indian/Alaska Native........ 2,326
Pacific Islander 166
Asian Indian....................... 1,750
Chinese 546
Filipino 19
Japanese 620
Korean............................. 1,055
Vietnamese......................... 1,224
Two or more races..................... 6,576

2   Vermont

Persons of Hispanic origin, 2004
Total Hispanic or Latino 5,124
   Mexican. 1,380
   Puerto Rican 2,140
   Cuban 211
   Other Hispanic or Latino 965

Marital status, 2000
Population 15 years & over 488,281
   Never married 130,371
   Married. 269,531
   Separated 6,348
   Widowed. 30,762
   Divorced 51,758

Language spoken at home, 2000
Population 5 years & over 574,842
   English only 540,767
   Spanish 5,791
   Other Indo-European languages 24,334
   Asian/Pacific Island languages. 3,015

Households & families, 2000
Households. 240,634
   with persons under 18 years 80,904
   with persons over 65 years. 54,149
   persons per household 2.44
Families. 157,763
   persons per family. 2.96
Married couples. 126,413
Female householder,
   no husband present. 22,272
One-person households 63,112

Nativity, 2000
Number of persons born in state 330,528
   percent of population. 54.3%

Immigration & Naturalization, 2004
Immigrants admitted. 790
Persons naturalized 419
Asylums granted 3
Asylums denied 0

Vital Statistics and Health

Marriages
2002 6,010
2003 5,988
2004 5,835

Divorces
2002 2,599
2003 2,493
2004 2,442

Births
2003 6,589
   Birthrate (per 1,000). 10.6
   Low birth weight (2,500g or less). 7.0%
   To unmarried mothers. 30.0%

2003, continued
   White. 6,413
   Black 54
   Hispanic 59
   Asian/Pacific Islander 119
   Amer. Indian/Alaska Native 6

2004 (preliminary). 6,565
   Birthrate (per 1,000). 10.6
   White. 6,383
   Black 58
   Hispanic 75
   Asian/Pacific Islander 112

Deaths
2002
All causes 5,075
   rate per 100,000. . . . . .823.1
Heart disease 1,370
   rate per 100,000. . . . . 222.2
Malignant neoplasms 1,224
   rate per 100,000. . . . . .198.5
Cerebrovascular disease. 335
   rate per 100,000. . . . . .54.3
Chronic lower respiratory disease 276
   rate per 100,000. . . . . 44.8
2003 5,112
   rate per 100,000. . . . . .825.7
2004 (provisional) 4,949

Infant deaths
2003 (provisional) 32
   rate per 1,000 . . . . .4.9
2004 (provisional) 30
   rate per 1,000 . . . . .4.6

Abortions, 2000
Total. 2,000
   rate per 1,000 women age 15-44. . . . . . . .12.7

Physicians, 2003
Total. 2,250
   rate per 1,000 persons. 363

Nurses, 2001
Total. 5,820
   rate per 1,000 persons. 949

Community Hospitals, 2003
Number. 14
Beds (x 1,000). 1.5
Patients admitted (x 1,000) 52
Average daily census (x 1,000) 0.9
Average cost per day $1,148
Outpatient visits (x mil). 2.2

Disability status of population, 2004
5 to 20 years 9.6%
21 to 64 years 13%
65 years and over 37.3%

Education

Educational attainment, 2004

Population over 25 years 417,159
  Less than 9th grade 15,389
  High school graduates only.......... 136,297
  Bachelor's degree only 82,211
  Graduate or professional degree...... 51,395
  Less than 9th grade percent 3.7%
  High school graduate or more 90.8%
  College graduate or more.............. 34.2%
  Graduate or professional degree....... 12.3%

Public school enrollment, Fall 2002

Total................................. 99,978
  Kindergarten through grade 8 68,034
  Grades 9 through 12 31,944
Enrollment, 2005 (projected) 93,700

Graduating public high school seniors

2004 (estimate)........................ 7,030

SAT scores, 2005

Average verbal score 521
Average math score 517
Percent of graduates taking test 67%

Public school teachers, 2004

Total (x 1,000) 9.0
  Elementary (x 1,000)..................... 4.7
  Secondary (x 1,000) 4.3
Average salary $42,000
  Elementary....................... $41,700
  Secondary........................ $42,300

State receipts & expenditures for public schools, 2004

Revenue receipts ($mil)................ $1,182
Expenditures
Total ($mil)........................... $1,206
  Per capita $1,948
  Per pupil $12,157

Institutions of higher education, 2004

Total..................................... 27
  Public..................................... 6
  Private................................... 21

Enrollment in institutions of higher education, Fall, 2003

Total................................. 37,915
  Full-time men 12,790
  Full-time women.................... 14,094
  Part-time men 3,655
  Part-time women.................... 7,376

Minority enrollment in institutions of higher education, Fall, 2003

Black, non-hispanic....................... 549
Hispanic 691
Asian/Pacific Islander 715
American Indian/Alaska Native............. 228

Earned degrees conferred, 2003

Bachelor's 4,545
Master's.............................. 1,449
First-professional......................... 248
Doctor's................................... 44

State & local financial support for higher education, 2003-2004

Full-time equivalent enrollment (x 1,000) ... 17.8
Appropriations per FTE................ $2,575
  as a percent of tax revenue.............. 3.0%

Social Insurance & Welfare Programs

Social Security benefits & beneficiaries, 2004

Beneficiaries
  Total............................. 110,000
  Retired & dependents................ 77,000
  Survivors........................... 14,000
  Disabled & dependents............... 20,000
Annual benefit payments ($ mil)
  Total............................. $1,117
  Retired & dependents................ $756
  Survivors............................ $179
  Disabled & dependents............... $182
Average Monthly Benefit
  Retired & dependents................ $945
  Disabled & dependents............... $848
  Widowed............................ $927

Medicare

Enrollment, 2001 (x 1,000) 90
  Payments ($ mil, est.) $400
Enrollment, 2003 (x 1,000) 93

Medicaid, 2002

Beneficiaries (x 1,000).................... 154
Payments ($ mil) $607

State Children's Health Insurance, 2004

Enrollment (x 1,000)...................... 6.7
Expenditures ($ mil)...................... $3.2

Persons without health insurance, 2003

Number (x 1,000)......................... 58
  percent............................... 9.5%
Number of children (x 1,000) 5
  percent of children 3.9%

Federal public aid

Temporary Assistance for Needy Families, 2004
Recipients (x 1,000)....................... 12
Families (x 1,000) 5

Supplemental Security Income, 2003
Recipients (x 1,000)....................... 13
Payments ($ mil) $57

Food Stamp Program, 2004

Participants (x 1,000) 43
Benefits ($ mil)........................... $40

Housing & Construction

Housing units
Total 2003 (estimate) 301,994
Total 2004 (estimate) 304,291
Seasonal or recreational use, 2003 46,000
Owner-occupied single-family, 2003 111,000
    Median value $138,457
Renter-occupied, 2003 67,000
    Median rent $624
Homeownership rate, 2003 . . . . 71.4%
Homeownership rate, 2004 . . . . 72.0%

New privately owned housing units, 2004
Number authorized (x 1,000) 3.6
Value ($ mil) $494
Started 2005 (x 1,000, estimate) 2.7
Started 2006 (x 1,000, estimate) 2.6

Existing home sales
2002 (x 1,000) 13.0
2003 (x 1,000) 14.5
2004 (x 1,000) 14.2

Government & Elections

State Officials 2006
Governor (name/party/term expires)
    Jim Douglas
    Republican - 1/07
Lieutenant Governor . . . . Brian Dubie
Secretary of State . . . . Deborah Markowitz
Attorney General . . . . William Sorrell
Chief Justice . . . . Paul L. Reiber

Governorship
Minimum age . . . . not specified
Length of term . . . . 2 years
Consecutive terms permitted . . . . . . not specified
Who succeeds . . . . Lt. Governor

State Legislature
Name . . . . General Assembly
Upper chamber . . . . Senate
    Number of members 30
    Length of term . . . . 2 years
    Party in majority, 2006 . . . . Democratic
Lower chamber . . . . House of Representatives
    Number of members 150
    Length of term . . . . 2 years
    Party in majority, 2006 . . . . Democratic

State Government Employees, 2004
Total 13,922
Payroll $50,706,900

Local Government Employees, 2004
Total 24,227
Payroll $71,167,440

Local Governments by Type, 2002
Total 733
    County 14
    Municipal 47
    Township 237
    School District 283
    Special District 152

Voting age population, November 2004
Total 482,000
    Male 233,000
    Female 249,000
    White 463,000
    Black 2,000
    Hispanic 3,000
    Asian 7,000

Presidential Election, 2004
Total Popular Vote 312,309
    Kerry 184,067
    Bush 121,180
Total Electoral Votes 3

Federal representation, 2006 (109th Congress)
Senator . . . . Jim Jeffords
    Party . . . . Independent
    Year term expires 2007
Senator . . . . Patrick J. Leahy
    Party . . . . Democrat
    Year term expires 2011
Representatives, total 1
    Democrats 0
    Republicans 0
    Other 1

Votes cast for US Senators
2002
Total vote (x 1,000) . . . . NA
Leading party . . . . NA
Percent for leading party . . . . NA
2004
Total vote (x 1,000) 307,000
Leading party . . . . Democratic
Percent for leading party 70.6%

Votes cast for US Representatives
2002
Total vote (x 1,000) 225
    Democratic . . . .
    Republican 73
Leading party . . . . Independent
Percent for leading party 64.3%
2004
Total vote (x 1,000) 305
    Democratic 22
    Republican 74
Leading party . . . . Independent
Percent for leading party 67.5%

Vermont 5

Women holding public office, 2006

US Congress 0
Statewide elected office. 1
State legislature 60

Black public officials, 2001

Total 1
  US and state legislatures 1
  City/county/regional offices 0
  Judicial/law enforcement. 0
  Education/school boards 0

Hispanic public officials, 2004

Total. 0
  State executives & legislators 0
  City/county/regional offices 0
  Judicial/law enforcement. 0
  Education/school boards 0

Governmental Finance

State government revenues, 2004

Total revenue ($1,000) $4,302,590
  Revenue per capita 6,928.49

General Revenue ($ per capita) $6,110.83
  Intergovernmental 2,117.42
  Taxes 2,844.96
    general sales .413.78
    individual income tax. 692.14
    corporate income tax 100.21
  Current charges. 589.24
  Miscellaneous .559.21

State government expenditure, 2004

Total expenditure (x $1,000) $3,913,616
  Expenditure per capita. 6,302.12
General Expenditure ($ per capita). $5,919.71
  Education 2,387.18
  Public welfare. 1,635.10
  Health 148.90
  Hospitals. 23.48
  Highways 408.66
  Police protection 111.24
  Correction 151.09
  Natural resources 135.99
  Parks & recreation. 20.47
  Governmental administration 218.72
  Interest on general debt 223.93

State debt & cash, 2004 ($ per capita)

Debt $4,085.57
Cash/security holdings. $8,434.55

Federal government grants to state & local government, 2004 (x $1,000)

Total. $1,423,455
By Federal Agency
  Defense $36,319

By Federal Agency, continued

  Education 109,905
  Energy 5,645
  Environmental Protection Agency 30,340
  Health & Human Services. 799,357
  Homeland Security. 7,509
  Housing & Urban Development 79,660
  Justice 40,844
  Labor 22,719
  Transportation 173,083
  Veterans Affairs. 3,187

Crime, Law Enforcement & Courts

Crime, 2004 (rates per 100,000 residents)

Property crimes 14,343
  Burglaries. 3,386
  Larcenies. 10,382
  Motor vehicle thefts 575
  Property crime rate. 2,308.2
Violent crimes. 696
  Murders 16
  Forcible rape. 152
  Robberies 76
  Aggravated assaults 452
  Violent crime rate 112.0

Police Agencies, 2004

Total agencies. 64
Total employees 1,409
  Male officers. 988
  Female officers. 77
  Male civilians. 114
  Female civilians. 230

Arrests, 2004

Total. 12,074
  Persons under 18 years of age 1,401

Prisoners under state & federal jurisdiction, 2004

Total prisoners. 1,968
  Percent change, 12/31/03 to 12/31/04 . . . . 1.2%
Sentenced to more than one year 1,451
  rate per 100,000. 233

Persons under sentence of death, 7/1/05

Total. 0
  White. 0
  Black 0
  Hispanic 0

State's highest court

Name . . . . .Supreme Court
Number of members 5
Length of term . . . . 6 years
Intermediate appeals court? . . . . no

Labor & Income

Civilian labor force, 2004

Total	353,000
Men	185,000
Women	169,000
Persons 16-19 years	21,000
White	343,000
Black	0
Hispanic	0
Asian	0

Civilian labor force as a percent of civilian non-institutional population, 2004

Total	70.8%
Men	75.9
Women	65.8
Persons 16-19 years	57.8
White	70.8
Black	0.0
Hispanic	0.0
Asian	0.0

Employment, 2004

Total	340,000
Men	177,000
Women	163,000
Persons 16-19 years	19,000
White	330,000
Black	0
Hispanic	0
Asian	0

Full-time/part-time labor force, 2002

Full-time labor force, employed	264,000
Part-time labor force, employed	71,000
Unemployed, looking for	
Full-time work	11,000
Part-time work	NA

Unemployment rate, 2004

Total	3.7%
Men	4.0
Women	3.4
Persons 16-19 years	11.8
White	3.7
Black	NA
Hispanic	NA
Asian	NA

Unemployed by reason for unemployment (as a percent of total unemployment), 2002

Job losers or completed temp jobs	53.8%
Job leavers	NA
Reentrants	NA
New entrants	NA

Labor unions, 2004

Membership	29,000
percent of employed	9.8%

Experienced civilian labor force by private industry, first quarter 2004

Total	242,878
Natural Resources & Mining	2,621
Construction	13,907
Manufacturing	36,395
Trade, transportation & utilities	57,313
Information	6,417
Finance	12,884
Professional & business	20,350
Education & Health	49,402
Leisure & hospitality	34,430
Other	9,159

Experienced civilian labor force by occupation, 2004

Management	8,450
Business & Financial	9,860
Legal	1,800
Sales	30,860
Office & Admin. Support	50,530
Computers & Math	6,350
Architecture & Engineering	5,930
Arts & Entertainment	4,380
Education	25,710
Social Services	7,130
Healthcare Practitioner & Technical	15,420
Healthcare support	8,390
Maintenance & Repair	12,150
Construction	16,200
Transportation & moving	17,100
Production	25,090
Farming, fishing & forestry	13,240

Hours and earnings of production workers on manufacturing payrolls, 2004

Average weekly hours	40.2
Average hourly earnings	$14.60
Average weekly earnings	$586.92

Average annual pay

2004	$33,274
change from 2003	3.7%

Household income

Median household income, three-year average, 2002-2004	$45,692

Personal income, 2004 ($ per capita)

In current dollars	$32,770
In constant (2000) dollars	$30,392

Poverty

Persons below poverty level, three-year average, 2002-2004	8.8%

Federal individual income tax returns, 2003

Returns filed	302,209
Adjusted gross income ($1,000)	$12,524,941
Total income tax paid ($1,000)	$1,444,968

Economy, Business, Industry & Agriculture

Fortune 500 companies, 2005 0

Patents issued, 2004 428

Bankruptcy cases filed, 2004 1,800

Business firm ownership, 2002

Women-owned.	18,989
Sales ($ mil)	$1,454
Black-owned.	211
Sales ($ mil)	$21
Hispanic-owned.	452
Sales ($ mil)	$38
Asian-owned	429
Sales ($ mil)	$72
Amer. Indian/Alaska Native-owned	300
Sales ($ mil)	$44
Hawaiian/Pacific Isl.-owned	NA
Sales ($ mil)	NA

Gross State Product, 2004 ($ mil)

Total Gross State Product	$21,921
Agriculture, forestry, fishing and hunting	289
Mining.	28
Utilities	637
Construction	1,054
Manufacturing, durable goods.	2,263
Manufacturing, non-durable goods	691
Wholesale trade.	1,108
Retail trade.	1,855
Transportation & warehousing	468
Information	830
Finance & insurance.	1,290
Real estate, rental, leasing	2,760
Professional and technical services	1,167
Educational services	406
Health care and social assistance	2,025
Accommodation/food services.	962
Other services, except government	533
Government	2,891

Establishments, by major industry group, 2003

Total.	21,831
Forestry, fishing & agriculture	144
Mining.	53
Construction	2,845
Manufacturing.	1,151
Wholesale trade.	873
Retail trade.	3,948
Transportation & warehousing	545
Information	501
Finance & insurance.	986
Professional/scientific/technical	2,010
Health care/social assistance	2,034
Accommodation/food services.	1,964

Annual payroll by major industry group, 2003

Total ($1,000)	$7,656,559
Forestry, fishing & agriculture	NA
Mining.	NA
Utilities	165,183
Construction	533,257
Manufacturing.	1,614,082
Wholesale trade.	424,519
Retail trade.	863,331
Transportation & warehousing	164,370
Information	248,219
Finance & insurance.	489,199
Professional/scientific/technical	485,060
Health care/social assistance	1,149,446
Accommodation/food services.	381,437

Agriculture

Number of farms, 2004	6,000
Farm acreage, 2004	
Total.	1,000,000
Acres per farm, 2004	195
Farm income, 2003 ($mil)	
Net farm income	$102
Debt/asset ratio	13.7
Farm marketings, 2003 ($mil)	
Total.	$482
Crops	79
Livestock	403

Principal commodities, in order by marketing receipts, 2003

Dairy products, cattle, greenhouse, hay

Federal economic activity in state

Expenditures, 2003

Total ($ mil)	$4,443
Per capita	$7,176
Defense ($ mil).	610
Non-defense ($ mil)	3,833

Defense department, 2003

Payroll ($ mil)	$136
Contract awards ($ mil)	$464
Grants ($ mil).	$20
Homeland security grants ($1,000)	
2004	$19,594
2005	$14,326

FDIC insured financial institutions, 2004

Number	19
Assets ($bil)	$7.9
Deposits ($bil)	9.0

Fishing, 2004

Catch (x 1,000 lbs)	0
Value ($1,000).	0

Mining, 2004 ($ mil)

Total non-fuel mineral production $69
Percent of U.S. 0.2%

Construction, 2003 ($ mil)

Total contracts (including non-building). . . $890
   residential.............................. 435
   non-residential 317

Establishments, receipts, payroll & employees, by major industry group, 2002

Mining 360
   Receipts ($1,000) $2,277,885
   Annual payroll ($1,000) $413,959
   Paid employees 9,418

Utilities 62
   Receipts ($1,000) .... NA
   Annual payroll ($1,000) $124,713
   Paid employees 1,767

Construction 2,715
   Receipts ($1,000) $2,253,071
   Annual payroll ($1,000) $495,252
   Paid employees 15,885

Manufacturing 1,176
   Receipts ($1,000) $9,660,529
   Annual payroll ($1,000) $1,757,617
   Paid employees 43,827

Wholesale trade 869
   Receipts ($1,000) $5,094,373
   Annual payroll ($1,000) $418,004
   Paid employees 10,792

Retail trade 3,946
   Receipts ($1,000) $7,623,872
   Annual payroll ($1,000) $820,807
   Paid employees 40,105

Transportation 539
   Receipts ($1,000) $405,598
   Annual payroll ($1,000) $134,309
   Paid employees 5,476

Information. 514
   Receipts ($1,000) .... NA
   Annual payroll ($1,000) $249,427
   Paid employees 7,341

Finance & insurance 943
   Receipts ($1,000) .... NA
   Annual payroll ($1,000) $477,325
   Paid employees 11,444

Professional, scientific & technical 1,998
   Receipts ($1,000) $1,100,405
   Annual payroll ($1,000) $476,690
   Paid employees 12,707

Health care & social assistance 1,999
   Receipts ($1,000) $2,526,933
   Annual payroll ($1,000) $1,084,885
   Paid employees 37,273

Accommodation & food service 1,950
   Receipts ($1,000) $1,154,048
   Annual payroll ($1,000) $357,265
   Paid employees 29,849

Communication, Energy & Transportation

Communication

Daily newspapers, 2004 8
Households with computers, 2003 ....66%
Households with internet access, 2003 ......58%

Energy

Electricity Consumption, 2001
Total (trillion Btu)........................ 164
Per capita (million Btu) 267
By source of production (trillion Btu)
   Coal .... < 0.5
   Natural gas 8
   Petroleum 89
   Nuclear electric power 44
   Hydroelectric power 9
By end-use sector (trillion Btu)
   Residential 48
   Commercial 33
   Industrial 31
   Transportation 52
Electric energy, 2003
   Production (billion kWh) 6
   Net summer capability (million kW) 1
Gas utilities, 2003
   Customers (x1,000)...................... 35
   Sales (trillion Btu)...................... 8
   Revenues ($mil) $63
Nuclear plants, 2003 1

Transportation, 2004

Public Road & Street Mileage 14,368
   Urban............................... 1,396
   Rural 12,972
   Interstate.............................. 320
Vehicle miles of travel per capita 12,649.0
Total motor vehicle registrations........ 523,212
   Automobiles........................ 280,158
   Buses 2,057
   Trucks 240,997
   Motorcycles 28,304
Licensed drivers 550,462
   19 years & under 23,641
Deaths from motor vehicle accidents 98

State Summary

Capital City....................Richmond
Governor.......................Tim Kaine
State Capitol
Third Floor
Richmond, VA 23219
804-786-2211
Admitted as a state 1788
Area (square miles)................... 42,774
Population, 2004 (est.) 7,459,827
Largest City..................Virginia Beach
Population, 2004................ 440,000
Personal income per capita, 2004
(in current dollars) $35,477
Gross state product ($ mil), 2004 ..... $329,332

Leading industries by payroll, 2003

Professional/Scientific/Technical, Manufacturing, Health care/Social assistance

Leading agricultural commodities by receipts, 2003

Broilers, cattle, dairy products, greenhouse

Geography & Environment

Total area (sq. mi.)................... 42,774
land 39,594
water 3,180
Federally-owned land, 2004 (acres) ... 2,534,178
percent............................9.9%
Highest point.....................Mt. Rogers
elevation (feet) 5,729
Lowest point ....Atlantic Ocean
elevation (feet) .... sea level
General coastline (miles)................. 112
Tidal shoreline (miles)................. 3,315
Capital City......................Richmond
Population 2000 198,000
Population 2004 192,000
Largest City..................Virginia Beach
Population 2000 425,000
Population 2004 440,000

Number of cities with over 100,000 population

1990 8
2000 8
2004 8

State park and recreation areas, 2003

Area (acres x 1,000)...................... 62
Number of visitors (x 1,000) 5,623
Revenues (x 1,000)................... $6,578
percent of operating expenditures......38.2%

National forest system land, 2004

Acres 1,664,000

Demographics and Characteristics of the Population

Population

1980 5,346,818
1990 6,187,358
2000 7,078,515
2004 (estimate)................... 7,459,827
persons per sq. mile of land............188.4
2005 (projection).................. 7,552,581
Male.......................... 3,702,570
Female........................ 3,850,011
2010 (projection) 8,010,245
2020 (projection) 8,917,395
2030 (projection) 9,825,019
Male.......................... 4,776,533
Female........................ 5,048,486

Metropolitan and Non-Metro. area population

	Metro	Non-Metro
1980	3,745,000	1,601,000
1990	4,483,000	1,704,000
2000	5,528,000	1,550,000

Change in population, 2000-2004

Number 380,797
percent............................5.4%
Natural increase (births minus deaths).. 181,484
Net internal migration 87,546
Net international migration 115,538

Persons by age, 2004

Under 5 years 498,386
18 years and over 5,654,927
65 years and over 846,921
85 years and over 102,561

Persons by age, 2010 (projected)

Total............................. 8,010,245
Under 5 years 535,955
5 to 17 years 1,344,229
18 and over 6,130,061
21 and over 5,765,154
65 and over 994,359
85 and over 135,299
Median age 37.2

Race, 2004 (estimate)

One Race
White......................... 5,502,331
Black or African American 1,482,963
American Indian/Alaska Native....... 24,314
Pacific Islander 5,476
Asian Indian...................... 80,530
Chinese 53,971
Filipino 50,546
Japanese 6,397
Korean.......................... 45,358
Vietnamese....................... 45,483
Two or more races.................... 115,214

2   Virginia

Persons of Hispanic origin, 2004

Total Hispanic or Latino 418,130
  Mexican. 110,522
  Puerto Rican 49,836
  Cuban 16,185
  Other Hispanic or Latino 45,343

Marital status, 2000

Population 15 years & over 5,623,628
  Never married 1,473,391
  Married. 3,132,361
  Separated 163,085
  Widowed. 348,665
  Divorced 506,127

Language spoken at home, 2000

Population 5 years & over 6,619,266
  English only 5,884,075
  Spanish 316,274
  Other Indo-European languages 195,846
  Asian/Pacific Island languages. 170,136

Households & families, 2000

Households. 2,699,173
  with persons under 18 years 968,736
  with persons over 65 years. 565,204
  persons per household 2.54
Families. 1,847,796
  persons per family. 3.04
Married couples. 1,426,044
Female householder,
  no husband present. 320,290
One-person households 676,907

Nativity, 2000

Number of persons born in state 3,676,255
  percent of population. 51.9%

Immigration & Naturalization, 2004

Immigrants admitted. 21,695
Persons naturalized 13,478
Asylums granted 450
Asylums denied 94

Vital Statistics and Health

Marriages

2002 62,650
2003 61,754
2004 61,990

Divorces

2002 30,818
2003 29,718
2004 29,411

Births

2003 101,254
  Birthrate (per 1,000). 13.7
  Low birth weight (2,500g or less). 8.2%
  To unmarried mothers. 30.4%

2003, continued
  White. 71,900
  Black 22,605
  Hispanic 10,689
  Asian/Pacific Islander 6,544
  Amer. Indian/Alaska Native. 177
2004 (preliminary). 103,915
  Birthrate (per 1,000). 13.9
  White. 73,953
  Black 22,899
  Hispanic 11,691
  Asian/Pacific Islander 6,911

Deaths

2002
All causes 57,196
  rate per 100,000. . . . . 784.2
Heart disease 14,952
  rate per 100,000. . . . . .205.0
Malignant neoplasms 13,602
  rate per 100,000. . . . . .186.5
Cerebrovascular disease. 3,960
  rate per 100,000. . . . . .54.3
Chronic lower respiratory disease 2,752
  rate per 100,000. . . . . .37.7
2003 58,415
  rate per 100,000. . . . . .790.9
2004 (provisional) 56,642

Infant deaths

2003 (provisional) 758
  rate per 1,000. . . . . .7.5
2004 (provisional) 741
  rate per 1,000. . . . . .7.1

Abortions, 2000

Total. 29,000
  rate per 1,000 women age 15-44. . . . . . . .18.1

Physicians, 2003

Total. 20,220
  rate per 1,000 persons. 274

Nurses, 2001

Total. 55,440
  rate per 1,000 persons. 770

Community Hospitals, 2003

Number. 84
Beds (x 1,000). 17.2
Patients admitted (x 1,000) 758
Average daily census (x 1,000) 12.0
Average cost per day $1,277
Outpatient visits (x mil). 11.2

Disability status of population, 2004

5 to 20 years 6.9%
21 to 64 years 11.4%
65 years and over 38.8%

Education

Educational attainment, 2004

Population over 25 years 4,790,386
  Less than 9th grade 269,575
  High school graduates only....... 1,268,833
  Bachelor's degree only 932,510
  Graduate or professional degree...... 632,277
  Less than 9th grade percent 5.6%
  High school graduate or more 88.4%
  College graduate or more............. 33.1%
  Graduate or professional degree....... 13.2%

Public school enrollment, Fall 2002

Total................................ 1,177,229
  Kindergarten through grade 8 831,504
  Grades 9 through 12 345,725
Enrollment, 2005 (projected) 1,193,200

Graduating public high school seniors

2004 (estimate)....................... 71,740

SAT scores, 2005

Average verbal score 516
Average math score 514
Percent of graduates taking test 73%

Public school teachers, 2004

Total (x 1,000) 98.7
  Elementary (x 1,000)................56.9
  Secondary (x 1,000) 41.7
Average salary $43,700
  Elementary $42,800
  Secondary......................... $44,900

State receipts & expenditures for public schools, 2004

Revenue receipts ($mil)............... $11,310
Expenditures
Total ($mil).......................... $12,012
  Per capita $1,631
  Per pupil $9,401

Institutions of higher education, 2004

Total.................................. 104
  Public............................... 39
  Private.............................. 65

Enrollment in institutions of higher education, Fall, 2003

Total............................... 424,316
  Full-time men 112,578
  Full-time women................... 144,155
  Part-time men 66,583
  Part-time women.................. 101,000

Minority enrollment in institutions of higher education, Fall, 2003

Black, non-hispanic.................. 76,729
Hispanic 13,272
Asian/Pacific Islander 21,262
American Indian/Alaska Native.......... 2,441

Earned degrees conferred, 2003

Bachelor's 34,657
Master's............................. 11,251
First-professional...................... 2,133
Doctor's.............................. 1,169

State & local financial support for higher education, 2003-2004

Full-time equivalent enrollment (x 1,000) ..257.7
Appropriations per FTE................. $4,571
  as a percent of tax revenue............. 6.5%

Social Insurance & Welfare Programs

Social Security benefits & beneficiaries, 2004

Beneficiaries
  Total........................... 1,114,000
  Retired & dependents.............. 757,000
  Survivors......................... 156,000
  Disabled & dependents............. 201,000
Annual benefit payments ($ mil)
  Total............................. $11,381
  Retired & dependents............... $7,408
  Survivors.......................... $1,987
  Disabled & dependents.............. $1,986
Average Monthly Benefit
  Retired & dependents............... $940
  Disabled & dependents.............. $898
  Widowed............................ $881

Medicare

Enrollment, 2001 (x 1,000) 910
  Payments ($ mil, est.) $3,900
Enrollment, 2003 (x 1,000) 946

Medicaid, 2002

Beneficiaries (x 1,000)..................... 665
Payments ($ mil) $3,018

State Children's Health Insurance, 2004

Enrollment (x 1,000)...................99.6
Expenditures ($ mil)...................$63.0

Persons without health insurance, 2003

Number (x 1,000)...................... 962
  percent............................ 13.0%
Number of children (x 1,000) 162
  percent of children 8.9%

Federal public aid

Temporary Assistance for Needy Families, 2004
Recipients (x 1,000)....................... 27
Families (x 1,000) 9

Supplemental Security Income, 2003
Recipients (x 1,000)...................... 134
Payments ($ mil) $587

Food Stamp Program, 2004

Participants (x 1,000) 486
Benefits ($ mil).......................... $476

Housing & Construction

Housing units

Total 2003 (estimate)	3,066,366
Total 2004 (estimate)	3,116,827
Seasonal or recreational use, 2003	66,000
Owner-occupied single-family, 2003	1,632,000
Median value	$162,080
Renter-occupied, 2003	841,000
Median rent	$751
Homeownership rate, 2003	75.0%
Homeownership rate, 2004	73.4%

New privately owned housing units, 2004

Number authorized (x 1,000)	63.2
Value ($ mil)	$8,094
Started 2005 (x 1,000, estimate)	51.8
Started 2006 (x 1,000, estimate)	50.6

Existing home sales

2002 (x 1,000)	150.1
2003 (x 1,000)	158.3
2004 (x 1,000)	186.0

Government & Elections

State Officials 2006

Governor (name/party/term expires)
Tim Kaine
Democrat - 1/10

Lieutenant Governor	Bill Bolling
Secretary of State	Anita Rimler
Attorney General	Bob McDonnell
Chief Justice	Leroy Hassell

Governorship

Minimum age	30
Length of term	4 years
Consecutive terms permitted	none
Who succeeds	Lt. Governor

State Legislature

Name	General Assembly
Upper chamber	Senate
Number of members	40
Length of term	4 years
Party in majority, 2006	Republican
Lower chamber	House of Delegates
Number of members	100
Length of term	2 years
Party in majority, 2006	Republican

State Government Employees, 2004

Total	119,317
Payroll	$404,881,342

Local Government Employees, 2004

Total	210,253
Payroll	$865,571,999

Local Governments by Type, 2002

Total	521
County	95
Municipal	229
Township	0
School District	1
Special District	196

Voting age population, November 2004

Total	5,364,000
Male	2,538,000
Female	2,826,000
White	4,101,000
Black	961,000
Hispanic	301,000
Asian	251,000

Presidential Election, 2004

Total Popular Vote	3,198,367
Kerry	1,454,742
Bush	1,716,959
Total Electoral Votes	13

Federal representation, 2006 (109th Congress)

Senator	George Allen
Party	Republican
Year term expires	2007
Senator	John W. Warner
Party	Republican
Year term expires	2009
Representatives, total	11
Democrats	3
Republicans	8
Other	0

Votes cast for US Senators

2002

Total vote (x 1,000)	1,489,000
Leading party	Republican
Percent for leading party	82.6%

2004

Total vote (x 1,000)	NA
Leading party	NA
Percent for leading party	NA

Votes cast for US Representatives

2002

Total vote (x 1,000)	1,516
Democratic	440
Republican	956
Leading party	Republican
Percent for leading party	63.0%

2004

Total vote (x 1,000)	3,004
Democratic	1,023
Republican	1,817
Leading party	Republican
Percent for leading party	60.5%

Women holding public office, 2006
US Congress 2
Statewide elected office...................... 1
State legislature 21

Black public officials, 2001
Total................................... 246
US and state legislatures 16
City/county/regional offices 130
Judicial/law enforcement................. 15
Education/school boards 85

Hispanic public officials, 2004
Total..................................... 1
State executives & legislators 0
City/county/regional offices 1
Judicial/law enforcement................. 0
Education/school boards 0

Governmental Finance

State government revenues, 2004
Total revenue ($1,000) $35,739,829
Revenue per capita 4,777.41

General Revenue ($ per capita) $3,739.04
Intergovernmental 833.84
Taxes 1,902.56
general sales 398.00
individual income tax............. 992.12
corporate income tax 56.43
Current charges..................... 597.80
Miscellaneous 404.84

State government expenditure, 2004
Total expenditure (x $1,000) $30,370,027
Expenditure per capita............. 4,059.62
General Expenditure ($ per capita).... $3,691.79
Education 1,377.90
Public welfare...................... 751.08
Health 96.83
Hospitals.......................... 262.80
Highways.......................... 331.17
Police protection.................... 73.45
Correction 162.53
Natural resources 24.24
Parks & recreation.................. 10.35
Governmental administration 134.42
Interest on general debt 96.50

State debt & cash, 2004 ($ per capita)
Debt $2,047.05
Cash/security holdings............. $7,705.20

Federal government grants to state & local government, 2004 (x $1,000)
Total............................. $7,991,079

By Federal Agency
Defense $105,144

By Federal Agency, continued
Education 821,824
Energy 39,084
Environmental Protection Agency ... 109,857
Health & Human Services......... 3,708,084
Homeland Security................. 234,418
Housing & Urban Development...... 652,819
Justice 217,658
Labor 267,791
Transportation 1,017,710
Veterans Affairs................... 20,100

Crime, Law Enforcement & Courts

Crime, 2004 (rates per 100,000 residents)
Property crimes 199,668
Burglaries......................... 28,793
Larcenies........................ 153,464
Motor vehicle thefts 17,411
Property crime rate............... 2,676.6
Violent crimes...................... 20,559
Murders.......................... 391
Forcible rape..................... 1,766
Robberies 6,906
Aggravated assaults 11,496
Violent crime rate 275.6

Police Agencies, 2004
Total agencies......................... 276
Total employees 22,105
Male officers..................... 15,120
Female officers................... 1,891
Male civilians.................... 1,424
Female civilians.................. 3,670

Arrests, 2004
Total............................... 267,765
Persons under 18 years of age 33,881

Prisoners under state & federal jurisdiction, 2004
Total prisoners..................... 35,564
Percent change, 12/31/03 to 12/31/04 .... 1.4%
Sentenced to more than one year 35,564
rate per 100,000..................... 473

Persons under sentence of death, 7/1/05
Total............................... 23
White.............................. 10
Black 13
Hispanic 0

State's highest court
Name .... Supreme Court
Number of members....................... 7
Length of term .... 12 years
Intermediate appeals court? .... no

6   Virginia

Labor & Income

Civilian labor force, 2004

Total	3,766,000
Men	1,975,000
Women	1,791,000
Persons 16-19 years	182,000
White	2,849,000
Black	681,000
Hispanic	223,000
Asian	192,000

Civilian labor force as a percent of civilian non-institutional population, 2004

Total	67.2%
Men	74.3
Women	60.8
Persons 16-19 years	43.9
White	67.2
Black	65.7
Hispanic	80.8
Asian	71.0

Employment, 2004

Total	3,619,000
Men	1,901,000
Women	1,718,000
Persons 16-19 years	162,000
White	2,764,000
Black	629,000
Hispanic	213,000
Asian	184,000

Full-time/part-time labor force, 2002

Full-time labor force, employed	3,058,000
Part-time labor force, employed	525,000
Unemployed, looking for	
Full-time work	128,000
Part-time work	NA

Unemployment rate, 2004

Total	3.9%
Men	3.8
Women	4.0
Persons 16-19 years	10.9
White	3.0
Black	7.7
Hispanic	4.7
Asian	4.2

Unemployed by reason for unemployment (as a percent of total unemployment), 2002

Job losers or completed temp jobs	46.1%
Job leavers	NA
Reentrants	NA
New entrants	NA

Labor unions, 2004

Membership	176,000
percent of employed	5.3%

Experienced civilian labor force by private industry, first quarter 2004

Total	2,800,574
Natural Resources & Mining	20,110
Construction	221,944
Manufacturing	297,927
Trade, transportation & utilities	628,250
Information	101,409
Finance	184,129
Professional & business	564,079
Education & Health	349,827
Leisure & hospitality	305,196
Other	122,560

Experienced civilian labor force by occupation, 2004

Management	138,580
Business & Financial	183,090
Legal	29,270
Sales	399,050
Office & Admin. Support	579,330
Computers & Math	164,870
Architecture & Engineering	77,440
Arts & Entertainment	43,270
Education	211,340
Social Services	38,510
Healthcare Practitioner & Technical	155,280
Healthcare support	69,160
Maintenance & Repair	157,220
Construction	198,730
Transportation & moving	241,780
Production	213,580
Farming, fishing & forestry	4,320

Hours and earnings of production workers on manufacturing payrolls, 2004

Average weekly hours	NA
Average hourly earnings	NA
Average weekly earnings	NA

Average annual pay

2004	$40,534
change from 2003	5.0%

Household income

Median household income, three-year average, 2002-2004	$53,275

Personal income, 2004 ($ per capita)

In current dollars	$35,477
In constant (2000) dollars	$32,903

Poverty

Persons below poverty level, three-year average, 2002-2004	9.8%

Federal individual income tax returns, 2003

Returns filed	3,431,766
Adjusted gross income ($1,000)	$180,639,507
Total income tax paid ($1,000)	$23,347,262

Economy, Business, Industry & Agriculture

Fortune 500 companies, 2005 18

Patents issued, 2004 1,181

Bankruptcy cases filed, 2004 42,100

Business firm ownership, 2002

Women-owned. 157,076
  Sales ($ mil) $22,139
Black-owned. 41,158
  Sales ($ mil) $3,497
Hispanic-owned. 19,017
  Sales ($ mil) $3,455
Asian-owned 30,470
  Sales ($ mil) $7,834
Amer. Indian/Alaska Native-owned 2,692
  Sales ($ mil) $444
Hawaiian/Pacific Isl.-owned 456
  Sales ($ mil) $172

Gross State Product, 2004 ($ mil)

Total Gross State Product $329,332
  Agriculture, forestry, fishing and
    hunting 1,377
  Mining. 1,314
  Utilities 5,384
  Construction 15,945
  Manufacturing, durable goods. 15,058
  Manufacturing, non-durable goods . . . 23,287
  Wholesale trade. 14,237
  Retail trade. 20,445
  Transportation & warehousing 8,206
  Information 18,396
  Finance & insurance. 22,215
  Real estate, rental, leasing 40,274
  Professional and technical services 33,911
  Educational services. 2,067
  Health care and social assistance. 17,000
  Accommodation/food services. 7,582
  Other services, except government 8,282
  Government 56,862

Establishments, by major industry group, 2003

Total. 183,468
  Forestry, fishing & agriculture 747
  Mining. 363
  Construction 22,038
  Manufacturing. 5,841
  Wholesale trade. 7,688
  Retail trade. 29,183
  Transportation & warehousing 5,067
  Information 3,859
  Finance & insurance. 11,065
  Professional/scientific/technical 23,661
  Health care/social assistance 15,731
  Accommodation/food services. 13,575

Annual payroll by major industry group, 2003

Total ($1,000) $106,077,785
  Forestry, fishing & agriculture 121,040
  Mining. 438,468
  Utilities 1,141,449
  Construction 7,223,660
  Manufacturing. 11,911,259
  Wholesale trade. 4,789,770
  Retail trade. 8,527,852
  Transportation & warehousing 3,358,576
  Information 7,380,667
  Finance & insurance. 9,154,098
  Professional/scientific/technical . . 18,890,334
  Health care/social assistance 11,689,858
  Accommodation/food services. 3,429,581

Agriculture

Number of farms, 2004 48,000
Farm acreage, 2004
  Total. 9,000,000
  Acres per farm, 2004 181
Farm income, 2003 ($mil)
  Net farm income $529
  Debt/asset ratio 9.8
Farm marketings, 2003 ($mil)
  Total. $2,227
  Crops. 695
  Livestock. 1,532

Principal commodities, in order by marketing receipts, 2003

  Broilers, cattle, dairy products, greenhouse

Federal economic activity in state

Expenditures, 2003
  Total ($ mil) $82,454
  Per capita $11,163
  Defense ($ mil). 32,684
  Non-defense ($ mil) 49,770
Defense department, 2003
  Payroll ($ mil) $14,187
  Contract awards ($ mil) $19,978
  Grants ($ mil). $64
  Homeland security grants ($1,000)
    2004 . . . . $61,902
    2005 . . . . $38,185

FDIC insured financial institutions, 2004

Number 140
  Assets ($bil) $221.2
  Deposits ($bil) 147.8

Fishing, 2004

Catch (x 1,000 lbs) 481,555
Value ($1,000). $160,285

Mining, 2004 ($ mil)

Total non-fuel mineral production $868
Percent of U.S. 2.0%

Construction, 2003 ($ mil)

Total contracts (including non-building) $14,970
   residential........................... 8,176
   non-residential 4,495

Establishments, receipts, payroll & employees, by major industry group, 2002

Mining 175
   Receipts ($1,000) $499,595
   Annual payroll ($1,000)............ $125,570
   Paid employees 2,731

Utilities 294
   Receipts ($1,000) .... NA
   Annual payroll ($1,000)............ $958,378
   Paid employees 15,097

Construction........................... 20,709
   Receipts ($1,000) $33,667,129
   Annual payroll ($1,000)......... $6,937,460
   Paid employees 211,849

Manufacturing 5,909
   Receipts ($1,000) $83,952,547
   Annual payroll ($1,000)......... $11,632,963
   Paid employees 311,787

Wholesale trade 7,712
   Receipts ($1,000) $69,267,796
   Annual payroll ($1,000)......... $4,503,110
   Paid employees 105,641

Retail trade 28,914
   Receipts ($1,000) $80,509,062
   Annual payroll ($1,000).......... $8,078,467
   Paid employees 401,921

Transportation........................ 4,955
   Receipts ($1,000) $7,137,609
   Annual payroll ($1,000)......... $2,504,902
   Paid employees 83,277

Information........................... 3,743
   Receipts ($1,000) .... NA
   Annual payroll ($1,000)......... $7,028,552
   Paid employees 130,939

Finance & insurance 10,555
   Receipts ($1,000) .... NA
   Annual payroll ($1,000)......... $8,175,722
   Paid employees 159,328

Professional, scientific & technical 23,152
   Receipts ($1,000) $40,683,149
   Annual payroll ($1,000)......... $17,555,444
   Paid employees 309,824

Health care & social assistance 15,444
   Receipts ($1,000) $28,199,263
   Annual payroll ($1,000)........ $10,983,448
   Paid employees 328,476

Accommodation & food service.......... 13,305
   Receipts ($1,000) $10,929,429
   Annual payroll ($1,000).......... $3,094,285
   Paid employees 256,341

Communication, Energy & Transportation

Communication

Daily newspapers, 2004 25
Households with computers, 2003 ....67%
Households with internet access, 2003 .....60%

Energy

Electricity Consumption, 2001
Total (trillion Btu)..................... 2,315
Per capita (million Btu) 322
By source of production (trillion Btu)
   Coal 482
   Natural gas 247
   Petroleum............................ 911
   Nuclear electric power 269
   Hydroelectric power 13
By end-use sector (trillion Btu)
   Residential 549
   Commercial 534
   Industrial 547
   Transportation 685
Electric energy, 2003
   Production (billion kWh) 75.3
   Net summer capability (million kW) 21.3
Gas utilities, 2003
   Customers (x1,000)................... 1,007
   Sales (trillion Btu)................... 134
   Revenues ($mil)..................... $1,360
Nuclear plants, 2003 4

Transportation, 2004

Public Road & Street Mileage 71,534
   Urban............................. 21,226
   Rural 50,308
   Interstate........................... 1,116
Vehicle miles of travel per capita....... 10,590.4
Total motor vehicle registrations...... 6,497,426
   Automobiles...................... 4,091,334
   Buses 18,199
   Trucks 2,387,893
   Motorcycles 75,457
Licensed drivers 5,112,523
   19 years & under 218,632
Deaths from motor vehicle accidents 925

State Summary

Capital City.........................Olympia
Governor................. Christine Gregoire
Office of the Governor
PO Box 40002
Olympia, WA 98504
360-902-4111
Admitted as a state 1889
Area (square miles) 71,300
Population, 2004 (est.) 6,203,788
Largest City......................... Seattle
Population, 2004................... 571,000
Personal income per capita, 2004
(in current dollars) $35,299
Gross state product ($ mil), 2004 ...... $261,549

Leading industries by payroll, 2003

Manufacturing, Health care/Social assistance,
Information

Leading agricultural commodities by receipts, 2003

Apples, dairy products, cattle, wheat

Geography & Environment

Total area (sq. mi.).................... 71,300
land 66,544
water 4,756
Federally-owned land, 2004 (acres) .. 12,949,662
percent...........................30.3%
Highest point...................... Mt. Rainier
elevation (feet) 14,410
Lowest point .... Pacific Ocean
elevation (feet) .... sea level
General coastline (miles).................. 157
Tidal shoreline (miles)................. 3,026
Capital City.......................Olympia
Population 2000 42,514
Population 2004 43,982
Largest City........................ Seattle
Population 2000 563,000
Population 2004 571,000

Number of cities with over 100,000 population

1990 3
2000 5
2004 5

State park and recreation areas, 2003

Area (acres x 1,000)...................... 259
Number of visitors (x 1,000) 44,991
Revenues (x 1,000).................... $15,720
percent of operating expenditures...... 32.7%

National forest system land, 2004

Acres 9,276,000

Demographics and Characteristics of the Population

Population

1980 4,132,156
1990 4,866,692
2000 5,894,121
2004 (estimate)..................... 6,203,788
persons per sq. mile of land.............93.2
2005 (projection)................... 6,204,632
Male...................... 3,086,443
Female........................ 3,118,189
2010 (projection)................... 6,541,963
2020 (projection)................... 7,432,136
2030 (projection)................... 8,624,801
Male...................... 4,272,591
Female........................ 4,352,210

Metropolitan and Non-Metro. area population

	Metro	Non-Metro
1980	3,322,000	810,000
1990	3,976,000	891,000
2000	4,899,000	995,000

Change in population, 2000-2004

Number 309,648
percent............................. 5.3%
Natural increase (births minus deaths).. 141,395
Net internal migration 52,965
Net international migration 112,580

Persons by age, 2004

Under 5 years 387,403
18 years and over 4,717,768
65 years and over 703,145
85 years and over 103,259

Persons by age, 2010 (projected)

Total............................. 6,541,963
Under 5 years 426,590
5 to 17 years 1,061,833
18 and over 5,053,540
21 and over 4,770,246
65 and over 795,528
85 and over 126,063
Median age 37.3

Race, 2004 (estimate)

One Race
White......................... 5,290,018
Black or African American 216,484
American Indian/Alaska Native...... 101,384
Pacific Islander 28,189
Asian Indian...................... 41,144
Chinese 75,257
Filipino 67,330
Japanese 34,011
Korean.......................... 47,809
Vietnamese...................... 56,079
Two or more races.................... 179,956

Persons of Hispanic origin, 2004

Total Hispanic or Latino	517,055
Mexican	418,027
Puerto Rican	14,769
Cuban	4,459
Other Hispanic or Latino	46,956

Marital status, 2000

Population 15 years & over	4,639,522
Never married	1,220,194
Married	2,565,656
Separated	74,232
Widowed	250,534
Divorced	528,906

Language spoken at home, 2000

Population 5 years & over	5,501,398
English only	4,730,512
Spanish	321,490
Other Indo-European languages	176,722
Asian/Pacific Island languages	242,836

Households & families, 2000

Households	2,271,398
with persons under 18 years	799,102
with persons over 65 years	463,007
persons per household	2.53
Families	1,499,127
persons per family	3.07
Married couples	1,181,995
Female householder, no husband present	224,618
One-person households	594,325

Nativity, 2000

Number of persons born in state	2,781,457
percent of population	47.2%

Immigration & Naturalization, 2004

Immigrants admitted	19,442
Persons naturalized	12,667
Asylums granted	255
Asylums denied	4

Vital Statistics and Health

Marriages

2002	39,518
2003	39,622
2004	40,169

Divorces

2002	28,023
2003	26,752
2004	26,674

Births

2003	80,489
Birthrate (per 1,000)	13.1
Low birth weight (2,500g or less)	6.0%
To unmarried mothers	28.8%

2003, continued

White	66,569
Black	4,029
Hispanic	13,307
Asian/Pacific Islander	7,833
Amer. Indian/Alaska Native	2,043
2004 (preliminary)	81,740
Birthrate (per 1,000)	13.2
White	67,157
Black	4,059
Hispanic	14,254
Asian/Pacific Islander	8,385

Deaths

2002

All causes	45,338
rate per 100,000	747.0
Heart disease	11,141
rate per 100,000	183.6
Malignant neoplasms	10,858
rate per 100,000	178.9
Cerebrovascular disease	3,753
rate per 100,000	61.8
Chronic lower respiratory disease	2,721
rate per 100,000	44.8
2003	45,964
rate per 100,000	749.6
2004 (provisional)	44,540

Infant deaths

2003 (provisional)	416
rate per 1,000	5.2
2004 (provisional)	444
rate per 1,000	5.4

Abortions, 2000

Total	26,000
rate per 1,000 women age 15-44	20.3

Physicians, 2003

Total	16,347
rate per 1,000 persons	267

Nurses, 2001

Total	45,170
rate per 1,000 persons	754

Community Hospitals, 2003

Number	85
Beds (x 1,000)	11.2
Patients admitted (x 1,000)	516
Average daily census (x 1,000)	6.8
Average cost per day	$1,827
Outpatient visits (x mil)	10.3

Disability status of population, 2004

5 to 20 years	6.4%
21 to 64 years	13.2%
65 years and over	39%

Education

Educational attainment, 2004

Population over 25 years 4,000,617
    Less than 9th grade 144,697
    High school graduates only......... 989,299
    Bachelor's degree only 815,568
    Graduate or professional degree...... 436,245
    Less than 9th grade percent 3.6%
    High school graduate or more 89.7%
    College graduate or more............. 29.9%
    Graduate or professional degree....... 10.9%

Public school enrollment, Fall 2002

Total............................. 1,014,798
    Kindergarten through grade 8 697,191
    Grades 9 through 12................ 317,607
Enrollment, 2005 (projected) 1,008,500

Graduating public high school seniors

2004 (estimate)........................ 60,410

SAT scores, 2005

Average verbal score 532
Average math score....................... 534
Percent of graduates taking test 55%

Public school teachers, 2004

Total (x 1,000) 52.9
    Elementary (x 1,000)...................29.3
    Secondary (x 1,000) 23.6
Average salary $45,400
    Elementary......................... $45,500
    Secondary.......................... $45,400

State receipts & expenditures for public schools, 2004

Revenue receipts ($mil)................. $8,758
Expenditures
Total ($mil)........................... $9,574
    Per capita $1,561
    Per pupil $7,904

Institutions of higher education, 2004

Total.................................... 81
    Public................................. 46
    Private................................ 35

Enrollment in institutions of higher education, Fall, 2003

Total................................. 353,198
    Full-time men 99,960
    Full-time women................... 122,484
    Part-time men 53,724
    Part-time women................... 77,030

Minority enrollment in institutions of higher education, Fall, 2003

Black, non-hispanic.................. 12,821
Hispanic 16,459
Asian/Pacific Islander 29,043
American Indian/Alaska Native.......... 5,792

Earned degrees conferred, 2003

Bachelor's 25,908
Master's.............................. 8,310
First-professional...................... 1,218
Doctor's................................ 663

State & local financial support for higher education, 2003-2004

Full-time equivalent enrollment (x 1,000) . 220.0
Appropriations per FTE................ $5,509
    as a percent of tax revenue.............. 7.0%

Social Insurance & Welfare Programs

Social Security benefits & beneficiaries, 2004

Beneficiaries
    Total............................. 913,000
    Retired & dependents............... 658,000
    Survivors......................... 114,000
    Disabled & dependents............. 141,000
Annual benefit payments ($ mil)
    Total............................. $9,833
    Retired & dependents............... $6,785
    Survivors.......................... $1,602
    Disabled & dependents.............. $1,445
Average Monthly Benefit
    Retired & dependents................ $993
    Disabled & dependents............... $906
    Widowed............................ $983

Medicare

Enrollment, 2001 (x 1,000) 746
    Payments ($ mil, est.) $3,200
Enrollment, 2003 (x 1,000) 775

Medicaid, 2002

Beneficiaries (x 1,000)................. 1,039
Payments ($ mil) $4,373

State Children's Health Insurance, 2004

Enrollment (x 1,000)....................17.0
Expenditures ($ mil)....................$39.7

Persons without health insurance, 2003

Number (x 1,000)...................... 944
    percent........................... 15.5%
Number of children (x 1,000) 125
    percent of children 8.4%

Federal public aid

Temporary Assistance for Needy Families, 2004
Recipients (x 1,000)...................... 137
Families (x 1,000) 56

Supplemental Security Income, 2003
Recipients (x 1,000)...................... 109
Payments ($ mil) $546

Food Stamp Program, 2004

Participants (x 1,000) 453
Benefits ($ mil).........................$455

Housing & Construction

Housing units
Total 2003 (estimate) 2,568,211
Total 2004 (estimate) 2,606,623
Seasonal or recreational use, 2003 54,000
Owner-occupied single-family, 2003. . 1,254,000
  Median value $200,235
Renter-occupied, 2003 845,000
  Median rent $734
Homeownership rate, 2003 . . . . 65.9%
Homeownership rate, 2004 . . . . 66.0%

New privately owned housing units, 2004
Number authorized (x 1,000) 50.1
Value ($ mil) $7,535
Started 2005 (x 1,000, estimate) 38.3
Started 2006 (x 1,000, estimate) 38.2

Existing home sales
2002 (x 1,000) 116.3
2003 (x 1,000) 132.3
2004 (x 1,000) 147.6

Government & Elections

State Officials 2006
Governor (name/party/term expires)
                Christine Gregoire
                Democrat - 1/09
Lieutenant Governor. . . . . Brad Owen
Secretary of State . . . . Patricia Elwood
Attorney General. . . . . .Rob McKenna
Chief Justice . . . . Gerry Alexander

Governorship
Minimum age. 18
Length of term . . . . 4 years
Consecutive terms permitted . . . . . . not specified
Who succeeds .Lt. Governor

State Legislature
Name . . . . Legislature
Upper chamber . . . . .Senate
  Number of members 49
  Length of term . . . . 4 years
  Party in majority, 2006 . . . . .Democratic
Lower chamber. . . . . . .House of Representatives
  Number of members 98
  Length of term . . . . 2 years
  Party in majority, 2006 . . . . .Democratic

State Government Employees, 2004
Total 112,738
Payroll $424,844,109

Local Government Employees, 2004
Total 291,568
Payroll $922,985,621

Local Governments by Type, 2002
Total 1,787
  County 39
  Municipal 279
  Township 0
  School District 296
  Special District 1,173

Voting age population, November 2004
Total 4,596,000
  Male 2,214,000
  Female 2,382,000
  White 3,792,000
  Black 141,000
  Hispanic 248,000
  Asian 404,000

Presidential Election, 2004
Total Popular Vote 2,859,084
  Kerry 1,510,201
  Bush 1,304,894
Total Electoral Votes 11

Federal representation, 2006 (109th Congress)
Senator. . . . . Maria Cantwell
  Party . . . . Democrat
  Year term expires 2007
Senator. . . . . Patty Murray
  Party . . . . Democrat
  Year term expires 2011
Representatives, total 9
  Democrats. 6
  Republicans 3
  Other 0

Votes cast for US Senators
2002
Total vote (x 1,000) . . . . NA
Leading party. . . . . NA
Percent for leading party . . . . NA

2004
Total vote (x 1,000) 2,819,000
Leading party .Democratic
Percent for leading party 55.0%

Votes cast for US Representatives
2002
Total vote (x 1,000) 1,739
  Democratic. 907
  Republican 779
Leading party .Democratic
Percent for leading party 52.2%

2004
Total vote (x 1,000) 2,730
  Democratic. 1,609
  Republican 1,095
Leading party .Democratic
Percent for leading party 58.9%

Women holding public office, 2006

US Congress 3
Statewide elected office. 2
State legislature 49

Black public officials, 2001

Total. 26
  US and state legislatures 2
  City/county/regional offices 12
  Judicial/law enforcement. 11
  Education/school boards 1

Hispanic public officials, 2004

Total. 14
  State executives & legislators 3
  City/county/regional offices 6
  Judicial/law enforcement. 0
  Education/school boards 5

Governmental Finance

State government revenues, 2004

Total revenue ($1,000) $35,085,947
  Revenue per capita 5,652.64

General Revenue ($ per capita) $4,060.21
  Intergovernmental 1,120.27
  Taxes 2,238.66
    general sales 1,357.04
    individual income tax. 0
    corporate income tax 0
  Current charges. 465.14
  Miscellaneous 236.14

State government expenditure, 2004

Total expenditure (x $1,000) $32,510,057
  Expenditure per capita. 5,237.64
General Expenditure ($ per capita). . . . $4,351.55
  Education 1,806.22
  Public welfare. 1,034.78
  Health 217.45
  Hospitals. 221.84
  Highways 322.33
  Police protection 39.18
  Correction 128.37
  Natural resources 98.05
  Parks & recreation. 17.07
  Governmental administration 99.56
  Interest on general debt 121.41

State debt & cash, 2004 ($ per capita)

Debt $2,541.28
Cash/security holdings. $10,778.73

Federal government grants to state & local government, 2004 (x $1,000)

Total. $9,082,685

By Federal Agency
  Defense $90,720

By Federal Agency, continued
  Education 713,947
  Energy 54,351
  Environmental Protection Agency . . . 106,550
  Health & Human Services. 5,151,472
  Homeland Security. 65,477
  Housing & Urban Development. 635,980
  Justice 157,451
  Labor 259,522
  Transportation 975,161
  Veterans Affairs. 11,728

Crime, Law Enforcement & Courts

Crime, 2004 (rates per 100,000 residents)

Property crimes 300,837
  Burglaries. 60,632
  Larcenies. 196,972
  Motor vehicle thefts 43,233
  Property crime rate. 4,849.2
Violent crimes. 21,330
  Murders. 190
  Forcible rape. 2,857
  Robberies 5,866
  Aggravated assaults 12,417
  Violent crime rate 343.8

Police Agencies, 2004

Total agencies. 247
Total employees 14,008
  Male officers 8,870
  Female officers 955
  Male civilians. 1,459
  Female civilians. 2,724

Arrests, 2004

Total. 216,541
  Persons under 18 years of age 35,285

Prisoners under state & federal jurisdiction, 2004

Total prisoners. 16,614
  Percent change, 12/31/03 to 12/31/04 . . . . 2.9%
Sentenced to more than one year 16,503
  rate per 100,000. 264

Persons under sentence of death, 7/1/05

Total. 10
  White. 6
  Black 4
  Hispanic 0

State's highest court

Name . . . . .Supreme Court
Number of members. 9
Length of term . . . . 6 years
Intermediate appeals court? . . . . .yes

Labor & Income

Civilian labor force, 2004

Total.............................. 3,240,000
  Men 1,746,000
  Women 1,494,000
  Persons 16-19 years............... 148,000
  White............................ 2,757,000
  Black 98,000
  Hispanic 216,000
  Asian 206,000

Civilian labor force as a percent of civilian non-institutional population, 2004

Total.................................. 67.8%
  Men 74.7
  Women 61.2
  Persons 16-19 years................. 43.6
  White............................... 67.7
  Black 70.6
  Hispanic 72.3
  Asian 67.1

Employment, 2004

Total.............................. 3,037,000
  Men 1,637,000
  Women 1,400,000
  Persons 16-19 years............... 116,000
  White............................ 2,589,000
  Black 90,000
  Hispanic 201,000
  Asian 195,000

Full-time/part-time labor force, 2002

Full-time labor force, employed 2,253,000
Part-time labor force, employed........ 618,000
Unemployed, looking for
  Full-time work..................... 180,000
  Part-time work...................... 46,000

Unemployment rate, 2004

Total.................................. 6.2%
  Men 6.2
  Women 6.3
  Persons 16-19 years................. 21.9
  White................................ 6.1
  Black 8.7
  Hispanic 6.9
  Asian 5.0

Unemployed by reason for unemployment (as a percent of total unemployment), 2002

Job losers or completed temp jobs 58.0%
Job leavers.............................. NA
Reentrants.............................. 25.7
New entrants .... NA

Labor unions, 2004

Membership 510,000
  percent of employed 19.3%

Experienced civilian labor force by private industry, first quarter 2004

Total............................. 2,133,055
  Natural Resources & Mining 69,474
  Construction 143,565
  Manufacturing...................... 254,487
  Trade, transportation & utilities 487,633
  Information 91,363
  Finance 147,805
  Professional & business 284,810
  Education & Health 296,800
  Leisure & hospitality................ 242,629
  Other.............................. 114,489

Experienced civilian labor force by occupation, 2004

Management......................... 80,490
Business & Financial................. 119,020
Legal............................... 20,890
Sales 294,420
Office & Admin. Support............. 444,430
Computers & Math 87,140
Architecture & Engineering 66,930
Arts & Entertainment................. 36,390
Education 159,130
Social Services 43,370
Healthcare Practitioner & Technical.... 123,820
Healthcare support 64,780
Maintenance & Repair 107,870
Construction 139,300
Transportation & moving 197,330
Production 157,100
Farming, fishing & forestry............... 390

Hours and earnings of production workers on manufacturing payrolls, 2004

Average weekly hours.................... 40.0
Average hourly earnings $18.27
Average weekly earnings $730.80

Average annual pay

2004 .... $39,361
  change from 2003 .... 0.9%

Household income

Median household income, three-year average,
  2002-2004........................ $48,688

Personal income, 2004 ($ per capita)

In current dollars.................... $35,299
In constant (2000) dollars $32,738

Poverty

Persons below poverty level, three-year average,
  2002-2004......................... 11.7%

Federal individual income tax returns, 2003

Returns filed...................... 2,808,556
Adjusted gross income ($1,000) ... $141,431,438
Total income tax paid ($1,000) $18,891,256

Economy, Business, Industry & Agriculture

Fortune 500 companies, 2005 9

Patents issued, 2004 2,442

Bankruptcy cases filed, 2004 40,100

Business firm ownership, 2002

Women-owned	137,396
Sales ($ mil)	$17,375
Black-owned	6,985
Sales ($ mil)	$1,056
Hispanic-owned	10,269
Sales ($ mil)	$1,548
Asian-owned	26,872
Sales ($ mil)	$7,533
Amer. Indian/Alaska Native-owned	5,734
Sales ($ mil)	$938
Hawaiian/Pacific Isl.-owned	739
Sales ($ mil)	$240

Gross State Product, 2004 ($ mil)

Total Gross State Product	$261,549
Agriculture, forestry, fishing and hunting	5,125
Mining	355
Utilities	2,612
Construction	12,513
Manufacturing, durable goods	16,006
Manufacturing, non-durable goods	6,949
Wholesale trade	16,112
Retail trade	18,871
Transportation & warehousing	7,330
Information	21,801
Finance & insurance	15,982
Real estate, rental, leasing	38,797
Professional and technical services	17,027
Educational services	1,293
Health care and social assistance	17,182
Accommodation/food services	6,472
Other services, except government	6,076
Government	37,109

Establishments, by major industry group, 2003

Total	167,272
Forestry, fishing & agriculture	1,669
Mining	178
Construction	21,958
Manufacturing	7,366
Wholesale trade	9,546
Retail trade	22,650
Transportation & warehousing	4,464
Information	3,117
Finance & insurance	9,768
Professional/scientific/technical	17,253
Health care/social assistance	16,771
Accommodation/food services	14,002

Annual payroll by major industry group, 2003

Total ($1,000)	$90,586,818
Forestry, fishing & agriculture	524,621
Mining	129,644
Utilities	333,461
Construction	6,336,822
Manufacturing	11,211,328
Wholesale trade	5,506,910
Retail trade	7,335,010
Transportation & warehousing	2,874,220
Information	8,915,397
Finance & insurance	6,023,382
Professional/scientific/technical . . .	8,016,773
Health care/social assistance	10,680,209
Accommodation/food services	2,790,176

Agriculture

Number of farms, 2004 35,000
Farm acreage, 2004

Total	15,000,000
Acres per farm, 2004	434

Farm income, 2003 ($mil)

Net farm income	$680
Debt/asset ratio	16.9

Farm marketings, 2003 ($mil)

Total	$5,345
Crops	3,818
Livestock	1,527

Principal commodities, in order by marketing receipts, 2003

Apples, dairy products, cattle, wheat

Federal economic activity in state

Expenditures, 2003

Total ($ mil)	$43,368
Per capita	$7,073
Defense ($ mil)	7,703
Non-defense ($ mil)	35,665

Defense department, 2003

Payroll ($ mil)	$4,774
Contract awards ($ mil)	$3,217
Grants ($ mil)	$56
Homeland security grants ($1,000)	
2004	$73,593
2005	$45,330

FDIC insured financial institutions, 2004

Number	98
Assets ($bil)	$78.5
Deposits ($bil)	87.4

Fishing, 2004

Catch (x 1,000 lbs)	454,747
Value ($1,000)	$175,081

Mining, 2004 ($ mil)
Total non-fuel mineral production $447
Percent of U.S. 1.0%

Construction, 2003 ($ mil)
Total contracts (including non-building) $12,788
   residential............................ 6,629
   non-residential 3,369

Establishments, receipts, payroll & employees, by major industry group, 2002

Mining.................................. 669
   Receipts ($1,000) $5,429,555
   Annual payroll ($1,000)........... $984,026
   Paid employees 22,187

Utilities 327
   Receipts ($1,000) .... NA
   Annual payroll ($1,000).......... $321,603
   Paid employees 5,617

Construction......................... 21,701
   Receipts ($1,000) $27,916,123
   Annual payroll ($1,000)......... $6,330,733
   Paid employees 167,874

Manufacturing 7,535
   Receipts ($1,000) $79,313,884
   Annual payroll ($1,000)........ $11,163,873
   Paid employees 265,010

Wholesale trade 9,670
   Receipts ($1,000) $84,634,499
   Annual payroll ($1,000)......... $5,156,988
   Paid employees 121,132

Retail trade......................... 22,564
   Receipts ($1,000) $65,262,333
   Annual payroll ($1,000)......... $6,860,587
   Paid employees 296,507

Transportation....................... 4,399
   Receipts ($1,000) $7,592,392
   Annual payroll ($1,000)......... $2,208,484
   Paid employees 65,315

Information.......................... 3,093
   Receipts ($1,000) .... NA
   Annual payroll ($1,000)........ $10,262,455
   Paid employees 101,636

Finance & insurance 9,534
   Receipts ($1,000) .... NA
   Annual payroll ($1,000)......... $5,404,736
   Paid employees 111,006

Professional, scientific & technical 16,963
   Receipts ($1,000) $16,730,409
   Annual payroll ($1,000)......... $7,566,562
   Paid employees 142,325

Health care & social assistance 16,493
   Receipts ($1,000) $24,707,761
   Annual payroll ($1,000)........ $10,328,590
   Paid employees 301,315

Accommodation & food service......... 13,699
   Receipts ($1,000) $8,642,681
   Annual payroll ($1,000).......... $2,571,978
   Paid employees 199,652

Communication, Energy & Transportation

Communication
Daily newspapers, 2004 23
Households with computers, 2003..........71%
Households with internet access, 2003 .....62%

Energy
Electricity Consumption, 2001
Total (trillion Btu)...................... 2,034
Per capita (million Btu) 339
By source of production (trillion Btu)
   Coal 100
   Natural gas......................... 323
   Petroleum........................... 843
   Nuclear electric power 86
   Hydroelectric power.................. 557
By end-use sector (trillion Btu)
   Residential 471
   Commercial 377
   Industrial 586
   Transportation 600
Electric energy, 2003
   Production (billion kWh) 100.1
   Net summer capability (million kW) 27.7
Gas utilities, 2003
   Customers (x1,000).................. 986
   Sales (trillion Btu)................. 132
   Revenues ($mil)................... $1,002
Nuclear plants, 2003 1

Transportation, 2004
Public Road & Street Mileage 81,216
   Urban............................ 20,124
   Rural 61,092
   Interstate........................... 764
Vehicle miles of travel per capita 8,834.2
Total motor vehicle registrations...... 5,535,236
   Automobiles...................... 3,034,253
   Buses 11,049
   Trucks 2,489,934
   Motorcycles 160,227
Licensed drivers 4,504,581
   19 years & under 179,183
Deaths from motor vehicle accidents 563

State Summary

Capital City...................... Charleston
Governor.................... Joe Manchin III
1900 Kanawha St
Charleston, WV 25305
304-558-2000
Admitted as a state 1863
Area (square miles)................... 24,230
Population, 2004 (est.) 1,815,354
Largest City...................... Charleston
  Population, 2004.................... 51,685
Personal income per capita, 2004
  (in current dollars) $25,872
Gross state product ($ mil), 2004 ...... $49,454

Leading industries by payroll, 2003

Health care/Social assistance, Manufacturing,
Retail trade

Leading agricultural commodities by receipts, 2003

Broilers, cattle, chicken eggs, turkeys

Geography & Environment

Total area (sq. mi.).................... 24,230
  land 24,078
  water 152
Federally-owned land, 2004 (acres) 1,146,211
  percent............................. 7.4%
Highest point.................... Spruce Knob
  elevation (feet) 4,861
Lowest point .... Potomac River
  elevation (feet) 240
General coastline (miles)..................... 0
Tidal shoreline (miles)....................... 0
Capital City...................... Charleston
  Population 2000 53,421
  Population 2004 51,685
Largest City...................... Charleston
  Population 2000 53,421
  Population 2004 51,685

Number of cities with over 100,000 population

1990 0
2000 0
2004 0

State park and recreation areas, 2003

Area (acres x 1,000)...................... 196
Number of visitors (x 1,000) 8,343
Revenues (x 1,000).................... $18,862
  percent of operating expenditures...... 61.0%

National forest system land, 2004

Acres 1,041,000

Demographics and Characteristics of the Population

Population

1980 1,949,644
1990 1,793,477
2000 1,808,344
2004 (estimate).................... 1,815,354
  persons per sq. mile of land............. 75.4
2005 (projection)................... 1,818,887
  Male........................... 887,970
  Female......................... 930,917
2010 (projection) 1,829,141
2020 (projection)................... 1,801,112
2030 (projection)................... 1,719,959
  Male........................... 845,670
  Female......................... 874,289

Metropolitan and Non-Metro. area population

	Metro	Non-Metro
1980	718,000	1,232,000
1990	653,000	1,140,000
2000	766,000	1,043,000

Change in population, 2000-2004

Number........................... 7,004
  percent........................... 0.4%
Natural increase (births minus deaths)... -2,044
Net internal migration 6,794
Net international migration 3,114

Persons by age, 2004

Under 5 years 101,109
18 years and over 1,430,713
65 years and over 278,354
85 years and over 32,535

Persons by age, 2010 (projected)

Total........................... 1,829,141
  Under 5 years 101,135
  5 to 17 years 281,176
  18 and over 1,446,830
  21 and over 1,380,755
  65 and over 292,402
  85 and over 40,569
  Median age 41.4

Race, 2004 (estimate)

One Race

White........................ 1,727,793
Black or African American 58,094
American Indian/Alaska Native....... 3,729
Pacific Islander 425
Asian Indian...................... 1,977
Chinese 1,430
Filipino 1,344
Japanese 397
Korean........................... 316
Vietnamese........................ 355
Two or more races.................... 15,075

Persons of Hispanic origin, 2004

Total Hispanic or Latino 10,935
   Mexican............................. 5,547
   Puerto Rican 2,647
   Cuba 479
   Other Hispanic or Latino 1,623

Marital status, 2000

Population 15 years & over 1,479,301
   Never married 326,926
   Married........................... 846,160
   Separated 22,190
   Widowed........................... 130,178
   Divorced 153,847

Language spoken at home, 2000

Population 5 years & over 1,706,931
   English only 1,661,036
   Spanish 17,652
   Other Indo-European languages 19,491
   Asian/Pacific Island languages........ 6,038

Households & families, 2000

Households......................... 736,481
   with persons under 18 years 233,906
   with persons over 65 years........... 201,399
   persons per household 2.4
Families........................... 504,055
   persons per family.......................2.9
Married couples.................... 397,499
Female householder,
   no husband present.................. 79,120
One-person households 199,587

Nativity, 2000

Number of persons born in state 1,342,589
   percent of population................. 74.2%

Immigration & Naturalization, 2004

Immigrants admitted...................... 583
Persons naturalized 237
Asylums granted 16
Asylums denied 0

Vital Statistics and Health

Marriages

2002 14,557
2003 13,659
2004 13,621

Divorces

2002 9,438
2003 9,335
2004 9,148

Births

2003 20,935
   Birthrate (per 1,000)....................11.6
   Low birth weight (2,500g or less)........ 8.6%
   To unmarried mothers................. 34.6%

2003, continued
   White............................. 20,005
   Black 722
   Hispanic 99
   Asian/Pacific Islander 156
   Amer. Indian/Alaska Native............ 25

2004 (preliminary)..................... 20,855
   Birthrate (per 1,000)....................11.5
   White............................. 19,992
   Black 673
   Hispanic 151
   Asian/Pacific Islander 170

Deaths

2002
All causes 21,016
   rate per 100,000.................... 1,166.3
Heart disease 6,189
   rate per 100,000.................... 343.5
Malignant neoplasms 4,652
   rate per 100,000.................... 258.2
Cerebrovascular disease................ 1,260
   rate per 100,000.....................69.9
Chronic lower respiratory disease 1,228
   rate per 100,000.....................68.2
2003 21,299
   rate per 100,000.................... 1,176.5
2004 (provisional) 20,584

Infant deaths

2003 (provisional) 153
   rate per 1,000 ....7.3
2004 (provisional) 135
   rate per 1,000 ....6.5

Abortions, 2000

Total................................. 3,000
   rate per 1,000 women age 15-44...........6.8

Physicians, 2003

Total................................. 4,168
   rate per 1,000 persons.................. 230

Nurses, 2001

Total................................. 15,850
   rate per 1,000 persons.................. 880

Community Hospitals, 2003

Number................................. 57
Beds (x 1,000)...........................7.8
Patients admitted (x 1,000) 296
Average daily census (x 1,000) 4.8
Average cost per day $993
Outpatient visits (x mil)....................5.8

Disability status of population, 2004

5 to 20 years 8.4%
21 to 64 years 21.5%
65 years and over 51.9%

Education

Educational attainment, 2004

Population over 25 years	1,232,821
Less than 9th grade	95,013
High school graduates only	504,520
Bachelor's degree only	126,137
Graduate or professional degree	75,166
Less than 9th grade percent	7.7%
High school graduate or more	80.9%
College graduate or more	15.3%
Graduate or professional degree	6.1%

Public school enrollment, Fall 2002

Total	282,455
Kindergarten through grade 8	200,002
Grades 9 through 12	82,453
Enrollment, 2005 (projected)	273,500

Graduating public high school seniors

2004 (estimate)	17,070

SAT scores, 2005

Average verbal score	523
Average math score	511
Percent of graduates taking test	20%

Public school teachers, 2004

Total (x 1,000)	19.9
Elementary (x 1,000)	13.7
Secondary (x 1,000)	6.1
Average salary	$38,500
Elementary	$38,200
Secondary	$39,000

State receipts & expenditures for public schools, 2004

Revenue receipts ($mil)	$2,728
Expenditures	
Total ($mil)	$2,785
Per capita	$1,538
Per pupil	$9,509

Institutions of higher education, 2004

Total	40
Public	18
Private	22

Enrollment in institutions of higher education, Fall, 2003

Total	100,242
Full-time men	33,958
Full-time women	40,527
Part-time men	9,751
Part-time women	16,006

Minority enrollment in institutions of higher education, Fall, 2003

Black, non-hispanic	4,634
Hispanic	912
Asian/Pacific Islander	1,055
American Indian/Alaska Native	377

Earned degrees conferred, 2003

Bachelor's	9,335
Master's	2,479
First-professional	471
Doctor's	160

State & local financial support for higher education, 2003-2004

Full-time equivalent enrollment (x 1,000)	69.5
Appropriations per FTE	$4,135
as a percent of tax revenue	9.3%

Social Insurance & Welfare Programs

Social Security benefits & beneficiaries, 2004

Beneficiaries	
Total	407,000
Retired & dependents	237,000
Survivors	71,000
Disabled & dependents	99,000
Annual benefit payments ($ mil)	
Total	$4,189
Retired & dependents	$2,268
Survivors	$905
Disabled & dependents	$1,016
Average Monthly Benefit	
Retired & dependents	$943
Disabled & dependents	$936
Widowed	$879

Medicare

Enrollment, 2001 (x 1,000)	340
Payments ($ mil, est.)	$1,800
Enrollment, 2003 (x 1,000)	347

Medicaid, 2002

Beneficiaries (x 1,000)	362
Payments ($ mil)	$1,578

State Children's Health Insurance, 2004

Enrollment (x 1,000)	36.9
Expenditures ($ mil)	$30.8

Persons without health insurance, 2003

Number (x 1,000)	296
percent	16.6%
Number of children (x 1,000)	34
percent of children	8.4%

Federal public aid

Temporary Assistance for Needy Families, 2004	
Recipients (x 1,000)	36
Families (x 1,000)	15
Supplemental Security Income, 2003	
Recipients (x 1,000)	75
Payments ($ mil)	$357

Food Stamp Program, 2004

Participants (x 1,000)	256
Benefits ($ mil)	$232

Housing & Construction

Housing units

Total 2003 (estimate) 862,280
Total 2004 (estimate) 866,944
Seasonal or recreational use, 2003 39,000
Owner-occupied single-family, 2003.... 387,000
    Median value $85,709
Renter-occupied, 2003 186,000
    Median rent $432
Homeownership rate, 2003 .... 78.1%
Homeownership rate, 2004 .... 80.3%

New privately owned housing units, 2004

Number authorized (x 1,000) 5.7
Value ($ mil)............................ $735
Started 2005 (x 1,000, estimate) 5.4
Started 2006 (x 1,000, estimate) 5.4

Existing home sales

2002 (x 1,000)...........................28.1
2003 (x 1,000)...........................28.9
2004 (x 1,000)...........................36.0

Government & Elections

State Officials 2006

Governor (name/party/term expires)
                Joe Manchin III
                Democrat - 1/09
Lieutenant Governor.........Earl Ray Tomblin
Secretary of State................ Betty Ireland
Attorney General.............Darrell McGraw
Chief Justice .... Joseph P. Albright

Governorship

Minimum age............................. 30
Length of term........................ 4 years
Consecutive terms permitted 2
Who succeeds................. Pres. of Senate

State Legislature

Name .... Legislature
Upper chamber ....Senate
    Number of members..................... 34
    Length of term..................... 4 years
    Party in majority, 2006 ....Democratic
Lower chamber............. House of Delegates
    Number of members.................... 100
    Length of term.................... 2 years
    Party in majority, 2006 ....Democratic

State Government Employees, 2004

Total................................. 37,583
Payroll........................ $111,412,488

Local Government Employees, 2004

Total................................ 217,422
Payroll........................ $749,415,162

Local Governments by Type, 2002

Total.................................. 686
    County................................. 55
    Municipal............................. 234
    Township 0
    School District......................... 55
    Special District 342

Voting age population, November 2004

Total............................. 1,395,000
    Male.............................. 676,000
    Female............................ 720,000
    White............................ 1,331,000
    Black 42,000
    Hispanic 5,000
    Asian 5,000

Presidential Election, 2004

Total Popular Vote 755,887
    Kerry 326,541
    Bush.............................. 423,778
Total Electoral Votes...................... 5

Federal representation, 2006 (109th Congress)

Senator.......................Robert C. Byrd
    Party .... Democrat
    Year term expires 2007
Senator....................... Jay Rockefeller
    Party .... Democrat
    Year term expires 2009
Representatives, total 3
    Democrats.............................. 2
    Republicans 1
    Other.................................. 0

Votes cast for US Senators

2002
Total vote (x 1,000) 436,000
Leading party.....................Democratic
Percent for leading party 63.1%

2004
Total vote (x 1,000) .... NA
Leading party........................... NA
Percent for leading party .... NA

Votes cast for US Representatives

2002
Total vote (x 1,000) 400
    Democratic........................... 264
    Republican........................... 136
Leading party.....................Democratic
Percent for leading party 66.0%

2004
Total vote (x 1,000) 722
    Democratic........................... 415
    Republican 303
Leading party.....................Democratic
Percent for leading party 57.6%

Women holding public office, 2006
US Congress 1
Statewide elected office...................... 1
State legislature 21

Black public officials, 2001
Total..................................... 19
    US and state legislatures 2
    City/county/regional offices 13
    Judicial/law enforcement.................. 3
    Education/school boards.................. 1

Hispanic public officials, 2004
Total...................................... 0
    State executives & legislators 0
    City/county/regional offices 0
    Judicial/law enforcement.................. 0
    Education/school boards.................. 0

Governmental Finance

State government revenues, 2004
Total revenue ($1,000) $11,633,343
    Revenue per capita 6,416.63

General Revenue ($ per capita) $5,316.13
    Intergovernmental 1,823.60
    Taxes 2,067.85
        general sales 563.36
        individual income tax.............. 589.20
        corporate income tax 100.12
    Current charges.................... 740.88
    Miscellaneous 683.80

State government expenditure, 2004
Total expenditure (x $1,000) $9,879,217
    Expenditure per capita............. 5,449.10
General Expenditure ($ per capita).... $4,718.85
    Education 1,621.44
    Public welfare..................... 1,265.56
    Health 158.69
    Hospitals...........................40.14
    Highways 523.39
    Police protection 32.30
    Correction 100.89
    Natural resources 102.05
    Parks & recreation..................31.19
    Governmental administration 245.14
    Interest on general debt 105.06

State debt & cash, 2004 ($ per capita)
Debt $2,617.42
Cash/security holdings.............. $6,833.64

Federal government grants to state & local government, 2004 (x $1,000)
Total $3,700,592
By Federal Agency
    Defense $70,638

By Federal Agency, continued
    Education 274,228
    Energy 14,033
    Environmental Protection Agency 68,857
    Health & Human Services. 2,117,589
    Homeland Security.................. 97,577
    Housing & Urban Development...... 175,777
    Justice 64,525
    Labor 58,461
    Transportation 431,228
    Veterans Affairs..................... 1,785

Crime, Law Enforcement & Courts

Crime, 2004 (rates per 100,000 residents)
Property crimes 45,497
    Burglaries......................... 10,932
    Larcenies.......................... 30,826
    Motor vehicle thefts 3,739
    Property crime rate................. 2,506.2
Violent crimes.......................... 4,924
    Murders........................... 68
    Forcible rape........................ 320
    Robberies 768
    Aggravated assaults 3,768
    Violent crime rate 271.2

Police Agencies, 2004
Total agencies........................... 342
Total employees 4,086
    Male officers....................... 3,080
    Female officers...................... 97
    Male civilians...................... 356
    Female civilians..................... 553

Arrests, 2004
Total................................ 30,257
    Persons under 18 years of age 1,940

Prisoners under state & federal jurisdiction, 2004
Total prisoners........................ 5,067
    Percent change, 12/31/03 to 12/31/04 .... 6.5%
Sentenced to more than one year 5,026
    rate per 100,000...................... 277

Persons under sentence of death, 7/1/05
Total.................................... 0
    White................................. 0
    Black 0
    Hispanic 0

State's highest court
Name .... Supreme Court of Appeals
Number of members...................... 5
Length of term .... 12 years
Intermediate appeals court? .... no

Labor & Income

Civilian labor force, 2004

Total	795,000
Men	425,000
Women	369,000
Persons 16-19 years	38,000
White	760,000
Black	21,000
Hispanic	0
Asian	0

Civilian labor force as a percent of civilian non-institutional population, 2004

Total	54.7%
Men	60.8
Women	49.1
Persons 16-19 years	36.3
White	54.7
Black	55.6
Hispanic	0.0
Asian	0.0

Employment, 2004

Total	753,000
Men	401,000
Women	352,000
Persons 16-19 years	32,000
White	723,000
Black	17,000
Hispanic	0
Asian	0

Full-time/part-time labor force, 2002

Full-time labor force, employed	635,000
Part-time labor force, employed	121,000
Unemployed, looking for	
Full-time work	42,000
Part-time work	NA

Unemployment rate, 2004

Total	5.3%
Men	5.8
Women	4.7
Persons 16-19 years	16.0
White	4.9
Black	15.5
Hispanic	NA
Asian	NA

Unemployed by reason for unemployment (as a percent of total unemployment), 2002

Job losers or completed temp jobs	46.9%
Job leavers	NA
Reentrants	26.5
New entrants	NA

Labor unions, 2004

Membership	99,000
percent of employed	14.2%

Experienced civilian labor force by private industry, first quarter 2004

Total	539,485
Natural Resources & Mining	23,740
Construction	31,868
Manufacturing	62,807
Trade, transportation & utilities	131,720
Information	12,006
Finance	28,354
Professional & business	56,851
Education & Health	103,845
Leisure & hospitality	65,820
Other	21,786

Experienced civilian labor force by occupation, 2004

Management	28,820
Business & Financial	18,710
Legal	5,840
Sales	74,950
Office & Admin. Support	115,730
Computers & Math	6,730
Architecture & Engineering	9,270
Arts & Entertainment	5,540
Education	40,190
Social Services	10,640
Healthcare Practitioner & Technical	44,970
Healthcare support	22,650
Maintenance & Repair	35,940
Construction	45,300
Transportation & moving	60,880
Production	46,030
Farming, fishing & forestry	NA

Hours and earnings of production workers on manufacturing payrolls, 2004

Average weekly hours	41.4
Average hourly earnings	$16.57
Average weekly earnings	$686.00

Average annual pay

2004	$30,382
change from 2003	3.7%

Household income

Median household income, three-year average, 2002-2004	$32,589

Personal income, 2004 ($ per capita)

In current dollars	$25,872
In constant (2000) dollars	$23,995

Poverty

Persons below poverty level, three-year average, 2002-2004	16.1%

Federal individual income tax returns, 2003

Returns filed	744,440
Adjusted gross income ($1,000)	$26,629,491
Total income tax paid ($1,000)	$2,790,795

Economy, Business, Industry & Agriculture

Fortune 500 companies, 2005 0

Patents issued, 2004 111

Bankruptcy cases filed, 2004 11,400

Business firm ownership, 2002

Women-owned. 31,301
   Sales ($ mil) $3,252
Black-owned. 1,475
   Sales ($ mil) $156
Hispanic-owned. 664
   Sales ($ mil) $187
Asian-owned 1,236
   Sales ($ mil) $731
Amer. Indian/Alaska Native-owned 405
   Sales ($ mil) $35
Hawaiian/Pacific Isl.-owned 11
   Sales ($ mil) $1

Gross State Product, 2004 ($ mil)

Total Gross State Product $49,454
   Agriculture, forestry, fishing and
      hunting 267
   Mining. 3,462
   Utilities 2,440
   Construction 2,150
   Manufacturing, durable goods. 3,028
   Manufacturing, non-durable goods 2,441
   Wholesale trade. 2,370
   Retail trade. 4,032
   Transportation & warehousing 1,610
   Information 1,323
   Finance & insurance. 1,964
   Real estate, rental, leasing 4,598
   Professional and technical services 1,957
   Educational services 234
   Health care and social assistance 4,757
   Accommodation/food services. 1,363
   Other services, except government 1,220
   Government 8,383

Establishments, by major industry group, 2003

Total. 40,376
   Forestry, fishing & agriculture 360
   Mining. 628
   Construction 4,395
   Manufacturing. 1,442
   Wholesale trade. 1,669
   Retail trade. 7,348
   Transportation & warehousing 1,458
   Information 723
   Finance & insurance. 2,144
   Professional/scientific/technical 2,963
   Health care/social assistance 4,623
   Accommodation/food services. 3,364

Annual payroll by major industry group, 2003

Total ($1,000) $15,247,779
   Forestry, fishing & agriculture 24,900
   Mining. 1,028,921
   Utilities 424,936
   Construction 876,019
   Manufacturing. 2,754,020
   Wholesale trade. 719,638
   Retail trade. 1,552,247
   Transportation & warehousing 511,729
   Information 437,006
   Finance & insurance. 687,859
   Professional/scientific/technical 763,734
   Health care/social assistance 3,178,791
   Accommodation/food services. 610,204

Agriculture

Number of farms, 2004 21,000
Farm acreage, 2004
   Total. 4,000,000
   Acres per farm, 2004 173
Farm income, 2003 ($mil)
   Net farm income $15
   Debt/asset ratio 8.4
Farm marketings, 2003 ($mil)
Total. $390
   Crops 73
   Livestock 317

Principal commodities, in order by marketing receipts, 2003

    Broilers, cattle, chicken eggs, turkeys

Federal economic activity in state

Expenditures, 2003
   Total ($ mil) $14,226
   Per capita $7,858
   Defense ($ mil). 510
   Non-defense ($ mil) 13,717
Defense department, 2003
   Payroll ($ mil) $316
   Contract awards ($ mil) $207
   Grants ($ mil). $26
   Homeland security grants ($1,000)
     2004 . . . . $25,270
     2005 . . . . $18,289

FDIC insured financial institutions, 2004

Number 72
   Assets ($bil) $19.8
   Deposits ($bil) 22.7

Fishing, 2004

Catch (x 1,000 lbs) 0
Value ($1,000). 0

Mining, 2004 ($ mil)
Total non-fuel mineral production $179
Percent of U.S. 0.4%

Construction, 2003 ($ mil)
Total contracts (including non-building). $1,697
   residential............................. 703
   non-residential 485

Establishments, receipts, payroll & employees, by major industry group, 2002

Mining 170
   Receipts ($1,000) $518,984
   Annual payroll ($1,000)........... $120,541
   Paid employees 2,668

Utilities 223
   Receipts ($1,000) .... NA
   Annual payroll ($1,000)........... $358,253
   Paid employees 6,189

Construction........................... 4,170
   Receipts ($1,000) $3,393,385
   Annual payroll ($1,000)........... $914,587
   Paid employees 29,255

Manufacturing 1,480
   Receipts ($1,000) $18,911,332
   Annual payroll ($1,000)......... $2,586,956
   Paid employees 67,319

Wholesale trade 1,699
   Receipts ($1,000) $10,924,279
   Annual payroll ($1,000)........... $669,680
   Paid employees 20,176

Retail trade 7,454
   Receipts ($1,000) $16,747,900
   Annual payroll ($1,000).......... $1,489,064
   Paid employees 89,340

Transportation........................ 1,477
   Receipts ($1,000) $1,927,398
   Annual payroll ($1,000)........... $472,752
   Paid employees 15,322

Information............................ 707
   Receipts ($1,000) .... NA
   Annual payroll ($1,000)........... $366,432
   Paid employees 12,673

Finance & insurance 2,103
   Receipts ($1,000) .... NA
   Annual payroll ($1,000)........... $653,027
   Paid employees 22,351

Professional, scientific & technical 2,940
   Receipts ($1,000) $1,860,522
   Annual payroll ($1,000)........... $702,492
   Paid employees 21,316

Health care & social assistance 4,669
   Receipts ($1,000) $7,631,590
   Annual payroll ($1,000).......... $3,078,885
   Paid employees 113,580

Accommodation & food service........... 3,310
   Receipts ($1,000) $1,974,851
   Annual payroll ($1,000)........... $555,598
   Paid employees 51,985

Communication, Energy & Transportation

Communication
Daily newspapers, 2004 20
Households with computers, 2003 .... 55%
Households with internet access, 2003 ..... 48%

Energy
Electricity Consumption, 2001
Total (trillion Btu)...................... 762
Per capita (million Btu) 423
By source of production (trillion Btu)
   Coal 872
   Natural gas......................... 152
   Petroleum........................... 215
   Nuclear electric power 0
   Hydroelectric power.................. 10
By end-use sector (trillion Btu)
   Residential 157
   Commercial 111
   Industrial 311
   Transportation 183
Electric energy, 2003
   Production (billion kWh) 94.7
   Net summer capability (million kW) 16.1
Gas utilities, 2003
   Customers (x1,000).................. 395
   Sales (trillion Btu)................. 59
   Revenues ($mil)..................... $463
Nuclear plants, 2003 0

Transportation, 2004
Public Road & Street Mileage 37,011
   Urban.............................. 3,191
   Rural 33,820
   Interstate........................... 555
Vehicle miles of travel per capita 10,897.5
Total motor vehicle registrations...... 1,396,420
   Automobiles....................... 740,834
   Buses 2,877
   Trucks 652,709
   Motorcycles 19,534
Licensed drivers 1,292,036
   19 years & under 67,104
Deaths from motor vehicle accidents 411

State Summary

Capital City. . . . . Madison
Governor. . . . . Jim Doyle
115 East State Capitol
Madison, WI 53707
608-266-1212

Admitted as a state 1848
Area (square miles) 65,498
Population, 2004 (est.) 5,509,026
Largest City. . . . . Milwaukee
   Population, 2004 584,000
Personal income per capita, 2004
   (in current dollars) $32,157
Gross state product ($ mil), 2004 . . . . . . $211,616

Leading industries by payroll, 2003

Manufacturing, Health care/Social assistance, Finance & Insurance

Leading agricultural commodities by receipts, 2003

Dairy products, cattle, corn, greenhouse

Geography & Environment

Total area (sq. mi.). 65,498
   land 54,310
   water 11,188

Federally-owned land, 2004 (acres) . . . 1,971,902
   percent. 5.6%

Highest point. . . . . Timms Hil
   elevation (feet) 1,951

Lowest point . . . . Lake Michigan
   elevation (feet) 581

General coastline (miles). 0

Tidal shoreline (miles). 0

Capital City. . . . . Madison
   Population 2000 208,000
   Population 2004 220,000

Largest City. . . . . Milwaukee
   Population 2000 597,000
   Population 2004 584,000

Number of cities with over 100,000 population

1990 2
2000 3
2004 3

State park and recreation areas, 2003

Area (acres x 1,000). 132
Number of visitors (x 1,000) 15,739
Revenues (x 1,000). $8,648
   percent of operating expenditures. 43.8%

National forest system land, 2004

Acres 1,527,000

Demographics and Characteristics of the Population

Population

1980 4,705,767
1990 4,891,769
2000 5,363,675
2004 (estimate). 5,509,026
   persons per sq. mile of land. 101.4
2005 (projection). 5,554,343
   Male. 2,748,295
   Female. 2,806,048
2010 (projection) 5,727,426
2020 (projection) 6,004,954
2030 (projection) 6,150,764
   Male. 3,034,459
   Female. 3,116,305

Metropolitan and Non-Metro. area population

	Metro	Non-Metro
1980	3,145,000	1,561,000
1990	3,298,000	1,593,000
2000	3,640,000	1,723,000

Change in population, 2000-2004

Number. 145,311
   percent. 2.7%
Natural increase (births minus deaths). . . 93,545
Net internal migration 15,381
Net international migration 39,044

Persons by age, 2004

Under 5 years 338,310
18 years and over 4,201,040
65 years and over 715,568
85 years and over 111,027

Persons by age, 2010 (projected)

Total. 5,727,426
   Under 5 years 367,567
   5 to 17 years 951,577
   18 and over 4,408,282
   21 and over 4,172,527
   65 and over 771,993
   85 and over 128,800
   Median age 38.1

Race, 2004 (estimate)

One Race
   White. 4,966,500
   Black or African American 327,626
   American Indian/Alaska Native. 51,463
   Pacific Islander 2,156
   Asian Indian. 19,403
   Chinese 12,775
   Filipino 4,953
   Japanese 2,497
   Korean 8,333
   Vietnamese. 4,975
Two or more races. 55,512

2   Wisconsin

Persons of Hispanic origin, 2004

Total Hispanic or Latino 234,453
   Mexican........................... 167,607
   Puerto Rican 32,672
   Cuban 2,435
   Other Hispanic or Latino 11,970

Marital status, 2000

Population 15 years & over 4,239,561
   Never married 1,153,161
   Married......................... 2,382,633
   Separated 50,875
   Widowed......................... 271,332
   Divorced 381,560

Language spoken at home, 2000

Population 5 years & over 5,022,073
   English only 4,653,361
   Spanish 168,778
   Other Indo-European languages 124,719
   Asian/Pacific Island languages........ 61,447

Households & families, 2000

Households........................ 2,084,544
   with persons under 18 years 706,399
   with persons over 65 years.......... 479,787
   persons per household 2.5
Families........................... 1,386,815
   persons per family....................3.05
Married couples.................... 1,108,597
Female householder,
   no husband present................ 200,300
One-person households 557,875

Nativity, 2000

Number of persons born in state 3,939,488
   percent of population 73.4%

Immigration & Naturalization, 2004

Immigrants admitted.................. 5,257
Persons naturalized 3,570
Asylums granted 18
Asylums denied .... NA

Vital Statistics and Health

Marriages

2002 34,241
2003 34,220
2004 34,056

Divorces

2002 17,471
2003 17,150
2004 16,802

Births

2003 70,040
   Birthrate (per 1,000)...................12.8
   Low birth weight (2,500g or less)....... 6.8%
   To unmarried mothers............... 30.4%

2003, continued
   White............................. 60,256
   Black 6,496
   Hispanic 5,539
   Asian/Pacific Islander 2,247
   Amer. Indian/Alaska Native.......... 1,054
2004 (preliminary).................... 70,154
   Birthrate (per 1,000)...................12.7
   White............................. 59,998
   Black 6,601
   Hispanic 5,888
   Asian/Pacific Islander 2,446

Deaths

2002
All causes 46,981
   rate per 100,000......................863.4
Heart disease 12,923
   rate per 100,000......................237.5
Malignant neoplasms 10,828
   rate per 100,000......................199.0
Cerebrovascular disease.............. 3,479
   rate per 100,000.......................63.9
Chronic lower respiratory disease 2,335
   rate per 100,000.......................42.9
2003 46,174
   rate per 100,000..................... 843.8
2004 (provisional) 45,613

Infant deaths

2003 (provisional) 451
   rate per 1,000 ....6.4
2004 (provisional) 413
   rate per 1,000 ....5.9

Abortions, 2000

Total................................ 11,000
   rate per 1,000 women age 15-44...........9.6

Physicians, 2003

Total................................ 13,769
   rate per 1,000 persons.................. 252

Nurses, 2001

Total................................ 49,610
   rate per 1,000 persons.................. 918

Community Hospitals, 2003

Number 121
Beds (x 1,000)..........................14.8
Patients admitted (x 1,000) 588
Average daily census (x 1,000) 9.2
Average cost per day $1,282
Outpatient visits (x mil)..................11.8

Disability status of population, 2004

5 to 20 years 7%
21 to 64 years 11.3%
65 years and over 35.2%

Education

Educational attainment, 2004

Population over 25 years	3,543,305
Less than 9th grade	137,617
High school graduates only	1,174,130
Bachelor's degree only	579,277
Graduate or professional degree	272,995
Less than 9th grade percent	3.9%
High school graduate or more	88.8%
College graduate or more	25.6%
Graduate or professional degree	7.7%

Public school enrollment, Fall 2002

Total	881,231
Kindergarten through grade 8	591,703
Grades 9 through 12	289,528
Enrollment, 2005 (projected)	858,700

Graduating public high school seniors

2004 (estimate)	62,270

SAT scores, 2005

Average verbal score	592
Average math score	599
Percent of graduates taking test	6%

Public school teachers, 2004

Total (x 1,000)	60.0
Elementary (x 1,000)	41.3
Secondary (x 1,000)	18.8
Average salary	$42,900
Elementary	$42,700
Secondary	$43,300

State receipts & expenditures for public schools, 2004

Revenue receipts ($mil)	$9,413
Expenditures	
Total ($mil)	$9,813
Per capita	$1,792
Per pupil	$10,293

Institutions of higher education, 2004

Total	68
Public	31
Private	37

Enrollment in institutions of higher education, Fall, 2003

Total	331,153
Full-time men	94,344
Full-time women	115,882
Part-time men	47,472
Part-time women	73,455

Minority enrollment in institutions of higher education, Fall, 2003

Black, non-hispanic	14,914
Hispanic	8,320
Asian/Pacific Islander	8,608
American Indian/Alaska Native	3,378

Earned degrees conferred, 2003

Bachelor's	29,645
Master's	8,288
First-professional	1,119
Doctor's	826

State & local financial support for higher education, 2003-2004

Full-time equivalent enrollment (x 1,000)	218.9
Appropriations per FTE	$5,941
as a percent of tax revenue	8.2%

Social Insurance & Welfare Programs

Social Security benefits & beneficiaries, 2004

Beneficiaries	
Total	937,000
Retired & dependents	685,000
Survivors	121,000
Disabled & dependents	132,000
Annual benefit payments ($ mil)	
Total	$10,000
Retired & dependents	$7,018
Survivors	$1,687
Disabled & dependents	$1,295
Average Monthly Benefit	
Retired & dependents	$979
Disabled & dependents	$894
Widowed	$968

Medicare

Enrollment, 2001 (x 1,000)	787
Payments ($ mil, est.)	$4,000
Enrollment, 2003 (x 1,000)	804

Medicaid, 2002

Beneficiaries (x 1,000)	716
Payments ($ mil)	$3,606

State Children's Health Insurance, 2004

Enrollment (x 1,000)	67.9
Expenditures ($ mil)	$93.7

Persons without health insurance, 2003

Number (x 1,000)	593
percent	10.9%
Number of children (x 1,000)	104
percent of children	7.7%

Federal public aid

Temporary Assistance for Needy Families, 2004

Recipients (x 1,000)	54
Families (x 1,000)	22

Supplemental Security Income, 2003

Recipients (x 1,000)	89
Payments ($ mil)	$398

Food Stamp Program, 2004

Participants (x 1,000)	324
Benefits ($ mil)	$269

Housing & Construction

Housing units

Total 2003 (estimate)	2,427,650
Total 2004 (estimate)	2,463,802
Seasonal or recreational use, 2003	155,000
Owner-occupied single-family, 2003	1,193,000
Median value	$131,908
Renter-occupied, 2003	646,000
Median rent	$595
Homeownership rate, 2003	72.8%
Homeownership rate, 2004	73.3%

New privately owned housing units, 2004

Number authorized (x 1,000)	40.0
Value ($ mil)	$5,783
Started 2005 (x 1,000, estimate)	36.7
Started 2006 (x 1,000, estimate)	35.8

Existing home sales

2002 (x 1,000)	105.5
2003 (x 1,000)	105.9
2004 (x 1,000)	116.8

Government & Elections

State Officials 2006

Governor (name/party/term expires)
Jim Doyle
Democrat - 1/07

Lieutenant Governor	Barbara Lawton
Secretary of State	Douglas La Follette
Attorney General	Peg Lautenschlager
Chief Justice	Shirley Abrahamson

Governorship

Minimum age	not specified
Length of term	4 years
Consecutive terms permitted	not specified
Who succeeds	Lt. Governor

State Legislature

Name	Legislature
Upper chamber	Senate
Number of members	33
Length of term	4 years
Party in majority, 2006	Republican
Lower chamber	Assembly
Number of members	99
Length of term	2 years
Party in majority, 2006	Republican

State Government Employees, 2004

Total	69,834
Payroll	$275,465,291

Local Government Employees, 2004

Total	31,470
Payroll	$90,925,427

Local Governments by Type, 2002

Total	3,048
County	72
Municipal	585
Township	1,265
School District	442
Special District	684

Voting age population, November 2004

Total	4,126,000
Male	2,017,000
Female	2,109,000
White	3,793,000
Black	195,000
Hispanic	203,000
Asian	85,000

Presidential Election, 2004

Total Popular Vote	2,997,007
Kerry	1,489,504
Bush	1,478,120
Total Electoral Votes	10

Federal representation, 2006 (109th Congress)

Senator	Herbert Kohl
Party	Democrat
Year term expires	2007
Senator	Russell Feingold
Party	Democrat
Year term expires	2011
Representatives, total	8
Democrats	4
Republicans	4
Other	0

Votes cast for US Senators

2002

Total vote (x 1,000)	NA
Leading party	NA
Percent for leading party	NA

2004

Total vote (x 1,000)	2,950,000
Leading party	Democratic
Percent for leading party	55.4%

Votes cast for US Representatives

2002

Total vote (x 1,000)	1,638
Democratic	677
Republican	889
Leading party	Republican
Percent for leading party	54.3%

2004

Total vote (x 1,000)	2,822
Democratic	1,369
Republican	1,381
Leading party	Republican
Percent for leading party	48.9%

Women holding public office, 2006
US Congress 2
Statewide elected office...................... 3
State legislature 34

Black public officials, 2001
Total................................... 33
   US and state legislatures 8
   City/county/regional offices 15
   Judicial/law enforcement.................. 5
   Education/school boards 5

Hispanic public officials, 2004
Total................................... 13
   State executives & legislators 1
   City/county/regional offices 5
   Judicial/law enforcement.................. 4
   Education/school boards 3

Governmental Finance

State government revenues, 2004
Total revenue ($1,000) $34,753,272
   Revenue per capita 6,314.18

General Revenue ($ per capita) $4,348.43
   Intergovernmental 1,241.19
   Taxes 2,296.20
      general sales 708.47
      individual income tax............. 954.07
      corporate income tax 123.91
   Current charges.................... 483.42
   Miscellaneous 327.63

State government expenditure, 2004
Total expenditure (x $1,000) $28,577,240
   Expenditure per capita............. 5,192.09
General Expenditure ($ per capita).... $4,503.82
   Education 1,643.36
   Public welfare.................... 1,073.56
   Health 117.09
   Hospitals......................... 145.30
   Highways 304.93
   Police protection 22.01
   Correction 166.92
   Natural resources 100.98
   Parks & recreation...................10.04
   Governmental administration 111.63
   Interest on general debt 149.32

State debt & cash, 2004 ($ per capita)
Debt $3,220.81
Cash/security holdings............. $15,083.69

Federal government grants to state & local government, 2004 (x $1,000)
Total........................... $7,483,990
By Federal Agency
   Defense $55,860

By Federal Agency, continued
   Education 619,511
   Energy 39,250
   Environmental Protection Agency ... 119,357
   Health & Human Services. 4,379,926
   Homeland Security.................. 39,835
   Housing & Urban Development...... 482,733
   Justice 113,030
   Labor 191,643
   Transportation 760,754
   Veterans Affairs.................. 36,092

Crime, Law Enforcement & Courts

Crime, 2004 (rates per 100,000 residents)
Property crimes 146,710
   Burglaries......................... 23,854
   Larcenies........................ 111,482
   Motor vehicle thefts 11,374
   Property crime rate................ 2,663.1
Violent crimes....................... 11,548
   Murders........................ 154
   Forcible rape..................... 1,136
   Robberies 4,067
   Aggravated assaults 6,191
   Violent crime rate 209.6

Police Agencies, 2004
Total agencies........................ 367
Total employees 17,977
   Male officers..................... 11,001
   Female officers.................... 1,838
   Male civilians..................... 1,790
   Female civilians.................... 3,348

Arrests, 2004
Total................................ 383,306
   Persons under 18 years of age 101,245

Prisoners under state & federal jurisdiction, 2004
Total prisoners...................... 22,966
   Percent change, 12/31/03 to 12/31/04 .... 1.6%
Sentenced to more than one year 21,540
   rate per 100,000..................... 390

Persons under sentence of death, 7/1/05
Total................................. 0
   White............................. 0
   Black 0
   Hispanic 0

State's highest court
Name ....Supreme Court
Number of members 7
Length of term .... 10 years
Intermediate appeals court? ....yes

Labor & Income

Civilian labor force, 2004

Total	3,071,000
Men	1,616,000
Women	1,456,000
Persons 16-19 years	186,000
White	2,846,000
Black	132,000
Hispanic	150,000
Asian	52,000

Civilian labor force as a percent of civilian non-institutional population, 2004

Total	71.8%
Men	77.2
Women	66.6
Persons 16-19 years	61.1
White	72.2
Black	63.4
Hispanic	75.8
Asian	72.7

Employment, 2004

Total	2,917,000
Men	1,526,000
Women	1,391,000
Persons 16-19 years	164,000
White	2,719,000
Black	110,000
Hispanic	134,000
Asian	50,000

Full-time/part-time labor force, 2002

Full-time labor force, employed	2,314,000
Part-time labor force, employed	547,000
Unemployed, looking for	
Full-time work	130,000
Part-time work	NA

Unemployment rate, 2004

Total	5.0%
Men	5.6
Women	4.4
Persons 16-19 years	11.9
White	4.5
Black	16.4
Hispanic	10.3
Asian	5.1

Unemployed by reason for unemployment (as a percent of total unemployment), 2002

Job losers or completed temp jobs	55.7%
Job leavers	NA
Reentrants	28.1
New entrants	NA

Labor unions, 2004

Membership	414,000
percent of employed	16.0%

Experienced civilian labor force by private industry, first quarter 2004

Total	2,258,717
Natural Resources & Mining	18,015
Construction	110,894
Manufacturing	494,881
Trade, transportation & utilities	520,578
Information	49,865
Finance	153,550
Professional & business	243,583
Education & Health	341,457
Leisure & hospitality	233,008
Other	82,120

Experienced civilian labor force by occupation, 2004

Management	97,150
Business & Financial	104,850
Legal	12,590
Sales	258,290
Office & Admin. Support	457,040
Computers & Math	47,400
Architecture & Engineering	47,510
Arts & Entertainment	32,660
Education	149,270
Social Services	31,530
Healthcare Practitioner & Technical	133,720
Healthcare support	77,870
Maintenance & Repair	106,350
Construction	119,440
Transportation & moving	224,000
Production	347,630
Farming, fishing & forestry	NA

Hours and earnings of production workers on manufacturing payrolls, 2004

Average weekly hours	40.3
Average hourly earnings	$16.19
Average weekly earnings	$652.46

Average annual pay

2004	$34,743
change from 2003	3.9%

Household income

Median household income, three-year average, 2002-2004	$47,220

Personal income, 2004 ($ per capita)

In current dollars	$32,157
In constant (2000) dollars	$29,824

Poverty

Persons below poverty level, three-year average, 2002-2004	10.2%

Federal individual income tax returns, 2003

Returns filed	2,589,845
Adjusted gross income ($1,000)	$117,029,363
Total income tax paid ($1,000)	$13,543,141

Economy, Business, Industry & Agriculture

Fortune 500 companies, 2005 10

Patents issued, 2004 1,975

Bankruptcy cases filed, 2004 27,700

Business firm ownership, 2002
Women-owned...................... 104,170
   Sales ($ mil) $17,582
Black-owned.......................... 6,687
   Sales ($ mil) $694
Hispanic-owned..................... 3,750
   Sales ($ mil) $975
Asian-owned 4,957
   Sales ($ mil) $1,533
Amer. Indian/Alaska Native-owned 2,530
   Sales ($ mil) $512
Hawaiian/Pacific Isl.-owned.............. NA
   Sales ($ mil) $4

Gross State Product, 2004 ($ mil)
Total Gross State Product $211,616
   Agriculture, forestry, fishing and
      hunting 3,101
   Mining............................... 302
   Utilities........................... 3,851
   Construction 9,370
   Manufacturing, durable goods........ 28,530
   Manufacturing, non-durable goods ... 19,155
   Wholesale trade.................... 11,580
   Retail trade....................... 13,902
   Transportation & warehousing 6,613
   Information 6,682
   Finance & insurance................ 15,601
   Real estate, rental, leasing 23,778
   Professional and technical services 8,618
   Educational services................ 1,517
   Health care and social assistance...... 16,968
   Accommodation/food services......... 4,505
   Other services, except government 4,712
   Government 22,719

Establishments, by major industry group, 2003
Total.............................. 142,220
   Forestry, fishing & agriculture 598
   Mining.............................. 164
   Construction 16,671
   Manufacturing...................... 9,766
   Wholesale trade.................... 7,377
   Retail trade....................... 21,372
   Transportation & warehousing 5,407
   Information 2,215
   Finance & insurance................ 9,003
   Professional/scientific/technical 11,259
   Health care/social assistance 13,540
   Accommodation/food services........ 13,307

Annual payroll by major industry group, 2003
Total ($1,000) $78,327,876
   Forestry, fishing & agriculture 114,740
   Mining............................ 134,555
   Utilities........................... 1,177,471
   Construction 5,279,693
   Manufacturing.................. 19,508,774
   Wholesale trade................. 4,839,902
   Retail trade..................... 6,267,618
   Transportation & warehousing 2,859,236
   Information 2,510,296
   Finance & insurance............. 6,771,928
   Professional/scientific/technical ... 4,071,106
   Health care/social assistance 11,355,611
   Accommodation/food services..... 2,181,337

Agriculture
Number of farms, 2004 77,000
Farm acreage, 2004
   Total........................... 16,000,000
   Acres per farm, 2004 203
Farm income, 2003 ($mil)
   Net farm income $1,626
   Debt/asset ratio 15.4
Farm marketings, 2003 ($mil)
Total................................ $5,876
   Crops............................. 1,782
   Livestock.......................... 4,094

Principal commodities, in order by marketing receipts, 2003
   Dairy products, cattle, corn, greenhouse

Federal economic activity in state
Expenditures, 2003
   Total ($ mil) $30,237
   Per capita $5,525
   Defense ($ mil)..................... 1,805
   Non-defense ($ mil) 28,432
Defense department, 2003
   Payroll ($ mil) $539
   Contract awards ($ mil) $1,271
   Grants ($ mil)......................... $59
   Homeland security grants ($1,000)
      2004 .... $51,343
      2005 .... $37,251

FDIC insured financial institutions, 2004
Number.............................. 308
   Assets ($bil) $118.4
   Deposits ($bil) 96.1

Fishing, 2004
Catch (x 1,000 lbs)..................... 3,856
Value ($1,000)....................... $3,133

Mining, 2004 ($ mil)

Total non-fuel mineral production $487
Percent of U.S. 1.1%

Construction, 2003 ($ mil)

Total contracts (including non-building). $9,966
   residential.......................... 5,368
   non-residential 2,491

Establishments, receipts, payroll & employees, by major industry group, 2002

Mining................................. 771
   Receipts ($1,000)............... $7,803,920
   Annual payroll ($1,000).......... $867,844
   Paid employees 19,775

Utilities 307
   Receipts ($1,000)...................... NA
   Annual payroll ($1,000)........... $896,457
   Paid employees 14,156

Construction........................ 16,207
   Receipts ($1,000).............. $23,477,496
   Annual payroll ($1,000)......... $5,254,483
   Paid employees 142,230

Manufacturing 9,915
   Receipts ($1,000).............. $124,664,004
   Annual payroll ($1,000)........ $19,334,385
   Paid employees 503,588

Wholesale trade 7,557
   Receipts ($1,000)............... $68,510,712
   Annual payroll ($1,000)......... $4,494,992
   Paid employees 112,763

Retail trade 21,360
   Receipts ($1,000)............... $59,978,700
   Annual payroll ($1,000)......... $6,013,140
   Paid employees 311,730

Transportation....................... 5,405
   Receipts ($1,000)............... $8,266,478
   Annual payroll ($1,000)......... $2,548,254
   Paid employees 87,628

Information.......................... 2,097
   Receipts ($1,000)...................... NA
   Annual payroll ($1,000)......... $2,231,978
   Paid employees 55,286

Finance & insurance 8,755
   Receipts ($1,000)...................... NA
   Annual payroll ($1,000)......... $6,073,101
   Paid employees 134,307

Professional, scientific & technical 11,240
   Receipts ($1,000)............... $8,961,379
   Annual payroll ($1,000)......... $3,750,486
   Paid employees 89,948

Health care & social assistance 13,369
   Receipts ($1,000)............... $24,053,322
   Annual payroll ($1,000)........ $10,656,199
   Paid employees 336,466

Accommodation & food service......... 13,268
   Receipts ($1,000)................ $6,885,765
   Annual payroll ($1,000).......... $1,954,391
   Paid employees 200,748

Communication, Energy & Transportation

Communication

Daily newspapers, 2004 35
Households with computers, 2003..........64%
Households with internet access, 2003 ......57%

Energy

Electricity Consumption, 2001
Total (trillion Btu)..................... 1,863
Per capita (million Btu) 345
By source of production (trillion Btu)
   Coal 495
   Natural gas........................... 363
   Petroleum............................. 668
   Nuclear electric power 120
   Hydroelectric power 21
By end-use sector (trillion Btu)
   Residential 401
   Commercial 313
   Industrial 729
   Transportation 422
Electric energy, 2003
   Production (billion kWh) 60.1
   Net summer capability (million kW) 14.3
Gas utilities, 2003
   Customers (x1,000)................... 1,699
   Sales (trillion Btu)..................... 255
   Revenues ($mil)..................... $2,153
Nuclear plants, 2003 3

Transportation, 2004

Public Road & Street Mileage 113,699
   Urban.............................. 21,980
   Rural.............................. 91,719
   Interstate............................. 743
Vehicle miles of travel per capita........ 9,853.0
Total motor vehicle registrations...... 4,705,069
   Automobiles...................... 2,591,731
   Buses 14,366
   Trucks 2,098,972
   Motorcycles 232,808
Licensed drivers 3,910,188
   19 years & under 222,291
Deaths from motor vehicle accidents 792

State Summary

Capital City...................... Cheyenne
Governor................. David Freudenthal
State Capitol Building
Room 124
Cheyenne, WY 82002
307-777-7434
Admitted as a state 1890
Area (square miles)................... 97,814
Population, 2004 (est.) 506,529
Largest City...................... Cheyenne
Population, 2004................... 55,362
Personal income per capita, 2004
(in current dollars) $34,306
Gross state product ($ mil), 2004 ...... $23,979

Leading industries by payroll, 2003

Mining, Health care/Social assistance, Retail trade

Leading agricultural commodities by receipts, 2003

Cattle, hay, sugar beets, sheep/lambs

Geography & Environment

Total area (sq. mi.).................... 97,814
land 97,100
water 713

Federally-owned land, 2004 (acres) .. 26,391,487
percent............................42.3%

Highest point.................... Gannett Peak
elevation (feet) 13,804

Lowest point .... Belle Fourche River
elevation (feet) 3,009

General coastline (miles).................... 0

Tidal shoreline (miles)...................... 0

Capital City..................... Cheyenne
Population 2000 53,011
Population 2004 55,362

Largest City..................... Cheyenne
Population 2000 53,011
Population 2004 55,362

Number of cities with over 100,000 population

1990 0
2000 0
2004 0

State park and recreation areas, 2003

Area (acres x 1,000)..................... 119
Number of visitors (x 1,000) 2,214
Revenues (x 1,000)..........................
percent of operating expenditures........ NA

National forest system land, 2004

Acres 9,238,000

Demographics and Characteristics of the Population

Population

1980 469,557
1990 453,588
2000 493,782
2004 (estimate)..................... 506,529
persons per sq. mile of land..............5.2
2005 (projection)................... 507,268
Male............................. 254,853
Female........................... 252,415
2010 (projection) 519,886
2020 (projection) 530,948
2030 (projection) 522,979
Male............................. 259,367
Female........................... 263,612

Metropolitan and Non-Metro. area population

	Metro	Non-Metro
1980	141,000	329,000
1990	134,000	319,000
2000	148,000	346,000

Change in population, 2000-2004

Number........................... 12,747
percent............................2.6%
Natural increase (births minus deaths).... 9,747
Net internal migration..................1,380
Net international migration 1,840

Persons by age, 2004

Under 5 years 30,867
18 years and over 389,597
65 years and over 61,113
85 years and over 7,374

Persons by age, 2010 (projected)

Total............................. 519,886
Under 5 years 32,671
5 to 17 years 83,602
18 and over 403,613
21 and over 384,520
65 and over 72,658
85 and over 10,123
Median age 39.5

Race, 2004 (estimate)

One Race
White........................ 480,064
Black or African American 4,448
American Indian/Alaska Native....... 12,224
Pacific Islander 358
Asian Indian...................... 180
Chinese 532
Filipino 782
Japanese......................... 407
Korean........................... 451
Vietnamese....................... 189
Two or more races...................... 6,180

Persons of Hispanic origin, 2004

Total Hispanic or Latino 33,011
Mexican........................... 21,893
Puerto Rican 1,107
Cuban 62
Other Hispanic or Latino 9,053

Marital status, 2000

Population 15 years & over 390,845
Never married 91,067
Married........................... 227,081
Separated 4,690
Widowed........................... 22,278
Divorced 45,338

Language spoken at home, 2000

Population 5 years & over 462,809
English only 433,324
Spanish 18,606
Other Indo-European languages 6,391
Asian/Pacific Island languages........ 2,117

Households & families, 2000

Households.......................... 193,608
with persons under 18 years 67,742
with persons over 65 years........... 40,335
persons per household 2.48
Families............................ 130,497
persons per family....................... 3
Married couples..................... 106,179
Female householder,
no husband present................. 16,837
One-person households 50,980

Nativity, 2000

Number of persons born in state 209,687
percent of population................42.5%

Immigration & Naturalization, 2004

Immigrants admitted..................... 295
Persons naturalized 146
Asylums granted 0
Asylums denied 4

Vital Statistics and Health

Marriages

2002................................. 4,755
2003................................. 4,689
2004................................. 4,740

Divorces

2002................................. 2,712
2003................................. 2,724
2004................................. 2,656

Births

2003 6,700
Birthrate (per 1,000)...................13.4
Low birth weight (2,500g or less)........ 8.9%
To unmarried mothers................ 32.6%

2003, continued
White............................. 6,299
Black 53
Hispanic 666
Asian/Pacific Islander 66
Amer. Indian/Alaska Native............. 290

2004 (preliminary)..................... 6,807
Birthrate (per 1,000)...................13.4
White............................. 6,359
Black 55
Hispanic 699
Asian/Pacific Islander 75

Deaths

2002
All causes 4,174
rate per 100,000.....................837.0
Heart disease 1,005
rate per 100,000.....................201.5
Malignant neoplasms 859
rate per 100,000.....................172.2
Cerebrovascular disease.................... 243
rate per 100,000.....................48.7
Chronic lower respiratory disease 324
rate per 100,000.....................65.0
2003 4,173
rate per 100,000.................... 832.5
2004 (provisional) 3,843

Infant deaths

2003 (provisional) 46
rate per 1,000 7
2004 (provisional) 62
rate per 1,000 ....9.2

Abortions, 2000

Total...................................... 0
rate per 1,000 women age 15-44..........0.9

Physicians, 2003

Total.................................... 963
rate per 1,000 persons................... 192

Nurses, 2001

Total................................. 3,780
rate per 1,000 persons.................. 765

Community Hospitals, 2003

Number................................ 23
Beds (x 1,000).............................1.8
Patients admitted (x 1,000) 53
Average daily census (x 1,000) 0.9
Average cost per day $943
Outpatient visits (x mil)....................0.9

Disability status of population, 2004

5 to 20 years 7.5%
21 to 64 years 13.3%
65 years and over....................... 38.6%

Education

Educational attainment, 2004

Population over 25 years 324,386
  Less than 9th grade 9,081
  High school graduates only 102,296
  Bachelor's degree only 55,809
  Graduate or professional degree 24,611
  Less than 9th grade percent 2.8%
  High school graduate or more 91.9%
  College graduate or more 22.5%
  Graduate or professional degree 7.6%

Public school enrollment, Fall 2002

Total 88,116
  Kindergarten through grade 8 59,926
  Grades 9 through 12 28,190
Enrollment, 2005 (projected) 83,400

Graduating public high school seniors

2004 (estimate) 5,730

SAT scores, 2005

Average verbal score 544
Average math score 543
Percent of graduates taking test 12%

Public school teachers, 2004

Total (x 1,000) 6.5
  Elementary (x 1,000) 3.2
  Secondary (x 1,000) 3.4
Average salary $39,500
  Elementary $39,600
  Secondary $39,500

State receipts & expenditures for public schools, 2004

Revenue receipts ($mil) $970
Expenditures
Total ($mil) $952
  Per capita $1,896
  Per pupil $10,413

Institutions of higher education, 2004

Total 9
  Public 8
  Private 1

Enrollment in institutions of higher education, Fall, 2003

Total 33,750
  Full-time men 9,655
  Full-time women 9,335
  Part-time men 5,150
  Part-time women 9,610

Minority enrollment in institutions of higher education, Fall 2003

Black, non-hispanic 315
Hispanic 1,428
Asian/Pacific Islander 261
American Indian/Alaska Native 601

Earned degrees conferred, 2003

Bachelor's 1,739
Master's 417
First-professional 104
Doctor's 56

State & local financial support for higher education, 2003-2004

Full-time equivalent enrollment (x 1,000) . . .22.2
Appropriations per FTE $11,358
  as a percent of tax revenue 14.7%

Social Insurance & Welfare Programs

Social Security benefits & beneficiaries, 2004

Beneficiaries
  Total 83,000
  Retired & dependents 60,000
  Survivors 11,000
  Disabled & dependents 12,000
Annual benefit payments ($ mil)
  Total $856
  Retired & dependents $598
  Survivors $141
  Disabled & dependents $117
Average Monthly Benefit
  Retired & dependents $955
  Disabled & dependents $896
  Widowed $947

Medicare

Enrollment, 2001 (x 1,000) 66
  Payments ($ mil, est.) $300
Enrollment, 2003 (x 1,000) 69

Medicaid, 2002

Beneficiaries (x 1,000) 59
Payments ($ mil) $280

State Children's Health Insurance, 2004

Enrollment (x 1,000) 5.5
Expenditures ($ mil) $5.2

Persons without health insurance, 2003

Number (x 1,000) 78
  percent 15.9%
Number of children (x 1,000) 15
  percent of children 12.5%

Federal public aid

Temporary Assistance for Needy Families, 2004
Recipients (x 1,000) 1
Families (x 1,000) . . . . NA

Supplemental Security Income, 2003
Recipients (x 1,000) 6
Payments ($ mil) $25

Food Stamp Program, 2004

Participants (x 1,000) 26
Benefits ($ mil) $25

Housing & Construction

Housing units

Total 2003 (estimate)	229,663
Total 2004 (estimate)	232,637
Seasonal or recreational use, 2003	15,000
Owner-occupied single-family, 2003	105,000
Median value	$116,360
Renter-occupied, 2003	53,000
Median rent	$494
Homeownership rate, 2003	72.9%
Homeownership rate, 2004	72.8%

New privately owned housing units, 2004

Number authorized (x 1,000)	3.3
Value ($ mil)	$525
Started 2005 (x 1,000, estimate)	2.2
Started 2006 (x 1,000, estimate)	2.3

Existing home sales

2002 (x 1,000)	10.6
2003 (x 1,000)	11.4
2004 (x 1,000)	13.2

Government & Elections

State Officials 2006

Governor (name/party/term expires)
David Freudenthal
Democrat - 1/07

Lieutenant Governor	(no Lt. Governor)
Secretary of State	Joe Meyer
Attorney General	Pat Crank
Chief Justice	William Hill

Governorship

Minimum age	30
Length of term	4 years
Consecutive terms permitted	not specified
Who succeeds	Sec. of State

State Legislature

Name	Legislature
Upper chamber	Senate
Number of members	30
Length of term	4 years
Party in majority, 2006	Republican
Lower chamber	House of Representatives
Number of members	60
Length of term	2 years
Party in majority, 2006	Republican

State Government Employees, 2004

Total	12,063
Payroll	$38,169,104

Local Government Employees, 2004

Total	60,649
Payroll	$164,472,319

Local Governments by Type, 2002

Total	722
County	23
Municipal	98
Township	0
School District	55
Special District	546

Voting age population, November 2004

Total	373,000
Male	187,000
Female	186,000
White	358,000
Black	3,000
Hispanic	20,000
Asian	2,000

Presidential Election, 2004

Total Popular Vote	243,428
Kerry	70,776
Bush	167,629
Total Electoral Votes	3

Federal representation, 2006 (109th Congress)

Senator	Craig Thomas
Party	Republican
Year term expires	2007
Senator	Michael Enzi
Party	Republican
Year term expires	2009
Representatives, total	1
Democrats	0
Republicans	1
Other	0

Votes cast for US Senators

2002

Total vote (x 1,000)	183,000
Leading party	Republican
Percent for leading party	73.0%

2004

Total vote (x 1,000)	NA
Leading party	NA
Percent for leading party	NA

Votes cast for US Representatives

2002

Total vote (x 1,000)	182
Democratic	66
Republican	110
Leading party	Republican
Percent for leading party	60.5%

2004

Total vote (x 1,000)	239
Democratic	100
Republican	132
Leading party	Republican
Percent for leading party	55.2%

Women holding public office, 2006

US Congress 1
Statewide elected office...................... 1
State legislature 13

Black public officials, 2001

Total................................... 1
US and state legislatures 0
City/county/regional offices 1
Judicial/law enforcement................. 0
Education/school boards................. 0

Hispanic public officials, 2004

Total................................... 3
State executives & legislators 1
City/county/regional offices 2
Judicial/law enforcement................. 0
Education/school boards................. 0

Governmental Finance

State government revenues, 2004

Total revenue ($1,000) $5,151,978
Revenue per capita 10,181.77

General Revenue ($ per capita) $8,025.96
Intergovernmental 3,906.33
Taxes 2,973.87
general sales 914.71
individual income tax................. 0
corporate income tax 0
Current charges..................... 241.13
Miscellaneous 904.63

State government expenditure, 2004

Total expenditure (x $1,000) $3,596,174
Expenditure per capita.............. 7,107.06
General Expenditure ($ per capita).... $6,295.46
Education 2,115.85
Public welfare..................... 982.96
Health 333.21
Hospitals.......................... 14.39
Highways 821.00
Police protection 60.47
Correction 179.85
Natural resources 353.53
Parks & recreation.................... 50.76
Governmental administration 241.23
Interest on general debt............... 95.12

State debt & cash, 2004 ($ per capita)

Debt $1,797.49
Cash/security holdings............. $22,865.03

Federal government grants to state & local government, 2004 (x $1,000)

Total............................ $1,635,620

By Federal Agency
Defense $1,985

By Federal Agency, continued
Education 118,905
Energy.............................. 6,540
Environmental Protection Agency 22,005
Health & Human Services........... 386,998
Homeland Security.................. 5,059
Housing & Urban Development....... 36,589
Justice 29,339
Labor 21,255
Transportation 252,575
Veterans Affairs.................... 1,159

Crime, Law Enforcement & Courts

Crime, 2004 (rates per 100,000 residents)

Property crimes 16,889
Burglaries........................ 2,738
Larcenies......................... 13,352
Motor vehicle thefts 799
Property crime rate................ 3,334.3
Violent crimes...................... 1,163
Murders.......................... 11
Forcible rape....................... 112
Robberies 67
Aggravated assaults 973
Violent crime rate 229.6

Police Agencies, 2004

Total agencies....................... 67
Total employees 1,966
Male officers..................... 1,176
Female officers.................... 103
Male civilians..................... 200
Female civilians................... 487

Arrests, 2004

Total................................ 35,849
Persons under 18 years of age 6,704

Prisoners under state & federal jurisdiction, 2004

Total prisoners....................... 1,980
Percent change, 12/31/03 to 12/31/04 .... 5.8%
Sentenced to more than one year 1,980
rate per 100,000..................... 389

Persons under sentence of death, 7/1/05

Total................................ 2
White.............................. 2
Black 0
Hispanic 0

State's highest court

Name ....Supreme Court
Number of members 5
Length of term........................ 8 years
Intermediate appeals court? .... no

Labor & Income

Civilian labor force, 2004

Total................................. 282,000
Men 151,000
Women 130,000
Persons 16-19 years................. 20,000
White............................. 270,000
Black 0
Hispanic 18,000
Asian 0

Civilian labor force as a percent of civilian non-institutional population, 2004

Total................................. 71.3%
Men 77.3
Women 65.3
Persons 16-19 years................. 59.7
White............................. 71.3
Black 0.0
Hispanic 71.7
Asian 0.0

Employment, 2004

Total................................. 271,000
Men 146,000
Women 125,000
Persons 16-19 years................. 18,000
White............................. 260,000
Black 0
Hispanic 17,000
Asian 0

Full-time/part-time labor force, 2002

Full-time labor force, employed 209,000
Part-time labor force, employed......... 50,000
Unemployed, looking for
Full-time work....................... 9,000
Part-time work........................ NA

Unemployment rate, 2004

Total................................. 3.8%
Men 3.4
Women 4.2
Persons 16-19 years................. 11.2
White............................. 3.5
Black .... NA
Hispanic 4.6
Asian .... NA

Unemployed by reason for unemployment (as a percent of total unemployment), 2002

Job losers or completed temp jobs .... NA
Job leavers.............................. NA
Reentrants.............................. NA
New entrants .... NA

Labor unions, 2004

Membership 18,000
percent of employed 8.0%

Experienced civilian labor force by private industry, first quarter 2004

Total................................. 178,280
Natural Resources & Mining 21,363
Construction 17,140
Manufacturing....................... 9,069
Trade, transportation & utilities 45,331
Information 4,253
Finance 10,184
Professional & business 14,390
Education & Health 20,393
Leisure & hospitality................. 28,787
Other............................. 7,370

Experienced civilian labor force by occupation, 2004

Management........................ 12,850
Business & Financial................. 6,140
Legal............................. 1,480
Sales............................. 22,300
Office & Admin. Support............. 34,990
Computers & Math 1,790
Architecture & Engineering 3,600
Arts & Entertainment................. 2,810
Education 16,260
Social Services 3,500
Healthcare Practitioner & Technical..... 10,360
Healthcare support 6,140
Maintenance & Repair 13,650
Construction 24,780
Transportation & moving 24,340
Production 12,120
Farming, fishing & forestry............... NA

Hours and earnings of production workers on manufacturing payrolls, 2004

Average weekly hours.................. 39.7
Average hourly earnings $16.58
Average weekly earnings $658.23

Average annual pay

2004............................... $31,210
change from 2003 .... 4.3%

Household income

Median household income, three-year average, 2002-2004......................... $43,641

Personal income, 2004 ($ per capita)

In current dollars.................... $34,306
In constant (2000) dollars $31,817

Poverty

Persons below poverty level, three-year average, 2002-2004........................... 9.6%

Federal individual income tax returns, 2003

Returns filed........................ 240,998
Adjusted gross income ($1,000) $11,092,479
Total income tax paid ($1,000) $1,469,968

Economy, Business, Industry & Agriculture

Fortune 500 companies, 2005 0

Patents issued, 2004 55

Bankruptcy cases filed, 2004 2,400

Business firm ownership, 2002

Women-owned. 12,945
   Sales ($ mil) $1,130
Black-owned 149
   Sales ($ mil) $10
Hispanic-owned. 1,320
   Sales ($ mil) $221
Asian-owned 401
   Sales ($ mil) $84
Amer. Indian/Alaska Native-owned 597
   Sales ($ mil) $60
Hawaiian/Pacific Isl.-owned . . . . NA
   Sales ($ mil) $1

Gross State Product, 2004 ($ mil)

Total Gross State Product $23,979
   Agriculture, forestry, fishing and
      hunting 356
   Mining. 5,997
   Utilities 1,108
   Construction 1,272
   Manufacturing, durable goods. . . . . NA
   Manufacturing, non-durable goods . . . . . NA
   Wholesale trade. 907
   Retail trade. 1,437
   Transportation & warehousing 1,390
   Information 417
   Finance & insurance. 678
   Real estate, rental, leasing 2,101
   Professional and technical services 697
   Educational services 46
   Health care and social assistance 1,063
   Accommodation/food services. 746
   Other services, except government . . . . . . NA
   Government . . . . NA

Establishments, by major industry group, 2003

Total. 18,917
   Forestry, fishing & agriculture 100
   Mining. 760
   Construction 2,575
   Manufacturing. 558
   Wholesale trade. 776
   Retail trade. 2,890
   Transportation & warehousing 760
   Information 355
   Finance & insurance. 898
   Professional/scientific/technical 1,618
   Health care/social assistance 1,558
   Accommodation/food services. 1,721

Annual payroll by major industry group, 2003

Total ($1,000) $5,370,514
   Forestry, fishing & agriculture . . . . NA
   Mining. 917,049
   Utilities 142,785
   Construction 502,115
   Manufacturing. 416,483
   Wholesale trade. 251,285
   Retail trade. 654,374
   Transportation & warehousing 230,877
   Information 128,799
   Finance & insurance. 265,863
   Professional/scientific/technical 236,430
   Health care/social assistance 811,305
   Accommodation/food services. 301,330

Agriculture

Number of farms, 2004 9,000
Farm acreage, 2004
   Total. 34,000,000
   Acres per farm, 2004 3,743
Farm income, 2003 ($mil)
   Net farm income $291
   Debt/asset ratio 9.7
Farm marketings, 2003 ($mil)
Total. $874
   Crops 150
   Livestock. 724

Principal commodities, in order by marketing receipts, 2003

     Cattle, hay, sugar beets, sheep/lambs

Federal economic activity in state

Expenditures, 2003
   Total ($ mil) $4,226
   Per capita $8,432
   Defense ($ mil). 374
   Non-defense ($ mil) 3,852
Defense department, 2003
   Payroll ($ mil) $279
   Contract awards ($ mil) $76
   Grants ($ mil). $19
   Homeland security grants ($1,000)
     2004 . . . . $18,809
     2005 . . . . $13,934

FDIC insured financial institutions, 2004

Number 44
   Assets ($bil) $5.7
   Deposits ($bil) 7.9

Fishing, 2004

Catch (x 1,000 lbs) 0
Value ($1,000). 0

Mining, 2004 ($ mil)

Total non-fuel mineral production $1,090
Percent of U.S. 2.5%

Construction, 2003 ($ mil)

Total contracts (including non-building). $1,028
   residential 421
   non-residential 272

Establishments, receipts, payroll & employees, by major industry group, 2002

Mining .... NA
   Receipts ($1,000) .... NA
   Annual payroll ($1,000) .... NA
   Paid employees .... NA

Utilities 97
   Receipts ($1,000) .... NA
   Annual payroll ($1,000) $134,477
   Paid employees 2,218

Construction 2,568
   Receipts ($1,000) $2,149,476
   Annual payroll ($1,000) $499,770
   Paid employees 17,319

Manufacturing 560
   Receipts ($1,000) $4,061,516
   Annual payroll ($1,000) $364,592
   Paid employees 9,608

Wholesale trade 789
   Receipts ($1,000) $3,331,043
   Annual payroll ($1,000) $227,499
   Paid employees 6,256

Retail trade 2,861
   Receipts ($1,000) $5,783,756
   Annual payroll ($1,000) $554,008
   Paid employees 28,796

Transportation 740
   Receipts ($1,000) $746,816
   Annual payroll ($1,000) $188,715
   Paid employees 5,865

Information 347
   Receipts ($1,000) .... NA
   Annual payroll ($1,000) $122,975
   Paid employees 4,217

Finance & insurance 882
   Receipts ($1,000) .... NA
   Annual payroll ($1,000) $227,308
   Paid employees 6,468

Professional, scientific & technical 1,592
   Receipts ($1,000) $654,070
   Annual payroll ($1,000) $231,531
   Paid employees 7,283

Health care & social assistance 1,546
   Receipts ($1,000) $1,621,193
   Annual payroll ($1,000) $689,585
   Paid employees 25,183

Accommodation & food service 1,742
   Receipts ($1,000) $984,684
   Annual payroll ($1,000) $270,423
   Paid employees 24,160

Communication, Energy & Transportation

Communication

Daily newspapers, 2004 9
Households with computers, 2003 .... 65%
Households with internet access, 2003 ..... 58%

Energy

Electricity Consumption, 2001
Total (trillion Btu) 439
Per capita (million Btu) 890
By source of production (trillion Btu)
   Coal 500
   Natural gas 104
   Petroleum 157
   Nuclear electric power 0
   Hydroelectric power 9
By end-use sector (trillion Btu)
   Residential 39
   Commercial 51
   Industrial 238
   Transportation 111
Electric energy, 2003
   Production (billion kWh) 43.6
   Net summer capability (million kW) 6.6
Gas utilities, 2003
   Customers (x1,000) 83
   Sales (trillion Btu) 13
   Revenues ($mil) $82
Nuclear plants, 2003 0

Transportation, 2004

Public Road & Street Mileage 27,594
   Urban 2,548
   Rural 25,046
   Interstate 913
Vehicle miles of travel per capita 18,485.0
Total motor vehicle registrations 640,914
   Automobiles 234,382
   Buses 2,976
   Trucks 403,556
   Motorcycles 30,615
Licensed drivers 380,180
   19 years & under 25,684
Deaths from motor vehicle accidents 164

United States Summary

Capital City................. Washington, DC
President..................... George W. Bush
The White House
1600 Pennsylvania Ave NW
Washington DC, US 20500
202-456-1414
Founded................................. 1776
Area (square miles) 3,794,083
Population, 2004 (est.) 293,655,404
Largest City......................... New York
Population, 2004................. 8,104,000
Personal income per capita, 2004
(in current dollars) $32,937
Gross state product ($ mil), 2004 ... $11,665,595

Leading industries by payroll, 2003

Manufacturing, Health care/social assistance,
Professional/scientific/technical

**Leading agricultural commodities by receipts,
2003**

Cattle, dairy products, corn, soybeans

Geography & Environment

Total area (sq. mi.).................. 3,794,083
land 3,537,439
water 256,645

Federally-owned land, 2004 (acres) . 653,299,090
percent............................. 28.8%

Highest point................... Mt. McKinley
elevation (feet) 20,320

Lowest point .... Death Valley
elevation (feet) .... -282

General coastline (miles)............... 12,383

Tidal shoreline (miles).................. 88,633

Capital City.................. Washington, DC
Population 2000 572,000
Population 2004 554,000

Largest City....................... New York
Population 2000 8,008,000
Population 2004 8,104,000

Number of cities with over 100,000 population

1990 190
2000 239
2004 251

State park and recreation areas, 2003

Area (acres x 1,000)................... 13,571
Number of visitors (x 1,000) 734,990
Revenues (x 1,000).................... $666,231
percent of operating expenditures...... 36.4%

National forest system land, 2004

Acres 192,830,000

Demographics and Characteristics of the Population

Population

1980 226,546,000
1990 248,709,873
2000 281,421,906
2004 (estimate)................. 293,655,404
persons per sq. mile of land.............. 77.4
2005 (projection)................. 295,507,134
Male........................... 145,113,237
Female......................... 150,393,897
2010 (projection) 308,935,581
2020 (projection) 335,804,546
2030 (projection) 363,584,435
Male........................... 178,562,747
Female......................... 185,021,688

Metropolitan and Non-Metro. area population

	Metro	Non-Metro
1980	172,335,000	54,211,000
1990	192,726,000	55,984,000
2000	225,968,000	55,453,000

Change in population, 2000-2004

Number 12,230,802
percent............................... 4.3%
Natural increase (births minus deaths) 6,901,163
Net internal migration 0
Net international migration 5,329,639

Persons by age, 2004

Under 5 years 20,071,268
18 years and over 220,377,406
65 years and over 36,293,985
85 years and over 4,859,631

Persons by age, 2010 (projected)

Total........................... 308,935,581
Under 5 years 21,426,163
5 to 17 years 53,005,348
18 and over 234,504,070
21 and over 221,214,985
65 and over 40,243,713
85 and over 6,123,458
Median age 37

Race, 2004 (estimate)

One Race
White........................... 236,057,761
Black or African American 37,502,320
American Indian/Alaska Native.... 2,824,751
Pacific Islander 505,602
Asian Indian..................... 2,245,239
Chinese 2,900,398
Filipino 2,148,227
Japanese 832,039
Korean 1,251,092
Vietnamese..................... 1,267,510
Two or more races.................. 4,438,754

2   US Summary

Persons of Hispanic origin, 2004

Total Hispanic or Latino 40,459,196
   Mexican........................ 25,894,763
   Puerto Rican 3,874,322
   Cuban 1,437,828
   Other Hispanic or Latino 3,084,069

Marital status, 2000

Population 15 years & over 221,148,671
   Never married 59,927,652
   Married...................... 120,194,565
   Separated 4,776,627
   Widowed...................... 14,678,687
   Divorced 21,559,356

Language spoken at home, 2000

Population 5 years & over 262,375,152
   English only 215,423,557
   Spanish 28,101,052
   Other Indo-European languages ... 10,017,989
   Asian/Pacific Island languages..... 6,960,065

Households & families, 2000

Households...................... 105,480,101
   with persons under 18 years 38,022,115
   with persons over 65 years....... 24,672,708
   persons per household 2.59
Families......................... 71,787,347
   persons per family....................3.14
Married couples.................. 54,493,232
Female householder,
   no husband present............. 12,900,103
One-person households 27,230,075

Nativity, 2000

Number of persons born in state ... 168,729,388
   percent of population 60.0%

Immigration & Naturalization, 2004

Immigrants admitted................. 946,142
Persons naturalized 537,151
Asylums granted 14,359
Asylums denied 2,440

Vital Statistics and Health

Marriages

2002 2,236,611
2003 2,224,000
2004 2,224,000

Divorces

2002 958,978
2003 .... NA
2004 .... NA

Births

2003 4,089,950
   Birthrate (per 1,000)....................14.1
   Low birth weight (2,500g or less)........ 7.9%
   To unmarried mothers................ 34.6%

2003, continued
   White......................... 3,227,755
   Black 599,414
   Hispanic 912,256
   Asian/Pacific Islander 221,247
   Amer. Indian/Alaska Native 42,647

2004 (preliminary)................. 4,115,590
   Birthrate (per 1,000).....................14.0
   White......................... 3,229,814
   Black 612,493
   Hispanic 944,993
   Asian/Pacific Islander 229,352

Deaths

2002
All causes 2,443,387
   rate per 100,000......................847.3
Heart disease 696,947
   rate per 100,000......................241.7
Malignant neoplasms 557,271
   rate per 100,000......................193.2
Cerebrovascular disease............ 162,672
   rate per 100,000.......................56.4
Chronic lower respiratory disease 124,816
   rate per 100,000.......................43.3
2003 2,443,908
   rate per 100,000...................... 840.4
2004 (provisional) 2,393,000

Infant deaths

2003 (provisional) 27,500
   rate per 1,000 ....6.7
2004 (provisional) 27,300
   rate per 1,000 ....6.6

Abortions, 2000

Total.............................1,313,000
   rate per 1,000 women age 15-44..........21.3

Physicians, 2003

Total............................. 774,849
   rate per 1,000 persons.................. 266

Nurses, 2001

Total............................ 2,262,020
   rate per 1,000 persons.................. 793

Community Hospitals, 2003

Number 4,895
Beds (x 1,000)......................813.3
Patients admitted (x 1,000) 34,783
Average daily census (x 1,000) 538.8
Average cost per day $1,379
Outpatient visits (x mil)................563.1

Disability status of population, 2004

5 to 20 years 6.5%
21 to 64 years 12.1%
65 years and over 39.6%

Education

Educational attainment, 2004

Population over 25 years 186,534,177
   Less than 9th grade 15,600,185
   High school graduates only. 55,055,121
   Bachelor's degree only 32,030,270
   Graduate or professional degree. . . . 18,381,134
   Less than 9th grade percent 8.4%
   High school graduate or more 85.2%
   College graduate or more. 27.7%
   Graduate or professional degree. 9.9%

Public school enrollment, Fall 2002

Total. 48,202,324
   Kindergarten through grade 8 34,135,225
   Grades 9 through 12 14,067,099
Enrollment, 2005 (projected) 48,375,400

Graduating public high school seniors

2004 (estimate). 2,757,540

SAT scores, 2005

Average verbal score 508
Average math score 520
Percent of graduates taking test 49%

Public school teachers, 2004

Total (x 1,000) 3044
   Elementary (x 1,000). 1782
   Secondary (x 1,000) 1265
Average salary $46,800
   Elementary. $46,400
   Secondary. $47,100

State receipts & expenditures for public schools, 2004

Revenue receipts ($mil) $452,795
Expenditures
Total ($mil). $471,965
   Per capita $1,623
   Per pupil $8,807

Institutions of higher education, 2004

Total. 4,236
   Public. 1,720
   Private. 2,516

Enrollment in institutions of higher education, Fall, 2003

Total. 17,329,462
   Full-time men 4,733,150
   Full-time women. 5,916,447
   Part-time men 2,656,398
   Part-time women. 4,023,467

Minority enrollment in institutions of higher education, Fall, 2003

Black, non-hispanic. 1,952,722
Hispanic 1,602,484
Asian/Pacific Islander 987,033
American Indian/Alaska Native. 162,997

Earned degrees conferred, 2003

Bachelor's 1,348,503
Master's. 512,645
First-professional. 80,810
Doctor's. 46,024

State & local financial support for higher education, 2003-2004

Full-time equivalent enrollment (x 1,000) 9,916.6
Appropriations per FTE. $5,716
   as a percent of tax revenue. 7.7%

Social Insurance & Welfare Programs

Social Security benefits & beneficiaries, 2004

Beneficiaries
   Total. 46,531,000
   Retired & dependents. 32,278,000
   Survivors. 6,510,000
   Disabled & dependents. 7,743,000
Annual benefit payments ($ mil)
   Total. $485,123
   Retired & dependents. $322,792
   Survivors. $85,828
   Disabled & dependents. $76,505
Average Monthly Benefit
   Retired & dependents. . . . . NA
   Disabled & dependents. . . . . NA
   Widowed. . . . . NA

Medicare

Enrollment, 2001 (x 1,000) 39,149
   Payments ($ mil, est.) $235,000
Enrollment, 2003 (x 1,000) 40,173

Medicaid, 2002

Beneficiaries (x 1,000). 49,755
Payments ($ mil) $213,491

State Children's Health Insurance, 2004

Enrollment (x 1,000). 6,058.9
Expenditures ($ mil) $4,600.7

Persons without health insurance, 2003

Number (x 1,000). 44,961
   percent. 15.6%
Number of children (x 1,000) 8,373
   percent of children 11.4%

Federal public aid

Temporary Assistance for Needy Families, 2004
Recipients (x 1,000). 4,723
Families (x 1,000) 1,966

Supplemental Security Income, 2003
Recipients (x 1,000). 6,902
Payments ($ mil) $34,696

Food Stamp Program, 2004

Participants (x 1,000) 23,819
Benefits ($ mil). $24,560

4   US Summary

Housing & Construction

Housing units
Total 2003 (estimate) 120,966,343
Total 2004 (estimate) 122,671,734
Seasonal or recreational use, 2003.... 3,757,000
Owner-occupied single-family, 2003. 58,809,000
   Median value $147,275
Renter-occupied, 2003 35,545,000
   Median rent $679
Homeownership rate, 2003 .... 68.3%
Homeownership rate, 2004 .... 69.0%

New privately owned housing units, 2004
Number authorized (x 1,000) 2,070.1
Value ($ mil) $292,414
Started 2005 (x 1,000, estimate) 1,658.0
Started 2006 (x 1,000, estimate) 1,614.0

Existing home sales
2002 (x 1,000) 5,631
2003 (x 1,000) 6,183
2004 (x 1,000) 6,784

Government & Elections

Federal Officials 2006
President (name/party/term expires)
          George W. Bush
          Republican - 1/09
Vice-President .... Richard Cheney
Secretary of State .... Condoleezza Rice
Attorney General .... Alberto Gonzales
Chief Justice .... John G. Roberts

Presidency
Minimum age 35
Length of term .... 4 years
Consecutive terms permitted 2
Who succeeds .... Vice-President

Federal Legislature
Name .... U.S. Congress
Upper chamber .... U.S. Senate
   Number of members 100
   Length of term .... 6 years
   Party in majority, 2006 .... Republican
Lower chamber... U. S. House of Representatives
   Number of members 435
   Length of term .... 2 years
   Party in majority, 2006 .... Republican

State Government Employees, 2004
Total 4,187,648
Payroll $15,477,521,408

Local Government Employees, 2004
Total 11,601,136
Payroll $40,437,397,482

Local Governments by Type, 2002
Total 87,525
   County 3,034
   Municipal 19,429
   Township 16,504
   School District 13,506
   Special District 35,052

Voting age population, November 2004
Total 215,694,000
   Male 103,812,000
   Female 111,882,000
   White 176,618,000
   Black 24,910,000
   Hispanic 27,129,000
   Asian 9,291,000

Presidential Election, 2004
Total Popular Vote 122,295,345
   Kerry 59,028,444
   Bush 62,040,610
Total Electoral Votes 538

Federal representation, 2006 (109th Congress)
Senators, total 100
   Democrats 44
   Republicans 55
   Other 1
Representatives, total 435
   Democrats 202
   Republicans 232
   Other 1

Votes cast for US Senators
2002
Total vote (x 1,000) 41,353,000
Leading party .... NA
Percent for leading party .... NA
2004
Total vote (x 1,000) 86,968,000
Leading party .... NA
Percent for leading party .... NA

Votes cast for US Representatives
2002
Total vote (x 1,000) 74,707
   Democratic 33,642
   Republican 37,091
Leading party .... Republican
Percent for leading party 49.6%
2004
Total vote (x 1,000) 113,192
   Democratic 52,745
   Republican 55,713
Leading party .... Republican
Percent for leading party 49.2%

Women holding public office, 2006

US Congress 81
Statewide elected office..................... 80
State legislature 1663

Black public officials, 2001

Total.................................9,061
   US and state legislatures 633
   City/county/regional offices 5,456
   Judicial/law enforcement.............. 1,044
   Education/school boards...............1,928

Hispanic public officials, 2004

Total................................. 4,651
   State executives & legislators 231
   City/county/regional offices 2,059
   Judicial/law enforcement............... 638
   Education/school boards............. 1,723

Governmental Finance

Federal government revenues, 2004

Total revenue ($1,000) $1,589,856,242
   Revenue per capita 5,424.22

General Revenue ($ per capita)....... $4,085.07
   Intergovernmental 1,345.93
   Taxes 2,025.98
      general sales 676.24
      individual income tax...............675.12
      corporate income tax 105.41
   Current charges......................391.82
   Miscellaneous 321.34

State government expenditure, 2004

Total expenditure (x $1,000) $1,406,039,800
   Expenditure per capita............. 4,797.08
General Expenditure ($ per capita).... $4,126.62
   Education 1,464.81
   Public welfare...................... 1,157.98
   Health 169.08
   Hospitals...........................137.92
   Highways 294.88
   Police protection.....................36.73
   Correction 134.13
   Natural resources 63.63
   Parks & recreation....................19.94
   Governmental administration 152.45
   Interest on general debt 112.19

State debt & cash, 2004 ($ per capita)

Debt $2,560.23
Cash/security holdings.............. $9,992.41

Federal government grants to state & local government, 2004 (x $1,000)

Total $460,152,282
By Federal Agency
   Defense $4,537,556

By Federal Agency, continued
   Education 38,757,134
   Energy........................ 1,847,718
   Environmental Protection Agency . 4,116,198
   Health & Human Services. 267,189,711
   Homeland Security............... 3,644,351
   Housing & Urban Development... 33,848,541
   Justice 7,155,656
   Labor 8,561,568
   Transportation 48,496,756
   Veterans Affairs.................. 654,107

Crime, Law Enforcement & Courts

Crime, 2004 (rates per 100,000 residents)

Property crimes 10,328,255
   Burglaries...................... 2,143,456
   Larcenies...................... 6,947,685
   Motor vehicle thefts 1,237,114
   Property crime rate................. 3,517.1
Violent crimes..................... 1,367,009
   Murders....................... 16,317
   Forcible rape.................... 94,635
   Robberies 401,326
   Aggravated assaults 854,911
   Violent crime rate................. 465.5

Police Agencies, 2004

Total agencies........................ 14,254
Total employees 970,588
   Male officers.................... 597,349
   Female officers.................... 78,385
   Male civilians.................... 111,750
   Female civilians.................. 183,104

Arrests, 2004

Total........................... 8,607,067
   Persons under 18 years of age 1,354,699

Prisoners under state & federal jurisdiction, 2004

Total prisoners.................... 1,496,629
   Percent change, 12/31/03 to 12/31/04 .... 1.9%
   Sentenced to more than one year 1,433,793
      rate per 100,000........................ 486

Persons under sentence of death, 7/1/05

Total................................. 3,415
   White........................... 1,553
   Black 1,432
   Hispanic 350

Country's highest court

Name ....Supreme Court
Number of members..................... 9
Length of term ....life
Intermediate appeals court? .... no

Labor & Income

Civilian labor force, 2004

Total	147,401,000
Men	78,980,000
Women	68,421,000
Persons 16-19 years	7,114,000
White	121,086,000
Black	16,638,000
Hispanic	19,272,000
Asian	6,271,000

Civilian labor force as a percent of civilian non-institutional population, 2004

Total	66.0%
Men	73.3
Women	59.2
Persons 16-19 years	43.9
White	66.3
Black	63.8
Hispanic	68.6
Asian	65.9

Employment, 2004

Total	139,252,000
Men	74,524,000
Women	64,728,000
Persons 16-19 years	5,907,000
White	115,239,000
Black	14,909,000
Hispanic	17,930,000
Asian	5,994,000

Full-time/part-time labor force, 2002

Full-time labor force, employed	112,700,000
Part-time labor force, employed	23,785,000
Unemployed, looking for	
Full-time work	7,063,000
Part-time work	1,314,000

Unemployment rate, 2004

Total	5.5%
Men	5.6
Women	5.4
Persons 16-19 years	17.0
White	4.8
Black	10.4
Hispanic	7.0
Asian	4.4

Unemployed by reason for unemployment (as a percent of total unemployment), 2002

Job losers or completed temp jobs	55%
Job leavers	10.3
Reentrants	28.3
New entrants	6.4

Labor unions, 2004

Membership	15,472,000
percent of employed	12.5%

Experienced civilian labor force by private industry, first quarter 2004

Total	106,446,187
Natural Resources & Mining	1,550,685
Construction	6,516,436
Manufacturing	14,178,971
Trade, transportation & utilities	24,810,489
Information	3,115,301
Finance	7,811,645
Professional & business	15,909,237
Education & Health	16,008,328
Leisure & hospitality	12,027,641
Other	4,263,948

Experienced civilian labor force by occupation, 2004

Management	6,085,780
Business & Financial	5,253,720
Legal	973,970
Sales	13,713,710
Office & Admin. Support	22,622,500
Computers & Math	2,932,790
Architecture & Engineering	2,385,680
Arts & Entertainment	1,645,870
Education	7,969,800
Social Services	1,680,750
Healthcare Practitioner & Technical	6,469,920
Healthcare support	3,307,150
Maintenance & Repair	5,246,720
Construction	6,303,180
Transportation & moving	9,597,380
Production	10,194,200
Farming, fishing & forestry	444,870

Hours and earnings of production workers on manufacturing payrolls, 2004

Average weekly hours	40.8
Average hourly earnings	$16.14
Average weekly earnings	$658.53

Average annual pay

2004	$39,354
change from 2003	4.3%

Household income

Median household income, three-year average, 2002-2004	$44,473

Personal income, 2004 ($ per capita)

In current dollars	$32,937
In constant (2000) dollars	$30,547

Poverty

Persons below poverty level, three-year average, 2002-2004	12.4%

Federal individual income tax returns, 2003

Returns filed	131,356,582
Adjusted gross income ($1,000)	$6,199,925,184
Total income tax paid ($1,000)	$795,529,497

Economy, Business, Industry & Agriculture

Fortune 500 companies, 2005 500

Patents issued, 2004 94,110

Bankruptcy cases filed, 2004 1,635,700

Business firm ownership, 2002

Women-owned. 6,489,483
   Sales ($ mil) $940,775
Black-owned. 1,197,988
   Sales ($ mil) $92,682
Hispanic-owned. 1,574,159
   Sales ($ mil) $226,468
Asian-owned 1,105,329
   Sales ($ mil) $343,322
Amer. Indian/Alaska Native-owned 206,125
   Sales ($ mil) $26,396
Hawaiian/Pacific Isl.-owned 32,299
   Sales ($ mil) $5,221

Gross State Product, 2004 ($ mil)

Total Gross State Product $11,665,595
   Agriculture, forestry, fishing and
      hunting 116,589
   Mining. 147,502
   Utilities 241,236
   Construction 541,414
   Manufacturing, durable goods. 862,611
   Manufacturing, non-durable goods . . 631,415
   Wholesale trade. 688,096
   Retail trade. 797,638
   Transportation & warehousing 338,643
   Information 547,191
   Finance & insurance. 972,393
   Real estate, rental, leasing 1,451,288
   Professional and technical services . . . 792,133
   Educational services 99,503
   Health care and social assistance 804,397
   Accommodation/food services. 308,058
   Other services, except government . . . 275,491
   Government 1,389,018

Establishments, by major industry group, 2003

Total. 7,254,745
   Forestry, fishing & agriculture 25,861
   Mining. 23,599
   Construction 732,175
   Manufacturing. 341,849
   Wholesale trade. 432,537
   Retail trade. 1,115,906
   Transportation & warehousing 202,673
   Information 140,027
   Finance & insurance. 460,591
   Professional/scientific/technical 780,870
   Health care/social assistance 716,350
   Accommodation/food services. 575,347

Annual payroll by major industry group, 2003

Total ($1,000) $4,040,888,841
   Forestry, fishing & agriculture 5,095,173
   Mining. 24,657,845
   Utilities 44,567,779
   Construction 252,939,518
   Manufacturing. 576,057,897
   Wholesale trade. 272,156,200
   Retail trade. 319,468,864
   Transportation & warehousing . . 142,748,785
   Information 204,024,231
   Finance & insurance. 392,873,188
   Professional/scientific/technical . 398,150,994
   Health care/social assistance 526,330,389
   Accommodation/food services. . . 139,189,908

Agriculture

Number of farms, 2004 2,113,000
Farm acreage, 2004
   Total. 937,000,000
   Acres per farm, 2004 443
Farm income, 2003 ($mil)
   Net farm income $59,229
   Debt/asset ratio 14.4
Farm marketings, 2003 ($mil)
Total. $211,647
   Crops 106,176
   Livestock 105,471

Principal commodities, in order by marketing receipts, 2003

   Cattle, dairy products, corn, soybeans

Federal economic activity in state

Expenditures, 2003
   Total ($ mil) $2,061,486
   Per capita $6,910
   Defense ($ mil). 319,507
   Non-defense ($ mil) 1,741,979
Defense department, 2003
   Payroll ($ mil) $122,270
   Contract awards ($ mil) $191,222
   Grants ($ mil). $3,156
   Homeland security grants ($1,000)
     2004 . . . . $3,050,076
     2005 . . . . $2,475,564

FDIC insured financial institutions, 2004

Number 8,975
   Assets ($bil) $10,104.6
   Deposits ($bil) 5,416.4

Fishing, 2004

Catch (x 1,000 lbs) 9,643,291
Value ($1,000). $3,652,281

Mining, 2004 ($ mil)
Total non-fuel mineral production $44,000
Percent of U.S. 100.0%

Construction, 2003 ($ mil)
Total contracts (including non-building).......
.... $526,996
  residential......................... 282,037
  non-residential 153,476

Establishments, receipts, payroll & employees, by major industry group, 2002

Mining 307
  Receipts ($1,000) $2,455,982
  Annual payroll ($1,000)........... $322,750
  Paid employees 6,964

Utilities 17,103
  Receipts ($1,000) $398,907,044
  Annual payroll ($1,000)........ $42,417,830
  Paid employees 663,044

Construction...................... 710,307
  Receipts ($1,000) $1,196,555,587
  Annual payroll ($1,000)....... $254,292,144
  Paid employees 7,193,069

Manufacturing 350,828
  Receipts ($1,000) $3,916,136,712
  Annual payroll ($1,000)....... $576,170,541
  Paid employees 14,699,536

Wholesale trade 435,521
  Receipts ($1,000) $4,634,755,112
  Annual payroll ($1,000)....... $259,653,080
  Paid employees 5,878,405

Retail trade 1,114,637
  Receipts ($1,000) $3,056,421,997
  Annual payroll ($1,000)....... $302,113,581
  Paid employees 14,647,675

Transportation..................... 199,618
  Receipts ($1,000) $382,152,040
  Annual payroll ($1,000)....... $115,988,733
  Paid employees 3,650,859

Information.......................... 137,678
  Receipts ($1,000) $891,845,956
  Annual payroll ($1,000)....... $194,670,163
  Paid employees 3,736,061

Finance & insurance 440,268
  Receipts ($1,000) $2,803,854,868
  Annual payroll ($1,000)....... $377,790,172
  Paid employees 6,578,817

Professional, scientific & technical 771,305
  Receipts ($1,000) $886,801,038
  Annual payroll ($1,000)....... $376,090,052
  Paid employees 7,243,505

Health care & social assistance 704,526
  Receipts ($1,000) $1,207,299,734
  Annual payroll ($1,000)....... $495,845,829
  Paid employees 15,052,255

Accommodation & food service......... 565,590
  Receipts ($1,000) $449,498,718
  Annual payroll ($1,000)....... $127,554,483
  Paid employees 10,120,951

Communication, Energy & Transportation

Communication
Daily newspapers, 2004 1,456
Households with computers, 2003 ....62%
Households with internet access, 2003 .....55%

Energy
Electricity Consumption, 2001
Total (trillion Btu)..................... 96,275
Per capita (million Btu) 338
By source of production (trillion Btu)
  Coal 21,905
  Natural gas 22,845
  Petroleum......................... 38,333
  Nuclear electric power 8,033
  Hydroelectric power................ 2,118
By end-use sector (trillion Btu)
  Residential 20,241
  Commercial 17,332
  Industrial 32,431
  Transportation 26,272
Electric energy, 2003
  Production (billion kWh) 3883.2
  Net summer capability (million kW) ... 948.4
Gas utilities, 2003
  Customers (x1,000)................. 62,610
  Sales (trillion Btu)................. 8,927
  Revenues ($mil)................... $72,606
Nuclear plants, 2003 104

Transportation, 2004
Public Road & Street Mileage 3,981,512
  Urban............................. 981,276
  Rural 3,000,236
  Interstate......................... 46,572
Vehicle miles of travel per capita....... 10,077.3
Total motor vehicle registrations.... 237,242,616
  Automobiles..................... 136,430,651
  Buses 795,274
  Trucks 100,016,691
  Motorcycles 5,780,870
Licensed drivers 198,888,912
  19 years & under 9,333,086
Deaths from motor vehicle accidents 42,636

Note: Rankings that are tied are listed alphabetically with the exception of the United States which is always listed as the final item in a group of ties.

1. Total Area (Square Miles)		2. Federally Owned Land, 2004	
* UNITED STATES	3,794,083	1. Nevada	84.5%
1. Alaska	663,267	2. Alaska	69.1
2. Texas	268,581	3. Utah	57.5
3. California	163,696	4. Oregon	53.1
4. Montana	147,042	5. Idaho	50.2
5. New Mexico	121,590	6. Arizona	48.1
6. Arizona	113,998	7. California	45.3
7. Nevada	110,561	8. Wyoming	42.3
8. Colorado	104,094	9. New Mexico	41.8
9. Oregon	98,381	10. Colorado	36.6
10. Wyoming	97,814	11. Washington	30.3
11. Michigan	96,716	12. Montana	29.9
12. Minnesota	86,939	* UNITED STATES	28.8
13. Utah	84,899	13. District of Columbia	24.7
14. Idaho	83,570	14. Hawaii	19.4
15. Kansas	82,277	15. New Hampshire	13.5
16. Nebraska	77,354	16. North Carolina	11.8
17. South Dakota	77,117	17. Michigan	10.0
18. Washington	71,300	18. Virginia	9.9
19. North Dakota	70,700	19. Florida	8.2
20. Oklahoma	69,898	20. Vermont	7.5
21. Missouri	69,704	21. West Virginia	7.4
22. Florida	65,755	22. Mississippi	7.3
23. Wisconsin	65,498	23. Arkansas	7.2
24. Georgia	59,425	24. South Dakota	6.2
25. Illinois	57,914	25. Wisconsin	5.6
26. Iowa	56,272	26. Minnesota	5.6
27. New York	54,556	27. Kentucky	5.4
28. North Carolina	53,819	28. Louisiana	5.1
29. Arkansas	53,179	29. Missouri	5.0
30. Alabama	52,419	30. Georgia	3.8
31. Louisiana	51,840	31. Oklahoma	3.6
32. Mississippi	48,430	32. Tennessee	3.2
33. Pennsylvania	46,055	33. New Jersey	3.1
34. Ohio	44,825	34. South Carolina	2.9
35. Virginia	42,774	35. Maryland	2.8
36. Tennessee	42,143	36. North Dakota	2.7
37. Kentucky	40,409	37. Pennsylvania	2.5
38. Indiana	36,418	38. Delaware	2.0
39. Maine	35,385	39. Indiana	2.0
40. South Carolina	32,020	40. Massachusetts	1.9
41. West Virginia	24,230	41. Texas	1.9
42. Maryland	12,407	42. Illinois	1.8
43. Hawaii	10,931	43. Ohio	1.7
44. Massachusetts	10,555	44. Alabama	1.6
45. Vermont	9,614	45. Nebraska	1.4
46. New Hampshire	9,350	46. Kansas	1.2
47. New Jersey	8,721	47. Maine	1.1
48. Connecticut	5,543	48. Iowa	0.8
49. Delaware	2,489	49. New York	0.8
50. Rhode Island	1,545	50. Connecticut	0.4
51. District of Columbia	68	51. Rhode Island	0.4

3. Cities with over 100,000 population, 2000			4. Cities with over 100,000 population, 2004		
*	UNITED STATES	239	*	UNITED STATES	251
1.	California	56	1.	California	62
2.	Texas	24	2.	Texas	24
3.	Florida	13	3.	Florida	17
4.	Arizona	9	4.	Arizona	9
5.	Colorado	8	5.	Colorado	9
6.	Michigan	8	6.	Virginia	8
7.	Virginia	8	7.	Illinois	7
8.	Illinois	7	8.	Michigan	7
9.	North Carolina	6	9.	North Carolina	7
10.	Ohio	6	10.	Ohio	6
11.	Connecticut	5	11.	Connecticut	5
12.	Georgia	5	12.	Georgia	5
13.	Indiana	5	13.	Kansas	5
14.	Massachusetts	5	14.	Massachusetts	5
15.	New York	5	15.	New York	5
16.	Tennessee	5	16.	Tennessee	5
17.	Washington	5	17.	Washington	5
18.	Alabama	4	18.	Alabama	4
19.	Kansas	4	19.	Indiana	4
20.	Louisiana	4	20.	Louisiana	4
21.	Missouri	4	21.	Missouri	4
22.	Nevada	4	22.	Nevada	4
23.	New Jersey	4	23.	New Jersey	4
24.	Pennsylvania	4	24.	Pennsylvania	4
25.	Oregon	3	25.	Oklahoma	3
26.	Utah	3	26.	Oregon	3
27.	Wisconsin	3	27.	Wisconsin	3
28.	Iowa	2	28.	Iowa	2
29.	Kentucky	2	29.	Kentucky	2
30.	Minnesota	2	30.	Minnesota	2
31.	Nebraska	2	31.	Nebraska	2
32.	Oklahoma	2	32.	South Carolina	2
33.	Alaska	1	33.	Utah	2
34.	Arkansas	1	34.	Alaska	1
35.	District of Columbia	1	35.	Arkansas	1
36.	Hawaii	1	36.	District of Columbia	1
37.	Idaho	1	37.	Hawaii	1
38.	Maryland	1	38.	Idaho	1
39.	Mississippi	1	39.	Maryland	1
40.	New Hampshire	1	40.	Mississippi	1
41.	New Mexico	1	41.	New Hampshire	1
42.	Rhode Island	1	42.	New Mexico	1
43.	South Carolina	1	43.	Rhode Island	1
44.	South Dakota	1	44.	South Dakota	1
45.	Delaware	0	45.	Delaware	0
46.	Maine	0	46.	Maine	0
47.	Montana	0	47.	Montana	0
48.	North Dakota	0	48.	North Dakota	0
49.	Vermont	0	49.	Vermont	0
50.	West Virginia	0	50.	West Virginia	0
51.	Wyoming	0	51.	Wyoming	0

5. Population, 1980		6. Population, 1990	
* UNITED STATES	226,546,000	* UNITED STATES	248,709,873
1. California	23,667,902	1. California	29,760,021
2. New York	17,558,072	2. New York	17,990,455
3. Texas	14,229,191	3. Texas	16,986,510
4. Pennsylvania	11,863,895	4. Florida	12,937,926
5. Illinois	11,426,518	5. Pennsylvania	11,881,643
6. Ohio	10,797,630	6. Illinois	11,430,602
7. Florida	9,746,324	7. Ohio	10,847,115
8. Michigan	9,262,078	8. Michigan	9,295,297
9. New Jersey	7,364,823	9. New Jersey	7,730,188
10. North Carolina	5,881,766	10. North Carolina	6,628,637
11. Massachusetts	5,737,037	11. Georgia	6,478,216
12. Indiana	5,490,224	12. Virginia	6,187,358
13. Georgia	5,463,105	13. Massachusetts	6,016,425
14. Virginia	5,346,818	14. Indiana	5,544,159
15. Missouri	4,916,686	15. Missouri	5,117,073
16. Wisconsin	4,705,767	16. Wisconsin	4,891,769
17. Tennessee	4,591,120	17. Tennessee	4,877,185
18. Maryland	4,216,975	18. Washington	4,866,692
19. Louisiana	4,205,900	19. Maryland	4,781,468
20. Washington	4,132,156	20. Minnesota	4,375,099
21. Minnesota	4,075,970	21. Louisiana	4,219,973
22. Alabama	3,893,800	22. Alabama	4,040,587
23. Kentucky	3,660,777	23. Kentucky	3,685,296
24. South Carolina	3,121,820	24. Arizona	3,665,228
25. Connecticut	3,107,576	25. South Carolina	3,486,703
26. Oklahoma	3,025,290	26. Colorado	3,294,394
27. Iowa	2,913,808	27. Connecticut	3,287,116
28. Colorado	2,889,964	28. Oklahoma	3,145,585
29. Arizona	2,718,215	29. Oregon	2,842,321
30. Oregon	2,633,105	30. Iowa	2,776,755
31. Mississippi	2,520,638	31. Mississippi	2,573,216
32. Kansas	2,363,679	32. Kansas	2,477,574
33. Arkansas	2,286,435	33. Arkansas	2,350,725
34. West Virginia	1,949,644	34. West Virginia	1,793,477
35. Nebraska	1,569,825	35. Utah	1,722,850
36. Utah	1,461,037	36. Nebraska	1,578,385
37. New Mexico	1,302,894	37. New Mexico	1,515,069
38. Maine	1,124,660	38. Maine	1,227,928
39. Hawaii	964,691	39. Nevada	1,201,833
40. Rhode Island	947,154	40. New Hampshire	1,109,252
41. Idaho	943,935	41. Hawaii	1,108,229
42. New Hampshire	920,610	42. Idaho	1,006,749
43. Nevada	800,493	43. Rhode Island	1,003,464
44. Montana	786,690	44. Montana	799,065
45. South Dakota	690,768	45. South Dakota	696,004
46. North Dakota	652,717	46. Delaware	666,168
47. District of Columbia	638,333	47. North Dakota	638,800
48. Delaware	594,338	48. District of Columbia	606,900
49. Vermont	511,456	49. Vermont	562,758
50. Wyoming	469,557	50. Alaska	550,043
51. Alaska	401,851	51. Wyoming	453,588

7. Population, 2000		8. Population, 2004	
* UNITED STATES	281,421,906	* UNITED STATES	293,655,404
1. California	33,871,648	1. California	35,893,799
2. Texas	20,851,820	2. Texas	22,490,022
3. New York	18,976,457	3. New York	19,227,088
4. Florida	15,982,378	4. Florida	17,397,161
5. Illinois	12,419,293	5. Illinois	12,713,634
6. Pennsylvania	12,281,054	6. Pennsylvania	12,406,292
7. Ohio	11,353,140	7. Ohio	11,459,011
8. Michigan	9,938,444	8. Michigan	10,112,620
9. New Jersey	8,414,350	9. Georgia	8,829,383
10. Georgia	8,186,453	10. New Jersey	8,698,879
11. North Carolina	8,049,313	11. North Carolina	8,541,221
12. Virginia	7,078,515	12. Virginia	7,459,827
13. Massachusetts	6,349,097	13. Massachusetts	6,416,505
14. Indiana	6,080,485	14. Indiana	6,237,569
15. Washington	5,894,121	15. Washington	6,203,788
16. Tennessee	5,689,283	16. Tennessee	5,900,962
17. Missouri	5,595,211	17. Missouri	5,754,618
18. Wisconsin	5,363,675	18. Arizona	5,743,834
19. Maryland	5,296,486	19. Maryland	5,558,058
20. Arizona	5,130,632	20. Wisconsin	5,509,026
21. Minnesota	4,919,479	21. Minnesota	5,100,958
22. Louisiana	4,468,976	22. Colorado	4,601,403
23. Alabama	4,447,100	23. Alabama	4,530,182
24. Colorado	4,301,261	24. Louisiana	4,515,770
25. Kentucky	4,041,769	25. South Carolina	4,198,068
26. South Carolina	4,012,012	26. Kentucky	4,145,922
27. Oklahoma	3,450,654	27. Oregon	3,594,586
28. Oregon	3,421,399	28. Oklahoma	3,523,553
29. Connecticut	3,405,565	29. Connecticut	3,503,604
30. Iowa	2,926,324	30. Iowa	2,954,451
31. Mississippi	2,844,658	31. Mississippi	2,902,966
32. Kansas	2,688,418	32. Arkansas	2,752,629
33. Arkansas	2,673,400	33. Kansas	2,735,502
34. Utah	2,233,169	34. Utah	2,389,039
35. Nevada	1,998,257	35. Nevada	2,334,771
36. New Mexico	1,819,046	36. New Mexico	1,903,289
37. West Virginia	1,808,344	37. West Virginia	1,815,354
38. Nebraska	1,711,263	38. Nebraska	1,747,214
39. Idaho	1,293,953	39. Idaho	1,393,262
40. Maine	1,274,923	40. Maine	1,317,253
41. New Hampshire	1,235,786	41. New Hampshire	1,299,500
42. Hawaii	1,211,537	42. Hawaii	1,262,840
43. Rhode Island	1,048,319	43. Rhode Island	1,080,632
44. Montana	902,195	44. Montana	926,865
45. Delaware	783,600	45. Delaware	830,364
46. South Dakota	754,844	46. South Dakota	770,883
47. North Dakota	642,200	47. Alaska	655,435
48. Alaska	626,932	48. North Dakota	634,366
49. Vermont	608,827	49. Vermont	621,394
50. District of Columbia	572,059	50. District of Columbia	553,523
51. Wyoming	493,782	51. Wyoming	506,529

9. Population, 2005†	
* UNITED STATES	295,507,134
1. California	36,038,859
2. Texas	22,775,044
3. New York	19,258,082
4. Florida	17,509,827
5. Illinois	12,699,336
6. Pennsylvania	12,426,603
7. Ohio	11,477,557
8. Michigan	10,207,421
9. Georgia	8,925,796
10. New Jersey	8,745,279
11. North Carolina	8,702,410
12. Virginia	7,552,581
13. Massachusetts	6,518,868
14. Indiana	6,249,617
15. Washington	6,204,632
16. Tennessee	5,965,317
17. Arizona	5,868,004
18. Missouri	5,765,166
19. Maryland	5,600,563
20. Wisconsin	5,554,343
21. Minnesota	5,174,743
22. Colorado	4,617,962
23. Louisiana	4,534,310
24. Alabama	4,527,166
25. South Carolina	4,239,310
26. Kentucky	4,163,360
27. Oregon	3,596,083
28. Oklahoma	3,521,379
29. Connecticut	3,503,185
30. Iowa	2,973,700
31. Mississippi	2,915,696
32. Arkansas	2,777,007
33. Kansas	2,751,509
34. Utah	2,417,998
35. Nevada	2,352,086
36. New Mexico	1,902,057
37. West Virginia	1,818,887
38. Nebraska	1,744,370
39. Idaho	1,407,060
40. Maine	1,318,557
41. New Hampshire	1,314,821
42. Hawaii	1,276,552
43. Rhode Island	1,086,575
44. Montana	933,005
45. Delaware	836,687
46. South Dakota	771,803
47. Alaska	661,110
48. North Dakota	635,468
49. Vermont	630,979
50. District of Columbia	551,136
51. Wyoming	507,268

† projected

10. Population, 2030†	
* UNITED STATES	363,584,435
1. California	46,444,861
2. Texas	33,317,744
3. Florida	28,685,769
4. New York	19,477,429
5. Illinois	13,432,892
6. Pennsylvania	12,768,184
7. North Carolina	12,227,739
8. Georgia	12,017,838
9. Ohio	11,550,528
10. Arizona	10,712,397
11. Michigan	10,694,172
12. Virginia	9,825,019
13. New Jersey	9,802,440
14. Washington	8,624,801
15. Tennessee	7,380,634
16. Maryland	7,022,251
17. Massachusetts	7,012,009
18. Indiana	6,810,108
19. Missouri	6,430,173
20. Minnesota	6,306,130
21. Wisconsin	6,150,764
22. Colorado	5,792,357
23. South Carolina	5,148,569
24. Alabama	4,874,243
25. Oregon	4,833,918
26. Louisiana	4,802,633
27. Kentucky	4,554,998
28. Nevada	4,282,102
29. Oklahoma	3,913,251
30. Connecticut	3,688,630
31. Utah	3,485,367
32. Arkansas	3,240,208
33. Mississippi	3,092,410
34. Iowa	2,955,172
35. Kansas	2,940,084
36. New Mexico	2,099,708
37. Idaho	1,969,624
38. Nebraska	1,820,247
39. West Virginia	1,719,959
40. New Hampshire	1,646,471
41. Hawaii	1,466,046
42. Maine	1,411,097
43. Rhode Island	1,152,941
44. Montana	1,044,898
45. Delaware	1,012,658
46. Alaska	867,674
47. South Dakota	800,462
48. Vermont	711,867
49. North Dakota	606,566
50. Wyoming	522,979
51. District of Columbia	433,414

† projected

	11. Metropolitan Area Population, 2000		12. Non-Metropolitan Area Population, 2000	
*	UNITED STATES	225,968,000	UNITED STATES	55,453,000
1.	California	32,750,000	Texas	3,160,000
2.	Texas	17,692,000	North Carolina	2,612,000
3.	New York	17,473,000	Georgia	2,520,000
4.	Florida	14,837,000	Ohio	2,139,000
5.	Illinois	10,542,000	Kentucky	2,069,000
6.	Pennsylvania	10,392,000	Pennsylvania	1,890,000
7.	Ohio	9,214,000	Illinois	1,878,000
8.	New Jersey	8,414,000	Tennessee	1,827,000
9.	Michigan	8,169,000	Mississippi	1,821,000
10.	Massachusetts	6,088,000	Missouri	1,800,000
11.	Georgia	5,667,000	Michigan	1,769,000
12.	Virginia	5,528,000	Wisconsin	1,723,000
13.	North Carolina	5,437,000	Indiana	1,691,000
14.	Maryland	4,911,000	Iowa	1,600,000
15.	Washington	4,899,000	Virginia	1,550,000
16.	Arizona	4,527,000	New York	1,503,000
17.	Indiana	4,390,000	Minnesota	1,456,000
18.	Tennessee	3,862,000	Arkansas	1,352,000
19.	Missouri	3,795,000	Oklahoma	1,352,000
20.	Wisconsin	3,640,000	Alabama	1,338,000
21.	Colorado	3,608,000	South Carolina	1,205,000
22.	Minnesota	3,463,000	Kansas	1,167,000
23.	Louisiana	3,370,000	Florida	1,145,000
24.	Connecticut	3,257,000	California	1,121,000
25.	Alabama	3,109,000	Louisiana	1,099,000
26.	South Carolina	2,807,000	West Virginia	1,043,000
27.	Oregon	2,502,000	Washington	995,000
28.	Oklahoma	2,098,000	Oregon	919,000
29.	Kentucky	1,973,000	Nebraska	811,000
30.	Nevada	1,748,000	Maine	808,000
31.	Utah	1,708,000	Idaho	786,000
32.	Kansas	1,521,000	New Mexico	784,000
33.	Iowa	1,326,000	Colorado	694,000
34.	Arkansas	1,321,000	Arizona	604,000
35.	New Mexico	1,035,000	Montana	597,000
36.	Mississippi	1,024,000	Utah	525,000
37.	Rhode Island	986,000	New Hampshire	496,000
38.	Nebraska	900,000	South Dakota	494,000
39.	Hawaii	876,000	Vermont	439,000
40.	West Virginia	766,000	Maryland	385,000
41.	New Hampshire	740,000	Alaska	367,000
42.	Delaware	627,000	North Dakota	358,000
43.	District of Columbia	572,000	Wyoming	346,000
44.	Idaho	508,000	Hawaii	335,000
45.	Maine	467,000	Massachusetts	261,000
46.	Montana	306,000	Nevada	251,000
47.	North Dakota	284,000	Delaware	157,000
48.	South Dakota	261,000	Connecticut	149,000
49.	Alaska	260,000	Rhode Island	62,000
50.	Vermont	169,000	District of Columbia	0
51.	Wyoming	148,000	New Jersey	0

13. Change in Population, 2000-2004		14. Persons per Land Square Mile, 2004	
1. Nevada	16.8%	1. District of Columbia	9074.1
2. Arizona	12.0	2. New Jersey	1172.8
3. Florida	8.8	3. Rhode Island	1034.1
4. Texas	7.9	4. Massachusetts	818.4
5. Georgia	7.8	5. Connecticut	723.1
6. Idaho	7.7	6. Maryland	568.7
7. Colorado	7.0	7. Delaware	425.0
8. Utah	7.0	8. New York	407.2
9. North Carolina	6.1	9. Florida	322.6
10. California	6.0	10. Ohio	279.8
11. Delaware	6.0	11. Pennsylvania	276.8
12. Virginia	5.4	12. California	230.1
13. Washington	5.3	13. Illinois	228.7
14. New Hampshire	5.2	14. Hawaii	196.6
15. Oregon	5.1	15. Virginia	188.4
16. Maryland	4.9	16. Michigan	178.0
17. New Mexico	4.6	17. North Carolina	175.3
18. South Carolina	4.6	18. Indiana	173.9
19. Alaska	4.5	19. Georgia	152.5
* UNITED STATES	4.3	20. New Hampshire	144.9
20. Hawaii	4.2	21. Tennessee	143.2
21. Minnesota	3.7	22. South Carolina	139.4
22. Tennessee	3.7	23. Kentucky	104.4
23. New Jersey	3.4	24. Louisiana	103.7
24. Maine	3.3	25. Wisconsin	101.4
25. Rhode Island	3.1	26. Washington	93.2
26. Arkansas	3.0	27. Alabama	89.3
27. Connecticut	2.9	28. Texas	85.9
28. Missouri	2.8	29. Missouri	83.5
29. Montana	2.7	* UNITED STATES	83.0
30. Wisconsin	2.7	30. West Virginia	75.4
31. Indiana	2.6	31. Vermont	67.2
32. Kentucky	2.6	32. Minnesota	64.1
33. Wyoming	2.6	33. Mississippi	61.9
34. Illinois	2.4	34. Iowa	52.9
35. Nebraska	2.1	35. Arkansas	52.9
36. Oklahoma	2.1	36. Oklahoma	51.3
37. South Dakota	2.1	37. Arizona	50.5
38. Vermont	2.1	38. Colorado	44.4
39. Mississippi	2.0	39. Maine	42.7
40. Alabama	1.9	40. Oregon	37.4
41. Michigan	1.8	41. Kansas	33.4
42. Kansas	1.7	42. Utah	29.1
43. New York	1.3	43. Nebraska	22.7
44. Massachusetts	1.1	44. Nevada	21.3
45. Iowa	1.0	45. Idaho	16.8
46. Louisiana	1.0	46. New Mexico	15.7
47. Pennsylvania	1.0	47. South Dakota	10.2
48. Ohio	0.9	48. North Dakota	9.2
49. West Virginia	0.4	49. Montana	6.4
50. North Dakota	-1.2	50. Wyoming	5.2
51. District of Columbia	-3.2	51. Alaska	1.1

15. Households, 2000		16. Persons Born in State of Residence, 2000	
* UNITED STATES	105,480,101	* UNITED STATES	168,729,388
1. California	11,502,870	1. California	17,019,097
2. Texas	7,393,354	2. Texas	12,970,203
3. New York	7,056,860	3. New York	12,384,940
4. Florida	6,337,929	4. Pennsylvania	9,544,251
5. Pennsylvania	4,777,003	5. Ohio	8,485,725
6. Illinois	4,591,779	6. Illinois	8,335,553
7. Ohio	4,445,773	7. Michigan	7,490,125
8. Michigan	3,785,661	8. Florida	5,231,906
9. North Carolina	3,132,013	9. North Carolina	5,073,066
10. New Jersey	3,064,645	10. Georgia	4,735,652
11. Georgia	3,006,369	11. New Jersey	4,490,524
12. Virginia	2,699,173	12. Indiana	4,215,694
13. Massachusetts	2,443,580	13. Massachusetts	4,196,702
14. Indiana	2,336,306	14. Wisconsin	3,939,488
15. Washington	2,271,398	15. Missouri	3,792,261
16. Tennessee	2,232,905	16. Tennessee	3,679,056
17. Missouri	2,194,594	17. Virginia	3,676,255
18. Wisconsin	2,084,544	18. Louisiana	3,546,980
19. Maryland	1,980,859	19. Minnesota	3,451,522
20. Arizona	1,901,327	20. Alabama	3,262,053
21. Minnesota	1,895,127	21. Kentucky	2,980,272
22. Alabama	1,737,080	22. Washington	2,781,457
23. Colorado	1,658,238	23. Maryland	2,610,963
24. Louisiana	1,656,053	24. South Carolina	2,568,954
25. Kentucky	1,590,647	25. Iowa	2,188,424
26. South Carolina	1,533,854	26. Oklahoma	2,158,827
27. Oklahoma	1,342,293	27. Mississippi	2,113,883
28. Oregon	1,333,723	28. Connecticut	1,940,576
29. Connecticut	1,301,670	29. Arizona	1,779,492
30. Iowa	1,149,276	30. Colorado	1,766,731
31. Mississippi	1,046,434	31. Arkansas	1,707,529
32. Arkansas	1,042,696	32. Kansas	1,600,274
33. Kansas	1,037,891	33. Oregon	1,549,044
34. Nevada	751,165	34. Utah	1,405,177
35. West Virginia	736,481	35. West Virginia	1,342,589
36. Utah	701,281	36. Nebraska	1,147,815
37. New Mexico	677,971	37. New Mexico	937,212
38. Nebraska	666,184	38. Maine	857,515
39. Maine	518,200	39. Hawaii	689,056
40. New Hampshire	474,606	40. Rhode Island	643,912
41. Idaho	469,645	41. Idaho	610,929
42. Rhode Island	408,424	42. New Hampshire	534,558
43. Hawaii	403,240	43. South Dakota	513,867
44. Montana	358,667	44. Montana	505,966
45. Delaware	298,736	45. North Dakota	465,667
46. South Dakota	290,245	46. Nevada	425,626
47. North Dakota	257,152	47. Delaware	378,840
48. District of Columbia	248,338	48. Vermont	330,528
49. Vermont	240,634	49. Alaska	238,613
50. Alaska	221,600	50. District of Columbia	224,352
51. Wyoming	193,608	51. Wyoming	209,687

17. Percent of Persons Born in State of Residence, 2000		18. Immigrants Admitted, 2004	
1. Louisiana	79.4%	* UNITED STATES	946,142
2. Pennsylvania	77.7	1. California	252,920
3. Michigan	75.4	2. New York	102,390
4. Iowa	74.8	3. Texas	91,799
5. Ohio	74.7	4. Florida	75,644
6. Mississippi	74.3	5. New Jersey	50,303
7. West Virginia	74.2	6. Illinois	46,314
8. Kentucky	73.7	7. Massachusetts	27,676
9. Wisconsin	73.4	8. Virginia	21,695
10. Alabama	73.4	9. Maryland	20,253
11. North Dakota	72.5	10. Washington	19,442
12. Minnesota	70.2	11. Arizona	19,297
13. Indiana	69.3	12. Michigan	18,334
14. South Dakota	68.1	13. Pennsylvania	18,232
15. Missouri	67.8	14. Georgia	16,286
16. Maine	67.3	15. Connecticut	12,138
17. Illinois	67.1	16. Minnesota	11,708
18. Nebraska	67.1	17. Ohio	11,599
19. Massachusetts	66.1	18. Colorado	10,923
20. New York	65.3	19. North Carolina	10,718
21. Tennessee	64.7	20. Nevada	8,758
22. South Carolina	64.0	21. Oregon	8,389
23. Arkansas	63.9	22. Missouri	6,782
24. North Carolina	63.0	23. Hawaii	6,347
25. Utah	62.9	24. Indiana	5,929
26. Oklahoma	62.6	25. Tennessee	5,620
27. Texas	62.2	26. Wisconsin	5,257
28. Rhode Island	61.4	27. Utah	4,255
* UNITED STATES	60.0	28. Kansas	4,041
29. Kansas	59.5	29. Iowa	3,984
30. Georgia	57.8	30. Rhode Island	3,689
31. Connecticut	57.0	31. Kentucky	3,624
32. Hawaii	56.9	32. Oklahoma	3,506
33. Montana	56.1	33. New Mexico	3,024
34. Vermont	54.3	34. Louisiana	2,998
35. New Jersey	53.4	35. Nebraska	2,954
36. Virginia	51.9	36. South Carolina	2,496
37. New Mexico	51.5	37. Arkansas	2,251
38. California	50.2	38. Idaho	2,229
39. Maryland	49.3	39. New Hampshire	2,198
40. Delaware	48.3	40. Alabama	2,139
41. Idaho	47.2	41. District of Columbia	2,110
42. Washington	47.2	42. Delaware	1,671
43. Oregon	45.3	43. Maine	1,264
44. New Hampshire	43.3	44. Mississippi	1,252
45. Wyoming	42.5	45. Alaska	1,219
46. Colorado	41.1	46. Vermont	790
47. District of Columbia	39.2	47. South Dakota	727
48. Alaska	38.1	48. West Virginia	583
49. Arizona	34.7	49. North Dakota	578
50. Florida	32.7	50. Montana	419
51. Nevada	21.3	51. Wyoming	295

19. Infant Deaths, 2004†		20. Infant Death Rate, 2004†	
* UNITED STATES	27,300	1. District of Columbia	11.0
1. California	2,781	2. Louisiana	10.0
2. Texas	2,334	3. Mississippi	9.2
3. New York	1,561	4. Wyoming	9.2
4. Florida	1,505	5. Maryland	8.7
5. Illinois	1,253	6. Alabama	8.6
6. Georgia	1,173	7. Arkansas	8.6
7. Ohio	1,120	8. North Carolina	8.5
8. North Carolina	1,022	9. Tennessee	8.5
9. Pennsylvania	1,002	10. Georgia	8.4
10. Michigan	997	11. South Carolina	8.4
11. Virginia	741	12. Indiana	8.3
12. Indiana	726	13. Oklahoma	8.2
13. Tennessee	675	14. Michigan	7.7
14. Maryland	657	15. South Dakota	7.7
15. Louisiana	653	16. Delaware	7.6
16. Arizona	626	17. Ohio	7.5
17. New Jersey	573	18. Kansas	7.2
18. Missouri	557	19. Missouri	7.2
19. Alabama	507	20. Virginia	7.1
20. South Carolina	476	21. Illinois	7.0
21. Washington	444	22. Florida	6.9
22. Colorado	442	23. Pennsylvania	6.9
23. Oklahoma	422	24. Idaho	6.8
24. Wisconsin	413	25. Arizona	6.7
25. Mississippi	391	26. Nebraska	6.7
26. Kentucky	348	* UNITED STATES	6.6
27. Minnesota	348	27. Colorado	6.5
28. Massachusetts	341	28. West Virginia	6.5
29. Arkansas	334	29. Alaska	6.3
30. Kansas	290	30. Kentucky	6.3
31. Utah	257	31. Nevada	6.3
32. Oregon	250	32. Texas	6.1
33. Connecticut	234	33. New Hampshire	6.0
34. Nevada	223	34. New Mexico	6.0
35. Iowa	198	35. New York	6.0
36. Nebraska	176	36. Wisconsin	5.9
37. New Mexico	170	37. Maine	5.8
38. Idaho	152	38. Connecticut	5.6
39. West Virginia	135	39. Oregon	5.5
40. Hawaii	95	40. Washington	5.4
41. New Hampshire	89	41. Hawaii	5.2
42. South Dakota	89	42. Iowa	5.2
43. Delaware	87	43. California	5.1
44. District of Columbia	82	44. Utah	5.1
45. Maine	81	45. New Jersey	5.0
46. Alaska	65	46. Minnesota	4.9
47. Wyoming	62	47. North Dakota	4.9
48. Rhode Island	59	48. Rhode Island	4.6
49. Montana	50	49. Vermont	4.6
50. North Dakota	40	50. Massachusetts	4.3
51. Vermont	30	51. Montana	4.3

† provisional

† provisional

21. Physicians per 1,000 Persons, 2003

1.	District of Columbia	768
2.	Massachusetts	443
3.	Maryland	414
4.	New York	391
5.	Vermont	363
6.	Connecticut	362
7.	Rhode Island	350
8.	Hawaii	310
9.	New Jersey	310
10.	Pennsylvania	295
11.	Minnesota	278
12.	Virginia	274
13.	Illinois	272
14.	Maine	267
15.	Washington	267
*	UNITED STATES	266
16.	Louisiana	265
17.	New Hampshire	263
18.	Oregon	262
19.	California	261
20.	Tennessee	260
21.	Colorado	255
22.	Ohio	255
23.	Delaware	253
24.	North Carolina	253
25.	Wisconsin	252
26.	Florida	248
27.	Nebraska	242
28.	Missouri	241
29.	North Dakota	241
30.	New Mexico	239
31.	Michigan	238
32.	South Carolina	230
33.	West Virginia	230
34.	Kentucky	227
35.	Montana	227
36.	Alaska	222
37.	Georgia	221
38.	Kansas	218
39.	Indiana	215
40.	South Dakota	215
41.	Alabama	212
42.	Texas	212
43.	Utah	212
44.	Arizona	209
45.	Arkansas	202
46.	Wyoming	192
47.	Iowa	188
48.	Nevada	185
49.	Mississippi	182
50.	Oklahoma	172
51.	Idaho	170

22. Nurses per 1,000 Persons, 2001

1.	District of Columbia	1,498
2.	Massachusetts	1,181
3.	South Dakota	1,114
4.	Pennsylvania	1,074
5.	Rhode Island	1,053
6.	Maine	1,043
7.	Iowa	1,030
8.	North Dakota	1,014
9.	Connecticut	953
10.	Vermont	949
11.	Minnesota	943
12.	Missouri	940
13.	Nebraska	928
14.	Wisconsin	918
15.	Delaware	913
16.	Kansas	913
17.	Ohio	912
18.	New Hampshire	889
19.	West Virginia	880
20.	North Carolina	878
21.	New York	868
22.	Kentucky	858
23.	Tennessee	850
24.	Montana	842
25.	New Jersey	840
26.	Michigan	839
27.	Illinois	837
28.	Louisiana	821
29.	Alabama	814
30.	Indiana	809
31.	Maryland	805
*	UNITED STATES	793
32.	Florida	792
33.	Mississippi	779
34.	Alaska	778
35.	Virginia	770
36.	Wyoming	765
37.	Colorado	756
38.	Washington	754
39.	Oregon	750
40.	Arkansas	737
41.	Hawaii	707
42.	Georgia	697
43.	South Carolina	693
44.	Oklahoma	660
45.	Arizona	657
46.	Idaho	636
47.	New Mexico	635
48.	Texas	607
49.	Utah	607
50.	California	536
51.	Nevada	517

23. Persons with Less Than 9 Years of School, 2004		24. High School Graduates or Higher, 2004	
* UNITED STATES	11,698,807	1. Minnesota	92.3%
1. California	2,250,737	2. Montana	91.9
2. Texas	1,381,348	3. Wyoming	91.9
3. New York	805,245	4. Nebraska	91.3
4. Florida	614,412	5. Utah	91.0
5. Illinois	503,482	6. New Hampshire	90.8
6. North Carolina	382,779	7. Vermont	90.8
7. Georgia	378,850	8. Alaska	90.2
8. Pennsylvania	327,176	9. Iowa	89.8
9. New Jersey	302,061	10. Washington	89.7
10. Tennessee	285,274	11. Kansas	89.6
11. Virginia	269,575	12. North Dakota	89.5
12. Kentucky	257,856	13. Connecticut	88.8
13. Arizona	254,306	14. Wisconsin	88.8
14. Ohio	232,970	15. Virginia	88.4
15. Michigan	219,304	16. Colorado	88.3
16. Indiana	198,283	17. Ohio	88.1
17. Louisiana	195,656	18. Hawaii	88.0
18. Massachusetts	195,532	19. Idaho	87.9
19. Alabama	175,932	20. Michigan	87.9
20. South Carolina	172,988	21. Missouri	87.9
21. Missouri	164,224	22. New Jersey	87.6
22. Maryland	153,071	23. South Dakota	87.5
23. Washington	144,697	24. Maryland	87.4
24. Mississippi	141,985	25. Oregon	87.4
25. Wisconsin	137,617	26. Indiana	87.2
26. Colorado	130,662	27. Maine	87.1
27. Arkansas	127,368	28. Massachusetts	86.9
28. Oklahoma	118,629	29. Illinois	86.8
29. Minnesota	116,802	30. Delaware	86.5
30. Nevada	105,776	31. Pennsylvania	86.5
31. Oregon	105,751	32. District of Columbia	86.4
32. New Mexico	105,733	33. Nevada	86.3
33. West Virginia	95,013	34. Florida	85.9
34. Connecticut	92,848	35. New York	85.4
35. Iowa	70,593	36. Georgia	85.2
36. Kansas	65,624	37. Oklahoma	85.2
37. Nebraska	46,676	* UNITED STATES	85.2
38. Hawaii	46,146	38. Arizona	84.4
39. Rhode Island	43,296	39. South Carolina	83.6
40. Utah	40,984	40. Mississippi	83.0
41. Idaho	36,703	41. New Mexico	82.9
42. Maine	36,040	42. Tennessee	82.9
43. New Hampshire	29,010	43. Alabama	82.4
44. South Dakota	22,879	44. Kentucky	81.8
45. North Dakota	22,426	45. California	81.3
46. Delaware	21,446	46. Rhode Island	81.1
47. District of Columbia	19,451	47. North Carolina	80.9
48. Montana	17,569	48. West Virginia	80.9
49. Vermont	15,389	49. Arkansas	79.2
50. Alaska	11,552	50. Louisiana	78.7
51. Wyoming	9,081	51. Texas	78.3

432

25. Persons with Bachelor's Degree or Higher, 2004		26. Average Public School Teacher's Salary, 2004	
1. District of Columbia	45.7%	1. Connecticut	$57,300
2. Massachusetts	36.7	2. District of Columbia	57,000
3. Colorado	35.5	3. California	56,400
4. New Hampshire	35.4	4. New Jersey	55,600
5. Maryland	35.2	5. New York	55,200
6. New Jersey	34.6	6. Michigan	54,400
7. Connecticut	34.5	7. Illinois	54,200
8. Vermont	34.2	8. Massachusetts	53,200
9. Virginia	33.1	9. Rhode Island	52,300
10. Minnesota	32.5	10. Pennsylvania	51,800
11. California	31.7	11. Alaska	51,700
12. Utah	30.8	12. Maryland	50,300
13. New York	30.6	13. Delaware	49,400
14. Kansas	30.0	14. Oregon	49,200
15. Washington	29.9	15. Ohio	47,500
16. Missouri	28.1	* UNITED STATES	46,800
17. Arizona	28.0	16. Georgia	46,000
* UNITED STATES	27.7	17. Indiana	45,800
18. Georgia	27.6	18. Hawaii	45,500
19. Illinois	27.4	19. Minnesota	45,400
20. Rhode Island	27.2	20. Washington	45,400
21. Delaware	26.9	21. Virginia	43,700
22. Hawaii	26.6	22. Colorado	43,300
23. Florida	26.0	23. North Carolina	43,200
24. Oregon	25.9	24. Wisconsin	42,900
25. Wisconsin	25.6	25. New Hampshire	42,700
26. Alaska	25.5	26. Nevada	42,300
27. Montana	25.5	27. Vermont	42,000
28. South Dakota	25.5	28. Arizona	41,800
29. Pennsylvania	25.3	29. South Carolina	41,200
30. North Dakota	25.2	30. Idaho	41,100
31. New Mexico	25.1	31. Florida	40,600
32. South Carolina	24.9	32. Texas	40,500
33. Nebraska	24.8	33. Tennessee	40,300
34. Ohio	24.6	34. Kentucky	40,200
35. Nevada	24.5	35. Maine	39,900
36. Texas	24.5	36. Wyoming	39,500
37. Michigan	24.4	37. Iowa	39,400
38. Iowa	24.3	38. Arkansas	39,300
39. Tennessee	24.3	39. Utah	39,000
40. Maine	24.2	40. Kansas	38,600
41. Idaho	23.8	41. West Virginia	38,500
42. North Carolina	23.4	42. Nebraska	38,400
43. Oklahoma	22.9	43. Alabama	38,300
44. Wyoming	22.5	44. New Mexico	38,100
45. Louisiana	22.4	45. Missouri	38,000
46. Alabama	22.3	46. Louisiana	37,900
47. Indiana	21.1	47. Montana	37,200
48. Kentucky	21.0	48. Mississippi	35,700
49. Mississippi	20.1	49. North Dakota	35,400
50. Arkansas	18.8	50. Oklahoma	35,100
51. West Virginia	15.3	51. South Dakota	33,200

27. Expenditures for Public Schools, per capita, 2004

1.	Illinois	$2,334
2.	Alaska	2,187
3.	Connecticut	2,142
4.	New York	2,046
5.	Vermont	1,948
6.	New Jersey	1,903
7.	Wyoming	1,896
8.	Michigan	1,880
9.	District of Columbia	1,869
10.	Minnesota	1,860
11.	Massachusetts	1,807
12.	Wisconsin	1,792
13.	Maine	1,716
14.	Texas	1,696
15.	Delaware	1,687
16.	Ohio	1,667
17.	California	1,657
18.	Georgia	1,648
19.	Indiana	1,644
20.	New Hampshire	1,632
21.	Virginia	1,631
22.	Maryland	1,627
*	UNITED STATES	1,623
23.	Pennsylvania	1,617
24.	New Mexico	1,608
25.	Colorado	1,599
26.	Rhode Island	1,594
27.	Washington	1,561
28.	West Virginia	1,538
29.	Nevada	1,516
30.	South Carolina	1,422
31.	Kansas	1,418
32.	Iowa	1,407
33.	Oregon	1,384
34.	Nebraska	1,373
35.	Louisiana	1,367
36.	Hawaii	1,347
37.	South Dakota	1,329
38.	Utah	1,319
39.	North Dakota	1,316
40.	Montana	1,312
41.	Missouri	1,288
42.	Florida	1,286
43.	Kentucky	1,263
44.	Idaho	1,244
45.	North Carolina	1,233
46.	Alabama	1,221
47.	Mississippi	1,178
48.	Oklahoma	1,163
49.	Arkansas	1,158
50.	Arizona	1,137
51.	Tennessee	1,079

28. Expenditures for Public Schools, per pupil, 2004

1.	District of Columbia	$14,621
2.	New York	12,408
3.	Connecticut	12,394
4.	Vermont	12,157
5.	New Jersey	11,847
6.	Massachusetts	11,445
7.	Alaska	11,432
8.	Rhode Island	10,976
9.	Maine	10,961
10.	Illinois	10,866
11.	Wyoming	10,413
12.	Delaware	10,347
13.	Wisconsin	10,293
14.	Ohio	10,102
15.	Pennsylvania	9,949
16.	New Hampshire	9,902
17.	Maryland	9,824
18.	Minnesota	9,513
19.	West Virginia	9,509
20.	Michigan	9,416
21.	Virginia	9,401
22.	Indiana	9,138
23.	Hawaii	9,019
*	UNITED STATES	8,807
24.	New Mexico	8,772
25.	Georgia	8,671
26.	Colorado	8,651
27.	Montana	8,631
28.	Oregon	8,575
29.	Kentucky	8,298
30.	Kansas	8,189
31.	Nebraska	7,947
32.	Washington	7,904
33.	California	7,860
34.	Louisiana	7,840
35.	Texas	7,698
36.	Iowa	7,696
37.	South Dakota	7,611
38.	Missouri	7,548
39.	North Carolina	7,511
40.	South Carolina	7,395
41.	Florida	7,181
42.	North Dakota	7,112
43.	Tennessee	6,983
44.	Alabama	6,953
45.	Idaho	6,779
46.	Arkansas	6,663
47.	Mississippi	6,556
48.	Oklahoma	6,405
49.	Nevada	6,177
50.	Arizona	5,595
51.	Utah	5,556

29. Social Security Beneficiaries, 2004		30. Medicare Enrollment, 2001†	
* UNITED STATES	46,531,000	* UNITED STATES	39,149
1. California	4,412,000	1. California	3,955
2. Florida	3,382,000	2. Florida	2,838
3. New York	3,045,000	3. New York	2,729
4. Texas	2,865,000	4. Texas	2,300
5. Pennsylvania	2,405,000	5. Pennsylvania	2,095
6. Ohio	1,951,000	6. Ohio	1,705
7. Illinois	1,884,000	7. Illinois	1,640
8. Michigan	1,716,000	8. Michigan	1,414
9. North Carolina	1,467,000	9. New Jersey	1,208
10. New Jersey	1,370,000	10. North Carolina	1,155
11. Georgia	1,192,000	11. Massachusetts	961
12. Virginia	1,114,000	12. Georgia	933
13. Tennessee	1,070,000	13. Virginia	910
14. Massachusetts	1,067,000	14. Missouri	867
15. Missouri	1,046,000	15. Indiana	858
16. Indiana	1,038,000	16. Tennessee	842
17. Wisconsin	937,000	17. Wisconsin	787
18. Washington	913,000	18. Washington	746
19. Arizona	888,000	19. Alabama	695
20. Alabama	884,000	20. Arizona	691
21. Kentucky	785,000	21. Minnesota	660
22. Minnesota	775,000	22. Maryland	655
23. Maryland	761,000	23. Kentucky	630
24. South Carolina	751,000	24. Louisiana	605
25. Louisiana	739,000	25. South Carolina	580
26. Oklahoma	623,000	26. Connecticut	516
27. Oregon	611,000	27. Oklahoma	511
28. Connecticut	584,000	28. Oregon	496
29. Colorado	571,000	29. Iowa	478
30. Arkansas	546,000	30. Colorado	476
31. Iowa	546,000	31. Arkansas	442
32. Mississippi	546,000	32. Mississippi	423
33. Kansas	447,000	33. Kansas	391
34. West Virginia	407,000	34. West Virginia	340
35. Nevada	341,000	35. Nebraska	255
36. New Mexico	304,000	36. Nevada	251
37. Nebraska	291,000	37. New Mexico	238
38. Maine	265,000	38. Maine	219
39. Utah	262,000	39. Utah	210
40. Idaho	219,000	40. New Hampshire	173
41. New Hampshire	219,000	41. Rhode Island	172
42. Hawaii	199,000	42. Idaho	169
43. Rhode Island	192,000	43. Hawaii	168
44. Montana	166,000	44. Montana	138
45. Delaware	149,000	45. South Dakota	120
46. South Dakota	140,000	46. Delaware	114
47. North Dakota	115,000	47. North Dakota	103
48. Vermont	110,000	48. Vermont	90
49. Wyoming	83,000	49. District of Columbia	75
50. District of Columbia	72,000	50. Wyoming	66
51. Alaska	63,000	51. Alaska	44

† x 1,000

31. Medicare Enrollment, 2003†		32. Medicaid Beneficiaries, 2002†	
* UNITED STATES	40,173	* UNITED STATES	49,755
1. California	4,078	1. California	9,301
2. Florida	2,921	2. New York	3,921
3. New York	2,763	3. Texas	2,953
4. Texas	2,390	4. Florida	2,676
5. Pennsylvania	2,110	5. Tennessee	1,732
6. Ohio	1,727	6. Illinois	1,731
7. Illinois	1,661	7. Ohio	1,656
8. Michigan	1,445	8. Georgia	1,637
9. New Jersey	1,220	9. Pennsylvania	1,627
10. North Carolina	1,205	10. Michigan	1,450
11. Georgia	974	11. North Carolina	1,355
12. Massachusetts	966	12. Massachusetts	1,066
13. Virginia	946	13. Washington	1,039
14. Missouri	884	14. Missouri	1,036
15. Indiana	878	15. New Jersey	954
16. Tennessee	872	16. Louisiana	899
17. Wisconsin	804	17. Arizona	878
18. Washington	775	18. Indiana	849
19. Arizona	729	19. South Carolina	809
20. Alabama	719	20. Kentucky	808
21. Minnesota	676	21. New Mexico	799
22. Maryland	674	22. Alabama	765
23. Kentucky	648	23. Wisconsin	716
24. Louisiana	620	24. Mississippi	712
25. South Carolina	606	25. Maryland	693
26. Connecticut	522	26. Virginia	665
27. Oklahoma	521	27. Oklahoma	631
28. Oregon	513	28. Minnesota	621
29. Colorado	493	29. Oregon	621
30. Iowa	482	30. Arkansas	579
31. Arkansas	453	31. Connecticut	479
32. Mississippi	437	32. Colorado	426
33. Kansas	394	33. West Virginia	362
34. West Virginia	347	34. Iowa	353
35. Nevada	274	35. Kansas	289
36. Nebraska	257	36. Maine	276
37. New Mexico	250	37. Utah	275
38. Maine	227	38. Nebraska	256
39. Utah	220	39. Nevada	202
40. New Hampshire	180	40. Hawaii	200
41. Idaho	178	41. Rhode Island	199
42. Hawaii	175	42. District of Columbia	193
43. Rhode Island	172	43. Idaho	176
44. Montana	142	44. Delaware	167
45. South Dakota	122	45. Vermont	154
46. Delaware	119	46. South Dakota	118
47. North Dakota	103	47. Alaska	110
48. Vermont	93	48. Montana	104
49. District of Columbia	74	49. New Hampshire	104
50. Wyoming	69	50. North Dakota	70
51. Alaska	48	51. Wyoming	59

† x 1,000

† x 1,000

33. Federal Govt. Grants to State & Local Governments,		34. Property Crime Rate, 2004†	
* UNITED STATES	$460,152,282	1. Arizona	5,340.5
1. California	54,534,048	2. District of Columbia	4,859.1
2. New York	50,008,574	3. Washington	4,849.2
3. Texas	27,792,386	4. Hawaii	4,792.8
4. Pennsylvania	19,915,826	5. Oregon	4,631.3
5. Florida	19,609,519	6. South Carolina	4,504.8
6. Illinois	16,531,175	7. Texas	4,494.0
7. Ohio	16,513,740	8. Louisiana	4,410.2
8. Massachusetts	13,876,126	9. Tennessee	4,306.5
9. Michigan	13,227,411	10. Georgia	4,265.9
10. North Carolina	12,574,492	11. Oklahoma	4,242.1
11. Georgia	11,758,731	12. Nevada	4,206.6
12. New Jersey	11,333,180	13. New Mexico	4,197.7
13. Tennessee	9,863,362	14. Florida	4,179.7
14. Washington	9,082,685	15. North Carolina	4,160.2
15. Maryland	8,836,910	16. Utah	4,085.6
16. Missouri	8,734,296	17. Alabama	4,025.0
17. Arizona	8,363,600	18. Arkansas	4,013.0
18. Virginia	7,991,079	19. Kansas	3,973.5
19. Louisiana	7,786,693	20. Colorado	3,919.3
20. Wisconsin	7,483,990	21. Missouri	3,903.5
21. Indiana	7,436,310	22. Ohio	3,673.2
22. Minnesota	7,208,781	23. Maryland	3,640.2
23. Alabama	7,007,819	24. Nebraska	3,520.6
24. Kentucky	6,743,285	* UNITED STATES	3,517.1
25. South Carolina	6,145,106	25. Mississippi	3,478.5
26. Colorado	5,643,498	26. California	3,419.0
27. Connecticut	5,555,683	27. Indiana	3,397.6
28. Mississippi	5,378,932	28. Alaska	3,382.8
29. Oklahoma	5,270,581	29. Wyoming	3,334.3
30. Oregon	5,184,929	30. Illinois	3,186.1
31. Arkansas	4,682,798	31. Delaware	3,163.9
32. New Mexico	4,662,536	32. Michigan	3,057.6
33. District of Columbia	4,204,862	33. Minnesota	3,039.0
34. Iowa	4,038,677	34. Montana	2,936.2
35. West Virginia	3,700,592	35. Iowa	2,905.3
36. Kansas	3,468,608	36. Rhode Island	2,884.1
37. Alaska	3,216,865	37. Idaho	2,794.4
38. Utah	2,947,857	38. Virginia	2,676.6
39. Maine	2,757,942	39. Wisconsin	2,663.1
40. Nebraska	2,530,936	40. Connecticut	2,627.2
41. Rhode Island	2,329,088	41. Kentucky	2,537.7
42. Nevada	2,321,630	42. West Virginia	2,506.2
43. Hawaii	2,158,313	43. Massachusetts	2,459.7
44. Montana	1,997,362	44. New Jersey	2,429.2
45. Idaho	1,994,706	45. Pennsylvania	2,415.0
46. New Hampshire	1,878,737	46. Maine	2,409.6
47. Wyoming	1,635,620	47. Vermont	2,308.2
48. South Dakota	1,620,407	48. New York	2,198.6
49. North Dakota	1,515,253	49. New Hampshire	2,040.1
50. Vermont	1,423,455	50. South Dakota	1,933.5
51. Delaware	1,241,092	51. North Dakota	1,916.6

† x $1,000

† per 100,000 residents

35. Violent Crime Rate, 2004†

1.	District of Columbia	1,371.2
2.	South Carolina	784.2
3.	Florida	711.3
4.	Maryland	700.5
5.	Tennessee	695.2
6.	New Mexico	687.3
7.	Louisiana	638.7
8.	Alaska	634.5
9.	Nevada	615.9
10.	Delaware	568.4
11.	California	551.8
12.	Illinois	542.9
13.	Texas	540.5
14.	Arizona	504.1
15.	Oklahoma	500.5
16.	Arkansas	499.1
17.	Missouri	490.5
18.	Michigan	490.2
*	UNITED STATES	465.5
19.	Massachusetts	458.8
20.	Georgia	455.5
21.	North Carolina	447.8
22.	New York	441.6
23.	Alabama	426.6
24.	Pennsylvania	411.1
25.	Kansas	374.5
26.	Colorado	373.5
27.	New Jersey	355.7
28.	Washington	343.8
29.	Ohio	341.8
30.	Indiana	325.4
31.	Nebraska	308.7
32.	Oregon	298.3
33.	Mississippi	295.1
34.	Montana	293.8
35.	Connecticut	286.3
36.	Virginia	275.6
37.	West Virginia	271.2
38.	Iowa	270.9
39.	Minnesota	269.6
40.	Hawaii	254.4
41.	Rhode Island	247.4
42.	Idaho	244.9
43.	Kentucky	244.9
44.	Utah	236.0
45.	Wyoming	229.6
46.	Wisconsin	209.6
47.	South Dakota	171.5
48.	New Hampshire	167.0
49.	Vermont	112.0
50.	Maine	103.5
51.	North Dakota	79.4

† per 100,000 residents

36. Incarceration Rate, 2004†

1.	Louisiana	816
2.	Texas	694
3.	Mississippi	669
4.	Oklahoma	649
5.	Georgia	574
6.	Alabama	556
7.	South Carolina	539
8.	Missouri	538
9.	Arizona	534
10.	Arkansas	495
11.	Delaware	488
12.	Florida	486
*	UNITED STATES	486
13.	Michigan	483
14.	Nevada	474
15.	Virginia	473
16.	California	456
17.	Idaho	454
18.	Colorado	438
19.	Tennessee	437
20.	Montana	416
21.	Kentucky	412
22.	Maryland	406
23.	South Dakota	399
24.	Alaska	398
25.	Ohio	391
26.	Wisconsin	390
27.	Wyoming	389
28.	Indiana	383
29.	Connecticut	377
30.	Oregon	365
31.	North Carolina	357
32.	Illinois	346
33.	New York	331
34.	Hawaii	329
35.	Pennsylvania	329
36.	Kansas	327
37.	New Mexico	318
38.	New Jersey	306
39.	Iowa	288
40.	West Virginia	277
41.	Washington	264
42.	Utah	246
43.	Vermont	233
44.	Massachusetts	232
45.	Nebraska	230
46.	North Dakota	195
47.	New Hampshire	187
48.	Rhode Island	175
49.	Minnesota	171
50.	Maine	148
51.	District of Columbia	NA

† per 100,000 residents

37. Civilian Labor Force, 2004

*	UNITED STATES	147,401,000
1.	California	17,551,000
2.	Texas	10,989,000
3.	New York	9,370,000
4.	Florida	8,411,000
5.	Illinois	6,386,000
6.	Pennsylvania	6,260,000
7.	Ohio	5,884,000
8.	Michigan	5,114,000
9.	Georgia	4,399,000
10.	New Jersey	4,388,000
11.	North Carolina	4,243,000
12.	Virginia	3,766,000
13.	Massachusetts	3,399,000
14.	Washington	3,240,000
15.	Indiana	3,160,000
16.	Wisconsin	3,071,000
17.	Missouri	3,017,000
18.	Minnesota	2,941,000
19.	Tennessee	2,894,000
20.	Maryland	2,883,000
21.	Arizona	2,778,000
22.	Colorado	2,525,000
23.	Alabama	2,179,000
24.	South Carolina	2,077,000
25.	Louisiana	2,058,000
26.	Kentucky	1,977,000
27.	Oregon	1,850,000
28.	Connecticut	1,790,000
29.	Oklahoma	1,714,000
30.	Iowa	1,620,000
31.	Kansas	1,480,000
32.	Mississippi	1,335,000
33.	Arkansas	1,308,000
34.	Utah	1,206,000
35.	Nevada	1,175,000
36.	Nebraska	990,000
37.	New Mexico	911,000
38.	West Virginia	795,000
39.	New Hampshire	724,000
40.	Idaho	706,000
41.	Maine	696,000
42.	Hawaii	612,000
43.	Rhode Island	562,000
44.	Montana	486,000
45.	South Dakota	431,000
46.	Delaware	426,000
47.	North Dakota	359,000
48.	Vermont	353,000
49.	Alaska	331,000
50.	District of Columbia	299,000
51.	Wyoming	282,000

38. Unemployment Rate, 2004

1.	District of Columbia	8.2%
2.	Oregon	7.6
3.	Alaska	7.5
4.	Michigan	7.0
5.	South Carolina	6.9
6.	Ohio	6.3
7.	California	6.2
8.	Mississippi	6.2
9.	Washington	6.2
10.	Illinois	6.1
11.	Louisiana	6.0
12.	Texas	6.0
13.	Arkansas	5.9
14.	Alabama	5.8
15.	New York	5.8
16.	Missouri	5.7
17.	New Mexico	5.6
18.	Pennsylvania	5.6
19.	Kansas	5.5
*	UNITED STATES	5.5
20.	Colorado	5.4
21.	North Carolina	5.4
22.	Rhode Island	5.4
23.	Idaho	5.3
24.	Indiana	5.3
25.	Utah	5.3
26.	West Virginia	5.3
27.	Kentucky	5.2
28.	Arizona	5.1
29.	Massachusetts	5.1
30.	Tennessee	5.1
31.	Wisconsin	5.0
32.	Connecticut	4.9
33.	Montana	4.9
34.	Oklahoma	4.9
35.	Minnesota	4.8
36.	New Jersey	4.8
37.	Georgia	4.7
38.	Maine	4.7
39.	Florida	4.6
40.	Iowa	4.6
41.	Maryland	4.2
42.	Nevada	4.2
43.	Delaware	3.9
44.	Virginia	3.9
45.	Nebraska	3.8
46.	Wyoming	3.8
47.	New Hampshire	3.7
48.	South Dakota	3.7
49.	Vermont	3.7
50.	Hawaii	3.4
51.	North Dakota	3.4

39. Average Hourly Earnings of Production Workers, 2004		40. Average Weekly Earnings of Production Workers, 2004	
1. Michigan	$21.53	1. Michigan	$912.87
2. Ohio	18.47	2. Ohio	770.20
3. Connecticut	18.35	3. Connecticut	767.03
4. Washington	18.27	4. Indiana	754.43
5. Indiana	17.92	5. Washington	730.80
6. Missouri	17.92	6. Missouri	720.38
7. Delaware	17.68	7. Louisiana	719.96
8. New York	17.29	8. Delaware	707.20
9. Maine	16.97	9. Massachusetts	694.18
10. Massachusetts	16.89	10. New York	686.41
11. Wyoming	16.58	11. West Virginia	686.00
12. Kansas	16.57	12. Iowa	682.37
13. West Virginia	16.57	13. Kansas	679.37
14. Kentucky	16.51	14. Kentucky	673.61
15. Maryland	16.48	15. Maine	672.01
16. Colorado	16.46	16. Colorado	664.98
17. Louisiana	16.40	17. Maryland	660.85
18. Wisconsin	16.19	18. New Jersey	659.71
19. Iowa	16.17	* UNITED STATES	658.53
* UNITED STATES	16.14	19. Wyoming	658.23
20. Minnesota	16.04	20. Minnesota	656.04
21. New Jersey	15.67	21. Wisconsin	652.46
22. Illinois	15.61	22. Illinois	640.01
23. New Hampshire	15.48	23. Nebraska	631.90
24. Utah	15.38	24. New Hampshire	619.20
25. California	15.35	25. California	614.00
26. Oregon	15.34	26. Pennsylvania	610.55
27. Nebraska	15.19	27. Oregon	599.79
28. Pennsylvania	15.15	28. Vermont	586.92
29. Montana	14.87	29. Utah	585.98
30. South Carolina	14.73	30. Nevada	585.46
31. Nevada	14.60	31. Alabama	584.66
32. Vermont	14.60	32. South Carolina	581.84
33. Georgia	14.53	33. Oklahoma	575.70
34. North Dakota	14.35	34. Arizona	575.10
35. Alabama	14.33	35. North Carolina	574.28
36. North Carolina	14.25	36. Idaho	573.08
37. Oklahoma	14.25	37. Georgia	569.58
38. Arizona	14.20	38. Montana	569.52
39. Idaho	14.15	39. Florida	568.82
40. Texas	13.98	40. North Dakota	563.96
41. Tennessee	13.85	41. South Dakota	561.12
42. Florida	13.84	42. Texas	556.40
43. Arkansas	13.49	43. Tennessee	554.00
44. Hawaii	13.48	44. Arkansas	538.25
45. South Dakota	13.36	45. Mississippi	526.11
46. New Mexico	13.13	46. New Mexico	519.95
47. Mississippi	13.12	47. Hawaii	510.89
48. Rhode Island	13.03	48. Rhode Island	510.78
49. Alaska	12.01	49. Alaska	487.61
50. District of Columbia	NA	50. District of Columbia	NA
51. Virginia	NA	51. Virginia	NA

41. Average Annual Pay, 2004		42. Median Household Income, 2002-2004†	
1. District of Columbia	$63,887	1. New Hampshire	$57,352
2. Connecticut	51,007	2. New Jersey	56,772
3. New York	49,941	3. Maryland	56,763
4. Massachusetts	48,916	4. Connecticut	55,970
5. New Jersey	48,064	5. Minnesota	55,914
6. California	44,641	6. Alaska	54,627
7. Maryland	42,579	7. Virginia	53,275
8. Delaware	42,487	8. Hawaii	53,123
9. Illinois	42,277	9. Massachusetts	52,354
10. Virginia	40,534	10. Colorado	51,022
11. Minnesota	40,398	11. Utah	50,614
12. Michigan	40,373	12. Delaware	50,152
13. Colorado	40,276	13. California	49,894
14. Washington	39,361	14. Washington	48,688
* UNITED STATES	39,354	15. Wisconsin	47,220
15. New Hampshire	39,176	16. Nevada	46,984
16. Alaska	39,062	17. Rhode Island	46,199
17. Pennsylvania	38,555	18. Illinois	45,787
18. Texas	38,511	19. Vermont	45,692
19. Georgia	37,866	20. Nebraska	44,623
20. Rhode Island	37,651	21. Michigan	44,476
21. Nevada	37,106	* UNITED STATES	44,473
22. Arizona	36,646	22. Pennsylvania	44,286
23. Ohio	36,441	23. New York	44,228
24. Oregon	35,630	24. Ohio	44,160
25. Hawaii	35,198	25. Missouri	43,988
26. Florida	35,186	26. Kansas	43,725
27. Tennessee	34,925	27. Wyoming	43,641
28. Missouri	34,845	28. District of Columbia	43,573
29. North Carolina	34,791	29. Georgia	43,217
30. Wisconsin	34,743	30. Iowa	43,042
31. Indiana	34,694	31. Indiana	43,003
32. Alabama	33,414	32. Oregon	42,617
33. Vermont	33,274	33. Arizona	42,590
34. Kentucky	33,165	34. Idaho	42,519
35. Kansas	32,738	35. Texas	41,275
36. Utah	32,171	36. South Dakota	40,518
37. Iowa	32,097	37. Florida	40,171
38. Maine	31,906	38. North Dakota	39,594
39. Louisiana	31,880	39. Maine	39,395
40. South Carolina	31,839	40. South Carolina	39,326
41. Nebraska	31,507	41. North Carolina	39,000
42. New Mexico	31,411	42. Tennessee	38,550
43. Wyoming	31,210	43. Oklahoma	38,281
44. Oklahoma	30,743	44. Alabama	38,111
45. West Virginia	30,382	45. New Mexico	37,587
46. Arkansas	30,245	46. Kentucky	37,396
47. Idaho	29,871	47. Louisiana	35,523
48. North Dakota	28,987	48. Montana	35,201
49. Mississippi	28,535	49. Arkansas	33,948
50. South Dakota	28,281	50. Mississippi	33,659
51. Montana	27,830	51. West Virginia	32,589

† three-year average

43. Personal Income, in Current Dollars, 2004†

1.	District of Columbia	$51,803
2.	Connecticut	45,398
3.	Massachusetts	41,801
4.	New Jersey	41,332
5.	Maryland	39,247
6.	New York	38,228
7.	New Hampshire	37,040
8.	Colorado	36,063
9.	Delaware	35,861
10.	Minnesota	35,861
11.	Virginia	35,477
12.	Washington	35,299
13.	California	35,019
14.	Alaska	34,454
15.	Illinois	34,351
16.	Wyoming	34,306
17.	Rhode Island	33,733
18.	Nevada	33,405
19.	Pennsylvania	33,348
*	UNITED STATES	32,937
20.	Vermont	32,770
21.	Hawaii	32,160
22.	Wisconsin	32,157
23.	Michigan	31,954
24.	Florida	31,455
25.	North Dakota	31,398
26.	Nebraska	31,339
27.	Ohio	31,322
28.	South Dakota	30,856
29.	Kansas	30,811
30.	Missouri	30,608
31.	Maine	30,566
32.	Iowa	30,560
33.	Texas	30,222
34.	Indiana	30,094
35.	Georgia	30,051
36.	Tennessee	30,005
37.	Oregon	29,971
38.	North Carolina	29,246
39.	Arizona	28,442
40.	Oklahoma	28,089
41.	Alabama	27,795
42.	Kentucky	27,709
43.	Louisiana	27,581
44.	South Carolina	27,172
45.	Idaho	27,098
46.	Montana	26,857
47.	Utah	26,606
48.	New Mexico	26,191
49.	West Virginia	25,872
50.	Arkansas	25,725
51.	Mississippi	24,650

† per capita

44. Personal Income, in Constant Dollars, 2004†

1.	District of Columbia	$48,044
2.	Connecticut	42,104
3.	Massachusetts	38,768
4.	New Jersey	38,333
5.	Maryland	36,399
6.	New York	35,454
7.	New Hampshire	34,352
8.	Colorado	33,446
9.	Delaware	33,259
10.	Minnesota	33,259
11.	Virginia	32,903
12.	Washington	32,738
13.	California	32,478
14.	Alaska	31,954
15.	Illinois	31,858
16.	Wyoming	31,817
17.	Rhode Island	31,285
18.	Nevada	30,981
19.	Pennsylvania	30,928
*	UNITED STATES	30,547
20.	Vermont	30,392
21.	Hawaii	29,826
22.	Wisconsin	29,824
23.	Michigan	29,635
24.	Florida	29,173
25.	North Dakota	29,120
26.	Nebraska	29,065
27.	Ohio	29,049
28.	South Dakota	28,617
29.	Kansas	28,575
30.	Missouri	28,387
31.	Maine	28,348
32.	Iowa	28,342
33.	Texas	28,029
34.	Indiana	27,910
35.	Georgia	27,870
36.	Tennessee	27,828
37.	Oregon	27,796
38.	North Carolina	27,124
39.	Arizona	26,378
40.	Oklahoma	26,051
41.	Alabama	25,778
42.	Kentucky	25,698
43.	Louisiana	25,580
44.	South Carolina	25,200
45.	Idaho	25,132
46.	Montana	24,908
47.	Utah	24,675
48.	New Mexico	24,291
49.	West Virginia	23,995
50.	Arkansas	23,858
51.	Mississippi	22,861

† per capita

45. Persons Below Poverty Level, 2002-2004[†]		46. *Fortune* 500 Companies, 2005	
1. Mississippi	17.7%	* UNITED STATES	500
2. Arkansas	17.6	1. New York	54
3. New Mexico	17.5	2. California	52
4. Louisiana	17.0	3. Texas	48
5. District of Columbia	16.8	4. Illinois	33
6. Texas	16.4	5. Ohio	30
7. West Virginia	16.1	6. Pennsylvania	27
8. Alabama	15.5	7. New Jersey	24
9. Kentucky	15.4	8. Michigan	22
10. Tennessee	14.9	9. Minnesota	18
11. North Carolina	14.8	10. Virginia	18
12. New York	14.4	11. Georgia	17
13. Montana	14.3	12. Connecticut	14
14. South Carolina	14.0	13. Florida	14
15. Arizona	13.8	14. North Carolina	14
16. California	13.2	15. Massachusetts	11
17. Oklahoma	12.6	16. Missouri	11
18. Illinois	12.5	17. Colorado	10
19. South Dakota	12.5	18. Wisconsin	10
* UNITED STATES	12.4	19. Washington	9
20. Florida	12.3	20. Tennessee	7
21. Maine	12.2	21. Indiana	6
22. Michigan	12.1	22. Kentucky	6
23. Georgia	12.0	23. Maryland	6
24. Oregon	11.7	24. Arkansas	5
25. Washington	11.7	25. Oklahoma	5
26. Rhode Island	11.3	26. Nebraska	4
27. Missouri	10.9	27. Arizona	3
28. Ohio	10.8	28. Nevada	3
29. Kansas	10.7	29. Alabama	2
30. Idaho	10.5	30. Delaware	2
31. Pennsylvania	10.4	31. District of Columbia	2
32. North Dakota	10.3	32. Idaho	2
33. Indiana	10.2	33. Iowa	2
34. Nevada	10.2	34. Kansas	2
35. Wisconsin	10.2	35. Rhode Island	2
36. Nebraska	9.9	36. Louisiana	1
37. Colorado	9.8	37. New Hampshire	1
38. Massachusetts	9.8	38. Oregon	1
39. Virginia	9.8	39. South Carolina	1
40. Hawaii	9.7	40. Utah	1
41. Iowa	9.7	41. Alaska	0
42. Utah	9.6	42. Hawaii	0
43. Wyoming	9.6	43. Maine	0
44. Alaska	9.2	44. Mississippi	0
45. Connecticut	8.8	45. Montana	0
46. Vermont	8.8	46. New Mexico	0
47. Maryland	8.6	47. North Dakota	0
48. Delaware	8.5	48. South Dakota	0
49. New Jersey	8.2	49. Vermont	0
50. Minnesota	7.0	50. West Virginia	0
51. New Hampshire	5.7	51. Wyoming	0

† three-year average

47. Patents Issued, 2004			48. Bankruptcy Cases Filed, 2004	
*	UNITED STATES	94,110	* UNITED STATES	1,635,700
1.	California	21,601	1. California	132,500
2.	New York	6,618	2. Florida	92,200
3.	Texas	6,239	3. Texas	92,200
4.	Michigan	4,122	4. Ohio	90,900
5.	Massachusetts	3,904	5. Illinois	81,300
6.	Illinois	3,754	6. New York	80,200
7.	Ohio	3,417	7. Georgia	79,800
8.	New Jersey	3,352	8. Michigan	63,000
9.	Pennsylvania	3,223	9. Tennessee	62,900
10.	Minnesota	2,996	10. Pennsylvania	59,100
11.	Florida	2,989	11. Indiana	55,700
12.	Washington	2,442	12. New Jersey	42,500
13.	Colorado	2,289	13. Alabama	42,400
14.	North Carolina	2,075	14. Virginia	42,100
15.	Wisconsin	1,975	15. Washington	40,100
16.	Oregon	1,967	16. Missouri	38,000
17.	Idaho	1,822	17. North Carolina	37,700
18.	Arizona	1,730	18. Maryland	32,000
19.	Connecticut	1,722	19. Arizona	31,800
20.	Georgia	1,492	20. Louisiana	30,200
21.	Indiana	1,485	21. Kentucky	29,300
22.	Maryland	1,436	22. Wisconsin	27,700
23.	Virginia	1,181	23. Colorado	27,400
24.	Missouri	895	24. Oklahoma	27,200
25.	Tennessee	874	25. Oregon	24,900
26.	Utah	784	26. Arkansas	24,200
27.	Iowa	736	27. Utah	21,300
28.	New Hampshire	681	28. Mississippi	21,200
29.	South Carolina	581	29. Nevada	19,400
30.	Kansas	540	30. Minnesota	19,100
31.	Oklahoma	490	31. Massachusetts	18,200
32.	Nevada	476	32. Kansas	16,300
33.	Kentucky	463	33. South Carolina	15,900
34.	Vermont	428	34. Iowa	13,000
35.	Alabama	412	35. Connecticut	11,800
36.	Delaware	406	36. West Virginia	11,400
37.	Louisiana	387	37. Idaho	9,700
38.	New Mexico	383	38. New Mexico	9,400
39.	Rhode Island	368	39. Nebraska	8,800
40.	Nebraska	229	40. Maine	4,600
41.	Arkansas	160	41. New Hampshire	4,500
42.	Mississippi	159	42. Montana	4,400
43.	Maine	138	43. Rhode Island	4,300
44.	Montana	131	44. Delaware	3,800
45.	West Virginia	111	45. Hawaii	3,500
46.	South Dakota	88	46. South Dakota	2,900
47.	Hawaii	86	47. Wyoming	2,400
48.	District of Columbia	80	48. North Dakota	2,300
49.	North Dakota	66	49. District of Columbia	2,100
50.	Wyoming	55	50. Vermont	1,800
51.	Alaska	49	51. Alaska	1,500

49. Gross State Product, 2004†

*	UNITED STATES	$11,665,595
1.	California	1,550,753
2.	New York	896,739
3.	Texas	884,136
4.	Florida	599,068
5.	Illinois	521,900
6.	Pennsylvania	468,089
7.	Ohio	419,866
8.	New Jersey	416,053
9.	Michigan	372,169
10.	Georgia	343,125
11.	North Carolina	336,398
12.	Virginia	329,332
13.	Massachusetts	317,798
14.	Washington	261,549
15.	Maryland	227,991
16.	Indiana	227,569
17.	Minnesota	223,822
18.	Tennessee	217,626
19.	Wisconsin	211,616
20.	Missouri	203,294
21.	Colorado	199,969
22.	Arizona	199,953
23.	Connecticut	185,802
24.	Louisiana	152,944
25.	Alabama	139,840
26.	Kentucky	136,446
27.	South Carolina	136,125
28.	Oregon	128,103
29.	Iowa	111,114
30.	Oklahoma	107,600
31.	Nevada	100,317
32.	Kansas	98,946
33.	Utah	82,611
34.	Arkansas	80,902
35.	District of Columbia	76,685
36.	Mississippi	76,166
37.	Nebraska	68,183
38.	New Mexico	61,012
39.	Delaware	54,274
40.	New Hampshire	51,871
41.	Hawaii	50,322
42.	West Virginia	49,454
43.	Idaho	43,571
44.	Maine	43,336
45.	Rhode Island	41,679
46.	Alaska	34,023
47.	South Dakota	29,386
48.	Montana	27,482
49.	Wyoming	23,979
50.	North Dakota	22,687
51.	Vermont	21,921

† in millions of dollars

50. Annual Payroll for Major Industry Groups, 2003†

*	UNITED STATES	$4,040,888,841
1.	California	520,597,420
2.	New York	332,635,342
3.	Texas	281,636,318
4.	Florida	202,370,528
5.	Illinois	201,040,291
6.	Pennsylvania	174,513,098
7.	Ohio	157,464,859
8.	New Jersey	154,521,098
9.	Michigan	143,974,115
10.	Massachusetts	127,099,808
11.	Georgia	116,311,049
12.	Virginia	106,077,785
13.	North Carolina	104,552,297
14.	Washington	90,586,818
15.	Minnesota	87,297,655
16.	Indiana	81,408,367
17.	Maryland	78,882,222
18.	Wisconsin	78,327,876
19.	Missouri	75,594,931
20.	Tennessee	73,203,638
21.	Connecticut	69,742,050
22.	Colorado	67,914,762
23.	Arizona	64,371,697
24.	Louisiana	47,137,015
25.	Alabama	47,070,000
26.	South Carolina	44,593,582
27.	Oregon	44,347,211
28.	Kentucky	43,768,132
29.	Iowa	35,989,231
30.	Kansas	34,040,946
31.	Oklahoma	33,555,356
32.	Nevada	31,331,904
33.	Arkansas	27,035,322
34.	Utah	26,788,628
35.	Mississippi	23,647,163
36.	Nebraska	23,091,980
37.	District of Columbia	22,456,247
38.	New Hampshire	18,846,455
39.	New Mexico	15,848,550
40.	West Virginia	15,247,779
41.	Delaware	15,079,817
42.	Maine	14,790,889
43.	Rhode Island	14,538,391
44.	Hawaii	14,138,996
45.	Idaho	13,106,885
46.	Alaska	8,694,257
47.	South Dakota	7,961,531
48.	Montana	7,727,630
49.	Vermont	7,656,559
50.	North Dakota	6,903,847
51.	Wyoming	5,370,514

† x $1,000

51. Number of Farms, 2004		52. Net Farm Income, 2003†	
* UNITED STATES	2,113,000	* UNITED STATES	$59,229
1. Texas	229,000	1. California	8,475
2. Missouri	106,000	2. Texas	5,939
3. Iowa	90,000	3. Nebraska	3,228
4. Kentucky	85,000	4. Georgia	2,971
5. Tennessee	85,000	5. Oklahoma	2,037
6. Oklahoma	84,000	6. Iowa	2,023
7. Minnesota	80,000	7. Arkansas	1,914
8. California	77,000	8. Florida	1,831
9. Ohio	77,000	9. Illinois	1,657
10. Wisconsin	77,000	10. North Carolina	1,629
11. Illinois	73,000	11. Wisconsin	1,626
12. Kansas	65,000	12. Alabama	1,604
13. Indiana	59,000	13. Minnesota	1,568
14. Pennsylvania	58,000	14. Missouri	1,539
15. Michigan	53,000	15. Ohio	1,470
16. North Carolina	52,000	16. Kansas	1,387
17. Georgia	49,000	17. Indiana	1,328
18. Arkansas	48,000	18. South Dakota	1,321
19. Nebraska	48,000	19. North Dakota	1,315
20. Virginia	48,000	20. Idaho	1,218
21. Alabama	44,000	21. Colorado	1,172
22. Florida	43,000	22. Mississippi	1,148
23. Mississippi	42,000	23. Pennsylvania	1,107
24. Oregon	40,000	24. Arizona	1,078
25. New York	36,000	25. Kentucky	864
26. Washington	35,000	26. New Mexico	716
27. South Dakota	32,000	27. Louisiana	711
28. Colorado	31,000	28. South Carolina	681
29. North Dakota	30,000	29. Washington	680
30. Montana	28,000	30. New York	597
31. Louisiana	27,000	31. Montana	576
32. Idaho	25,000	32. Virginia	529
33. South Carolina	24,000	33. Oregon	493
34. West Virginia	21,000	34. Tennessee	480
35. New Mexico	18,000	35. Michigan	444
36. Utah	15,000	36. Utah	368
37. Maryland	12,000	37. Maryland	327
38. Arizona	10,000	38. Wyoming	291
39. New Jersey	10,000	39. Delaware	156
40. Wyoming	9,000	40. New Jersey	127
41. Maine	7,000	41. Hawaii	122
42. Hawaii	6,000	42. Nevada	111
43. Massachusetts	6,000	43. Vermont	102
44. Vermont	6,000	44. Connecticut	93
45. Connecticut	4,000	45. Maine	84
46. Nevada	3,000	46. Massachusetts	40
47. New Hampshire	3,000	47. New Hampshire	17
48. Delaware	2,000	48. West Virginia	15
49. Alaska	1,000	49. Alaska	10
50. Rhode Island	1,000	50. Rhode Island	10
51. District of Columbia	NA	51. District of Columbia	NA

† in millions of dollars

53. Farm Marketing Receipts, 2003†		54. FDIC Insured Financial Institutions, Deposits, 2004†	
* UNITED STATES	$211,647	* UNITED STATES	$5,416.4
1. California	27,805	1. California	671.1
2. Texas	15,342	2. New York	637.6
3. Iowa	12,633	3. Texas	310.3
4. Nebraska	10,621	4. Florida	301.0
5. Kansas	9,046	5. Illinois	281.9
6. Minnesota	8,588	6. New Jersey	211.3
7. Illinois	8,290	7. Pennsylvania	210.7
8. North Carolina	6,916	8. Ohio	200.2
9. Florida	6,450	9. Massachusetts	172.7
10. Wisconsin	5,876	10. North Carolina	163.9
11. Washington	5,345	11. Virginia	147.8
12. Arkansas	5,298	12. Michigan	136.1
13. Georgia	5,246	13. Georgia	132.0
14. Indiana	5,162	14. Delaware	105.8
15. Missouri	4,973	15. Utah	102.0
16. Colorado	4,964	16. Wisconsin	96.1
17. Ohio	4,662	17. Minnesota	94.4
18. Oklahoma	4,526	18. Tennessee	90.2
19. Pennsylvania	4,266	19. Washington	87.4
20. South Dakota	4,018	20. Missouri	87.1
21. Idaho	3,953	21. Maryland	82.1
22. Michigan	3,821	22. Indiana	81.1
23. North Dakota	3,778	23. Connecticut	73.8
24. Kentucky	3,469	24. Colorado	64.5
25. Alabama	3,415	25. Alabama	62.6
26. Mississippi	3,411	26. Arizona	61.8
27. Oregon	3,284	27. Kentucky	56.9
28. New York	3,139	28. Louisiana	55.2
29. Arizona	2,586	29. South Dakota	53.3
30. Tennessee	2,339	30. Iowa	51.2
31. Virginia	2,227	31. South Carolina	48.1
32. New Mexico	2,140	32. Kansas	46.5
33. Louisiana	1,993	33. Oklahoma	46.3
34. Montana	1,892	34. Nevada	40.5
35. South Carolina	1,644	35. Oregon	39.2
36. Maryland	1,467	36. Arkansas	38.7
37. Utah	1,138	37. Mississippi	33.5
38. Wyoming	874	38. Nebraska	32.9
39. New Jersey	846	39. New Hampshire	29.4
40. Delaware	760	40. Hawaii	23.1
41. Hawaii	549	41. West Virginia	22.7
42. Maine	499	42. Rhode Island	19.9
43. Connecticut	485	43. District of Columbia	18.6
44. Vermont	482	44. New Mexico	18.2
45. Nevada	396	45. Maine	16.7
46. West Virginia	390	46. Idaho	13.8
47. Massachusetts	385	47. Montana	11.9
48. New Hampshire	150	48. North Dakota	11.4
49. Rhode Island	57	49. Vermont	9.0
50. Alaska	51	50. Wyoming	7.9
51. District of Columbia	NA	51. Alaska	6.0

† in millions of dollars

† in billions of dollars

55. Total Non-fuel Mineral Production, 2004†		56. Manufacturing Receipts, 2002†	
* UNITED STATES	44,000	* UNITED STATES	$3,916,136,712
1. California	3,620	1. California	378,661,414
2. Nevada	3,250	2. Texas	310,815,965
3. Arizona	3,000	3. Ohio	243,903,865
4. Texas	2,400	4. Michigan	221,433,262
5. Florida	2,220	5. Illinois	188,365,216
6. Georgia	1,830	6. Pennsylvania	181,462,443
7. Utah	1,740	7. Indiana	160,924,188
8. Minnesota	1,590	8. North Carolina	156,821,943
9. Missouri	1,540	9. New York	147,317,463
10. Michigan	1,530	10. Georgia	126,156,636
11. Pennsylvania	1,400	11. Wisconsin	124,664,004
12. Alaska	1,320	12. Tennessee	109,293,454
13. Ohio	1,090	13. New Jersey	96,599,807
14. Wyoming	1,090	14. Missouri	92,909,173
15. New York	1,060	15. Louisiana	89,540,799
16. Illinois	1,030	16. Kentucky	88,513,497
17. Alabama	982	17. Virginia	83,952,547
18. Virginia	868	18. South Carolina	81,132,781
19. North Carolina	822	19. Minnesota	80,623,873
20. New Mexico	811	20. Washington	79,313,884
21. Indiana	774	21. Florida	78,474,770
22. Colorado	762	22. Massachusetts	77,996,586
23. Kansas	741	23. Alabama	66,686,220
24. Kentucky	674	24. Iowa	65,042,043
25. Tennessee	660	25. Kansas	50,897,796
26. South Carolina	586	26. Arkansas	46,721,413
27. Montana	582	27. Oregon	45,864,552
28. Iowa	533	28. Connecticut	45,053,345
29. Arkansas	514	29. Arizona	41,910,739
30. Oklahoma	498	30. Oklahoma	39,924,050
31. Wisconsin	487	31. Mississippi	38,276,054
32. Maryland	478	32. Maryland	36,363,340
33. Washington	447	33. Colorado	34,661,144
34. Louisiana	364	34. Nebraska	30,610,970
35. Oregon	356	35. Utah	25,104,045
36. New Jersey	330	36. West Virginia	18,911,332
37. Idaho	322	37. Delaware	16,417,927
38. Massachusetts	221	38. New Hampshire	15,235,144
39. South Dakota	210	39. Idaho	15,174,196
40. Mississippi	189	40. Maine	13,851,915
41. West Virginia	179	41. Rhode Island	10,818,058
42. Connecticut	132	42. South Dakota	10,710,187
43. Maine	122	43. New Mexico	10,168,130
44. Nebraska	95	44. Vermont	9,660,529
45. Hawaii	75	45. Nevada	8,466,212
46. Vermont	69	46. North Dakota	6,856,653
47. New Hampshire	65	47. Montana	4,987,577
48. North Dakota	52	48. Wyoming	4,061,516
49. Rhode Island	37	49. Alaska	3,832,024
50. Delaware	21	50. Hawaii	3,460,199
51. District of Columbia	NA	51. District of Columbia	246,237

† in millions of dollars

† x $1,000

57. Manufacturing Payroll, 2002†		58. Households with Computers, 2003	
* UNITED STATES	$576,170,541	1. Utah	74.1%
1. California	66,468,561	2. Alaska	72.7
2. Ohio	35,301,070	3. New Hampshire	71.5
3. Texas	34,105,193	4. Washington	71.4
4. Michigan	33,171,232	5. Colorado	70.0
5. Illinois	29,841,718	6. Connecticut	69.2
6. Pennsylvania	27,520,049	7. Idaho	69.2
7. New York	25,373,757	8. Minnesota	67.9
8. Indiana	22,852,682	9. Maine	67.8
9. North Carolina	20,647,572	10. Oregon	67.0
10. Wisconsin	19,334,385	11. Virginia	66.8
11. New Jersey	15,877,239	12. California	66.3
12. Georgia	15,709,628	13. Nebraska	66.1
13. Massachusetts	15,573,734	14. Maryland	66.0
14. Tennessee	14,824,828	15. New Jersey	65.5
15. Florida	14,082,395	16. Vermont	65.5
16. Minnesota	14,077,260	17. Wyoming	65.4
17. Missouri	12,463,436	18. Iowa	64.7
18. Virginia	11,632,963	19. Arizona	64.3
19. Washington	11,163,873	20. District of Columbia	64.3
20. South Carolina	10,602,614	21. Massachusetts	64.1
21. Kentucky	10,077,029	22. Kansas	63.8
22. Connecticut	9,877,987	23. Wisconsin	63.8
23. Alabama	9,744,347	24. Hawaii	63.3
24. Iowa	8,125,864	25. Rhode Island	62.3
25. Oregon	7,173,223	26. South Dakota	62.1
26. Arizona	7,080,603	* UNITED STATES	61.8
27. Kansas	6,877,335	27. Nevada	61.3
28. Maryland	6,475,210	28. North Dakota	61.2
29. Louisiana	6,427,378	29. Florida	61.0
30. Colorado	6,323,772	30. Missouri	60.7
31. Arkansas	6,309,251	31. Georgia	60.6
32. Mississippi	5,476,928	32. Pennsylvania	60.2
33. Oklahoma	5,355,937	33. Illinois	60.0
34. Utah	4,001,272	34. New York	60.0
35. New Hampshire	3,421,148	35. Michigan	59.9
36. Nebraska	3,386,495	36. Indiana	59.6
37. Maine	2,627,814	37. Delaware	59.5
38. West Virginia	2,586,956	38. Montana	59.5
39. Rhode Island	2,294,561	39. Texas	59.0
40. Idaho	2,192,645	40. Ohio	58.8
41. Vermont	1,757,617	41. Kentucky	58.1
42. Nevada	1,642,783	42. North Carolina	57.7
43. Delaware	1,564,801	43. Tennessee	56.7
44. New Mexico	1,241,383	44. Oklahoma	55.4
45. South Dakota	1,096,775	45. West Virginia	55.0
46. North Dakota	757,012	46. South Carolina	54.9
47. Montana	638,834	47. Alabama	53.9
48. Hawaii	421,269	48. New Mexico	53.9
49. Wyoming	364,592	49. Louisiana	52.3
50. Alaska	362,220	50. Arkansas	50.0
51. District of Columbia	76,126	51. Mississippi	48.3

† x $1,000

59. Households with Internet Access, 2003		60. Electricity Consumption per capita, 2001[†]	
1. Alaska	67.6%	1. Alaska	1,164
2. New Hampshire	65.2	2. Wyoming	890
3. Colorado	63.0	3. Louisiana	784
4. Connecticut	62.9	4. North Dakota	640
5. Utah	62.6	5. Texas	564
6. Washington	62.3	6. Kentucky	462
7. Minnesota	61.6	7. Indiana	457
8. Oregon	61.0	8. Oklahoma	444
9. New Jersey	60.5	9. Alabama	435
10. Virginia	60.3	10. West Virginia	423
11. California	59.6	11. Arkansas	411
12. Maryland	59.2	12. Mississippi	410
13. Massachusetts	58.1	13. Montana	404
14. Vermont	58.1	14. Iowa	392
15. Maine	57.9	15. Kansas	387
16. Wyoming	57.7	16. Maine	382
17. Wisconsin	57.4	17. South Carolina	382
18. Iowa	57.1	18. Tennessee	382
19. District of Columbia	56.8	19. Idaho	379
20. Idaho	56.4	20. New Mexico	371
21. Rhode Island	55.7	21. Delaware	368
22. Florida	55.6	22. Nebraska	365
23. Nebraska	55.4	23. Minnesota	350
24. Arizona	55.2	24. Ohio	350
25. Nevada	55.2	25. Wisconsin	345
26. Hawaii	55.0	26. Georgia	343
27. Pennsylvania	54.7	27. Washington	339
* UNITED STATES	54.6	* UNITED STATES	338
28. Kansas	54.3	28. South Dakota	327
29. South Dakota	53.6	29. Missouri	322
30. Georgia	53.5	30. Virginia	322
31. New York	53.3	31. Pennsylvania	319
32. Delaware	53.2	32. Utah	318
33. North Dakota	53.2	33. North Carolina	316
34. Missouri	53.0	34. Michigan	312
35. Ohio	52.5	35. Illinois	309
36. Michigan	52.0	36. Oregon	307
37. Texas	51.8	37. Nevada	301
38. Illinois	51.1	38. District of Columbia	294
39. North Carolina	51.1	39. New Jersey	294
40. Indiana	51.0	40. Colorado	287
41. Montana	50.4	41. Vermont	267
42. Kentucky	49.6	42. Maryland	264
43. Tennessee	48.9	43. New Hampshire	256
44. Oklahoma	48.4	44. Arizona	255
45. West Virginia	47.6	45. Florida	253
46. Alabama	45.7	46. Connecticut	249
47. South Carolina	45.6	47. Massachusetts	242
48. New Mexico	44.5	48. Hawaii	230
49. Louisiana	44.1	49. California	227
50. Arkansas	42.4	50. New York	217
51. Mississippi	38.9	51. Rhode Island	215

† trillion Btu

61. Total Motor Vehicle Registrations, 2004		62. Automobile Registrations, 2004	
* UNITED STATES	237,242,616	* UNITED STATES	136,430,651
1. California	31,399,596	1. California	19,255,690
2. Texas	16,906,714	2. Texas	8,735,544
3. Florida	15,057,473	3. New York	8,548,783
4. New York	11,098,785	4. Florida	8,440,792
5. Ohio	10,636,290	5. Ohio	6,452,386
6. Pennsylvania	9,821,267	6. Pennsylvania	6,000,676
7. Illinois	9,231,541	7. Illinois	5,652,494
8. Michigan	8,398,621	8. Michigan	4,680,729
9. Georgia	7,882,365	9. Georgia	4,222,236
10. Virginia	6,497,426	10. Virginia	4,091,334
11. New Jersey	6,224,256	11. New Jersey	4,016,485
12. North Carolina	6,198,470	12. North Carolina	3,657,863
13. Washington	5,535,236	13. Massachusetts	3,504,943
14. Indiana	5,524,752	14. Indiana	3,067,260
15. Massachusetts	5,456,267	15. Washington	3,034,253
16. Tennessee	5,034,662	16. Tennessee	2,889,051
17. Missouri	4,812,096	17. Missouri	2,698,085
18. Wisconsin	4,705,069	18. Wisconsin	2,591,731
19. Minnesota	4,593,349	19. Maryland	2,547,973
20. Alabama	4,507,751	20. Minnesota	2,502,190
21. Maryland	4,119,664	21. Arizona	2,055,202
22. Arizona	3,776,114	22. Connecticut	2,047,031
23. Louisiana	3,766,793	23. Louisiana	1,973,399
24. Iowa	3,369,431	24. South Carolina	1,922,964
25. Kentucky	3,319,034	25. Iowa	1,882,364
26. South Carolina	3,257,072	26. Kentucky	1,881,213
27. Oklahoma	3,150,989	27. Alabama	1,693,741
28. Connecticut	3,041,592	28. Oklahoma	1,634,376
29. Oregon	3,003,227	29. Oregon	1,475,253
30. Kansas	2,346,522	30. Mississippi	1,123,242
31. Utah	2,084,424	31. Utah	1,036,674
32. Colorado	2,023,292	32. Arkansas	960,085
33. Mississippi	1,964,488	33. Colorado	894,582
34. Arkansas	1,917,503	34. Kansas	852,648
35. Nebraska	1,689,072	35. Nebraska	842,363
36. New Mexico	1,542,964	36. West Virginia	740,834
37. West Virginia	1,396,420	37. New Mexico	695,825
38. Idaho	1,344,124	38. New Hampshire	672,560
39. Nevada	1,281,424	39. Nevada	642,818
40. New Hampshire	1,178,312	40. Maine	608,700
41. Maine	1,068,064	41. Idaho	574,825
42. Montana	1,008,701	42. Hawaii	539,845
43. Hawaii	947,412	43. Rhode Island	531,872
44. South Dakota	841,167	44. Montana	433,160
45. Rhode Island	807,995	45. Delaware	422,755
46. Delaware	711,039	46. South Dakota	395,975
47. North Dakota	700,882	47. North Dakota	347,009
48. Alaska	659,981	48. Vermont	280,158
49. Wyoming	640,914	49. Alaska	255,068
50. Vermont	523,212	50. Wyoming	234,382
51. District of Columbia	238,802	51. District of Columbia	189,230

63. Motorcycle Registrations, 2004

*	UNITED STATES	5,780,870
1.	California	626,529
2.	Florida	461,935
3.	Ohio	298,652
4.	Pennsylvania	292,196
5.	Texas	286,992
6.	Illinois	276,122
7.	Wisconsin	232,808
8.	Michigan	228,856
9.	Arizona	209,048
10.	Minnesota	188,903
11.	New York	170,148
12.	Washington	160,227
13.	Indiana	153,566
14.	New Jersey	149,911
15.	Iowa	140,000
16.	Massachusetts	136,887
17.	Georgia	129,439
18.	Tennessee	108,659
19.	North Carolina	100,366
20.	Oklahoma	84,651
21.	Alabama	81,086
22.	Missouri	77,519
23.	Virginia	75,457
24.	Oregon	75,453
25.	Maryland	72,844
26.	New Hampshire	66,319
27.	Connecticut	64,754
28.	Kansas	61,678
29.	South Carolina	60,029
30.	Louisiana	55,846
31.	Kentucky	53,478
32.	Idaho	49,578
33.	Montana	47,967
34.	Nevada	44,823
35.	Utah	44,386
36.	Arkansas	43,668
37.	South Dakota	41,602
38.	Maine	38,712
39.	New Mexico	36,294
40.	Wyoming	30,615
41.	Nebraska	28,671
42.	Vermont	28,304
43.	Mississippi	27,162
44.	Rhode Island	26,506
45.	Hawaii	23,106
46.	Alaska	21,134
47.	North Dakota	20,953
48.	West Virginia	19,534
49.	Delaware	17,485
50.	Colorado	8,411
51.	District of Columbia	1,601

64. Vehicle Miles of Travel, per capita, 2004

1.	Wyoming	18,485
2.	Mississippi	13,588
3.	Oklahoma	13,450
4.	Indiana	13,113
5.	Alabama	12,926
6.	Georgia	12,668
7.	Vermont	12,649
8.	New Mexico	12,329
9.	Montana	12,116
10.	Tennessee	12,024
11.	North Dakota	11,978
12.	Missouri	11,830
13.	South Carolina	11,806
14.	Arkansas	11,567
15.	South Dakota	11,497
16.	Kentucky	11,414
17.	Maine	11,376
18.	Nebraska	11,324
19.	Delaware	11,233
20.	North Carolina	11,222
21.	Florida	11,214
22.	Minnesota	11,110
23.	Kansas	10,979
24.	West Virginia	10,897
25.	Idaho	10,775
26.	New Hampshire	10,658
27.	Iowa	10,594
28.	Virginia	10,590
29.	Texas	10,271
30.	Michigan	10,250
31.	Utah	10,247
*	UNITED STATES	10,077
32.	Arizona	9,982
33.	Colorado	9,974
34.	Maryland	9,947
35.	Oregon	9,905
36.	Wisconsin	9,853
37.	Ohio	9,744
38.	Louisiana	9,729
39.	Connecticut	9,072
40.	California	9,069
41.	Washington	8,834
42.	Pennsylvania	8,711
43.	Nevada	8,636
44.	Illinois	8,585
45.	Massachusetts	8,535
46.	New Jersey	8,374
47.	Rhode Island	7,845
48.	Hawaii	7,774
49.	Alaska	7,630
50.	New York	7,198
51.	District of Columbia	6,755